1996

W9-AFG-367

# INTRODUCTION TO A SPECIAL EDUCATION
## The Inclusive Classroom

# INTRODUCTION TO
# A SPECIAL EDUCATION
## The Inclusive Classroom

### Karen A. Waldron, Ph.D.

**Trinity University**
**San Antonio, TX**

**Delmar Publishers**

**An International Thomson Publishing Company**

Albany • Bonn • Boston • Cincinnati • Detroit • London • Madrid • Melbourne • Mexico City
New York • Pacific Grove • Paris • San Francisco • Singapore • Tokyo • Toronto • Washington

# NOTICE TO THE READER

Cover Design: J² Design

**Delmar Staff**

| | |
|---|---|
| Senior Editor: | Jay S. Whitney |
| Associate Editor: | Erin J. O'Connor |
| Production Coordinator: | Sandra Woods |
| Art and Design Coordinator: | Timothy J. Conners |

COPYRIGHT © 1996
by Delmar Publishers Inc.
a division of International Thomson Publishing Inc.
The ITP logo is a trademark under license.

Printed in the United States of America

For more information, contact:

Delmar Publishers
3 Columbia Circle
Box 15015
Albany, New York 12203-5015

International Thomson Editores
Campos Eliseos 385, Piso 7
Col Polanco
11560 Mexico D F Mexico

International Thomson Publishing Europe
Berkshire House 168-173
High Holborn
London WC1V7AA
England

International Thomson Publishing GmbH
Königswinterer Strasse 418
53227 Bonn
Germany

Thomas Nelson Australia
102 Dodds Street
South Melbourne, 3205
Victoria, Australia

International Thomson Publishing Asia
221 Henderson Road
#05-10 Henderson Building
Singapore 0315

Nelson Canada
1120 Birchmount Road
Scarborough, Ontario
Canada M1K5G4

International Thomson Publishing - Japan
Hirakawacho Kyowa Building, 3F
2-2-1 Hirakawacho
Chiyoda-ku, Tokyo 102
Japan

1  2  3  4  5  6  7  8  9  10  XXX  01  00  99  98  97  96  95

**Library of Congress Cataloging-in-Publication Data**

Waldron, Karen A., 1945-
    Introduction to special education: the inclusive classroom /
Karen A. Waldron.
      p.   cm.
Includes bibliographical references and index.
ISBN 0-8273-6076-2
1. Mainstreaming in education.    2. Mainstreaming in education-
-Case studies.    3. Special education.    4. Special education--Case
studies.    I. Title.
LC3965.W25    1995
371.9'046--dc20

95-31325
CIP
AC

# CONTENTS

## PART ▪ I

## INTRODUCTION,   1

## PART ▪ II

## COLLABORATION,   57

**P A R T   III**

**ASSESSMENT,   123**

**PART IV**

## CREATING THE TEACHING-LEARNING ENVIRONMENT, 237

# PART V

# TEACHING TECHNIQUES AND CURRICULUM MODIFICATION, 359

## Dedication

This book is dedicated to

*Burton Blatt,* who showed us that everyone matters, that specialness is a present from some to help all of us reach our potential. Burt took us to new legal and personal frontiers, teaching that risks are an imperative part of advocacy and change. While we mourn our loss of him, we carry his commitment in our hearts.

*Daniel D. Sage,* mentor and friend, whose knowledge of finance and law established the framework for inclusion. His personal leadership and ability to create leaders have molded the future of educational reform. From Washington to San Antonio, Dan never met a student he wouldn't teach for a lifetime.

Each of these men models the very essence of a *special* educator.

# LIST OF FIGURES AND TABLES

## FIGURES

TABLES

# PREFACE

*Introduction to a Special Education* is just that: A unique introductory college text to guide prospective special and regular educators toward understanding and meeting the needs of students with exceptionalities. This book maintains the critical information of the traditional introductory text: the history of special education, state and federal legislation, and the role of the courts. It elaborates the steps in the identification and assessment process as well as the development of an individualized educational program (IEP). It describes critical directions in special education, such as the least restrictive environment and the continuum of services. Through discussing movements such as the Regular Education Initiative, it traces how we arrived at the controversial sentiments of today. This text provides an objective overview of responses of experts who feel positively or negatively about directions toward inclusion.

Yet this book goes beyond conventional content. Instead of a chapter-by-chapter categorical review of characteristics of individual disabilities, it is written in an *integrated format* to match the placement of most students. Based on the premise that all students are special, that "good teaching is good teaching," it provides more than one hundred reproducible tables listing collaborative and teaching strategies to improve the education of everyone, including those traditionally not eligible for special services. It also incorporates techniques for students who demonstrate unique needs as a result of the disability. An additional text strength appears in the discussion of optimal ways to identify and assist students at-risk, with specific interventions included to avoid their eventual placement in special education. This book avoids the criticism that traditional texts provide background and characteristics of disabilities, but few practical ways to remediate or compensate for them. It includes countless teaching suggestions that are practical, inexpensive, and easily applied.

The critical issue of cultural diversity is considered throughout. An entire chapter discusses methods of identifying students with disabilities who are from different language and cultural backgrounds. A reproducible parent–interview form is included to help teachers, counselors, and school psychologists weigh the impact of diversity versus disability on student behaviors. Children of diversity, their needs, and specific teaching and intervention strategies are integrated throughout the text.

All of this critical content is developed within the context of the inclusive school. The purpose of this text is not to advocate for partial or full inclusion, since many factors and resources determine whether a particular student or teacher will be successful. The author's premise is that responsible inclusion can help improve the quality of education for all. When the needs of each student and the expertise of each teacher are considered individually, educators can create an environment where everyone can be successful. The text includes reproducible checklists to determine the existence of readiness factors before placing the student in an inclusive class. When educators work in teams to provide these supports, the student enters a supportive, ready environment.

*Introduction to a Special Education* contains two chapters that specify how educators can develop collaborative teams in their schools, combining efforts to help all students. Discussion includes steps for initiation and implementation of prereferral teams to identify students at-risk, as well as ongoing collaborative teams to support interventions with students with disabilities. The interactive role of parents, supportive professionals, and community representatives as involved team members underscores the concept of the "village" teaching the child. This text elaborates the changing role of regular and special educators working together to serve all students. Discussion of the co-teaching and consultation models demonstrates how adjustments in staffing patterns among teachers and paraprofessionals can result in improved programming for all students.

Often, prospective teachers feel the urgency of knowing specific methods for modifying curriculum and materials to meet the needs of students with disabilities. This understandable concern is addressed thoroughly in Chapter 13. Appearing after two full chapters on teaching techniques, ideas are practical and easily implemented across content areas without additional cost. The chapter also includes practical suggestions teachers can share with parents concerning ways to help students be successful in school and in homework completion.

Most importantly, this text is written for prospective and inservice educators, who need to feel that their concerns are understood and that content is directed toward daily practical application in their classrooms. In an interesting, highly readable fashion, *Introduction to a Special Education* takes place in Westside school district, where inclusion has just been mandated in a top-down dictate, to the alarm of teachers and administrators. Readers will meet Mort Stern, a caring but tired administrator who works through ethical and practical considerations of inclusion at Alyssa Jackson Elementary. Maura Hayes, a third-grade teacher, and Teresa Fuentes, a special educator, learn to collaborate as they adjust to the instructional needs of all students. Meanwhile, additional problems unique to secondary schools surface at Howard Apter High School. Principal Elena Cuellar and reluctant teacher John Robinson respond to instructional and behavioral demands in the midst of a number of students at-risk. In response, Dr. Andrea Mirales,

Special Education Director, initiates a series of inservices to guide teachers, administrators, and supportive personnel into responsible inclusion amidst school and community apprehensions. The reader joins these "real" educators with actual concerns as they take their journey toward equitable programming for all students.

## SPECIAL FEATURES

A number of features have been included in this text to make it readable, informative, and practical.

A **Foreword by Daniel D. Sage,** special education legislative and financial expert, sets the stage through a thoughtful discussion of the restructuring of the educational system toward unification of regular and special education.

**Tables and Figures** contain a complete listing of collaborative ideas and teaching strategies for immediate implementation. They can be found full-sized in the instructor's manual to be used as transparencies for class discussions.

**Realistic Case Studies** at the end of each chapter require readers to directly apply concepts discussed. Different case studies appear for elementary and for secondary levels of instruction and are easily identified by the icon in the margin.

**Readable Format** that takes place in a fictional, but realistic school district, makes the text particularly interesting to read. Supporting a problem-solving or role-playing format in class discussions, readers can take the viewpoints of specific educational characters depicted in the narrative. Examples of potential situations confronting educators appear in every chapter to encourage brainstorming and resolution through consideration of multiple perspectives.

**Summaries of Main Ideas** at the end of every chapter underscore and relate major concepts.

**My Portfolio Work Products** identified by the icon in the margin, appear throughout the text to provide visible examples for prospective teachers to consider in designing intervention programs to remediate or compensate for disabilities.

**Discussion of Multiple Teaching Models** provides readers with a variety of ways to instruct diverse learners.

**Identification of Disabilities Checklists** provide an extensive listing of specific behaviors that may indicate the presence of a disability. These checklists can be copied and used in schools to screen entire populations of students.

A **Glossary** of key terms as they appear as well as at the end of the book provides definitions of important concepts.

**Flash!™ for Windows™**, a computerized study guide with an interactive question and answer association program, allows readers to quickly and easily master the information and improve test-taking skills.

## ACKNOWLEDGMENTS

Without support of family and colleagues, no book comes to fruition easily. I am deeply indebted to the fine people who gave me invaluable assistance, including:

*Michael J. Kutchins,* my wonderful husband and in-resident computer expert, who spent so many personal hours on painstaking text design. His insights and humor made the entire writing process infinitely more enjoyable;

*Trinity University,* for affording the time and support that allowed me to concentrate on writing;

*Sonia Mireles,* Senior Secretary in Trinity's Department of Education, whose expert technical efforts throughout manuscript preparation were critical to its timely completion;

*Trinity students,* who provide a daily reminder that the future of teaching and education is very bright, indeed;

*Cha Karulak and the faculty and staff at Winston School, San Antonio,* for their provision of the outstanding samples of student work that appear throughout the text. Winston School is a tribute to the spectrum of services within inclusion, providing an additional place for students to thrive.

# FOREWORD

by DANIEL D. SAGE
Professor Emeritus
Syracuse University

Only a modest level of awareness is required to recognize that the enterprise of education, and the persons who are seriously engaged in the professions associated with schools, are currently being scrutinized and challenged. While those with an historical perspective might argue that this has always been the case, it is appropriate and important to at least identify the nature of the current discussion. Informed citizens of Western society have focused attention on the efficacy of existing systems of education and the quality of their outcomes. The apparently conflicting desires of society and expectations placed on our schools to achieve *excellence* (outcomes that meet the needs of an increasingly complex world) and *equity* (accommodating to an increasingly diverse population of students) present both policy makers and classroom teachers with a formidable challenge.

There appear to be two forces that are concurrently bringing focus to this challenge. One is perhaps best identified by the term *restructuring,* while the other has come to be associated with the label *inclusion.* Both terms suffer from ambiguity and multiple interpretations, but some general characteristics can be described which may help readers see the crucial relationships between the two forces and to see why the ideas and the advice laid out by Karen Waldron in the text which follows may be extremely valuable to their success as educators.

The literature on restructuring of education has for the past decade placed emphasis on the individual school site as the locus for organizational change, rather than the more centralized system. Within that setting, the focus for change has been the actual functions of teaching and learning. This entails the way learning time is distributed among whole-class instruction, small-group work, and individual study. It also emphasizes heterogeneity in the grouping of students, flexible scheduling, application rather than rote demonstration of knowledge, recognition of multiple intelligences, community-based learning, interaction with adult mentors, and the use of peer tutors.

For the professional life of teachers, restructuring has emphasized collaboration through the use of teams and co-teaching, moving away from the traditional practice of individual teachers "doing their thing behind a closed classroom door." The differentiation of teacher roles to include mentoring of novices, collegial planning, and the design and delivery of on-the-job staff development are among the many attributes that have come to be associated with the process of restructuring.

With the emphasis on site-based management, leadership and governance also has become more broadly participatory, involving teachers and parents to a greater extent in decision making, but also making school building principals more responsible and accountable for outcomes. The assessment of student outcomes calls for a focus on "authentic performance," rather than traditional emphasis on memorization of facts. Accountability depends on demonstrating the attainment of desired student outcomes, including active engagement in learning, critical and creative thinking, application of learning to life beyond school, as well as substantive knowledge about subjects of importance.

The quest for more inclusive schools has a number of dimensions. Inclusion of diverse populations of students within one unified system is intended to replace practices which segregate students, whether such segregation occurs *defacto* or by design. Schools that have cultural, ethnic, and racial diversity are living the value of inclusion. The issue of diversity within the dimension of student ability or disability is more recent and problematic. Professional educators as well as consumers of services for students with disabilities have by and large been satisfied and grateful that students with special needs were accorded mere access to education—any kind of education. Only more recently has the question of quality of special education been brought into focus. Analysis of the outcomes of special education programs has raised concern. In addition, the sociological parallels between the classification and separation of students by such attributes as ethnicity and by the seemingly less egregious attribute of disability, have drawn the attention of both professional and consumer stakeholders.

The concept of *least restrictive environment*, as a legal principle in the determination of appropriate educational programming for students with disabilities, has promoted the development and assurance of a continuum of services of varying intensity to accommodate their varying needs. However, as the numbers of students perceived as requiring such services has mushroomed, critics outside the system and policy makers within have expressed concern that special education has become too readily used as a convenient place to discard students who are difficult or unpleasant to teach. One aspect of this concern is that the regular education system is becoming unreasonably narrow and rigid in the type of students for whom it will accept responsibility. Another aspect is that the very existence of the parallel special system (the continuum) allows and even encourages regular educators to abdicate their normal responsibility.

Some observers have noted that inclusion, as a value and a policy goal, represents a culminating step in the evolutionary implementation of the principle of least restrictive environment. Earlier stages of this evolution (in the 1970's) saw the promotion of *mainstreaming* as a mechanism for bridging the gap between regular and special education. It was hoped that this would foster integration of students with disabilities into the regular stream of education. Proponents argued that the merger of the two parallel systems was both desirable and possible. However, it should not be assumed that there is conceptual equivalence among the terms that have been associated with the movement. *Mainstreaming* and *integration* both started with the existence of two separate systems of education and the assumption of inequity between the two. That is, integration involves allowing the lesser (special education) system members to join the more favored (mainstream) system, with the understanding that such *mainstreaming* is contingent upon demonstrating that participation will be in accordance with the standards of the dominant system. To be successfully mainstreamed the student must be ready to compete, in some fashion, within normal expectations of regular education. By contrast, *inclusion* implies the existence of only one unified educational system from the beginning, encompassing all members equitably, without regard for variations in their status. From this perspective there is no need for integration because there is no initial separation. All degrees of variation of students' needs and performances will be accommodated. Skeptics may note that such a view reflects only a utopian wish, and ambiguities abound as to the ultimate practical limits of *full* inclusion, but proponents argue that there are ways to work toward attaining it.

It is at this point that the forces pressing for *restructuring* and the forces pressing for *inclusion* come together. The total educational system cannot become truly restructured unless it becomes more inclusive in every sense. Conversely, inclusion for students with disabilities cannot be expected to work well in the existing system, but must depend on significant restructuring of education as we know it. In the final analysis, there is a co-dependency between the conceptual goals.

In the text that Karen Waldron has prepared, the practical considerations for working toward these goals are outlined with considerable detail. The day-to-day processes for creation of an inclusive environment, collaboration among professional personnel, assessment of diverse student needs, models of organization for instruction, and teaching techniques for diverse student populations are addressed. The focus is on the role of the teacher, in the classroom, surrounded by students with multiple dimensions of variability, truly "living in interesting times."

Special thanks to the reviewers who offered numerous valuable suggestions:

Reuben Altman, Ph.D.
University of Missouri-Columbia
Columbia, MO

David W. Anderson, Ed.D.
Bethel College
St. Paul, MN

Sylvia Artmann, Ed.D.
Dallas Baptist University
Dallas, TX

Nancy Belknap, Ed.D.
George Washington University
Washington, DC

Mack Bowen, Ph.D.
Illinois State University
Normal, IL

J. Perry Carter, M.Ed.
Richland College
Dallas, TX

Catherine J. Coggins, Ph.D.
Stetson University
DeLand, FL

Jack J. Hourcade, Ph.D.
Boise State University
Boise, ID

Melba Spooner, Ed.D.
University of North Carolina
    at Charlotte
Charlotte, NC

Jill Stanton, Ed.D.
University of Wisconsin-Stout
Menomonie, WI

Vicki D. Stayton, Ph.D.
Western Kentucky University
Bowling Green, KY

Terry L. Weaver, Ph.D.
Union University
Jackson, TN

# INTRODUCTION

# DIRECTORY

People you'll meet in Westside School District:

| | |
|---|---|
| Mort Stern | Principal, Alyssa C. Jackson Elementary School |
| Maura Hayes | Third-grade teacher, Jackson Elementary |
| Teresa Fuentes | Special education teacher, Jackson Elementary |
| Elena Cuellar | Principal, Howard Apter High School |
| John Robinson | Tenth-grade teacher, Apter High |
| Dr. Andrea Mirales | Director, Special Education |
| Alex Hamilton | Director, School Psychology |
| Mike Gonzales | Spokesperson, Westside Parent's Organization |
| Curt O'Hare | Conservative radio talk-show host |

# 1

# SPECIAL EDUCATION: THE HISTORICAL AND LEGAL INITIATIVE

A new era has begun in Westside School District. After two years of planning and numerous emotion-charged public hearings with parents, teachers, and administrators, Westside has adopted an inclusive model of serving students with disabilities. Under the new plan, students with mild to moderate disabilities will remain in "regular education" for their entire school day. Dr. Andrea Mirales, Director of Special Education, intends to include those with more severe disabilities in as many schoolwide academic activities as possible. They will participate in separate special education classes only when parents and teachers determine that their needs cannot be met without the intense involvement of specialists.

At most levels, Westside has not adopted the inclusion philosophy voluntarily. Perhaps parents of students with mild and moderate disabilities have been the most excited about seeing their children participate more fully in regular class activities. Yet, even these parents have expressed concerns that their children will not receive ongoing support of the Resource Rooms or Content Mastery Centers in which they previously participated and their special needs will now be forgotten. Parents of students with severe disabilities have been more difficult to convince, often because their anxiously voiced concerns mirror both extremes of the spectrum. Some of the parents fear inclusion, stating their children need to learn self-help and prevocational skills more than a strictly academic curriculum in which their transitional needs of the future would not be met. Other parents want full inclusion of their children now, citing gains in self-esteem and more normalized peer interactions as being critical. They are angry that they are expected to wait years before their children can partake of the same activities offered to the nondisabled.

Some of the most concerned parents raise different issues. Their children are not disabled, and they fear the possibility that teachers will spend so much time with the newly included students that they will have little time to spend with the gifted and "average" learner. This group of parents is so strong in their resentment of inclusion that their intimidating spokesperson, Mike Gonzales, has threatened to sue the district if instances of lowered educational standards are observed in local classrooms.

Teachers have had different, but equally strong, concerns. Regular educators feel a lack of preparation to teach students with disabilities. Most of them have attended colleges in which they were to take few, if any, special education courses. The concept of having students with more extreme needs in learning and behavior is very threatening. The number of students at risk in their classes seems to increase daily anyway, with concerns including abuse, gangs, and threats of youth violence. As one teacher noted, "We simply can't bring any more students with problems into our rooms. The children are already out-of-control." In the past, teachers felt some comfort in the supports of special education. Now they fear the removal of the safety net, which allowed them to send the more difficult students out of their rooms to the special education teacher down the hall.

Some also feel that fewer college students will choose to become teachers once they discover the increasing numbers of children at risk and adolescents in regular education. Across the state, few colleges have changed their traditional curriculum to a more inclusive approach, in which they would integrate methods for teaching children with special needs into all education courses. Instead, most continue to separate special and regular education courses, departments, and certification programs. The promise of well-trained inclusive teachers seems dim until the state education agency changes its policies and emphases.

Although usually knowledgeable in a variety of methods, special educators are not exempt from concerns. Previously, they often quoted Dr. Mirales's philosophy, "The purpose of special education is to put ourselves out of business." Now they're not so sure. What will their new business be? It is likely they will become supportive personnel in the developing collaborative relationships to which the district keeps referring. Does this mean they won't have their own classrooms? Will they wander to several regular education units each day, serving as tutors in support of other teachers' lesson plans? Within this structure, they fear what to them appears all too obvious: They may become second-class teachers, moving about to support "real teachers," working with some regular educators who have never wanted students with disabilities anyway. This sense of loss of control over their own professional identity is very threatening.

School administrators have their own apprehensions. While adopting an inclusion model was not mandated for each campus, the district has offered incentives for those schools electing to be part of the program. This policy is a result of the state education agency plan directing an increase in support of a school district's general education fund based on the number of schools in the district that normalize services to students with disabilities. Needless to say, the superintendent decided that accepting the state's offer would allow for increased flexibility in serving more students in the district, and each building principal has felt tremendous pressure to support the inclusion model.

When Mort Stern attended the district meeting for school principals, at first he was angered at the lack of input he and others had in this major policy change. In more than twenty years with the district, he had learned to accept change, wherever it was initiated. The only change he had rejected was when the superintendent had offered to "promote" him several times to the principalship of a middle school or high school. Mort loved Alyssa C. Jackson Elementary School, named after a woman raised in poverty who had refused to be overcome by race and gender discrimination, eventually becoming the first African-American mayor of the city. Grandfatherly, but wise, Mort most enjoyed the minutes he stole to visit personally in classes or one-on-one with his "children of color." Last year in one third-grade classroom there had been homicides against two children's parents. Mort had attended the funerals and appeared on local television stations to affirm his belief that his students could overcome this violence, that education was their opportunity.

Now his dilemma is a moral one. If he believes in equal opportunities for all children, why is he upset over his new charge to include all children in the same room? Does he really feel it won't work, or is he just getting older and avoiding confrontations these days? Luckily, the district has solved the decision part of the problem for him. He only wished the superintendent could change the attitudes of Jackson's teachers that easily.

Elena Cuellar's problem is quite different. She has been principal of Howard Apter High School for two years and is finally making progress. Her school was named after an astronaut as a reminder of the lofty goals neighborhood parents have for their children. Elena understands high school teachers: She herself came up "through the ranks." She realizes her teachers tend to be content-directed, with their frequent reminders, "I just want to teach English" and "Didn't these kids learn anything in elementary school?" Yet she has found them to be more caring than most people know. She has seen her teachers stay after school to meet with students having academic or personal problems. Teachers run school clubs that meet after-hours and on weekends, attend football and basketball games, and suffer the interminable curricular-change meetings, all without extra salary.

While the school has not changed its highly academic nature, faculty, parents, and students have labored to encompass students from lower-income families as they move into the more affluent neighborhood. The process has been ongoing, with Elena leading the battle to ensure equitable treatment for all students.

Similar to Mort, Elena's reaction toward including students with disabilities has caused her to wonder, "How much is too much?" When she met at length with her parent advisory group to discuss their concerns, Mike Gonzales requested this group be allowed to give final approval to curricular changes impacting the education of any students in the school. While she had been able to refer him to the School Board on this issue, she is concerned about the negativism she experienced. Mike is only one of the high-powered parents pressuring for more advanced placement courses, an expanded gifted/talented program, and more college advisement. Elena knows she will have to reflect a long time to find a way to meet everyone's needs.

None of these concerns had escaped the attention of the local media. Curt O'Hare is a popular radio host, listened to by most of the community members as they drive home each night. Very conservative, he is unbending in his traditional values and tends to have guests who are reactionary toward any type of community change. While his listeners view him as an eccentric because of the strength of his opinions, and they smiled with amusement some years ago when he was in a fistfight with another, more liberal, newscaster, they still listen. Every night.

Curt has a new issue these days: inclusion. "We all feel sorry for the plight of these kids, and they deserve a chance. But students with disabilities in a third-grade class all day? Or sitting in geometry? Come on now." His recent guests have been Mike Gonzales and his parent advisory group, fueling the fire.

The newspapers have tended to be more fair, explaining the changes, but always looking for sensational stories to sell papers. From parent interviews to requests to visit classrooms, the reporters always seem to be around on a "slow" news day. That is, when the state legislature isn't in session. The big news these days has been the near-bankruptcy of the state and the failure of the school finance system. As Mort and Elena started their school year, they were told they might not have enough money to pay their teachers and keep their schools open until the end of the year. Requests for smaller classes and money for increased supportive personnel likely will be viewed with amazement. How could demands be added to the system without additional money?

Miles apart, Mort and Elena both remember the Chinese curse, "May you live in interesting times."

# THE PAIN OF CHANGE

The pains Westside is newly experiencing have been felt across the country. The need for equity within a flexible educational structure that allows for differences is difficult in the best of circumstances. In an age of rejected bond issues, citizen concerns about raising taxes, and an overall sense that education is already into crisis management, it is difficult to increase expectations on an already overloaded system.

Yet, this is one of the most exciting times to be in education. With every claim that the system is not producing enough scientists, there follows a breakthrough in technology or medicine allowing for improved quality of life. The wonderful opportunities for women and minorities have grown tremendously, allowing previously excluded individuals to experience great personal success. Their stories almost always relate back to a teacher's influence or parents who encouraged a strong education. Living in interesting times may be more of a stimulus than a curse, urging everyone to stretch further to succeed in new areas. A fine education for all is the key.

**inclusion**—providing a normalized education experience for all children with disabilities.

**collaboration**—when educators interact to solve problems relating to student needs.

The goal of **inclusion**\* is to provide a normalized educational experience for all children with disabilities. For many students, this will mean their full-time instead of part-time participation in a regular education classroom, receiving supportive services through **collaboration** by educators. Many districts have adopted this model successfully, while others, such as Westside, are experiencing the pains of "paradigm shift" (Kuhn, 1970).

There are not many blueprints available for successful inclusive programs since variables such as administrative support, parental involvement, and teacher skills vary tremendously even within the same school district. Yet, there are individual schools that willingly include students with disabilities in all facets of school life. In these environments, teachers have the skills to work and succeed with all children, subsequently not feeling threatened by the presence of difference in their classrooms.

The purpose of this book is to provide the developing teacher and the practicing teacher with specific knowledge to be able to teach all children. Discussion will range from understanding how to work and plan with colleagues, to strategies for teaching academic skills more effectively to diversified groups of learners. The underlying premise of this text is that by improved understanding of how to meet varied students' needs, we will welcome them more fully into our classrooms.

\*Terms appearing in **color** are defined in page margins. The terms and their definitions also appear in alphabetical order in the glossary at the end of the text.

# EARLY PROGRAMMING FOR CHILDREN WITH DISABILITIES

As Westside and other districts wrestle with the logistics of developing an inclusive program, there is a mixed sense both of *deja-vu* and of change. The current ties to the history of special education are closely related to the humanitarian spirit of the early 1800s. Not only were there attempts to educate individuals with disabilities, but also a sincere belief by many reformers that despite differences in abilities, individuals with disabilities deserved to be treated with respect and dignity.

## The Nineteenth Century

special educator—a professional trained in meeting the needs of students with disabilities.

Initial records indicate that Jean Marc Gaspard Itard (1775–1838) may have been the first acknowledged **special educator**. A French physician specializing in causes and resultant conditions of hearing impairments, Itard is best known for his work with Victor, the "Wild Boy" who had been found wandering in the forests of France (Itard, trans., 1962). Itard was able to design educational methods training Victor in language and more appropriate behavioral responses. Despite the doubts of other professionals, Itard's successes indicated that individuals with disabilities could be educated and could demonstrate observable improvement in skills, an argument that was to become the basis for **advocacy** court cases in the 1970s.

advocacy—efforts, usually by parents or educators, to establish services for students.

Itard's student Edouard Seguin (1812–1880) designed teaching methods to improve the lives and learning of individuals with cognitive disabilities and formed the basis for the work of Maria Montessori (1870–1952). Both expressed the idea that despite differences in intellectual capacity, every child can be educated and can demonstrate some improvement in skills. Montessori expanded her work into early childhood education. The continued support of Montessori programs in the United States attests to the strength and positive outcomes of her methods.

"Certainly these were brilliant, dedicated people, but I'm not sure how all this history relates to what I'm doing with my third-graders," Maura Hayes notes.

There are general strategies that early leaders in special education found highly effective for teaching students with disabilities. Ironically, many of these instructional techniques are still used today (Table 1–1).

individualized instruction—teaching strategies based on the idea that a student's program should be tailored to meet the student's specific needs.

reinforcement—a consequence that encourages or discourages the continuance of a behavior.

life-skills training—teaching a student the skills needed to work and live independently.

Revolutionary for their time, these ideas supplied the foundation for current special education techniques. These early educational principles supported methods favored in current times: **individualized instruction** based on the needs of the child; sequencing educational tasks from the child's level to the more complex; providing stimulation through sensory experiences as a basis for more advanced learning; structuring the environment to optimize learning; provision of immediate **reinforcement**; and concentration on **life-skills training** to create later self-sufficiency. It is ironic that their early work indicated those practices educators and researchers are still finding the most effective.

### Table 1–1
### Educational Principles of Early Special Educators

1. Instruction should be individualized, based on the needs of the student.
2. Tasks should be analyzed into components and matched with student abilities.
3. Educational tasks should be sequenced from basic to complex.
4. Students should receive intensive guided and independent practice as they learn new skills.
5. From early schooling, teachers should provide ongoing sensory experiences and stimulation basic to more advanced learning.
6. Time on task is critical to learning. Even informal experiences should include reinforcement opportunities in areas such as language development.
7. Training should emphasize life skills to create independence in adulthood.
8. Immediate reinforcement underscores success in the learner.

Samuel Gridley Howe (1801–1876), an American colleague of Seguin's, was also a strong humanitarian and a pioneer in developing methods of working with the disabled. Later successes with Helen Keller were based on his early work with students who were deaf and blind. Besides his role in the foundation of the Perkins School for the Blind in Massachusetts, he also developed educational methods for work with the cognitively disabled. Others, such as Thomas Hopkins Gallaudet (1787–1851), developed strong residential

Traditionally, the concept of individualizing instruction to meet diverse needs has been an indicator of good teaching.

treatment programs for students who were deaf. He was later honored by the naming of Gallaudet University, a college for students who are deaf, which continues to be highly regarded for its outstanding academic programming and advocacy.

"Was there any programming for students with mild to moderate learning problems, the kind I see daily in my classroom?" Maura asks. Unfortunately not. Children with severe physical, sensory, and intellectual disabilities were recognized first historically, clearly because of the obvious presence of the disability, especially to the lay person. Greater public sympathy was expressed for individuals with sensory deficits, such as deafness and blindness (MacMillan & Hendrick, 1993). Because of these early emphases, even today the training for educators of students with visual and auditory impairments remains a separate program at universities. Often **service delivery** in the public schools has remained separate from both special and regular education. Historically, those students with mild differences, such as learning disabilities, were considered for services much later. Their presence in special education has become controversial and often litigious, likely because their disabilities are more subtle in manifestation, causing disagreements concerning appropriate placement and optimal **intervention methods**.

service delivery—providing instruction.

intervention methods—preventive, remedial, or compensatory efforts to educate students.

Historically, often it has been individuals with cognitive disabilities who have suffered the most exclusion from educational systems. For while the specialists of the 1800s, many of them physicians, were working through exciting new discoveries in teaching methods, most were kept at home with no education, often "closeted" by their families. As awareness broadened, residential institutions proliferated, with the goal of **habilitation** and eventual return to the community (MacMillan & Hendrick, 1993). This educational model gradually faded when the clients did not demonstrate easy improvement. With a changing philosophy over time, most institutions became basic care facilities with no education available and with no expectation that individuals with disabilities could benefit from an education. The notoriety of these facilities tended to be largely deserved. "Insane asylums" gave shelter, but rarely any care, and at times were places of extreme cruelty to their clients.

habilitation—efforts made to improve a student's skills and abilities.

## The Development of Separate Systems

"What about programs for students without disabilities?" interjects John Robinson. "I've always told my high school students the nineteenth century was a time when education flourished with strong support from parents and local communities."

It is true that the nineteenth century marked the growth of **common schools** for the general population of children, philosophically supporting the need to educate future generations. The mood in regular education was both inspir-

common schools—schools for the general population of children.

ing and exciting. The contrast between the development of regular and special education also became pronounced at this time. Individuals with disabilities were excluded because they were viewed as incapable of benefitting from the regular education system (Wolfensberger, 1971).

As the religious revival model of educational missionaries spread educational gospels through the end of the nineteenth century, a growing number of social workers started community homes for clients with psychiatric problems in more liberal cities, such as Boston. Yet, anger from neighbors and the general community demonstrated that public sentiment was largely in favor of continued isolation. As Burton Blatt and Wolf Wolfensberger so commonly noted in their later advocacy training, one seeking the ever-expanding institutions for individuals with disabilities need only look for the water tower in the most distant areas of town and the institution would be close by!

"It's really interesting to speculate at this point that special education might have developed in a different direction if individuals with disabilities had been included in the common schools and had not been placed in a separate system," comments Dr. Mirales.

So true. While only the more easily observed disabilities, such as behavioral disorders, developmental delays, deafness, blindness, and orthopedics, would have received programming, it is ironic that these children likely would have been mainstreamed wherever possible by their local community. The currently legislated **Individual Educational Plan (IEP)** created to meet specific child learning and behavioral needs, would have been informally designed for each child, with or without a disability, by a teacher in a small school setting who would have been forced situationally to use such "modern" ideas as peer tutoring and mastery learning.

**Individualized Educational Plan (IEP)**—specific goals, strategies, and evaluative measures meeting a particular child's learning and behavioral needs.

Perhaps because of the overwhelming nineteenth century needs to develop schools when few resources and numerous logistical problems were present, or because of the anticipated difficulties of teaching students with disabilities, rarely were these children included in the broad educational system.

## The Twentieth Century

"Happily, we're past that period. How did we initiate day programs for the disabled?" John asks.

As a result of the growing urbanization at the turn of the century, day-school programs began for people with mild and moderate disabilities. Children were classified by the nature of their disability and were grouped for instructional purposes, occasionally in a special class within a regular school, but usually in a separate building. A certain amount of **decentralization** occurred, keeping children with exceptional needs closer to their home communities, changing responsibility from state to local systems (Sage, 1970).

**decentralization**—keeping children with exceptional needs close to their home communities.

While the twentieth century brought a technological model to general education (Tyack & Hansot, 1982), a more humane approach re-emerged towards disabled citizens of all ages. The brutality and lack of human dignity forced upon the individuals with disabilities were tragically depicted in Blatt and Kaplan's brilliant pictorial essay, *Christmas in Purgatory* (1966), in which undercover photographs showed a shocked public audience the tortured lives of many in the institutionalized population. Willowbrook, in Staten Island, New York, as well as other institutions came under federal scrutiny and were closed until changes could be made. Numerous court suits followed, with Blatt and his colleagues testifying in support of initiating state laws to require not only safe shelter, but education as well.

Dr. Mirales interjects, "Where do the parents fit in? I know they've been central to the success of the special education movement."

True. The development of parental involvement differed between general and special education. For the able-bodied, as Tyack and Hansot (1982) note, "Education officials in the early stages of school-building traveled about from community to community to energize the local citizens" (p. 48). They created a mutual goal: "The best case for public education has always been that it is a common good: that everyone, ultimately, has a stake in education" (p. 260).

It required parental activism supported by a core of concerned professionals to initiate educational systems for students with disabilities. While parents of general education students had been encouraged to participate in the growth

Parents of students with disabilities have played a remarkable role in supporting their children's needs.

and improvement of the system, historically parents of students with special needs have had to advocate for education for their children. Education for the more seriously disabled often began with federal or state mandate initiated by parental litigation. The results of this adversarial process have created a "battleground of contending forces" (Tyack & Hansot, 1982) from which most administrators of special education programs have not since been able to remove themselves.

The trends in development of earlier educational systems continue today, with important implications for future generations. Little has been more significant than ongoing societal reactions in shaping special education as a parallel system. As Gartner and Lipsky (1987) note, "The origin, growth, and shape of special education have in many ways been defined by general education and the attitudes and behaviors of mainstream educators toward students with handicapping conditions" (p. 382).

labeling—figuratively attaching a name that categorizes a student as demonstrating a designated disability.

This pervasive societal attitude has been to view the system as functional and the student as dysfunctional (Skrtic, 1991). With the growth of bureaucracy and professionalism, a need to justify a parallel system of education has often driven the educational cart. The labeling of children into categories of dysfunction has often allowed their depersonalization both by legislators and educators, further avoiding consideration of the system as flawed and not the student. As we grow closer to changing the system to include rather than exclude children, we will need to embrace a new philosophy of designing instruction around the needs of each student as a unique person instead of attempting to fit all students into a predesigned program meeting bureaucratic requirements.

## THE IMPACT OF LAW

Dr. Mirales looks pensive. "I agree with the sentiment of all this, but the process is very difficult at times, especially with the increasing number of lawsuits Westside has been facing. Wherever did we develop this emphasis on litigation?"

### Litigation

Litigation supporting rights for the disabled has developed from a civil rights basis. While parental and professional attitudes allowed many to believe that children with disabilities should receive a separate but equal education, precedents were initially established by the *Brown v. Board of Education* decision

(347 U.S. 483). This important case underscored the significance of an education to the "life and minds" of children and recognized the inequality of a separate education.

As indicated in Table 1–2, there were a number of court cases that had direct impact on changing the direction of service delivery. Indicative of a new sensitivity to the relationship between culture and school performance, the courts worked to avoid overclassifying minority students as having disabilities. Responses ranged from *Hobson v. Hansen (1967)*, which prohibited the use of standardized tests to track students from nondominant cultures, to *Diana v. State Board of Education (1970)*, *Larry P. v. Riles (1971)*, and *Jose P. v. Ambach (1979)*, requiring assessment and instructional procedures to be more culturally relevant.

Following the precedent of the *Brown* decision, two key court cases established the right of students with disabilities to receive an education. The *Pennsylvania Association for Retarded Children (PARC) v. Commonwealth of Pennsylvania (1972)* decision (334 F. Supp. 1257) ruled that children with developmental disabilities could benefit from an education, requiring Pennsylvania schools to educate students previously claimed unteachable and excluded from their system. The following year, in the *Mills v. DC Board of Education (1972)* decision (348 F. Supp. 1257), the federal district court ruled that a school district could not exclude students from an education based on the amount of finances available, that students with disabilities should not have to wait for an education until typical students had been served.

In *Stuart v. Nappi (1978)* and *Honig v. Doe (1988)*, school districts were limited in their ability to expel students whose school infractions were linked to their behavioral disorders.

Particularly significant to the inclusion movement has been *Daniel R. R. v. State Board of Education (1989)*. This ruling established that if a student can receive a satisfactory education in the regular classroom, this must be deemed the appropriate placement. While placements should be determined on a case-by-case basis through an individualized educational plan, it is the burden of the district to establish that significant supplemental aids and techniques have been tried and the placement has been unsuccessful. Yet, the district need not go to extreme measures to support the student. Even if the academic setting is not optimal, if the nonacademic benefits such as improved self-esteem are successful, the placement should continue.

Subsequent court cases supported *Daniel R. R.*, adding that the district need not provide a full-time teacher to allow the student to remain in the setting (*Greer v. Rome City*) and that the courts should consider the effects of the inclusive placement on other students in the class (*Oberti v. Board of Education*). Yet, the overall response has been to require the school district to prove the student has been placed in the regular education environment with required supportive services, the effects on the student and peers, and the cost-effectiveness of the placement.

## Table 1–2
## Litigation Affecting Services for Individuals with Disabilities

| Court Cases | Rulings |
| --- | --- |
| *Brown v. Board of Education (1954)* | Children cannot be segregated in public schooling solely on the basis of race. Such segregation violates the equal protection clause of the Fourteenth Amendment to the U.S. Constitution by depriving them of equal educational opportunity. |
| *Hobson v. Hansen (1967)* | The use of standardized tests outside the cultural experiences of students to "track" them academically violates the equal protection clause of the Fourteenth Amendment. |
| *Diana v. State Board of Education (1970)* | California agreed to change the language used in special education assessment for Mexican and Chinese students, as well as to eliminate test items not culturally relevant. Tests would be developed more attuned to students' cultures. Students would be re-evaluated if their placement had been based on a diagnosis of cognitive disabilities. |
| *Larry P. v. Riles (1971)* | Rulings in the *Diana v. State Board of Education (1970)* case were extended to include African-American students. |
| *Pennsylvania Association for Retarded Children v. Commonwealth of Pennsylvania (1972)* | Pennsylvania agreed to provide a free, appropriate education for all students diagnosed as having cognitive disabilities, including preschool children, when such schooling generally was available. The definition of *education* was expanded to include a number of previously denied activities for students with cognitive disabilities. |
| *Mills v. D.C. Board of Education (1972)* | The District of Columbia agreed that students must have a scheduled hearing before exclusion from school or placement in a special setting. They cannot be excluded from school on the basis of a disability, such as a behavioral disorder. All students, regardless of a disability, have the right to a free, appropriate education. |
| *Wyatt v. Stickney (1972)* | State institutions must provide a meaningful education for children with disabilities in their care. Otherwise, child incarceration will be considered unlawful detention. |
| *Stuart v. Nappi (1978)* | Due process procedures must be followed before students can be expelled for disciplinary reasons. |
| *Jose P. v. Ambach (1979)* | Identification, evaluation, and instructional procedures used with students with disabilities must be appropriate to their bilingual backgrounds. |
| *Board v. Rowley (1982)* | The Supreme Court upheld the right of a board of education to deny additional services to a deaf student already enrolled in special education and achieving academically beyond the level of typical peers. The Court indicated that the law affords equal opportunity, but not maximum opportunity, to students with disabilities. |

*(Continued)*

**Table 1–2**   *(Continued)*

| Court Cases | Rulings |
|---|---|
| *Honig v. Doe (1988)* | A student cannot be expelled when the behavior is the outcome of a diagnosed disability. The school may initiate a short-term suspension when used judiciously. |
| *Daniel R. R. v. State Board of Education (1989)* | In a critical decision basic to the inclusion movement, the court ruled that if a student can receive a satisfactory education in the regular classroom, he or she must be educated there. In accordance with the Individuals with Disabilities Education Act (IDEA), even if the academic setting is not optimal for the student, the nonacademic benefits, such as improved self-esteem, support the placement. However, while the district must provide supplementary aids and accommodations in the regular classroom, the district need not provide every conceivable service or require teachers to devote all of their time to one student to the detriment of the rest of the class. |
| *Greer v. Rome City School Distirct (1992)* | The court held that before a student should be educated outside the regular classroom, the school district must consider the entire range of supplemental aids and services that would allow the student to participate in the regular education environment. Only when these supports are not enough for student success should the district consider a segregated placement. To do otherwise would be a violation of the provisions of the Individuals with Disabilities Education Act (IDEA). The court said that a school district cannot be required to provide a student with disabilities a full-time teacher, even if this would allow the student to remain in the regular education environment. |
| *Oberti v. Board of Education of the Borough of Clementon School District (1993)* | In deciding in favor of the parents in allowing a more inclusive placement for a student with severe intellectual and behavioral disorders, the court specified three factors to be considered when determining if a student can benefit from education in a regular education setting. The first involves the degree to which the district has attempted to modify the regular class. Next, the courts should consider the educational benefits the student would receive in the regular setting with those in the special class. Additionally, the courts should consider the effect of the inclusive placement on other students in the regular class. If a court determines that a student cannot be educated satisfactorily in the regular classroom, it should consider whether, when appropriate, the student participates maximally in school programs with typical students. |
| *Connecticut Association for Retarded Citizens v. State of Connecticut Board of Education (1993)* | This suit was brought by the parents of four students with cognitive disabilities. They wanted the lawsuit considered as a class action, on behalf of all such students, claiming their children had inappropriate access to special services in regular classrooms. The court refused the petition for change to a class action suit, noting |

*(Continued)*

**Table 1–2** *(Continued)*

| *Court Cases* | *Rulings* |
| --- | --- |
| | that appropriate educational placements for students with disabilities must be determined on a case-by-case basis. It underscored the IDEA requirement that every special education placement must be based on an individualized educational program (IEP). Significantly, the court determined that some students with disabilities may not benefit from full inclusion. |
| *Statum v. Birmingham Public Schools Board of Education (1993)* | The court affirmed the continued education of a student with severe disabilities in a regular kindergarten, despite the school district's petition to change the placement to a self-contained class. The court placed the burden of proof on the school district, noting officials had failed to prove the self-contained program would improve her education, that her IEP could not be enacted in the regular class, that other students would be adversely affected, and that costs would be prohibitive. The student was allowed to remain in the class for at least the remainder of the year. |
| *Sacramento City Unified School District v. Holland (1994)* | Upholding the placement of a student with a severe cognitive disability in a regular class, the court adopted factors to weigh when placing a student with disabilities: both academic and nonacademic benefits of the placement; the effect of the child on the teacher and peers; and costs resulting from the placement. |
| *Poolaw v. Parker Unified School District (1994)* | The court upheld the school district's recommendation to place a profoundly deaf student in a residential facility after it was determined that he had not benefitted enough from previous inclusive efforts involving intensive intervention to warrant a similar placement in another school district. |

## Legislation

As a result of these court cases, a number of federal laws resulted in establishing service delivery structures to children with disabilities, including guarantees of nondiscrimination and equal opportunity, personnel preparation, provision of capital funds and a series of discretionary grant programs, and research and demonstration projects (Gartner & Lipsky, 1987).

Table 1–3 presents an overview of important legislation that has supported the rights of individuals with disabilities. Early legislation supported funds for teacher training and support for state-operated and state-funded day and residential schools (Elementary and Secondary Education Act, 1965). Other legislation acknowledged the necessity of educating young children with disabilities in order to provide early intervention before problems became more severe (i.e., PL 90-538; PL 98-199; PL 99-457).

## Table 1–3
## Legislation Affecting Services for Individuals with Disabilities

| | |
|---|---|
| 1958 | PL 85-926: Grants to the state and to universities to encourage education of college professors to train teachers of students with cognitive disabilities. This law underscored funding by category of disability. |
| 1963 | PL 88-164: Funds for teacher training and for research and demonstration projects. Financial assistance in building facilities for the cognitively disabled and for community mental health centers. |
| 1965 | Elementary and Secondary Education Act (PL 89-10): Assistance was provided for local education agencies in state-operated and state-supported private day and residential schools. |
| 1968 | Handicapped Children's Early Education Assistance Act (PL 90-538): Grants for the development of model programs for birth through six years population. |
| 1970 | PL 91-230: Amendment to the Elementary and Secondary Education Act, consolidating all existing legislature into Title VI (Education of the Handicapped Act). Recognized learning disabilities as eligible for funding and expanded emphasis on programs for the gifted and talented. |
| 1973 | Vocational Rehabilitation Act: Section 504, The Bill of Rights for the Handicapped: Nondiscriminatory guarantees for school-age individuals and adults. Far-reaching rights in program access and employment practices for individuals with disabilities. |
| 1974 | PL 93-380: Amendment to the Elementary and Secondary Education Act that formed the foundation for PL 94-142. Umbrella legislation directing states to provide full education for students with disabilities, ages birth through 21 years, to guarantee their rights and parents' rights during the assessment process, and to place students in regular education classes whenever possible. |
| 1974 | Education of All Handicapped Children Act (PL 94-142): Combined all previous legislation and included consideration of outcomes from court cases concerning students with disabilities. Provided specifics of how to determine eligibility for services, design individual educational and behavioral programs, and ensure appropriate implementation. |
| 1984 | PL 98-199: Amended PL 90-538 (Handicapped Children's Early Assistance Act) to provide funds for planning statewide services for children with disabilities, ages birth through five years. |
| 1986 | PL 99-457: Amended the Education of the Handicapped Act to require states to provide services for preschool children and incentives to develop programs for the birth through two years population. |
| 1990 | The Americans with Disabilities Act (PL 101-336): Directed toward adults, attacking discrimination in the workplace. Employers cannot consider the disability when hiring. Required businesses with fifteen or more employees to provide specialized equipment for workers with disabilities. Underscored broad-based facilities access. |
| 1990 | PL 101-476: EHA was renamed Individuals with Disabilities Education Act, or IDEA. The definition of disability was broadened to include autism and traumatic brain injury. Additional related services were added, including therapeutic recreation, social work, rehabilitation counseling, and assistive technology. |
| 1994 | Congress began review of recommendation for IDEA's reauthorization, including a specification addressing the inclusion of students with disabilities in regular classrooms. |

The necessity of training teachers is critical to the success of working with students with disabilities. PL 85-926 (1958) and PL 88-164 (1963) provided grants to states and universities to train college professors, as well as teachers, and to establish research and demonstration projects.

Importantly, the Vocational Rehabilitation Act of 1973 prohibited agencies receiving federal assistance from discriminating against individuals with disabilities (Section 504). This act established programs for vocational rehabilitation and independent living, banned discrimination in the workplace, created a federal board to oversee access to transportation and public facilities, and required federal agencies and contractors to establish affirmative action policies. The *Rehabilitation Act* legislated the right for individuals with disabilities to receive equitable treatment in the community and established penalties for continued discrimination.

## The Education of All Handicapped Children Act

"What about PL 94-142?" asks John. "That's the law we hear about the most."

You're right. By far the most powerful law impacting the rights of children with disabilities in public schools has been The Education of All Handicapped Children Act, or PL 94-142. As amended by PL 101-476, the name was changed to the **Individuals with Disabilites Education Act (IDEA)**. The law eliminated the exclusion of children with disabilities from the education system, noting that no children would be considered uneducable. It also prohibited charging parents for educational services necessitated by the child's disabling condition and provided children with a free public education.

Walker (in Gartner & Lipsky, 1987) overviews six key principles underscoring the law:

1. access to the public education system;
2. individualization of service provision;
3. the concept of **least restrictive environment**;
4. the expanded scope of services to be provided by public schools, including procedural requirements;
5. general guidelines for identification of disabilities; and
6. primary state and local responsibilities for enactment of the law.

Dr. Mirales adds, "The individualized education plan (IEP) has become one of the most noticeable changes in programming for students with special needs. It requires a multidisciplinary individualized evaluation of the student to explore the nature of the disability. From there, a team of educators designs a plan to meet each student's educational needs. We discourage team members from relying on a single approach to teach students in a broadly defined category such as learning disabilities or hearing impairment. Instead, each student's unique needs should determine the nature of the plan and follow-up teaching procedures."

**Individuals with Disabilities Education Act (IDEA)**—formerly The Education of All Handicapped Children Act (PL 94-142); a law that eliminated the exclusion of children with disabilities from the education system.

**least restrictive environment**—the most normalized educational setting appropriate for a student.

## Normalization

normalization—the belief that all individuals with disabilities should be provided the opportunity to live as normally as possible in daily society.

Humane in its intent, IDEA was underscored by the philosophy of **normalization** earlier enacted in Scandinavia and Canada and espoused in the United States by Wolfensberger in the 1960s and early 1970s. Normalization is the belief that all individuals with disabilities should be encouraged and provided the opportunity to live as normally as possible in daily society. Artificial barriers created by lower societal expectations should be avoided, and individuals with disabilities should be permitted to be full participants in all social, educational, and vocational settings (Wolfensberger, 1971).

Interpretation of the normalization principle has varied. Educators disagree whether this philosophy means inclusion in every normalized societal setting, such as regular education classrooms, or whether it means providing for acceptance and support societally, although education or training programs may need to be in specialized settings away from the **mainstream** at times.

mainstream—the typical educational milieu.

Despite this disagreement, an outcome of the normalization philosophy within IDEA has been the concept of least restrictive environment, emphasizing the placement of students with disabilities in regular education settings whenever possible. Those students requiring additional assistance within the regular classroom receive supportive services allowing fuller participation. Such services range across a variety of areas, including speech and language therapy, psychological supports, and physical therapy. Students are placed outside the general education classroom only when their needs cannot be met adequately. This least restrictive emphasis has provided the framework for later expansion into a more inclusive system.

## Due Process

"As I participate in committee meetings, I hear a lot of discussion about parents' due process rights," observes John. "Exactly what do these include?"

due process—legal proceedings and policies that establish rules; in education, designed to ensure equal opportunities in education for all students with disabilities.

IDEA included due process procedures allowing parents to be an integral part of the assessment and placement process and establishing their rights as advocates for their child, including methods for legal appeal. To ensure the system was not abused, ceiling numbers for funding were established at 12 percent of the total school population to be eligible for services, with 2 percent defined as learning disabled. This latter figure became one of the most problematic as progressively more students qualified for services in this category (Gartner & Lipsky, 1987).

IDEA has had tremendous impact on the structure of the educational system. As Skrtic (1986) indicates, the special education/general education relationship was altered by extending certain constitutional rights and procedural safeguards, including due process, to the disabled and their families.

It is important to note that the law did not mandate the development of a separate educational system for disabled students (Gartner & Lipsky, 1987). Its designers did not anticipate the likelihood that the delivery system in public schools might develop as segregated services, keeping students isolated from the mainstream. However, because of a history of parallel rather than unitary structures in general and special education, a **continuum of services** was developed that often was delivered outside general education, in separate classrooms or even separate facilities. The assumption continued that there were distinct groups of children, with and without disabilities, requiring divided funding patterns, organization, and service delivery systems (Walker, 1987).

**continuum of services—** instructional and placement options available to serve students with disabilities.

The law has provided the basis for a dramatic increase in funds for programming for students with disabilities. Billions of dollars have been spent serving millions of students in special education since the passage of PL 94-142. All states have responded through the expansion of services and there has been a major philosophical shift toward the need to provide programming for students with disabilities. Parental rights have been guaranteed and most importantly, the need to educate all children has been acknowledged.

***Success of the Law***    "How well has all this worked?" asks Maura Hayes. "I have seen some of my third-graders blossom with the extra attention of special education, while other students are terribly embarrassed at having to leave the classroom in front of their peers."

Maura's question hits at the heart of the controversy. As increasingly more students qualify for services, questions about success of special education efforts during the past two decades have proliferated. In placement of students, disagreements have most often occurred regarding definitions and categories of disability as well as where students should receive services. An ever-increasing amount of referrals has brought a variety of concerns about how to best serve students, and if the prevalence of students at-risk is adding confusion to the numbers of students who actually have disabilities.

Numbers of children raised in poverty or lacking early stimulation are predicted to continue to increase into the next century, adding to the rosters of students with special needs (Reynolds, Wang, & Walberg, 1987; Yates, 1992). Chapter I programs have faced cutbacks in numbers of students served, excluding many students who require **remedial services**. Currently, these students are referred to special education. Ethnic minority children from nondominant-English homes increasingly attend schools that are unprepared to meet their needs. Emphasis on accountability and high standardized test scores has resulted in greater numbers of referrals of "low achievers" to special education, excluding their skill levels from test-score analyses that might reflect on teachers or districts. As educators become increasingly concerned about international competition and preparing students to keep up with rising standards, more students who do not perform at high achievement levels are categorized as learning disabled,

**remedial services—**efforts made to correct a deficiency through education.

cognitively disabled, or behaviorally disordered (Gartner & Lipsky, 1987).

IDEA states that removal from the regular education environment is to occur "only when the nature and severity of the handicap is such that education in regular education classes with the use of supplementary aids cannot be achieved satisfactorily."

Mort Stern asks, "Does this mean students who demonstrate extreme behavioral disorders resulting in aggressive acts towards peers or my faculty should be included? And what about those students with attention spans so brief that they frequently distract themselves and others? Or students whose learning progress is so slow that they constantly lag behind? How much inclusion is enough? How much is too much?"

## CONTINUUM OF SERVICES

pull-out—when a student leaves the regular classroom environment to go to another classroom or area for instruction.

The answers to Mort's questions and others will greatly depend on the skills and desires of the individual teacher and school district to accommodate students with disabilities into individual classrooms. As indicated in Figure 1–1, more than two-thirds of students with disabilities already are served primarily in regular education classrooms. The majority of special education services have been in the pull-out direction, in which students leave the room for one or more hours at a time to receive direct instruction in a specialized environment. Approximately one-fourth of students with disabilities attend separate, or self-contained, classes on their school campus, and only about 6 percent are placed in separate environments off the school campus, such

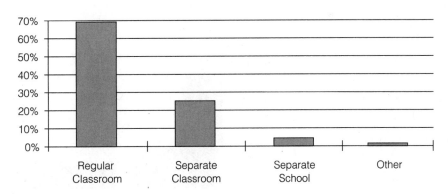

**Figure 1–1**   Special Education Placement Percentages (*Source:* Adapted from the 15th Annual Report to Congress, 1993)

as institutions, hospitals, or homebound settings (15th Annual Report to Congress, 1993).

Within these varied placements, the numbers of students served by category of disability is indicated in Figure 1–2. Of all students receiving special education services, one-half are learning disabled, by far the most frequent referral category. Slightly more than 2 percent of students referred demonstrated speech impairments, and 1 percent are diagnosed as cognitively disabled. Although understandably of concern to classroom teachers, fewer than 1 percent of students have serious behavioral disorders or other types of disabilities.

"How well have these students done with the traditional types of special education placements before inclusion?" asks John.

Despite extensive funding and special education supports, a large number of students have not graduated high school. As indicated in Figure 1–3, approximately one-third of students with learning disabilities or cognitive disabilities do not complete their schooling. Significantly, more than one-half of students with serious behavioral disorders do not graduate. The prognosis is poor for the success of students with disabilities who do not have high school diplomas and sufficient academic skills, especially in reading. When compounded by emotional problems or low adaptive skills common to students with cognitive disabilities, their ability to live independently and support themselves as adults is diminished.

"I'm bothered by the trend toward developing more pull-out programs," notes Dr. Mirales. "I've always felt that adapting the environment to the student through specialized intervention methods is more logical and sensitive than forcing the student to leave in failure. I've noticed that with increasingly more students being referred for special education services, we've concentrated too much on which type of classroom placement and too little on how to best teach students."

This is an interesting point. Placement continues to be a primary legal and

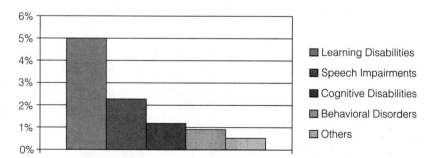

**Figure 1–2**  Disabilities of Students Receiving Special Education (Within Population of All Students Ages 6–17) (*Source:* Adapted from the 15th Annual Report to Congress, 1993)

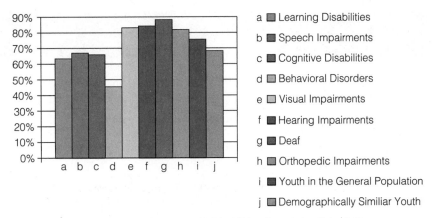

**Figure 1–3**   Percentages of Students with Disabilities Completing School *(Source: Adapted from Wagner, 1991)*

educational concern. The type of special education setting available often stems from an expansion of the continuum of services model (Deno, 1970).

Table 1–4 presents this expanded continuum, as well as the types of student disabilities served and teacher roles. It has been the framework for traditional service delivery to students with disabilities in most states and districts, providing a range of services from full participation in the mainstream environment to a totally segregated environment. At the most integrated level, students with the mildest of disabilities remain full-time in the regular classroom, with their education designed, managed, and monitored by their teacher. While most students enrolled in special education have participated in regular education for the majority of their day, they usually have required additional instruction by specialists, often because the regular education teacher has lacked the training or desire to work with atypical learners.

The next four levels of the continuum have been the most popular. The **Consulting Teacher** model has been effective with students who do not require extensive remedial or compensatory work, but need ongoing collaboration between specialist and generalist teachers to give them the supports to be successful in the mainstream. Without having to leave the classroom, teachers of gifted students with learning disabilities or of students with mild academic or behavior problems often are helped by consultants.

"Kara has been served by a Consulting Teacher for three years now," Mort reflects. "An extremely bright student, Kara has many **Attention Deficit Hyperactivity Disorder (ADHD)** behaviors. Without structure and teacher direction, I don't believe she'd ever start classwork with the necessary materials or be able to stay on task. The Consulting Teacher has advised Kara's teachers to avoid frustration and support organization by structuring Kara's assignments into smaller tasks and providing immediate reinforcement for work completion."

**Consulting Teacher**—educators who are trained to interact with and advise regular classroom teachers and others involved in instructing or working with exceptional children.

**Attention Deficit Hyperactivity Disorder (ADHD)**—a disorder characterized by difficulty in sustaining attention, impulsivity, distractibility, and excessive movement.

## Table 1–4
## Traditional Placements for Students Receiving Special Services

| Placement | Students Served | Educator Roles |
|---|---|---|
| *Full-Time Regular Class* | | |
| Total integration of students with disabilities | Students with mild learning, behavioral, and physical disorders | Regular teacher assumes full instructional responsibilities without requiring specialist assistance |
| *Regular Class/Consultation* | | |
| Students remain in class full time with occasional support | Students with mild/moderate learning and behavioral disorders | Specialist assists regular teacher in program design and implementation by meeting at scheduled intervals to discuss academic/behaviorial modifications |
| *Itinerant Teacher* | | |
| Students receive primary instruction in regular class, with additional therapy and specialized support as required | Students with disabilities in behavior, communication, vision and hearing, orthopedics | Specialist meets with student to provide training or therapy; specialist meets with regular teacher to design improved instructional materials and teaching strategies |
| *Content Mastery* | | |
| Students remain in regular class until requiring additional support to complete assignments/exams; students attend Content Mastery for modifications | Students with mild/moderate learning problems requiring immediate support to complete regular class assignments | Regular teacher provides lesson plans/exams to specialist who uses additional explanation or instructional resources |
| *Resource Class* | | |
| Students spend majority of day in class leaving for scheduled classes with specialist for academic/behavioral intervention | Students with mild/moderate learning and/or behavioral disabilities requiring academic remediation or support in communication, behavioral, or organization skills | Specialist meets with small groups of students for direct intervention; specialist consults with regular teacher or additional teaching strategies to support student success |
| *Self-Contained Class* | | |
| Students spend majority of day in segregated, special education unit on regular campus; may interact with typical students in unstructured activities or specified classes | Students with moderate/severe learning, behavioral, and/or physical disabilities | Specialist is full-day teacher; collaboration with regular teachers and school administrators for integration of students |
| *Special School* | | |
| Students attend all-day classes on a totally separate campus | Students with severe learning, behavioral, and/or physical disabilities | Specialist team provides complete instruction |

*(Continued)*

Table 1–4 *(Continued)*

| Placement | Students Served | Educator Roles |
|---|---|---|
| *Special School* | | |
| Students attend all-day classes on a totally separate campus | Students with severe learning, behavioral, and/or physical disabilities | Specialist team provides complete instruction |
| *Hospital/Homebound* | | |
| For a brief period, students unable to participate in regular/special education setting; receive instruction from specialist at hospital or home | Students undergoing medical treatment, recovery from accident or trauma, or physically or emotionally disabling condition | Specialist contacts teachers on regular/special campus for records and continuity of instruction; all teachers consult on student progress and optimal means of school reentry |
| *Residential Care* | | |
| Students live away from home and receive total schooling/therapy in special facility; may be integrated into community activities, (i.e. shopping, cultural events), but education is completely separate | Students with most severe/profound cognitive disabilities, behavior disorders, or multi-disabling conditions | Specialists/residence teams create total programs for self-help, language, behavioral, cognitive, and physical needs; provision of a non-academic curriculum to meet personal and social goals |

**Itinerant Teacher**—an educator trained to provide direct services to students with disabilities and their teachers, visiting them in their classroom on a regular basis.

The **Itinerant Teacher** model has served a different population of students in special education. Similar to the other less-segregated levels, the student receives the majority of instruction in the mainstream class. However, the student may have needs that cannot be met easily by nonspecialists, such as therapy or intensive individualization of instruction. For example, a student requiring speech and language therapy might meet in a small-group setting with a specialist outside the regular classroom several times weekly. Or an adolescent with a visual impairment would meet twice weekly with a mobility specialist to learn the most independent and expedient ways to walk around a new high school. As needed, each of these specialists contacts the student's classroom teacher to discuss follow-up techniques to allow for reinforcement and improved success in the regular education environment. Students with behavioral problems may meet with a psychologist or psychiatrist; those with physical disabilities, with a physical therapist; others with communications disorders, with a speech and language therapist.

**Content Mastery Center**—educational setting designed for students experiencing occasional difficulty in understanding the content or being able to perform assignments; this placement provides supportive instruction.

One of the settings that has gained widespread popularity in the Southwest has been the **Content Mastery Center.** Designed for students experiencing occasional difficulty in understanding the content or being able to perform assignments, this placement has provided supportive instruction. The student remains in the regular education class for the lesson taught to the large or small group. When the student requires additional clarification, is unable to read the text of the reinforcement assignment, or needs additional time

Popular in many regions, Content Mastery allows students to leave their classroom when they need one-on-one support from a specialist to fully understand the lesson.

or modifications to complete the exam, he leaves the room for the Content Mastery Center. The special education teacher at the center has a copy of the regular education teacher's weekly lesson plans for the student, as well as supplemental activities or the exam. Instructional resources, such as taped books, are also available for nonreaders. This model has been used extensively with middle and high school students and in some elementary schools after third grade, when the student has received primary reading and computational instruction. While initiated for special education students, a number of schools have expanded its use as a tutoring laboratory for any student experiencing difficulty (Waldron, 1992a).

"I visited a Content Mastery Center in Carrollton-Farmers Branch district in Texas," added Dr. Mirales. "I was surprised by the way students flowed between regular education and special education classes. Other schools in that region are now establishing these classes for nonspecial education students who need immediate support to understand the material. I just wish there were a way to provide these wonderful supports without students having to leave the room at all."

**Resource Room**—a separate classroom in which the student receives remedial or compensatory assistance from a specialist one to three hours daily.

Some students require more extensive support than Content Mastery and leave the class completely during instruction for a **Resource Room**. From one to three hours daily, students receive remedial or compensatory assistance from a specialist. In small groups, students work on academic and/or behavioral problems. Teresa Fuentes notes, "An important part of the success of this model at Jackson Elementary has been the ability of the regular and special education teachers to work together. If I know the grade-level curriculum and the teacher's approach as well as weekly plans, I can teach the students in a different way but still be sure they get all the information. It's when scheduling problems cause me to group students with different needs and grade levels in the same room that I have real problems. I try not just to tutor kids, but to teach them through their learning strengths—a challenge!" The Resource Room has been the most popular model in special education, especially for students with mild to moderate learning or behavioral disorders. At the secondary level, it has more recently been replaced at many schools by Content Mastery Centers because of students' needs to cover the same curriculum as their peers.

**self-contained**—a placement separate from the regular classroom in which the student spends most of the day with the special education teacher.

When this degree of intervention is not enough because of more extensive learning or behavioral problems, often students are placed in a **self-contained** unit, where they spend most of the day with the special education teacher, much less frequently participating in general education activities. Often this placement has been used with students with moderate to severe learning, behavioral, and/or physical disabilities. The specialist works with regular teachers and school administrators to integrate students in specified activities, such as lunch, recess, and concerts or field trips, as well as classes such as art, music, and physical education. Some students are included in academic classes, such as reading or social studies, as their skill level and/or behavior more closely matches that of others in those settings.

Elena interjects, "At the secondary level, we've been cutting back on the number of these special classes. While it's easier for us to meet students' specialized needs in a smaller group and with a specialist teacher, often the students are teased by their peers or treated as outcasts. Over the years we've also learned that placing students together because their behaviors are socially unacceptable removes them from the very role models they need. It's hard to learn how to behave appropriately if everyone in your class is inappropriate."

**special school**—a separate school campus for students with more severe disabilities.

Even more extreme is placement in the **special school** environment. Here the student demonstrates a more severe disability and rarely attends school on the regular education campus. Students in these segregated environments tend to have experienced failure within regular education. Often, they demonstrate a medical or multidisabling condition that requires intensive input by teams of specialists, making participation on a regular campus more difficult. Examples might include students with extremely physically aggressive behaviors, medically fragile conditions, or sensory disabilities, such as deafness or blindness, combined with severe learning and behavior problems. Frequently, instruction and therapy are the result of combined teams of specialists, therapists, and medical or psychological practitioners. Most of these students are integrated into the community for cultural, leisure, or vocational activities, but have little interaction with mainstream school campuses.

"These students will be among the most challenging as we move toward inclusive classes," John notes. "For example, we have a separate campus across town for students who have been expelled from their neighborhood school because of substance abuse, carrying weapons, and problems with the law. I know many of them are from problem homes and lack positive role models, but it is going to be difficult to expect teachers to welcome them back into classes. Yet, drop-out rates on their campus are high; and we know that with support we could really help some of these kids. It's a real dilemma."

**hospital-homebound**—students who are removed from their regular school environment for brief periods of time due to needed recovery from an accident, intensive medical treatment, or a physically or emotionally disabling condition.

**Hospital-homebound** students are removed from their regular school environment for brief periods of time. They may be recovering from an accident, receiving intensive medical treatment such as dialysis or chemotherapy, or suffering from a physically or emotionally disabling condition. The specialist meets with the student at the home or medical facility for continuity of academic instruction until the student can return to the regular or special school placement. It is important for teachers to work together to sustain the student academically and psychologically while undergoing treatment to make a smoother transition between environments. This placement is designed to be temporary.

**residential care facility**—placement that removes the student from home because of the assessed need for a totally therapeutic environment.

Placement in a **residential care facility** removes the student from home because of the assessed need for a totally therapeutic environment. This setting has most often been for students with severe cognitive disabilities, multidisabling conditions, or extreme behavioral disorders and few adaptive skills to support their independent functioning in society. The movement towards **deinstitutionalization** has dramatically changed the face of these facilities from large, impersonal, hospital-like buildings to community-based group homes with smaller numbers, warmer ambience, and more personalized attention. Emphasis on total programming has allowed for training in a variety of areas, from community survival skills, to personal hygiene and acceptable interactive behaviors. The curriculum is less academic than found in other settings.

**deinstitutionalization**—a movement toward removing individuals with disabilities from hospital-like buildings to community-based group homes.

The current trend towards an expanded concept of the least restrictive environment would change this continuum to bring more supportive service delivery directly to the regular classroom and would avoid many pull-out programs. Supporters of change express a desire to have special education students avoid missing valuable instruction in regular education and the potential embarrassment of their peers observing them leave the room. Fewer students would participate in separate classes and settings, the preferred location for instruction being the regular class, with modifications made only as necessary.

## SUMMARY

Chapter 1 described the exciting but painful changes special education is experiencing. It is set in the backdrop of Westside School District, a typical system whose administrators have decided to implement a more inclusive model of serving students with special needs. Westside officials have realized that many viewpoints will have to change, or at least to become more flexible, for students to experience success.

When considering the history of inclusive trends, attitudes of the nineteenth century are particularly important. Reformers such as Jean Marc Gaspard Itard (1775–1838), Edouard Seguin (1812–1880), and Maria Montessori (1870–1952), were pioneers who demonstrated that students with disabilities could be educated. Others such as Thomas Hopkins Gallaudet (1787–1851) and Samuel Gridley Howe (1801–1876) developed specific methods for intervention.

Despite burgeoning professional interest, most children with disabilities remained at home with no educational opportunities and little societal expectation that they would benefit from an education. Especially for individuals with cognitive disabilities, institutions expanded, becoming basic care facilities without the promise of habilitation. Many patients were treated with extreme cruelty, a trend that continued through the early twentieth century.

Common schools began their expansion, with parents encouraged to support the schools through involvement. Yet, educators did not allow students with special needs, such as the sensory, cognitively, or orthopedically impaired, to attend general education classes or schools. Parents of students with special needs were also excluded from the mainstream, cultivating a sense that they should hide or feel embarrassed about their children.

The twentieth century saw the development of community homes, with the continuation of institutions for individuals with cognitive and multiple disabilities living in extremely rural areas. Within cities, educators expanded day-school programs for the mildly and moderately impaired. Professionals encouraged parents in movements against cruel treatment of persons with disabilities.

Subsequent litigation became the signature of modern times, with key cases such as *Brown v. Board of Education; Pennsylvania Association for Retarded Children v. Commonwealth of Pennsylvania; Mills v. DC Board of Education* setting precedents that children with disabilities could and should benefit from an education. The *Vocational Rehabilitation Act of 1973* prohibited discrimination by agencies receiving public assistance.

The most powerful law appeared in 1974: The Education of All Handicapped Children Act (PL 94-142), later renamed the Individuals with Disabilities Education Act. Gains included access to the public education system; the preparation of individual education plans; expanded scope of services, with procedural requirements; general guidelines for identification of disabilities; primary state and local responsibilities for law enactment; and, importantly, the concept of least restrictive environment.

Chapter 1 discussed a number of problems with consistency in enacting the law, such as determining eligibility criteria and a tendency to exclude rather than include students in regular education classes. One of the most problematic areas was the determination of which environments are least restrictive for students with special needs.

The continuum of special education services has ranged from full participation in the regular education classroom to Resource and Content Mastery attendance or participation in more segregated placements such as special classes and schools. Most students have been forced to leave their regular classes, at times embarrassing themselves in front of their peers as well as missing valuable information, to attend special classes.

Is there a better way? Is there a chance of meeting students' needs to be educated together while not prioritizing the needs of some students over others? The remaining chapters will explore concerns and options as systems weave their way towards inclusive education.

## CASE STUDY: *Elementary*

Parents have been critical in determining educational directions for their children, usually because they know their children best and tend to be their strongest advocates. However, children and family situations differ, and parents don't always agree with administrative decisions, especially where change is involved.

**You are the parent of Brian, a third-grader in Maura Hayes's class this year. Brian is an average student, shy in his demeanor, the very kind of child whom you feel does not get enough attention in school these days. Brian's reading is fair, but not really fluent. His skills have not been strong enough to qualify him for the school gifted program, or weak enough to send him to the remedial teacher. As you've often said, "He just isn't special enough to anyone else." You are depending on Mrs. Hayes to work closely with him this year to give him the extra reading support he needs.**

**Now you've learned that the district has decided to include some students with disabilities in his class on a full-time basis. While Mrs. Hayes is a good teacher, she does not seem really enthused about this, and has shrugged and said, "We'll all have to work together to make it happen."**

**Although the program is to begin soon, no one seems to know all the details. You worry about this constantly and notice that Brian seems concerned about it too.**

These concerns are very common to parents of regular education students when they first hear about inclusion. Please respond to the following questions as a parent of a typical student.

1. What are your primary concerns about inclusion of students with disabilities in Brian's class?

2. What can the school do from the onset of the new inclusion program to make you and other parents more supportive?

3. What can Mrs. Hayes do to make the inclusion initiative work best with her students?

4. What kind of support must Mrs. Hayes have so you will be satisfied that Brian's needs can be met?

5. What can you do as a parent of a typical student to help inclusion work well for all the children in the class?

## CASE STUDY: *Secondary*

It was really difficult for your family when Katie was born with Down syndrome. She has done so well over these years, likely a result of all of the special programs, from speech and language therapy to Special Olympics.

At 15, she seems generally well-adjusted. Her academic levels have been higher than expected as a result of the intensive work you've done at home. She's reading at a sixth-grade level and her math computation is just slightly lower. She has been in self-contained special education classes for academic areas and for the past two years has participated in regular education for music and art.

Sadly, she has no friends in her non-special education classes. She does have a few friends in special education, but when she associates with them, typical students call her "Retard" and hurt her feelings. Lately she has been complaining more about being lonely.

Now you have a real dilemma. As part of the district's new inclusion movement, the counselor has suggested also placing Katie in regular education for English and history. He said she will be given help she needs to complete reading and writing assignments and she would remain full-time in the room to complete her work. While this sounds like a parent's dream after years of her attendance in special classes, you have some strong fears about the success of this placement.

---

As Katie's parent, develop a plan to enable you to allay these concerns and make the best decision about her academic placement. Respond to the following questions as you consider her options.

1. Your concerns for Katie are different since she has become an adolescent. What specific problems do you fear she may encounter in an inclusive classroom?

2. What will you do if you and Katie disagree on the better placement being special or general education?

3. Under the new plan, Katie will continue in special classes for science and math until her skills are strong enough for her to attend regular education in these areas. Will a partial integration into regular classes be confusing for her? Will she be embarrassed in front of peers as she returns to special classes for part of the day? How might the school handle this situation?

4. You are not an educator and do not understand how she will be able to keep up with her tenth-grade peers while reading on a sixth-grade level. How will you communicate this concern to her teachers without sounding negative and nonsupportive of their efforts?

5. What can you do to help Katie be socially integrated into the class so she can develop friends and not be stigmatized?

# 2

# THE INCLUSIVE ARGUMENT

In Mort's elementary setting as well as Elena's high school, the familiar concept of *mainstreaming* has encouraged placement of students with disabilities into regular education classes. "Hasn't mainstreaming worked?" asks John Robinson. "I'm confused about why we're moving toward inclusion since I've had some special education students in my classes for quite a while now."

Years of research have produced unclear results of the effectiveness of mainstreaming. Researchers have claimed a variety of outcomes: Some students demonstrated improved academic skills in general education classes, but were shunned socially by typical peers. Others stated that academic progress was minimal, but that students' self-concepts were strengthened by not experiencing the effects of segregation.

Additionally, the results of approximately thirty years of research into successful teaching methods for students with disabilities has been inconclusive, largely because researchers have emphasized the type of instructional placement of students (e.g., regular education class with resource vs. self-contained class) over what actually happens in the classroom. Often, issues such as specific teaching methods, grouping arrangements, and behavioral management structures were ignored in early research, while these issues likely are the very core of teaching-learning effectiveness (Waldron, 1992b). Therefore, specific methods of supporting mainstreaming in the regular classroom often have been lacking.

Maura Hayes adds, "Even with optimal supportive services and teacher involvement, some students have not performed well in general education. Often their extreme behaviors and academic skills are so far below those of their peers that we teachers lacked training to help them. We've had to return some students to self-contained classes to meet their needs. It's really frustrating when we feel we can't help them."

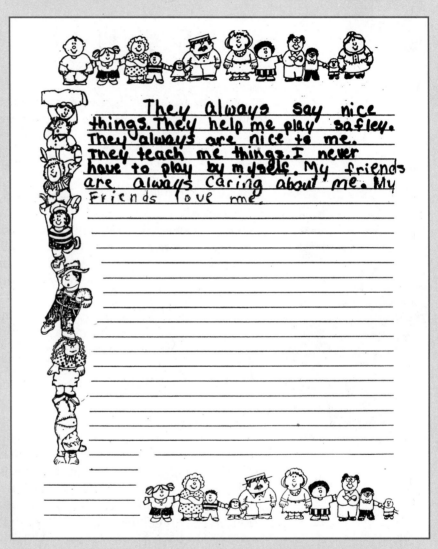

They always say nice things. They help me play safley. They always are nice to me. They teach me things. I never have to play by myself. My friends are always caring about me. My Friends love me.

These words were dictated to a classmate by a student with special needs who has been included in regular education for the first time. Reprinted with parental permission.

# THE REGULAR EDUCATION INITIATIVE

It is not surprising that as in many districts, Westside teachers and administrators are uneasy with reconceptualizing mainstreaming into inclusion. Mike Gonzales asks, "When did the change occur calling for a much greater inclusion of students with more disabilities in the regular classroom?"

The most noted change occurred in the mid-1980s, when a large cumulative body of research questioned the effectiveness of special education programming during the previous decade and called for a reassessment of educational service delivery based on a lack of excellence (Audette & Algozzine, 1992). Additionally, from a humane viewpoint, philosophical arguments of many special education professionals and parents found removal of students with special needs from regular education into segregated environments to be morally indefensible (Skrtic, 1991).

Former Assistant Secretary of Education Madeline Will presented some influential speeches and articles (1984, 1986) supporting a restructuring of general and special education. Whereas the two systems had developed in a parallel course with some interaction through mainstreaming, the new movement, called **Regular Education Initiative**, proposed their combination into one educational system for all children. This movement was not an extension of mainstreaming, but an attempt to totally redesign both the existing general and special education systems (Wiener, 1992).

**Regular Education Initiative—**national movement toward combining special and regular education into one educational system for all children.

This change would mean that instead of there being separate teaching and administrative staffs and funding sources, the systems would merge. All educators would become more responsible for students with disabilities, as well as those who are bilingual, or economically or socially disadvantaged. Rarely would students with special needs ever leave the classroom. This proposal prompted heated debate and became central to the current controversy over inclusion.

## Regular Education Initiative Proponents

Mike Gonzales contends, "As a parent of a gifted student, I can't understand how these changes will help him or anyone else."

"Mike, my office did some research on this for the superintendent," Dr. Mirales responds, "and I'd like to share with you what we found. Our chart for the next Board meeting (Table 2–1) states the primary arguments of supporters of the Regular Education Initiative. There are a number of issues advocated as reasons for placing students with disabilities in general education classes. Many of these concerns have the philosophical basis of the first point: that segregation of any student is indefensible, both morally and legally, which was the concept of separate not being equal underscored in

## Table 2–1
## Regular Education Initiative: Proponents' Arguments*

1. Exclusion of students from regular education classrooms is morally indefensible.

2. The existence of a separate special education system discourages regular education from taking responsibility for all students.

3. Labeling students makes it appear that the student or the disability is the cause of educational problems instead of the regular education system's limitations. Excluding students from the classroom supports this belief that any difficulties are their fault.

4. Regular educators have become increasingly threatened by students with disabilities in their classrooms. They need more exposure for both the teacher and student to experience success.

5. Years of separate programs have not demonstrated increased success in teaching academic skills to learners with special needs.

6. There is no need for all teachers to be trained to work with students with unique learning styles as long as these students are excluded from the regular classroom.

7. Good teaching methods are successful with all students. Students with disabilities may require adaptations of content or techniques, but can benefit from good teaching as much as typical students. Similarly, typical students can benefit from adaptations for students with disabilities.

8. Teaching all students in the same environment underscores the use of technology and expanded resources, benefitting everyone.

9. Separate systems require labeling of students. These labels are difficult to remove once they are assigned.

10. Far beyond original intentions, too many students have been labeled as "disabled." This excessive labeling has been true especially with students with learning disabilities.

11. Self–esteem of students is impaired by exclusion.

12. The ability of students to function in normalized adult environments is hindered by the lack of early interactions with typical peers.

13. Too much time is wasted in determining eligibility for services and too little time is spent actually serving students.

14. Special education programs are disjointed, often resulting in different administrators and funding sources based on categories of students served.

15. Pull-out programs fragment instruction for students, causing them to miss the very instruction they need in the regular education classroom.

*These arguments reflect the discussions of Skrtic, 1986, 1991; Audette & Algozzine, 1992; Reynolds, Wang, & Walberg, 1987; Gartner & Lipsky, 1987; Stainback & Stainback, 1984.

the *Brown vs. Board of Education (1954)* decision. While proponents acknowledge that many regular educators do not want students with disabilities in their classes, they point out that the existence of a separate system allows these teachers to give up their responsibility to teach children who may learn or behave differently, a form of **discrimination**."

**discrimination**—denying equal opportunity due to physical or personal characteristics.

Dr. Mirales is signifying the heart of the problem. Scholars such as Skrtic (1986) claim the current exclusive philosophy is supported by the tendency to identify the student as the cause of the problem, not the dysfunctional educational system. Students are assessed to examine the extent of their atypical behavior and then excluded by degree of assumed pathology, from mild (a Resource Room placement) to severe (a separate campus setting). This process allows the general educational organization to place blame on the students for learning or behavior problems and to relinquish responsibility for their education. Unfortunately, this process also prevents the system from examining its limitations and obligations to all students, freeing itself from accountability.

"Many teachers I talk to don't want kids with disabilities in their rooms," Mike responds. Because regular educators have been able to exclude many special education students from their classes, often they are threatened by the concept of inclusion. Uncertainty and discrimination are built on a lack

Socialization, resulting in improved self-esteem, is one of the most significant factors for educators favoring inclusion.

of positive experiences. Supporters of inclusion feel that giving these teachers more exposure to diverse learners would reduce their fears and allow them to experience unanticipated successes. Each success would then build on a willingness to work with a wider variety of students in the future.

Proponents note that many regular educators feel insecure in teaching students with disabilities because of a lack of training in specialized methods. They emphasize dual irony here: Little academic success has been demonstrated by these students in special education classes historically, even when taught by trained specialists, and the ability not to have these students in their classes negates any perceived need by regular educators to receive specialized training.

Supporters contend that "Good teaching is good teaching" for *all* students. The methods generalists currently find most successful in their classes will also work if adapted to individuals with special needs. They add that inclusion of learners with disabilities would necessitate increased **resources** to regular education classrooms and would encourage expansion of instructional technology as a viable support system.

**resources**—materials and equipment available for use.

Mort interrupts here. "My teachers won't easily accept these last points because they're feeling overburdened right now. But they might be more sympathetic to the feelings of the special education students. Do these students want to be included in regular education classes?"

A good question. The impact of a label of "disabled" tends to lower the **self-esteem** of students (Audette and Algozzine, 1992). As educators and parents can attest, once applied, these labels adhere with very strong glue, making them difficult to lose. There tends to be an erroneous public idea that students with disabilities do not know they are different, and that it is not as important to them to be included in school activities. Nothing could be further from the truth. From students who are severely impaired to those who are gifted or disabled, children and adolescents want to be like their peers and be accepted by them. Professionals in bilingual education often observe that children learn English most quickly on the playground instead of in the formal classroom. This occurs not so much because classroom instruction is poor, but because the need to be accepted by others is so strong that key words and terms in the new language are learned immediately to gain entrance to peer groups.

**self-esteem**—how a person feels about himself or herself.

Students with disabilities are similar in this respect. They want to be accepted, to belong, to be respected. It is not true that the more extensive the disability, the lower the appreciation students have of their own problems. Indeed, the more students are excluded because of their disabilities, the lower their esteem. The sense becomes that if everyone else feels one is not "normal," likely they are correct.

Stories abound of students attempting to disguise their differences through solutions such as painting over the glass doors in special education rooms, or completely refusing to attend special classes through fear their nondisabled peers would taunt them (Waldron, 1992a). While many students still are at the bottom of the "pecking order" in status in general education classes, they tend to prefer the social interactions with their peers over the embarrassment of separation.

"But educators are caring people who want students to feel good about themselves," observes Maura. "No one is doing this on purpose. How does this feeling of being *different* develop?"

Supporters of the Regular Education Initiative indicate that the appraisal process itself begins the stigma of separation. Because of the emphasis on meeting federal guidelines for program eligibility, assessment has almost taken on "a life of its own." Most often, students are extensively tested for hours by trained specialists such as school psychologists. These tests are usually administered in a separate room, or at times in a completely separate facility such as an appraisal center. Removal from familiar settings to a lengthy one-on-one interaction with a stranger often raises anxiety in a child or adolescent, who begins to ask, "What's wrong with me?" Even if a problem is not discovered, the student may feel that one exists.

When a student is placed in special education, only the parents and involved educators are supposed to know the diagnosis. Yet, the fact that the child leaves the regular education classroom in full observation of peers one or more times a day provides a label: *Different*. When the student returns from special education, again observed by peers, the class is usually involved in or completing an activity that the student has missed. Whether a pleasurable story enjoyed by classmates, or even a deskwork task involving practice, the perception is that the student is not smart enough to be involved. This sense becomes the basis for continued labeling. When assigned to a self-contained unit where there is little daily interaction with students in regular education, the student and peers expand their perception of deviance because the separation is more profound.

Dr. Mirales adds, "In our research, we were astonished to learn how the label 'learning disabled' has been the most extensively used, and perhaps, misused. States, and even geographically close school districts, differ in the interpretation of their assessments and the services for which individual students are eligible. Ysseldyke (1987) notes that more than 80 percent of the students in regular education could be classified as learning disabled by definitions in use. Based on this reflection, we could extrapolate that since the most popular model of service for the learning disabled is the Resource classroom, six out of thirty students might remain in the regular classroom as the other twenty-four leave for the Resource Room. Recently, I visited an elementary school where, because of scheduling, there were twenty-two students in the Resource Room during "language arts." The next room I visited was a regular fourth-grade class, where the teacher had twenty students!"

As noted in Table 2–1, proponents of the Regular Education Initiative underscore that too much time is spent determining whether students are eligible for services, and not enough attention focused on teaching to students' individual needs (Reynolds, Wang, & Walberg, 1987). While the necessity of meeting federal guidelines is paramount in most districts, the intent of IDEA has been to serve children. At times balancing what is required by the government with what is needed by the student has conflicted. Educators agree that students do not benefit by being labeled. Nor do they want to be. However, without the labeling process, the government has no basis for appropriating the resources to fund the programs.

Early supporters of normalization of environments for individuals with disabilities (Wolfensberger, 1971) noted how difficult it was for those who had been isolated as youths to function well interactively or in vocationally related tasks as adults. Indeed, the prime reason for workers with disabilities having problems or actually losing their jobs is their lack of socially acceptable personal habits and conversation. Since many of them have never been continuously exposed to normalcy, it is difficult for them to behave normally. Yet, to other workers, offensive habits are judged the result of the disability. Therefore, a person labeled "cognitively disabled" who also has received little social training and exposure to acceptable work standards will have his disability viewed as the cause of the inappropriateness instead of lack of instruction. Paucity of early interactions hinders success in normal adult environments.

Removing the sense of separatism of special education has been an important consideration of those supporting the Regular Education Initiative. This separatism is viewed as a hindrance at several levels. Pull-out programs cause a fragmentation of instruction. Not only does the student miss important information in the regular education classroom while attending a specialized setting, but also may work on academic tasks that have no relationship to what is otherwise being studied. Especially prevalent in Resource classrooms at the secondary level, where students are grouped together more for scheduling expediency than for commonality of academic or behavioral problems, special educators may teach a large-group lesson on spelling or vocabulary while a student's learning needs indicate an arithmetic disability. When not following the student's individualized plan, the teacher freely admits, "We cover math sometimes. We just can't do it all."

Even at the elementary level, this separate strain of instruction often occurs. One of Mort's best teachers, Teresa Fuentes, reports that in her Resource classroom she has students arriving simultaneously for individualized instruction in reading, handwriting, computation, and several areas of verbal language. "They don't even all come at the same time," she notes. "While they attend my class for at least an hour a day (and some for several hours scattered across the day), they arrive at different times during each hour, often disrupting others who are already at work. During my tenure at Jackson, my teaching load has increased from thirty to more than fifty students daily, and scheduling is a nightmare. So I small-group students according to areas affected by disability, such as phonics or math computation. I usually have about four groups working in different academic areas, plus a few students working by themselves because their needs are so unique. I circulate constantly and give brief directions or corrections to students, but I don't have time to provide the remediation they need. Some days I feel like I'm putting a band-aid on a broken arm instead of doing any real good."

So, the student gets further behind. Many regular and special educators in the same building share the instruction of the children but rarely, if ever, meet to discuss what they each are teaching and how they can coordinate instruction. The separatism of teachers at all instructional levels is profound. Articles describing means of collaborating appear frequently in lofty professional journals, but they rarely impact the people who need them most: teachers. Whereas the generalist teacher may feel threatened by instructing students with extreme learning and behavioral needs, often the specialist is threatened by sharing privileged information on remedial teaching strategies or **behavior management** techniques. Proponents of a unified system feel that it would force teachers to work together by sharing instead of separating students.

**behavior management**—skillfully directing a student's conduct in a positive direction.

Even at the administrative levels, separatism prevails. Funding sources are separate, with specialists often having more instructional materials, a teaching assistant, and greater opportunities for year-round schooling, field trips, and excursions. In a time of funding cuts for students in gifted/talented programs, as well as resource shortages for regular education classrooms, presumable additional funding sources make special education programs conspicuous to parents and other teachers in the building.

## Regular Education Initiative Opponents

"Dr. Mirales, in your research, surely you found a number of people who are opposed to inclusion," notes Mike. "I hear many negative comments about it from parents and teachers of students with disabilities, not just those in regular education."

"You're right, Mike. There are many strongly opposed to the momentum of the Regular Education Initiative. I've listed some of the negative viewpoints on another chart for our Board presentation. Opponents point out that the unique needs of learners with disabilities have not been served well in regular classes historically, and that if their needs had been better met there would not be as intense a need for the development of a separate system. In the past, it's true that students often failed or were ignored by teachers and peers. Some regular educators demonstrated an intolerance for difference (Kauffman, 1988). There is little to indicate that there has been significant enough change to demonstrate the possibility of success" (Kauffman, 1988; Council for Children with Behavioral Disorders, 1989).

Although the supporters claim it is important to have students placed in the least restrictive environment as a basis for normalization, opponents note that some children in special education may be more restricted. Historically,

## Table 2–2
## Regular Education Initiative: Opponents' Arguments*

1. Historically, needs of students with disabilities have not been met in regular education classes. This factor has underscored the special education movement.

2. Some students requiring special education will be more restricted in the regular education classroom, where they are rejected by others and fail to learn necessary academic and survival skills.

3. More than two-thirds of students with disabilities are already educated in regular education classes, often with support in a Resource class.

4. The long fought-after rights of parents and professionals may be lost by a re-integration of students into regular classrooms.

5. After years of effort and litigation, specific rights such as due process and individual education programs may be lost.

6. Special education funding is threatened by blending with regular education.

7. Additional monies to make the Regular Education Initiative work will not be available.

8. There are justifiable concerns regarding equity vs. excellence, wherein the education of average and gifted learners will become "watered-down" to meet the needs of learners with disabilities.

9. Regular educators have been missing from Regular Education Initiative planning. The majority of advocates have been vocal researchers and scholars from special education departments at universities.

10. The movement has been a "top-down" attempt at control from federal, state, and local agencies hoping to save money. Regular and special education teachers have not been included in planning efforts.

11. Most regular educators and administrators are not ready to meet the needs of students with special needs.

12. Regular educators are already overburdened.

13. Special educators are threatened by a lack of direction: Whom will they teach? Where will they instruct students? Will they be equal members in collaborative planning and implementation?

14. Community anger is continuing to accelerate at the perceived favoritism granted to students with special needs. Programming for these students is viewed as being at the expense of students in regular education.

15. Administrators and teachers are forced to defend special education students' participation in regular education classes to the broader community.

*These arguments reflect the discussions of Davis 1989; Skrtic, 1991; Kauffman, Gerber, & Semmel, 1988; Cruickshank, 1977; Hallahan & Kauffman, 1991.)

they have been rejected or ignored by peers and have failed to learn necessary skills for their own independence and well-being (Cruickshank, 1977).

Dr. Mirales comments, "I was really surprised to learn that more than two-thirds of students with disabilities are already educated in regular education, the majority receiving remedial or behavioral support in the Resource classroom." Opponents to the Regular Education Initiative add that while some students do receive instruction in self-contained units and separate schools, the majority of these students are below age 6 or are older teens, age groups where fewer integrated settings exist. Individuals served in these separate environments are ones whose disabilities are the most extreme and who would not have their extensive needs met easily in a regular education classroom.

"I can really understand some problems at the administrative level," Dr. Mirales adds. "There is also tremendous concern about the potential loss of services and funding for students with disabilities if the general and special education systems are blended (Skrtic, 1986). As we discussed in the history of special education, these programs were provided only after prolonged persistence by parents and professionals, often ending in the courtroom. It took years for learning disabilities to be recognized as a field, or for students with autism to receive the intense instruction they require. The type of teaching techniques research has demonstrated as effective for these groups may not be ones that the regular educator is comfortable using (such as daily drills to reinforce reading for students with learning disabilities, or redirection of students with autism who demonstrate inappropriate behaviors). The potential abolition of specialized service delivery systems would place students back into classrooms where they were poorly served initially."

Mike adds, "Some parents of students in special education are concerned about what would happen to hard-earned rights, such as due process procedures. If educators were to become involved in years of trying new ways of educating these students within the regular education classroom and if these methods were unsuccessful, what channels would remain open for parents to challenge the system? Many parents feel that supporting a system placing their children back into regular education would jeopardize their legal rights as child advocates while educators and researchers re-create efforts of the past twenty years in exploring the best teaching methods."

Additional concerns about the individualized education plan abound. One of the most significant outcomes of IDEA, this plan allows for careful consideration of the unique needs of each student with disabilities, based on assessment data, and parental and professional input. While it would be exciting for all students to have individually considered academic programs, educators gauge that outcome as unlikely because of time and expense. Parents and special educators fear that these plans are not an important part of the Regular Education Initiative and will be discontinued, causing students' unique learning needs to be overlooked in the regular classroom.

drills—repeated practice.

redirection—introducing a new behavior to guide the student toward the appropriate task.

inappropriate behaviors—actions that are not proper for the present circumstances.

Some parents and educators fear inclusion would result in funding cuts that would reduce the number of specilists working with students.

Those opposed to the initiative are also extremely concerned about what will happen to special education funding. Will it be placed in the general education fund as students participate full-time in these classes? Will it continue to be spent on students with certified needs or will it be spent in less significant areas? If the appraisal system is altered to avoid categorization of students, funding concerns will become even more pronounced with increasing possibility that monies will be used for students currently ineligible for services. Will the resources follow the student into the regular education classroom and be used for all students in that room or will resources be designated specifically for students with documented need? The fact that this question has not been suitably answered by supporters of the Regular Education Initiative is of dramatic concern to its opponents.

Elena Cuellar's concerns are also about money. "Typical of most high schools, we're supposed to teach everyone and everything," she notes. "Right now I have only two Content Mastery Centers and one Resource Room for students with academic problems. Students with extreme behaviors attend one of two self-contained units in the school, but usually only for part of the day. It's pretty apparent that the superintendent feels we'll save money by placing these students back in the regular education classes full-time, because we won't have to pay salaries for specialists to work with so few students. While the special education teachers will be used to consult with all teachers to help them with special students, he feels we can use some of the monies saved there for other programs such as AIDS prevention or substance abuse education. With so much to do in a school of 2,400 students, will we save money on inclusion?"

Elena's question triggers upset in most educators opposed to the progress of the Regular Education Initiative. They note that supportive services needed to make the changes work will actually be more, not less, expensive. With Apter High as an example, it would be physically impossible for the existing number of consulting special education teachers to support so many regular educators if students with disabilities were evenly placed among classes. To group students only within certain teachers' classes for ease of supportive services would simply re-create special rooms. Yet, in an age of funding cuts to education and observation by others of the large amounts of money dedicated to special education, it is unlikely that calls for increased funding would be met with sympathy in the educational or larger community. Many opponents feel the additional resources to make the initiative work rarely will be available (Kauffman, Gerber, & Semmel, 1988).

**equity vs. excellence**—the fear that the education of average and gifted learners will become "watered down" to meet the needs of atypical learners.

Another concern expressed by Elena's teachers involves the issue of **equity vs. excellence.** Since the addition of so many lower-income students with a previous lack of educational opportunity as well as the negative outcomes of poverty, the complexion of Apter High has been different. As recently as five years ago the primary concern was Apter's competition with Gateway High for the greater number of National Merit Finalists. Now Apter is struggling with the number of students not scoring high enough on the state-required achievement test to be able to graduate high school.

**tracking**—ability grouping.

The equity issue first became a reality when a number of parents of lower-achieving students complained about **tracking** in the school. Underscored by well-intentioned demands, schools were prompted to abandon the practice of ability-grouping, with concerns that it was another form of labeling that was difficult to escape. It seemed true that once placed in the lower track, students tended to stay there for years. While the arguments sounded humane and logical, most teachers found it much more difficult to instruct classes of students where the range of academic instruction varied from almost nonreaders to advanced readers. Since most of the research has dealt with programming at the elementary level, frequently concerns of high school educators have been overlooked (Schumaker & Deshler, 1988).

**heterogeneously**—grouping low and high achievers together.

John Robinson comments that whereas he used to have alternate books for his low-achieving English classes, since students have been grouped **heterogeneously**, all students are expected to cover the same curriculum from the same books. "I tend to water it down now," he complains. "My department chair recommended I use my students from the gifted/talented programs as tutors for students at risk. While this makes it easier for me, the students in gifted/talented have lost the enthusiasm they used to have and are bored. Frankly, so am I. We seem to be giving up the idea of academic excellence as our goal in education and replacing it with an acceptance of mediocrity in the name of fairness to all."

Educators like John are particularly concerned about the Regular Education Initiative and the reorganization of special education. Many teachers feel they are already overburdened by students with personal and family problems, that educators are being asked to cure society's ills. Frustrated by accusations that poor teaching is at the basis for lower student performance (Biklen & Zollers, 1986) and misconceptions that a combination of both equity and excellence is relatively easy to achieve, many regular educators are extremely opposed to the addition of increasingly more difficult learners to the classroom.

Teachers feel caught in a bind. Public pressures underscore the need to improve the academic levels of students. Yet teachers are being asked to accommodate more demanding students in their classes. With the inclusion of students with disabilities, overall **standardized scores** likely will decline even more. If teachers do not accept students at risk, they may be considered heartless and become the object of criticism about their inability to handle **diversity** (Davis, 1989). Teachers feel they will be blamed once again for failing to meet student needs.

Regular educators also tend to resent the **"top-down"** attempt to direct what happens in their classrooms. They note that the Regular Education Initiative has been forced on them by special education researchers and university faculty as well as by administrators who do not deal with difficult students daily. Already feeling unjustly criticized for their failure to impact illiteracy, drop-outs, and student scores, teachers complain that these additional special education mandates add more evidence that parents and other professionals are holding them responsible for broad-based problems outside their control (Davis, 1989).

John comments, "The school is only a reflection of the problems of larger society. When the family is healthy and supportive, the student learns more quickly and we can do our job. But when the home is dysfunctional or consumed by crises, the student is distracted from schoolwork and our job is incredibly difficult. Already we are overextended by the needs of regular education students who bring numerous problems. Please don't force us to add students with disabilities to our rooms. We're becoming overwhelmed."

Even opponents of the Regular Education Initiative acknowledge that these concerns can change with preparation of regular education teachers and administrators to meet the needs of students at risk. Yet they point out that such training would be extremely expensive and that there do not appear to be available funding sources. Since few schools will have enough special education teachers to **team-teach** with regular educators in each room, expanded training will be an important key to success. Currently, most teachers agree they are not prepared to deal with learners with disabilities.

Special educators also fear their loss of identity within the general education mainstream (Skrtic, 1991). Teresa Fuentes wonders what her new role will be outside the Resource class. "Direct teaching? If so, of whom—spe-

**standardized scores**—valid and reliable scores for which norms are available.

**diversity**—a characteristic that makes someone dissimilar or different.

**"top-down"**—directives from others who are perceived as having more input because of greater job status.

**team-teach**—to work together to instruct students.

cial education students or groups including non-disabled? Where will I teach? If we end pull-out programs, do I lose my room and have to travel all the time? Will I report to the special education supervisor or the principal? If I team-teach with regular class teachers, who directs the team? Who pays my salary, regular or special education?"

Mort and Elena also are concerned about how to guide community parents through the changes. Since the assumption is that services to the disabled will not be cut but will be enhanced, how will they explain this perceived programmatic favoritism? Will students with disabilities appear to receive more than typical students as they are instructed in regular education rooms, sparking additional jealousy, or will resources be reallocated, allowing their use with all students, initiating fears that special education students are being forgotten?

Additionally, the administrators will have to defend inclusive programs to concerned parents of students in regular education. It will be important for these parents to understand their children are not being forgotten and will not receive less attention. The principals themselves worry that perhaps they are asking too much of the teachers and that regular education students actually will receive fewer services than before because of the involvement of students with special needs in the classroom.

## INCLUSION

Despite these concerns of opponents of the Regular Education Initiative, an historical observation of the progress of litigation, changing sentiment, and mainstreaming make the current directions toward inclusion come as no surprise. "How is inclusion defined?" asks Maura. "At times we hear rumors that only students with mild and moderate disabilities will be placed in our classes. Then we hear that all special education students will be placed, even those with the most severe disabilities. Which of these is inclusion?" It depends.

Little has caused so much heated discussion and dissonance as the definition of inclusion and its subsequent translation into programming. Some proponents view the integration of students with mild and moderate disabilities into the educational mainstream as inclusion, while others call for a vastly more extensive integration of students with severe disabilities into regular education classrooms.

Table 2–3 outlines the four broad levels of inclusion from the initial proposals in the literature. The commonality of their responses is the belief that all students with disabilities should be served in their home schools on the same campuses as peers. Additionally, students not categorized as

**Table 2–3
Levels of Inclusion***

*Level I*

> Students with mild disabilities participate full-time in regular education classrooms. Students with moderate to profound disabilities attend separate classrooms on the regular education campus.
>
> (Lilly & Pugach; in Lilly, 1986)

*Level II*

> Students with mild and moderate disabilities participate full-time in regular education classrooms, with the elimination of all pull-out programs. Students with severe or profound disabilities would be served in a separate classrooms on the same campus.
>
> (Reynolds & Wang, 1983; Wang, Reynolds, & Walburg, 1987)

*Level III*

> All students participate in regular education classrooms except students with the most severe disabilities who would be in normalized and age-appropriate classroom on the same campus. Few students are excluded.
>
> (Gartner & Lipsky, 1987)

*Level IV*

> Despite the degree of disability, all students are fully included in general education classrooms. Specialists and teaching assistants provide support for students with the most severe disabilities within the classroom. The regular education teacher is responsible for structuring social interactions with typical peers.
>
> (Stainback & Stainback, 1984)

*At all levels, proponents of inclusion agree that pull-out programs for nonspecial education students should be eliminated. These students would be served in their regular classroom by visiting specialists.

disabled but who are currently served by remedial or compensatory programs would no longer leave their regular education classrooms to receive services. These students would remain full-time in their regular class while receiving additional assistance. Proponents note that staying with their class should remove some of the stigma these students feel from peer reactions as well as ensuring they do not miss important instruction while participating in pull-out programs.

MY PORTFOLIO

> Cat Party
> One of the cats was playing
> tug of war with the tablecloth.
> They were very funny and loud.
> I said "Everybody out", and gave
> them cat food. The party was over.
> The end of "Cat Party".

**Regardless of age or academic level, all students enjoy opportunities to demonstrate humor.** Reprinted with permission, Winston School, San Antonio.

However, based on the arguments of proponents and opponents presented earlier, the proposals for degree of implementation of the Regular Education Initiative differ dramatically (Skrtic, 1991). While the original direction of the initiative was to restructure special education so many more students with mild to moderate impairments would receive their instruction in regular education (Will, 1986; Audette and Algozzine, 1992), the question has become, "Which students with disabilities will most benefit from inclusion?"

Table 2–3 indicates the different levels of response. The least inclusive proposal places most students with mild disabilities in regular classes, but excludes those with moderate through severe disabilities, placing them in separate rooms within the regular school building (Lilly, 1986). This proposal is closest to the traditional manner of service delivery and is the easiest to implement in terms of using available special educators as support personnel and providing training in methods for regular education teachers to include these children.

More inclusive is the proposal to place students with mild or moderate disabilities in regular education classes (Reynolds & Wang, 1983; Wang, Reynolds, & Walberg, 1985). These students would be served totally in these settings, eliminating the need for pull-out programs. While students with organically based learning disabilities or moderately demonstrated behavioral disorders would not have been included in regular education rooms in the Level I proposal, they would be included here. Yet, proponents of both levels agree that there will be students with severe and/or multiple disabilities whose needs will not be served optimally in a mainstream environment. They feel that these students will need to participate full-time in separate settings.

Level III includes a more extensive involvement of severely impaired students in regular education. All students are included except those who are unable to be involved in academic or social interactions (Gartner & Lipsky, 1987). However, even these students would participate in nearby classrooms, which would be as normalized and age-appropriate as possible. Excluded students would be rare and even within special settings would be grouped according to instructional abilities.

**full inclusionists**—those who believe all students should participate in regular education classes.

The most extreme view is that of **full inclusionists,** who propose that all students should participate in general education classes. Claiming that to do otherwise would be to support a "dual system" for the most disabled, Level IV proponents propose the integration of even profoundly impaired students into totally normalized classes (Stainback & Stainback, 1984). This position has prompted the strongest reaction of implausibility from those opposed to the Regular Education Initiative. Yet parents and professionals supporting Level IV inclusion do acknowledge there are situations in which these students cannot be grouped with others because of instructional differences. Additionally, most often the student will be instructed by specialists other than the classroom teacher. However, the teacher will be responsible for fostering social integration with typical peers. Usually these interactions will not happen spontaneously but will require direct teacher intervention (Morsink & Lenk, 1992).

**intervention**—input directed toward change.

Dr. Mirales responds, "Most people in Westside would consider extensive inclusion as outrageous and impossible, but I have seen it work. The California Research Institute Model (Gartner & Lipsky, 1987) is my favorite for dealing with students with severe or profound disabilities. While not as extreme as the full inclusionists would like, the outcomes are really promising. Classes for students with extensive disabilities are on age-appropriate regular school campuses, making up between 5 and 20 percent of the total number of students. While these students are not placed full-time in regular education and they attend special classes, they participate in all the nonacademic functions of the school. Teachers and program coordinators plan opportunities for regular and special education students to interact so they will be frequently exposed to each other in as normal a setting as possible. There is a life-skills curriculum for students with disabilities so they can meet their own personal needs for independence. Students receive social skills training as they interact with others, allowing them to integrate new behaviors. The benefit to typical students in this program is their growing awareness and acceptance of differences in others. I know we will be starting at the basic levels of inclusion as we implement our program, but my long-term goal is much more integration into an accepting school and community environment."

While educators continue to be divided over the anticipated degree of inclusion, the trend is clear. Districts in many states have gone far in placing the greatest number of atypical students into general education as they feel can benefit. Others are developing their programs and wrestling with the difficult problems of Westside administrators, teachers, and parents.

# SUMMARY

The Regular Education Initiative has resulted from a sense that students need to be included, not excluded, and that there has been little demonstrated progress academically or self-conceptually as a result of separate systems. A number of ideas suggesting more inclusion of students with special needs are mentioned by Regular Education Initiative proponents. While the arguments are numerous, they list points such as overcoming the negative effects of labeling students, enabling general educators to deal with students with special needs, prior lack of success of special education programming, and the need to prepare students in normalized environments when young so they may be fully involved citizens when adults.

Yet, a number of researchers, educators, and parents have opposed the Regular Education Initiative strongly. They cite the historical inability and lack of desire of regular education to meet students needs, prompting litigation such as IDEA. They worry about loss of funding and parental rights, as well as individual educational plans, which demonstrated an attempt to meet student learning and behavioral needs. Importantly, they note that the initiative has originated in special education and most regular educators have not been trained to have students with special needs in their classes. How will teachers meet societal demands for excellence if they are expected to have vastly different levels of student academic and behavioral performance in their classes?

Supporters of inclusion differ in the extent of disability integrated into regular education classes. Some support placement only of students with mild disabilities in regular education, with students demonstrating more severe impairments participating on the regular education campus, but in separate classes. The continuum expands to include students with more severe impairments in regular classrooms on a part-time basis, to the full inclusionists, who would have all students participate full-time despite the degree of disability. The problem is how to incorporate students into classes where teachers and nondisabled peers are welcoming as well as competent in dealing with difference. Clearly, the debate continues.

The key has to be in collaboration of regular and special educators, parents, and administrators to work together to provide the best program to meet each student's unique needs. The following chapters will provide practical ways for special and general educators to work together toward this goal.

**CASE STUDY:** *Elementary*

These case studies describe difficult but typical problems prompted by the inclusion movement. They are intended to provide a basis for exploring your own feelings as well as a foundation for group discussion of possible ways to support success for administrators, teachers, and students.

**Cases aren't always about someone else. Sometimes they're about you. Mort was sensing that the hesitancy his teachers were feeling about embracing a more inclusive model at Alyssa Jackson was probably at least partly an outgrowth of his own concerns. He was feeling tired these days, and more than a bit overloaded. Yet he wouldn't even consider retiring until the district made him. This school with its wonderful children and teachers were his life.**

**Mort had won so many awards for pilot projects that other schools were afraid to tackle, such as the before- and after-school daycare to keep his children safe, and the widely publicized "Parents Training Parents" child abuse prevention program. Something in him said, "Take this and go with it. Become a model inclusion program for Westside." Something contradictory said, "New demands. Little money. Maybe the sentiment will pass." But he knew it wouldn't and that unless he emotionally and logistically embraced inclusion it couldn't succeed in his school.**

**As Mort discussed his concerns with his wife Cathy, she observed, "I remember the months of study and meetings you had before you started the other pilot programs. I think you're afraid to get into inclusion because you don't know much about it. That's probably smart; but since it's going to happen whether or not you support it, you'll probably feel better if you learn more about which kids are to be included and ways to make the changes work. Then, whether or not you pilot a districtwide program, at least you'll be more positive around your teachers and they'll feel your support and enthusiasm." As always, Cathy made sense.**

Develop a plan for Mort to expand his knowledge of inclusion. You might consider:

1. How will he get the information he needs? Whom should he contact and how should he proceed?

2. Should he act independently or involve his teachers as he learns about inclusion? If he does make them part of the process, which teachers and how many?

3. At this time, should he inform the Assistant Superintendent that he may be considering a pilot program at Jackson Elementary?

4. Specifically, from an administrative viewpoint, what does Mort need to know about inclusion to decide if he can support it enthusiastically and if it will work at his school?

Elena Cuellar's situation is different at Apter High School, but that's probably because high school teachers tend to react strongly to "top-down" mandates. While they have always been sympathetic to student needs, they don't like being told they have to have students with problems in their classes. "If the superintendent thinks it's such a good idea, let him try to teach these students to write a literate paragraph—no, change that to a literate sentence!"

John Robinson comments, "We're overloaded with problems at Apter. No training, no money for supports, and no more tracking (although it certainly was easier to teach homogeneous classes!). The community keeps complaining about how poorly we teachers are doing our jobs while everyone's happy to give us more problems and no raises!"

John's response strikes a common chord not only among Westside teachers, but among teachers across the country. Please respond to the following questions. Consider your feelings.

1. Should students with disabilities be included in regular education classes?

2. If so, what degree of inclusion is preferable in secondary school classes?

3. How can we balance the needs of the teachers not to become overwhelmed while providing the most normalized environment for all students?

4. What can Elena do at Apter High to change the growing negativism of her teachers and have them begin adapting to these "top-down" mandated changes?

# COLLABORATION

# 3

# ESTABLISHING THE COLLABORATIVE FRAMEWORK

The Annual Council for Exceptional Children Conference has been in town, and Dr. Mirales is feeling inspired. "I never seem to have time to reflect on what's happening in education," she notes. "I'm always in court or 'putting out fires' in the schools. Having a few days away from Westside concerns and talking with colleagues has given me some perspective about what's going on nationally. It's not just our district that's undergoing change pains. Everywhere, the word is *inclusion.* I'm glad Mort and Elena were at the sessions too. If they're sold on it, the other principals usually will follow their lead."

For all three administrators, the meetings posed more questions than answers. It was clear that individual teachers in regular education could not take on more students at risk and be expected to handle them alone. The idea of collaboration, of pairs or teams of teachers working together, was imperative. These teams would have to include regular and special education teachers working as equals. Inservice would be critical. The changing of attitudes would be at the core of school success.

Dr. Mirales understands that even more important than logistics is the creation of a vision of the way schools and classrooms can be. She needs both regular and special educators to realize that inclusion is not an extension of mainstreaming, that there will no longer be separate systems dividing responsibility for students, whether *Title, Chapter,* or *Special Education.* Breaking from tradition, within this vision there will no longer even be "regular education." There will simply be *education* for everyone (Sapon-Shevin, 1988). This new direction will be a merger of the best of all systems, embracing rather than excluding diversity.

# UNIFIED SCHOOLS

Unified School—schooling option in which students are considered special education for state and federal reporting and funding purposes, meeting legal requirements; yet in every other way they participate daily with their typical peers.

At the conference, Dr. Mirales was particularly taken with the "Unified School" options discussed by Leonard Burrello and Margaret McLaughlin (1993). Students would be considered special education for state and federal reporting and funding purposes, meeting legal requirements. Yet, in every other way they would participate daily with their typical peers. Dr. Mirales had decided to approach Mort and Elena to initiate this model.

mission statement—a declaration of the special function of a group; how a group perceives its duty.

anticipated student outcomes—expected results or achievement of a student.

The necessary school-site restructuring for Unified Schools seemed more approachable when considered in the steps proposed by Burrello and McLaughlin. First, teachers would be asked to develop a mission statement and goals for implementing inclusion in their school. Then they would specify anticipated student outcomes and means of establishing accountability. Dr. Mirales did not feel personally threatened by the decentralization of authority within the district, turning decisions regarding program design over to the schools. (Although she knew that this direction would not rest as easy with some of her administrative colleagues!) She felt the resistance towards inclusion had begun because of the "top-down" mandate from the superintendent's office. Clearly the best way to counter the strong opposition would be to allow site-based decision making at all levels of implementation. It was time to empower teachers to take charge of their own programs.

# DIFFERENTIATED STAFFING PATTERNS

The changes would be broad. Personnel concerns would range from altered school staffing patterns to expanded professional development opportunities. The entire curriculum would have to be reviewed to see what was really appropriate and what needed adaptation. Modifications of instructional arrangements would be at the heart of success. All of this was based on affording teachers the time and support to gain the excitement of going in a new direction.

One discussion at the conference had made particular sense to Dr. Mirales. Underscoring what experts had known for a decade (Reynolds & Wang, 1983), she had learned that current staff patterns both for regular and special educators had grown too rigid. Regardless of the school, all of her teachers were at identical levels of responsibility. They had their own rooms, their own students, and their own ways of doing things. Dr. Mirales was realizing that the district needed to change to differentiated functions and staffing patterns on a districtwide basis.

She would start by modifying this flat organizational structure. As part

site-based—taking place on the school campus.

of a site-based management plan, first she would ask all educators working on each campus to consider best alternatives for serving the children in regular education classrooms. "I know every teacher wants a room, a desk, and ownership of instructional methods, so this change may be difficult. If I can promise more support for working with students, at least some of the teachers will probably be willing to try." As part of the change, each school would be asked to develop a systematic approach for regular and special education teachers, school-based support staff, and district support staff (such as therapists and school psychologists) to work together instead of separately. The first questions would be about additional money, and the answer would not be popular. Maybe the challenge of fiscal cuts would be to provide a greater variety of services with improved quality. The key would be to have the teachers view this as a challenge instead of just one more burden.

As Dr. Mirales plans her role revisions, she may want to consider the model proposed by Birch and Reynolds (1982), in Table 3–1. While the model was originally designed for mainstreaming concerns of the 1980s, it is even more applicable to the inclusion movement of the 1990s. Several premises are basic to this plan. This educational system is totally unified. All special education and compensatory services for bilingual, disadvantaged, migrant, or limited-English proficient students are provided in the regular school building, most often in students' regular education classes.

## Table 3–1
## Redefinition of Educational Roles to Support Inclusion

| Level | Supportive Role |
|---|---|
| Fifth-Order | Research and development projects |
| Fourth-Order | Personnel preparation programs at colleges and universities |
| Third-Order | Regional and school district consultants (e.g., psychologists, behavior analysts, specialists for students with visual or hearing impairments) who support regular and special educators |
| Second-Order | Special educators and paraprofessionals who collaborate with regular teachers on each campus to provide supportive services for all students |
| First-Order | Regular educators who are prepared to work with all students |

(*Source:* Adapted from Birch & Reynolds, 1982)

## The Role of the Classroom Teacher

first-order level—trained teachers in regular education classes who are prepared to work with all types of students.

The heart of the program is at the first-order level, including trained teachers in regular education classes who are prepared to work with all types of students. To create a Unified School, it becomes necessary to "un-label" teachers rather than to label students (Sapon-Shevin, 1988). As schools move in the direction of avoiding categorization of students, they must also avoid categorization and labeling of educators. All teachers must have facility with instructing academics to all learners, in applying classroom management strategies, and in forming strong relationships between the school and family.

"While it may take time to develop these skills, I can see where teachers would be much more positive and less threatened by students with differences if they had confidence in their own abilities," notes Dr. Mirales.

supportive personnel—teachers who provide assistance to regular educators through direct in-class support by special and compensatory education teachers with additional expertise in teaching methods and curricular adaptations.

Additionally, this redesign would result in a change in roles of other instructional or administrative personnel, ranging across teachers of the learning disabled, speech and language pathologists, and among administrators such as building principals and curriculum supervisors (Birch & Reynolds, 1982). Their primary role change would be to become supportive personnel for regular educators, by providing resources and consultancy for

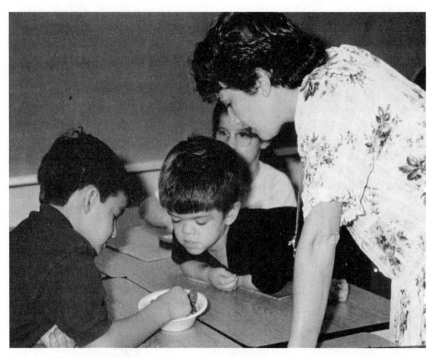

A re-definition of the role of personnel allows all teachers to interact freely with all children.

teaching a variety of learners in their classrooms. The demands of such a mental shift involve a personal redefinition of roles (such as the school principal changing from an instructional leader to an instructional enabler of teachers). Personnel such as school psychologists would no longer "own" the appraisal process, but would become interpreters of appraisal information into follow-up teaching strategies for the general education teacher. While this change of direction to supportive services might threaten many educators who have established their own "territory," it would be offset by the collaborative teamwork that finally encourages educators to work together instead of alone or competitively.

"These changes could be really positive if handled properly," comments Dr. Mirales. "For example, many Resource Room teachers complain about being isolated from colleagues, and most school psychologists feel frustrated by not being part of follow-up activities with the students they've tested. We'd have to provide as much retraining for these specialists as for generalist teachers to broaden their impact in the implementation process."

## Generalists and Specialists Working Together

second-order level—provides assistance to regular educators through direct in-class support by special and compensatory education teachers with additional expertise in teaching methods and curricular adaptations.

paraprofessionals—staff who assist the teacher in the classroom.

In Table 3–1, the **second-order level** provides assistance to regular educators through direct in-class support by special and compensatory education teachers with additional expertise in teaching methods and curricular adaptations. Along with **paraprofessionals**, these specialists are assigned to the building and work with a number of teachers and within a variety of classrooms. They allow for the intensive remedial or compensatory work needed by *any* children in the school, not only those labeled as special education. As will be noted, it is the support of these specialists in early intervention that prevents many students from needing special education at a later time.

The number of supportive staff available has been of growing concern to many educators in the move toward inclusion. Many regular education teachers want to team-teach with a specialist all day if any sizable number of students with disabilities are included in their classrooms, and want a full-time paraprofessional assigned to any student with severe disabilities so that the teacher is able to manage the entire group without undue distraction. Specialists tend to support this idea, since it would allow them to plan more extensively with the regular education teacher, would allot more time for them to work with any student in the class needing support, and would avoid their becoming harried by moving from class to class all day. Most importantly, both regular and special educators require a large number of supportive staff at the building level because they feel it would improve instruction for all students.

"There is a problem," admits Dr. Mirales. "I know that even with a redistribution of special education teachers and assistants, we cannot afford to have specialists all day in every class. What can we do?"

## Consultants

Dr. Mirales may want to consider the third-order level in Table 3–1. Historically, this model of school district or regional consultant staffs has been used in many rural districts where schools have been so geographically distant that it has been especially difficult to group students by disabilities because of transportation problems. States such as Vermont were early adopters of inclusion because of the costs and inconveniences of busing students to a centralized location, especially for low-incidence populations (Larson, McIntire, & Muoio, 1993). In some Vermont schools, facilitators, trained specialists, travel among schools to work with teachers concerned about individual students, supporting continued student participation in regular education. Additionally, regional teams funded by the school district and incorporating selected specialists consult on placement and instructional needs of students at risk.

"Although we're more urban, this system might work well for us, too," Dr. Mirales reflects. "We already have regional service centers to provide consultants in mobility training for students who are blind or have multiple disabilities. It might be more affordable to increase numbers of individual consultant hours for students with low-incidence disabilities. I really like the creation of districtwide teams of specialists for students with severe behavioral or learning disorders. The key would be to have the consultant or team on-call to any teacher who has greater needs than those easily handled by specialists or paraprofessionals at the building level. Some of these problems might be discussed by phone and not even necessitate a campus meeting." Additionally, these supportive services might include recommendations on individualizing instruction, selection of specialized materials, parental consultation, assessment concerns, and consultation with computer experts (Reynolds & Wang, 1983). Through a careful redesign at this level, all teachers might gain increased access to consultant services.

## The Role of the University

The fourth-order level and fifth-order level of redefining supportive roles in Table 3–1 involve college and university systems. Whether preparing preservice or inservice teachers, education departments will have to eliminate their own artificial divisions between regular and special education. Working together with state education agencies to design credentials preparing teachers to work with heterogeneous groups of students, higher education can provide a critical supportive function of personnel development. Additionally, through research and development, faculty can study areas of need indicated by districts and then disseminate their findings to practitioners for direct intervention, as indicated in the communications channel in Table 3–1.

areas of need—specific conditions in which there is a deficiency.

mentors—advisors.

professional development
schools—schools that implement the collaboration of school
and university educators
through mutual supports.

These final levels call for some reconsideration in higher education. At Trinity University, San Antonio, faculty work in schools weekly, share the concerns of regular and special educators, and collaborate on intervention teams to solve site-based problems. Master teachers in allied schools are daily mentors for preservice teachers. Instead of the university campus, the school becomes the primary training ground.

In the University of Vermont model, faculty provide inservice activities for teachers and supportive staff of entire schools based on grants. In conjunction with school district personnel, faculty also train paraprofessionals at workshops, expanding the skills of supportive staff in the classroom.

Topics for university research might be selected based on expressed needs of teachers, who tend to be practical by nature because of their demanding interactions with students daily. Through involvement with these educators on the "firing lines," faculty can select areas directed toward the solution of field-based problems. The integration of a redefined university role in strengthening direct services enhances specialized service provision to all students, including those at risk.

"I've been hearing a good deal about professional development schools," notes Mort. "How do they work?"

Professional development schools, Table 3–2, implement the collaboration of school and university educators through mutual supports. Preservice

## Table 3–2
## Characteristics of Professional Development Schools

- The university and school work closely together, including joint planning and problem-solving.

- Combined goals are clearly specified and include academic skills improvement for children while preparing university students with state-of-the-art methods in teaching.

- University faculty and teachers become equal partners on collaborative teams in schools.

- Mentor teachers in schools work with university students, modeling and sharing practices.

- Instead of the university campus, the school becomes the primary training ground.

- University faculty and teachers jointly present seminars for university students and colleagues in schools.

- Universities assist training paraprofessionals in schools.

- Teachers express needs for areas of research.

- University faculty share research results through dissemination of new ideas.

- Evaluation of program success is continuous, involving input from teachers, university faculty, students, children and their families.

Professional development schools provide benefits both for preservice teachers and their students.

teachers enrolled in the university program benefit by working with teachers and students in allied schools. Instead of the traditional student teaching program, they may participate in public or private classrooms from their earliest entry into the Education Department program. In this manner, they understand the real world of teaching, the problems and successes encountered daily by educators, and their own preferences for teaching-learning environments.

University students are placed with model classroom teachers, often developing a mutually supportive relationship within the most realistic training opportunity. Frequently, they work with teams of educators, attend staff meetings, and not only learn optimal instructional methods from their mentor teachers, but are part of curriculum teams and involved in meetings with specialists and parents.

To further support the model, at times university faculty and participant teachers present seminars collaboratively for university students and colleagues, demonstrating close ties between environments. Instead of being involved only a few times each semester for formal observations of student work, professors visit the schools frequently and become part of the school culture. They may participate on school planning teams to discuss program development or methods of integration of all students into the classroom. They should not be viewed as the experts but as equal members of each team.

# PREREFERRAL

"I like the idea of redefining our roles as professionals," notes Elena. "That makes good sense and certainly is more cost-effective; but, I'm unclear about which students would receive specialized services as we expand the program. With the problems they bring to school these days, it seems like half of our high school students could be considered eligible."

Elena is correct in observing that many students are at risk, but do not fall within the traditional categories for services. Before any program can serve students adequately, involved educators must identify the students at-risk and their specific needs.

## Traditional Assessment Practices

Historically, this process has involved only those students severe enough to be under consideration for special education services. Usually the process has been initiated by a parent or teacher referring a student for formal assessment by a specialist, often a school psychologist. This assessment takes one or more lengthy sessions, customarily in a setting removed from the student's classroom or even more disruptively, from the school. Not only is this method of assessment potentially unreliable, based on one or two isolated observations of a student under pressure, but it is also expensive, since it requires the time of a well-trained professional, both for testing and subsequent report writing.

While the educational goal of this assessment is to determine the student's learning/behavioral strengths and problem areas to provide supportive instruction, the legal goal has been to demonstrate that the student meets eligibility requirements within a category of disability. The natural outcome of this process has been labeling of students with any variety of names (learning disabled, severely behaviorally disordered) and then placing them in a prescribed setting or unit for students with that type of disability. This structure has not been flexible enough to accommodate students who may need a different type of instruction than that offered in the unit, and often has resulted in lack of successful intervention.

segregation—separating because of differences.

Additionally, funding has underscored rigidity. Traditionally, a student has had to be labeled to be funded for services. In many states, the type of unit, such as self-contained or resource, and the amount of time spent there by the student, have determined the amount of fiscal support. Some state departments continue to provide more money for students placed in self-contained units than in inclusive classes, rewarding segregation and discouraging districts from placing students in general education. More supportive of integration, others provide local districts with money to spend on individual students regardless of the placement. Therefore, a student needing the additional supports of a reading specialist or therapist would not receive less funding because of full-time participation in a regular classroom (Larson, McIntyre, & Muoio, 1993).

· These broadened funding directions are allowing educators to rethink assessment and placement. While it may always be necessary to substantiate the presence of disabilities to receive financial support, it may not be mandatory to have such intense and elaborate assessment procedures. It is more cost-effective and educationally sound to identify student problems early and to provide intervention immediately than to wait until the student has a major problem and then deal with crisis management. Often the decision to refer a student for an evaluation for possible enrollment in special education is tantamount to a decision to assign that student to special education (Ysseldyke, Thurlow, Graden, Wesson, Algozzine, & Deno, 1983).

prereferral—early intervention in response to an observable, developing problem; may preclude the need for later placement in special education.

screening—testing students in a variety of subject areas to identify those who may need special services.

Early intervention in response to an observable, developing problem may preclude the need for later placement in special education. The purpose of prereferral is to solve a small problem before it becomes a greater one, avoiding the necessity of ultimately referring students for special education services. The appropriate timing of prereferral screening and intervention helps ensure that indepth assessment is limited to those students with clearly identifiable disabilities (Reynolds, Wang, & Walberg, 1987).

A number of factors have initiated the change in attitude from referring students out of the regular classroom for special education services. Primarily the increasing numbers of students with problems entering our schools, ones whose needs are extreme enough to require some degree of special services, have increased dramatically.

Maura Hayes notes, "By traditional standards, almost one-half of my third-graders would qualify for pull-out services. Many of my colleagues at the high school would lose an even greater number because of substance abuse and gang involvements. In the last fifteen years, I have had more and more students suffering the effects of poverty and lack of stimulation, poor nutrition, exposure to disease, and lack of hygiene, and from homes that are abusive, neglectful, and violent. Even when the parents are supportive (and I'm grateful for those who are!), many children are victims of poor prenatal care and low birthweight. The attention deficits are rampant and there's so much innate distractibility at times that my room reverberates. So many of my students have these problems that it's obvious I can't send them all out of the room."

With a burgeoning number of societal problems, teachers like Maura strongly agree on one point: No educator can work alone and be expected to solve the extreme situations impacting students' abilities to learn. The "lonely teacher" and even the "lonely principal" are outdated traditions in American education. Not just a trend, the new direction has become increased collaboration between regular educators, specialists, administrators, and parents. Ranging across grade levels or content areas, as well as specific areas of expertise, professionals working together have become the best support for students with extreme needs.

Because of additional demands of adolescents, many educators at the secondary level have found the collaborative approach mandatory. Content teachers may have 120 to 150 students in their rooms each day, rarely interacting with each class for more than fifty minutes. During a period in their lives in which students are developing their identity and need guidance to form healthy relationships and avoid pitfalls, this system creates a sense of anonymity instead of caring.

When teams of teachers work together with the same group of students daily despite content area differences, they come to know their students and can more easily determine those at risk for failure. By brainstorming ideas with other educators and with the family, they can redirect students earlier and can impart the sense of caring so desperately needed by young people.

"This sounds good, but how do we create these teams? With so many students in my English classes, how will I identify those at risk?" asks John Robinson.

## PLANNING TEAMS

Teams of educators directed toward identifying developing student problems and recommending specific techniques for intervention are at the heart of successful inclusion. No one can expect teachers to be effective if large numbers of students with extreme behavioral disorders or attentional and learning problems are placed in their classes, or if they have not received intensive training in meeting exceptional needs. Identifying students early and designing educational support strategies are critical. Two issues are pivotal: developing a team of professionals who can work together, and educating all involved educators in the symptoms of students at risk.

Who participates on these **planning teams**? It depends on the needs of teachers and students on each campus, Table 3–3. Yet, informed regular educators are the key to successful intervention. Their involvement helps to establish "ownership" by the general education system for all students and their input provides important ongoing information about the success of alternate teaching methods. Since the ability of team members to have an impact is largely dependent on their interactive skills with other teachers, some faculties, such as those using **Teacher Assistance Teams** (Chalfant & Pysh, 1989), often elect several teachers from various grades or disciplines. The regular education teacher requesting help with a particular student joins the team for as long as the assistance is needed. Depending on the needs of the child, the team may have additional members, such as principals, special educators, and parents. Many teachers respond best to this type of team because it consists primarily of regular educators who can relate to the situation of having to problem-solve within the regular classroom. The threat factor of having a specialist or expert give advice from a different background disappears as teachers work together to brainstorm ideas. However, if a student's needs are unusual or extreme, the appropriate specialist is asked to join the team as an equal member in order to suggest intervention techniques or to recommend supplemental programs.

**planning teams**—groups of educators directed toward identifying developing student problems and recommending specific techniques for intervention.

**Teacher Assistance Teams**—teachers work together to brainstorm ideas; the regular education teacher requesting help with a particular student joins the team for as long as the assistance is needed.

**Table 3–3**
**Planning Team Membership**

| *Members may include, but should not be limited to:* | *When behavioral or family problems exist for an individual student, the team may want to add:* |
|---|---|
| • Regular education teachers from various grades and disciplines | • The school counselor |
| • The classroom teacher requesting assistance | • A school or counseling psychologist |
| • A special education teacher, to serve as a consultant | • A community social worker or representative of child protective services |
| • Parents or involved family members | • The school nurse |
| • A school administrator | |

Teacher Resource Model—a consultant trains selected regular classroom teachers and building-level special educators to provide inservice training, ongoing consultation, and technical assistance to regular classroom teachers with students at risk.

at risk—refers to children who do not demonstrate disabilities, but who for environmental or biological reasons may develop such delays.

Mainstream Assistance Team—consultants visit the classroom to help guide teachers through identifying student problems, analyzing intervention strategies, and providing feedback.

In the Teacher Resource Model for prereferral at the secondary level (Maher, in Nelson & Smith, 1991), a consultant trains selected regular classroom teachers and three building-level special educators to provide inservice training, ongoing consultation, and technical assistance to regular classroom teachers with students at risk. The "trainer-of-trainers" model for inservice delivery has been found effective in providing the total faculty of involved schools with expertise in behavior management strategies and alternate techniques for instructing academic areas (Waldron, 1980). With the addition of ongoing support from the team, Maher (in Nelson & Smith, 1991) found that two participant high schools were able to significantly reduce their need to refer students to special education, and that teachers reached their goals with 85 percent of students at risk.

The Mainstream Assistance Team (Fuchs, Fuchs, & Bahr, 1990) also uses specialists and a multidisciplinary team. Consultants play a more direct, ongoing role in this model, where they visit the classroom to help guide teachers through identifying student problems, analyzing intervention strategies, and providing feedback. The teachers reported the greatest success when they had the ongoing consultant available in addition to the school-based team. Although this model may be expensive for many districts to implement, it holds promise as an extension of the university-school collaborative discussed earlier.

Regardless of the model selected by any campus, the regular educators participating should want to be on the team, be flexible in considering programming activities, be able to work well with others, and not be hesitant to have specialist members join the team to solve difficult problems. The type of specialist will vary, but may include educators with specific skills in working with bilingual students or students with disabilities. Additionally, counselors, psychologists, social workers, and medical staff may be asked to participate on the team if a student is experiencing personal or family adjustment problems.

## Roles of Team Members

"Exactly what do these teams do?" Maura asks. "I'm afraid I'll be asked to have more difficult third graders in my room and also be required to attend extra meetings and do more paperwork. If I have a student with learning or behavior problems, is this going to be as much work as those placement teams for special education?"

multidisciplinary teams—fulfill legal placement and review requirements for students in special education.

Planning teams should not be confused with multidisciplinary teams, which have traditionally fulfilled legal placement and review requirements for students in special education. While those teams met occasionally, often only annually, to discuss a particular student, the planning teams meet on an ongoing basis to solve daily problems for teachers in the school, Table 3–4. Their function is to create a nonthreatening support system to help regular

## Table 3–4
## Purposes of School Planning Teams

Planning teams should not be confused with multidisciplinary teams meeting to place students in special education.

The most important goal of the team is to identify and assist students at risk in the regular classroom before their problems worsen and they require special education services.

*Other purposes include:*

- Meeting on an ongoing basis to solve daily student problems for teachers in the school
- Providing a nonthreatening support system to help teachers with individual students demonstrating learning or behavior problems
- Observing students in the classroom and discussing results with the referring teacher
- Meeting with parents and/or related specialists as needed to form a team approach to working with the student
- Establishing behavioral and learning goals for the student
- Helping the referring teacher design an intervention plan
- Evaluating the effectiveness of the plan on an intermittent basis after its implementation
- Modifying the plan as necessary until the student has demonstrated adequate progress

education teachers instruct students demonstrating learning and/or behavior problems (Andringa & Keller, 1991).

If these teams become bureaucratic, causing extensive paperwork or time involvement, they cannot be successful. In many settings, the teacher calls a meeting of the team and describes the problems observed. The team leader or members may informally observe the referred child, and parents and/or specialists may be asked to attend subsequent meetings, based on the needs of the student. Together with the referring teacher, the team sets behavioral and learning goals and designs an intervention plan with suggestions for the teacher.

## Team Planning Time

Most of the individual teachers are pleased about the direct, professional support and advice the team provides. When the teacher feels the student has demonstrated significant improvement, she no longer meets with the team.

The team meets regularly, weekly if possible, to discuss the cases referred to them and to consider the effectiveness of the interventions suggested. Teachers must have released time from instructional responsibilities to meet on these teams. Teachers participating as ongoing team members should have additional meeting time beyond their personal conference planning period. At the elementary level, this might be arranged by their sharing at least a half-day a week when their own students are involved in a block of time scheduled for physical education, art, music, or library. Teachers whose students are experiencing problems could schedule a meeting with the team during this several-hour period when their own class is least likely to be affected by their absence.

At the secondary level, team members might teach one fewer class than their colleagues. Their meeting periods could be scheduled to coincide. Within the "rotating class times" many secondary schools have adopted, other teachers in the school would be free during this meeting period to discuss problems and progress of students at risk.

"I still have the same concerns as Maura," John Robinson notes. "It looks like if I have students with academic and behavioral problems, our only meeting time will come out of my planning time and I'll be working later after school or nights at home."

Certainly these concerns are valid, but there are several additional options. In some regions of Denmark, schools close for instruction mid-day on Friday. This time is delegated for teacher inservice, curricular planning, and team consultation on individual students.

Following this model, to avoid parental anxiety about unsupervised students at home, schools can coordinate with community agencies such as the YMCA to sponsor after-school programs on the campus. High-school students can work in programs for elementary and middle-school students. Those who prefer could participate off-campus in a variety of vocational and mentoring locations, exposing them to potential job futures. Others could support social service agencies by working at shelters or in programs for the disadvantaged.

If the district or community is opposed to the half-day planning time, school can close one hour earlier a few days each week, with on-campus activities for students, ranging from arts involvements to intramurals. While currently some high schools have students enroll in an extra class period during the school day for participation in extra-curricular activities, these activities could take place after school hours as they have done traditionally to avoid any loss of academic time. If school is dismissed earlier and students participate in organized functions, teachers can rotate their meeting schedule so part of the faculty will always be available to oversee concurrent student activities, while others are free to attend planning and implementation meetings.

If educators are asked to attend weekly meetings after school hours or during their vacations (whether on the traditional or year-round calendar), they should be paid for their time. To avoid this additional cost, many districts might look at the teacher's expenditure of time more creatively. For example, administrators may consider which time-consuming tasks teachers are asked to perform during the school day that could be performed by

Children can participate in a variety of activities while their teachers collaborate in meetings.

paraprofessionals. From supervising lunchrooms to monitoring students or performing "bus duty," staff can be trained for these tasks in order to allow teachers to concentrate on instructional planning. (In Ireland, often educators are free to plan their own time around teaching, including leaving the building without the demeaning "permission" required in so many American schools. This allows teachers to consider themselves professionals and to establish their schedules more flexibly for meeting with other teachers.) Usually, the best plan for released time to collaborate with peers is suggested by educators at individual schools. Even within districts, this emphasis on site-based management should allow for the creation of a variety of plans.

## Team Membership

"I've read a report by John Stager about the Massachusetts Department of Education plan, and I really like the flexibility of their Teacher Support Teams," Dr. Mirales comments. "Their in-school team meets weekly with teachers of students experiencing academic, emotional, or attendance problems. They also ask teachers to discuss any students at risk of pregnancy, suicide, violence, substance addiction, or family abuse or neglect. They include on the team a member from the same cultural or language background as the student in order to be sure the student's needs are really understood. That would be so helpful for us, not only for our African-American students and our children who speak Spanish, but for the new minorities in our district. We now have Hmong students from Laos and Eastern European students who are beginning a new wave of immigration through our church and synagogue sponsorships."

The Massachusetts plan also includes parents and students in collaborative efforts as part of an attempt to build communication between school and family. Parental input is invited throughout the process in developing strategies to help students. If parents are not satisfied that the support team's interventions are working, they have the right to refer the student for special education evaluation.

The teams also consider a series of concerns for improving the education for all students in the school through discussing topics such as:

- how to vary instructional strategies to support teachers and students;
- effective behavioral management;
- grouping students;
- enhancing school climate;
- modification of existing school policies; and
- improvement of social and health services to students and their families (Stager, 1990).

procedural follow-up—the involved teacher has ongoing contact with a member of the Teacher Support Team.

**Procedural follow-up** is part of this system, where the involved teacher has ongoing contact with a member of the Teacher Support Team.

Within this plan educators recognize that while the team members should have broad areas of expertise, they need ongoing training in specified areas as well as support on a district or regional basis. As requested, selected inservices and consultation time from other professionals add to team skills in dealing with individuals or groups of students. Members receive compensatory time or stipends for after-school meetings. Additionally, team ideas are expanded beyond the boundaries of an individual school campus. Regional newsletters and publications containing innovative teaching and behavioral management strategies are circulated to all teachers, introducing them to new ideas. As Ernest Boyer (1993) noted, "We know what works. Now we just need to look at our most successful schools and spread the word."

## SUCCESSFUL COLLABORATIVE PRACTICES

Inclusion is based on professionals working together. To move towards cooperative intervention, teachers must be willing to share their knowledge and lessen their feelings of being threatened by working together with others having a variety of expertise. They must get rid of any feelings of competition and develop a spirit of camaraderie, putting the success of the student at the center of their efforts.

## Selecting Members of the Planning Team

"How would we select members of the planning team?" asks Elena. "A few teachers would jump at the chance and some others would feel it a burden; but most would hesitate, not knowing if they had expertise or time." Possible criteria for establishing team membership are listed in Table 3–5.

*Classroom Experience.*  Chalfant, Pysh, and Moultrie (1979) note that previous classroom experience is an important factor in establishing the credibility of team recommendations. An educator with successful front-line teaching usually carries more status among peers than external consultants who may not be as familiar with daily problems in the classroom.

*Knowledge of Curriculum and Materials.*  This background should include a broad awareness of varied curricula and materials to suggest adaptations for effective inclusion of learners with differences (Larson, McIntire, & Mouio, 1993). At the secondary level, this need implies the participation

---

**Table 3–5**
**Selection Criteria for Collaborative Team**

*Team members should have:*

- Classroom experience

- Knowledge of curriculum and materials

- Interest and ability in assessing learning and behavior problems

- Knowledge of techniques for individualizing instruction

- Specialized skills

- Input from individuals of the same culture, language, and background as the student being discussed

- Strong interpersonal skills, allowing them to communicate well with colleagues, students, and parents

- Excitement about the prereferral model and interest in helping teachers

- Input from family members

- Involvement of the student in goal-setting and plan implementation

(*Sources:*  Adapted from Chalfant, Pysh, & Moultrie, 1979; Muoio, in Larson, McIntire, & Muoio, 1993)

of at least one team member knowledgeable of curriculum in the content areas where the student is experiencing difficulties, such as biology or English. In many schools where integrated curricula have been implemented, a curriculum committee member might be included on the team, not only to recommend modifications, but also as a liaison between teams to consider the unique needs of some students as additional changes are designed.

***Assessment Skills.***  One or more team members should also possess skills in assessing learning and behavior problems. While an indepth individualized assessment will be conducted for those students ultimately referred for special education, the prereferral goal is to recognize the symptoms of academic and behavioral difficulty early enough to remediate or compensate for problems, altogether avoiding the need for special education assessment.

"Why can't all of us become aware of symptoms that place a student at risk?" asks Maura. The long-term direction will be to train all teachers in the school to look for indicators of developing problems, but the immediate purpose is to have team expertise in listening to teachers describe problems and being able to identify causes. By being part of these discussions, other team members will experience a broadening of their own skills in assessment. When the student is presenting unique or extreme problems beyond the diagnostic capabilities of the existing team, members may decide to involve external assessment specialists from the district. When the team makes the request for additional input, they usually are more supportive of specialist recommendations.

***Knowledge of Individualized Instruction.***  As noted in Table 3–5, team members should also be conversant in methods of individualizing instruction in the regular education classroom. Such awareness goes far beyond technical knowledge of instructional strategies. It underscores a willingness to adapt to learners with unique needs. An attitude of flexibility is critical to successful inclusion of students with disabilities. Planning teams that espouse adaptability can create this same sense in the teachers with whom they confer.

***Specialized Skills.***  "Clearly, I'm most concerned in knowing how to teach the students with weak skills," notes John. Members who possess strong technical knowledge skills in academic remediation and behavioral management will serve a critical team function. Many regular education teachers lack knowledge of remedial teaching or behavioral management methods to help a student reading three years below grade level, or one who refuses to complete assignments. While inservices and change toward more practical skill delivery in university training programs will have to be instituted to make inclusion work, a teacher with a problem cannot wait, needing an answer immediately. There must be suggestions on workable solutions for team credibility to be established. One or more members should be selected for strengths in academic remediation and behavioral management, relying on external members if student needs are unique, (such as blindness or multidisabling conditions).

Some teams consist entirely of regular educators, and others routinely include a site-based special education teacher with a history of gaining the confidence of colleagues and an ability to design remedial and behavioral programs for individuals and groups of students. From the onset, team members should understand each other's roles and vocabularies (Morsink & Lenk, 1992). For example, when dealing with regular education teachers, specialists should not use terms such as **aphasia** or **conduct disorder** to describe students. Such vocabulary will only serve to underscore differences in teacher training and to signify that the specialist is the expert, possessing a body of knowledge outside that of other educators. Instead, the meeting should be conducted by a regular education team leader who asks the specialist to describe the specific learning and/or behavioral problems demonstrated by the student. Selecting vocabulary common to all educators, parents, and students (if present), the specialist should explain the nature of the problem and specific intervention techniques that should work in the regular education classroom. In this manner, others at the meeting will respect the involvement of the specialist without being threatened.

***Multicultural Concerns.*** Even well-regarded specialists are not always aware of the unique needs and difficulties experienced by language-minority children. Educators must be more concerned about diversity. Allen and Turner (1990) predict that by the twenty-first century, more than one-third of all Americans will belong to an ethnic or racial minority group.

In the past, students with limited English proficiency were overreferred to special education settings, resulting in a number of lawsuits and subsequent court orders, such as *Diana v. California State Board of Education.* As a backlash to the many student placements that had demonstrated **cultural bias,** data collected by the California State Department of Education has indicated the subsequent trend of under-identification of minority students who require specialized services (Olson, 1991).

"It's a pretty evident problem in my Resource class," Teresa Fuentes notes. "During my early teaching years, most of my students were minority and the bias seemed clear, especially because of lack of bilingual programs and teachers who spoke anything but standard English. Now that more minority students are in general education classes, their teachers call on me for help all the time with their Spanish-speaking children because I'm bilingual. When I work with the students I find that many of them do have learning or behavioral problems that are not being addressed. I don't want these students segregated again into special education, but I'm worried about their falling between the cracks since they get so little support."

---

aphasia—a disability in which the student has difficulty understanding or speaking oral language.

conduct disorder—students who exhibit bold, negative actions and behaviors.

cultural bias—prejudging a student's abilities based on preconceptions or stereotypes regarding cultural background.

Teresa's concerns are supported by annual statistics. Yates (1992) notes that the largest language minority group is Spanish-speaking, comprising more than two-thirds of the entire language minority population in the United States. Yet, there has been no indication that teachers who speak Spanish, the very individuals who may be best equipped to understand students' cultural and linguistic needs, will increase proportionately.

The non-Hispanic population of immigrants is expected to be approximately 100,000 by the year 2000, including 82,000 Indochinese (Baca & Cervantes, 1989). Additionally, immigrants and refugees continue to enter the United States from countries such as Vietnam, Laos, Cambodia, Hungary, Romania, Bulgaria, Russia, China, Japan, and India, increasing the variety of languages spoken in schools. It is startling to consider that ten different languages are represented by the Indochinese refugees alone. The number of Asian-Americans has more than doubled since 1980 (Yates, 1992).

While most would assume that Native Americans are fluent in English, this is not true for many, who are isolated from mainstream educational experiences and may lack essential vocabulary (Hoover & Collier, 1991). While the linguistically different language spoken by many African-Americans was intensely considered in the 1960s and 1970s, many schools now ignore these concerns because of the more immediately impactful problems of immigrant students. Additional problems, such as low self-esteem, and subsequently the **self-fulfilling prophecy** of lower achievement by many African-American students have also been put aside (Howard & Hammond, 1985). As with the Hispanic population, there is an underrepresentation of African-American teachers to understand student needs and to act as role models.

"Then what do we do?" asks Teresa. "Clearly I can't work with every student I'd like to, nor meet with every teacher. How can we meet so many differing needs?"

As a planning team is formed to consider students at risk, individuals must be included with backgrounds similar to those of students. Teresa is best placed on the team when she understands the culture, language, and educational needs of the student being discussed. If no educator is available who fully appreciates the needs of a student, then a community member from a similar background should be included on the team, as well as the adults in the family.

Often the outcomes of this expansion outside the school are more far-reaching than anticipated. For example, when including representatives from community agencies such as Jewish Family Services to help the assimilation of children from countries such as Russia, the breadth of assistance usually is expanded to social services, helping the family get settled in a new home with furniture from volunteers, support in finding jobs, and a general orientation to the community. All of these services promote the well-being of the child because of the improved adjustment of the family. Especially at the secondary level, where students are most sensitive to lack of friends as they immigrate

**self-fulfilling prophecy—** brought to fulfillment as an effect of having been expected or predicted.

and often cannot communicate in English, a kindred community can become the new family. In light of this, each school district should have a listing of services available to families from culturally and linguistically different backgrounds, as well as whom to contact to include representatives on school-based teams as students first enter the school community, avoiding their becoming at risk at a later time.

***Communication Skills.*** Personality and communication skills are also critical variables in selection of team members. Whether interacting with teachers who may feel overwhelmed by student behaviors, with parents who may be reluctant participants, or with students who do not appreciate a need for change, there must be a demeanor of understanding and support. Within a school, the best candidates are those teachers who have demonstrated previous success through cooperation with colleagues on varied projects or committees or who have been approached by other teachers for help in solving academic and behavioral problems with students.

***Supportive of Team Goals.*** Most importantly, team members need to be excited about the model established at their school and desirous of working hard to make it successful (Chalfant & Pysh, 1989). No member should be forced to be on the team because of possession of expertise in a particular area. Participation should be entirely voluntary. Administrators can best encourage support of qualified teachers by demonstrating a positive attitude themselves, by reducing team member classloads, and by promoting the follow-up implementation of team recommendations.

***Parental Input.*** "What about the parents?" asks Dr. Mirales. "While we have some who would be really happy for any support we can give them, there are others who will avoid recognizing that their child has any problem. We see this especially at the high school level when teachers become concerned because of a change to a rough peer group or suspected drug use. Many parents want to ignore these problems, hoping they'll go away. How can we expect educators to spend time meeting to intervene with the student if we don't have parental backing to implement changes?"

This point expresses well the frustration many educators feel about working with nonparticipatory, or overtly negative, families. However, there are two potential approaches to take when proceeding with the planning team process despite potential lack of parental support. The first is to assume that parents will want to be part of the process. They should be contacted by the counselor or a designated teacher when their child is to be discussed by the team. They should be told that while the problem is not yet extreme, some teachers are concerned and would like to meet with the parents to stem the problem before it becomes a major concern. Most parents care deeply about their children and if the situation is presented with a "let's work together" attitude, will attend a meeting with the team to discuss the problem and brainstorm initial interventions. The parent should be treated as an equal member of the team whose expertise is in knowing the child best. If the parent leaves the initial meeting secure in the knowledge that the school is an ally, ensuing interactions will be far easier.

There are parents who will not respond to requests to be part of the process. While a few may be verbally negative in their attitude, more will be non-participatory. However, lack of involvement does not tie the hands of the planning team to the same degree that it would the special education referral team. Since this process is more informal and is dedicated to solving problems in their earliest stages, teachers are considering best educational and management strategies to be used in the classroom. Although these discussions would be enhanced by parental input, they do not necessitate it. Teachers do not require formal parental permission to initiate differentiated teaching methods such as individualized instruction or remedial instruction in the general classroom.

"That does make it easier," interjects Dr. Mirales. "What about parents like Mrs. Williams who don't want their children served in the regular education classroom, but want to place them in special education for as much of the day as possible? She would never agree to the types of modifications of a planning committee."

It is important to remember that legally parents can request assessment of their child for special education placement at any time. If they wish to omit the prereferral process completely, that is their right. However, with the national move toward inclusion, it would be educationally negligent not to inform a parent of the school's willingness to place the student in the regular education classroom. Parents should be encouraged to try this option first, assured they will have input to the team, and they can maintain the right for a special education referral at any time. Usually this gives them a sense of security while demonstrating that the district is doing everything possible to ensure as normalized an education as possible with typical peers.

***Student Involvement.*** Students can be your greatest ally, and it is important to include them in the prereferral process as much as possible. Most students do not want to leave the room frequently or permanently to attend special classes away from their peers. This sense of difference is intensified as they progress in elementary grades, and is especially true at the secondary level, reinforcing educators' desires to place the student in regular education. Once they realize they are eligible to remain in the classroom, often students encourage their parents to support this placement. It is important for the counselor or a designated team member to discuss programming options openly with the student. It is at the discretion of the team if they want the student at some of their sessions or if the student will benefit most from conferences with individual team members. The best way to make this decision is to ask the students directly how they would like to have input into their own programming.

## Selecting the Team Leader

"Who runs the team?" asks John. "There must be a coordinator to organize member's work, their meetings, and follow-up."

team leader—the person who coordinates the team and runs the meetings.

This important function is carried out by the **team leader.** Participation of team members with a variety of skills is important, but selection of a good team leader is critical. Table 3–6 lists some of the characteristics and duties of the prereferral leader. The method of designation will differ with the school. Some principals prefer appointing a team leader with whose work they are familiar, such as a vice-principal, counselor, or teacher. Other schools select leaders by rank or longevity at the school. In other cases, they are chosen by election of the prereferral team members. The latter method seems most supportive of team cohesion and willingness to support leader efforts.

As noted by Chalfant, Pysh, and Moultrie (1979), there are characteristics of the team leader that are critical to the success of the prereferral process. The leader should be strongly committed to the concept of assisting learners with special needs to be successful in the regular classroom. If the attitude of the team leader is ambivalent or apathetic, the rest of the team may be swayed in a similar direction or they may sense that their own efforts are being thwarted.

The leader should have the ability to direct others, demonstrating strong interactive skills with a sense of humor and perspective. She should be able

---

**Table 3–6**
**Characteristics of Effective Team Leaders**

*Team leaders should:*

- Be committed to the concept of placing students in the least restrictive environment

- Understand group dynamics

- Be willing to coordinate team efforts and follow-up

- Foster collaboration in team meetings

- Encourage referrals of students at risk

- Establish case priorities

- Schedule meetings

- Verify specific actions to be taken on team recommendations

- Ensure follow-up takes place

(*Source:* Adapted from Chalfant, Pysh, & Moultrie, 1979)

to work with groups of teachers, understanding the dynamics of school inter-action, never allowing a teacher to "lose face" in the eyes of colleagues. The leader should understand the need to call meetings only when necessary, to make these sessions as brief as possible, and to avoid all unnecessary paperwork.

As coordinator of group efforts, the leader should be sure that work is dis-tributed fairly, with no one member assigned overburdening numbers of stu-dents to consider. The leader should encourage open discussion in nonthreatening meetings, directing the group to heed all important rec-ommendations.

Specific duties include encouraging referral of students experiencing academic or behavioral difficulties and talking with faculty and parents about presenting problems. The team leader then establishes case priorities, ensuring that students demonstrating the most extreme problems are han-dled first. (Such behaviors might include indicators of suicide, drug use, depres-sion, or physically aggressive behaviors potentially injurious to the students or classmates.)

The regular classroom teacher's sense of urgency about the student should also be considered. If the teacher feels a personal sense of anger or frustration, indicating that the student is ruining the educational process for the class, team consideration of the problem might be prioritized. By meet-ing initially with the educator or parent concerned about student progress, the leader should be able to determine the urgency of the situation.

The team leader must be able to schedule meetings in a professionally con-siderate manner and should initiate a meeting as soon after the referral as possible, always respecting the schedules of team members. Except for infrequent emergencies, the leader should notify teachers days in advance of the meeting so that they can arrange to be there without disrupting other planned activities. The leader should work with involved team mem-bers and administrators to arrange blocks of common meeting times dur-ing the day, making before- or after-school sessions unnecessary.

To demonstrate the importance of team member decision making, the leader should conduct meetings so recommendations are stated in a form under-stood by all, that educators responsible for working with the student, such as regular classroom and bilingual education teachers, understand fully what they are to do to help the student, and when the next meeting concerning the student will be held to measure progress. It is critical that the leader con-duct follow-up discussions at subsequent meetings to ensure student progress and teacher satisfaction.

"Is the role of team leader a great deal of extra work?" asks John. It is work, often with unknown variables and requiring time and organizational skills. However, it does not have to be *extra* work. The team leader should receive additional released time from teaching and other committee responsibilities to be effective. Individuals enjoying leadership, group interaction, and making an impact will find tremendous satisfaction in this role.

# SUMMARY

Chapter 3 discussed the benefits of collaboration of educators working together in pairs or teams to resolve the learning and behavioral problems of students at risk. A central goal would include having all students remain with peers in regular education classes wherever possible, while providing teacher supports for success.

Westside officials considered the broad series of changes necessary to create an inclusive environment and selected site-based management as a means of countering opposition to modifications superimposed by districtwide administrators. Structured on Birch and Reynolds's model (1983), a series of differentiated staffing patterns would be selected by the educators at each school, redefining teacher-teacher and teacher-student instructional arrangements.

Faculty in each school would consider the best alternatives for serving students in regular education classrooms. Their plan should include ways that regular and special education teachers, school, and districtwide support staff could work together instead of separately. Regular education teachers would receive training in working with all types of students, while the additional range of instructors and administrative personnel would play a supportive role. It is important to note that supportive does not mean subordinate. Truly collaborative teamwork would require all educators to work together instead of separately or competitively.

Rarely will resources be available to fund ongoing specialist support in every classroom, especially for the participation of students with low-incidence disabilities. Consultants may provide this support by visiting schools on an individually scheduled basis or regional teams funded by the school district can meet with regular education teachers to confer on specific learning, behavioral, or social problems.

Colleges and universities are encouraged to become part of the collaborative structure by preparing all preservice teachers, not only specialists, to work with students with disabilities. Developing teachers can be trained in district classrooms under the guidance of a mentor teacher. Their university faculty can be part of school planning and intervention teams, working as equal members with teachers and support personnel. Additionally, university research can be directed more completely toward solving field-based problems encountered in schools daily.

Prereferral is critical to successful intervention with students at risk. Whereas traditional assessment involved the review only of students severe enough to be considered for special education services, prereferral seeks to identify student problems much earlier and to provide intervention immediately. By educators working together to solve a small problem before it becomes greater, often they can avoid the need for an eventual special education placement.

A primary reason for the current emphasis on prereferral has been the dramatic increase in numbers of students with problems entering schools today. The spread of substance abuse and violence, as well as the increase in societal expectations for the schools to overcome the effects of poverty and lack of stimulation, have made it impossible for educators to ignore children's needs. Because no one teacher working alone can be expected to handle these problems, collaboration within teams of educators has become mandatory to develop the best intervention strategies.

These planning teams consist primarily of regular educators, with specialists, administrators, parents, and students participating as appropriate. In the Teacher Assistance Team model (Chalfant & Pysh, 1989), the faculty elects several teachers from varied grades and disciplines as team members. In the Teacher Resource Model (Maher, in Nelson & Smith, 1991), a consultant trains selected regular classroom teachers and specialists to provide inservices, consultation, and technical assistance directed towards students at risk. The referring teacher requesting help with a particular student remains a team member as long as assistance is needed. Consultants play a more direct role in the Mainstream Assistance Team (Fuchs, Fuchs, & Bahr, 1990), visiting individual classrooms to work with teachers on specific problems.

Critical issues in success of planning teams include the absence of bureaucracy and paperwork, released time from instructional and logistical responsibilities, and scheduled times for meeting periods. Often the time factor is the most difficult, forcing schools to become more flexible through early dismissal or supervised after-school activities for students. In the absence of funds to pay team members for additional time involvements, districts can train paraprofessionals to perform many of their supervisory or monitoring tasks.

While planning team emphasis is on regular classroom teachers sharing and solving problems with specialist input as needed, collaboration with school or community individuals from the same language and cultural background is critical to be sure that the student's needs are really understood. Members also seek parental input to develop appropriate intervention strategies. Where appropriate, students are welcome to meet with the team as a whole or with individual members to become participants in their own goal-setting and change process.

Selection of team members to collaborate in the intervention process is critical. Chapter 3 discussed optimal criteria for team membership. Factors such as previous classroom experience contribute to credibility, while knowledge of varied curricula and material and an ability to individualize instruction allow programming for unique student needs. One or more members should have skills in assessment of behavior and learning problems. Importantly, other members should be aware of teaching and behavioral management strategies for students at risk. If student needs are extreme, specialists should be included on the team. Individuals with cultural and language backgrounds similar to the student's should be included from the school and community. Members can contribute most positively and experience the regard of others when strong communication skills allow them to interact easily and when they are excited about the intervention model at their school, evidencing a positive attitude. Most parents want to be part of interventions on their child's behalf and are eager contributors to the team process. When reluctant, their children may encourage them to become more involved in the school, usually because of a desire to remain in the regular education classroom and avoid special education placement.

The significance of a strongly directed team leader was underscored in this chapter. To be effective, the leader should be strongly committed to the concept of assisting learners with special needs to be successful in the regular classroom, especially through supporting their teachers' efforts. Qualities such as leadership, interactive skills based on humor and perspective, and consideration of team members' schedules are critical. The leader should also distribute work fairly among members, establish case priorities based on degree of urgency, and ensure that all members understand fully what they are to do to help the student be successful.

The key to successful collaboration lies in special and regular educators working together with the student's successful integration as the goal. Chapter 3 emphasized that the planning team is a critical aspect of successful intervention with learners at risk. The full role of the most important team member, the regular classroom teacher who will implement the plan, will be discussed in Chapter 4.

CASE STUDY: *Elementary*

Teresa has been a strong supporter of inclusion, but she's starting to have some second thoughts. With the changes in staffing patterns at West-side, her role as a special educator would be altered dramatically. Instead of having classes of students in her Resource Room, she would be traveling to regular educator's classes to give them support for their teaching. While in the past she has felt isolated from other educators at times, she's not sure that she won't be losing more than she's gaining by being in someone else's classroom.

Sensing Teresa's feelings, Maura is concerned that Teresa has shared teaching responsibilities when they work collaboratively with the third-grade class. Since Teresa will work with her for 1 1/2 hours each day during language arts, together they can reach more children if they plan and work cooperatively. The key will be to make both teachers feel it is their class and their room.

---

Maura has four students in the third-grade class who are significantly below others in reading and written expression.

1. Describe the type of small-group support Teresa can provide in the classroom if the skills being taught are too difficult for these students.

2. If Teresa and Maura were to share the large- and small-group teaching for 1 1/2 hours each day, what are ways they can divide instruction so teaching will become more creative and fun for them as well as their students?

3. As Teresa designs her involvement in the inclusive school, she realizes teachers are most threatened by students with behavioral problems. What are ways she can support a broader number of teachers in the school as they include these students in their classes?

## CASE STUDY: *Secondary*

Teachers at Apter High have decided to restructure so that teams of area teachers will work with the same "core" of 120 students daily. Regardless of their content area, they feel this change will allow them to get to know students better, identify students at risk sooner, and plan with each other more closely.

As the new structure evolves, John sees the opportunity to develop a stronger prereferral process within each core. For stability and continuity, he wants to have one or two educators from a core become permanent prereferral committee members for any students potentially at risk within their assigned student group. As noted in Table 3–2, the other members of this committee would change as a particular student was referred by core teachers.

1. Who  should be the permanent prereferral committee members? What guidelines should John recommend so their time commitment will not become overwhelming?

2. Two of the content area teachers in John's core do not feel the need for prereferral teams to discuss individual students. They believe their meetings twice-monthly to discuss curriculum and the general progress of students in their core is enough. They fear too many meetings.

   a. Are they right?
   b. What can John suggest to modify the structure so these teachers become supportive?

3. When a student first appears at risk and core teachers indicate the need to call a prereferral team meeting,

   a. Who should be asked to attend?
   b. Are parents included at the first session or later?
   c. How will team members obtain any background information or records on the student? Should they discuss this information at the first meeting or later?

# 4

# FROM COLLABORATION TO INCLUSION

The significance of collaboration between regular and special educators had become very apparent to teachers in Westside. Alex decided to explore the specifics of team member roles and strategies during his next inservice.

"We've discussed the ongoing prereferral team leader and members, but what about the referring teachers, the ones who are going to have to implement the plan? What are their responsibilities?" Maura asks.

Districts implementing inclusion have learned that the key to success is in the hands of the regular classroom teacher, who must be able to identify and then intervene effectively with students who behave or learn differently. However, as noted in Table 4–1, their initial

---

**Table 4–1**
**Role of Regular Education Teacher in the Collaborative Process**

*Regular educators should:*

- Be aware of symptoms and behaviors of students at risk

- Meet with the collaborative team leader to discuss concerns with specific student

- Meet with the collaborative team and present the case

- Help determine the best case manager to interact with family, student, and/or social services

- Brainstorm plans for intervention with other members of the collaborative team

- Implement the plan recommended by the team

- Report progress and ongoing concerns to the team at subsequent meetings

involvement is as a participant in the team process. Their attitude of acceptance or rejection of team efforts will "make or break" successful inclusion of students in their classroom.

Regular education teachers need to be aware of the identifying characteristics of students experiencing personal or academic problems. While most would have little difficulty noticing an explosive child, the more subtle signs, such as withdrawal or loss of friends, must become equally significant. It is extremely important that teachers recognize these indicators early, before it becomes necessary to refer the student for special education services.

The concerned teacher contacts the prereferral team leader directly, presenting problems and discussing the urgency of the situation. The teacher next meets with the core prereferral team, describing concerns. At this meeting, the team can decide additional members to add, considering the student's other teachers, necessary specialists, parents and community members, and the student.

"So the basic team is in place and doesn't have to be reinstated each time," Maura notes. "That makes it a lot easier if teachers know in advance whom to contact with a problem."

Exactly. Time is a critical factor. Regular educators should not allow student behaviors and their own level of frustration to worsen. As soon as possible, the entire team should be convened, with the referring teacher reviewing student behaviors and requesting assistance on developing and implementing a plan. As members brainstorm ideas, a case manager should be appointed to orchestrate team efforts so follow-up procedures are not fragmented. At times, this case manager will be the referring teacher or someone familiar to the student. However, when specialist or social services interventions are necessary, such as in suspected instances of child abuse, the case manager might be another involved member, such as the school counselor or vice-principal.

Most often classroom modifications are suggested by the team. If the teacher is not aware of remedial strategies or extensive behavioral management techniques, an assigned special education teacher may provide ongoing support through a consultation model, suggesting specific interventions and meeting with the classroom teacher on a scheduled basis to provide support. When students demonstrate low-incidence disabilities, such as deafness or blindness, the school district or regional service center may be asked to include an expert on the team for initial programming considerations as well as for subsequent consultation with the teacher.

At a predetermined time, the team reconvenes and the teacher presents a report on progress and continuing concerns in plan implementation. The case manager discusses related services and their success, giving all involved team members the opportunity to comment on any ongoing problems. They discuss additional intervention strategies. If necessary, they determine a meeting time to provide follow-up, or request that the teacher contact the leader if additional problems arise.

# COLLABORATING EFFECTIVELY WITH THE PLANNING TEAM

Regular education teachers need the ongoing involvement of their colleagues to be most effective. Intervention teams in Illinois found their initial role was to serve more as a support team for teachers than as an actual change agent for students (Andringa & Keller, 1991). While some of this support occurs outside committee sessions through discussion of specific implementation strategies, most of it occurs during meetings. Table 4–2 lists some of the factors found to be most effective in productive collaborative sessions.

***Common Goals.***  Throughout the design of intervention for students at risk, it is critical that all educators be committed to a common goal of providing the best education possible in the least restrictive environment (Anderlini, 1983). In doing so, they should show respect for individual differences in physical appearance, race, sex, disability, ethnicity, religion, socioeconomic status, or ability (West & Cannon, 1988).

***Student-Centered Program.***  The concern cannot be how to get rid of a problem, but instead, how to help involved educators and students alike be most successful. Basic to this goal is the "adhocratic" spirit advocated by Skrtic

---

**Table 4–2**
**Factors in Effective Collaboration**

*Team members should:*

- Be committed to a common goal of providing the best education possible in the least restrictive environment

- Design the program to meet unique needs of each student

- Share insights and expertise

- Practice effective communication with a limited use of technical language

- Include at least one member of similar cultural background to the student

- Promote high expectations for students with disabilities

- Engage in conflict resolution through active listening

- Receive training in remedial teaching strategies and behavioral interventions

- Include family and community members, where appropriate

- Have full awareness of team operating procedures

(*Sources:* Adapted from Chalfant & Pysh, 1989; Skrtic, in Thousand, 1990; Morsink & Lenk, 1992)

(in conversation with Thousand, 1990). With this attitude, instructional programs are designed around the needs of the student instead of the bureaucratic structure, which first creates the program and then tries to make students fit into the standardized mold. Proceeding with a student-centered instead of a **program-centered approach** allows team members to view each student as unique instead of as a member of a problem group. This very concept takes educators away from an historic tendency to label students.

For example, if Maura approaches the team with concerns about a nine-year-old student who acts aggressively toward others, has no friends, and calls out frequently in class, it would be inappropriate for her team members to attempt to categorize this student as behaviorally disordered (or more specifically, conduct disordered) and to discuss what they have done with students demonstrating similar behaviors in the past. Such initial labeling with a subsequent attempt to provide services has been the direction of special education placement for years. The goal is not to label at all, but to examine *why* the student is behaving in this manner (Problems at home? Models of aggression as appropriate? Low self-esteem? Peer group?) and how to combine the expertise of concerned adults in changing the behavior before it becomes habitual. Such considerations mandate a **child-centered approach.**

***Shared Expertise.***  In discussions regarding this student, the traditional role of the expert superimposing a plan is inappropriate. All members of the team have been chosen for their expertise and should be regarded as equally competent in problem-solving (Thousand, Villa, Paolucci-Whitcomb, & Nevin, 1992). The language arts teacher who has just finished a successful unit needs to be given the opportunity to share his workable solution of using **contingencies** with this student. Concerned because the child has begun to demonstrate these behaviors at home since parents experienced a difficult divorce, the mother needs to discuss what has and has not been effective. The counselor should consider whether individual sessions or ones with peers will be best in improving the child's self-esteem. Participants need to be able to put aside their traditional roles through sharing information and competencies (Lyon & Lyon, 1980). In this way, there will be no jealous guarding of expertise but the development of a spirit of camaraderie that will help Maura impact the child's behavior.

***Effective Communication.*** Researchers and practitioners alike agree that **effective communication** among team members is at the core of significant intervention (Anderlini, 1983). **Active listening** to each other can result in brainstorming of new ideas. Part of this listening includes nonjudgmental paraphrasing and summarizing ideas for personal and group clarity, ongoing verbal and nonverbal feedback, and crediting others for their ideas and accomplishments (West & Cannon, 1988). Educators need to avoid specialized vocabulary that might set them aside from others. They should maintain good relationships with all team members through showing

---

**program-centered approach—** instruction is designed to meet general programmatic goals.

**child-centered approach—** instruction is designed to meet the needs of the children.

**contingencies—**effective consequences used to deter or encourage certain behaviors.

**effective communication—** interactions that produce the intended results or outcomes.

**active listening—**a technique in which people show interest and understanding in what others are saying; often exhibited by using eye contact and gestures of acknowledgment.

respect for others' ideas and remaining nonthreatening in questions, earning the trust of their colleagues (Chalfant & Pysh, 1989).

In the instance of Maura's disruptive student, it would be fairly easy to communicate even nonverbally to the mother feelings by team members that the child's behavior is her fault. Likely, the mother would feel threatened and become defensive about her own actions, undercutting the team concern of how to intervene best with the child. Alternately, if the approach becomes one of "What can *we* do to help her?," the mother understands the goal of the group, is not threatened personally, and becomes an integral part of the process, appreciative of the school's support.

**Understanding of Varied Cultural Backgrounds.**  If the family is from a culture different from the majority of the school, the team must be open to discussion and input from members of similar backgrounds to understand the problem. Not only will this expand their own experiences, but it may help them appreciate the reasons for the child's behavior. However, it is important for the group not to develop alternate **stereotypes**, concluding that the student is incapable of responding properly because of ethnicity or language differences. Such an attitude may prevent the development of appropriate behaviors by a reverse bias of lowered expectations.

**stereotypes**—critical judgment; categorizing expectations based on generalizable preconceptions about specific groups.

"I know exactly what that means," comments John Robinson. "Several years ago I was supervising a student teacher in my high school English classes. She was really a good teacher in terms of lessons she planned and her interest in the students. But she was terrible with discipline and the classes were becoming progressively more disruptive when she taught. Well, one day a fight broke out between two students, one of them Caucasian and the other African-American. They had been clowning around and it had just gotten out-of-hand when she didn't stop it early enough. She sent both boys to the principal's office and went there after class to follow up on a punishment. She reprimanded the African-American student for his participation and sent him back to class. Then she recommended the other student for on-campus suspension for his involvement. Yet both boys had been involved equally in starting the fight.

"That night at home I received a call from the African-American student's mother. She told me how her son had come home gloating that he had gotten away with his fighting and the other student had been punished. She was really angry. She was so right when she asked why her son had not been equally suspended for his role. She wanted to know if the student teacher's expectation was that African-American students could not behave properly, therefore not benefitting from the same punishment as other students when breaking school rules. The mother said that she expected her son to attend graduate school some day and allowing him to misbehave was going against his valuing education as important.

"When I discussed it with the student teacher the next day, she was horrified. It was clear that she had not realized she was stereotyping students, but had done it subconsciously. While there was no good way to remedy this situation except to equalize the punishment after the fact, I think she learned a powerful lesson."

In John's example, it became necessary for someone close to the student to point out what had happened, not unusual when educators have not had a previous opportunity to analyze their own thoughts or feelings about a situation. When working as a team trying to help students at risk, members can only benefit from support and explanation from others who can better understand the student's background and needs.

***High Expectations.*** Ethnic and racial differences are not the only reasons expectations are fixed by stereotypes or prejudices. Bogden and Biklen (1977) discuss the attitude of "handicapism," which has encouraged a sense that some individuals are second-class and unable to benefit from services and has been at the core of the development of a separate special educational system.

Gartner and Lipsky (1987) note that the perception of the outcomes of disability adversely affects educators' expectations regarding the academic achievement of these students. This attitude not only serves to separate them from other students, but involves them in a "watered-down" curriculum, excuses them from local and national academic standards and tests applied to other students, at times gives them grades they have not earned, and often results in their receiving different diplomas than peers. These lowered expectations have also resulted in state departments of education, school districts, and even the courts excusing students considered disabled from the social and behavioral standards established for other students.

The positive outcomes of effective schools should be accessible to all students (Gartner & Lipsky, 1987). If teachers can develop an attitude that students are more alike than different, that the child comes before the disability

When teachers view students as more alike than different, inclusion becomes easier.

(e.g., "a student with a learning disability," instead of a "learning disabled student"), they will begin to expect common codes of conduct from all students and to adapt instead of dilute the curriculum. They will become powerful models for these attitudes for their typical students, encouraging a more extensive acceptance of all students in their classrooms.

***Conflict Resolution.*** Difficult issues may cause conflict in the collaborative process. Since long-term success with all students is based on the ability of team members to work together positively, any conflictive situations should be handled immediately without allowing emotions to escalate and influence future teamwork. The skills of the team leader will be of paramount importance as conflicts arise. The leader should not just placate, but be sure that active listening continues as the group reaches to understand the thoughts of each member. The initial sense of group cohesion and respect will support these efforts.

Basic to successful conflict management is an understanding of the underlying causes of disagreement. If Maura's student has become extremely disruptive to the class and the accelerated use of contingency management has been ineffective, she may feel upset if the group conclusion is to continue in the same direction. Fundamental to her unhappiness is that she is threatened by a student she cannot control, that she has already attempted what the team is recommending, and essentially, no team member really understands the situation or how deeply it is upsetting her. If another teacher at the meeting suggests the student is not so difficult in his class and Maura just has not found the correct contingencies to change the student behavior, she is likely to respond in anger, suggesting that this other teacher might like to have the student all day since he is having such strong success.

"You're right about that," admits Maura. "The one thing I can't stand in my classes is when students don't follow the rules. I think you've understated my anger if another teacher insinuated that I just hadn't tried hard enough or been clever enough to come up with the right management system.

"What would work for me is if the committee commiserated with my frustration, asked me what I had tried and why I felt it hadn't worked. If we couldn't brainstorm anything I felt was better, I would want the option of asking other educators more expert than we are in behavior management, or of working more closely with the student's parents to develop a total plan for home and school." Maura has asked herself what would work if team efforts-to-date had been ineffective, and has come up with some viable solutions.

During conflict management in the meetings, the person most upset is often the teacher or parent primarily responsible for the student. The team must anticipate teacher concern and in each situation ask how they can be most supportive. As Maura was able to develop a plan to meet her own needs, most educators can give direction to the process if they feel group follow-up support instead of disagreement.

*Staff Training.* Knowledge of best teaching and behavioral management techniques is also critical. For staff to generate workable intervention strategies, they need to be trained. Such training takes administrative support through providing time and resources for educators in the district. In reviewing the effectiveness of twenty-three prereferral teams in impacting student behavior, Chalfant and Pysh (1985) noted that twenty-one teams (91 percent) cited support from the building principal as a key factor. In their later review of ninety-six teams in seven states, they note a 63.9 percent decrease in the number of inappropriate referrals and an 88.7 percent rate of successful interventions (Chalfant & Pysh, 1989).

*Family-Community Involvement.* While the inclusion of families and community members has been mentioned earlier in team formation, the importance of their input must be underscored. In their study of an Illinois school district, Andringa and Keller (1991) found that 30 percent of student referrals across the district were from **dysfunctional** families. If the family chooses to participate with educators and community representatives, such as those from social services, their membership on the team can critically underscore success with the child since the functioning of the entire family will be affected.

dysfunctional—abnormal; not providing the nurturing and support needed by family members.

*Team Operating Procedures.* The final requirement is for team members to be well-trained in operating procedures. This allows for support of follow-up intervention. The case manager should fully understand the responsibilities. The regular education teacher should be aware of whom to contact if team recommendations are not working. The parent should have a designated person to call, such as the counselor or case manager, if disruptions have occurred at home or if the student's behaviors are worsening. Members should be aware of the length of time before they reconvene to discuss plan effectiveness. Organization with substance is an excellent underpinning for success and allows the regular education teacher to appreciate that assistance will be ongoing.

# SELECTING THE APPROPRIATE REGULAR EDUCATION ENVIRONMENT

As discussed in Chapter 2, the concept of least restrictive environment for students with disabilities has been one of the most hotly debated issues both in general and special education. With the emerging philosophy of inclusion, the debate has continued, especially in the midst of the reality of placement of individual students.

nurturing attitude—encouraging and warm disposition.

"Certainly I can relate to that," comments Mort Stern. "At Jackson our teachers tend to have a very **nurturing attitude,** maybe even more so than in a lot
of schools. Yet, I find it's difficult to place certain students because the
teachers are afraid of the disruptions to the entire class. With school starting immediately, I'm feeling pressured because I still haven't found a classroom for several students. How can I decide the best teacher for these
kids?"

Mort's situation is not unusual. Understandably teachers are reluctant to
welcome students who may make their total-class instruction difficult, or whose
needs they may view as time-consuming. Yet, placement in segregated
special education classes for all or part of the day forces these students to be
removed from the very environments they need for normalized experiences.

In too many regions, special educators have determined the need for inclusion without so much as a discussion of the initiative with their regular education colleagues. Yet, they expect all educators to embrace the concept.
Lieberman (1985) compares this trend as similar to "a wedding in which we,
as special educators, have forgotten to invite the bride." Before success can
take place, there are some necessary factors that will make regular educators more supportive, resulting in teachers willing to instruct students with
learning and behavioral differences.

## Factors Supporting Successful Inclusion

As indicated in Table 4–3, one of the most significant ways to impact regular education teacher attitudes has been discussed earlier in this chapter: the
successful use of the collaborative team with a membership of predominantly

**Table 4–3**
**Factors Supporting Successful Inclusion**

*Inclusion requires:*

- Successful use of collaborative planning teams, including educators, parents, student, community members

- Small class size

- Continuous, rather than isolated, staff train- ing in intervention strategies

- Available consultants

- Specialized equipment, media, and comput- ers

- Review of previous assessment and pro- gramming records

- Additional teaching assistants

(*Source:* Waldron, 1995)

general educators. This team promotes the concept that students at-risk or demonstrating disabilities are everyone's responsibility. Once teachers realize there is an organized "safety-net" in the school, often they are less threatened by having these students in their classes.

There are additional factors that will encourage teacher flexibility in allowing students to be placed in the least restrictive environment possible (Waldron, 1995). **Small class size** allows all students to receive attention, quelling teacher concerns about a minority of students monopolizing their time. Continuous teacher training for improved intervention strategies is more effective than the "one-shot deal" approach currently enacted by many districts. Consultants should be available to teachers daily, not just during collaborative team meetings. Additionally, specialized equipment, media, and computers with **adaptive software** should become part of the learning environment. The teacher should be aware of any factors in the student's environment that will impact classroom learning and behavior. They should have available all assessment and previous programming records if the student has been in special education. If the student's needs are more extreme, the district should supply **teaching assistants** to work to meet the needs of specific students, such as through the creation of braille materials to support a student who is blind.

"We could do many of these at Jackson," Mort interjects, "although factors such as smaller classes, the purchase of computers, and the provision of teaching assistants are district decisions. It sounds as if the teachers need my support and I need the school district's."

Exactly. The attitude and expectations of the principal are reflected in the teachers. If Mort regards inclusion as a positive instead of negative challenge and encourages teachers through technical means as well as interest and praise, their attitude will be more open to change. Humor and reassurance as the process is implemented will have a far-reaching effect in developing a good *esprit de corps* in the school.

"Since he heard about the inclusion discussion, Curt O'Hare has been after me to be on his radio show. I hadn't formulated my thoughts or gotten a strong enough pulse from teachers' comments to feel secure talking to the public, so I've been avoiding him. Is this the time?"

Probably not. The best time to meet with groups of parents and community representatives is when the framework is firmly established within the school, any major problems have been solved, and the resources are in place. However, including several involved parents and community members as you develop the program is a very good idea, since their input will be invaluable in understanding community needs and anticipating concerns. After the program has been carefully planned and initiated, along with a parent and community spokesperson, district officials will want to publicize the program and answer questions and concerns. In meetings with parents or during media coverage, it is important to explain the goals of inclusion and how the district will support success for all children. Administrators and

**small class size**—limited number of students in class; allows all students to receive attention.

**adaptive software**—computer programming made to suit a particular need.

**teaching assistants**—people trained to support instruction in an educational situation.

teachers will want to solicit their direct support and ask parents to encourage their children to assist in program success.

"I'm concerned about the parents' representative, Mike Gonzales, who is loudly expressing concern about inclusion lowering the standards for all students," reflects Dr. Mirales. "I'm worried about the hostility he always seems to generate in the community as well as a potential law suit, which would really tie our hands and be very expensive."

It is a rare district that has the support of all parents or that does not experience real anger from some parents. Instead of being afraid of the response of certain groups, it is better to include them in the design of the program. Mike is concerned that inclusion will mean the loss of educational resources for his son, who is extremely gifted. He feels he is being a good parent by opposing anything that would diminish his own son's schooling. If invited to be part of the process where he can see that improving education for other students need not detract from his son's education, he may be satisfied or even supportive. He would be a very powerful spokesperson on local media in persuading other parents to adopt the program. If he is too hostile to be a contributing group member during planning sessions and you cannot risk his destroying the process, you may want to include a few members of the regular education parent community who are well-regarded but nonhostile.

While a recent emphasis on litigation has encouraged its use as a threat, it is important for educators to realize the courts continue to place students

A student should be placed in an inclusive classroom only after readiness is established.

in regular education initially and only change to a more segregated environment when all reasonable supports have failed. It is likely that even an irate parent will not change this trend.

## Readiness in the Classroom

As in most areas of education, the success of any program is dependent on what takes place between teachers and students in the classroom. Before placing a student in a particular environment, educators should ask themselves a series of questions to be sure both teachers and students can be successful. Tables 4–4 through 4–10 are checklists to be used in making inclusive placements. They contain a series of critical necessities for all involved individuals, from the regular education teacher and students to the building administrator and involved parents. These checklists encompass the areas noted in Table 4–3 and provide an easy mechanism for checking which specific factors for successful inclusion have been met. They can be used as a guide before placement occurs or as an indicator of areas of concentration if the student has already been placed.

In most areas, the *Yes* column should be checked, indicating the classroom is providing appropriate supports. When an area has not been accomplished, such as consideration of previous appraisal records, the teacher should enter the date of anticipated completion of the records review in the *In Progress* column. When *No* has been marked, the collaborative team considering placement of the child should discuss if this factor is important enough to warrant an alternative placement. All educators should realize the goal is not just to place the student, but to have the student be successful in the placement. The areas on the checklist are divided by individual responsibilities and are those that research and practice have indicated as significant in attaining this success (Christensen, Ysseldyke, & Thurlow, 1989; Dardig, 1981; Morsink & Lenk, 1992; Waldron, 1992b).

***The Regular Education Teacher.*** The key to successful inclusion lies in the preparedness of the regular education teacher. Table 4–4 includes characteristics of regular educators that are conducive to the success of the student. The teacher must want to have the student and be able to devote time to meeting special academic and remedial needs. A **pupil-teacher ratio** should be set at a level where the teacher feels capable of responding to all students in the class without ignoring the needs of the larger group. This point is extremely important to most teachers who tend to try to be very fair in apportioning their time among class members. They and their students easily can begin feeling resentful of any child who demands an inordinate amount of time, removing the teacher's attention from others. However, there is no exact ratio that would allow every teacher to work successfully with all students. Factors such as the extent of the integrated student's instructional and behavioral needs and

**pupil-teacher ratio**—the comparative number of students for whom a teacher is responsible.

## Table 4–4
## Checklist for Successful Inclusion: The Regular Education Teacher

| Yes | No | In Progress | |
|---|---|---|---|
| | | | Wants to have the student in class |
| | | | Has received training in a variety of behavioral management strategies |
| | | | Has received training in teaching students requiring academic remediation |
| | | | Is aware of methods of social integration, encouraging the student to have genuine friendships with typical peers |
| | | | Is knowledgeable of the student's background, skill levels, and learning/behavioral goals |
| | | | Has available all assessment and previous programming records if the student has been in special education |
| | | | Has consultants with specialized expertise available for necessary support |
| | | | Allows students to complete assignments at different rates and academic skill levels |
| | | | States classroom rules clearly, yet enforces them flexibly, allowing success of students with attentional problems |
| | | | Modifies the physical environment to accommodate student needs (e.g., nondistractible study areas; ease of access for students with physical/sensory disabilities) |

the amount of one-on-one attention required are better determinants on an individual case basis. Many districts have solved this problem by assigning a teacher assistant to work specifically with a student with more extreme disabilities, freeing up the teacher to attend to the entire class.

Teachers are most successful when they fully understand students' backgrounds and needs. Many students have a previous history of school assessment and goal-setting, especially if they have been in special education. Before the student attends the class, the school should make all records available to the regular education teacher. If the child has been in special classes, the specialist teacher should provide information about student skill levels and programming and behavioral management techniques that have been successful. A regular educator who is fully informed about a new student's background is more confident, does not need to try things that have not worked before, and progresses more quickly toward academic and behavioral goals.

As noted earlier, teachers need training in specialized techniques and curricular and materials modification before they can be successful with students who learn differently. If John has a student in his English class who reads four years below expectancy and subsequently lacks writing skills, neither the student nor John can be successful unless John is knowledgeable of remedial teaching skills.

On the checklist for successful inclusion, the most important consideration before student placement is a well-trained teacher. This teacher allows students to complete their work at different rates or provides assignments at varied academic levels, underscoring student ability to complete the task.

There are modifications that the teacher cannot do alone. John's student, reading years below expectancy, may need more substantial supports than shortened assignments. High interest-low vocabulary reading materials can provide him the information without forcing John to spend inordinate amounts of time in preparation; or, a specialist teacher can work with a small group including the student and any others significantly low in reading, while John instructs the rest of the class. The small-group work with the specialist should take place within the classroom only as needed so students no longer have to miss primary instruction by attending a separate setting. Before a student is placed in a regular education classroom, the teacher and planning team should determine which modifications will be necessary for success. The student will stand the greatest chance of success when these supports are in place. Consultants with specialized expertise must continue to be available as student and teacher needs evolve.

Few things upset a teacher more than a student who refuses to follow class rules. As part of preplacement training, the teacher should receive instruction in a variety of behavioral management strategies. Most importantly, the teacher will learn how to state and post rules clearly from the beginning of the year, enforcing them with specified consequences. Maura's third-graders need to understand acceptable behaviors. Yet a **hyperactive** student will not have the same level of control as a typical student. Through training and support of specialists like Teresa, she will learn how to establish **individual contracts** and enforce rules flexibly, allowing for student differences.

No student should be placed in a classroom where the teacher is unsure of how to encourage social integration with peers. Yet, few tasks are more difficult. If the student has a mild, less noticeable difference, such as a learning disability, integration is easier. When a student has a sensory loss, such as deafness or blindness, often typical peers are uncertain as to how to

**hyperactive**—excessive movement that usually interferes with a student's learning ability.

**individual contracts**—agreements with the teacher in which the student promises to perform or behave a certain way in exchange for an agreed-upon reward from the teacher.

act and tend to ignore their classmate. It becomes the teacher's responsibility to ensure that all students are accepted and respected. Otherwise, the newly integrated student will concentrate more on exclusion from the group than on learning academic work. Part of the teacher's readiness training must encompass methods of social integration.

*readiness*—the background skills necessary to perform task.

**The Student.**  It is as important to review the readiness of the student for inclusion as much as of the teacher. These behaviors are listed in Table 4–5. It is natural for any student who has a history of failure in regular education to be skeptical about the possibility of personal success. A student's desire to participate may be based on perceived future opportunities to accomplish general goals for the class and to be respected by peers. If the teacher communicates acceptance and expectations for acceptable achievement, the student will work hard to prove the teacher correct. Often this sense of mutual cooperation toward a common goal is the foundation for teacher-student positive interactions.

*flexible rules*—regulations that are capable of modification to suit the needs of the student and teacher.

While the teacher needs to set **flexible rules** and be trained in behavior management, with direction the integrated student needs to be able to behave appropriately, be nondisruptive toward others, and follow teacher

**Table 4–5**
**Checklist for Successful Inclusion: The Student at Risk**

| Yes | No | In Progress | |
|---|---|---|---|
| | | | Wants to be in the regular classroom |
| | | | Understands class rules and routines |
| | | | Attends to task long enough to complete modified assignments |
| | | | Reacts appropriately to peers socially |
| | | | Responds correctly to verbal and/or written directions |
| | | | Does not disrupt the classroom environment for others |
| | | | Has the opportunity for frequent interactions with teachers and peers |
| | | | Is able to meet behavioral expectations of the environment |
| | | | Has the opportunity to be actively involved in class lessons |

rules. Often a student's behavioral skills cannot be fully predicted on a pre-placement checklist. They are dependent on teacher training and personal flexibility as well as student abilities to integrate and respond to class rules. If the student has participated previously in special education, the specialist teacher will be an important resource in discussion of best management systems. Otherwise, the behavioral area should be one of ongoing discussion by the planning team supporting the regular educator, so the student's behavior does not detract from academic success.

Contrary to teacher fears, not every student at risk is distracting to others. Often students learn to become passive to avoid the personal embarrassment of displaying weak skills to classmates or because they do not know how to respond socially. If the student is asked to do work she is capable of completing, she becomes an **active learner**. If she is placed in a group with others working on an academic project, she becomes part of their goal accomplishment.

**active learner**—a student who shows genuine involvement and understanding during the lesson.

**socially appropriate**—acceptable based on the norms of society.

To be included fully, she needs to be able to react to peers in a **socially appropriate** manner. "This is really a problem at times," Maura reflects. "I had a student last year who wanted very badly to be part of the group. He had no friends in class, but it was easy to see why. He was loud and disruptive and said things that hurt other students' feelings. He was very bright, but never understood how to act properly if he wanted others to like or respect him."

Many students who are unaccepted by others would really like to behave appropriately. However, for many reasons, ranging from a neurology that drives their body like a highly tuned engine or previous exposure to aggressive role models, these students are inappropriate in their actions around others. Along with the student, the teacher and class can take some responsibility for improving the student's behaviors. However, at this decision point, the student's potential for acceptance and ability to work with others should be considered carefully with the goal of placement in the setting where suitable social behaviors will most likely occur.

*Typical Peers.* As indicated in Table 4–6, peers in a class have a supportive role in making inclusion work. It is unrealistic to expect them to take the lead without teacher direction and guidance. As a student with a disability is placed in a regular class, the teacher, and when possible, the student, should discuss with the class the nature of the disability. For example, if a hearing-impaired student is to join the class, the teacher might discuss generally the nature of a hearing loss and how it could impact the student's class involvement. Many teachers have found it helpful to use media support, showing the class a video about the disability. The student may want to have others try her hearing aid so they become more relaxed about the disability. If the student joins the class at the beginning of the year, the teacher could discuss the nature of other disabilities as well, avoiding "singling out" one student.

If the disability is a sensory impairment and the student will be present, the teacher should ask him in advance if it will be acceptable to discuss the

## Table 4–6
## Checklist for Successful Inclusion: Typical Peers

| Yes | No | In Progress | |
|-----|-----|-------------|---|
| | | | Have been informed about the nature of any disabilities of newly included students |
| | | | Are encouraged to incorporate the student with a disability in their friendship groups |
| | | | Have been told how they can assist the student in participating in class activities |
| | | | Feel free to ask questions about the student's behaviors or how they can assist the student's inclusion in their class |

disability with the class. Often the student is pleased to join in the open discussion and to answer questions. Younger students tend to be more open about allowing others to try any supportive equipment they may need, such as a wheel chair or a brailler. Once typical peers are given the opportunity to understand that the disability is not something to fear, they begin to accept the student more readily.

"How do I prepare my high school students to accept a student who can't read the text?" asks John. Particularly as students become older or when they have academic or behavioral problems, they are not as open to a general discussion by the teacher with their peers. They find these discussions embarrassing and the basis for being singled out as different. It may be far better for the teacher to assume a leadership position initiating class activities incorporating these students. When students are performing a group project, John can appoint the student to a particular role in which he feels the student can be successful. If the student is not being accepted socially, John might have her work in pairs or small groups with a variety of other students to develop patterns of acceptance. In all instances, emphasis should be placed on the student's capability, not disability, so that peers will become more inclusive naturally.

*The Specialist.*  The availability of specialist support may be the critical variable for successful inclusion. As indicated in Table 4–7, before placement, a specialist with expertise in areas of student disability should be a member of the planning team, giving input into the design of the intervention plan. During meetings, the specialist should discuss the student's areas of difficulty and programming needs in nontechnical language with educators and parents. The specialist's role in program implementation is crucial, since she

## Table 4–7
## Checklist for Successful Inclusion: The Specialist

| Yes | No | In Progress | |
|-----|----|----|---|
| | | | Possesses expertise in areas of student difficulty/disability |
| | | | Supports collaborative team efforts in designing student intervention plan |
| | | | Consults effectively with individual educators in plan implementation |
| | | | As appropriate, teaches collaboratively with the regular education teacher in the inclusive classroom |
| | | | Discusses the student's problems and programming with educators and family members, without the use of technical vocabulary |

becomes the supportive educator responding to specific needs by the team. At times she may best be a consultant, meeting weekly with the regular education teacher. Other times, collaboration with the regular education teacher is more appropriate. When there are lingering concerns, she may serve as a case manager to discuss ongoing concerns with the parents and student directly. Any of these roles may be appropriate for the specialist based on the needs of the student and teacher. However, before making the regular education placement, the specialist should work together closely with the team and teacher to determine what the best intervention role should be.

The school district must make a commitment to provide specialists for the regular classroom teacher. If a student needs more extensive assistance to be successful, such as individual work with the specialist, every attempt should be made to provide supports at the time of placement. District officials should be aware that a teaching assistant is not an educational specialist. Assistants do not have the training to design intervention strategies and should not be used in place of specialists.

***The School/District Administrator.*** These considerations lead naturally to the function of school and districtwide administrators, listed in Table 4–8. As in any leadership position, the attitude of the individual often leads to programmatic success or failure.

"I'm really aware of that," comments Mort. "I admit that my own feelings were mixed when the superintendent told us the district was adopting

| Table 4–8 |
| :-- |
| **Checklist for Successful Inclusion: The School Administrator** |

| Yes | No | In Progress | |
| :-- | :-- | :-- | :-- |
| | | | Encourages inclusive placements |
| | | | Supports the acquisition of resources to support student success in regular education classes |
| | | | Acts as a liaison with central office personnel to ensure districtwide support for students at risk |
| | | | Provides opportunities for inservice training for all teachers in the school |
| | | | Explains goals of inclusive programming to parents and community organizations |

inclusion and we needed to make it work. As I've studied its success in other districts, I've seen its potential to be very strong. My own turning point came when I visited inclusive classrooms in nearby districts and talked with teachers who discussed their own initial hesitations, but who were now really excited about having integrated students whom they never felt would succeed in their classrooms. Their enthusiasm was infectious. I really hope to see Jackson's regular and special education teachers feeling the same way in the next few years. I'm excited and personally challenged."

Within his school, Mort will be responsible for initiating the planning team to identify and intervene with students at risk. He should work with the team at their request, listening to their concerns and supplying information or specialist supports for individual children. He might provide opportunities for teachers to visit same-level classrooms in inclusive schools in other districts to view first-hand the possibilities for success. Mort's teachers need to view him as their liaison to available district resources. He becomes their spokesperson in obtaining the daily supports to make their teaching successful with a variety of learners. By providing them this sustenance, he allows them the time and freedom to concentrate on their teaching role. Teachers should never have to struggle to obtain the resources they need for successful instruction. Administrators should work to obtain supports so teachers will not be distracted from their primary work in the classroom.

Dr. Mirales's role is broader than Mort's. As special education director, she is the districtwide facilitator of program logistics as well as supportive resources, such as providing specialist teachers. She can perform school-based needs assessments on individual campuses to determine areas where the general faculty want additional training before implementing inclusion. Then she can provide opportunities for inservice training for all teachers in the school.

Dr. Mirales is not alone in directing the success of this program. She needs to collaborate with administrators in regular education, such as Elena and Mort, to spread her enthusiasm and support into their schools. When Mort's teachers need specific resources, he should be able to contact Dr. Mirales to expedite the system. As he is the promoter of his teachers' requests, so she must be his liaison in the central office.

As part of this integrated system, the collaborative skills discussed in the previous chapter become as critical for administrators as for teachers. At a districtwide level, Dr. Mirales may want to initiate a planning team consisting of herself, school principals, and a teacher and parent from each involved campus. When the programs in these pilot schools have proven successful, several of these team members may meet with planning teams in additional schools to help them establish their own inclusive systems.

Once the initial collaborative administrative team has been working smoothly, they can meet with parents and community groups to explain inclusive programming, responding to questions and concerns. By this time, ownership of successful inclusion should belong to a number of individuals. It is not Dr. Mirales's program, but a districtwide attempt to treat all students more equitably. No one person should receive praise or blame. Instead, everyone is working together toward a common goal.

*Parents of Students at Risk.*  Whether their children are typical or disabled, all parents have a contributory role in making inclusion work. As noted in Table 4–9, educators should include parents in placement decisions from the

**Table 4–9**
**Checklist for Successful Inclusion: Parents of Students at Risk**

| Yes | No | In Progress | |
|-----|-----|-----|-----|
| | | | Have been invited to participate in collaborative meetings regarding placement of their child |
| | | | Are included in decisions about placement changes |
| | | | Have been asked to support school efforts by encouraging the child's success in the regular education classroom |
| | | | Are given specific methods to use at home to enhance child's academic and behavioral needs |

| | | | Table 4–10<br>Checklist for Successful Inclusion: Parents of Typical Students |
|---|---|---|---|

| Yes | No | In Progress | |
|---|---|---|---|
| | | | Have had the goals of the inclusive program explained to them in parent meetings |
| | | | Have had the opportunity to ask questions of teachers and administrators regarding classroom changes |
| | | | Have been requested to support the inclusive concept and to encourage their children to assist in program success |

onset. Parents of students at risk should meet with the planning committee to consider the appropriate environment before any placement changes occur. While some may express hesitation about a less restrictive setting, it is important for committee members to encourage them to support their child's success. Many parents respond well when the teacher or specialist meets with them after the placement and suggests specific activities they can do at home to underscore classroom learning. This encourages them to become part of the process.

***Parents of Typical Students.*** All parents should be part of placement considerations, as indicated in Table 4–10. While the need to ensure privacy prevents their involvement on the planning committee for students with disabilities, they should understand the broader goals of inclusion. District and school administrators should explain the program and answer questions at parent meetings. They might discuss specific ways parents can discuss inclusion at home with their children so typical students can assist in program success.

## Curricular Considerations

Muoio (in Larson, McIntire, & Muoio, 1993) adds questions concerning curricular modification for successfully adapting the teaching-learning situation. She emphasizes that these should not be used as a basis for excluding students for whom the standard curriculum is difficult, but as a point of reflection for educators in deciding the extent of modification necessary. Her questions appear in Table 4–11.

**Table 4–11**
**Questions for Curriculum Modification**

1. Can the student participate in this classroom activity in the same manner as typical students?

2. Can the student participate, with adaptive materials available to facilitate full involvement?

3. Can the student participate, but with an emphasis on different skill areas, such as communication, motor, and social development?

4. Can the student be part of the group, but work on a different activity, designed to meet an individual educational goal?

5. Can the student be working in another part of the classroom on an activity to meet individual goals?

6. Can the student do an out-of-class activity that is relevant to individual educational priorities and to classroom expectations?

(*Source:* Adapted from Muoio, in Larson, McIntire, & Muoio, 1993)

The goal of these curricular considerations is to normalize the classroom experience as much as possible for students with disabilities. It can be time-consuming for teachers to have to make curricular adaptations and exclusionary for students not to participate as fully as possible. Therefore, it is in the best interests of both for students to work within the typical curriculum wherever appropriate.

However, sometimes the student cannot be successful without additional supports, including adaptive materials, such as computers, tangible objects, or media. These needs should be predetermined by the classroom teacher or indicated by consultant specialists so the student is not left with a sense of failure and forced to be a nonparticipant in a group activity. Supportive educational materials often can be obtained from the **regional service center** or from **media/materials centers** in many school districts. (Specific suggestions for curricular and materials modification are discussed in Chapter 13.)

**regional service center**—federally and state-funded resources and consultants available to educators in a designated geographic area.

**media/materials centers**—a library of supportive educational materials.

**peer interaction skills**—ability to act reciprocally and appropriately with peers.

At times, the student may not be able to complete the group task fully, but can work on related skill areas of need, such as involvement in discussions or social activities. Since improvement of **peer interaction skills** is a critical part of many students' plans, their involvement provides opportunities for reinforcement.

If the curricular emphasis is academic instead of social and the student is unable to complete group assignments because of skills deficiencies, he may be part of the group physically while working on an individualized educational task supporting remedial or compensatory skills. Especially at the secondary level, it is unlikely there would be only one or two students

With corrections, the student writes, "A 17-year-old boy set a school on fire. The fire fighters were taken to put it out. Why do you think he did it?" Part of the curriculum should support student integration of responses to difficult social problems. Reprinted with permission, Winston School, San Antonio.

completing differentiated assignments, since academic skills may range across such a broad spectrum of abilities.

"This is certainly the case in my English classes," reports John. "Even before discussions about inclusion I've had to prepare alternate assignments for a number of students. The first year I did this I thought it was a waste of time, but I've saved the assignments in my file drawer and use them every semester. Interestingly enough, many of the students requiring curricular modifications are not even in special education or considered at risk by the school. They are most often students who never mastered basic skills."

An important outgrowth of considering the needs of students who learn differently is that the curriculum and methods can be very useful with a broad number of students. Sometimes a student has needs that cannot be met by the larger group activity and require placement in another part of the room. If there are any peers requiring reinforcement in similar areas, they can work with the student to avoid a sense of isolation. If not, these activities can be carried out when the entire class is performing individual desk-work so the isolation does not become obvious.

"What about the students with more extreme needs?" asks Teresa Fuentes. "Should I continue to work with them in my Resource classroom?"

*The goal of inclusion is to have students in the general education classroom as much of the day as possible.* Therefore, it would be far better if you worked with the student in that environment, even if the task were one totally different from the group. The key would be to relate the content matter of the skill you teach as closely as possible to the curricular topic of typical students in the room. In this manner, the student does not receive diluted content, is not embarrassed in front of peers by leaving the room, and stays current with large-group activities.

# CO-TEACHING

cooperative teaching (co-teaching)—based on regular and special educators jointly planning, teaching, and evaluating all learners in the integrated classroom.

"We've been discussing supportive services in the classroom," comments John. "Aren't there any ways to have direct services through the assistance of others who have more expertise in working with students at risk?"

Considerations about how to help students most directly and expeditiously have resulted in development and expansion of **cooperative teaching (co-teaching)** strategies. When students bring a diversity of needs that go beyond the ability of individual teachers to manage comfortably, sharing ideas and unique skills with colleagues has become a highly successful way to implement interventions.

Beyond allowing teachers to use their expertise effectively, there are additional benefits to co-teaching (Bauwens, Hourcade, & Friend, 1989). When students transition from special to regular education, teachers must carefully adapt curriculum, instruction, and materials to their needs. The special educator is present to provide these supports as the student adjusts to the regular classroom.

Additionally, co-teaching provides a proactive basis for the prereferral process. If any student demonstrates learning or behavioral problems, a specialist is present to modify instruction and provide additional reinforcement as needed. Early intervention stems later problems.

Co-teaching is based on regular and special educators jointly planning, teaching, and evaluating all learners in the integrated classrooms. Preferred models appear in Table 4–12 (Bauwens & Hourcade, 1991; Adamson, Matthews, & Schuller, 1990). However, adaptations are limitless, dependent on teacher and student needs for the teaching-learning environment, as well as available resources. Co-teaching motivates teachers through shared enthusiasm and encourages them to creatively assess their own situation and possibilities.

As indicated in Table 4–12, teachers may want to divide teaching responsibilities based on knowledge of, or certification in, a specified content field. When students demonstrate unique learning and behavioral needs, clearly the teacher with the most related training will direct their primary instruction. In this model, the special educator can broaden the extent of skills groups to incorporate any student in the class who may be experiencing difficulty learning a concept. Some regular educators also enjoy the challenge of teaching skills. Where students have differentiated levels of performance,

| Table 4–12 |
| --- |
| **Co-Teaching Models** |

- Teachers divide content into areas of preference and expertise, each selecting the specific information to teach the entire class or small group.

- Regular educator presents content, with special educator teaching subsequent skills groups for any students needing additional explanation or reinforcement.

- Each teacher instructs a skill group until mastery is attained.

- One teacher presents information initially, while the second teacher provides additional information and paraphrasing for reinforcement.

- One teacher works with individual students using alternative techniques and methods.

- Teachers alternate teaching the low-performing group.

- One teacher takes responsibility for presenting academic information while the other teaches and reinforces social, behavioral, and organizational skills that reinforce interactive and study habits.

(*Sources:*  Adapted from Bauwens & Hourcade, 1991; Adamson, Matthews, & Schuller, 1990)

co-teaching may involve each teacher training groups of students in prerequisite areas. In some classrooms, teachers alternate these groups so they have an opportunity to work with all students.

When large-group instruction is appropriate, one teacher may want to present information initially, while the second paraphrases or discusses ideas for reinforcement. During this model, the teacher not leading the discussion may provide behavioral reminders to students or oversee their individual work to ensure they are understanding the concepts.

Bauwens and Hourcade (1991) offer important suggestions for procedural considerations during co-teaching. In advance, teachers should decide the model to be used for a particular unit or lesson, concerning which teacher will provide specified information. Scheduling is critical to smooth organization. Together teachers should determine behavioral rules and techniques for handling discipline problems. They should delegate paperwork responsibilities and acquisition of materials and equipment. When issues such as monitoring student progress and communicating with parents are discussed initially, later miscommunication can be avoided. Planning time is critical to co-teaching implementation.

"I'm not sure where to start with all this," comments Maura. "Teresa and I have talked about co-teaching next year. Where would we start in our planning?"

Planning is the key. From the start, co-teachers need to decide when they can meet. If no shared time is present immediately, at first, some plan over lunch or meeting a few times a week. Then, for the next school year, they schedule concurrent conference periods. As their program develops and they work together daily, they flexibly shift and plan for future classes as they gauge the effectiveness of their instruction. However, there should always be a specified block of time, since casual planning may result in a lack of definition of roles.

Friend and Cook (1992) emphasize additional important considerations. From the start, teachers should discuss their goals for instruction and the degree to which they believe individual students can meet them. They should jointly determine classroom routines such as turning in assignments, leaving the room, and specific behaviors they find particularly disruptive.

These open discussions allow teachers to appreciate each other's personal needs from the onset. Differences will occur when people work together closely, but feelings of mutual appreciation and respect will support flexibility and cooperation.

Part of positive interactions clearly rests on both teachers feeling equally empowered in the classroom. Special education teachers should never be treated as paraprofessionals. Their job is to share teaching responsibilities, not to spend hours at the copy machine or running errands. Their expertise is invaluable in working with students at risk and can be underutilized if they are not viewed as equals.

# TEACHERS AS CONSULTANTS

Maura continues, "I'm concerned about how I'll be able to work with my students the rest of the day when Teresa isn't present in my classroom. I'm really busy now. If I have a few more students with disabilities next year, how will I be able to handle them without her full-time support?"

It would be optimal if all teachers could have a colleague in their classes for the entire day. However, since funds rarely are available, they must consider additional options for providing teacher support. When included students require one-on-one support or when the teacher has a number of students performing at different levels, schools may prefer paraprofessionals to provide instruction under teacher guidance.

Additionally, Resource and Content Mastery teachers can serve a significant consultancy role so that the teacher can continue to instruct all students appropriately. Adamson, Matthews, and Schuller (1990) suggest a range of consultation services that lend support. They suggest the consultant assist the regular teacher in selecting academic and behavioral intervention strategies. The specialist can model these methods in the regular classroom in order to gauge their effectiveness.

Regular educators may not have time to adapt or obtain materials and equipment. They may not have supplementary materials available at different levels. They may be unclear as to ways of measuring student progress and programming effectiveness. The specialist can provide very appreciated consultation and hands-on effort in these areas.

Again, teachers should plan when to meet for consultation. Follow-up procedures should be established to assure methods are successful and to make changes where problems arise. Teachers appreciate the ongoing support of a specialist who works flexibly and cooperatively.

To provide these services, the special education teacher should have an extra conference period or time otherwise allotted within the schedule to meet with regular educators and to gather or modify supplementary materials. The balance of time spent between co-teaching and consultancy should provide rewarding results for everyone.

## SUMMARY

Initially, Chapter 4 considered the role of the regular educator in the collaborative process. As the educator responsible for implementing the intervention plan, the regular educator needs to be concerned with a variety of factors and to complete a series of steps to work successfully with students at risk.

The regular educator should be aware of the behaviors indicating a student is experiencing academic or behavioral problems and meet with the planning team to discuss concerns. After the team considers the best intervention strategies to use with the student, the most important part of the process begins as the regular educator implements the plan. Team members meet on a scheduled basis to discuss student progress and reconsider areas of ongoing concern.

Regular educators need this ongoing support of their colleagues to be successful with students at-risk. This chapter discussed factors allowing for effective collaboration within the team so that the process will flow smoothly. All educators on the team should be committed to the same goal: providing the best education for the student in the least restrictive environment. The student's unique needs should direct suggestions for remedial or intervention programs. Educators should attempt to avoid categorizing or labeling students and placing them in classrooms that fit their concept of where students with disabilities should be.

As part of collaboration, teachers should share their expertise with other team members. From teachers to counselors to parents, each member presents unique insights and awareness about the student's background and behaviors. If the student is from a culture different from the majority of the school, the team should include at least one member from similar background to avoid either ignoring significant factors or creating stereotypes of expected behaviors.

As part of effective collaboration within the team, members should be involved in active listening, crediting each other's ideas, and respecting viewpoints. Specialized vocabulary should be avoided. When conflictive issues based on varied viewpoints do enter the process, the team leader should respond quickly, ensuring that active listening continues. If previous groundwork has created a sense of respect, the group will usually resolve conflicts more quickly because of mutual regard and direction toward a common goal. Additionally, members should be well-versed in team operating procedures, avoiding conflict because of lack of role clarification. Within specified parameters, the case manager should be available to families and the regular educator should be aware of whom to contact if team recommendations are unsuccessful.

However, the most well-considered planning teams cannot be successful if certain variables are not in place to make inclusion work effectively. These factors include small class size; continuous teacher training; specialized equipment; availability of previous assessment records; and additional teaching assistants. District administrators must work together with teachers to be sure that these supports are in place.

Chapter 4 contains a series of checklists to be used in making inclusive placements. They contain a number of critical necessities that should be in place before the student enters the regular classroom. While it is unlikely that all these supports will be in place before every placement occurs, they provide a reminder of specific variables for consideration. In completing the checklists, teachers should enter the date of anticipated achievement of each factor not in place. If a major variable seems unlikely for attainment at any near-future time, such as the regular educator wanting to have the student in his class, the team may want to consider an alternative placement.

Co-teaching has been one of the most effective instructional approaches for inclusion. Based on regular and special educators jointly planning, teaching, and evaluating all learners in an integrated classroom, it provides strong supports both for teachers and students.

The most successful co-teaching models have included: teachers' selection of which areas they will teach to the entire class or small group; flexible moving between skills groups by both teachers; one teacher presenting the lesson with subsequent explanation and reinforcement by the co-teacher; one teacher working with individual students using alternative techniques and methods; or one teacher assuming responsibility for presenting academic information while the other reinforces social, behavioral, and organizational skills supportive to learning.

While specialists cannot be in the regular classroom during the entire day, they can serve as consultants for students with disabilities. In this role they suggest an array of possible teaching and behavioral management strategies, modeling these methods directly with the student to gauge effectiveness. Additionally, they can obtain and modify materials and suggest ways to evaluate student progress. They should schedule time to assist teachers with students at risk so future problems are avoided. With these supports, the classroom teacher should always have a specialist immediately available to assist with planning and intervention strategies.

"Where do we go from here?" asks Dr. Mirales. "I'm excited by the possibilities, ready to approach Mort and Elena to start the collaborative teams in their school, and willing to ask the associate superintendent to pull together as many district resources as possible. How do we start?"

You already have. Administrative enthusiasm means administrative support, both at the district and site level. In explaining the concept of inclusion, you need to share your vision of how schools can be when all students work together in one system toward the primary goal of an excellent and equitable education. While the following chapters will provide practical implementation techniques, ranging from understanding assessment data to specific teaching methods, educators' anticipation and expectation that inclusion will succeed are among the most critical variables for success.

## CASE STUDY: *Elementary*

The following case studies describe situations faced by students at risk, requiring collaborative teamwork for support. In your consideration of the optimal ways of handling these problems, you will want to rely on many of the concepts discussed in the chapter for developing cooperative intervention strategies.

**Whenever Mort feels any hesitation about inclusion of students with disabilities in general education, he always reminds himself of Kaitlyn. A beautiful little girl who has made everyone around her smile with her own endearing nature, she had suffered brain damage as the result of an automobile accident when not wearing a seatbelt.**

**Kaitlyn's intelligence is significantly below her chronological age, and she demonstrates some fine and gross motor problems, resulting in poor development of handwriting and an awkwardness of gait when she walks. Despite all her problems, and her clear realization that she is different from her peers, she brings out the warmth in others with willingness to try tasks that are extremely difficult for her.**

**In first and second grade she had been enrolled in special education classes for all academic work, participating with typical peers only in art and music. She is just beginning to read at a first-grade level and her arithmetic computation skills are only slightly higher. Her attention span lasts ten to twelve minutes before she begins looking around the room at others.**

**Intuitively, Mort has realized that Kaitlyn can be successful in a regular education classroom with the right teacher and good supports. He also knows that without careful preparation before placement, her needs won't be met and faculty and parents will be upset, threatening placements of other students in the future.**

Inclusion of students such as Kaitlyn begins even before the regular education placement, as her collaborative team considers the variables necessary for success.

Review Table 4–3, Factors Supporting Successful Inclusion, and respond to the following questions:

1. Who should be included on her collaborative planning team?

2. What type of teaching techniques will regular education faculty need to know in order to be successful with her?

3. What kind of educational consultants and teaching assistants will best support her classroom teachers?

*Continued*

Review Tables 4–4 through 4–10, Checklists for Successful Inclusion, and consider the following questions:

4. Which educators or family members will be most necessary to consult in completing these checklists for Kaitlyn?
5. How can the checklists be used throughout the year to measure her success and to consider additional modifications that may be necessary?
6. How will you discuss Kaitlyn's needs with her typical classmates without embarrassing her or making her feel different?

## CASE STUDY: *Secondary*

Mai (16) and Sheng (14) are Taiwanese students who entered Apter High School several months ago. Recent immigrants to the United States, they and their parents speak only Taiwanese and read and write Chinese. There are no teachers or students at Apter who are conversant in either language.

Mai is a very shy young woman who appears intelligent, but does not interact academically or socially with any other students, likely because of her inability to communicate in English. Her teachers have tried grouping her with others during assignments, and she sits there quietly but nonresponsively. She does not enter discussions, answer questions, or complete class or homework reading assignments. At lunchtime she sits by herself in the cafeteria, rarely eating, watching other students. She goes home on the bus daily, involved in no after-school activities. She rarely smiles and recently has seemed more depressed and withdrawn than ever.

Her brother Sheng also presents a dilemma for teachers. Demonstrating the same language differences as Mai, he has a very short attention span, especially when others are doing deskwork he is unable to complete. Lately he has had occasional outbursts where he breaks a pencil or kicks a book. The other students do not like to be around him because he yells at them in Taiwanese and then laughs, or tries to distract them through aggressive body movements they find threatening. Similar to his sister, he has developed no friends and has an inability to communicate verbally with peers and teachers.

Both parents are laborers who have received immigration visas through a local church. While several church members speak Taiwanese, they have not been responsive to calls from the school because of their own busy work schedules.

*Continued*

Regardless of the ethnic background, Mai and Sheng present problems common to educators as non-English speaking students enter schools. Because of the social pressures, these problems are even more pronounced when they appear at the secondary level.

Design a plan to formalize the collaboration process to integrate these students into the school community, both academically and socially. In developing your planning team, you might consider:

1. Who should the team members be, based on those most likely to have strong impact on these students' lives?

2. What are the goals for each student that you hope to achieve through collaboration?

3. Who might be an effective team leader? Why?

4. Will any specialists be needed on the team?

5. How will you involve the parents?

6. Will you include the students as team members?

7. Will you consider the students' needs separately or together in team meetings, since different sets of teachers are involved?

8. What are some initial suggestions you would bring to the team if you were asked to brainstorm solutions to Mai's and Sheng's difficulties?

PART

III

# ASSESSMENT

# THE ASSESSMENT PROCESS

It was back to school in Westside District. After long discussions with Dr. Mirales, both Mort and Elena had agreed to work with their faculty teams to develop model inclusive schools this year. They had responded positively to the idea of collaboration among educators and families and felt that regardless of the speed of the change, everyone would benefit by working together more closely.

Each building had developed teams of regular and special educators, as well as administrative and district representatives, to determine the best direction for their campus. John Robinson had surprised everyone by volunteering to represent teachers in his content area. "For a long time now, I've been feeling powerless to actually teach English to my students. Maybe it's time to make some changes." No one questioned Maura Hayes's or Teresa Fuentes's desire to be on the Jackson team. "Regular education and special education teachers have been *us* and *them* for too long. Hopefully, this is our chance to work together."

Whether at the secondary or elementary level, everyone needed more training. The two planning teams had attended summer meetings to understand the collaborative model and their individual and group roles. They had developed goals for specific outcomes of inclusion at their schools and then had designed follow-up sessions for all teachers and staff. The initial program was to be voluntary, allowing families the right to choose the classroom setting for their child and teachers to decide how to make their individual rooms more accepting of students with differences.

Mort and Elena knew the program could only be successful if specific teacher needs were met. Toward this end, they asked all personnel to complete questionnaires stating areas in which they felt competencies or concerns about working with learners with special needs. Several areas were underscored by almost everyone. In addition to wanting to learn more extensive teaching methods, they felt uncertain about assessment: How would they identify student difficulties early enough to initiate the prereferral process and prevent larger problems from developing? What should they look for to know that students require more formal testing by school psychologists? If students were assessed formally, would there be any way of not only helping teachers understand implications of test results, but translating them into more effective classroom methods? Understandably, assessment and appropriate follow-up teaching were the major concerns.

With the support of Dr. Mirales, the principals decided to initiate a series of inservices. The first would consider formal and informal assessment methods, with emphasis on what the results would mean to teachers. Additional inservices would consider teaching methods effective for all children in inclusive classrooms.

## ASSESSMENT AND THE IEP PROCESS

Mort and Elena had approached Alex Hamilton, director of pupil appraisal services for Westside, to design inservices for their faculties. Alex was known for his creative but practical style in working with teachers. They appreciated his special ability to interpret assessment data into workable classroom techniques. This skill had been developed in his eight years of teaching and subsequent ongoing participation in implementing educational plans with students long after many school psychologists would have considered their role completed.

"Kids are fun," he noted, "and I would never know how successful our staff's appraisal had been if I didn't try to use some of the methods they suggested. We use labels or special education categories only in paperwork to meet federal funding requirements. Otherwise, our sense is that children are children first, and if we're having trouble teaching them, we just need to keep looking for the right way. How can we not be creative when an eight- year-old is telling us he'll probably never learn to read? Or a teenager feels excluded from peers just because she happens to be blind? Every time our assessment gets to the root of the problem and we develop a workable solution, we get really excited."

Alex and his staff were so enthused that they began work on the inservices immediately. At the first session, participants showed a varied degree of knowledge of assessment purposes, and the presenting team realized they needed to define words and terms that were frequently confused, as well as to fully explain the process.

"I hear the terms *assessment* and *testing* interchangeably," observed John. "How are they different?"

**testing**—the acquisition of data or information in specific areas of concern.

**Testing** is the acquisition of data or information in specific areas of concern. For example, if a parent observes that his youngest daughter has been slower than his older children in **developmental motor activities** such as standing and walking, he may request that a test be given to be sure that her problems are not serious, that she is only mildly delayed. Or a ninth-grade teacher may be concerned that one of his students is not reading on level. He would request academic testing to be sure the student is not experiencing learning problems. In both situations, specific standardized tests are administered to consider whether the problem is severe enough to warrant concern.

**developmental motor activities**—functions of motion that normally develop in a sequence, such as standing and walking.

**assessment**—collecting a broad variety of data that provides an extensive picture of the student's achievement and behavior.

**Assessment** is much more encompassing than testing. It includes collecting a broad variety of data that provide a more complete picture of the student's achievement and behavior. This information is used to assist in placing the student in the most appropriate setting, designing teaching strategies, and measuring ongoing success.

**formal assessment**—use of specific standardized tests to determine performance levels or the existence of a disability.

Not all data can be gathered from **formal assessment**. Often, it involves consideration of the student's interaction with peers, and may be best

**informal assessment**—use of nonstandardized information, such as curriculum-based measures and student work products, to determine performance levels.

**portfolio**—a selection of representative work compiled over an extended period to indicate gains in student performance.

obtained by informal observation in the regular education classroom. At other times, it necessitates examining a student's ability to be successful in a focused course of content study. To best serve this purpose, an informal assessment is appropriate, such as having a student perform mathematics problems from the text. Or, it may include considering a portfolio of student performance, comparing early and later work products. Assessment involves finding out what we need to know to program successfully for the student. This information may be gathered formally or informally.

Maura noted, "We've had some discussions on the prereferral process and collaborative teams recently, and I've come to believe that these are at the heart of inclusion. I'm confused. Where does assessment fit in?"

A good question. Prereferral and planning team efforts are an attempt to meet students' needs early in their educational experience, when they first demonstrate academic or behavioral difficulties. As noted in Chapter 3, educators, parents, and at times, students and involved specialists and community representatives meet to discuss their observations and concerns and to design an intervention program. Prereferral is a form of prevention. Often, this collaborative process is highly successful and obviates the need to refer students for formal assessment or for special education services, hence the term *prereferral*.

## The Formal Referral Process

**referral**—a request for consideration of special services.

Sometimes the student's needs are more extreme or the collaborative team has been unable to create an optimal intervention plan and needs more information to design a successful program. At this time, the student receives a referral for a more formalized evaluation. The referral process involves assessment to determine eligibility for special education based on an individualized educational plan including goals, objectives, specific services, and means of evaluation. This referral often originates from teachers who have become frustrated by lack of success, from parents who have not observed progress, from others in a position to note little improvement in skills or behaviors, and at times from the involved student.

It is at this point that prereferral ends and the formalized referral process begins, considering the appropriateness of special education supports.

**procedural safeguards**—precautions taken to protect the rights of students and their families during referral for special education assessment and programming.

*Referral Stages.* Lerner (1994) describes the stages of this process. During the initial referral stages, a plan is designed, specifying the kind of assessment needed and who will be responsible for its acquisition. Additionally, procedural safeguards are enacted, which protect the rights of students and their families. These include written parental consent for assessment to take place, as well as allowing parents to view all results while maintaining confidentiality of records for the school and family. When appropriate staff and test instruments are available, assessments are carried out in the student's

parental consent—permission from the parents for special education assessment.

confidentiality—privacy and secrecy, restricting sharing of information without approval.

impartial hearing—an appearance before a judge in which no party has undue advantage.

assessment stages—the steps taken to determine a student's abilities.

trained assessors—people educated in the process of testing students.

observe—to watch student and document specific occurrences of a particular behavior.

native language and findings are reported in that language. Formalized tests selected are to be free of racial or cultural bias. Additionally, the family has the right to an **impartial hearing** if they disagree with outcomes from the assessment.

## Assessment Stages

The **assessment stages** begin with a multidisciplinary evaluation by specialists, often involving formal testing. Frequently, specialists involved in the evaluation include **trained assessors**, such as school psychologists or diagnosticians; experts in the suspected disability area, such as learning disabilities or behavioral disorders; and speech and language therapists. In addition to collecting formal test data, team members often **observe** students informally during class, examine daily work, review records and academic history, and obtain developmental background information from parents.

The assessment team prepares a report after they have collected this extensive information. The report gives the diagnosis (e.g., severe behavioral disorder; specific learning disability) and the data to substantiate the disability. All observational and medical data are included, along with how this data is affecting the student's school performance. Finally, the team notes whether

After working individually with students, specialists can provide valuable teaching information from assessment data.

the student is eligible for special education support services, based on the diagnosis.

A member of the assessment team, such as the school psychologist, discusses the results of the assessment at a meeting with the student's teachers, parents, a school administrator, experts invited by the parents or school, and where appropriate, the student. This group most often becomes the IEP **committee.**

"There seem to be a number of school-based teams or committees," John notes. "How does the assessment team differ from the IEP committee?"

The assessment team includes only those involved in gathering information about the student. Once assessment is completed, this team turns over responsibility for the child to the IEP committee, which will initiate follow-up work with the child, such as the design of **supportive services.** These committee members are the individuals who will be responsible for implementing and monitoring the **intervention plan.**

At the IEP meeting, committee members write an individualized education program (IEP) to support the student's improved school achievement or behavior. The IEP is the bridge between assessment and intervention. It includes a description of the student's academic and behavioral performance as a notation of problem areas. The dates for providing services are included, often with the consideration that the committee will formally meet at that time to consider extending support to the student. Next, the plan contains annual behavioral and academic goals, including **short-term objectives** to reach these goals. This goal-setting with specific objectives is critical so educators and parents can express how they will evaluate the success of the intervention plan.

The IEP also includes the specific services the student will receive, such as speech or language therapy. It often notes strategies for teaching the student, such as use of a contingency management program. Importantly, the plan indicates the type of participation the student will have in regular education, such as full inclusion without supports or assisted instruction by a resource teacher for a specified number of hours each day. An important aspect in current IEPs is the strong attempt to design a program allowing the student's participation in the regular education for the majority of the day. The plan's evaluation criteria include procedures for determining its effectiveness in meeting objectives.

## Intervention Stages

After the committee writes and approves the IEP, the **intervention stages** follow. This is the teaching time, the critical period when the student receives academic and/or behavioral assistance, and specialists and generalists work together to support improved learning and behavior. The student is placed in the setting specified in the IEP and receives direct instruction by

**IEP committee**—team that reviews special education assessment data, and plans and evaluates the effectiveness of subsequent interventions.

**supportive services**—special services, such as physical therapy, occupational therapy, and speech therapy, that may be appropriate for a student.

**intervention plan**—steps of action to be taken to interrupt the current pattern of behavior or learning taking place.

**short-term objectives**—smaller steps within goals, to be worked on and achieved in a short span of time, such as 3 to 6 months.

**intervention stages**—the teaching time; the critical period when the student receives academic and/or behavioral assistance, and specialists and generalists work together to support improved learning and behavior.

one or a team of educators. If the goals and objectives have been well-planned, the teaching directions are clear. The most effective teaching strategies and methods to use with students with disabilities will be discussed in following chapters.

**evaluation stage**—teachers review stated objectives and the student's success in meeting them.

The **evaluation stage** is important also. During the evaluation, teachers review stated objectives and the student's success in meeting them. Often goals are measured annually as a mark of program effectiveness. Yet, many teachers have found it far better to conduct a continuous evaluation of student efforts throughout the intervention period instead of at the end. Such ongoing evaluation allows the teacher to change methods or to request specialist input if the student is not successful in meeting goals.

## ASSESSMENT AUDIENCES

Alex added, "Today as we focus on the assessment part of this process, we have to consider that each of us may want different information about the academic or behavioral appraisal of the same student. This has become really clear to me as I participate on IEP committees and observe members be satisfied or unhappy with conclusions and follow-up programming."

To make this point, Alex had participant teachers compile a list of information they need appraisal staff to provide them to make an assessment beneficial. The teachers were surprised to find that, based on their own educational specialties or teaching fields, even among themselves they wanted to know different things. "After an appraisal, I need to know if the student can do the work in my classroom without absorbing all my time, and if he can behave himself without disrupting others," Maura noted. "I also could really benefit from specific remedial strategies to understand how to teach him."

"At the high school level, I have the same concerns as Maura, with a few more," John added. "Will the student be able to handle a college-bound curriculum, or will modifications have to be made? Are his academic skills so low that he won't be able to use the same textbook, take the same exams, or benefit from class lectures and discussions? How can teachers help the student gain socially appropriate behaviors so he can be accepted by peers?"

"This is really interesting," commented Teresa. "As a resource teacher, I have related but different needs than Maura and John from assessment information. To develop an appropriate remedial teaching strategy, I'm always concerned about the student's best **learning modality**: visual, auditory, or motor. I've tried to find out whether the learning problems stem from difficulties with word or number perception, or from a basic language disability. When I consult with other teachers, I ask myself how to interpret assessment

**learning modality**—the means through which a student best learns: visually, auditorily, or motorically.

information into successful objectives for their classes. Before today I assumed they wanted to know the same things I did from testing results."

"Exactly," responded Alex. "When assessors select which tests to give or write reports, often we assume others want to know what's important to us. As a result, at times we don't give enough information to answer the questions of everyone reading the reports. I never realized the different concerns of others, even beyond teachers, until I read Carl Smith's (1992) comments. I have some charts to show you with the varied questions about assessment that come from different audiences, based on his paper and on my own additional observations."

From the questions in Tables 5–1 through 5–6, it becomes clear that regular and special educators differ in what they want to know from student assessments. As Maura indicated, she is most concerned with students' academic and behavioral skills and their ability to perform at the same level as the rest of the class. Answers to these questions can allay any threat that teachers may have about being overwhelmed by students whose performance is dramatically different.

As indicated in Table 5–1, teachers usually concern themselves with immediate issues (Smith, 1992), such as how to support students in learning tasks through remedial strategies and activities. Regular educators want to know how similar students will be to peers in their ability to complete assignments, follow lectures, and adhere to rules. They also are concerned about ways they can help assessed students interact better with peers in order to gain group acceptance.

Regular educators are not concerned with categorizing or labeling students. Many times the scores school psychologists spend hours computing

---

**Table 5–1**
**Assessment Information: The Regular Educator**

*Regular education teachers want to know:*

- What are the student's academic levels? Will he or she be able to read the text?

- If the student is below grade level academically, what are remedial strategies I should use in my teaching?

- What alternate activities can I use to teach the student curricular content information?

- Will the student be able to follow classroom rules and avoid disruptive behaviors?

- What are appropriate behavior management strategies?

- How socially appropriate are the student's behaviors? Are there ways to improve peer interactions and acceptance?

are of little interest to them. Their main concern is how to make inclusion work for all students in their classes. Recommendations for facilitation tend to be far more important than test scores.

Specialists may have different concerns when reviewing test reports, as Table 5–2 indicates. They want to understand the underlying cause of the problem to devise remedial or compensatory strategies. They are concerned that students be placed in the appropriate setting and that necessary learning supports be provided to help students succeed in the general education curriculum. Specialists are often responsible for interpreting the data and suggesting the service model to the collaborative team, including the need for consultants, team teachers, or modified intervention or materials. Often they are responsible for supporting the regular education teacher in making inclusion work.

"As an administrator, I've always had to be concerned whether assessments met legal guidelines, such as following the review process appropriately, and including parental permission and input all along the way," noted Mort, "and obviously these are still important considerations. In an inclusive school, I can see where the issues are broader than that."

"Absolutely," added Elena. "At the high school, teachers and parents are concerned about curriculum appropriateness for the assessed student: Do we have to alter the content or just the way it's taught? Based on the diagnosis, I would have to know how to support a placement when teachers, parents, and other community members ask questions or voice concerns. For example, I can already feel Mike Gonzales's distress when a special education student with academic or behavioral problems is included in his son's class."

"At all levels, we'd have to consider the resources necessary to help all students be successful," Mort observed. "Will specialists and adaptive materials be available to meet assessed needs? We'll have to develop a

**Table 5–2**
**Assessment Information: The Special Educator**

*Special education teachers want to know:*

- From the assessment, what is the student's diagnosed problem?
- What is the underlying cause of the problem?
- What are the specific learning strengths and areas of difficulty?
- What kind of special education model is most appropriate to meet the student's needs?
- In the regular education classroom, what kind of supports will the student need (e.g., untimed tests, teaching assistant, shortened assignments)?

## Table 5–3
## Assessment Information: School and District Administrators

*Administrators want to know:*

- Did the review process and appraisal follow legal and district guidelines?

- Is the curriculum appropriate for the student's assessed learning needs?

- If the diagnosis indicates severe learning or behavioral problems, how can I best support the student's regular class placement when talking to teachers, parents, and community representatives?

- What resources will be necessary for the student to succeed in the inclusive classroom? Are these resources available? Affordable?

- Are specialists available to provide consultants or direct services for inclusive classrooms?

- Are regular education teachers satisfied that they can meet the student's learning needs?

direct line to the administration or regional service centers to obtain supports for students with low-incidence disabilities. As indicated in Table 5–3, the primary objective for administrators has to be how to prepare regular education teachers with the skills and supports to make inclusion work."

"So our concerns are the same, Mort," observed Teresa. "We both have to help regular education teachers be successful. What about parents? Don't they have other concerns about assessment results? I've seen a lot of anxiety and tears when students' disabilities are first noted. I've also watched parents support or disrupt their child's program based on their understanding and approval of what we're doing."

"Many of you have children," commented Alex. "If your child had been experiencing academic or behavioral problems, you would probably be very concerned. In that situation, what would you need to know that would help you understand and deal with the problem?"

As the discussion continued, participants compiled a series of questions parents would want answered. As listed in Table 5–4, their primary concerns would include appropriateness of the placement to meet the student's assessed needs and whether or not the student would experience success.

Alex pointed out that parents are frequently more concerned with the long-term progress of their child. Is college in the future, or vocational training in high school? What marketable skills will the student have? Based on assessment and placement, will their child have skills to participate in a competitive work environment?

"Sally Smith (1992) notes how paradoxical it is that the recent movement has been to create an environment that is highly interesting to students," Alex observed. "Certainly, interest and motivation are of concern to parents, but often are not at the top of their list. Parents want their children to

**Table 5–4**
**Assessment Information: Parents**

*Parents want to know:*

- Based on assessment data, what is the best placement for my child?

- Will resources such as assistants, specialists, and modified materials be available in the regular classroom?

- Will my child be able to go to college?

- Will my child develop the skills to get a good job?

- How can my child obtain literacy and computational skills despite the existence of a disability?

demonstrate skills in reading, math, and science. Especially when students' needs are more extreme, parents tend to be more long-term with their questions, because their final goal is independence for their child. They want to know if resources, ranging from personnel to adaptive materials, will be available to underscore academic and personal success.

"Too often we leave out the child," he mused, "the very person who is the most frustrated and yet who has expended the most effort to overcome the problem. How can we subterfuge the reason for the assessment or not explain the results to the person most involved?" He asked teachers to consider the varied expectations and concerns a student would have during testing and regarding the specific outcomes.

As indicated in Table 5–5, they decided that students are concerned about academic and social issues, with the latter growing more important as they become older. Much of their self-esteem is based on their ability to be successful in their classes, ranging from performing on level in reading

**Table 5–5**
**Assessment Information: Students**

*Students want to know:*

- Can I learn to read (write, compute) like other students?

- How can I make (keep) more friends?

- How can I be an important part of social and academic activities at school?

- Will I have to leave the room to get special help?

- Will I go to college? Find a good job?

and computational skills to being an integral part of school activities, such as plays, art projects, and physical education.

More immediate to their concerns than their parents', students crave friends and social acceptance much as any child does. They may not have the social skills to make friends easily and are concerned about anything that will make them look foolish or different, such as leaving the room for special education services. As adolescents, they may refuse to wear hearing aids or participate in supportive remedial training for fear they will not gain admission into a peer group. As they progress through high school they may have serious concerns about their own future job potential, beginning to demonstrate some of the concerns of their parents.

"Another group with different responses are community members," Elena added. "Because many of them are parents of children in our schools, they share those concerns we mentioned. When they wear their business and economic hats as potential employers or retirees, they want their money well-spent. They are concerned about overall achievement levels and whether or not our students will compete in the workplace. They tend to be more interested in the performance of groups of students and the school as a whole than with individuals. If a student's behavior seems disruptive to the group, there often is less tolerance because they are more concerned with overall group progress. The assessment data they question relates to how academically strong student performance is and whether students achieving below mean levels are indicative of weaknesses at our school or in the system. They ask questions about the relevance of curricular content, but also about overcoming any academic problem areas early in the student's schooling."

Inservice participants began to realize that there is no one goal for assessment, that anticipated outcomes are a result of the individual's role in the

---

**Table 5–6**
**Assessment Information: Community Members**

*Community members want to know:*

- Will the student be able to compete in the workplace?

- Do assessed problem areas indicate weaknesses in the total educational system?

- How can problems in learning and behavior be discovered easily enough to avoid their developing into lifetime disabilities?

- Does the curriculum contain practical information to help the student become a productive citizen?

- Are the student's assessed needs so extreme that they will hinder the teacher's ability to teach other students in the class?

educational process, from regular or special educator to administrator, parent, student, or community representative. Importantly, they realized that their concerns might not be the only concerns. While school psychologists and administrators are most involved with test data indicating a diagnostic category for placement and funding, parents wanted to know causality and implications for an independent future life. Teachers are more concerned with the intermediary steps: What is the diagnosis and what can we do to assure the development of strong adaptive behavior allowing for an independent future? The community wants tangible results, while students ask to feel good about themselves and their own abilities, both academic and social.

## REFERRAL

processing skills—the ability to interpret incoming stimuli into usable information.

"Once you realize each of us wants some different information from assessment," Alex summarized, "it becomes clear that we need to consider the questions as we make the referral. Do we need to know if the student will be able to read from the textbook, if he has a learning disability in receptive language, or if his intellectual **processing skills** will require more concrete methods of teaching? Each of these questions requires a different type of assessment to be answered, along with different professionals to conduct the assessment. If we perform the wrong type of assessment, the information will be of little use, and our questions about programming will go unanswered."

If inclusion is to work effectively, the teacher must know how to instruct the student. While everyone's concerns are important, assessment should first consider the questions of regular educators in how to improve the academic and/or behavioral performance of the student. Teachers should be very specific in the questions they need answered when they refer students.

"That's where I can see some problems," commented John. "We've been discussing collaboration and the prereferral process recently, with the emphasis on avoiding referrals. I think it will feel like a failure to me if I have to have a student tested because I haven't seen any success in my efforts or from the planning team's suggestions. It would seem as if I were turning him over to someone else because we weren't smart enough to figure out what he needed."

Most teachers do feel somewhat threatened when they refer a student. What if the problem is so basic that they should have been able to handle it? Or what if the appraisal results indicate they should teach using some remedial methods in which they have not been trained?

The important thing to note is that recommending a student for assessment does not mean the process operates without the involvement of the referring teacher. Additionally, it is not an adversarial process where professionals work separately and compete for the diagnosis or design of the best IEP. The concept of the multidisciplinary team means all educators bring their own expertise to the assessment, plan together, diagnose together, and design an intervention plan together. The same collaborative structure that was so critical to prereferral of high-risk students only gains in importance when a referral has to be made.

## LEVELS OF ASSESSMENT

Not all assessments are the same, because not all teachers need the same information. Yet there are general levels of assessment, based on the sophistication of the required information and the need to translate it into teaching methods. Moran (1976) presents a solid framework for teachers to judge which level is most appropriate for their informational needs.

### The Academic Functioning Level

academic functioning level—the instructional level of the student in each subject area.

The **academic functioning level**, Table 5–7, is the most fundamental in information gathering as well as closest to the teacher's daily instruction. "I want you to consider an actual student whose needs fall into this category of appraisal," interjected Alex. "Some of you at Jackson Elementary will remember Miguel, a fourth-grader last year, in Carrie Stevens's class. There were a number of observable behaviors that were lowering his school performance. His oral and reading vocabulary are poor, and he tends to understand things very literally. He has poor sentence syntax, both in speaking and writing. His sight word vocabulary is low, although he improves his word analysis when allowed to use phonics.

| Table 5–7 I. Academic Functioning Level of Assessment | |
| --- | --- |
| *Outcomes* | *Programming* |
| Description of skills and deficiencies in reading, arithmetic, written expression | Academic remediation in areas below expectancy |

"While his math computation is good, his problem-solving is poor. The combination of verbal and written language problems along with reading comprehension and math reasoning had been causing him to achieve far below the rest of the class."

"I really learned a lot from this experience," Carrie reflected. "I called Alex to start the IEP process for a formal assessment of Miguel's academic work. I was concerned because he seemed to be falling further behind the class daily. When Alex asked me what information I needed from the assessment, I was surprised because I had thought all assessments were the same once a student was referred. I told him that I really just needed to know what Miguel's strengths and weaknesses were in his academic areas and in language. Then I would need some help developing teaching techniques to improve his skills.

IQ (intelligence quotient)—a number that indicates intelligence as measured on a standardized instrument.

"I was annoyed at first when Alex told me that, unless considered as a special education candidate, Miguel probably didn't need a formal assessment with IQ (intelligence quotient) testing and all that. Alex said that he would help me pull together the information I had and would call in specialists if I felt I needed more input."

Alex asked Carrie to collect samples of Miguel's daily written work in spelling, creative expression, arithmetic computation and problem solving, and science and social studies. She also compiled his standardized test scores and percentiles, including answer sheets containing his work. When noticing the particularly low scores in language on the standardized tests, Carrie recalled how Miguel's spoken vocabulary was very weak, how he seemed to have problems selecting appropriate words and expressing himself in sentences.

"Once Alex and I began this process, I began to listen more closely to Miguel when he spoke. His sentences were very short and he rarely used descriptive words. He tended to gesture a lot and to allow others to finish sentences for him. Yet, I could tell he wasn't a slow child. He was always curious about what we were doing and especially loved science. He was the first one to volunteer to participate in our experiments."

hands-on activities—lessons that include the student's getting involved actively.

As Carrie became more aware of Miguel's learning styles, now noticing his enjoyment of hands-on activities, she realized he was also a good artist. At times when he had difficulty writing a story, he drew an elaborate picture with fine details to illustrate his meaning. She realized that very likely his problems in reading comprehension were a result of poor vocabulary and weak verbal skills.

"It made sense to me that if he had poor skills in verbal language, he would have poor skills in reading comprehension, since the vocabulary was even more sophisticated. If he couldn't express himself well in speaking, how could he express himself well in writing, since he had the added concerns of spelling, punctuation, and handwriting? His rote skills, such as phonics and math computation were at grade level. He had the most difficulty with activities involving language use and comprehension."

With Alex, she reviewed his formal record file and discovered the primary language spoken at home was Spanish. Miguel had started school in a bilingual education program in another district, and teacher comments were positive about his language progress. However, he had changed schools three times since then and had not continued bilingual education after first grade. "What a shame," Carrie noted. "With all the disruptions going on in his young life, his language skills were never given a chance to develop. No wonder he's had problems."

This information still did not tell Carrie how to teach him. "I knew he needed hands-on instruction, but I still needed more specifics."

Carrie contacted Teresa Fuentes, whose training as a resource teacher had included remedial reading and arithmetic instruction. Teresa administered an indepth reading test, a diagnostic arithmetic test, and tests of verbal receptive and expressive language, as well as written expression.

"The results confirmed everything Carrie knew from her informal data gathering," Teresa commented. "But they also showed us the individual areas in which he was stronger or weaker. Based on the test results, the bilingual education teacher and I met with her weekly for the remainder of the year, loaning her remedial language materials and suggesting specific strategies and activities to help Miguel. It was interesting and fun for all of us, especially since he's improved so much."

Teachers have numerous daily opportunities to gather informal assessment data on their students.

Carrie's questions about Miguel's learning had been on the academic level and did not require sophisticated indepth testing. She found that her own ability to gather data informally was at the core of being able to help him. When she considered her own concerns, such as discovering remedial materials and techniques, she realized her best help would come from collaboration with specialists such as Teresa.

As educators develop more prereferral teams to identify and serve students at risk in the early stages of problem development, they may not even need to refer students such as Miguel. The process of records review and study of student daily schoolwork may indicate appropriate outcomes at this level. The key will be to train all teachers to use the information already available to them in making a diagnosis. Teachers should never doubt their own abilities. They are often in the best position to achieve an accurate assessment of student achievement.

modality processing level—considers how the student performs psychomotor or information processing.

## Modality Processing Level

As indicated in Table 5–8, the second level of assessment, modality processing level, considers how the student performs psychomotor or information processing. The inherent goal is to find the student's best learning style, based on perception and language skills (Moran, 1976). While educators often question the applicability of such testing to their remedial work with students, others find the information useful for subsequent placement and programming decisions.

"Ernie is a good example of a student who benefitted from this type of referral," reflected Alex. Last year in seventh grade, his homework and test grades began to drop considerably. While his records showed that he had never been an exceptionally strong student, former grades of B and C in elementary school now were often D's. He was in danger of failing English when his teacher and parents agreed that a formal referral for special education

**Table 5–8**
**II. Modality Processing Level of Assessment**

| Outcome | Programming |
| --- | --- |
| Indicate students' optimal learning style through assessing language and perceptual-motor skills | Design of specialized techniques to improve receptive, inner, or expressive language, and to teach academic skills through remedial or compensatory approaches |

assessment was necessary. His teacher felt she could not reach him effectively after trying many classroom modifications and meeting with the school planning team. It just seemed that things were going on that she needed to understand to really be able to help him."

When a teacher has not received enough information from a first-level referral of the type Carrie conducted on Miguel or unsuccessfully has attempted

MY PORTFOLIO

Assessment should include consideration of a student's stronger areas of performance to determine a mode for optimal expression. (Can you interpret the student's written words as he describes *The Great Kapok Tree*, by Lynne Cherry? Yet his pictures wonderfully describe the essence of the story.) Reprinted with permission, Winston School, San Antonio.

a number of remedial teaching strategies, it is important to make a referral for more indepth assessment. Additionally, some teachers refer at this point when they need to know a student's learning strengths and problem areas to program successfully. Usually a referral at this level indicates the anticipated need of special support services to help the student be successful.

At the second level, tests are usually administered by a specialist trained in perception and communication disorders. An assessment team might include a school psychologist and a language therapist, both of whom would administer and interpret the tests. Additionally, regular and special education teachers would be invaluable members who would give input on informal observations, daily work products, previous history, and the success of specialized teaching techniques and activities that had already been attempted. The testing is directed towards finding the underlying cause of academic difficulties and designing a remedial program to help the student overcome or compensate, based on individual learning style.

Since problems often occur in perception of school information, it is important initially to rule out the existence of vision and hearing problems. Many parents believe they have had their child's vision and hearing tested through the school or during pediatrician's visits. They may not realize these are only perfunctory screenings, not intended to replace indepth exams. Whenever a sensory problem is suspected, a student's vision should be examined by an **ophthalmologist** and hearing examined by an **audiologist**. While other professionals may provide good exams, often they are not as thorough or as extensive.

**ophthalmologist**—a doctor who treats the diseases and functions of the eye.

**audiologist**—a specialist who assesses hearing acuity at different frequency ranges and decibel levels.

**modality testing**—assessing through which modality the student best learns.

Once testing indicates that the student does not have vision or hearing problems, the **modality testing** should take place. This type of assessment includes areas such as discrimination and sequencing of letters in words, figure-ground abilities, visual memory, eye-hand coordination, directionality, laterality, understanding of spatial relationships, speech articulation, understanding and use of vocabulary, and communications skills in verbal and written expressive language as well as receptive language. While these are only examples of possible assessment areas, students are tested selectively based on informal information provided by teachers that may indicate a particular type of problem.

Although some teachers might question the application of these perceptual and language outcomes to their classrooms, in situations such as Ernie's, they can provide critical understanding of reasons for lowered academic performance.

"First our staff school psychologist ruled out behavioral upset or interpersonal problems at school and home, since these can have a similar impact," Alex noted. "Then she tested Ernie for perceptual and language problems. The results showed he reads extremely slowly because of problems in visual discrimination of letters: He was having problems perceiving differences between letters such as *m/n*, *h/l*, and *o/c*. He also tended to missequence letters as he read them, such as reading "board" for "broad" or "trucky" for "turkey." Obviously these problems were affecting not only his reading rate, but the accuracy of information he obtained from reading. When she tested his language skills, she found he had additional problems with auditory memory, having difficulty recalling specific information discussed in class."

"Why hadn't I noticed these problems when I had him in third grade?" asked Maura. "I'm more than a little embarrassed because I like to think that I'm observant of students' learning problems."

"In many ways you probably didn't notice these perceptual or language behaviors because you're such a hands-on teacher: nothing to feel bad about. I've been in your room, and your students are always involved in learning centers, watching videos, listening to tapes, and taking part in discussions. In your class, Ernie was able to get the information he needed because you taught him through a variety of learning modalities. He may never have been a strong student, but he never appeared to be a weak one either because you always provided alternative ways for him to learn the information."

"What happened in middle school?"

"I can answer that," reflected John. "We secondary teachers have a really broad curriculum to cover and tend to rely much less on hands-on experiences than elementary teachers. We lecture, have discussions, and assign reading to be performed in and out of class. Independent reading and recalling information heard in class are the two primary ways most of us require students to learn. If he has problems in those areas, basically he has no way to learn the information if we don't provide him alternatives."

John's observations are correct. After the assessment, when Ernie's teachers became part of the IEP team, they worked together with a specialist to design alternate materials and teaching strategies to reach him. During his study hall, they also had him work daily with the reading teacher to improve his skills.

Clearly, it was most important to teach him the remedial skills he needed to improve his reading and avoid future failure. We also had the district language specialist attend meetings with his regular teachers to discuss ways of supporting classroom lectures and expanding group discussions so he would retain verbal information.

"It was interesting that at the end of the school year his teachers reported not only that Ernie's performance had improved but that they were incorporating suggestions from the specialists into their daily teaching with the entire class. Maybe one result of inclusion is that we learn how to teach all of our students better."

Many teachers feel this second-level assessment level will not give them information they can use. The example of Ernie is important in underscoring how the combined expertise of teachers and assessment specialists can determine the cause of a problem as well as remedial and compensatory strategies to allow the regular educator to work successfully on a daily basis. If assessment results had stopped at the stage of reporting problems in auditory memory and visual perception, there would have been little of concrete importance for teachers to use in working with Ernie. Understanding how his perceptual and language deficits have resulted in school failure and ways of working to overcome them can result in success for him in the future.

Many school psychologists are not trained in designing activities and teaching strategies for the classroom, thereby frustrating educators who need workable ideas to use daily with the student. The importance of the IEP team is that it allows members to share their expertise, ranging from explaining the cause of the problem to brainstorming intervention strategies.

## Cognitive and Behavioral Functioning Level

**cognitive functioning level**—the student's ability to use logic and analysis, to associate and categorize information to perform inductive and deductive reasoning.

**behavioral functioning level**—the student's ability to demonstrate predetermined appropriate behaviors individually and in group settings.

**learning aptitude**—ability to learn or understand new information.

**inductive**—pulling separate facts together to prove a general statement.

**deductive**—reasoning from a known general statement to an unknown.

"Unfortunately, there are a number of students whose difficulties stem from deficits in reasoning and problem-solving or from behavioral disorders. After the planning team has met to design and implement programs for these students, frequently they call our appraisal office for additional testing and supports."

As indicated in Table 5–9, the cognitive and behavioral functioning level of assessment often includes IQ and learning aptitude measures considering the student's ability to use logic and analysis, to associate and categorize information to perform inductive and deductive reasoning (Moran, 1976). While consideration of behavioral factors has been important at all assessment levels, there tends to be more overlap at this level, often requiring the use of specialized affective instruments. While school psychologists and language specialists usually administer most tests, related assessment may be required from neurologists, psychiatrists, physical therapists or others.

"We haven't talked much about testing for students with behavioral disorders," interjected Mort. "Can you give us an example of the type of testing or outcomes for these students?"

### Table 5–9
### III. Cognitive and Behavioral Functioning Level of Assessment

| *Outcomes* | *Programming* |
| --- | --- |
| Measure of learning aptitude (logic, analytic abilities) | Teaching strategies emphasizing categorization and relationships among concepts. Activities involve association and classification, ranging from concrete objects to abstractions. |
| Assessment of emotional status and affective problems that impact academic performance and interpersonal relationships | Interventions planned to decrease behaviors detrimental to self or others |

"There are lots of examples," responded Alex, "but the one that comes to mind caused so much community grief for Elena and all of us."

"Of course," said Elena, shaking her head. "I can relate that story by heart. Let's call her Ann. She was a really intelligent junior, in all advanced classes, poised, and extremely interactive with adults, seeming sophisticated beyond her years. She was always surrounded by other students and was the leader of her peer group. Certainly not the type of young woman whom you would ever feel had behavioral problems, even if you were her teacher or school principal.

"I started to receive concerned calls from parents of her friends, first one, and then several more. She was saying cruel things to one about the other, lying beyond proportion. While normally I would refer this to one of our school counselors, I became involved when parents reported incidents of physical fights between boys in her group. The parents had observed her "going with" a few boys at once, usually best friends. She would criticize one to the other, destroying the boys' friendship, and would actually goad them into fighting over her, always when she was in their presence. The situation began to escalate at teenage parties. One night several boys, drinking underage, fought at a party. One boy's jaw was broken, the other's shoulder dislocated. While the parents were furious with their sons, they called me when they learned that once again Ann had instigated the argument, trying to decide which one she would prefer as her boyfriend.

"Our planning team was baffled by her behaviors until we started to read informal notes from teachers in her records and to observe her behaviors more closely with peers on a daily basis. Records indicated she had always interacted beyond her years on a surface level with teachers. However, she had been caught lying to them on numerous occasions, usually talking herself out of any punishment. Her parents were cooperative with the school, but reported they had not observed deceptive behavior at home.

"Two current teachers noted she always has a few boyfriends, but they were younger than she, and as parents had reported, had been close friends until their association with Ann. At after-school activities, sponsors indicated she was the leader of her small social group, often scolding members and directing their behaviors, but outside the earshot of the teacher.

"From these behaviors we realized she was extremely manipulative both of adults and peers, but had learned enough social behaviors to be skillfully deceptive and to get away with hurting others. She was actually a status member of her peer group, enjoying her position of telling friends what to do and having boys fight over her. We felt she had become a powerful young woman whose own emotional needs were exerting a very bad influence on other teenagers. Feeling foolish that she had taken all of us in for so long, we called Alex's office for an appraisal."

Alex continued, "The family interview was very interesting. Ann answered most questions, even those directed toward her parents. She sat next to her father, arm on his, as he basked in her exemplary academic performance at school. When her mother admitted often Ann was cruel to her younger sister, this year a freshman, Ann whispered to her father, who then contradicted the mother's comments. Ann and her father repeated this behavior several times.

"Indepth psychological assessment indicated Ann is a gifted student, certainly something we already knew. Affective measures indicated she has a Borderline Personality Disorder, needing to feed her self-esteem through success at manipulating people. She has no remorse at hurting others and does not have a strong sense of conscience that what she is doing is wrong. Apparently, when her more attractive sister started attending the same school, she was spurred to even greater attempts to prove her worth to the boys in the school. She had divided and conquered close friends and even her parents without any concern for the consequences of her behavior. The more they fought over her, the greater her personal esteem."

Elena added, "I never expected the parents to follow through with the psychiatric counseling we suggested, but they had received enough calls from other parents and were afraid that she would be involved in activities in which someone else would be hurt. She currently meets weekly to review her behaviors with her school counselor and a teacher she selected. These meetings were difficult for her at first, as she seemed embarrassed about their open discussions of her peer and adult interactions. Now she seems much happier since all of her teachers are working together to build up her self-esteem."

With behaviors such as Ann's, in which sophisticated testing into cognitive and behavioral aspects of the student are required to discover the problem, this third level of diagnosis is best. While obvious in some situations, Ann's harmful behaviors were subtle enough in their causality that it took a team of teachers, assessment personnel, and parents to work through the actual problem and devise an intervention plan. Similarly, when a student presents problems that cannot be managed by daily observation and trials at varied intervention methods, higher-level assessments may be required. The most intense appraisals should be made when other options have been exhausted, when the student acts out or withdraws from classroom activities, or when academic work does not improve despite teacher intervention methods. In these instances, usually **clinical assessment** is necessary.

**clinical assessment**—assessment performed in a professional setting.

# THE REGULAR EDUCATOR'S ROLE IN ASSESSMENT

Alex reflected, "I've tried to describe assessment as a team effort. For years the appraisal staff was guilty of overassessing students, taking them to an isolated setting outside the classroom, at times even to another building, to administer our 'magic.' We reported the results of our findings back to teachers, often restating what they already knew in a professional jargon that they couldn't understand. Justifiably, we lost credibility with a lot of educators who feel this lengthy process didn't benefit them in their teaching of the student.

"A coin has two sides, and I hear about the appraisal problems faced by my staff. Many times they will be completing the IEP process, offering their observations and suggestions, and then have teachers give them information that would have eased or lessened the assessment process considerably if the school psychologist had been aware of it initially. If assessment is going to be part of our newly developing collaborative process, we have to work together from the beginning."

Alex is right. Before the assessment begins, the teaching and appraisal staff at each school should share information and devise a list of issues to be reviewed about the student for the outcomes to provide valuable information. Most of the concerns and information will come from the teachers at this point because of their previous interactions with the student. Table 5–10 lists suggested components for successful teacher referrals.

***Anticipated Outcomes.*** As discussed earlier, different people need different information from an assessment. In Ernie's case, his middle school teachers wanted to know why his skills were so low and what additional classroom interventions they could implement to help him. Specialists wanted to know specific remedial and compensatory strategies that might support perceptual or language deficiencies. His parents asked what they could do to help him at home. With these concerns in mind, the school psychologist can

---

**Table 5–10**
**Teacher Referrals**

*Teacher referrals should include:*

- A statement of the information the teacher hopes to learn from the assessment

- Informal observations of the student's classroom behaviors

- Samples of written work

- A review of previous school records

- A description of work habits, including observations and notations of specific areas of academic or behavioral difficulty

- Previous intervention strategies, methods, and materials used successfully with the student

direct the assessment toward answering as many of these questions as possible.

*Informal Behavioral Observations.* The teacher is in the best position to observe a student daily in the learning milieu and note behaviors that may be interfering with learning. Does the student have a short attention span? Seem distractible? Respond impulsively rather than reflectively? Appear attention-seeking? Have many friends? Participate easily in group activities? Demonstrate fluctuations in mood or work productivity? Withdraw at times? A discussion of ongoing behaviors in addition to the school psychologist's observation of the student in the classroom provides an invaluable context for getting the "whole picture" of what may underlie the problem.

*Daily Work Products.* While an assessment instrument can provide good insights into student expertise in a number of arithmetic subareas, students' daily classwork may provide even more substantial supportive information into making the correct diagnosis. For example, Ernie's problems in sequencing letters and numbers may not be in evidence as much when computing from printed problems on the diagnostic test page. Yet, a review of his daily work products may provide more opportunities for him to confuse "486" with "468" as he independently writes out all of the problems and solutions. Similarly, concerns, such as organization of thoughts for written essays or even spelling and handwriting difficulties, are often most evident in classwork and homework, affording valuable information in the assessment.

*Records Review.* In advance of the assessment, a team member, such as the referring teacher, counselor, or school psychologist, should take the responsibility for a careful review of previous school records. Attendance and health records are as important as test scores for providing a picture of where the student may have encountered environmental impediments to his learning progress (Moran, 1978).

In Miguel's situation, a thorough records review provided important answers to many questions. His teacher learned he spoke Spanish at home and had changed schools frequently, including leaving a bilingual education program. His family had relocated the most often during instruction in phonics and sight words, critical building-blocks to reading. His standardized test scores substantiated a verbal and written language problem. Added to her observations of his classroom behaviors and work samples, the teacher received enough information to organize supports for a successful intervention.

Do a student's attendance records indicate major numbers of absences causing the loss of important classroom content? Do health records note frequent allergies or bouts with otitis media, possibly resulting in hearing problems and subsequent difficulties learning phonics? Has the child's behavior suffered from upheaval caused by family moves or other disruptions such as

otitis media—middle ear inflammation that may cause fever and pain, and subsequently affect hearing; impact may reduce student's ability to use phonics in learning to read.

divorce? The informal comments written by previous teachers can provide invaluable insights.

**Work Habits.** Beyond classroom behaviors that interfere with learning are a series of organizational habits that may have direct impact on a student's productivity and content area competence. Does the student record assignments daily on a sheet or in a notebook? Come to class with books and other materials? Complete homework correctly? Seem rested? Organized? Work independently?

Many students with disabilities demonstrate a sense of confusion and disorganization, greatly hindering their ability to be successful. These organizational behaviors are especially important at the secondary level with increasing teacher expectations for student independence in completing tasks both in and out of class. If a student comes to class having lost the homework or not having allotted enough time to complete a major assignment satisfactorily, secondary teachers tend to be less forgiving than elementary teachers.

"Very much so," responded John. "In our defense, it's also understandable. An adult's professional success is closely related to being places on time, ready to get started, with materials and background information about the job. If a student comes to class unprepared, we're not doing him a favor by allowing this behavior to continue. Work habits are part of what we teach in school."

No one can argue with John's point. Therefore, as a teacher refers a student for assessment, it is critical to include a description of any of these organizational behaviors that present a problem to future success.

**Previous Intervention Strategies.** Any educator who has worked on a planning committee knows the frustration of working with the team to devise an intervention plan, only having the student's teacher respond, "I tried that and it didn't work." During the referral for special education, it is extremely helpful to share previous attempts at modifying the classroom, both giving insight into why these attempts did not work and avoiding the IEP team's consideration of them as viable.

"I can see where this sharing would be particularly important as we emphasize a prereferral process in the future," observed Alex. "For example, when Ernie's problems started in middle school, the planning team met with his teachers and discussed logical interventions to improve his academic skills. His teachers tried these but did not feel that the changes were significant. Then they referred him for an indepth assessment.

"Because of thorough background information given by his teachers, the school psychologist and language specialist knew which interventions had failed and were able to include these considerations in their assessment. They were able to select the best level of assessment, since Ernie's teacher had already collected information suggesting the need to go beyond an assessment of basic academic functioning. When they tested Ernie at the next level of modality

A teacher can be far more successful with a student by knowing which techniques, such as contingency reinforcers, have worked in the past.

processing, they found he had perceptual and language problems that had gone previously undetected. They were able to provide new intervention ideas in their follow-up report because they were fully aware of what had been tried previously."

If teacher referrals for assessment include a review of methods and materials used successfully in previous interventions, they provide a basis for future work with the student.

## SUMMARY

This chapter discussed the assessment process and how it can be orchestrated to produce positive outcomes both for educators and students. Understanding the difference between testing and assessment is a critical element. Testing is the acquisition of data or information about specific areas of student performance. Often this is accomplished by the administration of a series of formal or informal measurement instruments. Assessment is more encompassing and includes collecting a broad variety of data to provide a total picture of student achievement and behavior. The usual purpose of assessment is to determine the most appropriate instructional setting, to design intervention strategies, and to measure student ongoing success.

While previous chapters discussed the concept of prereferral, this chapter described the formal referral process for assessment, used when prereferral has not been effective or when the student demonstrates more extensive academic and behavioral problems requiring specialist assistance. Lerner's (1993) stages of formal referral present a good framework for conceptualizing this process. Specialists perform a multidisciplinary evaluation of student academic performance and behaviors. In addition to formally testing the student, they often observe him informally in class, examine daily work products, review previous records and academic/behavioral history, and obtain background history from parents.

After specialists write a report discussing assessment results, they meet with teachers, parents, and school personnel to discuss their findings. This group then becomes the IEP committee, which will initiate follow-up work with the student and recommend provision of supportive services. The IEP is a plan of goals and objectives, specification of specialist supports, intervention strategies for use in the classroom, and methods of evaluating success.

Once the plan is approved, the next stage in the formal referral process involves intervention of specialists and generalists to teach the student. Educators provide the classroom setting and instructional methods suggested in the IEP. As the process continues, involved educators consider its success in improving student performance.

The chapter discussed the concept that different individuals, from educators to the family, often want different types of appraisal information about the academic and behavioral performance of the student. Regular education teachers require input about the student's ability to be successful in their classes. Specialists are more concerned with causality of the problem and designing remedial techniques. Administrators tend to be more process-directed, concerned with following district guidelines and ways to prepare regular education teachers to work with the student. Parents want to understand the nature of the problem and what services the school will provide. Students tend to tie self-esteem issues to assessment results, wanting to be as similar as possible to their peers in achievement and behavior.

As Moran (1976) noted, not all assessments are alike. To receive the most appropriate information, teachers must learn to request the correct type of assessment. The most fundamental assessment is at the academic functioning level, where educators gather information already available on the student and do not require formal testing. This information may include daily work samples in varied academic areas, standardized test scores, attention to language and behavioral patterns as the teacher and peers interact with the student, and a review of records describing previous performance and family background. When the teacher and specialist interact in analyzing this information they are often able to assess the problem accurately and to design an appropriate intervention plan based on available data.

The second level of assessment considers how the student performs psychomotor or information processing, with the goal of finding the optimal learning style, based on perception and language skills. Teachers should make this type of referral when they have not received enough information from the records gathered in an academic assessment or their remedial strategies have not been effective. Testing is conducted and interpreted by trained specialists such as school psychologists and language therapists. The goal at this assessment level is to find the underlying cause of academic problems and to formulate a remedial program to help the student overcome or compensate for a disability, based on individual learning style. Once this information is obtained, the IEP team works together with a specialist to develop alternate teaching strategies and materials. They also select the most appropriate classroom for placement.

There are students whose disabilities are more extreme, often based on deficits in reasoning and problem-solving or from behavioral disorders. Their assessment is the most extensive, usually including IQ and learning aptitude measures as well as personality tests. Causality of the problems may be subtle, requiring a team of teachers, assessment personnel, and parents to work together toward the correct diagnosis and preparation of follow-up interventions.

Regardless of the level of assessment, teachers can provide appraisal staff with important information which underscores collaboration in helping the student. Referrals should include a statement of the information needed by the teacher as a result of the assessment. In this way, specialists can be sure they are meeting teacher goals by selecting the correct form of appraisal. Teachers should describe students' informal behaviors in the classroom, such as inattention or withdrawal, to alert examiners to information that may not be apparent during the testing session. Daily work products portray ongoing problems in completing class assignments, adding valuable information to the assessment process. Educators should review previous student records to learn about family background, attendance and health history, and previous referrals for special education services. Teachers should provide descriptions of organizational behaviors which may interfere with learning, such as not bringing assigned materials or homework to class, losing assignments, and an inability to work independently. Additionally, they should discuss teaching strategies which have already been tried but have proven ineffective with the student, allowing the team insights into student responses.

CASE STUDY: *Elementary*

Lettie has become more withdrawn in fifth grade this year, staying away from most interactions with peers and teachers. You notice that her reading seems slower than other students', and that she writes in a labored manner, expressing her ideas in a disjointed fashion. While she is not a particularly distractible student, her attention span is short for academic tasks, and she looks up frequently from her work. Recently she has refused to read aloud even in small groups.

You see some worrisome behaviors. Lettie talks to almost no one and turns students down when they ask her to play at recess or to be part of their academic group in class. Her mother says she goes directly home from school and sleeps for hours, waking for dinner, homework, and going to bed early. She no longer plays with children in the neighborhood. She told her mother that her friends are "boring" and she doesn't intend to see them again. On weekends she stays inside and watches television. Both you and her mother are concerned about her behavior and decide to have her assessed to discover the problems.

1. Based on the levels of assessment discussed in Tables 5–7 through 5–9, what type(s) will you recommend for Lettie? Why?

2. As a regular educator, what information from the assessment will be of greatest use to you? What type of information will her mother want to know? Since you will need to share the test results with Lettie as well, what may her concerns be?

3. Once assessment is completed, what steps will you take to help Lettie overcome her problems?

4. For optimal assistance, which specialists may you need to involve?

**CASE STUDY:** *Secondary*

Jake has entered the "rebellious stage" of adolescence. He seems to be acting out against everything in which his parents believe. Coming from a family with traditional values, in early middle school he began wearing an earring and "punk" hairstyles. Now in eighth grade, the ring is in his nose and his hair is partially orange. His primary vocabulary exists of expletives when talking to friends.

Jake has not demonstrated too many negative behaviors at school. While not particularly motivated or involved in class discussion, he keeps up with in-class assignments and homework. While he tries to avoid teachers, when involved in conversations he is generally polite.

Jake's parents report different behaviors at home. He yells at them and is rude, sarcastically responding to their advice or even informal conversations. He has begun to stay out beyond curfews, hanging out with high school students who drive. Several families of neighbors recently requested he and his friends not hang out in front of their homes because they are a "bad influence" on younger children.

His parents are very concerned about his behavioral changes and have requested an assessment by the school. You want to assure them that it's only a stage, but you're not sure.

1  What type of assessment should the school perform? When conducting an interview with the parents and with Jake, what questions should they ask to determine potential reasons for changes in his behavior?

2. Because of their specific concerns, what questions will Jake's parents add to Table 5–4 to provide them more extensive information?

3. Similarly, what assessment information will his teachers want to add to Table 5–1 as he enters high school next year?

4. How can the school collaborative team work together with you and Jake's parents to give optimal support? What can you do in the classroom to help?

# 6

# FROM ASSESSMENT TO INTERVENTION

With a clearer understanding of their roles, the Westside teachers felt more confidence in their ability to approach the assessment process. Yet, they expressed uncertainty about methods of collecting assessment information and relating it directly to teaching.

Maura observes, "I have some concerns about how to observe academic or behavioral problems accurately so I can explain them to my colleagues, both during the prereferral and referral processes. I can tell other teachers a student seems hyperactive or her classroom effort is diminishing, but I'm not sure they'll really understand what I mean so they can give me helpful suggestions."

Maura is underscoring an important area of assessment: classroom observations. Yet, often the potential significance of observing the student in the actual learning environment is diminished because these observations are unfocused or random or because the results may not indicate clearly whether behaviors have changed after intervention. If the purpose and method of observation are planned carefully in advance, subsequent data can be among the most powerful in initiating and measuring the intervention process.

# GOALS FOR CLASSROOM OBSERVATIONS

There are broad goals and individualized objectives behind most successful observations. As listed in Table 6–1, goals vary based on the type of information needed by the collaborative or assessment team. The overall purpose of observing students is to provide more information, enhancing the team's effectiveness with student placement and intervention decisions. Within this broad purpose, the general goals listed in Table 6–1 can provide invaluable information about the student's daily performance (Taylor, 1989).

**Initial Identification of Problems.** This use of observation provides a mechanism for screening students who may be starting to experience difficulties. The teacher should note any students whose behaviors or academic performance vary from the expected level of the group. Behaviors, such as inability to finish assignments, refusal to complete homework, or lack of friends and peer involvements, signify developing problems the teacher should discuss with the school prereferral committee. If the teacher observes an increase in these behaviors after trying early intervention, she should refer the student for more indepth assessment in academic or behavioral areas.

**Determination of Student Academic and Behavioral Needs.** The classroom observer does not look solely at a student's problems but at accomplishments as well. What skills does the student possess in the areas under observation? How far is the student from full mastery of critical tasks? In other words, what are the **entry level behaviors** the student demonstrates in areas under observation? Knowledge here provides the teacher with information concerning where to begin instruction or whether additional evaluation is necessary.

**entry level behaviors**—how a student behaves or performs before the intervention strategies are implemented.

---

**Table 6–1**
**Goals for Classroom Observations**

*Goals should include:*

- Initial identification of problems
- Determination of student academic and behavioral needs
- Noting effective teacher techniques
- Decisions regarding appropriate student placement
- Monitoring success of intervention program

(*Source:* Adapted from Taylor, 1989)

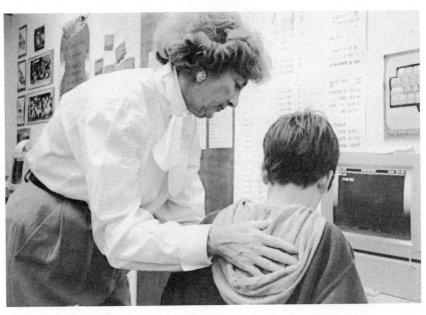

Teacher observation of student success in daily efforts underscores programmatic success.

***Recording Previously Attempted Teaching and Management Techniques.*** It is important to provide the collaborative and assessment teams with information regarding teaching strategies that have been successful or have failed with the student. If the observer notes the student becomes aggressive with others when she cannot perform her work, the follow-up recommendation would be to be sure she is only given work with which she can be successful. If the student is inattentive in the larger group when working on subjects requiring concentration, such as arithmetic or foreign language, she might be directed to complete these in a less distractible area such as a study carrel.

***Decisions Regarding Optimal Placement.*** Watching the student's performance in the teaching-learning milieu provides critical information toward understanding student needs. Once the observer notes student behaviors and successful intervention strategies, she can work with the collaborative team to determine the best teachers and classrooms for placement. Optimally, the student can remain in the current instructional unit, without being removed from teachers, friends, and daily routines and expectations. However, if the student's problems are more extreme and initial interventions have failed, she may need to participate in another setting. While inclusion calls for placement in the regular classroom setting wherever possible, not every teacher can teach every student. Therefore, when examining observed behaviors and learning characteristics to make placement decisions, it is better for the team to consider the needs of the student, the teacher, and peers.

***Monitoring the Success of the Intervention Program.*** Even after placement considerations are concluded, observation has another important goal, that of evaluating programming effectiveness. The observer should consider a series of issues. Are the revised teaching strategies working? Have the changes resulted in improved student performance? Is the teacher interacting well with the student? Has student behavior improved? Are peers responding well? Whether the student has remained in the same instructional setting or moved to a new classroom, observation continues to be important in gauging programmatic success.

# GUIDELINES FOR OBSERVATIONS

"I can appreciate these goals for observations," notes John. "But I rarely have time to do them myself, and I'm concerned about the potential disruptions caused by other adults in the classroom. Especially at the secondary level, students don't seem to miss much. I can see them doing their own observations while I'm trying to teach. It won't take them long to figure out who's being watched and to tease that student. Is there any way we can make the process less disruptive?"

John expresses the concerns of many teachers about having other adults in the classroom and ruining total class response to the lesson. Yet, without observations the data will be incomplete concerning students at risk. Table 6–2 includes a number of suggestions observers have found helpful in avoiding disruptions.

It is important to discuss the goals of the observation with the regular education teacher in advance so both will agree on desired outcomes. Additionally, the teacher should set the time of day when the student will be performing the behaviors most important to the observation (e.g., during lectures, group interactions) and when another adult will be least distracting to the class.

The guidelines in Table 6–2 underscore the need for the observer to become a quiet member of the setting as quickly as possible. Entering the room after the lesson has begun or moving around while the teacher is directing instruction will serve only to attract student attention. Selecting the observation site in advance and having a few other available seats requires planning but ensures a quieter involvement.

Students will look for something to discuss with the new class member. The observer should not be wearing distracting clothing or jewelry and should avoid traits such as gum-chewing or carrying food or beverages into the room.

**Table 6–2**
**Guidelines for Classroom Observers**

*Observers should:*

- Discuss the goals of the observation with the regular education teacher in advance of the visit

- Have the teacher decide the time of day the student will most likely demonstrate the behaviors under observation

- Enter the room as quickly and quietly as possible

- Sit where the student can be observed as easily and unobtrusively as possible

- Not make conversation or eye contact with any students in the room

- Avoid clothing or traits that attract attention

- Arrive at the scheduled time

- Discuss observation findings with the classroom teacher

(*Source:* Adapted from Broaden, in Hall, 1975)

off-task behavior—when attention is distracted from the activity or task at hand; results in nonproductive classroom time.

Doing so engages the students in conversation ("I like your vest"; "Can I have some of that coffee?"; "Hey, how come she can chew gum and I can't?"). Seasoned observers know how alluring eye contact can be in initiating conversation. Students will notice any glances in their direction and will try to interact with the adult, resulting in **off-task behavior**. The observer should try to look around the room, not focusing attention on any one student or suggesting a desire to interact. A shake of the head or an "I'm busy" comment usually is enough to deter the more persistent students.

"How do you keep them from knowing which student is being observed?" asks John. "It's really embarrassing for the student when others are aware and teasing."

The key is in not initiating the observation until the class has settled into their routine and has lost interest in the visiting adult. While this may take ten or fifteen minutes after class begins, with the support of the regular education teacher engaging students in the assignment of the day, the observer has more latitude to look at the specified student. The teacher and observer might decide in advance the tasks in which the student should be involved in order to gain most information and to draw attention away from any individual.

Some students will require observations over several class periods or days. Unless performance on a variety of specific tasks is important, the appearance of the observer at the same time each session will diminish student interest as the observer is no longer new to the environment. If the observer returns periodically to consider student progress, with the support of the teacher, she becomes an accepted class member and less likely to cause distractions.

"As a special educator, I frequently do these observations for prereferrals as well as students being assessed for supportive services," notes Teresa. "One time I went back to a certain class often enough that the students reported to their teacher 'She's ba-ack' when I entered the room. They even invited me to their holiday party!

"I have found it helpful to observe two students at once unless I'm recording numerical data. For example, when a collaborative team wants me to observe one student, I may ask the teacher if there is anyone else starting to demonstrate problems or whom they might refer soon. By situating myself in the room where I can see both students, the rest of the class has a harder time focusing on any one peer and I can provide additional information on a student about whom the teacher may be concerned."

Teresa's latter idea is particularly important. The observer is only an invited guest into the classroom and should demonstrate visiting behaviors. It is inexcusable to miss a scheduled observation or to arrive late, disrupting the class. Accordingly, any information gathered should be shared with the teacher immediately as well as with the school-based team that requested the observation. If there are to be several visits, the observer should overview findings after the initial visit to be sure she is collecting the observational data the teacher needs.

## STAGES OF ASSESSMENT

"How do you actually conduct an observation?" asks Maura. "I'm asking because the day may come when I want to collect my own information on a student without bringing other teachers into my classroom."

### Baseline Data

baseline data—collection of facts taken, usually through observation and assessment, before intervention strategies are implemented, with the purpose of determining effectiveness of the intervention.

There are several stages when educators are assessing students informally through methods such as observation. Noted in Table 6–3, the first involves collecting baseline data concerning where the student is performing academically or behaviorally before any intervention occurs. To gain accurate information at this starting point, the teacher should know which specific behaviors are of interest and look for them in the setting where they normally occur (Jobes & Hawthorne, 1977). This initial observation should provide a

**Table 6–3**
**Types of Data Collection**

| Approach | Characteristics |
|---|---|
| Baseline Data | Observation of student's skills and behaviors before any intervention. |
| | Provides data against which to compare the later success of teacher interventions. |
| Intervention Data | Measurement of effectiveness of teacher intervention and classroom modifications. |
| | Indicates which antecedents and consequences have greatest impact by comparison of the frequency of negative behaviors with the initial number in the baseline data collection. |
| Generalization Data | Observation of positive changes in student behavior in a different environment than the one in which they were learned. |
| | If changes have not occurred in the new setting, teachers can use the same interventions and consequences as in their classrooms. |

(*Source:* Adapted from Jobes & Hawthorne, 1977)

clear picture of the student's skills and behaviors as a starting point against which to compare future changes. Without assessment prior to intervention, there is no way to accurately measure effectiveness.

For example, if Shane is a student in Maura's class and has been having difficulty participating in group projects because of aggression, Maura will need to change his behavior as quickly as possible. However, to establish the most effective intervention she needs to have an idea of which behavioral management technique has the strongest long-term impact. In collecting baseline data, Maura or another observer counts the number of times Shane is verbally or physically aggressive in a specified time period when working with others. During this data collection, it is important that the teacher instruct as she does normally, not providing **antecedents** or **consequences** to change the behavior unless it is extreme at that moment. The purpose of baseline data is to provide a foundation for comparison of current student behaviors before and after teacher interventions. After several such initial baseline data collections, the teacher should average the number of occurrences to obtain an idea of the **norm**.

antecedents—things that happen before or prior to a behavior.

consequences—things that happen as a result of behavior.

norm—average or normal.

## Intervention Data

intervention data—a collection of facts that substantiates which antecedents and consequences are most effective in shaping student behaviors in the desired direction.

As indicated in Table 6–3, the next stage is to collect **intervention data** to substantiate which antecedents and consequences are most effective in shaping student behaviors in the desired direction. Maura might try verbal comments with Shane before he begins working with others, directing him to avoid specified physical or verbal aggressions. ("You will keep your hands on your desk at all times and touch no one"; "You will not speak to anyone in the group without my approval.") The observer records the number of times Shane demonstrates aggressive acts. After several observations, the average number of occurrences is compared to the original baseline data to see if the specific intervention is being effective.

While researchers often suggest an average trial of three to five days to measure intervention success (Jobes & Hawthorne, 1977), instances such as Shane's, in which a student negatively impacts others, may necessitate a shorter trial. If Shane did not respond during an entire day of teacher **verbal redirections**, Maura might want to add a more powerful intervention, such as **time out**, isolating Shane from the group as a consequence for aggression. When he returns to group participation, she can remind him again of appropriate behaviors through antecedent comments and remove him immediately in response to aggression. Comparing the number of aggressive instances within this framework with the number at baseline would be a good indication of intervention effectiveness.

verbal redirections—verbally guiding the student back to on-task, purposeful behavior.

time out—isolating the student from the group as a consequence.

## Generalization Data

generalization data—information indicating how well modified behavior continues in other environments.

As listed in Table 6–3, the third type of data is **generalization data**, which ensures the application of changed behaviors to alternate environments. No intervention is fully successful unless the student uses it appropriately in a variety of situations. There are settings, such as other classrooms, in which Maura can anticipate that Shane's behavior should improve once it has been established in her room. Research has indicated that students tend to best generalize changes in behavior when new settings are similar to the environment where the behavior was first learned (Kennedy & Thompson, 1967; Walker & Buckley, 1968). However, if Shane continues his aggressions against others, his teachers in that setting should use the same stimuli and consequences that have been effective for Maura to affect change. Collaborative teams of teachers meeting to discuss students at risk are particularly effective in situations such as this, since they can share data about the student and cooperate to ensure that generalization occurs.

Additionally, Maura's goal is not only to have Shane stop his aggressive behaviors in classes, but also in the cafeteria and on the playground. Since these settings tend to be less structured, they are at higher probability for problems with generalization of behaviors. She should observe his behaviors

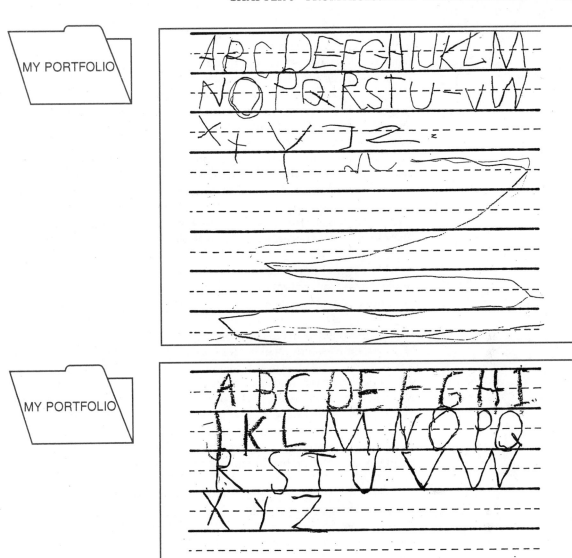

MY PORTFOLIO

MY PORTFOLIO

Even a short period of time between observations can demonstrate improved student performance. Reprinted with permission, Winston School, San Antonio.

initially in these settings to compare the frequency of aggression with that in the classroom. Then, after intervention in class, she should informally note whether his behaviors have improved in unstructured environments, in other words, whether they have been generalized. If she realizes that he has not corrected his aggressive tendencies outside the classroom, she should initiate another intervention in this setting, such as discussing with him the preferred behaviors and following through with an immediate consequence for any aggressive outburst.

"There's an academic type of response generalization that I'm concerned about," notes John. "When I teach my students a new skill, ranging from spelling or vocabulary to grammar, I want them to use it independently in writing papers and completing projects in English and other subjects. I often hear history and science teachers complain that no one has taught the student to write well, and it concerns me. Often students seem to master the skill, but in isolation."

John's frustration is shared by many teachers, especially at the secondary level, since they do not want to reteach skills that should have been not only mastered by students, but integrated into their schoolwork. Therefore, it is important to continuously assess generalization of skills to intervene wherever necessary.

When John assigns an essay for his class to write, he should tell them in advance that he is measuring their ability to avoid sentence fragments, an area they have been studying in grammar. He should alert them to proofread their work carefully to be sure no fragments have been included. When he reads their papers, he will note the success of students' integration of the concept. However, true generalization will not have occurred until students edit their work for this and other areas studied without being alerted by the teacher. When they independently perform the task in other classes, generalization will have occurred.

To encourage this, he can ask other content area teachers to note errors in writing when they grade students' papers. The teachers can list these errors both for the students and John so concentrated effort will continue to encourage generalization across other subject areas.

# RECORDING DATA

While most teachers try to informally observe changes in student behavior, they usually do not measure these changes in any systematic way. As a result, they may not have a complete understanding of how well their intervention techniques are working. For example, when Shane acts aggressively, if

verbal reprimands—being told the behavior is inappropriate

Maura responds with **verbal reprimands**, it might appear informally that her method has worked. Likely Shane would look at her and then his peers for their response, and stop the aggressive behavior. Maura would feel that immediate verbal responses after the behavior are the best way to handle Shane.

However, if Maura collects data in a more systematic way, she might find that the opposite is actually true. What if Shane's misbehavior is an attempt to gain attention? Through Maura's response he learns that by being aggressive he gains not only her attention, but that of the entire class. Quite a reward! If she or a classroom observer had measured the length of the intervals between aggressive outbursts when she verbally reprimanded him and contrasted this data with the intervals after a stronger, less public consequence such as time out, she might find that her scolding did not have a long-term effect although it had appeared initially to have the immediate impact she wanted.

Most teachers avoid collecting and recording data because they feel it is too time-consuming and their efforts are better spent in teaching. Indeed, an overly cumbersome system might cause rather than solve problems. If data recording is convenient, however, and provides useful information to help the teacher evaluate student behaviors, it can serve an important function. The teacher should consider when it is best to have an outside observer record the data. If the class is large or the teacher feels too busy to record accurately, she should contact a special educator or counselor to perform the observation.

## Student Work

"How do I know the type of data to record?" asks John. "I'm not a researcher and I'm not sure where to proceed from here."

One of the best ways to collect baseline, intervention, or generalization data is to examine student work products carefully. This is the easiest type of data analysis, since it is part of teachers' routine teaching responsibility. In the example earlier, initially John read students' papers and noted a number of incomplete sentences in their writing. His observation was that the entire class could use some instruction in this area, but that two particular students made so many of these errors that clearly they would require more intensive intervention. Noting how many sentence fragments were in all student's papers and comparing this with the number included after instruction would be time-consuming. Since he is most concerned about the performance of two students, he might note the total errors they produce and contrast this with numbers in later papers. As the year progresses, at random intervals, he might count numbers of incomplete sentences these two students write to gauge how well they have integrated his instruction.

MY PORTFOLIO

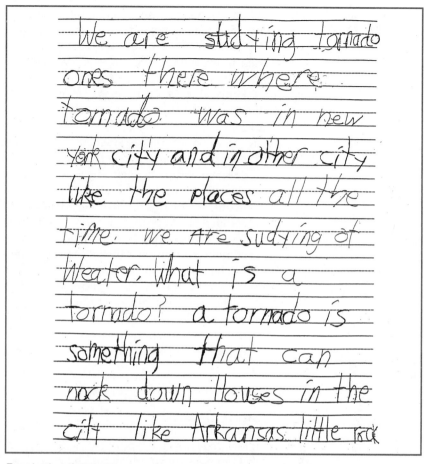

We are studying tornado ones there where tornado was in new york city and in other city like the places all the time. we Are sudying of Weater. what is a tornado? a tornado is something that can nock down Houses in the city like Arkansas little rock

Examination of student work products can demonstrate a variety of learning needs. This student has difficulty organizing ideas and writing them in correct syntax. Reprinted with permission, Winston School, San Antonio.

## Event Recording

**event recording**—making a tally each time the behavior being observed occurs.

Frequently used by teachers, **event recording** requires the teacher to make a tally each time the behavior being observed occurs. It is used to measure the frequency of the behavior at baseline, before the teacher initiates any intervention and later, during intervention and generalization periods, to be sure the behavior is changing. Event recording is best when behaviors have a discrete beginning and ending, not if the student performs the behavior at an extremely high rate (e.g., clicking a pen) or for a long period of time (e.g., looking around the room at peers) (Taylor, 1989). Both Shane's aggressive behaviors and the sentence fragments written by John's students could be tallied easily by event, or frequency, recording. While many teachers record numbers of inappropriate behaviors by hash marks on a paper, others mark a piece of tape on their wrist, move paper clips, or most conveniently, wear a wrist counter (Jobes & Hawthorne, 1977).

Teachers need observe students for only brief periods daily. They should observe them during the same time or content period so that the demands of the task are similar and there are no extraneous factors influencing students' responses.

## Duration Recording

"What if one of my students misbehaves or becomes apathetic over a longer period of time. How do I assess degree of change?" asks Maura. "For example, Casey is a student in my class who has a history of depression. She becomes easily overwhelmed by any academic task that appears difficult, and she refuses to continue. At that point, she puts her head down on the desk and becomes totally nonresponsive to me and the assignment."

In this instance, it is better for Maura to measure on-task than off-task behaviors because it will be easier to motivate Casey and keep her working than to get her to begin again once she has stopped. The first step for Maura is to establish an observation goal to determine how long Casey works successfully on a subject, such as phonics, without feeling overwhelmed.

Maura records Casey's baseline data as shown in Table 6–4. Her behavioral intervention plan might include discussing the problem with Casey and

### Table 6–4
### Comparison of Baseline and Intervention Data

*Casey: Baseline Data*

|  | Monday | Tuesday | Wednesday | Thursday | Friday |
|---|---|---|---|---|---|
| Minutes to Complete Phonics | 4 | 6 | 5 | 6 | 5 |

*Casey: Intervention Data*

|  | Monday | Tuesday | Wednesday | Thursday | Friday |
|---|---|---|---|---|---|
| Minutes to Complete Phonics | 5 | 8 | 8 | 9 | 7 |

duration recording—keeping track of the amount of time spent involved in a specific behavior.

instructing her to raise her hand when her work becomes too difficult. Casey should continue at the task until Maura comes to her desk to explain the material. As a reinforcement at the end of the day Casey would be able to earn a personally motivating reward, such as reading a book of her choice for each minute of phonics spent on-task (without head on desk) after she indicated the work had become difficult.

Casey's **duration recording** during intervention might appear as noted in Table 6–4. Maura and she would continue to work toward the goal of twenty minutes, the entire phonics period. As this goal is approximated, Maura can move toward generalization of Casey's on-task behavior by changing to a different reward for continuing to work during arithmetic.

The example of Casey demonstrates how Maura can use duration recording to measure a behavior that takes place across extended time periods. The steps in combining data collection and intervention are easy to implement. Maura observes specific behaviors impacting Casey's learning and emotional status. She decides they are serious enough to warrant teacher attention and begins by collecting baseline data. During this stage Maura selects the subject area and time of day for observation to avoid introducing other factors, such as differing content areas, selecting a time that would not allow full demonstration of the behaviors under observation. After assuring herself that the phonics assignment is at Casey's instructional level and should challenge but not frustrate her, Maura counts the amount of time Casey remains working. After a week of data collection, Maura introduces her intervention plan, which involves an alternative, more appropriate action for Casey when she becomes overwhelmed, along with a desired reward for reinforcement. Then Maura records how long Casey remains on task with the intervention. Importantly, she performs her observation during the same subject and time of day as she collected baseline data. She then compares the results to ensure that the intervention plan is working. After a week of data collection, if the data were not demonstrably different from the initial observation, Maura could change the intervention or **reinforcement** and continue observing and recording.

reinforcement—providing a consequence for a particular behavior; may be positive or negative.

latency recording—noting the amount of time a student takes to respond to a particular stimulus.

interval recording—the teacher divides the observation period and notes the appropriateness of student behaviors within subunits of the total time.

momentary time sampling— the teacher observes a student at a given time to note if specified behavior is occurring.

There are a number of other systems teachers can use for observing specific student behaviors. **Latency recording** involves noting the amount of time a student takes to respond to a particular stimulus, such as teacher directions to begin work or to cease an undesirable behavior. During **interval recording** the teacher divides the observation period and notes the appropriateness of student behaviors within subunits of the total time. For example, when his students are completing a group project, John might divide a ten-minute time period into five two-minute intervals and note whether a certain distractible student is paying attention. Similarly, **momentary time sampling** allows the teacher to observe a student at a given time (e.g., every two minutes) to note if the specified behavior is occurring (Taylor, 1989).

While each of these three systems can provide useful information, they tend to be more time-consuming for teachers, potentially drawing their attention away from the rest of the class to observe a few students. Additionally, they may require a cue to signal the time to record, alerting students and disrupting the lesson. If these methods are to be used, it is better to have another teacher, such as a special educator, conduct the observation so the class is not disrupted.

# FORMAL STANDARDIZED TESTS

However methodical, there are times when teacher observations cannot provide enough information, or when they indicate the need for more indepth assessment. When students are being considered for support by special education services, formal testing is required in order to document the existence of a disability and to meet state and federal guidelines. While the use of standardized instruments has been the subject of controversy, most discussions have been concerned with the degree of relevance of results as they pertain to individual students, especially those from culturally or linguistically different backgrounds. Assessment experts agree no one test should form the basis of a **diagnosis**. Any test is only a small sample of a student's behavior at one moment in time (Lerner, 1993). In addition to teacher observation, a variety of formal and informal assessment tools are necessary to understand the needs of the student.

diagnosis—determining the nature of the problem by examination or assessment.

## Test Selection

When standardized tests are administered, it is important that strict guidelines are followed to ensure meaningful results. Educators should select a particular **instrument** because it meets the criteria listed in Table 6–5.

instrument—in assessment, the chosen test.

*Validity.* A test is **valid** when it measures accurately what it is supposed to measure. Often, educators are most concerned with **content validity**, or a test's provision of an adequate sample of skills, abilities, or attributes in a specified area. For example, in selecting an instrument to assess arithmetic skills for third-graders, Maura should consider including a range of basic computation skills from initial addition and subtraction to multiplication, and even some division. This broad spectrum allows her to assess the needs of students across a variety of arithmetic competencies, from basic to advanced. She would not select a test with fewer items in basic computation and many in fractions and decimals, since this content would not be appropriate for her curriculum and grade level. Similarly, understanding that students' abilities to analyze and solve word problems are critical in arithmetic

valid—measures accurately what it is supposed to measure.

content validity—a test's provision of an adequate sample of skills, abilities, or attributes in a specified area.

## Table 6–5
## Guidelines for Standardized Test Selection

- The test should be valid.

- It should be reliable.

- The test should have been standardized on a larger sample, with characteristics similar to the current population.

- The test manual should be easily readable and contain age and grade norms for student results, as well as percentile ranks and standard scores for comparative purposes.

- The test should be easy to administer and score.

- Time requirements for administration and scoring should be minimal.

- Results of the instrument will provide important insights into the student's learning and behavior.

- Test results should be easily interpreted.

- Teachers should be able to apply results toward meaningful instruction.

application, she wants an instrument that includes problem-solving questions involving one to three mathematical operations. Tests comprised solely of computational problems or emphasizing too few or too many operations would not be suitable for her assessment needs.

reliable—provides results consistent with the individual's performance over an extended time.

"practice effect"—once a student takes a test a number of times, or even more than once in a brief time period, it becomes unreliable, because of familiarity with the questions.

*Reliability.* A test is considered **reliable** when it provides results consistent with the individual's performance over an extended time period. Reliability should demonstrate similar outcomes from an individual on the same instrument after multiple administrations. Frequently, these samples are obtained by using a variety of forms of the same test so the **"practice effect"** does not elevate scores artificially.

"I can even gauge reliability on my own tests in class," John notes. "If I have a student who normally performs extremely well and has a low score on an exam, I find it's usually a result of one or more factors outside the student's ability. If others also perform poorly, I can see the test was too difficult and I may want to grade on a curve. Or sometimes, like the rest of us, the student may have had a bad day, or just not be feeling well. It isn't fair to penalize a normally hard worker when this happens, so I may decide to lower the impact of that particular test on this student's final average by providing a chance to submit additional work or take another exam. The purpose of testing should be to get an accurate measure of a student's ongoing abilities and performance, not to penalize them." During formal assessment, John's attitude toward consistency and fairness is very important in gauging a student's actual ability level.

norm-referencing—information on the population used as the standardization group when a specific test was developed.

*Standardization.* The manual should contain information about the standardization group during test **norm-referencing**. How large was the group of students who initially took this test to validate the items? Were they of similar age, gender, and grade levels? Was their socioeconomic background varied? Were there a sufficient number of students to represent the racial and ethnic characteristics of this school district? If so, was there a varied level of performance correlated to gender, race, ethnicity, or socioeconomic background? For the test to be useful, it should be representative of students in the teacher's classes.

test manual—information and directions concerning an evaluation instrument.

***Test Manual.*** While many educators review only the directions for test administration in the test manual, they should acquaint themselves with the full breadth of information available to support their interpretation of results. Most manuals contain validity and reliability information as well as a description of the group on which the test was normed. Additionally, educators can compare the student's score with those of others of similar age and grade level to ascertain strengths and problem areas. Many manuals contain percentile ranks or scaled scores, indicating the student's relative rank on a national comparison basis.

***Ease of Administration.*** Tests do not need to be complex to be effective. While certain tests mandate specialized training, well-designed instruments provide clear directions for administration and scoring. All potential examiner concerns should be answered in the manual, minimizing the degree of individual interpretation necessary and lowering the possibility of testing error. Instructions should be written without use of professional jargon or assumptions about the examiner's background.

Standardized tests can provide important background information for student placement.

***Time.*** No teacher has extensive time to spend administering a standardized test to individuals or small groups of students. Even when specialized personnel such as school psychologists are available, time-consuming instruments tend to tire students and lessen reliability. Therefore, it is extremely important that educators note in advance test length and consider how it relates to their own time constraints and student attentional abilities. While many instruments are divided into series of subtests, making it possible for students to take a short break, or even to continue at another time, this is not advised if the teacher wants a true indicator of student performance. Some assessment personnel feel that when tired or inattentive, students demonstrate the behaviors most difficult for teachers to manage and give the examiner a clearer picture of what happens in the classroom as the day progresses. However, the purpose of assessment is to obtain a true picture of students' academic and affective behaviors to determine the best educational responses. This insight is best obtained when students are not worn out or distracted by taking an overly-long test.

***Student-Centered.*** In some school districts, pupil appraisal personnel have a standard battery of tests they administer to all students who are referred for assessment. Usually these instruments have been selected because they meet state guidelines for determining eligibility for services. However, optimal test selection should be based on the needs of the student. Aside from those areas of assessment required to meet state mandates, only those measures that provide further insights into the student should be administered to avoid over-testing.

***Ease of Interpretation.*** Appraisal specialists and regular educators appreciate instruments that give results that are easily analyzable. If a test takes a long time to score or requires sophisticated expertise to interpret results, inaccuracies may result. Because the nature of some cognitive and psychological tests may dictate a degree of complexity to achieve desired information, these instruments should always be administered and scored by trained specialists. It becomes the responsibility of the specialist to interpret results carefully into language the classroom teacher and parents can understand to appreciate the nature of the learning or behavioral problem.

interpret—rephrase for practical use.

***Usefulness in Intervention.*** Maura comments, "Often I find even if the results of formal testing indicate a problem, I'm not sure how to translate assessment into the work we do in class. Isolated test results showing a perceptual problem don't tell me if the child can be successful in our basal reader. It's hard to group the student or even to determine my goals if I just have standardized test scores." Maura's concerns are typical of many teachers who struggle to relate traditional psychometric evaluations to specific classroom goals and intervention strategies. The purpose of assessment is the design of appropriate instruction. Therefore, if teachers are more directly involved

psychometric—measuring mental processes.

in the evaluation process, their awareness of student learning styles, rates, and academic levels increases.

As discussed in Chapter 5, the regular classroom teacher may want different questions answered from an assessment than do others involved with the student. A skill, such as auditory discrimination of sounds and words, may be correlated with academic success and provide important information for the school psychologist. Yet, the teacher may be more concerned with the student's ability to understand and respond appropriately to verbal information in a classroom environment where **extraneous stimuli** are present, such as other students talking. Eligibility for special education usually requires consideration of national norms. Data providing the student's comparative performance within national norms for auditory discrimination would be of interest to the teacher but would not provide the information she really needs to change the environment or teach the student. Teachers feel the need to assess the variables required for academic success, not areas that may be related but do not demonstrate a daily impact on student performance (Jobes & Hawthorne, 1977).

extraneous stimuli—external distractions.

## INFORMAL ASSESSMENT

"It may sound odd coming from the director of appraisal services, but I think educators rely too much on standardized tests for information, and then are dissatisfied because they haven't learned everything they needed to know," commented Alex. "They tend to feel the test companies are the experts and teacher measures just aren't as good. Yet, when I look at some teacher-created tests, I realize often they provide much more practical information for teaching than do standardized tests."

Alex is suggesting the primary reason why teachers should consider informal assessment an important indicator of student performance. Informal measures may be more useful for the teacher. Often they test students on the materials and procedures they use daily in the classroom. There are a variety of types of informal assessment instruments, ranging from informal tests to curriculum-based assessment, portfolios, **criterion-referenced tests**, and **diagnostic teaching**. Informal measures may be designed commercially, although many teachers prefer to create their own so they have control over content and can better observe students' abilities to follow classroom procedures and to work with available materials.

criterion-referenced tests—assessment of a student's performance that is not based on comparison to other students, but to an absolute level of mastery.

diagnostic teaching—planning activities based on the needs of the students.

Researchers view teacher involvement in evaluation as a key to better linkage between assessment and instruction (Airasian, 1991; Fuchs, Fuchs, & Fernstrom, 1992; Gable, Hendrickson, Meeks, Evans, & Evans, 1990). As Heiss (1977) notes, "The more nearly the assessment of learning approximates the context in which the learning problem was found, the greater the degree of success in matching instructional planning to instructional assessment." His observation reflects generalized teacher dissatisfaction with evaluations that remove the student from critical environmental factors in the classroom that may be part of the reason for lowered student performance (e.g., distractions caused by the presence of other students; space restrictions resulting in too close a proximity to others).

Often informal measures lack certain advantages of standardized tests. They have not been normed on large populations of students and have not been examined for validity and reliability. Since most teachers are not measurement experts, some of their test questions may be too difficult or easy or may reflect only factual recall instead of higher cognitive processes. If the student has been referred for assessment for potential special education placement, state guidelines usually mandate use of standardized instruments.

On the other hand, informal tests are less expensive and are usually administered during class periods. Additionally, teachers have more flexibility in designing their own tests. "So true," comments John. "Anyone who has taught a class of adolescents knows they arrive the first day of school with a range of reading levels that may span many years. I need to see who can read my textbooks, who can write well, and who has higher level thinking skills that will encompass some abstract ideas we'll be studying. I also want to know who the weaker readers and writers are, and who will need directed questions in order to approach higher-order thinking.

"To find out this information, I give a simple reading-thinking-writing pretest. The first day of class, I have students read a brief chapter in their text, one which is similar to the type of reading they'll be doing for the rest of the year. Then I have them answer four or five questions about the meaning of the reading selection. I write these questions myself, since I have found that the ones in the text may not be varied enough in their conceptual levels. Only one of my questions is factual. The second involves a main idea of the passage, and the rest emphasize higher cognitive responses, such as evaluation of what is said or generalization of concepts to other situations.

"Based on this simple informal test, I get lots of information. Sometimes I have a student who cannot even complete reading the passage and I know I'll need specialist help to teach her basic decoding skills. Or, if she hasn't finished because she was inattentive, I'll have to consider how to redirect her as I teach. From reading students' written work I find out each individual's ability to use correct grammar, syntax, and vocabulary. Often I "red flag" common errors and can get an initial picture of what I'll have to teach or review for writing instruction. I also get an overview of their cognitive levels by studying which questions they were able to answer appropriately. Not only does this set the stage for my lesson planning, but it helps me decide the types of questions to ask individual students during class discussions so that they can answer and not be embarrassed. Then I can work to take them to the next level of thinking as the term progresses."

decoding skills—the ability to interpret letters into meaningful words.

syntax—the meaningful arrangement of words in a sentence.

MY PORTFOLIO

> A long time ago
> thare lived a vary yuong
> Butif women see was
> maired her husbend
> was In the army
> he liket it she wusint
> to hapy about hem being
> In the army But wen
> veat nom came he
> told his wife he hud
> to go and if he wer to
> tie to find a uttue man
> 3 monts in to the wor
> she got a leter confermiy
> his dern she crid over and
> over she couldent stup
> and every night ent ell
> she died shed cried and
> tuke a hour to remeber
> him When she died
> a lot of peple reder
> hering her sprit say
> my nusband my husb
> and if you ever her
> tha yel now its her

Informal assessment of student work at the beginning of the year can indicate necessary teaching directions. After reading a story, a middle school student wrote the above essay. With corrections, it reads: "A long time ago, there lived a very young, beautiful woman. She was married. Her husband was in the Army. He liked it. She wasn't too happy about him being in the Army. But when Vietnam came, he told his wife he had to go and if he were to die, to find another man. Three months into the war, she got a letter confirming his death. She cried over and over. She couldn't stop. And every night until she died she cried and took an hour to remember him. When she died a lot of people remembered hearing her spirit say, "My husband! My husband!" And if you ever hear that yell now, it's her."
Reprinted with permission, Winston School, San Antonio.

It is exciting to consider what teachers can learn from one informal test if they consider their goals and needs carefully. John wants to find out students' conceptual levels, so he avoids the tendency to ask only factual questions or to use the text questions at the end of the chapter because they are too limited. He is able to observe students as they read and write, informally gauging their attentive abilities. He is even able to get information on their written composition skills through a sample of their work. The message is that all teachers can obtain the information they need from assessment if they consider their own purposes before selecting or designing the instrument.

Teacher flexibility is a strong advantage of informal measures. If John observes a few students who need more time to read or prepare answers to questions, he can extend the time they are allowed to complete the task. If they are inattentive, he can direct them to work in a less distractible area of the room so that they can concentrate better. If they need a break, he can allow them to resume testing at another time. While he makes note of these differing needs, he permits the students' academic and behavioral requirements to drive the testing situation, not the opposite, as is too often the case. If he finds that a student cannot read the book, he provides a text with a lower reading level, allowing the student success while measuring skill levels. The very nature of informal tests encourages the teacher to use a variety of materials and procedures (Lerner, 1993).

## Guidelines for Informal Measures

Whether teachers use their own informal tests or commercial ones, they should plan in advance to obtain the information they need for improved intervention. Table 6–6 includes a series of guidelines for educators in administering informal tests.

***Assess Deficient Skills.***  When John tests his class informally, he is interested in screening for any academic or behavioral tendencies that would impact student work. He is able to judge more proficient learners and those who need additional remedial help. Yet, while John has been able to identify these students, he must administer additional measures to determine which specific skills are present or absent.

For example, if Sandy reads slowly and barely finishes the assignment, John may assume she has problems with **word analysis**, but he needs more specific information to be able to help her. He might ask her to stop by his room before or after school and to read aloud for him so he can note where her problems lie. She may never have mastered phonics, may have a poor sight word vocabulary, or have difficulty with syllabication. Once he analyzes where her specific **skill deficits** are, he can request support from the school reading specialist or special education teacher in order to have her be successful in his class (Lerner, 1993).

word analysis—use of strategies such as phonics or structural clues (prefixes, suffixes, or syllables) to obtain word meaning.

skill deficits—areas that lack specific ability.

| Table 6-6 |
| :--- |
| **Guidelines for Administering Informal Tests** |

*Guidelines should include:*

- Assessment of skills that appear deficient
- Estimation of difficulty level and change to easier material if required
- Typical classroom conditions
- Combination of informal observation with test results
  (*Source:* Lerner, 1993)
- Materials availability at a variety of levels
- Selection of time least disruptive to remainder of class
- Selection of time when student is most attentive
- Recording and interpretation of test results immediately

difficulty level—the skill level necessary to complete the work successfully.

***Estimate Difficulty Level.*** It may be difficult for the teacher to guess a student's performance level when beginning assessment. When teachers begin administration of informal tests, they should estimate the difficulty level. Then, if the student is unable to respond at grade level, the teacher should present progressively easier material, moving downward until the student is able to perform the task. In this way, a true estimate of student skill levels can be achieved (Lerner, 1993).

***Present Typical Classroom Conditions.*** Many teachers prefer informal instruments because they can administer them to individuals or small groups in the actual classroom environment. Teachers should approximate the student's daily learning conditions as closely as possible in order to learn the most from assessment (Lerner, 1993).

"I can see where this would be important," notes Maura. "Sean is so highly distracted by any movement around him that he stops his work, loses his place, and just watches what's going on. If he were assessed in one of those small testing rooms at Jackson, it would be much more difficult to note that his inattention is the real problem in class." Teachers should observe and test students in the classroom whenever possible.

***Combine Observation and Assessment.*** Earlier discussion in this chapter emphasized the importance of observation as an assessment tool. Whether teachers use formal or informal tests, they should carefully observe student behaviors during testing as well as during daily work and interactions with others. Tests cannot take the place of careful observations. Their purpose is to provide additional information about the student's skill levels and learning styles. Educators will receive the most comprehensive information by combining a number of assessment modes.

***Have a Variety of Materials Available.*** It is every teacher's unlikely dream that students come to class able to complete assigned work because of skills at grade level. Unfortunately, rarely is this true, especially in classrooms where students may have a number of academic disabilities or behavioral problems interfering with learning. Therefore, to assess students' mastery levels accurately, educators should have available a wide spectrum of materials at varied grade levels. At the elementary level, for reading assessment the teacher might have a number of basal readers at different levels, or math work ranging across a spectrum of skills.

"I finally have worked out a comfortable system for informally assessing my third-graders' reading levels at the beginning of the school year," notes Maura. "I set aside basal readers ranging from primer to fifth grade in case I need them handy. I have each student come to my desk and read aloud for just a few minutes from a third-grade passage. If the student encounters problems, I move her down to the lower-level basal until she reaches her **instructional level**. This tells me which reader she'll need in class.

"Just like John does with his secondary students, I've prepared a series of several questions for each passage, ranging across cognitive levels. The way the student responds tells me how strong her reading comprehension is, as well as her ability to answer different types of questions in class. Although I don't have a great deal of time with each student, I can assess different basic reading skills during this informal pretest. If I find any area with a number of problems, I can assess it more indepth at another time or ask Teresa to help me, since she's more expert at this. The chart I use to record students' reading problems is in Table 6–7.

"I like this chart because it allows me to easily list all students' appropriate basals and reading comprehension levels, based on the questions they answer most correctly. Also, I can check any problem in basic decoding that may cause the student to read slowly or with lowered comprehension. After this initial **pretest**, I can assign the best text and place students in small instructional groups in which they need additional work, in areas like phonics. This skills summary helps me plan my goals for individual students because I can see where they need more skill-building."

***Avoid Disrupting Large Group.*** It is important that teachers select a time of day for informal assessment when it has the least impact on disrupting the routine of the entire class. As Maura and John have described with their informal reading inventories, when teachers are assessing all students, it is easier to schedule one or two class periods in which everyone is involved or performing alternate tasks. However, if the teacher is concerned only with a few students, assessment may need to be done at alternate times.

"Exactly," notes Maura. "While I'm hearing individual students read and I'm recording their errors, I have the rest of the class give me additional samples of their work in other areas. For example, I have all students complete

**instructional level**—the level at which the teacher should present lessons; the student should experience success as well as learning.

**pretest**—test to determine how much the student already knows about a skill; used to determine where to begin teaching.

**Table 6–7**
**Informal Reading Inventory**

**Directions:** For each student, record the basal reader name and level where he or she makes no more than 3 oral reading errors per page. Check any decoding column where the student experiences problems and may need further assessment or remedial teaching.

| Name | Text Level | Phonics | | | | Sight Words | | Structural Analysis | Comprehension | | |
| | | Conso-nants | Vowels | Blends | Digraphs | At Level | Below Level | Compds., Affixes, Syllables | Lit. | Interp. | Eval. |
| --- | --- | --- | --- | --- | --- | --- | --- | --- | --- | --- | --- |
| | | | | | | | | | | | |
| | | | | | | | | | | | |
| | | | | | | | | | | | |
| | | | | | | | | | | | |

inventory—test including a sampling of skills across a variety of areas.

splinter skills—student knows certain operations well but has never learned others completely.

an informal math inventory at their desk. I've included an example of this in Figure 6–1. When they finish this computational inventory, I give them a quick break and then an inventory with arithmetic word problems. On this informal arithmetic inventory, I have a variety of problems ranging in difficulty from first to fifth grade. While I'm not including every skill, I have a sample of math operations the students should have mastered by now, as well as a few above grade level for my stronger mathematicians. I find that many students have splinter skills in math computation, where they know certain operations well but have never learned others completely. After this informal math assessment, I can formulate small groups for students with similar remedial needs and can teach certain skills more intensely. That way students will be able to catch up with their peers and continue to more advanced levels. Administering this informal math inventory really lets me help students who tend to fall behind and always suffer from not having learned the basics.

"On a different day, when I'm recording students' reading skills, I have all students do a writing sample on a topic I select. Like John, the writing

Addition

| | | | | |
|---|---|---|---|---|
| 14<br>+3 | 48<br>+68 | 68<br>+75 | 48<br>6<br>39<br>+27 | 788<br>+97 |

Subtraction

| | | | | |
|---|---|---|---|---|
| 5<br>−2 | 29<br>−10 | 614<br>−398 | 822<br>−708 | 4091<br>−3285 |

Multiplication

| | | | | |
|---|---|---|---|---|
| 27<br>×20 | 67<br>×93 | 413<br>×398 | 674<br>×503 | 708<br>×967 |

Division

| | | | | |
|---|---|---|---|---|
| 8÷2 | 48÷6 | 847÷7 | 9062÷23 | 4913÷13 |

Figure 6–1   Informal Arithmetic Inventory

sample gives me the chance to observe not only students' grammatical skills, but their conceptual and organizational abilities. In this way, I'm gathering a tremendous amount of information on each student and my screening for problems is complete." Maura's informal assessment works well because it allows her to plan her teaching goals for the entire class.

If she did need to further assess some students who newly entered her class or for whom she needs more indepth information, most often she can look for alternate time periods, such as during lunch, before, or after school.

Since students and teachers usually resent missing subjects such as physical education, music, and art, these time periods should only be used for assessment when absolutely necessary. Attempting to test during recess or periods especially important to students may result in loss of their attention and motivation.

"What about secondary teachers?" asks John. "My lunch period may be different than the student's and my room is usually full of others wanting help or just to talk before or after school." When there is no time to assess beyond regular classroom screening, teachers should ask the specialists in their building for support. If educators are team-teaching the class, one can continue with the lesson while the other takes the student aside. If the teacher does not have the time or indepth assessment skill, the special educator should conduct the assessment in a quiet location to allow classroom teaching to continue.

*Select Time Students Are Most Attentive.*  When performing informal assessments, mornings are usually best since students may be more alert. If students demonstrate Attention Deficit Hyperactivity Disorder (ADHD), teachers should assess over briefer periods of time in situations in which students are not distracted by excessive stimuli. Many students have difficulty concentrating after recess periods or physical education, requiring time to reintegrate into an academic environment. Additionally, teachers should indicate to students that concentration will be required, allowing a short break before beginning, and redirecting students if their attention wanders.

**Attention Deficit Hyperactivity Disorder (ADHD)**—a conduct disorder characterized by difficulty in sustaining attention, impulsiveness, and hyperactivity.

*Record Data Immediately.*  As suggested by Maura's informal reading inventory assessment sheet in Table 6–7, there should be a formalized way of recording even informally collected data. As during observations, teachers should record information as quickly as possible so that student behaviors are not confused or forgotten. If students complete work products, such as the informal arithmetic inventory or a written response to questions, teachers should review these immediately to use the information in setting up groups and formulating goals for instruction.

# TESTING PRACTICES

"What about the tests we give as the semester progresses?" asks John. "While I need initial information for grouping and material selection, what should I do to assess students as the year continues?"

"That's a really interesting question, and one that most of us take for granted," Alex responds. "We assume the best way to find out if students are learning anything is to give them traditional tests on content. I read an interesting study done at the University of Kansas (Putnam, 1992), where a number of seventh-grade and tenth-grade regular education teachers in Kansas, Florida, and Indiana were interviewed about their testing practices. In their English, social studies, science, and mathematics classes, all of these teachers had students with mild disabilities.

"Teachers reported they gave an average of eleven tests a grading period, and that almost half of a student's grade was based on test scores. An adolescent enrolled in four content-area classes would average forty-four tests in a forty-five day grading semester. Since most students additionally take foreign language, the number is probably even higher. Only a quarter of the teachers provided any instruction in test-taking strategies or skills. These usually included training students to answer easy questions first, to eliminate difficult ones, and to read directions carefully. While a number of teachers said they would provide alternate testing procedures, such as having the exam read aloud to the student or permitting the student to refer to notes, they reported doing this only once or twice a school year. No wonder students with disabilities struggle so much, when many of them can't read the exam or don't know how to organize their time or review their work."

In a survey of middle school and high school teachers, Cuthbertson (1980) asked teachers "When you are evaluating a response on a test, what can cause the student to lose points?" High school teachers most often responded that it was sloppy writing. Middle school teachers noted poor spelling, sloppy writing, and answering with incomplete sentences. Ironically, students with special needs may be penalized when they have mastered the content on the test, but lack technical writing skills. These outcomes are important for teachers to consider in supporting students in doing well.

Special and regular educators need to work together to train students in strategies that can be used in most test-taking situations. These include:

1. planning and using time wisely;
2. reading all directions and questions carefully;
3. attempting to answer all questions; and
4. asking for clarification when the student does not fully understand the question (Putnam, 1992).

SCORER—acronym standing for steps of a test-taking system.

A more global test-taking system may result in student generalization across content area classes. For example, SCORER (Carman & Adams, 1972) includes the following steps:

S—Schedule your time;
C—Clue words;
O—Omit difficult questions;
R—Read carefully;
E—Estimate your answer; and
R—Review your work.

This approach has been successful with students with learning disabilities as well as students with poor reading comprehension skills. It is important that teachers provide direct instruction in each of these steps as well as encourage practice on classroom tests if students are to generalize to other content areas.

# CURRICULUM-BASED ASSESSMENT

curriculum-based assessment (CBA)—a procedure that uses curricular content as a basis for determining students' instructional needs.

A significant development in relating assessment directly to instruction has occurred through the use of curriculum-based assessment (CBA) practices. CBA is a means of evaluating the instructional needs of students, both at elementary and secondary levels. It is not one clear-cut method, but any procedure that uses curricular content to determine students' instructional needs. Three characteristics are evident in CBA measures:

1. assessment materials are derived from the current curriculum;
2. measurement is ongoing; and
3. information from the assessment is used to make instructional decisions regarding how to best teach the student (Tucker, 1987).

Teachers design students' current curriculum and materials into assessment measures instead of using traditional achievement tests which may be less applicable to information taught in class.

Many educators feel CBA is the most acceptable means of assessment because it focuses on the curriculum students must master, provides a rationale for placing individual students in the appropriate level of the curriculum, and is a mechanism for ongoing measure of student progress in that curriculum (Reisberg & Wolf, 1988). Follow-up interventions based on CBA can be directly related to students' specific needs in developing skills and awarenesses mandated by the curriculum. CBA is often used to collect data about students' initial performance level in an academic subject in order to design objectives. As the teacher instructs in curricular content, student progress is measured as an indicator of success.

"At times I've seen teachers a lot happier with the results of their own assessment of students from curriculum and materials than from standardized measures normally used by school districts," observed Alex. "Many of the positive aspects of informal assessment are combined with content directly applicable to their teaching. They can perform indepth observations of the student working under typical classroom conditions, and have a variety of materials available at different grade levels. They note behaviors which may be important to their later success with this student, such as attention span or distractibility."

The benefit of CBA over informal testing is that it provides ongoing assessment instead of intermittent review. Teachers can observe student behaviors and academic responses continuously as they implement different interventions. As discussed earlier in this chapter, if they record initial data on students and carefully monitor changes after teaching has occurred, they will have an excellent sense of which techniques are most effective. Some practitioners prefer informality, despite their inclusion of data. They decide how to design and administer tests based on the curriculum and how to use subsequent information in developmental or remedial instruction.

As listed in Table 6–8, there are some commonly followed steps in implementing curriculum-based assessment in the classroom (Fuchs, Fuchs, & Hamlett, 1990). Initially the classroom teacher examines the curriculum in order to list the skills sequentially that the student needs to master. For example, Maura's third-grade curriculum might emphasize reading comprehension competencies ranging from recall of facts to understanding main ideas or evaluating the correctness of information. John's curriculum might include literary genre and different writing styles of great authors. In both cases, teachers list the specific objectives students need to master to accomplish curricular goals. This provides a teaching framework and a structure for building skills hierarchically.

Next, the teacher creates a way of observing or measuring the student's skill levels. Maura can create a series of questions ranging from factual to evaluative information that would be asked regarding specified material in her basal reader. John may list specific literary genre from his curriculum and consider different writing styles. Individually, the students complete these tests or answer teacher questions aloud in order to indicate their initial instructional level.

---

### Table 6–8
### Steps in Implementing Curriculum-Based Instruction

1. Teacher examines curriculum and lists sequence of skills to be mastered.
2. Teacher develops own procedure or test to measure each skill or short-term objective.
3. Student completes test, demonstrating skill levels.
4. Teacher instructs student on unmastered skills.
5. Teacher observes and measures student progress continuously during instruction.
6. When student masters skill, teacher measures the next skill in sequence and begins instruction.

(*Source:* Adapted from Fuchs, Fuchs, & Hamlett, 1990)

The teacher then teaches the information. Different from common classroom procedures, in curriculum-based assessment the teacher observes and measures student gains continuously. Some students may take tests daily in areas such as spelling, arithmetic, or science. Or teachers may ask questions of them frequently to assess in specific areas such as reading comprehension skills. Many teachers record student growth on graphs to have precise indicators of progress. When the student has mastered the skill to the teacher's level of satisfaction, they begin instruction in the next skill in the hierarchy, followed by ongoing measurement of gain in that skill area.

Some types of CBA are more formalized and incorporate standardized procedures for designing, administering, and using information from curriculum-based tests. One of the most promising formalized models is **Curriculum-Based Measurement (CBM)** (Fuchs & Fuchs, 1988). Based on extensive research (Deno 1985, 1986; Shinn, 1989), CBM is a more prescribed system of appraisal than many of the other CBA measures. While most types of CBA examine students' mastery of short-term behavioral objectives, CBM considers the entire year's curriculum for its pool of measurement items. The **long-term goal** is for the student to achieve success in all areas of the grade-level curriculum. Instead of an exhaustive list of questions on individual skills, there are sample questions on many skills across the curriculum. Teachers use standardized procedures in designing questions and to administer and score tests. Results are recorded carefully to judge broad skills achievement during the year.

While CBA and CBM are logical approaches to relating assessment to instruction, their major drawbacks are requirements for time and expertise in assessment (Reisberg & Wolf, 1988). Developing and administering tests is time-consuming for teachers, many of whom are already overly burdened. Often teachers do not view themselves as measurement experts, and have problems standardizing test instruments. Additionally, curricula and materials changes, such as with the adoption of new texts, require that previously used tests must be redesigned. However, curricular-based measures can be successful if teachers work in a team to create assessment instruments, or if a consulting teacher is available for support in design, administration, and analysis.

curriculum-based measurement (CBM)—prescribed system of appraisal that considers students' long-term goals.

long-term goal—an objective set to work toward over a length of time.

## PORTFOLIO ASSESSMENT

authentic assessment—assessment based on examples of students' work in a particular subject area over an extended period of time.

"I've been hearing a good deal about **authentic assessment** as a means of evaluating student work. Exactly what is this type of assessment and how does it work? Is it primarily for elementary school? When is it more appropriate for use than standardized or short-answer tests?" asks John.

The goals of authentic writing assessments have been to incorporate writing experiences into the teaching of all subject areas, from language arts and English to mathematics, science, and history. Whether students are describing themes from a short story they have read or explaining the important variables in a math problem, they write. Many teachers believe that this process is superior to multiple-choice formats because it forces students to be more analytical and to support their responses (Chapman, 1990).

Although writing assessment has been popular among many educators, it has been expanded into **portfolio assessment**, which allows for a broader demonstration of student skills. Initially, a portfolio was a system for organizing evidence of the literary progress of individual pupils. Often expanded beyond writing, it has become a collection of selected examples of students' work in a particular subject area. It demonstrates the type and quality of work a student produces at a particular point in time, and often provides comparative data when similar assignments are assigned during the year. It allows the teacher and student to consider mastery of skills continuously as a means of evaluating progress (Idol & West, 1993).

"What goes into a portfolio?" asks John. "I can see saving examples of student essays, but I tend to keep these anyway. What can I add to motivate the students and myself to make this meaningful?"

**portfolio assessment**—assessment based on examples of students' work in a particular subject area over an extended period of time.

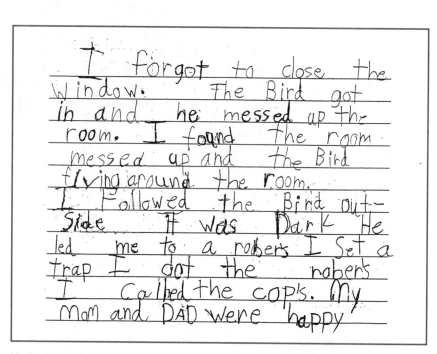

My Portfolio Work Products showing creativity are perfect components of a portfolio.
Reprinted with permission, Winston School, San Antonio.

Teachers can add anything they and the students feel is a valid indicator of their work. There is no typical portfolio, but researchers (McRobbie, 1992) find that there are some common characteristics of successful portfolios: They include work over an extended time period, selected by the student, with teacher guidance. The student writes an introduction explaining why the particular pieces were selected, as well as a summary statement about what was learned as the student compiled and later analyzed portfolio contents.

Teachers should encourage students to select their best products of work-in-progress. As teachers, students, and parents analyze these efforts, they can determine what the student has learned, skills that have developed, and problems that still exist. It is important to review student work as it is placed in the portfolio, not solely at the end of the year. In this way it fulfills its function for ongoing assessment and becomes a basis for creating new instructional objectives and methods.

Table 6–9 indicates some items that might appear in a student's portfolio. The contents are limited only by teacher and student imagination. Teachers may prefer to place the contents in a file folder, a six-pleat accordion file, or any other container which suits their needs. Contents may range from more traditional writing samples to auditory or visual tapes (Morton, 1991). Students enjoy personal photographs or pictures they have drawn, as well as comments on their own work. In organizing the portfolios, teachers may want to place student work products in different sections than conference notes or graphs and charts demonstrating academic or behavioral changes. They should determine in advance who the audience will be for the portfolio, in order to be sure nothing is included which would invade the student's privacy or personal wishes. Tests and graded worksheets should not be included.

**Table 6–9
Portfolio Contents**

Portfolios might include, but are not limited to:

| | | |
|---|---|---|
| • Journal entries | • Attitude and interest surveys | • Conference notes |
| • Samples of student's best efforts | • Student self-assessment | • Interviews |
| • Audiotapes of student's reading | • Writing samples | • Teacher observations |
| • Pictures | • Photographs | |
| • Graphs and charts of student gains | • Videotapes | |
| | • Posters | |

(*Sources:* Adapted from Morton, 1991; McRobbie, 1992)

"This sounds like one more thing for me to do," comments John. "How do I prevent this from becoming really time-consuming?"

Collecting items for the portfolio should not be time-consuming, but part of classroom routine. The teacher develops guidelines in advance to indicate the types of assignments included. Then students take over the work, considering which efforts they want in their portfolio and placing the material directly there as they complete it. Teachers do need to take the time to read or view the material to assess ongoing skill development, but they would do this with any work produced by students, regardless of portfolio involvement (Morton, 1991).

## Goals of Portfolios

It is important for teachers to use portfolios for assessment, not merely as folders for collection of student work products. Portfolios can be designed in any content area, both at elementary and secondary levels. They fulfill a number of assessment purposes when used correctly, as indicated in Table 6–10. Educators should be aware that portfolio use not only supports evaluation of students' instructional growth, but improves classroom affect as students take pride in observing their own development and achievement.

---

**Table 6–10**
**Goals of Portfolio Assessment**

*Portfolios:*

- Function both as a teaching tool and a means of assessment

- Allow teachers and students to gather work products demonstrating current instructional level

- Monitor student progress over an extended period of time

- Provide student work products as ongoing evidence of learning

- Demonstrate students' analytical skills

- Train students to assess themselves

- Indicate to students that process is important, not only final products

- Permit teachers to compare a student's performance with that of peers

- Can be used with an entire class without drawing attention or teacher time to one student

- Support the use of a variety of teaching-learning approaches

- Encourage teachers to reflect on their own instructional methods

- Support collaboration between teachers and students

Optimally, teachers should initiate portfolio use at the beginning of the academic year, so they will have a clear measure of student skill levels. They can use this information to develop teaching goals for individual students and groups. For example, if John decides to explore students' speaking skills, he might give them a class session to organize their thoughts and prepare a five-minute oral presentation on a topic he suggests, or one of interest to them. If he were teaching history or science, he would relate the topic to those content areas. The next day, students would audio-tape their presentation. The teacher and class would listen to these tapes critically, commenting on areas of strength or needing development. John would make notes about skill needs for individuals, later turning these into teaching goals. Students could write down their responses to their own tapes and areas they would like to improve this academic year. They would then place the tapes and written reflections in their portfolios. John would teach to the areas in which he noted student skill-building needs, using assessment as a basis for instruction. During the year, as specific skills were being taught, students would tape additional presentations for their portfolio. At designated periods, students and teachers would collaborate in comparing earlier and later tapes, setting new instructional goals.

Collaborating with students in assessing their work products also allows teachers the opportunity to gauge individual analytical skills and encourage critical review of personal efforts. Additionally, teachers are training students in assessing themselves, in critically considering their own work products as indicators of growth. Whereas students typically regard the rapid completion of academic assignments as their goal, the need to reflect upon the progress of their work impacts their attitude. They learn process can be as important, and sometimes more important, than the final product.

Portfolios can provide strong performance indicators of the academic levels of students with disabilities. They allow teachers the opportunity to compare individual student work with that of peers and to determine basic skills that may require remediation. Since all students in the class will be placing selected work in portfolios, the student with special needs does not draw away attention or require additional teacher time at the expense of others.

In addition to assessment and instructional benefits, teachers often report they tend to become more creative when developing portfolio assignments, since they must go beyond traditional workbook pages. With pleasure, they discuss having students keep journals, write stories about photographs they have taken, or design posters to support political opinions. In mini-conferences, they encourage students to reflect on their own work and to discuss its improvement. Such student reflection often initiates teacher reflection about instructional methods and anticipated student outcomes.

# SUMMARY

This chapter discussed a variety of ways classroom teachers can gather their own assessment data and relate it directly to their subsequent work with students. Classroom observations are a primary method of information gathering, but only if teachers set their purposes and plan their methods carefully in advance. A number of goals for classroom outcomes were listed, including identification of learning or behavioral problems, to determine student needs for intervention. Ongoing observation allows for making optimal decisions regarding student placement, the effectiveness of specific teaching techniques, and the success of the total intervention program.

The classroom teacher cannot always perform observations, due to time constraints of the demands of working with the entire class. In this instance, a specialist teacher or school psychologist will visit the room to observe specified students. Chapter 6 included guidelines for observers to follow so that they do not disturb the class or bring undue attention to the student. It is important for the observer and regular classroom teacher to agree on the goals of the observation in advance. They should also consider logistics, such as the optimal time of the visit and where the observer can sit unobtrusively. The visitor should avoid eye contact and conversation with any student as well as any clothing or behavior that would draw personal attention. Immediately after the visit, the observer should discuss findings with the teacher and collaborative team members, arranging for additional observations if necessary.

The chapter reviewed ways of collecting and recording data through methods such as observation. The initial step involves baseline data, which indicates where the student is performing academically or behaviorally before any intervention occurs. The teacher should focus on the specific behaviors of interest and observe them in the setting where they normally occur. Once a baseline has been established, teachers collect intervention data as they try different techniques to change student behaviors. They compare the number of times the behaviors occur after teacher intervention with the number during baseline to see if the technique being observed has been successful. Importantly, teachers then observe for generalization data, noting whether the intervention has resulted in behavioral change in a variety of settings or situations outside the initial environment.

To accurately observe change, teachers need to become familiar with some basic data recording techniques. Methods should be convenient and not disrupt the teacher's involvement with the entire class. One of the best ways to collect baseline, intervention, and generalization data is from examination of student work products and how they change after teacher instruction. When students are misbehaving in class, educators may want to use event recording, noting changes in frequency of behaviors between baseline and intervention. This type of recordkeeping is most effective when behaviors have a discrete beginning and ending. When the behavior under observation continues over a longer period of time, duration recording is more effective. Here, as baseline data, the educator notes the amount of time a student behavior persists initially and then how long after intervention. A comparison of results indicates the effectiveness of the intervention.

Observations cannot always provide enough information about academic and behavioral needs of students. Especially when a student's needs are extreme enough to require assessment for special education services, formal testing is required. Because no one test can form the basis of a diagnosis, a number of standardized tests should be used. In selecting these instruments, certain guidelines should be followed. Tests should be valid and reliable, and should have been standardized on a large population with characteristics similar to the current sample. They should be easy to administer and score, not requiring extensive time or expertise in interpretation. Importantly, teachers should be able to use the results to design meaningful followup instruction.

Educators will not want to use formal tests exclusively. Often informal measures provide more useful information because they test students on materials, academic, and behavioral demands faced daily in the classroom. While they may be designed commercially, most teachers prefer to create their own. These are less expensive, can usually be administered during class periods, and allow teachers flexibility in content design. However, informal tests do have some drawbacks. They may not be valid or reliable, and test questions may be too difficult or too easy. Teacher-created tests usually lack standardization and are not acceptable for making legal placement decisions about most students.

Chapter 6 included a series of guidelines for administration of informal tests. Teachers should assess for specific skills which may be deficient, in order to plan subsequent instruction for individual students. During informal assessment, they should have a variety of materials available at a spectrum of levels, allowing them to estimate students' instructional level, but to change to easier or more difficult material if student needs dictate. The setting for testing should approximate the student's daily learning environment and most alert time of day. Teachers should always avoid disrupting the larger class in order to gain information on individuals, requesting assistance from the special educator if disruption appears inevitable.

Curriculum-based assessment (CBA) is a method for evaluating instructional needs of students by deriving assessment materials from curricular content. Measurement is continuous, and information from the assessment provides a basis for making decisions on how best to instruct students. Many educators regard CBA favorably because it focuses on specific material the students need to learn, allows for student placement in the most appropriate level of the curriculum, and provides a mechanism for ongoing assessment of student success. Within CBA teachers can record baseline and intervention data on student change, observing which teaching techniques are most effective.

Through a planned sequence of steps, CBA is the basis for providing information for curriculum-based instruction. Teachers review the curriculum and list the skills to be mastered. They develop the test to measure each skill or curriculum objective. Students complete the test, provide baseline data for teacher intervention. The teacher then provides instruction on unmastered skills, continuously observing and measuring student progress, noting the effects of different teaching techniques. When the student masters the skill, the teacher measures student performance on the next skill, records data, and begins instruction. In this method, assessment is linked directly to intervention.

Portfolio assessment has provided success for many educators. Portfolios contain a collection of selected examples of student work in a particular subject area. When collected continuously throughout the year, contents demonstrate students' ongoing mastery of skills with an emphasis on improving quality. Portfolio contents are not limited to written assignments, but may include any type of material selected by the students as indicative of their work. Portfolios function not only as assessment but as instructional tools, monitoring student progress in response to specific teaching techniques, thereby encouraging educators to reflect on their methods. They can be used with the entire class and allow teachers to compare peer products without drawing attention to particular students. They provide an assessment method that allows teachers, students, and parents to measure tangible progress across the year.

## CASE STUDY: *Elementary*

**Miguel is a student in your fourth-grade class who is experiencing a variety of academic and behavioral problems. He reads approximately two years below grade level, with particular problems in word analysis and memory for whole words you have studied many times. While he says he enjoys arithmetic, his skills are spotty since he lacks recall of a number of basic facts that you have reviewed frequently.**

**Frequently, Miguel's attention wanders away from his deskwork. He looks around the room constantly and talks to anyone seated near him. You stand close to his desk and redirect him often. Yet, as soon as you leave the proximity, he returns to off-task behavior.**

**You have decided to meet with the collaborative team of teachers to discuss how to proceed with Miguel since he is falling further behind daily. You know that you will have to collect more specific information if they are going to be able to help you.**

1. Based on the information studied in this chapter, decide the best informal appraisal methods to use to arrive at the most complete picture of Miguel's learning and behavioral problems. (For example, should you use informal inventories, curriculum-based assessment, portfolios, or other means of assessment?) Note why you have selected these particular methods for Miguel.

2. Design a system for collecting baseline, intervention, and generalization data on the following:

   a. strong and weak areas in Miguel's decoding skills in reading, including word analysis and whole word recall;
   b. Miguel's basic computation skills;
   c. Miguel's attention span during reading and math activities;
   d. the frequency with which he talks to other students.

3. Note any areas in which you may have to recommend formal assessment. Why might informal assessment not provide enough information in these areas?

**In collecting assessment data, often needs vary at the secondary level. Teachers have five or six classes daily, lasting less than an hour. There are well over 100 students each day and teacher planning time is limited. Therefore, it can be particularly difficult to assess the needs of students. Yet, it is extremely unfair to ignore learning and behavioral differences that impact their performance.**

Please answer these questions to design a program to informally assess students in your content area.

1. To be successful, what basic skills should students possess as they enter your class?

2. Describe informal inventories you would create to measure initial skill levels the first week of school.

3. After informal screening, you find six students in your class seem considerably low in academic skills necessary for success.

   a. How will you test these students more extensively to determine the specific areas in which they need remedial instruction?
   b. At what point would you decide to refer any of these students for formal testing?
   c. If you need more support from other educators, when would you contact

      (1) the school counselor?
      (2) the school psychologist?
      (3) the special education teacher?

# 7

# ASSESSING STUDENTS FROM DIVERSE LINGUISTIC AND CULTURAL BACKGROUNDS

"I really like the informal assessment methods we discussed, especially portfolios and curriculum-based measures," observed Mort. "In most situations, we should be able to select those students at risk for academic failure or those with more severe problems that may require special education support. How do we avoid referring students who are not disabled at all but who are from culturally and linguistically different backgrounds? Language and behavioral differences often limit their achievement. As a result, any number of academic areas are affected, particularly those dependent on speaking, understanding teacher lectures, directions, reading, and writing. Students may appear to have behavior problems when the real problem is they're not adjusting well to classroom rules and demands."

Mort's concern is critical to appropriately assessing and working with students from minority backgrounds. Historically, the misdiagnosis and subsequent overrefferral of these students for special education placement has led to lawsuits and court orders (e.g., *Diana v. California State Board of Education*). As a result, some researchers fear that many districts have shifted from overidentification of minorities to underidentification, lowering student eligibility for supportive services that may be critical to their success (Vasquez-Chairez, 1988). It is imperative that teachers become aware of the diagnostic and instructional needs of students from diverse cultural backgrounds so they may refer appropriately.

# RELATIONSHIPS BETWEEN CULTURE AND BEHAVIOR

Every person experiences the impact of culture throughout a lifetime. For years, those who lived in minority cultures were called "culturally deprived," an irony for the many who experienced rich involvements, languages, and experiences. One may mature in a culture different from the mainstream without having experienced any particular deprivation.

"As I travel, I'm often fascinated by the way so many American families and neighborhoods do manage to keep their cultures," comments Elena. "On a recent trip to California, within a few days I visited Korean, Chinese, Taiwanese, and Japanese markets and restaurants. There was a religious celebration by Orthodox Jews, and at the same time several streets away there was a Mexican fiesta. My initial stereotype was that I was in new immigrant neighborhoods, but when I inquired I learned that many of these families had been here for generations. The location, whether Minneapolis, Chicago, or New York, doesn't appear to matter. Most people seem to integrate their **cultural identity** into a sense of positive self-esteem. It adds to their experiences and gives them a sense of group belonging."

cultural identity—the feeling of belonging to a group with the same cultural background and having some of the same characteristics of that group.

It also may give them and their teachers some unexpected outcomes at school. Figure 7–1 on page 201 depicts the factors impacting the classroom success of students from diverse cultural backgrounds. While there are numerous concerns, they fall into three basic groups: the family, the student, and the teacher.

## The Family

The cultural beliefs of the family are an outgrowth of the broader culture to which the family belongs. They have a direct influence on the values of the parents and subsequently their expectations for their children. For example, if competition is not valued, the child will not respond to the teacher's rewarding the "best" or "fastest" in the class. If cooperation is valued, the student may sublimate personal efforts into group success, not wanting to be singled out as extraordinary for individual accomplishments. If contemplation is valued more than speed, the student may not perform well on timed tests. If the family's cultural beliefs are different from or in conflict with those encouraged by the school and larger community, they will impact the student's social and educational success (Sugai, 1988). If there are a number of students from the same cultural background, a community resource person from that culture should be asked to develop a list of characteristics children may demonstrate in the school environment. This list may be shared with educators in the district to help them better understand which behaviors are based on beliefs of the primary culture.

In any culture, family values and expectations shape child-rearing practices. Some cultures tolerate more extreme, acting-out behaviors from children, while others demand respect and immediate obedience. Some teach their children not to make direct eye contact or to confide in adults. Some children learn to demand that their needs be met immediately, while others assimilate the need to quietly acquiesce to others. While students from majority backgrounds demonstrate this spectrum of behaviors as well, their responses usually fit into teacher expectations at some level. When teachers lack understanding of the student's culture and cannot communicate fully because of language differences, they feel more threatened by differences emanating from the family.

As in the majority culture, minority members may vary in their response to the presence of a disability in a child. Some respond with guilt and shame, blaming the immediate family for having caused the problem in some way. Others deny the existence of a problem, especially if it is not immediately visible to others, such as a learning disability or behavioral disorder. Others value the child's uniqueness and seek help in supporting success and growth.

However, as newcomers to the system, minority parents may not be as aware of available services or how to access them. Some children may receive no assistance until they enter first grade, although a disability has been present from birth. If the parents are not knowledgeable about the existence of services or the bureaucracy is overwhelming to them, especially if they are non-English speaking, the child may have lost supports during the most critical periods of intellectual, physical, and social development.

"My husband is a nurse at St. Gregory's Hospital," commented Elena. "They've started a wonderful program over there, similar to the Canadian and Scandinavian Visiting Nurses. To make sure all new parents are aware of available support services, whenever they deliver an infant who is disabled or at risk for a major type of problem, such as drug withdrawal or developmental delays based on low birthweight or a difficult birth, they assign a nurse and social worker to the family. Hospital staff form their own collaborative team, very similar to the ones we've been starting in our schools, and they divide responsibilities to help the family. They may visit the family in the home to check on the baby's progress or to be sure that no abuse or neglect is occurring, especially when it's teenage or drug-addicted parents. The social worker contacts community agencies to provide ongoing supports as the child gets older.

"While this system is wonderful for any family, it's especially helpful for those who are non-English speaking or from different cultures as they might not do this easily on their own. Just a few weeks ago, a Korean family initially felt overwhelmed and helpless when they had a Down syndrome baby. Joe became their caseworker, contacted the local support organization, and two parents even visited the mother and baby in the hospital. At one month, the baby and her parents will begin participation in the local program. By the time the baby begins school officially, she will have progressed so much further than if the parents had been asked to cope alone with an unfamiliar system."

The student's degree of success throughout school will depend heavily on the attitude of the family toward the disability. When teachers meet parents who seem confused or unable to cope with their child, it is critical that they work together with the family to ensure classroom success through positive interactions and the availability of supportive services.

## The Teacher

As indicated in Figure 7–1, in any classroom the teacher's attitude is critical to success. Nowhere is this more apparent than when working with

Teacher understanding of student needs can result in increased student motivation to perform.

**Family and Cultural Variables**

Cultural Beliefs
Family Values and Expectations
Child-rearing Practices
Family Response to Child's Disability

| **Student Variables** | **Teacher Variables** |
|---|---|
| Mastery of Prerequisite Skills | Understanding of Student's Culture |
| Ability to Communicate in English | Acceptance of Diversity |
| Social-Interactive Skills | Understanding of Disability |
| Impact of Disability | Ability to Communicate |

Figure 7–1   Factors Affecting Classroom Success (*Source:* Adapted from Sugai, 1988)

students from diverse cultural and linguistic backgrounds. Not only must teachers be willing to accept diversity, but they must understand it. They must become aware of the degree of students' academic and behavioral responses caused by cultural differences versus the presence of a disability. Since teachers make the majority of referrals and are the catalysts for change when students are experiencing problems, they must be well-informed about cultural differences and desirous of helping students regardless of background.

Educators must also be able to understand the nature of disabilities and those developmental and remedial teaching strategies most appropriate to support students. Teachers who have negative attitudes toward students from different cultures or with disabilities cannot expect to be successful with many students they will encounter in the inclusive classroom. Students will model their responses on those of the teacher and, often at young ages, develop a personal attitude based on what they observe daily. If a teacher acts frustrated or upset in not communicating easily with a non-English speaking student or one with a learning or behavior problem, peers will believe it acceptable to define this student as difficult and not accept him fully into the larger group. Since a student demonstrating differences usually enters a classroom with few friends, a negative or unresponsive attitude by the teacher may further hinder chances of becoming part of a supportive peer group.

*The Student.* Figure 7–1 lists the student variables heavily affecting successful classroom integration. Students need the prerequisite academic skills to be successful. If they cannot read the text, compute the arithmetic facts, or write with intact grammar and syntax, they will be at a disadvantage. Students with limited English proficiency may be far removed from reading and writing fluently as they newly develop their spoken language. The presence of a disability may serve to slow their academic progress. Their success depends on teacher knowledge of instructional methods to increase verbal, reading, and writing skills. If prerequisite knowledge is lacking, the prereferral committee should determine which supports will help the student catch up with peers most quickly and provide these services in the regular classroom whenever possible. Many times this program development relies strongly on students and teachers working closely with the bilingual education teacher or consultant.

Students will need social skills to interact with peers and adults successfully. Some of the cultural values and expectations may hinder their involvement. As Sugai (1988) notes, if the social difficulties students demonstrate are cultural in nature, educators must teach an expanded repertoire of behaviors to provide opportunities for success without forcing students to sacrifice their individual uniqueness.

"These behaviors are best taught by other students," notes John. "Adolescents are so attuned to appearance, ranging from hairstyle to shoes. When a newly immigrated student enters the school, peers are likely to exchange mocking glances if the dress is different or the student isn't 'with-it' in body language and behavior. The tried-and-true method of assigning one or more students in each class to help the student really works! While teachers may be concerned about academic and logistical guidance, supportive peers will encourage the student to dress in a more stylish way or change some behavior that is unacceptable to the larger group. It's really important to select peer helpers who are positive models and give good guidance. Although I often wish students cared less about externals, it does make me feel good when I see a new student being accepted by the larger group."

When students from culturally and linguistically different backgrounds experience a disability, the impact may be even more powerful than in students from majority backgrounds. If the student is being introduced initially to peers, the disability may result in additional isolation during a period when the student craves acceptance. The nature and severity of the condition as well as student, teacher, and peer attitudes will determine the degree of acceptance. If the student has learned to accept and compensate for the disability, others will also be more at ease. If the student appears unapproachable or behaves in an aggressive or demanding manner, peers will practice avoidance.

## PREREFERRAL

"Why do we always hear the best way to learn a language is to be immersed in it?" John asked. "No one can dispute the logic that you'll learn increasingly quickly the more you're exposed to a language, especially when you have to develop survival skills in social situations to meet your needs or avoid being embarrassed. Consider the pressures that puts on the young person! Last year we enrolled two brothers from Mexico, a freshman and a junior. They knew no English when they entered the school, and although we paired each of them in class with another student who spoke Spanish, they have been effectively cut off from class lectures and texts as well as from extracurricular activities. They're learning English, but won't be able to participate in coursework for some time yet, and by then the older boy will be finished with school. We're becoming concerned about his younger brother, who's been hanging around with a gang. I guess he needed a group to accept him."

John's story underscores researchers' concerns (Cummins, 1984; Tikunoff, 1985; De George, 1989). Whether in elementary or secondary grades, students with limited English proficiency are called upon to develop a myriad of skills immediately, to be academically and socially successful. They must develop interpersonal facility in a foreign environment where they are observed closely by peers. Yet, often they do not understand the new cultural-interactive rules they must follow. Regardless of the level of their skills in their native language, they are expected to meet spoken and written language requirements in English immediately. They must master subject area content, technical reading and writing skills, and develop the differing academic language abilities required by each subject area. When students lack strong speaking, reading, and writing skills in their own language, this new task becomes daunting, if not impossible. Learning subject matter at the same time they are acquiring English results almost automatically in their falling behind English-speaking peers. These students have been placed in personal and instructional situations that are far more difficult for them than for students with English proficiency.

## Prereferral Concerns

There are a number of questions the prereferral team must consider to obtain information on background variables in the student's life that may be impacting school performance. These questions are listed in Table 7–1. Ranging from physiological factors in early childhood to school attendance and language functioning, they provide a framework for information-gathering to obtain a complete picture. Has the family experienced frequent moves, affecting school attendance, and subsequently learning basic skills? Other questions consider academic and behavioral problems the student may be demonstrating. Are responses indicative of cultural variables, adjustment factors, or a learning or behavioral problem?

Additionally, the team should consider the type of assessment necessary to provide information not apparent from educators' observations. If the student's needs are extreme, the team may refer immediately for assessment

## Table 7–1
## Prereferral Concerns

The prereferral team should ask the following questions:

1. Were there variables in the student's early development that may have affected school performance (e.g., low birthweight, high fevers, trauma, surgeries, vision or hearing problems)?

2. Has the family moved frequently? Are previous school records available?

3. Has the child attended school regularly? If not, what were the causes of absences?

4. Has the student been enrolled in any special school programs, such as bilingual education, compensatory reading, or special education? Are records from these programs available?

5. How long has the family resided in the United States? Have there been any stressful situations that may be related to a lack of opportunity for the student (e.g., poverty, inability to speak the language)?

6. What language is spoken in the home between parents? Between parents and child? Between siblings?

7. Is the student exposed frequently to books and reading activities? If so, in which language?

8. At school, what language does the child speak to teachers and peers?

9. What are the student's spoken and written proficiency levels in the dominant language?

10. What are the student's spoken and written proficiency levels in English?

11. What types of previous language intervention has the student received?

12. Are student language behaviors typical of students who are learning a second language, or do there appear to be other factors present limiting the student's ability to learn English (e.g., the presence of a disability)?

13. Are the student's social behaviors appropriate to the school setting? If not, are differences a result of cultural variations or behavioral problems?

14. Are student behaviors appropriate to his or her dominant culture?

15. What specific behaviors is the student demonstrating that are disruptive to the class?

16. What academic problems is the student demonstrating?

17. Does the student require indepth special education testing at this point?

18. Do the student's learning needs require curricular and/or instructional accommodations?

19. Are the teachers familiar with teaching techniques, remedial and compensatory strategies to help this student?

20. What additional information is necessary to provide an accurate teaching plan for the student?

(*Source:* Adapted from Garcia & Ortiz, 1988)

for special education services. Usually members prefer to recommend curricular and instructional modifications for teachers to implement, monitoring success continuously. In these instances, teachers must become familiar with remedial, compensatory, and specialized language techniques to meet students' needs. Clearly supportive personnel, such as bilingual education and special education teachers, must become part of the team and consult with the teacher frequently on instructional methods.

## Assessment of Learning Problems

"When they have a learning disability or a developmental delay, the task is worsened considerably," reflected Mort. "When students have so many social and academic skills to learn, how do you determine whether they have a disability as well?"

Early awareness that there may be a problem provides the opportunity to initiate a prereferral intervention. Ortiz, Wilkinson, and Rivera (1991) found this stage to be critical in avoiding inappropriate referrals. In their study over a two-year period, of the 100 requests for assistance with language minority students, 73 percent were resolved by regular classroom teachers or additionally using available school and community supports. In contrast, Reynolds (1984) noted that 70 to 90 percent of referrals for special education assessment resulted in placement in special education.

Prereferral intervention for culturally diverse students has a number of advantages. It allows teachers to determine the specific types of assistance they need to keep the student in the mainstream, avoiding a pull-out program. Because the focus of academic and behavioral interventions is the regular education classroom, teachers will improve their abilities to work with a variety of students. This skills improvement will affect the planning and teaching of other committee members who have students from similar backgrounds. Importantly, inappropriate and segregated placements can be reduced (Sugai, 1988).

# DEVELOPMENTAL VARIABLES

"What information should the prereferral team consider when designing a program for students from minority cultures?" asks John. "We need to be sure we get the information we need quickly and easily to ensure student success."

An important aspect of the prereferral process involves meeting with parents and obtaining information about the student's background that would

PARENTAL INFORMATION FORM

Name _____    Date of Birth _____

School _____    Grade _____ Age _____

Home Address _____

_____    Phone _____

Person Interviewed _____    Relationship _____

Interviewer _____    Position _____

A. Pregnancy and Birth

1. Mother's health during pregnancy:    Good _____ Fair _____ Poor _____
2. Describe any physical problems. _____

_____

3. Labor and Birth:  Complicated _____    Uncomplicated _____
   Describe any problems: _____
4. Was the baby premature?  Yes _____  No _____
   If so, how early was the baby born? _____
5. Did the baby breathe immediately? Yes _____ No _____
   If not, describe the circumstances. _____
6. How much did the baby weigh at birth? _____

B. Early Development

1. Age of walking without support: _____
2. Age when first used words: _____    Sentences: _____
3. Illnesses during childhood: _____
4. Instances of high fever: _____
5. Describe accidents and hospitalizations: _____
6. Describe any medical factors that may have impacted the student's school performance negatively:
      Vision _____    Hearing _____
      Injury _____    Illnesses _____
      Nutrition _____    Allergies _____
      Other _____
7. Compared with brothers and sisters or others his age, is this student different? If
   so, describe how.

_____

C. Experiences

1. Have there been factors in the student's previous schooling that are related to
   current learning problems?
      Poor attendance (Reasons?) _____
      Frequent family moves _____
      Lack of opportunity to attend quality schools _____
2. List previous schools the student has attended.

   |          School          |          Address          |
   |--------------------------|--------------------------|
   |                          |                          |
   |                          |                          |
   |                          |                          |
   |                          |                          |

3. Where was the student born? _____
   If not in U.S., how long has the family lived in this country? _____
4. Father's occupation: _____
   Mother's occupation: _____

Figure 7–2    Interviewing Families from Diverse Backgrounds

Figure 7–2   *(Continued)*

---

D. Language
  1. What language does the family speak at home? _____
  2. What language does the family prefer the student to use at school? _____
  3. How long has the student been exposed to English? _____
  4. In previous schools, has the student been enrolled in bilingual education? _____

E. School
  1. Describe any problems the student has experienced in previous schooling. _____
  _____
  2. How have these been handled? _____
  _____
  3. Has the student ever been tested for special education services?
  Yes _____ No _____
  If so, describe testing results. _____
  _____
  4. Discuss any special education services the student has received. _____
  _____
  5. How motivated is your child to do well in school?
  Very motivated _____ Sometimes motivated _____ Rarely motivated _____
  6. What things do you feel the school can do to help your child be successful? _____
  _____
  7. Are you willing to meet with your child's teachers to discuss how the school and home can work together to help your child? Yes _____ No _____

---

assist in programming. Data collected will allow educators to go beyond surface indicators that a problem may exist and to examine the young person as a student first, de-emphasizing cultural differences.

Figure 7–2 contains a questionnaire to be used by prereferral committee members when they meet with parents from culturally and linguistically different backgrounds. The questions vary in their intent, ranging from physiological problems in early childhood to prior school attendance, language proficiency and previous school difficulties. Since some of the information is personal, it is best if one team member, such as the school counselor, meets with the parents individually to show respect for privacy and to avoid parental embarrassment at larger group discussions. If the parents do not speak English, a native speaker should conduct the interview. The initial questions regarding pregnancy and childbirth should be asked clinically. If the parent shows discomfort or does not want to answer them, the interviewer should move on immediately to Section B, discussing ages of developmental milestones such as walking and talking.

Both Sections A and B explore prenatal and developmental factors that may indicate the presence of a disability (e.g., low birthweight, injuries, lack of oxygen). While previously educators may have attributed student behaviors such as inattention to a language difference, after noting an early developmental history that included a difficult birth or febrile seizures, they may consider the possibility that physiological trauma has been responsible.

In Figure 7–2, Section C includes questions about previous schooling experiences that may relate to current problems. Has there been a history of poor school attendance or frequent family moves, either of which would have interrupted the continuity of schooling? A listing of previous schools attended allows the current school to request records and track the student's progress. If the family is new to the United States and has not been able to find employment, with permission the school may contact social services or local religious organizations to help the family become settled. Such supports will help the student's progress in school.

Section D of the interview form considers language factors that impact instruction. Concerns such as degree of previous exposure to English at home and school, as well as participation in bilingual education programs, will help the prereferral committee with intervention strategies. Questions in Section E include family attitudes towards success in school as well as the student's previous participation in special education or supportive programming. Additional indepth testing may be avoided if information from previous assessments is available. As part of the interview, it is also important to consider the family's expectations of the school so responsibilities will be clearly defined and miscommunication avoided.

## ASSESSING STUDENTS WITH BEHAVIORAL DISORDERS

"What do we do when it's not a learning problem, but a behavior problem the student demonstrates?" asks Elena. "Most of our teachers try any number of academic interventions when the student isn't learning the material. When students are disruptive to the class, ignoring or defying rules and expected behaviors, teachers tend to refer them immediately. Usually they request the student remain in a more restrictive setting such as a self-contained unit until demonstrating improved behaviors. My experience is that teachers will be patient and explore working with any type of disability longer than a behavioral one, probably because of the impact on the class."

Elena is correct in her observations. There is a great potential for overreferral of students from minority backgrounds because they may not understand the demands and requirements of the educational setting. Sugai (1988) notes that when educators do not consider the impact of culture on behavior, often there are four outcomes: minority students may be judged as having a disability when none exists; they are viewed as less competent by peers; teachers are unclear about when to refer students appropriately for special education assessment; teachers continue to be bothered by student behaviors without understanding them.

Migrant and immigrant children are often referred almost immediately as they enter the classroom since teachers are concerned about their lack of acceptable behavior. Yet, often these students have been given neither the opportunity nor the time to adjust to a new system. Those experiencing the greatest number of family moves may require the most teacher encouragement to adapt because of the upheaval that has become part of their lives.

Any students from a differing culture must be taught skills necessary to underscore success in a new environment. There has to be a complete understanding between the teacher and student on acceptable behaviors. When the student is non-English speaking, teachers should have a native speaker explain classroom rules and discuss teacher expectations. Only after students fully understand the rules and permissible behaviors should the teacher initiate the referral process. Teachers should not refer students for assessment for special education placement until they have tried all other avenues of intervention.

## Prereferral for Behavioral Problems

When educators have discussed classroom rules and appropriate behaviors and the student's behavior remains disruptive to personal or group learning, they should convene the prereferral committee. It is important for team members to examine their individual biases and stereotypic expectations as they consider behaviors of students from minority groups. It is an interesting phenomenon that prejudice may cause opposite expectations. For example, one teacher may stereotype students from a particular ethnic background as behaving disrespectfully. When a student from that minority group misbehaves the first time, through expectations heightened by bias the teacher may overreact, attempting to stem the behavior before it worsens. Another teacher with the same feelings may not respond at all to the behavior because of the assumption that the student cannot control or change the behavior because of membership in that particular ethnic group. Neither teacher response is correct.

Table 7–2 contains a number of questions for consideration by the prereferral committee when students from culturally different backgrounds present behavioral problems. Adapted from Sugai (1988), these questions provide an organizational framework for considering the student more objectively. The first two questions consider the individuals most bothered by the behavior and whether the behaviors occur predominantly in the presence of one teacher. Responses will indicate to the team the intended audience for the misbehavior and might cull out the purpose (e.g., attention by peers or parents).

The team should next consider the nature of the troublesome behavior and how different it is from that of others in the class. This concern may be the most important, as teachers compare the student's behavior to two peer groups: the majority peer group and the culturally similar peer group. Such a

## Table 7–2
## Behavioral Referrals of Minority Students

The prereferral committee should consider:

- Who views the behaviors as troublesome (e.g., teachers, peers, administrators, parents)?

- Have referrals been made by more than one teacher?

- What is the specific behavior causing problems?

- Is this student's behavior different from that of others in the class? From a culturally similar peer group?

- Does the behavior interfere with the student's learning? With the class's learning?

- Is the behavior destructive or injurious? To whom?

- Does the behavior interfere with peer relations? Adult relations?

- Have there been dramatic changes in student behavior over a relatively brief period of time?

- Have there been any major recent life changes in the student's family?

(*Source:* Adapted from Sugai, 1988)

comparison allows educators to avoid expectations of behaviors for students in a particular group and more objectively observe how students in that group behave in a specified environment. If this student's actions are considerably different, educators may assume a problem exists.

The prereferral team should consider the impact of the behavior next. Is learning interrupted for the student or class? Does the action result in injury to self or others, or in the destruction of property? Subsequently, have peer and adult relations been affected? It is obvious that when student behavior is so extreme as to potentially harm the student or others, it must be controlled immediately and the student removed temporarily from the situation until appropriate interventions are determined.

The final two questions on Table 7–2 consider causes for misbehaviors. Educators will view the situation quite differently if the student has always acted this way or caused similar problems. However, if the situation is atypical for the child and has developed recently, a single causal factor may be indicated. The team should discuss with the family any major life events that may have caused strong behavioral changes.

## Functional Analysis

The classroom observation techniques discussed in Chapter 6 can be particularly successful in studying problem behaviors of students from culturally

functional analysis—examination of a problem within the context of the classroom to determine necessary changes to impact student behavior.

diverse backgrounds. The teacher should carry out a functional analysis, or examination of student behavior, teacher behavior, the setting, and consequences. By examining the problem in context, educators are able to objectify what is actually occurring and examine how the setting, teacher behaviors, and consequences can be changed to impact student behavior. Figure 7–3 is an adaptation of a simplified functional analysis format form by Sugai (1988). In using this form, the observer divides a sheet of paper into five columns.

The first two columns include the time, subject area, and activity when the behavioral problem occurs. This information is important because misbehaviors may tend to surface at a particular time each day (e.g., late afternoon when medication has lost its effectiveness), during a certain subject in which the student experiences difficulty, or a certain activity that may be too difficult or unstructured for the student to perform easily.

During the initial observations, the antecedent to the problem behavior may not be obvious, and the observer should note the exact behavior and any consequences from the teacher or peers (e.g., the teacher sent the student to time out; peers laughed). However, once the behavior has appeared

Observer _____

Student _____

Setting Characteristics:

| Date/Time | Subject/Activity | Antecedents | Behaviors | Consequences |
|-----------|------------------|-------------|-----------|--------------|
|           |                  |             |           |              |

Figure 7–3   Functional Analysis Format (*Source:* Adapted from Sugai, 1988)

in context, the observer should consider any actions or occurrences that preceded it and look for these in the future as indicators that the student may behave inappropriately once again.

It is important for the observer to state the exact behavior interfering with the student's or class's learning. Labeling behaviors with words such as *hyperactive* or *aggressive* does not provide specific enough description for intervention to be successful. It is far easier to change the behavior of a student who stops working when the teacher asks the class to read independently than that of an "unmotivated" student. Educators can redirect a student who begins to talk with others during small group assignments more easily than a student who is described as "inattentive." One of the benefits of the functional analysis format is that it encourages specificity in describing behaviors. When the prereferral committee meets to discuss intervention strategies, they can respond more successfully by changing student behaviors instead of student labels.

If the behaviors appear across the day at a variety of times, it may not be possible for an external observer to be present because of time constraints. In this situation, the teacher may be the best observer because of consistency and duration of time spent with the student. While the concurrent demands of other students may distract the teacher's full attention away from the individual student, once teachers become aware of common antecedents precipitating a student's inappropriate behaviors, they can look for these indicators to signal a developing problem.

"I can really appreciate that," reflects John. "Last year Leila had so many problems when she entered my class. She spoke little English and seemed exceptionally shy. She had been in the U.S. briefly and was from a tradition and religion that dictated different customs and dress. She was extremely cooperative and even began making a few friends, students interested in her background. However, at times she refused to work. She just wouldn't do anything. When I asked her why, she acted shy and wouldn't discuss it with me.

"I began observing her behaviors more carefully, looking for antecedent reasons for her work refusal. I noticed she was most cooperative when I taught the class as a whole, but stopped working when I gave small-group assignments. When I called a family conference to discuss her behavior, her father met with me and immediately understood the problem. Culturally, she was to avoid interactions with male students. As long as I taught the class as a whole, there was no problem; but her tradition did not allow her to interact with boys after puberty. Her father explained that in our city the only private schools for girls had been of different religions. When registering her in public school, her parents had directed her to follow the tradition despite the presence of boys in the class.

"With the father's permission I called a meeting of all her teachers. He met with us, explaining traditional customs and answering questions about how the teachers could adapt to family needs. Everyone seemed satisfied, even intrigued by the new challenge. Since then I've assigned her to work in pairs or small groups with girls only, and there have been no more problems. You can tell she's happy to have the pressure removed from her. It was such a simple solution to what seemed to be a difficult problem."

Leila's lack of involvement was problematic for John because her behavior did not seem justified when he compared her with her peer group, American students in an English class. In the case of students from different backgrounds from the mainstream, it is important also to compare them with a culturally similar peer group. When this is impossible, as in Leila's case, a carefully completed functional analysis, noting behaviors, antecedents, and consequences can indicate the locus of the problem. When discussed with family members or others from the culture, the reason for the difficulty may become immediately clear.

Importantly, it also becomes apparent when the problem is not cultural. It is equally significant when a student's behavior does not agree with norms for culturally similar peers. This conclusion should be made from teachers' comparisons of peer behaviors observed in class, from discussions with the student's other teachers, the family, and other adults from the student's native culture.

Once the conclusion is reached about the relationship between the culture and the behavior, the prereferral team chooses a course of action. Even if the behavior can be explained by cultural variables, it must be modified if it is disruptive to student or class learning. After reviewing the patterns established in the functional analysis, the team can suggest classroom modifications and direct intervention strategies to change the student's behavior. The student should be taught a broad repertoire of skills to increase success without sacrificing individual cultural differences (Sugai, 1988).

## ASSESSING LANGUAGE PROFICIENCY

Maura interjected, "I find that managing a student's behavior is so much easier when I have a grasp on their abilities to understand and use English. Unless I'm sure of their language skills, I know that I'm potentially inviting failure and related problems each time I give a student with limited English proficiency an individual or group assignment. To date my only method has been trial-and-error with work on different informal inventories or curricular materials. When the student performs poorly, often becoming frustrated, I know the assignment is too difficult. Surely there must be a better way to assess language functions."

trial-and-error—making attempts that are steered by failures and successes.

Teachers should observe students from non-English backgrounds carefully as they begin schooling. Regardless of their native language or culture, all students lacking verbal, reading, and writing skills are at risk for failure unless adequate supports are provided. Based on information deemed most important to the teacher, there are a few highly effective ways of assessing students' language capabilities.

Formal assessment instruments alone rarely provide a solid picture of students' skills. There is a lack of norm-referenced instruments appropriate for assessing students with limited English proficiency, since the majority of standardized tests are in English. Optimally, assessment should include performance measures in the native language as well as English, to determine students' knowledge level as well as their ability to be successful when participating in an English-speaking classroom. Measures in the native language would indicate whether any learning deficits present are attributable to a disability. If none appear and the only problems apparent are on tests requiring knowledge of English, educators can emphasize improving students' second-language acquisition while fostering their native language, thereby encouraging the development of academic skills in both languages (Ortiz & Wilkinson, 1991).

## The POWER Model

POWER model—a tool used to determine students' spoken and written language skills; based on a comparison between skills in the native language and English.

The POWER model designed by Fradd and Bermudez (1991) is an excellent tool in determining students' spoken and written language skills. It is based on a comparison between skills in the native language and English, providing an excellent source of information for teachers trying to assess a student's knowledge and competencies.

This model is particularly beneficial because it examines student skill levels both in English and the student's native language. Measuring competencies in both languages is important because it provides the opportunity for students to demonstrate their true competencies without language becoming a barrier. For example, if a teacher observes newly enrolled students with limited English proficiency, they may appear disinterested in class discussions and unable to complete assignments. They may seem less competent than their English-speaking peers and have difficulty demonstrating what they actually know (Fradd & Weismantel, 1989). When teachers provide opportunities for students to actively use their native language in planned activities, students usually become very excited and may behave in an enthusiastic, take-charge manner adults have not seen demonstrated earlier.

A bilingual educator or translator should perform the observation of designated student assessment activities both in the native language and in English. Results of performance in both languages should be compared, providing important information, such as academic skill levels, personal interests, and future goals.

In their development of this model measuring competencies in two languages, Fradd and Bermudez (1991) adapted the assessment areas in Table

**Table 7–3**
**Observing Language Functions**

| Language Function | Behavior Observed | Activity |
|---|---|---|
| Interactional | Initiates conversations with peers; gets along with others; able to understand listener's perspective | Student role-plays helping a friend. |
| Instrumental | Student tries to accomplish a task such as obtaining an object (e.g., school supplies, books) | Student describes an object not present. |
| Personal | Student expresses feelings and opinions on an issue | Ask the student to discuss whether or not it is important to stay in school and to go to college. |
| Regulatory | Student gives directions for completion of a task | Student teaches adult or peer how to play a game. |
| Heuristic | Student's manner of generating questions when problem-solving | Student interviews peer or adult to care for pet when student visits relatives. |
| Imaginative | Student creates original story | Given a topic or situation, student creates a story. |
| Informal | Student describes situations, noting cause and effect relationships | Student explains school project; student gives specific information about concepts learned at school. |

(*Source:*  Adapted from Fradd & Bermudez, 1991)

7–3 (Halliday, 1978). Measuring these language functions requires student active involvement, at times in contrived situations. It is important to design activities that allow students to demonstrate logical, academic, and interpersonal skills. An interpreter with an understanding of the student's dominant culture can discuss with the prereferral team which of the student's behaviors are related to cultural background.

The activities listed in Table 7–3 are only examples of problem-solving situations allowing students opportunities to demonstrate their capabilities to adults. These activities should be changed to accommodate students' immediate needs and areas in which teachers need more appraisal. However, it is better to have a formulated activity with the goal of measuring a specific language function than to casually observe the student and hope that certain situations occur to demonstrate the behavior under consideration.

For example, the interactional language activity noted in Table 7–3 encourages the student to role-play how to help a friend. This task requires not only language proficiency, but social and logical ones basic to problem-solving. It would be difficult for teachers informally observing a student at recess or changing classes to note this interactive experience in a natural setting. It is likely that the very cause of the problem, limited English, would prevent the student from interacting with others easily. If the student did interact with peers who speak the same native language, the teacher would have to be fluent to attach any meaning to the conversation. Even if the teacher were to overhear the discussion, the topic might not provide the opportunity to gauge logic skills.

The use of a predesigned activity also provides opportunities for comparison of the student's skill performance in English versus the native language. The quality of student output during the activity should be measured initially, but then continuously over a period of time so educators can gauge improvement in English-language proficiency. It is important to be aware of students' beginning levels so appropriate instructional activities can be planned.

The POWER model is based on the concept of development of English proficiency as progression from the limited amount of English a beginning student would speak, including single words and short, memorized phrases. Students with these minimal skills are at the novice level.

As students move to more creative use of language, such as the ability to meet personal needs and initiate conversations outside those earlier rote patterns, they enter the intermediate level. Students have not fully understood correct use of English grammar at this point, at time combining words in an unlikely syntax. This level emphasizes meeting survival needs.

Moving to the advanced level, also referred to as the expanded level, for school-aged children requires the production of grammatically correct sentences in past, present, continuous present, and future tenses. The speaker should be able to relate a larger quantity of information, not limited to brief sentences for survival. The speaker should be able to have expanded discussion about a central topic, elaborating on ideas and creating sentences as the interaction continues. The exception to these extended discourses is for preschool children whose sentence length and use of modifiers such as adjectives and adverbs is not normally developed into expanded patterns at a young age. They would be expected to speak in age-appropriate grammatical patterns, including the use of common errors such as overgeneralization of rules to past tenses and plurals (e.g., *goed* for *go; mouses* for *mice*.)

Students functioning at the superior level use language in an easier, fluent manner, able to initiate and elaborate on ideas cohesively. Their language is easily understood by others as they incorporate colloquialisms and interact in expanded conversations in any area. Even if they show other signs of fluency in English young children should not be expected to discuss abstract topics since they will not develop that ability for many years. It is important for teachers to be aware of students' language and cognitive capabilities at a given age, so they develop a personal norm for gauging abilities.

Regardless of the level of proficiency and the exposure to others speaking English, students will require additional activities to introduce vocabulary and syntactical patterns and to reinforce speaking, reading, and writing skills. Fradd and Bermudez (1991) encourage the use of developmental language activities and experiences for all students with limited English proficiency, but especially for those experiencing learning and behavioral disabilities.

The most extensive of these activities involve integrated problem-solving activities similar to those in the initial assessment, allowing students to use language as a tool for expanding their critical thinking skills. Beyond assessment, the model encourages the use of **whole language activities, cooperative learning**, and an **integrated curriculum** that relates the reading and writing process. The implementation of these processes will be discussed in later chapters.

**whole language activities—** lessons based on the integration of writing, reading, and oral language skills.

**cooperative learning—an** approach based on children working in teams combining students with disabilities with typical peers.

**integrated curriculum—com-** bining the content areas within a meaningful context.

**Student Oral Proficiency Scale—**an instrument used to measure students' abilities to use English in five areas: comprehension, fluency, vocabulary, pronunciation, and grammar.

## Student Oral Proficiency Scale

An additional measure for considering level of spoken language is the **Student Oral Proficiency Scale** (Development Associates, 1988). Adapted from an oral language matrix developed by the San Jose Unified School District, California, it is used to explore students' abilities to use English. A holistic matrix, it considers students' total competence in oral communication, based on their performance in five categories: comprehension, fluency, vocabulary, pronunciation, and grammar. Within each of these categories, students' proficiency levels are rated, ranging from Level 1 (minimal ability to comprehend or express meaning ) to Level 5 (communicates as well as a native speaker). The five subscores are combined to determine a total communication score. This matrix should be administered as soon as the limited English proficient student enrolls in school. It should be reviewed by the prereferral committee as they determine optimal instructional placements for the student, and can become the basis for developing goals and objectives to improve oral language skills. It should be completed again at the end of the school year, the results forming a comparison with the initial scale to determine growth and areas still needing improvement.

## Reading Skills Rating Scale

The assessment of student reading skills in English and in the native language is a complex process. Since receptive and expressive spoken language precede reading, no effort should be made to emphasize reading until a modicum of oral language is attained. Educators can initiate measuring students' abilities to analyze situations literally and inferentially by asking a series of

Name _____ Grade _____ Language Observed _____

School _____ Date _____

DIRECTIONS: For each of the five categories below at the left, mark an X across the box that best describes the student's abilities.

| Category | Level 1 | Level 2 | Level 3 | Level 4 | Level 5 |
|---|---|---|---|---|---|
| Comprehension | Cannot understand even simple conversation. | Has great difficulty following what is said. Can comprehend only "social conversation" spoken slowly and with frequent repetitions. | Understands most of what is said at slower-than-normal speed with repetitions. | Understands nearly everything at normal speed, although occasional repetition may be necessary. | Understands everyday conversation and normal classroom discussions with difficulty. |
| Fluency | Speech is so halting and fragmentary as to make conversation virtually impossible. | Usually hesitant; often forced into silence by language limitations. | Speech in everyday communication and classroom discussion is frequently disrupted by the student's search for the correct manner of expression. | Speech in everyday communication and classroom discussion is generally fluent, with occasional lapses while the student searches for the correct manner of expression. | Speech in everyday conversation and in classroom discussions is fluent and effortless, approximating that of a native speaker. |
| Vocabulary | Vocabulary limitations are so extreme as to make conversation virtually impossible. | Misuse of words and very limited vocabulary make comprehension quite difficult. | Frequently uses the wrong words; conversation somewhat limited because of inadequate vocabulary. | Occasionally uses inappropriate terms or must rephrase ideas because of inadequate vocabulary. | Use of vocabulary and idioms approximates that of a native speaker. |
| Pronunciation | Pronunciation problems are so severe as to make speech virtually unintelligible. | Very hard to understand because of pronunciation problems. Must frequently repeat to be understood. | Pronunciation problems necessitate concentration on the part of the listener and occasionally lead to misunderstanding. | Always intelligible, though one is conscious of a definite accent and occasional inappropriate intonation patterns. | Pronunciation and intonation approximate a native speaker's. |
| Grammar | Errors in grammar and word order are so severe as to make speech virtually unintelligible. | Grammar and word order errors make comprehension difficult. Must often rephrase or restrict what is said to basic patterns. | Makes frequent errors of grammar and word order that occasionally obscure meaning. | Occasionally makes grammatical or word order errors that do not obscure meaning. | Grammatical usage and word order approximate a native speaker's. |

Signature of Rater _____

FIGURE 7–4    Student Oral Proficiency Scale (*Source:* Adaptation of the Student Oral Language Matrix [SOLOM] from the San Jose [California] Unified School District; Development Associates, Inc., Arlington, Virginia 1988).

probe questions following a reading assignment. Some questions might include the following (Maryland State Department of Education, in Pierce & O'Malley, 1992):

**Knowledge**
Who was the main person in this text?
Where and when did this story take place?

**Comprehension**
What was the main idea of the reading?
Retell the story in your own words.

**Analysis**
How does _____ compare with _____?
What evidence supports_____?

**Synthesis**
What will happen next in the story?
What would you suggest as a solution?

**Evaluation**
Do you agree with_____?
What would you have done if you were in the character's place?

The teacher should have a standard for evaluation of student performance. Table 7–4 is an expansion of a scale for measuring students' ability to

### Table 7–4
### Evaluating Reading Outcomes for Culturally Diverse Students

| Reading Task | Independently | With Assistance | Unable to Perform |
|---|---|---|---|
| Understands literal meaning | | | |
| Draws inferences from reading | | | |
| Sequences events correctly | | | |
| Compares/contrasts characters and events | | | |
| Predicts upcoming story and event outcomes | | | |
| Uses personal experiences to evaluate ideas and events | | | |

(*Source:* Adapted from Vygotsky, 1978)

perform reading tasks (Pierce & O'Malley, 1992), using the criteria developed by Vygotsky (1978). Teachers rate students' responses to the probe questions at one of three levels: independently, with assistance, or unable to perform task. Use of this scale provides an indicator of students' reading comprehension levels in English and/or their native language. They can begin at the current student level and work to increase comprehension through class discussions and carefully planned questions about material read.

Teachers can also use this information as a basis for gauging students' cognitive levels when asking questions in class. Knowing a student tends to understand at a literal or an inferential level allows the teacher to formulate questions about not only reading material, but also information covered in class discussions, so the student can answer capably, while always attempting to move students to the next level.

## Literacy Development Checklist

"I'd like to share an excellent checklist that I've been using with my students for the last two years," noted Maura. "While it was initially given to me by the bilingual education teacher so we could jointly monitor the improvement made by students with limited English proficiency, I've been using it with all my students. When I first started teaching, I felt reading was an 'either/or' process: Either a student could read or not. I've observed this isn't really accurate. Learning to read is a fluid process that develops over a period of many years. It requires the student's and teacher's active involvement to develop not only good skills but good reading habits. The checklist provides a way for us to monitor reading progress together."

*Literacy Development Checklist*—a checklist of reading processes, such as skills, interests, applications, and strategies, that can provide valuable information to a teacher about a student's reading skills.

Figure 7–5 contains a *Literacy Development Checklist* by Pierce and O'Malley (1992), based on materials developed by the National Council of Teachers of English and The Writing Lab of the University of New Hampshire. While its use is recommended for students with limited English proficiency, as Maura noted, it can provide valuable information about all students. For each quarter of the year, the teacher marks whether a student has mastered a skill or reading application, uses it effectively at times, or needs more instruction.

The *Reading Skills* section considers the extent to which the student is able to perform a number of skills critical to reading. These skills are arranged in sequence of difficulty, with comprehension of oral stories at the easiest level, extending through understanding of reading vocabulary and fluency of decoding, or word analysis. Subsequently, students should be able to comprehend material they read at a literal and then inferential level.

Once a student learns basic skills, the checklist can be use to record manifestations of *Interest* in reading. Does the student read a variety of types of books independently and for pleasure? Teachers should be particularly proud of their teaching when they develop lifetime readers, young people

| Student _____ | Teacher _____ | | | |
|---|---|---|---|---|
| School _____ | Academic Year _____ | | | |
| MARK:      E—Effective      S—Sometimes Effective | N—Needs Work | | | |
| Reading Processes | Quarter | | | |
| | 1 | 2 | 3 | 4 |
| I. READING SKILLS | | | | |
| Comprehends oral stories | | | | |
| Reading vocabulary | | | | |
| Fluent decoding | | | | |
| Literal comprehension in reading | | | | |
| Inferential comprehension | | | | |
| II. INTEREST | | | | |
| Initiates own reading | | | | |
| Shows pleasure in reading | | | | |
| Selects books independently | | | | |
| Samples a variety of materials | | | | |
| III. APPLICATIONS | | | | |
| Participates in language experience story development | | | | |
| Participates in reading discussion groups | | | | |
| Writes appropriate dialogue journal entries | | | | |
| Chooses books of appropriate difficulty | | | | |
| Uses reading in written communication | | | | |
| IV. READING STRATEGIES | | | | |
| Monitors attention | | | | |
| Notices miscues that interfere with meaning | | | | |
| Infers meaning based on: | | | | |
| Word clues | | | | |
| Sentence structure | | | | |
| Story structure | | | | |
| Prior experience | | | | |
| Summarizes main ideas or key events | | | | |
| Links details to main ideas | | | | |
| Remembers sequence of events | | | | |
| Predicts conclusions | | | | |
| Requests help if needed | | | | |

**Figure 7–5   Literacy Development Checklist** (*Source:* Adapted from materials developed by the National Council of Teachers of English and by The Writing Lab of the University of New Hampshire [in Pierce & O'Malley, 1992]).

who will thrive through imagination and discovery. When students enjoy selecting books and are willing to read across content areas, they broaden their own education extensively.

The *Application* section indicates the manner in which students use reading as participants in group learning activities, such as language experience, story development and discussions. Do they expand information they read into their own expression through journal entries and writing assignments? Are they able to write in varied formats and genre as extensions of reading activities?

The use of appropriate *Reading Strategies* for full comprehension allows students to understand and recall important, sophisticated information. What inferences are underscored by sentence and story structure? Is the student able to rely on knowledge learned through previous experiences to add meaning to current selections? What are the main ideas? How are they related? Importantly, teachers should encourage students to use logic and analysis as keys to comprehension, always requesting help when needed.

Since students require years to acquire the skills on the Literacy Development Checklist, teachers might view the categories as long-term goals and pass sheets on to teachers in higher grades as students progress. Many of these skills are not fully developed until the secondary level, making this a useful tool for older students.

Regardless of age or grade level, it provides a logical series of skills for students with limited English proficiency as it lists those literacy behaviors that develop from first exposure to reading in a non-native language to those anticipated over a period of years. As teachers check the degree of mastery on a quarterly basis, goals for the next term are indicated. All teachers who work with the student can share this information to view the student's progress in their content area. The form provides important information to the prereferral team as they meet to consider areas of emphasis in the student's curriculum.

## ASSESSING STUDENTS FROM DIVERSE CULTURAL BACKGROUNDS

"While a number of our students are learning English as a second language, there are others who are English-dominant but whose cultural or economic background differ from majority students," Mort observes. "How do we vary assessment for these students?"

While students with limited English proficiency clearly require alternative skills assessment measures, English-speaking students from diverse cultural or economic backgrounds also demonstrate exceptional needs. When designing assessments, it is best to include the needs of this broader group so that an accurate indicator of all students' academic levels will be provided. Assessment personnel must consider a number of factors: differences in students' prior knowledge base for experiences measured; their ability to use test format or strategies to increase their score; their ability to meet time limitations on subtests; their understanding of teacher pronunciation in oral directions or actual test items; and their own articulation of responses or ability to express answers (Garcia & Pearson, 1991).

There are a number of alternative literacy measures that can be used to determine reading and writing skill levels. Table 7–5 lists effective methods that can be used to collect alternative assessment information from students. Summarized by Garcia and Pearson (1991) a number of these measures were discussed in Chapter 6 as means of gathering authentic or "situated" information grounded in the daily reality of students and their teachers (Garcia & Pearson, 1991). They can be used with individual students or with the entire class, allowing students from diverse cultural and linguistic backgrounds to fit more easily into the classroom structure and to demand less teacher time than if they required unique assessment measures.

When a student has limited English proficiency as well, those measures testing academic knowledge and skills should contain samples both in English and in the student's native language, allowing for comparison. The bilingual education teacher can analyze the communication skills in the native language. If no bilingual services are available at the school, another bilingual adult should review the results and discuss them with the regular classroom teacher.

anecdotal records—observations of a student written in a narrative form.

For students from different cultural backgrounds, the use of anecdotal records noted on Table 7–5 may include a teacher's ongoing record of student development, such as a checklist of students' skills at the beginning of the year, with dates added as they gain mastery. Often these records create a positive response from educators, students, and parents, since they demonstrate

## Table 7–5
## Alternate Assessment Measures

When assessing students from diverse cultural backgrounds, educators should include:

- anecdotal records
- story retellings
- oral miscue analysis
- self-assessment
- teacher-student interactions
- informal reading and math inventories
- portfolios
- curriculum-based assessment

(*Source:* Adapted from Garcia & Pearson, 1991)

what students can do, instead of what they cannot do, and they provide a record of ongoing development (Garcia & Pearson, 1991).

Teacher-student interactions are an important source of assessment information. Varying from informal conversations to asking the student questions regarding reading material, the teacher observes for student ability to integrate information. However, in the multicultural classroom, teachers should be aware of how the student's background may influence these interactions. For example, in some cultures it is considered rude to make eye contact, or even to interact too informally, with adults. If the interactions deal with literary materials, it may be the first time a student has been asked to consider written information and its application to life situations. Educators then must sort out academic skill levels from cultural responses. It is important for teachers to ask probing questions instead of ones that can be answered with a "yes" or "no" response. Expanded responses clarify more completely the extent of student knowledge.

Some educators enjoy using story retellings to assess comprehension (Morrow, 1989). Instead of retelling a story they have read, cultures such as Native American often enjoy creating their own stories and relating them to others. When students have limited English proficiency, they should be allowed to intersperse words from their native language in order to aid elaboration, or even tell the story completely in their dominant language. The presence of another student or teacher to act as interpreter allows the entire class an enriched opportunity.

"I had a really meaningful experience with retellings," reflected John. "I had been unable to gauge the potential of an African-American student in my freshman English class last fall. He was failing, largely because he slept through classes, did no homework, and had low grades on exams. The obvious conclusion was that he couldn't do the work. But occasionally he would make really insightful comments, indicating that he did have good comprehension.

"I had the students create their own stories about the one thing in their lives that had impacted them the most. They then told the stories to small groups of two or three other students, a technique that I hoped would encourage even shy students to participate. Martin's story was about his daughter! She had been born to his 15-year-old girlfriend the previous year, and the mother had quit school to be with the baby. While she lived at home, her own mother insisted that she would have to meet all of her own and the baby's expenses. So Martin worked: all night, every night. No wonder he slept through classes! As he talked about his daughter, Martin was emotional and proud, making everyone laugh as he described exactly how she toddled as she was learning to walk. That one story told me more about Martin that anything else could have.

"With Martin's permission, the counselor and I contacted community social services to give support to his young family, so he would work evenings and weekends, but not nights. They persuaded Martin's girlfriend to return to school and enrolled the baby in a daycare program. Martin even brought the baby to the class holiday party, where the students gave her some toys as a surprise gift. The challenges to his future will be tremendous; but he has demonstrated a strength of character that none of us would have realized without that story!"

As discussed in Chapter 6, informal reading and math inventories can provide information about basic skill levels as well as the appropriate instructional levels of classroom materials. If educators are listening to students read aloud, they should include an **oral miscue analysis**, where they note word attack and analysis skills, repetition or omission of words and sounds, use of phonics and syllabication, and substitutions. Comprehension is more important than pronunciation, and teachers should emphasize content understanding over ability to decode words. Students may skip reading words aloud because they cannot pronounce them. However, they may understand their meaning (Garcia & Pearson, 1991).

The use of portfolios in multicultural classrooms allows both students and teachers to observe work progress and language development. Students should be encouraged to take pride in their efforts through pleasure of completing the task. Many cultures are not competitive and the promise of a high grade does not provide intended motivation. Similarly, public demonstration of student efforts, such as displaying work on bulletin boards, will discourage students from backgrounds where the group outcome is more important than the individual product.

"How can I know this if I'm personally from a background where these motivations usually work?" asks Maura.

The earlier recommendation to include at least one adult from a similar environment on the prereferral team will help teachers understand how student acculturation may differ from that of their own experiences. Additionally, they can attune teachers to emotional and academic supports that will be well-received. Many times the teacher need only ask the student how he would like to be rewarded for his efforts in order to discover the best motivations and reinforcements. A type of **self-assessment**, usually verbal, can be extended to assessment of specific work products. The student can explain why he answered the question in a specific way or can expand on the nature of the response. Through these interchanges, teachers can gain understanding of student reasoning abilities and cultural influences on analysis.

Table 7–6 includes a number of ways that educators can create a classroom environment that is conducive to accurate assessment of students from varied cultural and linguistic backgrounds. When teachers create a **risk-free environment**, they encourage students to take chances, to not be afraid that others will laugh at them or tease them. Risk-free classrooms have a relaxed affect felt immediately by visitors. Students work together and help each other succeed. Competition is a means to improving a performance of individuals and groups, not a method for creating winners and losers. Students are

---

**oral miscue analysis**—observations about how a student uses word attack and analysis skills, repetition, omission, and substitutions of words and sounds, use of phonics and syllabication.

**self-assessment**—students evaluate their own work.

**risk-free environment**—an atmosphere in which students feel free to take chances and are not afraid others will laugh at them or tease them.

## Table 7–6
## The Assessment Environment

*Teachers should:*

- create a risk-free affect in their classrooms

- motivate students to participate in activities for enjoyment and learning, not for competition

- provide assessment and instructional tasks that emphasize what the student can do successfully

- assess continuously

- observe students informally, so students do not know they are being assessed

- observe students in a variety of settings

- use both formal and informal methods

- not rely solely on any one measure for accuracy, but on combined results from a variety of instruments

- teach test-taking strategies

- make recommendations based on an understanding of cultural variables

(*Source:* Adapted from Garcia & Pearson, 1991; Piece & O'Malley, 1992)

motivated to perform tasks because the process is fun, not because the product must be perfect. Within this setting, whether using portfolios, curriculum-based assessment, formal and informal methods, it is important to provide instructional tasks that indicate what the student can do successfully. Such emphases allow students to feel pride in work products and avoids lowered self-esteem.

Assessment should be continuous, at times students not even realizing that their work is under scrutiny. Similarly, educators should observe students in a variety of settings, ranging from deskwork activities to recess or interactions with others outside class. Such assessment requires the use of a variety of the methods discussed above, from observation to student completion of formal tasks. Teachers should not rely on any one measure alone to provide accurate information, but on a combination of information from all sources.

When teachers administer formal group tests, they should teach test-taking strategies that may not be part of the student's background. Time-budgeting among test items, initial completion of items the student can do easily, and concentration on task through avoidance of distractions are just a few topics that may enhance skills.

"The type of test is also really important," comments Maura. Students have to learn early that multiple choice items require different mental sets than short-answer tests, and certainly, than essays. For example, they need to learn to eliminate responses that are clearly incorrect among choices. On the other hand, they have to know which specific ideas to select for short-answer tests and how to organize and expand upon their ideas in essays. Sometimes students know the answer, but they don't know how to respond to the question."

scantron tests—machine-scored answer sheets.

John added, "At the secondary level, scantron tests offer all types of additional problems, although some teachers like them because of their ease in scoring. If you think it's difficult to explain test-taking strategies to students from differing cultures or languages, it's more overwhelming to try to teach them how to complete these answer sheets. And how do you keep students with perceptual problems in reading from losing their place on the test page or record booklet? One line skipped and they fail. I'm on a personal campaign to have teachers stop using these at our school."

test anxiety—a fear of taking tests.

Any educator who has ever experienced test anxiety personally can empathize with a student from a minority background or culture who is not only trying to decide what the answer is, but almost more importantly, how to record the information. Such added concerns detract from content knowledge as the reason for the assessment and place undue emphasis on test logistics. For this reason, whenever possible teachers should teach test-taking skills they can avoid these problems by relying on the measures listed in Table 7–5.

## FROM ASSESSMENT TO INTERVENTION

"We've talked a good deal about ways to perform assessment," observed Alex, "but not about how to use this information for programming. Let's discuss how to organize instruction for students from different cultural backgrounds."

Baca and Cervantes (1989) provide a series of guidelines for programming for students from minority backgrounds who require academic and behavioral support both for disabilities and for language differences. For optimal instruction, they strongly advocate combining native language and culture with English as a Second Language (ESL) programming support. As indicated in Table 7–7, they suggest directions for educators to follow.

English as a Second Language (ESL)—programming support for non-native speakers as they learn English.

### Preparation for Success

The first series of guidelines in Table 7–7 involves setting the stage for successful intervention. All educators on a campus should meet and discuss their goals in providing services for students who are bilingual/multicultural as

### Table 7–7
### Programming for Bilingual Students with Disabilities

Preparation for programming should include:

- a well-considered sense of direction for faculty working with bilingual students with disabilities
- a belief by all staff that programming can be effective in improving achievement levels
- strong leadership by administrators
- high expectations both for teachers and students in the program
- respectful treatment of all students, languages, and cultures
- establishment of effective and cooperative interactions with the home

Instruction should include:

- a focus on students' abilities and learning styles
- native language and ESL training in all programming, as appropriate
- ongoing development of students' skills in native language to the cognitive and academic levels needed for achieving similarly advanced skills in English
- monitoring of student progress in both languages, providing ongoing feedback
- direct teaching and consultation by bilingual and special educators

(*Source:* Adapted from Baca & Cervantes, 1989)

well as disabled. They should list the specific needs for their school, often different from others even in the same city (e.g., size of population served; degree of community supportive services available; specific cultures and languages represented).

As part of developing their mission, staff must believe they can be effective in teaching children with varied but intense needs. In small teams they should visit schools where innovative programming has been successful, allowing them to engender new ideas in their own environment. Administrators should invite faculty from these effective programs to provide inservice training, sharing their excitement and successes. Teachers training other teachers can impart critical awareness and spark new ideas, fostering collaboration.

When developing any new program, the attitude of the administrator is critical to success. "I can attest to that," observed Mort. "I remember my own hesitation when we started developing inclusive programs in our district. Until I was convinced that I could initiate a strong one at Jackson, even that I wanted to initiate one, I was very unenthused. Not surprisingly, my faculty, usually innovative and excited about programming, followed my lead. We all thought of reasons why inclusion was bad, until we considered the opposite: exclusion of the very children who seemed to need us the most. Once we decided to develop a model program, there's been no stopping us. The teachers still amaze me with their creativity and enthusiasm. After that first step, it's been surprisingly easy for us to ask ourselves how to expand even further to include students from a variety of cultures and languages."

Mort and his teachers are a team, but he is the leader. The mood of the school citizens, its teachers, students, and staff, is formulated daily by the positive or negative attitude he imparts. When the principal and other district administrators believe that all children can be successful, regardless of their linguistic or cultural background, the students themselves feel they can be successful. When respect for difference is part of the attitude of the adults of the school, students have powerful models.

An important aspect of the collaborative spirit is the school and home working together to support student success. When a child begins to have academic or behavioral difficulties, the family should be contacted immediately to help stem the problem. Obviously, the traditional practice of complaining to parents about the student and asking them to take care of the problem will not be successful. As educators must work together to solve the multitude of problems students may carry with them to the classroom, they require parental help. Optimally, parents should meet with the prereferral team, discuss their personal observations and concerns about the child, and indicate which of the behaviors demonstrated may be cultural in nature. They should work with educators to develop an intervention plan. Instead of continuing the often divisive nature of school-home interactions, healthy interchanges engender a cooperative relationship.

## Designing the Instructional Program

The guidelines in Table 7–7 include important suggestions when programming for bilingual or multicultural students with disabilities. The previous sections of this chapter emphasized methods of obtaining specific assessment information so the nature of the disability can be accurately understood. It is critical that educators rely on the results of the assessment to indicate future directions in programming. All too often personnel gather valuable data on students only to file it away from use by the very educators who need to intervene. Assessment conclusions and recommendations should be carefully reviewed by the prereferral team. Based on diagnosed skills and perceived learning needs, the student's program should then be developed, including specific learning goals, teaching methods and activities, as well as continuous evaluative strategies to assure the student is progressing successfully.

Assessment measures discussed earlier allow for determination of oral and written language skills both in the student's native language and

Teachers can continually assess student progress through informal observations of skill development.

English. It is important that subsequent interventions also include instruction in both languages so the student may continue learning academic information while improving skills. Primary language instruction is particularly important as a means of preparation to attain advanced levels of English. Secondary students particularly risk slowing their development of abstract thinking skills if teachers wait for them to fully develop English.

At the same time, educators must meet students' needs for special education resources. Some students will require skill-building activities to improve reading, computation, and written expression. Others will need behavioral interventions such as contingency contracts and clearly delineated consequences. Educators may begin to rely more on hands-on lessons requiring active student involvement, as well as media and computers.

To meet the multifaceted needs of bilingual students with disabilities, staff appropriately trained in ESL and special education will need to work together to provide a rich curriculum of basic skill-building within a multicultural context.

"How can this be accomplished, especially at the secondary level?" asks John. "It seems that placing all these demands on a teacher would be overwhelming and nonproductive."

John is right as long as schools continue to rely on the traditional model of a single teacher in a classroom instructing all students on the same information, from the same text, requiring the same responses on exams. Inclusion will not work well for any student within this framework, regardless of native culture or dominant language. When these additional variables are introduced, inclusion will be impossible without differentiated instruction.

Emphasizing time on task and task completion for all, a team of teachers must assign work at the student's cognitive and skill level, including supportive personnel such as the ESL teacher when students speak little English. The ESL teacher does not have to be present for the entire lesson as an attempt to teach in a parallel manner, but can serve as a consultant to the regular educator, providing supportive materials and tapes in the native language and meeting with the student at assigned times to discuss information and measure progress. Similarly, the special educator may teach small groups of students within the regular classroom when specialized skills training is necessary. At other times, the specialist can provide texts with important information highlighted or taped for students with disabilities. The specialist can work with the regular educator to shorten exams or to provide alternate testing, such as through extended time or oral administration. The key to successful instruction will be flexible interactions by educators to meet student needs as indicated in assessment data.

## SUMMARY

This chapter included discussion of a variety of ways to assess students from diverse linguistic and cultural backgrounds. Often these students experience limitations due to language and behavioral differences that impact their understanding of class lectures, discussions, and reading assignments. Others appear to have behavior problems when in actuality they have not adjusted to classroom expectations. These students suffer from inappropriate referrals for special education since the nature of the problem is often difficult for educators to discern.

In considering the behaviors a student brings to the classroom, it is necessary to consider the impact of the culture on the family, the student, and subsequently, the teacher. Family values and expectations shape child-rearing practices, especially behavioral expectations, such as aggression or acquiescence. These behaviors may not fit teacher and peer expectations in an academic setting. When the student has a disability, parents may not be aware of how to avail themselves of services, allowing the disability to negatively impact the student over a period of years. Their attitude toward the disability will impact how positively they regard systemic intervention by the school.

The teacher's attitude is equally critical. Does the teacher understand and accept diversity? Is there a positive or negative attitude toward students from different cultures or with disabilities? This attitude will serve as a model for other students and form the basis for interactions between the teacher and the family unit.

Student factors such as mastery of prerequisite academic skills, English proficiency, and ability to cope with a disability will impact classroom success. Do students have the social skills to interact with peers and adults successfully, or must they learn an expanded repertoire of behaviors?

The importance of the prereferral process is apparent in avoiding over-referrals to special education. Teachers and peers must not expect non-native speakers to be able to meet spoken and written language requirements in English immediately. They must be allowed to progress in learning using their own language, while at the same time developing receptive and expressive language skills in English. Teachers aware of a potential problem should initiate a meeting, allowing the committee to consider optimal intervention before the student experiences failure.

Parents should complete a questionnaire considering developmental, educational, and linguistic variables that may be impacting the student's performance (see Figure 7–2). Results will help determine if a disability is present or if problems may be attributed to other factors. The questionnaire can provide the basis for understanding the student more fully.

When student behaviors are of concern, the team should consider their perceived cause and audience, how the student differs from others of similar cultural backgrounds, and the impact of the behavior on the student and others in the class. An observer or the classroom teacher can then conduct a functional analysis of the problem: What content area or activity normally prompts the misbehavior? Is there a particular antecedent or precipitating event that causes the student to act inappropriately? What is the specific nature of the misbehavior? What consequences are normally imposed? How does the student react?

Upon discussion of the results of the functional analysis, the team should determine how to modify the behavior. Curtailing antecedents that appear to initiate the behavior or changing the consequences may obviate the problem completely.

An important aspect of assessment for students from linguistically different backgrounds is the determination of students' spoken and written language skills, both in their native language and in English. The chapter includes several successful models, such as POWER, where problem-solving situations are created, allowing students to demonstrate their linguistic and logical capabilities in both languages. Another model, the Student Oral Proficiency Scale, rates students' competence in English, on a matrix considering comprehension, fluency, vocabulary, pronunciation, and grammar. A scale to rate student understanding of a series of reading passages includes probe questions considering knowledge base and different levels of comprehension. Students are rated as being able to perform independently, with assistance, or with extreme difficulty. This information allows the teacher to assess fairly the need for intervention.

The Literacy Development Checklist can be used with all students as a determinant of student skill levels and interest in reading. Observations include the manner in which the student uses reading as a basis for participating in group language activities and writing assignments. The use of appropriate reading strategies, such as inferences based on word clues, sentence structure, and prior experience, alerts the teacher that the student possesses skills to acquire more sophisticated content knowledge. The checklist can be placed in the student's file to demonstrate linguistic gains over a period of years.

While these instruments are successful for students with limited English proficiency, there should be additional informal assessment measures for students from diverse cultural backgrounds. Anecdotal records may include a teacher's continuous report of student progress. They include a record of what the child can do, receiving a positive response from educators and parents as growth continues.

Ranging from informal conversations to direct questions, teacher-student interactions provide an observation point to measure student integration of information. Others enjoy story retellings, where a student creates or shares cultural or personal stories, interspersing native words as elaboration. Additionally, informal reading and math inventories provide information about basic skill levels, indicating which instructional materials may be the most appropriate. Portfolios provide another method of observing progress and language development. They encourage students to take pride in personal accomplishment, minimizing competition with others.

Educators should create a classroom environment that is risk-free, motivating students to attempt new tasks and support each other. Assessment should be continuous, informal wherever possible, and take place across a variety of settings.

When formal tests are deemed necessary, teachers should teach test-taking strategies in advance, including methods of approaching different types of exams, time-budgeting, and organizing responses. Students with disabilities may have additional problems with scantron tests or formats that may distract from test content, such as unclear directions.

Once teachers complete assessment, it is critical that they use the information to design effective interventions for student success. Before intervention even begins, faculties can insure success through deciding their goals for providing services for students who are bilingual/multicultural as well as disabled. They should visit other schools where programming has been successful and attend inservices engendering new ideas and intervention strategies.

The school administrator should function as a positive instructional leader, modeling inclusion of all students, regardless of their background.

The collaborative spirit must include families and community representatives.

When intervention begins, the prereferral team should review conclusions and recommendations from the assessment in order to design teaching and behavioral strategies. They should develop goals, teaching methods and activities, and methods of evaluation. Special educators and bilingual education teachers should play important roles in methods selection. When necessary, the student should continue to receive instruction in the native language as well as English so that cognitive and content skills will not be lost.

Students requiring special education supports should receive them in the regular classroom. The special teacher may work with students in small-group skill-building activities at times, and serve as a consultant to the classroom teacher at others, providing not only suggestions for instruction, but modified materials to underscore success.

## CASE STUDY: *Elementary*

Yolanda is a new student in third grade at Jackson Elementary. Recently, she has moved from Mexico with her mother and two younger brothers, joining her father, who has been working in the United States for a few years. Yolanda does not speak English and has been having a difficult time coping in school since she also is moderately hearing impaired. Her Spanish is difficult for even the bilingual teacher to understand, because Yolanda mispronounces many sounds based on her hearing loss. She does not know any sign language and does not read Spanish except for a few consonant and vowel sounds.

Her teacher, Maura Hayes, is concerned because Yolanda often comes to school without her hearing aid. When she does wear it, Maura suspects the batteries have not been changed frequently enough. The family does not have a phone and seems to be avoiding any contact with the school. Yolanda watches the other children perform schoolwork but seems bewildered by her own work. She is friendly to the teacher, but sits passively as others work in groups or complete assignments.

"I'm really getting frustrated with this situation," notes Maura. "I know I'm supposed to be understanding of diversity and all that, but we're wasting everyone's time. What can I do?"

1. To help Maura understand the variety of factors impacting her and Yolanda, review Figure 7–1. Placing yourself in the position of (a) the family, (b) Maura, and (c) Yolanda, consider the variables that may be affecting their behavior at this time.
2. As Maura refers Yolanda to the prereferral team, plan their course of action to help her.
3. Clearly, Maura cannot be helpful until she has a better idea of Yolanda's verbal skills in Spanish. Modify the activities suggested in Table 7–3 to help the bilingual teacher evaluate Yolanda's Spanish.
4. How can Maura help Yolanda make friends and adjust socially?

## CASE STUDY: *Secondary*

"Since we've been discussing assessment of kids from different backgrounds, I can't stop thinking about Sergei," John noted. "He's the one who arrived last year from Russia with his parents and older brother.

"I thought we would be all right with his transitions since he's been learning to speak English pretty quickly. He seems very bright. He's been able to follow along in some of our class discussions and his reading skills are developing, although I'm never sure how much he actually understands from the text. I try to include him in small-group discussions, both to improve his English and reinforce meaning for him.

"I'm really concerned about his behavior. Most of the time he's absolutely obnoxious to me and everyone else in the class except a few gang members who love to encourage him.

"Unfortunately, his early English included many profanities. I can't believe the names he's called me and others during class. I've sent him to the office so many times that they've asked me to keep him in class because he's rude to the secretaries.

"Recently he and some gang members were picked up by the police for harassing and threatening some shoppers downtown. I'm really concerned that weapons will be involved next time.

"His parents seem like good people. With an interpreter, they've met with his teachers at school. But they work all the time and just aren't there to provide supervision. They say they can't control him. What can we do?"

---

You are part of the prereferral team convening about ways to help change Sergei's behavior. But first the committee must understand him better.

1. Who should be the other members of the prereferral committee to affect Sergei most effectively?
2. Which questions from Table 7–1 will provide you with the most input? From whom will you get this information?
3. How can you use the information gained from questions in Table 7–2 to plan your intervention?
4. What can John do to immediately change Sergei's behaviors in class? What can the school and family do to involve him with a positive peer group, removing him from gang influence?

# CREATING THE TEACHING- LEARNING ENVIRONMENT

# 8

# DIAGNOSTIC TEACHING

The Westside school year was well underway. From the superintendent to district parents, all were observing carefully as Jackson Elementary and Apter High School initiated inclusion. As always, there had been some surprises, both in positive and negative directions. Faculty had benefitted tremendously from the inservice training sessions with Alex and his appraisal staff, becoming more enthusiastic about their abilities to meet the academic needs of all students in the school. Although many viewed elementary and secondary schools as very different, Mort and Elena had realized early that there were great similarities in shaping their programs. They had met frequently to strategize methods of making inclusion work in their schools.

They visited with school principals and teachers in other districts to share their experiences and adapt successful program models to Westside. They met with teachers in their own schools who had volunteered to be on prereferral teams and organized inservice training in methods of successful collaboration. From the beginning of the school year, the prereferral teams met weekly, encouraging colleagues to refer students with potential problems before special education services became necessary.

The good news was that many teachers embraced the inclusive philosophy and were willing to have students with special needs in their classrooms. The bad news was that a number of others viewed the program warily or were openly negative, indicating that they did not want students with learning and behavior problems. The more extreme the student's disability, the louder the outcry from these teachers.

Mort and Elena were surprised by the number of parents who also viewed inclusion with suspicion. Mike Gonzales, the parents' spokesperson, continued his diatribe with anyone who would listen. Unfortunately he was most vocal at PTA meetings and on Curt O'Hare's radio show. The parents who supported inclusion were much quieter, volunteering their efforts at the school and encouraging full participation of their children in classroom and extracurricular activities. Yet even they were skeptical at times, the most common concern being that regular classroom teachers were not giving their children the full attention and remediation necessary.

"We need a positive attitude injection," Elena noted. "While our school year is progressing better than I expected, I'm concerned about the growing negativism based on a small group of parents and teachers. We need to give some new life to our program or clearly it will fail."

"Agreed," reflected Mort. "I think teachers and parents are losing confidence about what's happening in the classroom. It's become apparent that a 'quick fix' hasn't occurred and that we're going to have to find out what teachers feel they require to be successful. If we can meet whatever needs they have through training and ongoing supports, likely they'll express more assuredness about working with students with exceptionalities. Hopefully the spinoff will be that the parents will gain trust in placing their child in the regular classroom."

Mort and Elena distributed a needs survey to teachers and staff at their schools, asking for specific information about what information and supports they needed to work with students with special needs. They were surprised that even teachers who were negative towards inclusion responded with enthusiasm and worthwhile suggestions. The results of the surveys were summarized by the Inclusion Committee at each school, consisting of regular and special educators, an administrator, and a parent.

Despite anticipated elementary-secondary differences, teachers responses were very similar across grade levels. Commonly, teachers indicated that they wanted more information about ways of identifying specific problems, ranging from vision and hearing to learning disabilities and behavior. However, the most frequently stated need was for specific intervention techniques that can be used in the regular classroom setting. In comments added to the survey, one teacher wrote, "I just need to feel that I know what I'm doing with every student, regardless of their learning and behavior. Once I feel in charge, I'll view inclusion as a challenge, not a burden."

# IDENTIFICATION OF SPECIFIC DISABILITIES

Mort and Elena decided to contact Alex Hamilton again to provide teachers with specific "red flags" that would signal a student with problems. They asked him to work together with Teresa Fuentes so she could provide follow-up intervention strategies found successful for students needing specific skills or behavioral strategies. While in the past they would have expected Alex and Teresa to work separately, each sharing their expertise with audiences of teachers, Mort and Elena had learned the benefits of professionals working together on a first-hand basis. The brainstorming sessions they had held as a team in initiating inclusion had benefitted both of them by providing the opportunity to exchange ideas and cooperatively build a program for the district. As the school year started, they had observed enthusiastic prereferral teams meet with parents and concerned professionals to provide supports for students with problems, while Inclusion Committee members were synergistic as they discussed new directions in their schools. The message was clear: *Educators can be far more successful working together than working alone.*

Alex and Elena decided to create a series of checklists for teachers at Jackson and Apter to use in identifying students with disabilities. They were sensitive to Westside's decision to label students as little as possible, but also understood that combining behaviors commonly found together in certain problem areas such as visual or language impairments would allow educators to identify existing problems impacting school performance. They encouraged teachers to seek input from other professionals such as physicians, psychologists, and language therapists whenever it would help them work with the student.

"That's so important," observed Mort. "Inclusion has never meant removing supports from students. It involves providing them in as normalized an environment as possible. If teachers are attuned to the signs indicating a problem is present, they can arrange for special services, helping the student and themselves."

## Visual Disabilities

The group reviewed the initial checklist on visual disabilities in Table 8–1. "I've found that once alerted to the behaviors, teachers are the strongest source of referral of students with visual disabilities," comments Teresa. "Often parents don't note the signs because they see their children informally, with lots of unstructured activities going on at the same time. If the child sits too close to the television, they may claim that it's a habit he's developed. If headaches or nausea are present, they may feel that he's upset over something. All of us, parents and teachers alike, tend to overlook signs of visual disabilities in younger children, since we tend to feel they won't have problems until they're older."

### Table 8–1
### Identification of Visual Disabilities

|  | Yes | No |
|---|---|---|
| 1.  Sensitivity to light |  |  |
| 2.  Eyes turn inward or outward |  |  |
| 3.  Eyes appear red or watery |  |  |
| 4.  Works with head close to paper or book |  |  |
| 5.  Squints when looking at distant objects, such as overhead projector |  |  |
| 6.  Complains of headaches or nausea |  |  |
| 7.  Irritability after sustained period of reading at desk or from blackboard |  |  |
| 8.  Has problems coordinating movement of both eyes |  |  |

(*Sources:*  Adapted from Mann, Suiter, & McClung, 1987; Koenig & Holbrook, 1989)

"Ironically, the reverse happens when students enter secondary school," notes Alex. "Often teachers feel that any vision problems would have been detected earlier and they don't consider that a student who squints when looking at overhead transparencies may be having trouble seeing the information. When observing red eyelids, adults may feel the student needs more sleep or has allergies."

While most adults wear glasses as a correction for visual disabilities that developed gradually, they may not realize that a number of students have difficulty seeing correctly from birth and cannot perform well academically as a result. It is important to note that few students report their own vision problems in elementary grades, since they are accustomed to seeing things imperfectly and do not realize anything is wrong. If a student develops a far-distance acuity problem gradually and reports difficulty seeing the blackboard, he should be tested immediately by a specialist. School districts should inform parents never to ignore a student complaint about a physical problem.

Teachers and parents should be aware that muscular coordination of both eyes is important for correct vision. In the past, many have believed that an eye might turn inward or outward if a student were tired. "Absolutely not the case," responds Alex. "While an eye may tend to turn more often if the student is fatigued, this only allows us to evidence the problem more easily. An eye turning at any time indicates a need for a complete eye exam.

"Some students experience strabismus—the eyes stay crossed permanently. It is imperative that parents are informed to take their child to an ophthalmologist as early as possible to prevent progressive blindness in the less dominant eye. Physicians frequently prescribe a patch over the stronger eye, forcing the weaker eye to improve. They may also require eye exercises for better muscular coordination. In extreme cases, surgery may be indicated. However, surgery should be performed before the child is seven. After this age, too much damage may have occurred for successful correction."

Another misconception is that once correction of any vision problem has occurred, the student will be able to perform academic work at grade level. If a child has missed initial reading instruction, especially in areas such as letter and word or number identification, he has to be re-taught this information. Now he should be expected to learn more quickly and efficiently with improved vision. However, unless teachers provide remedial skills training in deficient academic areas, the student will not only progress more slowly than peers, but may never perform well at higher academic tasks because of missed skills in early academic instruction.

## Hearing Impairments

"Is the same true for students with hearing impairments?" asks Maura. Absolutely. However, hearing problems are more difficult to detect. As indicated in Table 8–2, several of the indicators of a hearing loss overlap with characteristics of other types of disabilities. For example, if a student frequently requests repetition of information from the teacher or peers or does not make sense when answering questions, a hearing problem, a language problem, or both hearing and language problems may be present. Difficulty in learning phonics may also be a result of a learning disability based on poor auditory discrimination of sounds or problems associating sounds and symbols.

Sadly, many students with undetected hearing losses may be judged as slow learners, or even as cognitively delayed, because of the inadequacy of their responses to classroom instruction. While these students may lack a number of higher abstract concepts, most often this is due to missed verbal instruction or conversations. While parents and teachers identify profound losses in any area of disability more easily, mild to moderate problems in "hidden areas" such as hearing are difficult to detect. While a child's inability to attend to loud noises behind him may signal a hearing loss, his difficulty responding to sounds at higher frequency levels may go unnoticed. Teachers should be observant for students who have frequent allergies, since resultant conditions such as otitis media, or middle-ear infections, may cause the accumulation of scar tissue if untreated. Accumulation of this scar tissue may result in a hearing loss, particularly at higher frequency levels. Unfortunately, since the consonant sounds of the alphabet fall in the higher frequency range, children with a history of ear infections often have problems learning phonics,

**Table 8–2**
**Identification of Hearing Disabilities**

|  | Yes | No |
|---|---|---|
| 1. Stares at the face of the person speaking |  |  |
| 2. Turns one ear to the speaker |  |  |
| 3. Speaks in a voice which is too loud, soft, or monotonic |  |  |
| 4. Asks to have information repeated |  |  |
| 5. Frequently turns to peers to ask questions regarding directions/information |  |  |
| 6. Does not make sense when answering questions |  |  |
| 7. Difficulty in learning phonics |  |  |
| 8. Problems identifying rhyming words |  |  |
| 9. Frequent allergies, ear infections |  |  |
| 10. Fails to answer to name from behind |  |  |

(*Sources:* Adapted from White, 1981; Mann, Suiter, & McClung, 1987)

since they do not hear the sounds clearly. To date, these outcomes are untreatable. Therefore, it is important for teachers to alert parents and the school nurse if they encounter students with chronic untreated allergies or infections.

## Speech Disorders

As noted in Table 8–3, there are a number of identifying characteristics for students demonstrating speech problems. These behaviors are more obvious than many other disabilities, if teachers listen carefully to students' speech patterns. While many adults find sound distortion and substitution engaging in young children, students themselves often are embarrassed by their inability to produce sounds correctly. **Stuttering** is a source of concern to many children, and often their concentration on their own speech patterns only results in additional stress.

stuttering—a language disorder in which the student repeats words or parts of words involuntarily.

"At the secondary level, it's often really difficult to detect speech problems when first encountering students," notes John. "They don't speak! I guess because of a history of others making fun of them, they've learned to be quiet to avoid negative attention. On that checklist I see behaviors such as *Speech is difficult to hear* and *Voice is soft*. So true. I've found that instead of asking them to speak louder during responses in class, if I strike up a casual con-

**Table 8–3**
**Identification of Speech Impairments**

|  | Yes | No |
|---|---|---|
| 1.  Speech is difficult to hear |  |  |
| 2.  Sounds or words are distorted (e.g., *bring/bwing*) |  |  |
| 3.  Substitutes one sound for another (e.g., *same/thame*) |  |  |
| 4.  Omits sounds (e.g., *plant/pant*) |  |  |
| 5.  Labored speech production |  |  |
| 6.  Unusual pitch, bringing attention to speaker |  |  |
| 7.  Uses "baby-talk" |  |  |
| 8.  Stutters or stammers, repeating or prolonging sounds or words |  |  |
| 9.  Voice is so soft that it is difficult to hear |  |  |
| 10.  Voice is excessively loud |  |  |
| 11.  Speech production is labored |  |  |
| 12.  Voice quality is unusual (hoarse, nasal, guttural, breathy) |  |  |

(*Sources:*  Adapted from Mann, Suiter, & McClung, 1987)

versation with them when they're alone I can usually find out pretty quickly if their timidity is due to a speech disability."

It is important for educators to realize that a speech problem may be the first indicator of a hearing loss. Since students reproduce sounds as they hear them, if their hearing is faulty, often speech problems result. In this instance, the student's primary area of difficulty is not speech, but hearing, a disability that must be treated by specialists before either speech or hearing will improve. The more intense the hearing loss, the more intense the resultant speech problems. Therefore, when a student demonstrates differences in speech production, he should be examined by a hearing specialist, as well as speech and language personnel.

## Language Disabilities

Speech disabilities involve difficulties in producing sounds normally. Language disabilities are much more encompassing, including disorders in a number of areas of communication, such as delayed speech, or problems in vocabulary retrieval, word meanings, sentence syntax, concept formation,

## Table 8–4
## Identification of Receptive and Expressive Language Disabilities

|  | Yes | No |
|---|---|---|
| 1. Appears confused during conversations and class discussions (receptive) |  |  |
| 2. Has difficulty understanding directions (receptive) |  |  |
| 3. Does not recognize familiar sounds (e.g., phone ringing; dog barking) (receptive) |  |  |
| 4. Seems unable to classify common objects by category (e.g., bread and milk as food) (receptive) |  |  |
| 5. Fails to associate commonly encountered objects, people, or situations (e.g., mother and child) (receptive) |  |  |
| 6. Difficulty understanding meaning of words describing spatial position (e.g., around, through) or describing time (e.g., later, after) (receptive) |  |  |
| 7. Problems understanding words with multiple meanings, even when used in context (e.g., wait, weight) (receptive) |  |  |
| 8. Difficulty interpreting body language from others (e.g., facial expressions) (receptive) |  |  |
| 9. Below expectancy in reading comprehension (receptive) |  |  |
| 10. Problems interpreting cause-effect relationships in social situations (receptive) |  |  |
| 11. Frequently does not recall common vocabulary (receptive/expressive) |  |  |
| 12. Difficulty explaining ideas clearly (receptive/expressive) |  |  |
| 13. Asks questions or makes comments that do not relate to the topic or are nonsensical (receptive/expressive) |  |  |
| 14. Speaks in short phrases, avoiding adjectives and adverbs (expressive) |  |  |
| 15. Problems expressing self in writing (expressive) |  |  |
| 16. Unable to describe familiar past experience or story (expressive) |  |  |
| 17. Frequently repeats words or ideas (expressive) |  |  |

(*Sources:* Adapted from Lerner, 1993)

and language comprehension (Lerner, 1993). The impact of language problems can be overwhelming for some students, who demonstrate difficulties in understanding what they hear or read, or in expressing themselves verbally and in writing.

oral receptive language disability—a language disorder in
which the student has difficulty
understanding spoken lan-
guage.

Language problems, commonly referred to as aphasia, can cause a number of academic problems at any grade level. As noted in Table 8–4, an **oral
receptive language disability** may result in students' lack of understanding of class discussions or lectures, as well as specific directions. Teresa adds,
"I was so embarrassed several years ago when I missed some of the signs
of a receptive language disability in one of my students. While I normally
consider myself a patient person, I had experienced a really rough day and
overreacted when Blake, a boy in my Resource class, didn't follow my
directions about putting his materials away properly. In my upset, I started
to list for him the number of times recently that he had ignored me or not
listened when I had asked him to do something. As I went through the list,
I realized that Blake was demonstrating classic signs of a language problem.
His quivering face told me that he really wanted to please me! I felt terrible
for days."

Children such as Blake are often called lazy, and scolded by parents
and teachers alike for not listening. It is imperative to identify them early so
they do not become belligerent teenagers who respond to adult negations
by their own hostility, or experience lowered self-esteem because of constant
criticism.

Difficulties in understanding information usually result in problems
with cognitive integration, in which the neurological system relates incoming and outgoing information. For example, when Teresa directs Blake, "Put
your book up on the shelf; put your materials back in the learning center;
put your completed math assignment in the box behind my desk," she is giving a very complex message. Not only must Blake relate words such as "shelf"
and "learning center" to the objects or locations they represent, but he
must perform some action to demonstrate his understanding. If he has
problems interpreting the initial spoken directions, he will have problems
integrating each behavior into previous experiences, the very basis for cognition, or thinking. Amidst three directions are subconcepts that Teresa is taking for granted that Blake understands. Is his math assignment completed?
If he follows all other directions but does not understand that he cannot move
until his work is done, he will experience her disapproval. Does he understand *behind* the desk, versus *in front of* or *on* the desk? The latter problem
of spatial confusion is one often encountered by students with language problems.

Blake's teachers need to understand that he may have additional integration
problems when trying to associate objects or ideas commonly encountered
together, blocking relationships between concepts. Additionally, he may have
difficulties categorizing even common objects, such as dogs and cats as animals, or tables and chairs as furniture. Teachers should make immediate note
of any students demonstrating problems with association and/or classification since these abilities are critical for development of higher cognitive
processes.

Other students have problems expressing themselves verbally. While they
do not stutter or misarticulate sounds, they may have difficulty recalling

common vocabulary or arranging words correctly in sentences. When they speak in sentences, usually they avoid descriptive words such as adjectives and adverbs, or make grammatical errors such as using incorrect past tense (*taked, catched*) or plurals (*mouses, womans*). As teachers listen carefully, they will hear these students speak in incomplete sentences or favor certain general words that they use frequently instead of vocabulary to more precisely express their meaning.

"I found these word retrieval problems particularly evident in a high school student I tested a few years ago," commented Alex. "She was very attractively dressed and had a good deal of poise. Her teachers claimed she seemed unable to express her ideas in speaking or writing, having a paucity of vocabulary. When I visited with her in the classroom, initially there was no indication that she had any problem. I asked her if she had taken a summer vacation with her family. She responded that she had. They had gone 'far away, to the other side of the world.' When I asked her what she had done while she was on vacation, she responded that she had seen 'lots of old places.' She couldn't remember or name any of them! No wonder she was having problems in school. As we talked, I noticed she had certain pet phrases similar to 'the other side of the world' that she used whenever she couldn't recall specifics to discuss general meaning. Because she was so socially graced otherwise, she seemed to fit in well until you listened to her."

It is clear that students with problems expressing themselves verbally also will have difficulties in written expression, since so many additional skills

MY PORTFOLIO

Written after his visit to a football stadium, this student demonstrates problems expressing ideas. A corrected paragraph reads, "I learned a lot of things. I learned that the goals (they) are yellow (and) green. And I learned that they have sweats. And I learned that their lockers are wood. And I learned a lot of other things, but it would take me years." Comments such as "... but it would take me years," are global statements students often use when they do not have the ability to retrieve vocabulary or organize thoughts into cohesive sentences when expressing themselves. Reprinted with permission, Winston School, San Antonio.

are required. When Alex's student completes an essay about her summer vacation, she will write the generalities she discussed orally. In addition, she will have to recall how to use punctuation and spelling correctly, accurate grammar in her sentences, and organization of her ideas into cohesive paragraphs. The task may be overwhelming for her, far surpassing her capabilities.

Teachers may have more difficulty identifying students with language disorders at the secondary level, where greater class enrollments dictate a longer time period to know individuals. An informal writing assignment the first few days of school can provide a mechanism for more immediate identification. When a student writes essays with inadequate content or expression of ideas, teachers should discuss the paper directly with the student to determine if it is lack of writing skills or verbal skills that are at the core of the problem. Too often the more serious underlying verbal language problem is ignored while teachers concentrate on the more obvious writing problem.

## Visual Perception and Memory

"I'm glad to see visual and auditory perceptual problems included in the identification of disabilities checklist," observed Teresa. "Years ago, educators were so concerned when students reversed letters in their reading or writing or couldn't blend sounds into words. Then we moved on to different issues in reading and don't seem as much concerned about perception any more. However, the problem hasn't gone away and frequently I work with students who have undiagnosed perceptual problems. We're calling them *dyslexic* these days, but doing very little to remediate or compensate for some very real problems blocking their reading development."

visual perception—analyzing and giving meaning to visual information

vision—a measure of acuity, or how accurately a person takes in raw visual stimuli from the environment.

It is important for educators to distinguish between **visual perception** and **vision**. Vision is a measure of acuity, or how accurately a person takes in raw visual stimuli from the environment. Basically, it measures how well one's eyes work in comparison with others. Does this individual have the same clarity of focus and detail of objects at a distance of 20 feet that others do? Do near-point vision, muscular balance, and depth perception function accurately? Vision brings raw data to the brain, but does not analyze its meaning. The behaviors noted in Table 8–1 are indicators of vision problems in students.

On the other hand, visual perception involves analyzing and giving meaning to visual information. The millions of bits of raw data seen across the room comprise a person, a specific object, or the homework assignment written on the blackboard. While most people have no problem determining differences between large or distinctly different objects, some do have trouble distinguishing between similar shapes, such as the letters *i/l; c/o; m/n; n/h*. Clearly, this type of difficulty lessens word analysis skills since students are unable to determine which letter they are reading.

## Table 8–5
## Identification of Disabilities in Visual Perception and Memory

|  | Yes | No |
|---|---|---|
| 1. Problems distinguising between similar-appearing letters and numbers (e.g., *i/l; c/o; m/n; b/d; 3/8; 1/7*) (discrimination) |  |  |
| 2. Missequences letters in words (e.g., *broad/board; pre/per; scald/sclad*) |  |  |
| 3. Unable to relate the letter with the correct sound in studying phonics (sound-symbol association) |  |  |
| 4. Confused and distracted when completing work on a crowded page (figure-ground) |  |  |
| 5. Skips words or lines of print when reading (spatial) |  |  |
| 6. Misjudges amount of remaining space for writing letters or numbers on a line (spatial) |  |  |
| 7. Difficulty staying on line when writing (spatial) |  |  |
| 8. Problems reading and spelling non-phonetic words (memory) |  |  |
| 9. Difficulty copying from blackboard or overhead projector without looking frequently from blackboard or projector to paper (memory/spatial) |  |  |

(*Sources:* Adapted from Waldron, 1992a; Scruggs & Mastropieri, 1992)

visual-spatial perception—the ability to correctly perceive the spatial arrangement of objects or symbols such as letters and numbers.

Others have problems with visual-spatial perception, impacting their reading of letters such as *b/d, p/q, m/w,* or of words such as *was/saw, now/won,* and *no/on.* These difficulties also may cause a student to omit small words (*the, an, of*) and punctuation, or even skip complete lines of print in reading. When writing, students may misformulate letters or misjudge the amount of remaining space on a line, providing output that is extremely difficult for teachers to read. One of the most difficult tasks for students with visual-spatial problems to perform is the copying of information from a blackboard, an overhead projector, or even a textbook on their desk.

"This explains a problem Mark is having in my class," comments John. "I've noticed that he reads slowly, finishing assignments after others. I've stopped having him read aloud because he is so slow and halting that it's painful. He's a sophomore in high school and can't stay on a line when he does a writing assignment. His spelling is really poor, very phonetic. When he copies a homework assignment from the board or takes class notes from the overhead, I've noticed that he rarely gets everything written down, and even when he does it's not always accurate. I felt sorry for him a few weeks ago when

MY PORTFOLIO

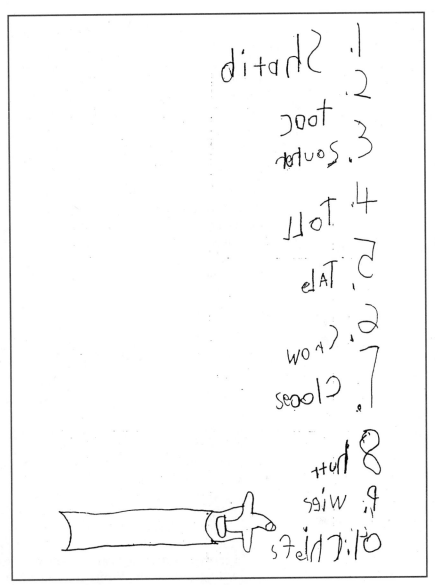

Visual-spatial problems such as this example of "mirror-writing" can slow student progress immensely. The actual words dictated by the teacher are as follows: (1) shouted; (2) took; (3) sooner; (4) told; (5) tale; (6) grow; (7) closes; (8) hurt; (9) wise; (10) chiefs. In addition are problems with auditory discrimination of sounds and letter reversals. Reprinted with permission, Winston School, San Antonio.

he copied the homework pages as *432 to 440,* when the assignment was for pages *423 to 440.* He lost quite a bit of credit because he didn't complete the entire assignment. Since then I've been giving assignments orally as well and checking what Mark writes down to be sure its correct."

John has noted an additional visual perceptual problem that strongly impairs reading: visual-sequencing difficulties. Mark missequenced number order, causing him to misunderstand the assignment. Many students with this problem also missequence letters in words, resulting in such perceptions as *board* for *broad* and *brefore* for *before*. As in the latter example, since many words do not make sense after missequencing occurs, reading comprehension is affected as much as word analysis. Students such as Mark read much more slowly than others as they experience these problems, since they are trying to analyze words properly amidst difficulties with visual discrimination and sequencing of letters.

Another area impacted strongly is visual memory. When a student misperceives a word originally, it is almost impossible to recall it correctly on the next reading assignment or spelling test. Students with visual discrimination or sequencing problems lack a great number of **sight words** that most students commit to memory easily because of frequency of occurrence. Even as a high school student, Mark's visual perceptual problems cause him to look back and forth between the blackboard or overhead projector and his desk as he spells words letter-by-letter that his peers committed to memory years ago. It is no wonder that he makes mistakes often.

**sight words**—words a reader commits to memory rather than having to sound them out each time they are encountered.

## Auditory Perception and Memory

As some students incorrectly analyze information they see, so do others incorrectly process what they hear. The previous discussion about differences between vision as an acuity process and visual perception as a contextual, analytical process mirror the differences between hearing and auditory perception.

**Hearing** is the process by which individuals take in millions of bits of raw auditory stimuli and convert them to sound. **Auditory perception** is the process by which sound gains meaning, such as a passing train or a telephone ringing. While few individuals have problems identifying a train, many have problems identifying differences between similar sounds or blending sounds into the meaningful units of words.

**hearing**—the process by which individuals take in raw auditory stimuli and convert them to sound.

**auditory perception**—the process by which sound gains meaning.

Students with difficulties in auditory discrimination have problems learning to read and spell. Many schools rely extensively on phonics as a basis for reading instruction. While phonics must be part of every student's reading development, it should not be the only method taught for word analysis. If students cannot perceive sound differences correctly, they require a more visual approach.

Students' spelling should be observed carefully for sound substitutions that may indicate auditory discrimination problems. When the teacher looks at the word, sound confusion may not be readily apparent. However, if the teacher says the word aloud the way the student has written it, the inaccuracy may be readily apparent, such as when the student writes *funicha* for *furniture* and *cul* for *call*.

## Table 8–6
## Identification of Disabilities in Auditory Perception and Memory

|  | Yes | No |
|---|---|---|
| 1. Problems perceiving differences between similar sounds (discrimination) |  |  |
| 2. Difficulty learning phonics (discrimination) |  |  |
| 3. Cannot blend letter sounds or syllables into words (blending) |  |  |
| 4. Does not pay attention to speaker when there is background noise in room (figure-ground) |  |  |
| 5. Difficulty following directions (memory/sequence) |  |  |
| 6. Does not say names of days, months, seasons in correct order (memory/sequence) |  |  |
| 7. Difficulty repeating story events or steps in a procedure in correct order (e.g., science procedures, steps in calculating math problems, chronology of history) (memory/sequence) |  |  |
| 8. Unable to recall most information presented in class lectures (memory) |  |  |

(*Sources:* Adapted from Klumb, 1992; Waldron, 1992a)

**sound-symbol association**—the ability to match the correct sound and letter.

Another perceptual difficulty is **sound-symbol association**. While the student does not have problems discriminating between sounds, he has difficulty matching the correct sound and letter. He tends to rely on visual memorization, learning phonics only through ongoing repetition and practice involving reading and writing more than listening. Usually the student's reading rate is slow as he tries to associate sound with symbol.

Other students have problems blending letter sounds or syllables into words, although the sounds themselves may be correct. "That's a really baffling problem," notes Maura. "In last year's third grade, Elda was my weakest reader. She had no difficulties discriminating letter sounds or applying them to word analysis. But constantly she became stuck on the individual sounds and just couldn't blend them into meaningful words. I felt so frustrated when she would say *r-u-n* by sounds and then blend them into *rat*, or *tr-ee* and say *track*. Her only method of word attack was to read the beginning sounds and guess from the initial letter."

**auditory sequencing**—recalling multiple units of information in the correct order.

Teachers are also frustrated by another auditory perception problem, most often when they give oral directions. Students with **auditory sequencing** problems have extreme difficulty recalling multiple units of information in the

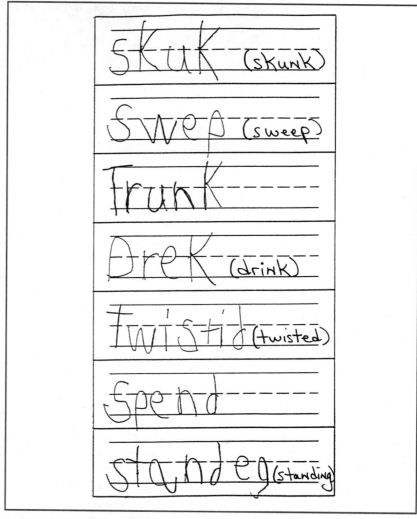

Auditory discrimination problems can lessen students' abilities to isolate specific sounds accurately. Reprinted with permission, Winston School, San Antonio.

correct order. As noted earlier, students with receptive language problems experience difficulty understanding and responding to oral directions, when the auditory difficulty is specific to sequencing, it is the order that tends to be confused.

Students with sequencing problems will also have difficulty recalling stories read to them, especially when the order of events is important. They tend to have problems remembering the names of days, months, and seasons in the correct order. The difficulty may be very pronounced in arithmetic because orally presented word problems require a careful resequencing of information after listening to the entire problem. The student may concentrate on ordering facts as he hears them instead of integrating them into the total solution. When secondary students attempt to order procedural steps correctly in science or recall the chronology of historical occurrences, they may experience difficulty. While the teachers may feel the student is not attending, in actuality the disability is preventing a correct response.

## Behavioral Disorders

Teachers often feel that behavioral problems are easy to detect, since they pose so many interruptions to the teaching day. This tends to be especially true for students demonstrating verbal or physical aggression or outbursts resulting in general disruptions. However, there are many behaviors that go unheeded by teachers because they are not readily visible. Table 8–7 includes a number of behaviors that may indicate students are experiencing problems. Ones such as withdrawal from peers, lack of involvement in schoolwork, as well as chronic unhappiness should receive as much concern as acting-out behaviors. Ongoing anxiety or extreme sensitivity to criticism should be noted as well. If teachers observe a student who newly associates with gang members or is at risk of substance abuse, they should respond before the situation worsens. Students who break school rules or are truant need intervention before negative behaviors become an extreme problem. The prereferral committee, including the student and parents, should convene as these problems become obvious to determine reasons for the behaviors and to plan intervention strategies.

"I can support a quick response to these behaviors," observes John Robinson. "Two years ago we didn't have any formal mechanisms such as a prereferral committee in place to support students if they were having problems. It was up to individual teachers to do something, if they were aware of what was happening and took the time.

"A few of us commented about Mindi, a junior, whose behavior had started to change. She was newly dating a boy who was always in trouble and had already been arrested for dealing drugs. We weren't sure how to handle this situation, but one of the teachers decided to talk to her and express concerns about the fact that Mindi's schoolwork was deteriorating and that she always seemed tired. Mindi became belligerent and told the teacher that it was none of her business! This was so unlike her previous behavior that the teacher decided to call Mindi's parents. They indicated that they hadn't noticed anything but that they would talk to Mindi.

"No one else intervened and by summer, Mindi was in the hospital recovering from a cocaine overdose during which she had actually experienced seizures. She's been in and out of rehabilitation since, but still hangs around with the same boy, is often truant, and her grades are terrible. Now

## Table 8–7
## Identification of Behavioral Disorders

| | Yes | No |
|---|---|---|
| 1. Withdraws from others | | |
| 2. Shy and nonassertive among peers | | |
| 3. Pervasive sense of unhappiness | | |
| 4. Cries easily | | |
| 5. Does not perform tasks requested by teacher | | |
| 6. Quick-tempered; responds easily with anger or frustration | | |
| 7. Destructive of own or others' property | | |
| 8. Verbally aggressive toward peers or teacher | | |
| 9. Physically aggressive toward peers or teacher | | |
| 10. Lacks motivation for school-related tasks | | |
| 11. Belongs to a gang | | |
| 12. Often truant | | |
| 13. Friends have negative moral and ethical values | | |
| 14. Substance abuse | | |
| 15. Does not show remorse for hurting others or breaking school rules | | |
| 16. Excessive "daydreaming" or absentmindedness | | |
| 17. Overly influenced by peers | | |
| 18. Highly nervous or anxious | | |
| 19. Unusual fears about people or situations | | |
| 20. Overly reactive to criticism | | |

(*Sources:* Adapted from Klumb, 1992)

her parents and teachers are really concerned, but it may be too late. If we had reacted more seriously to her early behaviors and convened a prereferral committee meeting, her teachers, counselor, and parents would have understood the depth of concern and reacted more strongly from the beginning. I really believe that if she had realized how negatively her behaviors were being perceived by significant adults in her life, she might have reconsidered the path she was taking."

"How do you decide when the behaviors on that checklist are problematic?" Elena asked. "Obviously, gang involvements, substance abuse, and destructive behaviors have to be handled quickly. Especially when dealing with teenagers, we find most students experience some of the other behaviors occasionally, such as lack of motivation, daydreaming, anxiety, and anger. When should we intervene?"

Educators should intervene when the behaviors begin to occur frequently instead of occasionally, or when they mark a distinctive change in the student's usual behavior. As John described Mindi, she had not been in difficulty before changing her peer group. When her negative behaviors were first noticed, her teachers should have met to discuss potential causes. If behaviors are beginning to have a negative impact on the student individually or on the classroom environment, educators must take note before events progress out-of-hand.

Sometimes students are in crisis temporarily, such as when their parents experience a divorce. During these changes at home, it is normal for students to be depressed and anxious, often withdrawing from peers or experiencing angry outbursts. Working with families to provide emotional supports for students during these difficult times helps ensure that behavioral changes will not be permanent. When changes are in response to negative life events, students should not be considered to have a behavioral disorder. However, they should receive help through the crisis so the problems do not become permanent.

## Motor Integration Disabilities

Table 8–8 includes a number of behaviors indicating problems with motor and integration skills that may affect schoolwork. Many teachers tend to overlook the importance of motor and integration proficiency as a basis for learning academics. Through involvement of fine and gross motor skills, laterality, or spatial and temporal competence, this experiential base is critical to a variety of school-related skills. While it is obvious that fine motor skills are required for appropriate handwriting, they also are essential for visual tracking of information on a page. The combination of fine and gross motor skills allows for balance and coordination.

Integration of time relationships not only results in improved understanding of the environment, but also of the intent of language. Academic areas ranging from literature comprehension to mathematics, science, and history rely on temporal clarity for meaning.

Teresa adds, "Most of us integrate time so easily that it's hard to realize the impact of a problem in this area until we observe it in students. They may not know the days of the week, months or seasons of the year in correct order. While usually they can tell you if it's morning or afternoon, their guess about the hour is often way off. They have difficulty comparing fixed time intervals, such as noon and midnight. Older students become embarrassed when they can't tell you the date or even the year, and they may lack a sense

## Table 8–8
## Identification of Motor and Integration Disabilities

| | Yes | No |
|---|---|---|
| 1. Problems distinguishing between left and right (laterality) | | |
| 2. Appears awkward or uncoordinated in body movements (coordination) | | |
| 3. Walks or runs with an awkward gait (balance/coordination) | | |
| 4. Accident-prone (balance/coordination) | | |
| 5. Difficulty holding pen, pencil, or crayon correctly (fine motor) | | |
| 6. Poor handwriting (fine motor) | | |
| 7. Difficulty using scissors (fine motor) | | |
| 8. Frequently drops things (fine motor) | | |
| 9. Tries to fit large objects into small spaces (spatial) | | |
| 10. Difficulty drawing human body with parts in correct position or in correct size relationship (body image) | | |
| 11. Problems understanding concepts of time, space, and geography (spatial-temporal) | | |
| 12. Difficulty telling time (temporal) | | |

(*Source:* Adapted from Mann, Suiter, & McClung, 1987)

of chronology for personal and historical events. While they may hear about concepts such as decades and centuries, they almost never really understand their significance. It's no wonder so often these students have poor judgment about how long it will take them to prepare for an exam, complete a homework assignment or a long-term project, since their sense of time is distorted. Frequently they are late, having misjudged preparation or travel time. When these behaviors carry over to the work environment they lower the student's dependability on the job."

Similarly, students must integrate space. **Spatial assimilation** allows students to write and compute properly, to manipulate the body and objects correctly in the surrounding environment, and to understand relationships among distances in mathematics, science, and geography. It is important to identify students experiencing difficulty in these areas so that compensatory skills can be taught as early as possible.

"I can certainly see the necessity for training at the secondary level," commented John. "As teens begin to drive, their spatial judgment is critical for

**spatial assimilation**—allows students to write and compute properly, to manipulate the body and objects correctly in the surrounding environment, and to understand relationships among distances in mathematics, science, and geography.

From an early age, motor skills have a strong impact on a student's ability to learn.

preventing accidents. When a student has poorly integrated spatial awareness, he tends to follow others too closely or to misjudge, especially in emergency situations. He gets lost easily. Coupled with the usual adolescent attitude
of invulnerability and a tendency to drive much too quickly, a student
with spatial problems may be dangerous to himself and everyone else."

## Attention Deficit Disorder

"What about Attention Deficit Hyperactivity Disorder? How do students with
this condition differ from students with behavioral problems?" asks Maura.
Attention Deficit Disorder, with or without hyperactivity, is an ongoing condition developed before the age of seven. Neurological in its basis, it is a grouping of behaviors which, when appearing together, directly affect the student's
performance in a number of areas. Instead of the student lacking in attention, as the name indicates, he pays attention to an overload of irrelevant stimuli at once, distracting him from the information upon which he should be
focusing. The student also tends to behave impulsively, rarely regarding consequences of his behavior. Table 8–9 lists additional characteristics which appear
in many students with Attention Deficit Disorder.

**Table 8–9**
**Identification of Attention Deficit Disorder**

| *Inattention* | Yes | No |
|---|---|---|
| 1. Often fails to pay attention to details or makes careless mistakes in schoolwork | | |
| 2. Often has difficulty sustaining attention in academic tasks or play activities | | |
| 3. Often does not seem to listen, even when addressed directly | | |
| 4. Often does not follow instructions correctly or fails to finish schoolwork (not a result of oppositional behavior or an inability to understand directions) | | |
| 5. Often has difficulty organizing school tasks or activities in general | | |
| 6. Often avoids tasks that require sustained mental effort, such as school assignments and homework | | |
| 7. Often loses things necessary to complete tasks or to participate in activities, such as assignments, books, papers, toys | | |
| 8. Often distracted easily by extraneous stimuli, such as movement, noises, and others present | | |
| 9. Often appears forgetful in daily activities, such as lessons and group work | | |

| *Hyperactivity-Impulsivity* | Yes | No |
|---|---|---|
| 1. Often fidgets with hands and feet or appears to squirm in seat | | |
| 2. Often leaves seat in class or in other situations where remaining seated is appropriate and expected | | |
| 3. Often demonstrates inappropriate, excessive movements, such as running and climbing; adolescents may demonstrate or express feelings of restlessness | | |
| 4. Often has difficulty playing or participating in leisure activities quietly | | |
| 5. Often seems driven to move or "on the go" | | |
| 6. Often talks incessantly | | |
| 7. Often blurts out answers prematurely, before questions are completed | | |
| 8. Often has difficulty awaiting own turn | | |
| 9. Often interrupts others when speaking or intrudes without asking | | |

*(Continued)*

**Table 8–9** *(Continued)*

> \*\*Attention Deficit Hyperactivity Disorder, Combined Type is present when at least six symptoms of inattention and at least six symptoms of hyperactivity-impulsivity have been present for at least six months.
> \*\*Attention Deficit Hyperactivity Disorder, Predominantly Inattentive Type is present when at least six symptoms of inattention have been present for at least six months.
> \*\*Attention Deficit Hyperactivity Disorder, Predominantly Hyperactive-Impulsive Type is present when at least six symptoms of hyperactivity-impulsivity have been present for at least six months.
> (*Source:* Adapted from the American Psychiatric Association, 1994).

The primary types of Attention Deficit Hyperactivity Disorder are included in the *Diagnostic and Statistical Manual of Mental Disorders, 4th Ed.* (DSM-4) (American Psychiatric Association, 1994). The first section of Table 8–9 lists the characteristics of students who demonstrate predominantly the inattentive type. Its diagnosis is dependent on six or more of these symptoms of inattention having been demonstrated for at least six months.

The second section of Table 8–9 lists the characteristics of the predominantly hyperactive-impulsive type. This diagnosis is appropriate if six or more of these symptoms have been demonstrated for at least six months.

Among children and adolescents, the most common type of Attention Deficit Hyperactivity Disorder combines these behaviors. It is diagnosed by the presence of six or more symptoms of inattention and six or more symptoms of hyperactivity-impulsivity, having persisted for at least six months.

Some of the symptoms should have been present before age seven. Behaviors should be present in two or more settings, such as at school and at home. There should also be clear evidence that their impact has significantly impaired student functioning in social, academic, or occupational settings (American Psychiatric Association, 1994).

When considering the characteristics on the list, clearly teachers are aware of the impact of these behaviors on the learning of individual students and on the class. A student who is distracted easily by auditory or visual stimuli, who wanders around the room, or behaves impulsively and without regard for consequences may frustrate even the most well-intended educators.

Teresa adds, "There are two major behaviors in this disorder that we tend to attribute to other causes: short attention span and disorganization. We just want the student to pay attention longer, forgetting that most often he'd like to focus more on his work if he were able. This concentration factor may require us to change his desk area to a less distractible corner of the room or to shorten his assignments. When we make these minor modifications, we're often surprised at how well the student performs.

"When disorganization forces students to forget or lose their homework, not to bring assigned materials, and to have poor study habits, often teachers and parents become angry, as if the student is doing it on purpose. When we require students to carry assignment sheets home and ask their parents to help them organize materials for the next day's classes, usually we're pleasantly surprised."

Teresa's conclusions are very important here. Students with Attention Deficit Hyperactivity Disorder are not demonstrating these behaviors on purpose. They want to be like everyone else, but their body has taken control and they need intervention to be successful. Once adults identify the disorder, they tend to be more understanding of the reasons for students' behaviors and can begin to provide supports instead of blame.

Parents and teachers alike should exercise caution in categorizing students as having Attention Deficit Hyperactivity Disorder. Many young children have short attention spans and difficulty concentrating. Part of their school acculturation is to reduce impulsivity, avoiding classroom interruptions. They need to learn a variety of behaviors, ranging from staying in their seats to listening to others as they speak. A student who has not yet mastered these skills simply may not have been exposed to them sufficiently.

Regardless of the area of disability, teachers should adapt instructional techniques and the classroom environment to meet students' varied learning and behavioral needs. They should discuss specific behaviors needing reinforcement and avoid using labels to describe children. Such labels encourage treatment of students as if they have a pre-existing condition for

When teachers positively redirect distracted students to their work, the learning environment is enjoyable for both.

which educators hold no responsibility or cure. When this attitude is prevalent, teachers tend to blame students for disabilities instead of helping them (Skrtic, 1991).

## INVOLVEMENT OF PROFESSIONALS

"I can see where identification of students with learning and behavioral differences is critical if we are going to help them," commented Maura. "Once we've noticed some of the behaviors on the checklist, to whom do we refer students?"

Maura's question poses an important concern, because educators can only help students if they refer them to appropriate professionals. Figure 8–1 includes a listing of specialists who may be helpful when a referral is indicated.

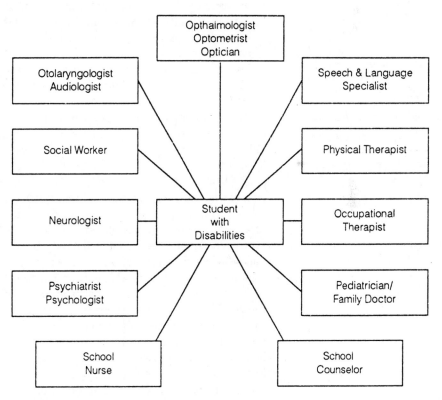

Figure 8–1    Specialists Involved in Student Referrals

family practice physicians—generalist doctors who deal with all aspects of medicine.

ophthalmologists—physicians concerned with eye diseases and conditions, as well as ongoing health of the eye.

optometrists—trained to deal with measurement and correction of visual disorders, not diseases; not a medical doctor.

opticians—concerned with correct eye function; trained to prescribe series of eye exercises to help improve areas such as muscular balance and coordination; not a medical doctor.

otologist—a physician who diagnoses and treats conditions and diseases of the auditory system.

otolaryngology—the study of ear, nose, and throat diseases.

audiologists—nonmedical specialists who test hearing acuity to ensure normal range accuracy.

Traditionally, **family practice physicians** have been viewed as generalists. However, increasingly they have been expected to possess specialist knowledge in areas such as developmental delays, and psychiatric and biochemical disorders (Lerner, 1993). Along with pediatricians, who specialize in child treatment, they are often the first professional to whom parents turn when they suspect a problem. Is the child developing normally? Are his balance and coordination adequate? Why does he refuse to go to sleep at night? Why is he talking at a much later age than his sister did? He seems to move around a great deal: Is he hyperactive?

When a vision problem is suspected, an eye specialist should be consulted. While there is often overlap among procedures used by the several types of eye specialists, parents and professionals should carefully review the needs of the child as they seek intervention. **Ophthalmologists** are physicians who are concerned with eye diseases and conditions, as well as the ongoing health of the eye. When adults are unsure of the nature of the vision problem, or if they note indicators of problems such as muscular imbalances or recurrent infections, they should take the child to the ophthalmologist for a complete exam.

**Optometrists** are not physicians and deal with the function of the eye instead of its diseases. They are involved in measurement and correction of visual disorders, usually through prescribing glasses or exercises to enhance eye use on a daily basis. **Opticians** serve a related function in examining for functional abnormalities. They may prescribe series of eye exercises to help improve areas such as muscular balance and coordination.

There are several specialists who deal with hearing problems. The **otologist** is a physician who diagnoses and treats conditions and diseases of the auditory system. A related medical specialty is **otolaryngology**, commonly called "ear, nose, and throat." Parents should consult this specialist if their child has recurrent infections and allergies, potentially causing hearing loss.

**Audiologists** are nonmedical specialists who test hearing acuity to ensure that the child's hearing is in the normal range. Using equipment such as an audiometer, they measure the ability to hear the loudness and pitch of sounds commonly encountered in the surrounding environment and importantly, in human speech. They are also able to test the ability to hear in situations where the level of background noise differs. This information is important for students who may be able to hear in a quiet environment, but experience problems with the addition of surrounding noise such as conversations in the classroom.

While nurses in many school districts provide vision and hearing screenings to indicate the need for more extensive testing, these exams should not be viewed as definitive since they may overlook some students with sensory losses. Even if the school has provided screening tests, teachers should rely more on their own observational abilities. If they note a child with the characteristics on the checklist, they should pursue indepth testing by a specialist to be sure that the problem is discovered.

**Speech and language specialists** diagnose and provide remediation for a variety of communication disorders. Speech assessment involves testing for abnormalities in areas such as sound production, articulation, and voice quality. Language appraisal includes consideration of communication abilities receptively and expressively. The specialist considers a breadth of areas, such as vocabulary, syntax, and use of grammatical rules, as well as the ability to understand and express concepts. Because of the frequency and potential impact of these disabilities, school districts employ speech and language specialists not only to assess students, but to provide direct remediation. While traditionally they have removed students from regular classes to attend small group therapy sessions, specialists are changing the way they deliver services, adapting to the inclusive classroom. Once students have been referred and deemed eligible for services, specialists have been working with them directly in the inclusive environment. Additionally, these specialists have become consultants for regular education teachers in providing speech and language-based activities to enhance student learning throughout the day.

When students demonstrate problems with motor and integration skills or behaviors indicative of Attention Deficit Disorder or a learning disability, parents may refer them to a **neurologist**. During the exam, the neurologist looks for the patient's response to sensory stimuli, level of performance of reflexive behaviors, and motor responses to perception and stimulation tasks. The physician tests for abnormalities in brain activity and may further examine body biochemistry and endocrinology. Often neurologists detect **"soft signs"** when students demonstrate a learning disability. Such signs may include delayed language development, lack of motor coordination, visual-motor problems, mild tremors, and hyperactivity. Parents and teachers should refer students for neurological assessments only when the information gained from the diagnosis will help them better understand or work remedially with the student. Often these exams are time-consuming and expensive and educators are not sure how to apply the results to academics. If the outcomes will be accompanied by recommendations for tangible activities that will improve student skills and performance, then a neurological exam should be considered.

When motor disabilities are impairing student mobility, input from a **physical therapist** may be helpful. Employed by many school districts, clinics, and hospitals, these professionals assess the motor abilities of the student and provide input for educators on appropriate body positioning, exercise for specific problem areas, and the correct use of adaptive equipment. Often they meet with the student several times weekly and provide direct therapy to enhance equilibrium, movement, spatial awareness and integration, limb facility and extension, as well as the reduction of any pain that may be

---

speech and language specialists—diagnose and provide remediation for a variety of communication disorders.

neurologists—specialists trained to diagnose problems with motor and integration skills or behaviors.

"soft signs"—observable indicators that neurological problems may be present.

physical therapists—professionals who assess the motor abilities of the student and provide input for educators on appropriate body positioning, exercise for specific problem areas, and the correct use of adaptive equipment.

present. They provide ongoing consultation with parents and teachers regarding follow-up exercises and physical activities to support student gains outside therapy sessions.

**occupational therapists—**specialists who works with the family to determine the behaviors the student must master to facilitate participation in daily life.

When the student needs support to be involved in family living activities, the school may contact an **occupational therapist**. This specialist works with the family to determine the behaviors the student must master to facilitate participation in family life. For young students, toileting and feeding issues may be important; for older students, mobility in adaptive equipment on the job may be considered. The therapist works with teachers on any problems they may be having in equipment or positioning that will allow the student to participate more fully in the classroom.

**psychiatrists—**medical specialists who examine the relationship between psychodynamic and organic factors, considering how the physiological aspects of an individual student may interface with psychological behaviors and experiences.

When emotional factors appear to be the cause of behaviors disruptive to the student or peers' learning, the school may refer the student for psychological or psychiatric services. As medical specialists, **psychiatrists** examine the relationship between psychodynamic and organic factors, considering how the physiological aspects of an individual student may interface with psychological behaviors and experiences. While referring a student to a psychiatrist should never be considered a decision to medicate before a diagnosis of the difficulty, these physicians do administer medications if they feel the cause of the problem is organic or the student will not be able to control behaviors otherwise (e.g., severe depression; psychosis). Psychiatrists provide ongoing therapy to the student and family to enhance their understanding of the causes of the problems and how they can work as a supportive unit.

**psychologists—**nonmedical specialists who work with students and their families to uncover the reasons for behaviors and ways to redirect student actions productively.

**school psychologists—**psychologists who perform primarily assessment functions, identifying learning and behavioral differences that may be contributing to school-related problems.

Similar to psychiatrists, **psychologists** work with students and their families to uncover the reasons for behaviors and ways to redirect student actions productively. As nonmedical specialists, they differ from psychiatrists in not prescribing medication and in emphasizing more immediate behavioral changes to allow students to better adapt to their environment. Many districts employ **school psychologists**, who perform more assessment than therapeutic functions, identifying learning and behavioral differences that may be contributing to school-related problems. Traditionally, they have been part of the formal assessment process for special education, determining students' eligibility for services. After assessment, often they have consulted with the classroom teacher on ways of restructuring the classroom environment to support student needs. It is likely that the functions of the school psychologist will shift as school districts move towards an inclusive model. Their diagnostic and therapeutic skills will become supports much earlier in the process, as school psychologists become members of prereferral teams and consult with educators, parents, and students. Instead of spending much of their time writing assessment reports, they may be intervening to provide direct counseling for students experiencing difficulties.

**school counselor—**works directly with individuals and groups of students, as well as serving as a liaison with families; primary function is to guide towards responsible decision-making.

Also facing a redefinition of traditional roles is the **school counselor**. In many schools, currently counselors spend the majority of their time fulfilling logistical roles, particularly at the secondary level where they may be respon-

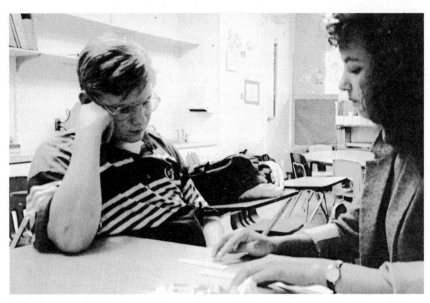

Even during academic work, teachers can counsel students informally.

sible for scheduling academic classes for the entire school. With the inclusive emphasis on early identification and intervention, their counseling skills may be better served in working directly with individual and groups of students, as well as serving as a liaison with families.

school nurse—nurse in a school setting who is responsible for administration of medications, catheterization, and consulting with teachers, parents, and community social services on health issues pertaining to the students.

The role of the school nurse has grown in responsibility as increasing numbers of students with health-related problems have become members of regular education classrooms. Ranging from administration of medications to catheterization, the nurse consults with teachers and parents on health issues, which may affect school performance. As issues of liability have become a greater concern, often the nurse is responsible for assuring that physician's directives are followed accurately. With secondary students, the nurse supports public information programs, such as prevention of infectious diseases and substance abuse.

social workers—professionals who are involved with families needing school and community support in areas such as counseling, social services, and health care.

Social workers are involved with families needing school and community support in areas such as counseling, social services, and health care. Most often they are contacted initially by the special education teacher, counselor, or nurse who has observed child or family problems that extend beyond the educational parameters of the school (e.g., evidence of child abuse; concerns about immunizations; needs of students living in foster homes). Social workers can be members of prereferral teams, assuring coordination between school and community services when increased family supports will positively affect the progress of the student.

## CLINICAL TEACHING

"I feel more secure now in being aware of specific behaviors indicating the need for a referral and knowing the best professionals to involve," commented Maura. "How can we use this information most successfully in teaching our students?"

It is important for educators to note the entire purpose of assessment is to understand the learning or behavior problem, and to use information gathered in developing an intervention plan to help the student. The steps in clinical teaching are listed in Table 8–10.

The initial step of observing student behaviors that may indicate a problem has been discussed extensively in this chapter. The critical nature of identification of academic and behavioral difficulties must be underscored, since educators cannot address an unidentified problem. The second step is to perform the assessment to obtain useful data for planning.

Once this data has been obtained, the planning stage begins. Educators must use assessment results to design individual objectives and teaching strategies to encourage positive academic and behavioral changes. Student needs should indicate which teaching techniques and materials are used. Teachers must avoid returning to traditional techniques that have not worked previously with this student.

"We had a real problem in that area at Jackson," laughed Mort. "We had an incredible overload of phonics books, ordered by two teachers who subsequently left the school. They must have been phonics zealots! At first we thought it was funny, but I found that no matter which classroom I visited, all the teachers were teaching reading exclusively by phonics.

---

### Table 8–10
### Steps in Clinical Teaching

1. Student academic performance or behavior indicates that a problem may be present.
2. Diagnostic team assesses the student for learning and behavior problems.
3. Educators use assessment data to design objectives and a teaching plan unique to the student.
4. The teacher implements the plan through ongoing daily instruction.
5. Educators evaluate the plan's success by observing positive changes in academics and behavior.
6. The plan is modified wherever necessary.
7. Educators continually evaluate student performance and adjust the curriculum and teaching methods.

It didn't seem to matter if a student's testing had indicated a visual learning style or a poor record of learning auditorily. We used phonics. It was only at a faculty meeting when Teresa reviewed the assessment results of a number of our students and asked teachers how they were using differentiated instruction that they looked a little sheepish. Since then we've expanded our basal readers, ordered a few series of linguistic readers, lots of multisensory materials, as well as video and audio tapes. We've begun to look at the needs of the individual child. Phonics is still taught daily as a basis for reading. Yet our expanded, eclectic program now has something for everyone. When assessment results indicate a child who learns differently from the norm, our program is so broad that we already have something in place."

eclectic—based on integration of a variety of approaches.

Mort's teachers are now at the stage of implementing the student's plan through ongoing daily instruction. The role of the regular educator is most critical at this point. The teacher must be familiar with input from the collaborative and assessment teams in order to instruct the student successfully. A thorough knowledge of remedial and compensatory techniques is also imperative, along with an understanding of specific behavioral intervention techniques. If the teacher does not understand the appropriate ways to instruct this student there is little chance of success.

"I guess even I'm starting to come around a bit," noted John. "I've really been opposed to teaching students with special needs, primarily because I haven't been sure that I can do it. I've learned that good teaching is good teaching, and if I'm open to adapting what I normally do, all of my students learn."

John has noted the prime ingredient of inclusion: good teaching for all students. When students with special needs attend regular classrooms, it is not necessary to eliminate teaching methods that have worked successfully with students previously. It only becomes necessary to adapt these methods. Teachers who have taught well before inclusion will have the least difficulty adapting to inclusion.

The next step in clinical teaching is evaluative. Teachers can best note growth through observation. Is the student reading more fluently? Is he able to perform addition, or calculus, problems more successfully? Does he now participate in group work without disturbing others? Does he submit assignments on time? Is he more easily able to make friends? While formal exams provide checkpoints to measure competencies, often they do not offer a broad indicator of student growth. Areas such as behavioral interventions are best evaluated by observed changes in personal and group functioning.

When the plan is not successful, it is important to modify wherever necessary. Educators must consider *why* the interventions have not worked. Were assignments at too high a difficulty level? Expectations too great? Is the student embarrassed at reading as part of a group? Was the plan reliant on organizational skills beyond the student's capability?

Additional modifications are then made to alter classroom teaching and behavior management interventions until they are successful. The teacher may decide to have the student read aloud to only one peer initially, or shorten assignments for more successful completion. If areas such as organization are problematic, the teacher may provide an assignment sheet to be signed daily by both the student and parent.

Clinical teaching necessitates the continual evaluation of student success and the adjustment of curriculum and teaching methods to ensure learning. If the regular educator finds that modifications have not been effective, it will be necessary to meet with the collaborative team to gain their input. Ongoing evaluation is the most important step in clinical teaching because it insures a fluid, flexible, and student-centered process.

# TASK ANALYSIS

skill-based—directed toward developing skills at the appropriate level for completing of school tasks.

content-based—directed toward developing content knowledge at the appropriate level for integrating curricular information.

The process of moving into effective clinical teaching is based on an understanding both of the curriculum and the student. Many states adopt curricula for their students from a series of formulated objectives of content that should be taught in a specified grade. These objectives may be skill-based (*The student will be able to divide words into syllables with 90 percent accuracy*) or content-based (*The student will be able to list the causes of the Civil War*). Teachers then set about to teach the skill or content area to students in fulfillment of curricular requirements.

Many schools have established their own curricular committees made up of teachers who devise series of teaching strategies and activities to help colleagues with successful implementation. Yet, even with their own school as the focus, often educators overlook the differentiated learning and behavioral styles of students with special needs. A careful task analysis relating curricular and learner needs can insure success.

## Task Analysis of the Curriculum

A curriculum is a holistic compilation of information and skills that are intended to be taught as a unit. Yet, often students are not prepared to learn all aspects of the unit, lacking proficiency and information in certain required areas. Therefore, teachers cannot assume that a state or locally adopted curriculum is appropriate for everyone.

"I'm concerned about our high school teachers," reflects Elena. "So many of them haven't had any special education training. Where do they begin when they review their annual curriculum?"

The first step involves analyzing the specific aspect of the curriculum under consideration. What does it require the student to learn? What prerequisite skills should the student have in order to be successful? What will be the order of information presented? How will successful completion of the task be indicated?

Lerner (1993) suggests four steps for analyzing skills required in the curriculum. The first involves the design of the **behavioral objective** describing the task to be learned. Examples include:

behavioral objective—a description of the task to be learned including specific behaviors demonstrating its acquisition.

1. Students will be able to use syllables in dividing words they read and spell.
2. Students will identify and correct sentence fragments in their writing.

Once they have defined the task, they should list skills the student must develop to meet objectives. It is important to list these skills sequentially so teachers can observe most easily those skills students have mastered. Examples include:

1. *To divide words into syllables correctly, students need to be able to apply phonics appropriately, to divide compound words, prefixes, and suffixes; to identify sound units within words.*
2. *To identify sentence fragments, students must be able to note that a complete sentence has at least a subject and verb. They need to identify phrases and clauses that express incomplete thoughts because either the subject or verb is missing. They must proofread each sentence they write to ensure they have included a subject and verb and have written a complete thought.*

The next step in analyzing the curriculum involves informal assessment of students to determine which skills they can already perform. It makes no sense pedagogically to have students repeat information they already know. On the other hand, often students cannot progress toward mastery of curricular objectives until they receive remedial teaching of basic skills required for task mastery.

**Table 8–11**
**Steps for Analyzing Curricular Skill Requirements**

Educators should:

1. clearly describe the learning task through behavioral objectives
2. list and sequence all the skills the student must demonstrate to meet objectives
3. assess informally to determine which skills the student has already mastered
4. in sequence, begin teaching the next skill in the hierarchy.

(*Source:* Adapted from Lerner, 1993)

The final step in analyzing curricular skills involves direct instruction. The teacher must begin teaching the next skill in the hierarchy. No skills required for task mastery should be omitted. While educators may believe that students who lack skills will improve automatically through exposure during class discussions, instead students tend to fall further behind. Content areas such as mathematics and foreign language are particularly hierarchical in skill requirements, making it especially difficult to progress without a firm grasp of lower-level skills. Teaching of differentiated skills may require homogeneous grouping, so that all students in the class can progress from their initial level of understanding to mastery of curricular information.

## Task Analysis of the Learner

As discussed, an analysis of curricular tasks indicates what information and skills need to be taught. The purpose of analyzing the learner is to determine specific abilities the student must have in order to accomplish the task. These abilities relate to functions such as the way the student understands and processes information, physical strengths and limitations, required classroom behaviors, and motivation demonstrated toward learning the task. The teacher's goal is to assure from the beginning of the curricular unit that individual students are capable of learning the information, avoiding potential student and teacher frustration.

Table 8–12 includes a list of issues teachers should review when analyzing specific skills required in the curriculum. Initial concerns require care-

### Table 8–12
### Analyzing the Learner's Ability to Complete Curricular Tasks

Educators should ask:

1. What learning abilities does the student need to perform the task?

| | |
|---|---|
| Expressive language _____ | Memory _____ |
| Receptive language _____ | Problem-solving _____ |
| Reading _____ | Physical mobility _____ |
| Writing _____ | Long attention span _____ |
| Vision _____ | Hearing _____ |

2. Is the student required to shift from one of these abilities to another? If so, which ones? _____
3. What skill level is required for success? _____
4. What personal behaviors are required for the student to successfully complete the task? _____

ful examination of learners' language, cognitive processing, physical, and academic abilities. Can students understand the information during class discussions? Are they able to express their own ideas regarding the content? Have students integrated and recalled past experiences in order to improve understanding of current information? Are students reading and writing sufficiently well enough to be successful in teacher assignments? Are there sensory limitations in vision or hearing that may hinder student involvement and understanding? Do students have mobility limitations that will keep them from participating actively?

Once teachers have examined learning skills and disability areas presented by students, they should match them with skills required for success in curricular subareas. For example, a student with a visual impairment will not be able to read and respond to a short story assignment unless modifications such as an audiotape or braille copy are provided. A student with limited cognitive skills will not be able to respond easily to arithmetic word problems requiring several levels of operations unless the task is simplified.

Educators should establish a skill level for acceptable performance. If a teacher requires perfection, students with disabilities may not be able to succeed in that classroom. However, as is more commonly the norm, if teachers are flexible in their expectations, all students will experience a modicum of success.

Students' personal behaviors also strongly affect their task performance. Are they motivated? Do they attend to task? Are abilities in concentration and attention strong enough to support task completion? Can students participate in group discussions and decision-making? Are social skills acceptable to peers in group assignments?

## Integrating Curricular Tasks with Learner Characteristics

This step is the most important in performing successful task analyses. Teachers must blend their awareness of the skills sequence in a content area with an understanding of students' capabilities to perform those skills. Sometimes there is no common ground and a teacher realizes that a particular student is not going to be able to master a skill at that point in time. Yet, the teacher can set eventual skill accomplishment as a long-term goal.

"I can understand that," responds Maura. "Last year I had a student who was barely reading at a kindergarten level, just identifying a few consonants and vowels. Most of the rest of the class was moving on toward syllabication skills. Assessment results indicated that the student had a severe auditory processing disability and was going to require a good deal of specialist assistance to even complete first-grade skills by the end of the year. Considering the tasks required in reading for readiness to study syllabication, we realized that there was no way this student would accomplish the class goal.

"We worked it out to everyone's benefit. Teresa came to our room and included him in a small group of learners who needed additional teaching and remediation across beginning reading skills. She provided lots of reinforcement for all of them. His skills and everyone else's increased substantially. I certainly haven't given up on the goal of all of the students gaining fluency through syllabication skills. I've just had to delay it for awhile."

Usually knowledge of the curriculum and student abilities results in a modification of the task rather than omission. If Maura's student had been reading one grade level higher, possessing skills in phonics and sight word recognition, she could have introduced him to compound words, prefixes and suffixes as whole units. While the student would have spent part of his day learning and practicing remedial skills, he would have benefitted from initial teaching with the more advanced group. Then, as basic information was integrated, he could have moved on at a later time towards the achievement level of his peers.

Specificity is the key for successful integration of task requirements with learner capabilities. Noting the sequence of steps and developmental skills required and combining them with knowledge of student functioning levels provides a basis for making appropriate decisions about how to best teach the student.

## SUMMARY

Chapter 8 dealt extensively with identification of specific types of disabilities. Table 8–1 provided a comprehensive overview of behaviors indicating the need for referrals for vision and hearing examinations by professionals. Identification and remediation of these problems usually result in improved school performance. Many times students are not aware of sensory difficulties because of their personal adjustment to seeing and hearing in a particular manner. Yet when modifications are made their performance may improve dramatically. Parents and educators should never ignore a complaint about a physical problem such as a child not being able to see the blackboard or hear the teacher.

Visual impairments such as muscular imbalances can result in reading disabilities because students are unable to track a line of print or sequence letters correctly. Strabismus syndrome requires early surgery to prevent blindness in the less dominant eye. Teachers should be aware that an eye should never turn inward or outward, even if the student is fatigued.

Hearing losses can be easily confused with characteristics of other disabilities. The student may be judged as a slow learner because of difficulties dealing with abstractions. He may seem to not pay attention or ask for repetition of directions from classmates. In others, hearing losses may be the cumulative result of a series of middle ear infections in early childhood, resulting in difficulty learning phonics. At times hearing losses are indicated by speech problems, as the student repeats sounds exactly as he hears them.

Speech disorders are often marked by sound distortions and substitutions. Conditions such as stuttering or unusual voice quality may bring undue attention to the speaker. More obvious than other hidden disabilities, the student may become quiet, especially during adolescence, to avoid embarrassment. Early intervention by a language therapist may be very helpful in training appropriate patterns and overcoming the problems. Therapists often can work directly in the classroom as well as provide teachers with information on how they can assist the child in overcoming the problem.

More encompassing than speech, language is the basis of communication. Disorders may involve areas such as problems in word retrieval and meaning, sentence syntax, concept formation, and language comprehension. Verbal receptive disabilities impair students' abilities to understand class lectures and discussions, as well as teacher directions. Expressive problems impact their recall and use of vocabulary and syntax in sentences. These students have difficulty explaining ideas, usually demonstrating a paucity of adjectives and adverbs, as well as a tendency to use short phrases instead of sentences.

Logically, when students have difficulty understanding spoken language, they have problems understanding what they read. Similarly verbal expressive problems are also demonstrated in written expressive difficulties. Students tend to have language input and output problems in both verbal and written language. When the additional symbolic requirements of reading and writing are considered in addition to those of verbal language, the added difficulties become apparent.

Other students may have problems in visual perception, or the interpretation of information seen. Some students confuse similar-appearing letters, while others missequence letter order. Some have difficulty tracking a line of print, while others have problems copying correctly from a blackboard or overhead projector. Visual perception problems clearly affect the student's memory. When the visual input is incorrect, the student recalls information as he has seen it. In this way, word recall and analysis skills are strongly impacted.

Similarly, some students experience auditory perceptual problems, or difficulty understanding correctly information that they hear. They may be unable to discriminate between similar sounds. Or their problem may be in blending sounds or syllables into words. Both of these problems negatively impact a student's use of phonics in beginning reading and result in both reading and spelling problems. They may missequence information they hear, such as chronological events in a story or the months of the year. These misperceptions of auditory information result in faulty memories of information presented in lectures and class discussions.

Teachers are all too aware of many of the symptoms of behavioral problems, especially those indicated by aggressive or destructive behaviors. Many other students have "quiet" problems that may go unnoticed because they are nonintrusive. These students may withdraw from peers or be unmotivated to complete schoolwork. They may be highly anxious or self-critical. Those who are overly influenced by peers should be of particular concern, since they tend to join gangs and experiment with drugs and alcohol.

Besides the obviously important reaction to gang involvement, truancy, and substance abuse, educators should intervene when less apparent behaviors mark a distinctive change in the student's usual behavior. If students are going through a temporary family crisis, such as parental divorce or loss of job, teachers and parents should work together to stabilize the environment so that student responses do not escalate into behavioral problems.

Motor skills are basic to the development of academics. They include fine and gross motor skills, important to appropriate interpretation of developmental experiences. This understanding supports language use and comprehension. Laterality and spatial integration are important not only to body posturing but to understanding left and right, a skill critical to reading and writing. Spatial assimilation allows students to write and compute, to move the body in the environment, and to understand distance relationships in science, mathematics, and geography.

Integration of time also supports understanding of language and its application to literature, mathematics, science and history. Students with temporal difficulties tend to have problems across content areas in associating and applying information to their daily experiences. They may also have problems judging the amount of time it takes to complete assignments, especially those requiring continual preparation.

Lastly, Attention Deficit Hyperactivity Disorder (ADHD) was considered. A neurological disorder, ADHD includes a series of behaviors that direct the student to focus on irrelevant stimuli instead of the primary learning task. He may also demonstrate a shortened attention span, impulsivity, low frustration tolerance, and visual or auditory distractibility. The student tends to be disorganized, resulting in lost materials and assignments as well as poor planning skills.

While students may demonstrate ADHD behaviors without having a disability, they normally have lowered academic and social performance because of the interference with school-related demands. It is important to note that ADHD is not an emotional disorder, but a syndrome of behaviors over which the student has little control.

After the discussion of identification of disabilities, Chapter 8 included consideration of appropriate professionals for referral once symptoms are noted. Ranging across specialties, the purpose of referral is to assess the presence of the disability as well as means of helping the student through direct intervention. Ranging from audiologists to ophthalmologists, and psychiatrists to psychologists, it is imperative that educators work collaboratively with other professionals for support in overcoming or compensating for the problem.

Additional discussion included clinical teaching, involving steps that begin with observation and assessment of student academic and behavioral performance and rely on the use of assessment data to design a teaching plan unique to the student. The teacher implements the plan through daily instruction, followed by evaluation of its effectiveness and modification wherever necessary. Continual evaluation and teaching adjustments follow as the student progresses in academic and behavioral changes.

Finally, Chapter 8 included discussion of the process of successfully implementing task analysis in order to successfully teach students with disabilities. The process involves three steps: analysis of skills students must demonstrate to meet curricular objectives, analysis of skills possessed by the learner, and integration of curricular tasks with learner characteristics.

This sequence allows educators to realistically appraise curricular requirements for all students with a degree of skill specificity not normally considered. Additionally, while teachers may tend to classify students by those who can and cannot complete the task, this analysis process encourages them to look at each child as a unique individual with certain skills and limitations. The final stage of meshing the student and the curriculum encourages teachers to consider flexible ways of including students with disabilities in an educational process from which they may previously have been excluded. Once expectations increase, often performance improves as well.

## CASE STUDY: *Elementary*

Marcus is a third-grade student who is reading significantly below grade level. His teacher has noted that he demonstrates the following types of problems:

- missequences letter order in spelling and number order in computations;

- asks peers about directions she has just given orally;

- has poor recall of vocabulary he has heard;

- has difficulty with phonics, especially blending sounds together;

- has problems with reading comprehension;

- reads with head close to the paper, yet tends to skip lines of print;

- is easily distracted by visual stimuli; and

- is a poor listener during class discussions.

---

1. Refer to Tables 8–1 through 8–9. From the listed characteristics, what are some potential problem areas Marcus's teacher might suspect?

2. To which professionals should his teacher refer him for follow-up assessment?

3. Which of the behaviors he demonstrates may be having the greatest impact on his reading performance?

4. How can his teachers work together to provide for his needs in the regular classroom so he receives reading assistance and does not fall dramatically behind?

**CASE STUDY:** *Secondary*

As the result of a serious car accident with her friends last year, Rose has suffered a severe head trauma. Physicians indicate a resultant loss of short-term memory for rote tasks and a difficulty associating and classifying information into concepts. She cannot deal with abstractions without experiential learning. She has most difficulty learning abstract concepts in history, science, and mathematics. She does not understand inferential material in readings.

While everyone has been kind and supportive, Rose considers herself "stupid" since the accident, and refuses to attempt any schoolwork she feels may be too difficult. As her teacher, you find it increasingly important to use a task analysis procedure to teach her successfully.

1. Based on your content area, select one of the following topics. List and sequence all the skills necessary to understand the concepts:

   Mathematics: Estimation
   Science: Photosynthesis
   History: The growth of slavery before the Civil War
   Foreign Language: Verb conjugations in present, past, and future tenses
   English: Recognizing and avoiding comma splices (run-on sentences) in writing assignments

2. List ways you can teach this content to Rose, employing methods that are concrete instead of abstract.

3. How will you improve her esteem during these activities so she regains confidence in her ability to perform well in school?

**9**

# MODELS FOR GROUPING AND INSTRUCTION

"I'm most concerned about what actually goes on in the classroom during inclusion," commented John. "While we've talked a great deal about identifying disabilities and analyzing both the learner and assignment for a match, I need more specifics about how we teachers can help students succeed in the regular class."

Teaching and learning in the classroom are the core of effective inclusion. Despite good intentions and the indepth planning by teams of educators, the factors that students and teachers bring to the setting determine degrees of success.

# STUDENT FACTORS

From their review of research, Scruggs and Mastropieri (1992) suggest eight general areas in which students should perform acceptably to be successful in the regular education classroom. Listed in Table 9–1, the level of performance of these factors impacts the ease with which students are accepted by teachers and peers, as well as personal outcomes as students work toward goals.

## Attention

Specific characteristics of Attention Deficit Hyperactivity Disorder were enumerated in Chapter 8. These behaviors can be categorized as indicating deficient attention span, visual or auditory distractibility, impulsivity, disorganization, and/or excessive movement. Attention to task has been described as the most critical behavioral variable in learning (Hewett, 1968).

"So true," comments John. "Every educator has felt the frustration of trying to teach a student who isn't reading the material or following the discussion, but instead seems compelled to look around the room. Sometimes I just want to hold the student's head where it should be, but then I know that even then I couldn't control eye movements that would be darting everywhere!"

John's upset is obvious to all teachers. It is clear that students with longer attention spans and fewer responses to distractible stimuli will learn more information quickly in the mainstream environment.

**Table 9–1**
**Success in the Inclusive Classroom—Student Factors**

Student factors include:

- ability to attend to task
- short- and long-term memory and ability to use memory strategies
- intellectual abilities
- expressive and receptive language skills in verbal and written areas
- academic skill levels
- study and organization skills
- social and behavioral adeptness
- degree of motivation

(*Source:* Adapted from Scruggs & Mastropieri, 1992)

# Memory

Students with good memory for previously encountered vocabulary and concepts are strong candidates for success in inclusive environments. Since much learning is based on recall of previous experiences and the ability to assimilate new input, strong short-term and long-term memory skills facilitate the process tremendously. Many students with disabilities suffer from poor memory, hindering their retention and integration of information across a broad spectrum, including academic and social skills. If students do not recall information that teachers assume has been learned, they may be missing the basic skills to support learning new concepts.

# Learning Differences

When students perform poorly in memory tasks, often it is because they lack basic ability in associating and classifying experiences into meaningful concepts. Students with learning disabilities, cognitive delays, and behavioral disorders often have core problems integrating information from their academic and social environments (Scruggs & Mastropieri, 1992). The more extreme the intellectual delay, clearly the more impactful will be outcomes on student performance, especially in academic areas.

# Language Skills

Student abilities to understand and use spoken language underscore their abilities in reading and writing. When a student experiences confusion during class discussions, not recalling specific vocabulary or misinterpreting the syntax of information, outcomes will be affected in learning the information correctly. When information is in print, its difficulty is compounded by demands for student word analysis and recognition of the symbolic code used in writing. Students with problems in listening comprehension often experience problems in reading comprehension.

Similarly, some students have difficulty expressing themselves verbally, through disabilities in word retrieval, sentence syntax, or organization of ideas. Clearly they experience even more difficulties when they attempt to write their ideas for class assignments. They are expected to use grammar, punctuation and spelling correctly while selecting appropriate vocabulary and organizing a series of ideas. The additional variables result in more difficulty in writing, even beyond those in verbal expression.

"That's really interesting," reflects John. "Especially at the secondary level, teachers tend to rely on reading and lecture as primary teaching methods, the two areas in which most students have the greatest difficulty. I can see where the degree of anticipated student success in the inclusive classroom hinges primarily on the student's ability to understand and use verbal and written language correctly."

## Academic Skill Levels

Another important prerequisite for success is achievement of basic skill levels in reading, writing, spelling, and arithmetic. Everyone experiences frustration when students are placed in a third-grade or tenth-grade class without being able to complete assignments. The student feels less able than peers and the teacher struggles to provide training in skills critical to task performance. Students cannot learn algebra without being able to perform basic arithmetic functions. They cannot conjugate verbs in a foreign language if their verbal skills in their dominant language are underdeveloped. The closer the skill levels of students with disabilities approximate those of peers, the more likely the success of the inclusive placement.

## Study and Organization Skills

While educators often focus most on in-class performance factors, there are planning skills that students must perform independently to support school outcomes. Students who allow themselves adequate time to prepare for exams and homework assignments and who bring necessary materials to school possess the bases for success. They should know which notes to record during discussions and how to prepare for a variety of types of exams. These skills are particularly necessary in secondary school, where teachers with differing demands require diverse responsibilities. The more of these competencies students possess, the more likely they will perform capably in the inclusive classroom.

## Social and Behavioral Factors

Despite the school's emphasis on academic areas, students concentrate most heavily on social outcomes. Every student wants to be appreciated and accepted by peers. To gain approval, students need to act appropriately around others, dress within acceptable limits, and demonstrate ease of participation within peer culture.

Teachers are concerned with students' behaviors as they affect the classroom environment. Overt demonstrations of aggression or withdrawal disrupt the behavioral balance of the class. Teachers and peers both object to extreme degrees of attention being focused on students who do not practice self-control. Students with acceptable behaviors derived from an understanding of personal limits are admitted quickly to full class participation.

Student motivation is a critical variable for success.

Those with more serious behavioral infractions tend to alienate others from including them.

## Motivation

Degree of motivation is the final criterion affecting success in the inclusive classroom. When a student wants to learn, teachers and peers try harder to provide successful experiences. Too often students with disabilities lack motivation because of past failures. They are afraid to try and fail again. As a result, they may not complete assignments or choose to participate fully in group assignments. It becomes extremely important for teachers to provide stimulating lessons or incentives to reinitiate their active participation in the learning process.

# TEACHER FACTORS

The relationship between educators and their students is tremendously interactive. Teachers bring as many critical variables to the teaching-learning situation as do their students. Listed in Table 9–2, it is the combination of these factors in any classroom that determines the level of successful interactions.

## Attitude

Student attitudes and teacher attitudes are intricately related in every classroom. Student motivation to try in difficult classroom situations is affected greatly by teacher outlook. Does the instructor want to teach students with learning and behavioral differences? Usually the answer is a resounding "NO!" because of the additional work diversity brings to the classroom. Yet, confronted with the knowledge that personal efforts will afford the student an opportunity to be successful in a normalized environment, many teachers are willing to try despite reservations.

In the world of the classroom, the teacher is always the central character. If the teacher's attitude is positive, upbeat, and carries with it the expectation that all students will be successful, the feeling is contagious and encourages even the most cautious student to take risks.

"I saw this just recently in my own room," noted Maura. "Kristi had been diagnosed as having delayed cognitive skills years ago, and her parents and teachers had taken this to mean that she would never learn very much,

---

**Table 9–2**
**Success in the Inclusive Classroom—Teacher Factors**

Teacher factors include:

- attitude toward teaching all students
- motivation to make inclusion work
- willingness to collaborate with other professionals
- flexibility in adapting methods and curricula to meet individual learner needs
- ability to handle demands of the classroom environment (Doyle, 1980):
  - multidimensionality
  - simultaneity
  - immediacy
  - unpredictability
  - history

especially in academic areas. Previously, she had been in a full-time self-contained unit except for art, music, and physical education. When Mort wanted to place her in my room all day this year, I really hesitated. I love kids, but I just didn't want to overextend myself by having a student who takes my time away from others.

"I really would have failed with Kristi, except for Teresa's help. She comes into my room every morning for 90 minutes during reading groups. At first I thought she would just be working one-on-one with Kristi. But Teresa asked if I had any other low readers, even those not qualified for special education services. I certainly do! Now she teaches skills such as phonics and sight words to a group of seven every day. Students that I rarely was able to teach directly are receiving her full attention and are moving along very rapidly. And Kristi is blossoming! She's getting attention, learning to read, and doesn't stand out as different."

"What do you do the rest of the day when Teresa isn't in the room?" asks Alex.

"She leaves me assignments and materials for Kristi, ones I've also started to use with other students performing at lower academic levels. When I realized her need for support in math, I spoke to the collaborative committee and I now have a teaching assistant who comes to my room three days a week to conduct small group activities with Kristi and four other students. Teresa provides the assistant with the materials and direction, and I supervise the instruction. It's been working really well. Ironically, I'm now grateful for Kristi's being in my room because she's brought with her so much additional assistance that otherwise would not have been available."

## Motivation

Maura has become motivated to make inclusion work because she has seen how successful it can be. When teachers develop this positive attitude, they share it with students and together develop a sense of camaraderie. When Maura tries harder, so will Kristi and her peers. Kristi's parents will become more supportive of the school and teacher as they feel her happiness, acceptance, and improvement in skills.

## Willingness to Collaborate

"There's a critical factor here that can't be overlooked," comments Mort. "Maura is willing to collaborate with other educators to make inclusion work. I realized that we were taking a tremendous risk in placing Kristi in her class. Kristi's academic skills are extremely low and she has never before fully participated in regular education. Maura was hesitant, as were Kristi's parents, about how successful we would be.

"Despite Maura's great teaching skills, she's only one person and did not have extensive time to focus on an individual child to the detriment of other students. Her willingness to meet with the collaborative committee of other teachers and to design an intervention plan was the first step. But then she welcomed Teresa into her room, consulted with her weekly, and was not threatened by suggestions. She has taken the lead in supervising the teaching assistant as they develop a math program. She was willing to realize that she needed help and to go to others for support."

Without collaboration, inclusion cannot work. Ironically, many teachers in traditional settings complain that working all day by themselves in student-centered environments deprives them of the intellectual stimulation they need as individuals. Interacting and problem-solving with other teachers provides them with new ideas as well as personal support. Willingness to collaborate with others is one of the most important underpinnings of successful teaching in modern times.

## Knowledge of Curricular Adaptations and Teaching Modifications

As teachers engage in the collaborative process, they bring many strengths from a variety of experiences and backgrounds. As a regular educator Maura understands her curriculum and the essential elements that she must teach annually. She is aware of techniques to instruct the larger group and activities to reinforce their learning.

Teresa brings different strengths as a special educator. Likely not as involved in broad-based curricular demands, she is trained in selecting those areas of the curriculum that students with special needs can learn more readily. She knows specialized teaching techniques and how to highlight important information and provide more practice for those who need extensive reinforcement.

As will be discussed, when teachers formulate a team they share their curricular and methodological expertise to reach all students.

## Managing the Demands of the Classroom Environment

Whether or not students with disabilities enter the classroom, teachers are bombarded daily with a series of demands. Noted by Doyle (1980), classroom settings are directed by a series of factors that strongly impact student-teacher interactions. To maximize instructional effectiveness, teachers must learn to manage this combination of attributes.

**Multidimensionality** describes the coexistence of many tasks and events occurring simultaneously in the same classroom. Students arrive with dif-

multidimensionality—the coexistence of many tasks and events occurring at the same time in the same classroom.

ferent levels of basic skills and motivation. Daily and semester schedules must be met, shortages of materials require sharing, and supplies and records need organization (Waldron, 1992b). The teacher's ability to anticipate problem areas, such as unavailable equipment or student outbursts, determines the success of the lesson despite the addition of the unexpected.

simultaneity—the teacher's ability to direct and monitor a number of ongoing variables at any one time.

**Simultaneity** involves the teacher's ability to direct and monitor a number of ongoing variables at any one time. Are the students in the skills group working or talking? What additional input does the research group require to complete its task? Is Michael getting ready to fight with Marcos? Why is Katie reading a novel? How can Jason's attention be redirected to the text? Teachers must be able to attend to a multitude of simultaneous variables through skills in "overlapping," or multi-processing of events (Kounin, 1977).

immediacy—the occurrence of classroom demands that require quick responses, not always allowing for full reflection.

**Immediacy** describes the teacher's frequent feeling that "Nothing ever happens slowly in my classroom." Classroom demands occur rapidly, rarely allowing time for teacher reflection. Seldom permitting the luxury of considering the most appropriate reaction, teachers are expected to respond almost reflexively, but always correctly. Most demands are in response to questions, or offering praise and reprimands. However, at times students can "drop a bombshell" in the midst of the classroom environment.

"I can attest to that," responds John. "I was having a very hectic preholiday Friday, when my students and I were both anticipating a break. We were in the midst of a group assignment I had tried to make particularly motivational in order to keep students on task during a distracting day. One of my students was quietly uninvolved and I went over to his desk to redirect him. He responded that he was having difficulty concentrating, and without further explanation, this normally quiet young man confided that he was concerned that his girlfriend might be pregnant!

"I knew I was the first person in whom he had confided and I needed to make a really well-considered response and to suggest some things he might do. At the same time, those other factors of multidimensionality and simultaneity you described were well underway. I had two students lined up behind me to ask questions, we were supposed to be returning to large-group discussion, and there was an argument escalating into a fight between two highly aggressive students. What to do?" (See Case Study: Secondary at the end of the chapter for additional discussion.)

unpredictability—occurring unexpectedly.

John's dilemma describes another variable well-known to seasoned teachers: **unpredictability**. Despite the best of plans and most well-run of classrooms, situations occur that demand immediate attention. Which event should the teacher handle first? What can wait? As more students with disabilities enter classrooms already unpredictable by nature, teachers need a sense of self-confidence in their own abilities to handle a variety of situations.

publicness—being on display; having one's behaviors judged by others.

Doyle (1980) adds **publicness** to important interactive factors. The teacher is "on display" to make fair, appropriate responses and decisions, despite the existence of other classroom attributes such as immediacy and unpredictability. In areas such as teaching quality and behavior management procedures, educators are observed, and often criticized, by students and teacher colleagues.

**history**—the interactive patterns that develop as the year progresses.

The last environmental factor, **history**, describes the interactive patterns that develop as the year progresses. Are students and faculty adversarial in their interactions, or is there a sense of mutual respect? Has the class developed a cohesive bonding, where students help each other work toward common goals, both educational and personal? From the first session, all classroom participants develop roles that are mutually impactful on the teaching-learning progress of the year.

# INSTRUCTIONAL MODELS

**instructional models**—styles of teaching based on student learning styles, the demands of the content, and teacher preference.

There are a number of **instructional models** that teachers may find successful in their classroom. Model selection is based on student learning styles, the demands of the content, and teacher preference. When a regular and special educator are co-teaching, they can modify these models to meet their individual strengths (e.g., one may prefer teaching content in a direct instruction format while the other works with reinforcement activities for learners with special needs).

# THE DIRECT INSTRUCTION MODEL

**direct instruction model**—teaching style in which the teacher reviews previously learned material, states objectives for the lesson, presents new material, provides guided practice with feedback, provides independent practice with feedback, and reviews all concepts before beginning any new material; most effective in teaching skills that can be broken up into discrete segments.

Studies on effective teaching have supported the usefulness of the **direct instruction model**. Rosenshine and Stevens (1986) list six steps to guide teachers in working with students. Included in Table 9–3, these stages provide a framework for instructing students towards mastery learning.

Direct instruction is most effective in teaching skills that can be broken up into discrete segments (Gunter, Estes, & Schwab, 1990). Many students with disabilities benefit from the guided practice as they integrate new information. As indicated by Scruggs and Mastropieri (1992), explicit teaching requires less reliance on students to transfer learning independently between settings. Many students with language processing problems have difficulty with **discovery learning**, or requirements to assess what is to be learned and how to learn it. They perform far better with guided and independent practice activities until they have mastered skills enough to move on to the next level.

**Table 9–3**
**The Direct Instruction Model**

Teachers should:

1. review previously learned material
2. state objectives for the lesson
3. present new material
4. provide guided practice with feedback
5. provide independent practice with feedback
6. review all concepts before beginning any new material

(*Source:* Adapted from Gunter, Estes, & Schwab, 1990)

discovery learning—understanding through integrating varied experiences, arriving at new concepts gradually as a result of independently understanding relationships among ideas.

"I'm a little unclear about how to use this model in my classroom," comments John. "When is it appropriate? How do I keep the students involved and interested?"

Because much of the direct instruction model relies on rote practice, educators can use it most effectively when emphasizing skill building. John will find it very useful when teaching a lesson on written grammar, while

Direct instruction enhances student learning through teacher explanation and modeling.

he would use a different model to conduct a class discussion on a short story. Similarly, in teaching phonics and sight words in beginning reading, as well as in math, foreign language, and science laboratory procedures, the guided reinforcement inherent in this model is highly effective.

## Review

In beginning to teach new information through direct instruction, the teacher needs to review supportive information to be sure the student is ready to learn the next concept. If John is going to teach a lesson on avoiding sentence fragments in written composition, he would begin by reviewing the previous lesson on identifying subjects and verbs in sentences. He would check homework accuracy, being sure that students had mastered the information necessary to support the lesson of the day. Before introducing new concepts, he would reteach any information on which students had demonstrated difficulty. Review provides the opportunity for students to refocus on the content while assuring the teacher that they have mastered prerequisite information.

If instructors are beginning a new skill, they should administer a pretest to the class. Gifted students who indicate information mastery should move on to more advanced areas, not being required to sit through instruction on information they already know. Students who do not have prerequisite skills should practice content basic to the new area before beginning advanced instruction.

## Statement of Objectives

Many times teachers have important objectives in mind, but do not share them with students. Teaching and learning are intricately interwoven processes, requiring that the instructor and the learner both are aware of desired outcomes. Sharing objectives with the learner assures that there is a mutual understanding of the meaning of successful performance.

John might note to his students that his goal is that every sentence they write impart a complete thought, based on using a subject and verb properly. Then the class might discuss the importance of this objective to their ability to communicate their ideas accurately. If students feel the objective will be of benefit to them directly, often they are more motivated to complete the assignment.

## Presentation of New Material

Clearly of most concern to teachers, this element involves the actual teaching of new information. The steps for impactful teaching are listed by

Gunter, Estes, and Schwab (1990), and included in Table 9–4. While they can be used in preparation for teaching individual lessons, they are best considered before beginning a new unit of content study.

Chapter 8 included discussion of beginning the lesson with a thorough task analysis of the content as well as the learner's needs. Too much information or too high a level of difficulty confuses the learner. Thorough consideration of curricular demands and learning styles allows for better consideration of individual differences.

The teacher should organize material into main points and subareas, emphasizing primary information, then questioning students in its relationship to their past experiences. When there are a number of skills involved, the teacher should divide them into segments and teach them in sequence. A student should not progress to the next higher concept until demonstrating mastery of more basic concepts. If the class is divided in its ability to progress, the teacher might form **skill groups** for intensive reinforcement of prerequisite information.

**skill groups**—a number of students collected together for intensive reinforcement of prerequisite information.

As the teacher begins instruction, she should provide background information about the theme to be covered, as well as motivation for new content. For example, John might provide the class a series of sentence fragments that are humorous because of the lack of clarity of their meaning. Students would then be able to understand that their writing might be similarly misunderstood without improved syntax.

Teachers should carefully emphasize those ideas critical to the unit or lesson, limiting their number. Teachers should combine a series of teaching methods, ranging from discussions and questions, to use of technology,

---

**Table 9–4**
**Steps in Teaching New Information to Students**

Teachers should:

1. perform a task analysis, comparing academic content requirements with learner abilities
2. organize material from general to specific
3. divide skills into basic segments and present them in sequence
4. provide background information as motivation for new content
5. select main points or steps, limiting their number
6. provide examples to support main ideas
7. continuously question students to measure their understanding
8. summarize main ideas and use them as a starting point for future lessons

(*Source:* Adapted from Gunter, Estes, & Schwab, 1990)

demonstrations, and experiential learning. Since lectures often result in passive, apathetic students, teachers should have students performing motivational activities wherever possible to support both comprehension and memory.

## Guided Practice with Feedback

John's students will not learn to write well without frequent practice. It is important that this practice be supervised, or guided, by a teacher reflecting on how well objectives are being met. As lessons and units progress, teachers need to provide thoughtful questions to gauge how well students are understanding the information.

During this step, the teacher should look for confusion about the task, without becoming upset with students who are not integrating the information or who have not understood directions. Teachers should immediately correct any student errors they observe so students do not continue to reinforce incorrect information. If there are students who require far more practice than others, teachers should include small-group instruction, programmed learning materials, additional individualized materials, and computer-assisted instruction (Gunter, Estes, & Schwab, 1990).

## Independent Practice with Feedback

Once students have understood the concepts in the lesson, teachers should allow adequate time to practice the information for long-term comprehension and memory. Students can perform reinforcement activities individually or in small groups, while the teacher circulates around the classroom, monitoring student efforts. It is important to check student work consistently during this independent period so students do not reinforce errors through practice. Continuous assessment is particularly important if the students are completing worksheets, since there are many opportunities for students to incorporate errors. Teachers should review several initial worksheet problems as part of the guided practice step so students can view the correct process before they begin working on their own.

As the teacher oversees student work during independent practice, she should stop at desks of students who seem to be unclear about the information or performing their work with hesitation. If she determines a student has not clearly understood the concept, the **teachable moment** is usually the immediate one. She should review the information with an individual or small group of students who are experiencing any difficulty. They should then return to the guided practice stage, where the teacher provides reinforcement activities for the steps where the student encountered difficulty. Once students

teachable moment—an immediate opportunity to explain a concept.

MY PORTFOLIO

$3 \times 8 = 40$
✗$3 \times 5 = 15$
✗$3 \times 10 = 30$
✗$3 \times 3 = 9$
✗$3 \times 6 = 18$
✗$3 \times 1 = 3$
✗$3 \times 4 = 12$
$3 \times 7 = 38$
✗$3 \times 2 = 6$
$3 \times 9 = 43$

✗$3 \times 8 = 24$
✗$3 \times 5 = 15$
✗$3 \times 10 = 30$
✗$3 \times 3 = 9$
$3 \times 6 = 15$
$3 \times 1 = 4$
✗$3 \times 4 = 12$
✗$3 \times 7 = 21$
✗$3 \times 2 = 6$
✗$3 \times 9 = 27$

Student independent practice affords teachers the opportunity to observe areas for future skill-building. Reprinted with permission, Winston School, San Antonio.

demonstrate that they have thoroughly integrated the information, they should return to independent practice.

As a follow-up step, students should complete additional independent activities for homework. It is important that the teacher note a student comfort level with the concepts before assigning independent practice to be done at home. Students tend to become frustrated when they are asked to practice new information that is unclear to them. Often they ask others, such as parents and peers to help them, and they may not be practicing the information in the way the teacher intended. Teachers should allow students to begin homework completion before they leave class, ensuring that all students are prepared to do the homework independently. Teachers should never assign homework that includes new information that has not been studied and practiced in class.

## Review with Feedback

Skill review begins with checking homework daily before proceeding to the next concept. If students are insecure in their skill knowledge, it is important to review the information and provide more practice. If teachers ignore homework review, students may not feel their independent efforts are important and may perform carelessly or try to get by without doing homework at all.

John may require students to write several paragraphs on an assigned topic, reminding them to check their written work for sentence fragments. When checking the assignment the next day, he might have students exchange papers with peers, proofreading each other's assignments after discussing the grammatical errors they are seeking. Peer review allows for concept reinforcement in an applied manner, as well as providing immediacy of response to student efforts.

Often teachers set aside their own personal needs during evenings and weekends to grade student homework. Understandably this process necessitates a several-day delay in returning assignments. To their dismay, often teachers find that students have forgotten the homework information in the interim. For teachers and students both, it is far better to review the information immediately, allowing the teaching-learning process to progress.

In addition to homework review, students benefit from weekly and monthly review of critical skills information. In unit teaching, review may involve relating central ideas as the unit progresses and then as it ends, allowing students to understand relationships among concepts.

## CLASSROOM DISCUSSION MODEL

classroom discussion model—
teaching-training structure in
which discussion stimulates
consideration of multiple
answers to the same question
and may lead to additional considerations not in the initial
questions; the purpose is to consider a wealth of responses and
expand one's original ideas
through contemplating ideas
offered by others.

The direct instruction model is most effective for teaching content that can be divided into a sequence of skills, with critical emphasis on review and practice of information that needs to be committed to memory. However, a **classroom discussion model** may be most appropriate when subject matter is complex, requiring analysis for interpretation instead of rote recall of discrete skills.

While direct instruction relies on correctness of a limited number of responses, discussion stimulates consideration of multiple answers to the same question. Opposing views may be equally acceptable when supported by data or the use of logic. Ideas discussed may lead to additional considerations not in the initial questions. The purpose is not to find the precise response, but to consider a wealth of responses and expand one's original ideas through contemplating ideas offered by others.

The discussion model provides stronger support for student recall of content, since it requires students to clarify and better understand information covered in class. This process is better for long-term retention of important vocabulary and concepts.

The steps in the classroom discussion model are listed in Table 9–5 and are discussed here.

## Teacher Preparation

The multitude of demands affecting the classroom at any given moment requires teacher attention to be in many places. Often it is impossible for teachers to maintain the concentration required to design varied questions because their attention is directed toward a student need or behavioral problem. It is critical for teachers to read material carefully before presenting the lesson and to consider questions in advance so discussions will be productive.

## Preparing Questions

Teachers should design questions purposefully before beginning the lesson. **Questioning** is one of the most important skills in good teaching, allowing teachers to discern knowledge students already possess as well as directing them toward the development of new ideas. Teachers should avoid overreliance on factual questions instead, asking higher-level questions to prompt fuller student comprehension and application of information.

Table 9–6 distinguishes between categories of questions and their characteristics. **Convergent questions** are directed toward factual, "right or wrong" responses, usually with only one correct answer. In contrast, **divergent questions** are more open-ended, permitting multiple answers, generating

**questioning**—prompting student comprehension and application of information by asking for responses and directing students toward the development of new ideas.

**convergent questions**—factual, "right or wrong" responses, usually with only one correct answer; encourage little classroom interaction.

**divergent questions**—open-ended responses, permitting multiple answers, generating discussion, and encouraging creativity and critical thinking.

---

**Table 9–5**
**The Classroom Discussion Model**

Teachers should:

1. read the material thoroughly and design thoughtful questions
2. cluster and sequence the questions before the discussion
3. introduce new or difficult vocabulary in reading selections
4. have students read the material and design their own questions
5. conduct the discussion in a facilitative manner
6. with students, review the discussion points and questions they found particularly significant

(*Source:* The Great Books Foundation, in Gunter, Estes, & Schwab, 1990).

### Table 9–6
### Categories of Questions

| Convergent | Divergent |
| --- | --- |
| • require specific "right or wrong" responses | • multiple answers anticipated |
| • encourage factual, concrete answers | • encourage creative, critical thinking |
| • only one answer considered correct | • open-ended, allowing contemplation |
| • encourage little classroom interaction | • encourage broad classroom interaction |

(*Source:* Adapted from Frazee & Rudnitski, 1994)

discussion, and encouraging creativity and critical thinking (Frazee & Rudnitski, 1994).

Consideration of ideas of others relies on teacher willingness to ask a variety of types of questions, not only those emphasizing factual recall. If there is only one correct response to content information, such as that measured by objective tests, then the discussion model may not be appropriate. However, when factual questions serve a supportive function as a basis for divergent considerations, they can encourage inferential and evaluative thinking.

Ironically, many educators use convergent questions, they prefer the teaching-learning environment resulting from divergent questions. The classroom tends to be more exciting and supportive of student involvement when responses to questions require exploration instead of memorization.

Table 9–7 contains a listing of types of convergent and divergent questions. Convergent questions typically require lower-level thinking skills, while divergent progress to higher-level processes (Frazee & Rudnitski, 1994).

"I think it's important not to be too stereotypic in our considerations of these questions," reflects Maura. "Knowledge of specific facts may be lowest on the mental processing scale because it doesn't require creative use of information. But my third-graders will really be in trouble if they don't master phonics or basic math. Secondary school teachers rely on us to give them a factual basis so they can perform higher operations."

"It's true in my area too," notes John. "If students can't write a complete sentence or incorporate the elements of a good paragraph, they'll never reach their creative writing potential. I'm sure Hemingway mastered all the basics of written composition before he wrote *The Old Man and the Sea*."

Maura and John are making a critical point. All types of questions serve important purposes when supporting needs of the learner and the content

### Table 9–7
### Types of Questions

| Convergent | Divergent |
|---|---|
| • Ask students for their **knowledge** of specific facts (What? Who? When? Where?)<br>• Require students to provide a **summary** of information, based on conclusions from facts<br>• Present situations for the **application** of information to solve problems or add new ideas | • Encourage **analysis** to infer beyond stated information<br>• Allow for **synthesis** of information and development of creative insights<br>• Present situations for student **evaluation** as the basis for forming their own ideas and opinions |

(*Source:* Adapted from Frazee & Rudnitski, 1994)

area. Every high school teacher continues to require student command of some factual information basic to the content area, whether algebraic formulae or conjugations of verbs in Spanish. Students will not be able to conquer advanced information without a strong factual basis. However, teachers must be alert to the tendency to ask factual questions exclusively. Once students have mastered content basic to their subject area, they should be asked questions that allow them to infer beyond the basics and apply the information creatively.

The convergent questions listed in Table 9–7 trace the progression of questions from the lowest level of specific factual recall to the highest level of evaluation based on previous experiences. Second-level questions require a summary of information, deriving concepts based on the facts. Questions such as *What is the main idea?* or *What would a good title be for this story?* typify teachers' efforts to have students expand factual information into more global summaries.

Higher-level convergent questions may require students to apply information from reading or discussions into solving problems. Basing their solutions on facts presented, students learn they can take stated information and use it in real-life situations. *How much money would John save by taking out a three-year loan instead of a five-year loan on a new car? How does the principle of "supply and demand" affect the price of items you buy for holiday presents?*

Noted in Table 9–7, divergent thinking requires analysis of situations or problems encouraging students to infer information not stated specifically in their reading. In all content areas these encourage comparison and contrast between new concepts as well as between those in the student's previous experience. *What would people's concerns have been when they first heard that the stock market had crashed? How does poetry differ from prose?*

As noted in Table 9–7, questions requiring synthesis encourage student originality and creativity in responses. Given a thorough understanding of the material read, students are asked to consider new alternatives, to go beyond the usual summaries of existing information. Gifted students particularly enjoy these questions, since they allow them to synthesize information and to predict outcomes they may not have considered previously. *How can we lessen the incidence of crime among youth in our society? What will have to occur in research and in public sentiment in order to develop gene therapy?*

The most sophisticated questions occur at the evaluative level, where students are asked to formulate their own opinions, based on interpretation of given information. Do points discussed fit into their moral and ethical structure? What personal choices would they make based on the information they read? This level of questioning is extremely important in allowing students to integrate material into their personal view of the world. Since many young people actually develop their ideas as they express them verbally, they need to consider questions that initiate ongoing reflection. *How do you feel about abortion? Do you believe the girl was right or wrong when she stole to feed her sick brother?*

***Methods for Optimal Questioning.***  Teachers need to consider not only what information they are seeking when they ask questions, but also appropriate ways to ask questions during class. The previous discussion of six distinct types of questions indicates teachers must choose the type of questions that best meets their goals in teaching.

Cognitive levels of students dictate that certain types are more appropriate than others for individual students. Due to age or developmental delays, some students may not be able to deal with abstract concepts. Initially, teachers should direct factual and summary questions to these students to ensure they acquire basic knowledge as well as to include them in class discussions. However, teachers should work constantly to move students to the next higher level of questioning. This is best done through practice in small groups or individually before the student is called upon in the large group.

"It's not really that difficult, either," responds Maura. "At the beginning of this year it was apparent during our math exercises that Kendra had learned to memorize facts in addition, subtraction, and multiplication. She even became the expert when others couldn't remember facts immediately. We all said she was really good in math. But I noticed that she has almost no ability to apply the usage of her factual knowledge to problem solving. On our trip to the county fair she couldn't even count her change correctly when she bought her lunch! Since then we've been doing math problem solving every day, based on real-life situations. She's even more excited now that she's beginning to see a use for all this factual knowledge.

"I've expanded these exercises to the entire class so I'm sure I reach everyone. And after I found that application questions were too easy for my gifted students, I started giving them problems at higher levels. They're comparing which math operations to use most expediently, deciding which information is critical to answering the questions, and finally using estimation correctly to predict the correctness of their outcomes. It took that one experience with Kendra to convince me that I was too limited in my questioning. Since then, everyone has benefitted."

***Phrasing Questions Clearly.*** To obtain thoughtful answers, teachers should pose thoughtful questions. When teaching to the large group, they should ask one question at a time, encouraging all students to feel they are responsible for the answer. For higher-level, divergent questions, teachers might indicate to all students that they should be "question-ready," by a comment such as, "This is a really important question because it forces us to draw major conclusions from the story we've been reading," or "Listen up! This is a tough question, but I know you can answer it."

After asking the question of the large group and pausing for their reflection, the teacher should then say the name of the student she wishes to have respond. Subsequently, she should repeat the question one more time, assuring that the student has been attending and is focused on the issue at hand.

Traditionally, some teachers have felt that they could force all students to attend more closely or embarrass those who are inattentive by calling the student's name after the question has been asked. This method penalizes everyone. Even the best students daydream at times, and no student ever appreciates ridicule in front of the group by having to acknowledge not having heard the question. Student attitude toward teachers may become more wary and less positive if there is a sense that questions are being used to discipline instead of to support learning.

***Allowing Response Time.*** There is a tendency in many classrooms for teachers to ask the question and call on the first students raising their hands. Generally teachers know the type of answers they are looking for when they generate questions. However, students cannot anticipate a teacher's specific question, and once the question has been asked, they need time to consider their response.

Several problems occur when teachers do not pause long enough after inquiries. They discourage more reflective students from even considering answers because they have already accepted another student's response. Students learn that the teacher wants an immediate answer and likely will not call on them because they have not raised their hand. As a result, a few students may answer questions all the time and carry the class discussion, encouraging passive learning by their peers.

Allowing students five seconds or longer to consider responses encourages increased student participation and more complex, considered responses. Teachers also learn that once a student who rarely participates answers a question correctly, the likelihood of that student asking and answering additional questions increases. The purpose of questioning is to direct students in

Allowing students the time they need to respond and practice can result in their successful learning experiences.

considering information in a new manner, not for the teacher to receive quick responses. Pausing and allowing students to think supports teaching-learning goals.

***Inclusive Questioning.*** In the inclusive classroom, all students participate in discussions to their capability level. This involvement requires teacher awareness of each student's cognitive ability in order to pose questions at the appropriate level. When selecting a particular student to answer a question, the teacher should believe that the student has the ability to offer a considered response. To avoid embarrassment and anxiety, teachers should never call on a student whom they do not believe can answer the question.

Some of the best responses are obtained during small-group work. Teachers can provide a series of questions aimed at student capability levels and content to be reinforced, whether homogeneously or heterogeneously grouped. In this less-threatening atmosphere, often students are more willing to take risks by proffering an answer of which they are unsure of.

Whether conducting large or small groups, teachers should beware of the tendency to call upon higher achievers exclusively. While the class may move more quickly, there will be many students who will not have integrated the information and who require more extensive discussions.

## Clustering and Sequencing Questions

As part of the stages of the classroom discussion model listed in Table 9–5, teachers should cluster and sequence questions carefully before the discussion begins (Gunter, Estes, & Schwab, 1990). Depending on the amount of review required, they may want to ask a few factual questions first, ensuring student recall of information necessary to the day's lesson.

To cluster questions for student integration of major concepts, teachers need to design encompassing questions covering an entire issue or concern, followed by more specific questions that will combine to allow students to answer the broader issue.

Often these clusters begin by focusing on a broad question at the application level of difficulty. There should be more than one acceptable answer to this basic question in order to promote heated discussion. *Why was Gatsby great? Why did some slaves choose to stay on plantations even after their freedom had been granted? What impact is the drug trade having on the daily lives of the lower and middle class in Colombia?*

Because these questions are extremely broad and encompassing by nature, they are an indicator of the teacher's goal for student awareness from the discussion. The teacher should not ask a general question of the class and await answers, but should provide a series of more specific queries that lead students to a response to the broader question. *How does Fitzgerald describe*

*Gatsby's clothes, lifestyle, mannerisms? What did the slaves have to lose once they left the plantations? Are significant numbers of lower and middle class Colombians using drugs themselves or are the drugs primarily for export?* These are just a few of the follow-up questions in the cluster that will cause students to reach their conclusions about the central question.

It is important to note that although these follow-up questions may be specific, they are not necessarily lower-level or factual. In themselves, they require summary and application of information previously studied. Importantly, teachers can lead students through the hierarchy of questions listed in Table 9–7 to accomplish their goal of having students integrate and evaluate a broader issue.

## Student Preparation

As noted in Table 9–5, the next step in the Classroom Discussion Model involves the students reading the material. Before having them read independently, teachers should introduce any vocabulary words with which the students may be unfamiliar. These words usually fall in two categories: words that are difficult to decode or analyze and ones whose meaning will be unclear because of lack of previous experience with the concept. For example, if Maura's students have not yet mastered word analysis through use of syllabication, a word such as *concentration* or *interesting* may be difficult for them to decode, although likely they would know the meaning once they read the word. On the other hand, while they might be able to decode the words *prod* and *bicker*, they would have difficulty defining their meaning. At the secondary level, content words requiring comprehension of specific processes (e.g., *coagulation* in a science experiment or *simile* in reading about poetry) may require both decoding and explanation before students can attain full meaning from the selection.

The teacher should direct students to formulate several questions as they read the material. Initially, students may tend to create only factual questions because they are easier to ask and answer. However, teachers should instruct students to ask interesting questions that go beyond stated facts. They can model for students questions that are more interpretive and applied, motivating more thorough consideration of content. Students will also be encouraged when they learn they will have the opportunity to ask these questions of their peers.

## Conducting the Discussion

It is important to provide a framework for discussions, where students are aware both of the process and structure for their participation. Students should be instructed that they will each have the opportunity to present their ideas but they must never speak until recognized by the teacher or group leader. Teachers should emphasize the importance of listening to each other without interruption.

During the discussion, teachers should ask a variety of the types of questions noted, wait an adequate amount of time for student responses, then call on several students for their answers. Allowing a number of students to respond to the same question provides a basis for additional discussion and makes students realize there may be other opinions than their own that are equally acceptable. This awareness is particularly important with students whose conceptual processes are egocentric, causing them to believe that their belief in an opinion justifies its correctness, even without factual substantiation. If others offer alternate views and support them well, the student gains an appreciation of the need for more indepth background information to discuss ideas fully.

### Review of Ideas Discussed

The final step in the discussion model is a review and summary of major points considered. If students have provided specific information supporting the main idea in the cluster of questions, the teacher should present an overview of how the specific ideas lead to the general conclusion. It is important that students leave a discussion with an awareness of the relationship among concepts and how they can integrate information learned into their own lives.

As teachers review the process, it is very motivational when they refer to comments made by specific students during the discussion. Such responses provide reinforcement for students to participate in the future.

## GROUPING FOR INSTRUCTION

paired learning—two students work together on a particular task.

Regardless of the instructional model, students working together can support each other while learning important academic and social skills. However, group learning or paired learning must be carefully structured so students are task-centered and productive. The instructor's decision about the type of grouping arrangement depends on a variety of factors.

As listed in Table 9–8, there are a series of questions teachers should ask when they create student groups in the inclusive classroom. If academic remediation is the basis for the group assignment, homogeneous groups may be best, where students have the opportunity to use materials at their level and reinforce skills needed by everyone in the group. Maura might form these groups during reading, where some students work together on

**Table 9–8**
**Designing Effective Student Groups**

Teachers should ask:

- Is the goal to academically or socially integrate students, or both?

- Is group *process* or group *product* the goal?

- Is the academic assignment reliant on all students being at the same skill level to complete the task?

- If students are at differing skill levels, will they all be able to contribute to group outcomes?

- Are there behavioral characteristics that will prevent some students from working well with others?

- Are students from a variety of social, ethnic, and linguistic backgrounds grouped together?

- Do members of the group understand the assignment and their individual roles?

- Have I taught students in the group how to listen to each other?

- Do members show respect for each other's opinions? Skill levels? Differences?

phonics activities, some participate in pairs at the sand table to reinforce basic sight words they have not mastered, and others read aloud to each other from more advanced texts. Similarly, during arithmetic, some students might be practicing in pairs with flash cards, reinforcing multiplication facts. Others would be in small groups as she explained the steps in long division.

Skill groups are critical for providing additional practice so that students have a firm basis for advancing to higher-level tasks. Because the inclusive classroom encompasses students at a variety of academic levels, skill grouping affords the opportunity for all students to progress. It is a much more powerful teaching arrangement than teaching to the "golden mean" of large-group performance, or relying only on curricular content without taking varying student levels into account. In this instance, the goal involves both individual and group product, since skill reinforcement is critical.

Other times, social integration of students is the goal. In this instance, group process becomes of paramount importance. Integration for social purposes is appropriate when there are students with behavioral disorders or inappropriate behaviors who can benefit from interaction with positive peer role models. It is important to instruct these students on acceptable behaviors before they become group members so that they gain respect and not alienate peers. If they possess certain characteristics antithetical to positive interactions, such as verbal and physical aggression, they should begin groupwork paired with others who will not tolerate this behavior. The teacher can have these students earn the right to work in pairs or larger groups by demonstrating

"golden mean"—the average.

nonaggressive behaviors. It is critical that group participation be earned by increasingly appropriate behaviors. Peer responses and behavior management structure can be powerful tools is shaping student responses. The student should not be permitted to return to group membership until demonstrating behaviors appropriate to learning.

Behavioral problems can be avoided when members have a clear idea of the assignment and their roles in the group. If the teacher has structured and explained the task clearly, students will move into group work with a sense of purpose. If they are unsure about the exact nature of the assignment or what they can offer in its completion, they tend to use peer proximity as a distraction. Teachers should initiate groups with clearly defined questions and student awareness of where to obtain the responses (e.g., research, text, discussion).

The group leader should be versed in questions to ask others, maintenance of group attention to task, and anticipated outcomes. Other members should be assigned specific responsibilities, such as recording information or sharing conclusions with the larger group after task completion. When members feel the purposefulness of the activity and their specific part, they tend to work together toward the shared goal.

In selecting members for each group, teachers should mix students together from a variety of social, ethnic, and linguistic backgrounds. When they have positive experiences working together toward a goal, students form the bases for commonalities and friendships. It is difficult for students to discriminate against others when they have friends in that minority group.

Beyond basic behavioral standards, there are valuable skills that can be taught through group participation. Students can be taught to demonstrate respect for each other's opinions when teachers expect good listening skills. Educators should instruct students that they may only participate when called upon by the group leader. At other times, they are to look at the person speaking and reflect on the ideas without interrupting by speaking or being off-task.

Teachers should instruct students that others' opinions are valuable, and that if there is disagreement all students will be able to interject their views. When they realize they will have the opportunity to discuss differing viewpoints, often students are more willing to wait their turn and not to be derogatory towards others' ideas.

Similarly, students must learn to appreciate that peer skill levels differ. By its very name and nature, the inclusive classroom is accepting. Some students will be more advanced academically than their peers. Under no circumstances should they be allowed to tease others or become arrogant about their own abilities. When students at lower skill levels offer ideas in a group discussion, they deserve the same respect and degree of listening that they must give others. Teachers can model these behaviors in their daily teaching, as well as enforce them during groupwork.

# COOPERATIVE LEARNING

One of the most popular directions in establishing alternate grouping arrangements has been cooperative learning (Johnson & Johnson, 1975, 1986; Slavin, 1983, 1991). It originated as an attempt to develop interracial relationships and social acceptance through structuring the classroom so students were reliant on each other to attain group goals (Lloyd, Crowley, Kohler, & Strain, 1988). Over recent years, variations have been used to attempt solutions for a number of educational problems.

There are an extensive variety of cooperative learning methods, the choice impacting success in a given classroom. Students work together in small groups, usually heterogeneous, to support each other's academic learning. Two concepts are basic: group goals and individual accountability (Slavin, 1991). In a typical setting, after group participation students are tested individually to measure their gains from group learning. Student progress may be noted by comparing their improvement from their own previous work or to a fixed standard (Lloyd, Crowley, Kohler, & Strain, 1988). Teachers note individual mastery and combine the results within each group. Subsequently, groups receive rewards based on the total result of individual accomplishments by all members.

All cooperative learning techniques rely on the concept of interdependence. Students are responsible for others' successful learning as well as their own. Emphasis is on individual accountability. The only way that a team can perform successfully is if all members master the objectives of the lesson.

Equal opportunity for success is based on the ability of all students to contribute to team success by improving their own past performance. In this way, all levels of learners are encouraged to increase their skills without penalizing lower achievers.

The concept of team rewards is based on combined outcomes of individual members, not competition with other teams. It is possible for every team or no team to win an award or certificate based on the improvement of individual members. Differing from traditional types of competition between groups based on achievement of the highest total score, cooperative learning encourages higher-achieving students to accept working with lower-achievers and to encourage their academic growth.

Research studies on cooperative learning (Lloyd, Crowley, Kohler, & Strain, 1988; Johnson & Johnson, 1989; Slavin, 1991) have provided important information regarding its effectiveness. Impact appears to be greatest on improving self-esteem and the ability to work together with others. Studies indicated that peer response to students with disabilities tends to improve (Madden & Slavin, 1983; Johnson, Johnson, Warring, & Maruyama, 1986). Cooperative settings appear to have significantly more influence on social behavior than individualized or competitive settings.

**individual accountability—**each member of the group has a certain responsibility toward the group.

**interdependence—**students are responsible for others' successful learning as well as their own.

**equal opportunity for success—**the ability of all students to contribute to team success by improving their own past performance.

**team rewards—**reinforcers based on combined outcomes of individual members, not competition with other teams.

Research reviews do not demonstrate a significant impact by cooperative learning on academic achievement (Lloyd, Crowley, Kohler, & Strain, 1988). Indeed, Cosden, Pearl, & Bryan (1985) found that groups combining male peers with students demonstrating learning disabilities had lower scores in academic areas than when students worked individually. Females in the study did not significantly differ between their performance in cooperative learning groups and individually.

Before teachers embrace cooperative learning to the exclusion of other grouping models, more research needs to be done on ways of improving its academic success. Additionally, researchers should continue to explore answers to questions such as the following:

1. Does the emphasis on heterogeneous grouping in cooperative learning detract from the development of specific skills needed by individual students?
2. Do students with disabilities in the mild and moderate range benefit more than students with severe disabilities who are placed in cooperative learning groups?
3. Is cooperative learning detrimental to the learning advancement of gifted students, slowing their motivation and academic progress?
4. Is there an optimal mix of the amount of time students should spend daily in cooperative groups versus in large-group and individual work?

## Grouping Structures

"I can see where it would be counterproductive to group in the same pattern all the time," reflects Maura. "The students would be bored, and frankly, so would I! What are some student combinations that would allow me teaching flexibility?"

Kagan and Kagan (in Sharan, 1994) expand cooperative learning groups to be responsive to a great variety of teaching objectives. Based on the belief that there is a strong association between what students do and what they learn, they rely on a sequence of social interactions, or group structures. They note, "Because these structures have different learning outcomes, the teacher who knows and uses a range of structures can efficiently produce specific academic, cognitive, and social outcomes among students" (p. 115). The more group structures a teacher masters, the more options for creating groups to support learning objectives.

Before selecting a specific group structure, Kagan and Kagan (1994) suggest teachers ask questions concerning:

1. What kind of cognitive development is my goal?
2. What kind of social skills am I trying to develop?

**Table 9–9**
**Overview of Selected Cooperative Learning Groups**

| Structure | Description | Outcomes |
|---|---|---|
| Roundrobin | In turn, each student shares information with teammates. | Expressing ideas and opinions. Getting aquainted. |
| Send-a-Problem | Each student writes a review problem on a flash card. Teammates attempt to solve it. Questions are then given to another group. | Mastery. Review. Practicing skills. |
| Brainstorm | Students work together to generate ideas on a particular problem or concept. | Reasoning. Knowledge. Sharing information. |
| Three-Step Interview | Pairs of students interview each other, then share information with the larger group. | Sharing personal information. Listening. Participation. |
| Cooperative Review | Students work together on a series of educational games to review the week's work. | Review. Checking for comprehension. |
| Numbered Heads Together | The teacher asks a question. After students consult to be sure everyone knows the answer, one student is called upon. | Review. Knowledge. Checking for comprehension. Tutoring. |
| Inside-Outside Circle | Students stand in two concentric circles, facing a partner. Students use flash cards or answer teacher questions. Then they rotate to a new partner. | Review. Checking for comprehension. Tutoring. |
| Spend-a-Buck | Each student receives four quarters (votes) and decides how to "spend" them on a particular situation. Group tally determines the decision. | Conflict resolution. Consensus-building. Decision-making. |
| Partners | Students work in pairs to create or master new content. They consult with a pair from another team. They then meet with the other partner pair in their own team to share information learned or products created. | Communication. Mastery and presentation of new material. Concept development. |
| Pairs Check | Within groups of four, students work in pairs, in which one solves a problem while the other coaches. After every two problems, the pairs check results with each other. | Practicing skills. Review. |
| Think-Pair-Share | The teacher provides a topic with questions. Students think independently about topic, then pair with another student to discuss it. They share their conclusions with the class. | Reasoning. Application to experiences. |
| Co-Op Co-Op | Students work in groups, producing a product they share with the entire class. Each student's contribution is included. | Planning. Decision-making. Application. Synthesis. Presentation skills. |

*(Continued)*

**Table 9–9**    *(Continued)*

| Structure | Description | Outcomes |
|---|---|---|
| Group Investigation | After identifying a topic, students organize into research groups to gather data. They combine information into a group report. | Planning. Decision-making. Analysis. Synthesis. Presentation skills. |
| Roundtable | Within teams, students exchange information by writing one answer as a paper and pencil are passed around the group. More than one paper can be used at once. | Assessing prior knowledge. Practicing skills. Review. |
| Blackboard Share | A student from each team solves a problem, writes an opinion, or shares information on the board. | Sharing information. Problem-solving. |
| Group Processing | Students analyze their ability to work together as a group. They review each member's participation. They discuss how to improve group functioning in the future. | Communication skills. Problem-solving. Team-building. |

(*Sources:* Adapted from Kagan, S. & Kagan, M., in Shlomo Sharan (Ed.), 1994; Pierce, 1992)

3. Where will this grouping structure best fit in the lesson?
4. What kind of curriculum will it support?

These considerations allow teachers to choose the best grouping arrangements to meet the objectives for their daily lesson.

It is important that teachers select the structure from Table 9–9 that best supports their outcomes so that there is not a mismatch between lesson objectives and student learning. For example, if the teacher wants all students to gain in the ability to discuss ideas and opinions to a small group, the Roundtable structure will provide this opportunity. On the other hand, if skill-building in specific areas is the objective, the Pairs Check will be more effective. When outcomes require teams sharing their information with the entire class, the Blackboard Share is excellent.

## Cooperative Learning and Gifted Students

"These groups sound really interesting," notes John. "I'm concerned about gifted students not having their needs met adequately in these groups. What do I say to Mike Gonzales when he complains to me about his son being in a group with students of far lower potential?"

Cooperative learning structures were designed to be heterogeneous to encourage acceptance of diversity. However, they should not be used exclusively, to the detriment of students who will benefit from advanced work. John's observation is important: If Greg Gonzales is reading from books below his level and is not pursuing challenging work then cooperative learning may not be beneficial to him.

Matthews (1992) underscores that teachers must be aware of potentially negative responses to cooperative learning on the part of gifted students. During her interviews, they reported feeling frustrated in cooperative learning groups because peers with lower academic skills were inattentive or had difficulty understanding material gifted students had learned easily. They resented taking time away from their own schoolwork and reported difficulty explaining material to others when its meaning was "obvious." Gifted students reported feeling used by teachers. None indicated gaining a clearer understanding of material they taught others in cooperative learning groups.

Johnson and Johnson (1989) discuss group structures as supporting positive social interactions among students by having all members share equally in the teacher's response to the final product. Yet, gifted students disagreed with this in Matthews's (1992) study. They said that when some group members do not complete their work or do so with less quality, the gifted tend to dominate the group or do all the work themselves while peers become uninvolved.

Gifted students appear more enthusiastic about cooperative learning when grouped homogeneously with gifted peers. Willis (1990) suggests that they

From an early age, gifted students should be nurtured to develop a love of learning.

seem to be more humble and less individually dominant when working closely on a goal with students who are strong academic learners, acknowledging more easily that group members are good at different things. They tend to feel that efforts are more equally shared when in groups with gifted peers than with peers less academically able.

"Does this indicate that cooperative learning should not be used with gifted students?" asks John.

It appears that teachers should design groups carefully when they are including gifted students, not expecting one student to teach information to others at the expense of personal learning. If a student has mastered the information, she should move on to more advanced content with other learners who are similarly ready. No student should be required to become a surrogate teacher at personal expense.

Inclusion is not intended to penalize any students, including gifted ones. It is important that teachers remember this as they design lesson objectives. For example, if Greg would benefit from working with a gifted peer on a research report, John should choose the Think-Pair-Share grouping model noted in Table 9–9, allowing two gifted students to work together and relate their findings to the class. In this way, everyone benefits. Greg and his classmate are motivated and progress at their own rate while other students benefit from the results by learning new information.

# PEER TUTORING

**peer tutoring**—a method for providing one-to-one instruction in which peers work individually with students with disabilities to help them learn, practice, or review academic information.

"I keep hearing about peer tutoring," notes Teresa. How does it work in the inclusive classroom?"

**Peer tutoring** is a method for providing one-to-one instruction. Peers work individually with students with disabilities to help them learn, practice, or review academic information (Lerner, 1993). Typical tasks include writing spelling words, arithmetic facts, or reading aloud. The tutor verifies the correctness of the response and encourages the peer to make changes or modifications when necessary.

In their review of the literature on peer-mediated interventions, Lloyd, Crowley, Kohler, and Strain (1988) note that there are additional social outcomes to this academic support system. They discuss the related peer manager aspects, such as the modification of academic-support behaviors, including working quietly and independently, completing homework, and raising hand to gain teacher attention.

Peer tutoring holds promise for supporting the needs of varied learning styles and academic levels in the same class. Students needing more reinforcement and practice are afforded extended opportunities through peer support. This method also serves to provide teachers with additional classroom help.

However, as indicated in the literature review by Lloyd, Crowley, Kohler, and Strain (1988), before embracing peer tutoring in the inclusive classroom, more research needs to be done concerning whether peer tutors themselves benefit from instructing their classmates and if they are able to be effective teachers. Some of the complaints voiced by gifted students about cooperative learning may be relevant in their feeling of being used by teachers and not advancing their own work.

Maura notes, "In my class, I have found that the best pairing of students doesn't occur between an advanced student and a peer with substantially poorer skills, but between two students who are at approximately the same skill level. For instance, recently I've been having Kevin work with Jeremy on learning multiplication tables. Jeremy is just beginning multiplication, while Kevin is moving on to higher facts. But although we covered basic tables in Kevin's group earlier this year, he didn't master them and clearly needs more practice before he can proceed further. It's been a perfect pairing: Jeremy has a severe learning disability and trouble making friends, and Kevin needs the practice as well as a sense of being important and successful. They're both learning and seem to be enjoying the process."

"We're trying a more formalized peer tutoring program at Apter this year, largely a result of inclusion," adds Elena. "We've found that tutoring among peers in the same class can work well, as Maura noted, especially if both students are close in their skill development. Adolescents can be cruel to each other, and a number of teachers noticed the tutors becoming bored with the arrangements, especially if they were to work with the same peer over an extended period.

"As a result, we've created a schoolwide program, in which students interested in being peer tutors at their own grade or lower grade levels can sign up to work daily during their study hall. We're expanding this through the Honor Society and our student volunteer group, the Apter Angels, so that students can fulfill their required service hours by working weekly after school or during lunch with a student needing academic support. It's been fun to watch the positive outcomes when students choose to tutor a peer instead of being forced."

As Elena indicates, peer tutoring programs can be creative and flexible, with positive outcomes for everyone. The underlying concept of the inclusive school being a team effort is critical to students learning to help each other.

# SUMMARY

Chapter 9 included discussion of critical variables supporting the inclusive classroom as a positive learning environment. Eight student factors underscoring personal success include the following:

1. extended attention to task, including the ability to ignore distractions and control impulsive behaviors;
2. short- and long-term memory for previously taught information, supporting integration and retention of academic and social skills;
3. ability to associate and integrate information basic to academic and social skills development;
4. skills in understanding and using spoken language well, critical foundations for reading and writing comprehension;
5. accomplishment of basic skills in reading, writing, spelling, and arithmetic, basic to development of more advanced skills;
6. study and organization skills, supporting preparation for assignments and exams;
7. appropriate social behaviors, allowing for acceptance into the peer culture; and
8. motivation to be successful in the regular education classroom, promoting intense efforts to learn material and become full group participants (Scruggs & Mastropieri, 1992).

Similarly, a number of teacher factors underscore success in the inclusive setting:

1. attitude toward students with learning and behavioral differences, modeling acceptance;
2. motivation to make inclusion work, encouraging teachers to try harder to accept diversity;
3. willingness to collaborate with other educators to design programs for students with disabilities;
4. knowledge of curricular adaptations and teaching modifications, allowing for alternate teaching methods; and
5. managing multiple demands of the classroom environment to maximize instructional effectiveness.

The latter issue of daily demands on the teacher included the following factors: multidimensionality, requiring the ability to handle a number of tasks and events, with skill in anticipating problems before they occur; simultaneity, demanding the direction and monitoring of a number of variables at any one time; immediacy, when classroom events occur rapidly and require immediate response; unpredictability, when unanticipated situations require appropriate teacher action; publicness, the problem of always being observed by students and professionals, open to criticism if behavior is ever in question; and history, describing the interactive processes that develop over time, resulting in mutual respect or adversarial behaviors (Doyle, 1980).

Chapter 9 included discussion of instructional models supportive of teaching students with a variety of learning styles. The Direct Instruction Model is most effective in teaching skills that can be broken up into discrete segments. Steps in this model include:

1. review of information from the previous lesson, supporting mastery of prerequisite knowledge;
2. sharing lesson objectives with the learner, ensuring awareness of anticipated outcomes;
3. presentation of new material;
4. guided practice with feedback, affording opportunity for reinforcement with teacher supervision; and
5. review of knowledge of current information before teaching new skills.

Step 3 involves teacher organization of relationships between current and previously studied information, accompanied by an analysis of requirements of course content and skills of the learner. Teachers should combine a series of methods, ranging from discussions and questions, to use of technology, demonstrations, and experiential learning.

The Classroom Discussion Model is most appropriate with complex subject matter that requires analysis and allows for a variety of responses. It supports student recall of content because it is based on clarity and understanding . Steps include the following:

1. teacher reading of material and formulation of questions before meeting with students;
2. incorporation of a variety of questions, emphasizing divergent ones that allow for creativity and critical thinking;
3. clustering and sequencing questions carefully before discussion begins;
4. students reading the material after teachers introduce any potentially problematic vocabulary;
5. teachers or group leaders conducting the discussion, asking questions requiring thoughtful responses; and
6. reviewing of the major ideas discussed so that students can understand relationships among concepts.

Chapter 9 contained discussion of effective methods of grouping students for instruction. In designing groups to include students with disabilities, teachers should consider a series of issues, such as whether their objectives are academic or social and if the group process or product is the most important outcome. They should review student skill levels and behaviors, and ensure that all members understand group rules such as listening and demonstrating mutual respect.

While arrangements such as Cooperative Learning have been popularly received, teachers should look to the benefits for all students in the group in order to determine the optimal grouping method. Peer tutoring allows students to work together towards skill reinforcement. It may be most beneficial to both students if their skills levels are approximately even. Some schools may formalize a peer tutoring program to assure that all students' needs are met and that tutors are selected because of their willingness to work with others.

CASE STUDY: *Elementary*

After the discussion of effective teaching models and ways of grouping students, Maura has decided to try some new instructional arrangements in her classroom. She is especially concerned about three students and how to include them effectively in groupwork:

Sharon has low cognitive and academic skills. She thinks on a very concrete level in response to questions. Her decoding and reading comprehension skills are approximately two years below peers and she has difficulty completing reading assignments without extensive time. She has good interactive behaviors, and although she behaves immaturely at times, is accepted by peers. Maura wants to have her be able to offer as much as others in the group and to keep up with discussions despite her low academic skills.

Marty is the class clown. He constantly seeks attention by making inappropriate comments and sounds, usually getting reinforcement from the reactions of peers. His reading and other academic skills are slightly below grade level, but when he concentrates heavily he can usually keep up with other students. Maura's primary concerns have been grouping him with peers whom he may distract or find distracting.

Jorge is highly gifted but does not have many friends. He loves to read and work on computers, but reacts with genuine panic, almost immobilizing him, when asked to share information with the class. Peers tend to make fun of him because of his lack of social skills. He then becomes more embarrassed and withdrawn. Maura would like to have him share his knowledge more comfortably, as well as to make friends and be accepted.

Assuming that Maura's class is typical, there will be a variety of intellectual, academic, and behavioral levels among the remaining twenty-eight students.

1. Describe the types of grouping arrangements you would use when having each of the three students discussed above work with their peers. Include when you would use homogeneous and heterogeneous groups. Refer to Table 9–9 to select different types of groups that might work for these students.

2. In her grouping arrangements, how should Maura handle differences in intellectual levels, such as Sharon being at a concrete level and Jorge being more abstract?

3. How can Maura best provide Sharon with questions that will encourage her to move beyond the concrete level of thought? How can she

*Continued*

deal with Jorge's desire to read and learn beyond the realm of others while ensuring him group interactions that are so important to his social development?

4. How can she control Marty's behavior in the group so he concentrates and learns the information without distracting himself and others?

## CASE STUDY: *Secondary*

John is still reflecting on the incident in his classroom where a normally quiet student confided that he was concerned about his girlfriend's possible pregnancy. While he discussed the issue briefly with the young man and advised him to talk to the school counselor, John is concerned that he did not respond fully enough to really be of help.

"My main problem at that time was keeping the class going on a preholiday Friday. We were in the midst of a group assignment when the student confided in me. With students lined up to talk to me and an argument developing into a fight between members of rival gangs, I felt like I was in the middle of a city street waiting to be run over! I had to handle too many things at once!

"The last time this happened, during large group discussion of an essay on outcomes of eating disorders, one of my students confided that she was bulemic! I didn't know if I should continue the discussion of the essay or her particular problem, since I didn't want to upset her by asking inappropriate questions. I didn't say much, but continued on with the lesson."

John is concerned with how to deal with extreme personal problems that a student discusses for the first time. However indirectly the problem is stated, he knows that the student is asking for help. However, classroom circumstances may make the teacher less able to provide necessary assistance.

1. What should John, or any teacher, do when a student confides an extremely personal fact one-on-one to the teacher during class?

2. What should teachers do when a student confides in the entire group? Discuss how to handle the situation when it arises in class. What are additional ways of supporting the student afterwards and of preventing peers from spreading gossip about the problem?

*Continued*

3. What other adults should be involved when a student voices a problem? How can John structure their involvement without embarrassing the student?

4. Discuss specific ways of handling the potential pregnancy and bulemia situations previously discussed.

# 10  MODIFYING INSTRUCTION FOR STUDENTS WITH SPECIAL NEEDS

"I'm really excited about the inservice today," Maura commented to Alex. "These last months have been interesting, setting up collaborative teams in our building and initiating your assessment suggestions. Recently, I've started using group work much more on a daily basis and the students seem to be really motivated. My classroom is more fun these days!

"I have to admit that I still need lots more teaching strategies. How do I improve students' basic skills in interesting ways? How do I increase their understanding of what we cover in class? How can I teach reading and math so students retain the information permanently?"

John added, "You're not alone in needing techniques. Most of the teachers at the secondary level feel the same way. We're pressed with the urgency of teaching curricular content, preparing all students with learning strategies they can use in college, as well as increasing skills. In addition to the students with learning disabilities who are full-time in my classes these days, I've volunteered to have a student who has a history of some real behavioral problems. Maybe I'm crazy, but I thought she would be a real challenge for me and would add a new dimension to our class. So I hope this inservice gives us techniques I can use with a variety of students."

# MOTIVATING STUDENTS

"I appreciate all the confidence you're placing in me today," observed Teresa. "I've been compiling teaching techniques since Westside decided to adopt inclusion, and I'm really happy to share them with you. I've always felt that regular teachers are on the "firing lines" daily while the rest of us work to support you. Your job is the most difficult because you have the responsibility for making inclusion work.

"Let's start by discussing how to motivate students. As Maura mentioned, watching kids become excited about learning in our classrooms motivates us as well. Actually, it's an affective cycle where our enthusiasm spreads to create more situations for learning. Everyone benefits and students and teachers all feel better about coming to school every day.

"Since students with disabilities have failed so much, often they are the least motivated to try harder, fearing greater failure. As a result, they tend not to be risk-takers. The research literature has a number of things we can do to motivate them."

When considering learners who refuse to try, teachers should assess student academic levels to be sure students possess skills at a level where they are able to complete assigned work (Licht, 1983). This concern is true especially if students have learning disabilities, cognitive deficits, or a history of behavioral problems that interfered with early schooling. Beginning with daily work products, teachers should cross-compare student work across all members of the class to be sure everyone is capable of completing the assignment. If students feel they cannot be successful, they will not make the effort.

Once the teacher is sure a student can do the work, the techniques listed in Table 10–1 should motivate all students in the class. As Klumb (1992) notes, "The three basics of motivation seem to be achieving success, receiving feedback, and personal involvement in the learning process" (p. 17). When students feel they are in an environment where they can be successful, that their efforts are not only acceptable but important to the class, they try harder.

Part of this sense of acceptance is that students receive praise for trying. When teachers grade student work only on the acceptability of the final product, they discourage students with learning problems who may feel their work will never meet teacher expectations. Indeed some students realize they cannot even complete the work in the amount of time allowed, so there is no reason to begin or care about the effort. When teachers compliment students on their initiative, on their attention to task, and sometimes even for attempting an assignment that may be difficult for them, students realize it is their ongoing work that matters, not only whether the final product is perfect.

closure—finality; drawing an activity or lesson to an end.

However, all students appreciate a sense of **closure** to their efforts. Teachers should assign work that has a final product. If involved in a large-

**Table 10–1**
**Techniques for Motivating Students to Learn**

Teachers should:

- create a caring, risk-free environment for all students

- vary methods of teaching

- incorporate interesting activities

- use humor and surprise

- allow for student choice within activities

- provide opportunities for students to be actively involved, not just listening and reading

- praise and reward effort, not only perfect work products

- organize lessons and assignments so students can create finished products

- allow students to select their own work for display

- help students attribute positive outcomes to their own degree of effort, not to "luck"

- direct students in establishing short- and long-term goals. Reward accomplishments immediately

(*Source:*  Adapted from Klumb, 1992).

group discussion, at the end of class the teacher can summarize important concepts developed through student input. If reading or writing in content areas is involved, students should be able to complete their work by the end of the class period. Even unit work that extends over a period of days or weeks should consist of a series of specific objectives each attainable within class time. Teachers may need to create shorter assignments or select less extensive aspects of unit work for students who require more time to complete their efforts.

Teachers also motivate when they vary their methods. Trying something different is stimulating both to instructors and students, making the lesson more interesting. Particularly successful are using fun activities, humor, and suspense. Students enjoy a new challenge or just something out of the ordinary.

"I can really relate to that," commented John. "I became tired of teaching *Moby Dick* every year, but it's in the curriculum and I haven't had much choice. On the way to work one morning I was in a mood for something to motivate *me*. So when I got to class, I asked each student to write several situations in the novel from the viewpoint of the whale. Then we had a role-playing situation in which students volunteered to read their dialog as if it were actually part of the novel. We laughed a lot and enjoyed a book that had become tedious to us. When Mark left the room, he said, "Mr. Robinson, I've never seen you laugh so hard! That was a great class!" I guess what you were saying about enthusiasm being infectious really can happen."

Part of the success of John's lesson was that he provided the opportunity for students to become actively involved in the class, a variation on the traditional lecture and reading activities performed in many high schools. When they have the opportunity to discuss their ideas, to simulate situations, to employ creativity, students enjoy the process and are willing to try harder.

They also enjoy the element of choice. "Really?" asks Maura. "Whenever I tell my students to write about something of particular interest to them, or an exciting or meaningful situation, they usually moan and can't think of anything. What am I doing wrong?"

Students tend to prefer choice within a limited structure. Maura might have more success directing them to write about an interesting event that happened to them over the weekend, or something they observed on a class field trip. Narrowing the choices actually gives students a direction they welcome instead of an open time and situational framework that may provide an overwhelming number of situations. Students with limited conceptual skills are especially appreciative of direction since otherwise they may have difficulty understanding the assignment.

Another motivational tool is displaying student creative work. While traditionally teachers have posted worksheets and pictures on room bulletin

MY PORTFOLIO

> A gost!
> But then ti faded away. I remeber my mom saying there was a mysterious woman that livd in my house for the day. I was scard. My mom said go to your room I had got in big trubl. I quietly wabkt in my room. I saw my bruther no wunder he left wen I was telling abuat the gost. my bruther got in big trubut.

A creative topic affords students a good opportunity to discuss their ideas. Reprinted with permission, Winston School, San Antonio.

boards, most often they have selected what they considered that student's best effort, often identical and indistinguishable from the work of peers.

"Sounds like brown turkeys with colorful fan tails before Thanksgiving," notes Maura. Exactly. Either it is difficult to tell which picture belongs to any individual student because the products all look alike, or it is easy to tell because one or two are so different, often because the child had a difficult time with the task and the awkward attempt is posted. When the latter happens, rarely is that student satisfied as he compares his weaker effort with that of his peers, knowing that everyone perceives his picture of lesser worth.

As discussed previously, when dealing with development of student portfolios illustrating progressive growth in student efforts, it is best to allow students to select their favorite work product for display in the classroom. The room takes on a more interesting flavor when different types of work from a variety of projects and subjects is evident. Importantly, students are motivated to work their hardest to produce something *they* feel worthy of display.

Often, working together with peers also provides motivation, especially when the student feels he is accepted as a competent group member. When group outcomes involve a product observable to others, such as a play for the class or even just the leader presenting ideas discussed, each student feels a pride in accomplishment. For many students with disabilities, there are additional social outcomes when interacting with peers that allow for modeling appropriate behaviors and making friendships.

**attribution training—understanding exactly why efforts succeeded or failed.**

Teachers can encourage students to appreciate results of personal efforts through the use of **attribution training**, or understanding exactly why their efforts succeeded or failed. Typically when students perform poorly on an assignment, they claim that it happened because they are "dumb" or "stupid." When they are successful, they claim that the task is "too easy" or that they are "lucky." Either they tend to self-characterize or to externalize instead of examining those personal attributes that influenced their performance (Scruggs & Mastropieri, 1992).

Teachers can help students consider what specific things they did that underscored their success or caused problems in a particular assignment. For example, if Mark fails an examination, John can discuss with him those behaviors that should be attributed to Mark's lack of success. In their conference, Mark learns his not having carefully read the material, having allotted too brief an amount of time for studying, and having stayed up very late the night before to try to cover the information are the reasons for his failure. Before the next exam, John can suggest to Mark that he can take control of his performance in advance by changing these behaviors. He and Mark can create a study schedule to review information each night during the week of the test. Mark can ask questions in class concerning any material he reviews that is unclear to him. John can remind Mark and his classmates of the importance of a good night's sleep on concentration and memory.

# TEACHER BEHAVIORS AFFECTING STUDENT PERFORMANCE

During a time when they are challenged by parents and under public scrutiny for producing tangible outcomes, teachers may feel overwhelmed and powerless. It is important for educators to realize that despite many extraneous variables and pressures, they can have a strong impact on how well every student does in class.

Factors affecting student success are not new to education, nor are they difficult or expensive. However, it is important for teachers to review them in their daily interactions with students to assure they are maximizing student success. These factors are listed in Table 10–2 (Rosenshine & Stevens, 1986; Klumb, 1992).

Students need to know those behaviors that are supportive of their success. Teachers are in the best position to provide continuous feedback about a range of student academic and social behaviors. Ongoing feedback is far more impactful than responding after students have failed or performed poorly. At that time, change is less likely because of discouragement and subsequent lack of motivation. For example, if Maura observes Carl interrupting other students' comments during group assignments, insisting that his own viewpoint be heard, she should take him aside immediately and discuss with him the impact his lack of listening is having on others in the group. Suggesting that others will not want him to work with them in the future if this behavior continues may be enough to initiate his self-monitoring of interruptive behavior.

---

**Table 10–2**
**Teacher Behaviors Affecting Student Performance**

Teachers should:

- provide continuous feedback and reinforcement
- afford equal response opportunities for all learners
- vary difficulty level of questions
- maximize student time on task
- have high expectations for low achievers
- give assignments in which learners can be successful
- have students participate in discussing learning difficulties, selecting their remedial work, and continuously evaluating their success
- employ interesting methods and materials, and offer rewards for effort and persistence

(*Source:* Adapted from Rosenshine & Stevens, 1986; Klumb, 1992).

Reinforcement should be continuous as well. Many students with disabilities are concrete and immediate in their needs for teacher response. Praise for a good question, permission to take a quick break for a drink of water, or an actual reward for hard work serve to improve student efforts and support integration of those behaviors most important to learning.

Teachers need to call on all learners to respond, not permitting advanced students to dominate discussions. Allowing equal opportunity for all learners to respond creates a sense that everyone is important and has something to contribute to the classroom.

Few factors in the teaching-learning environment are more important than the amount of time students are directly engaged in acquiring new information. Currently schools tend to be overwhelmed by nonacademic activities, ranging from discouraging gang membership to sponsoring drug awareness and suicide prevention programs. No one would argue that these programs are critical to guiding youth through very risky times. Yet teachers must remember that their primary concern on a daily basis is to educate students academically.

"We hope to see some changes in the roles of our ancillary personnel that will help in that regard," interjects Alex. "For example, my school psychologists are excited by the possibility of performing fewer assessments and spending more time directly engaged in counseling students. Because of the pre-referral process we discussed earlier, we hope students will need special education testing and placement less frequently because teachers are identifying and helping them before their problems become severe.

pull-in programs—educators work with special education students in the regular classroom.

Since the advent of inclusion, **pull-in programs** have flourished. As they enter regular classrooms to teach students with disabilities, many special education teachers are now allowed by state policy to work with noncategorized students in the class. When regular educators determine that a student is below expectancy in important academic skills they can ask the special educator to include that student in a skill-building group. In many situations, this results in additional support in reading and arithmetic, helping nonspecial education students keep up with classmates and avoid eventual special education placement. Such supports help provide learning opportunities at a variety of levels as well as increase on-task time for students.

Teresa comments, "All too often, when a student is labeled as requiring special education, an indelible scarlet *S* appears on the forehead. Unfortunately, it may remain there for the student's entire schooling. Teachers expect students with a poor achievement history to be poor achievers. While this premise may seem appropriate, the impact of the human tendency to view convictions of others as true needs to be examined.

"If I've been called names because I've failed, I begin to believe those names as I continue to fail. Then a syndrome sets in, where I don't try because I'll fail. Why embarrass myself more than I need to? If my teachers exclude me from more difficult assignments, they are indicating that my diagnosis of potential failure is correct. Why don't I look for friends who fail also and we can do other things, since school just isn't our place?"

Students' expectations of their own abilities can be changed, but it requires the efforts of many, especially if there is a long history of failure. When teachers say, "This work is hard (difficult, tough), but I believe you can do it," they indicate their belief in the student. If the student fails, there is an external reason: Even the teacher said it was difficult. If the student succeeds, there is an enhanced sense of accomplishment of a task that was acknowledged to be difficult. Students are aware quickly of how teachers feel about them, based on attitude and expectation. They try harder when others support their feelings of potential success.

In the creation of strong expectations for all students, there should be a realization of current skill levels and objectives for "next steps" on the learning hierarchy, based on a developmental curriculum. When teachers assign the same work to all students in the class, they are assuring that some students will fail while others will be bored.

Ironically, if students are to meet their own and others' expectations for success, there may need to be a modification of assignments so that they are working at their conceptual and skill levels.

Students should always be aware of the objectives for their instruction. What skills need to be developed further? What remedial work will support

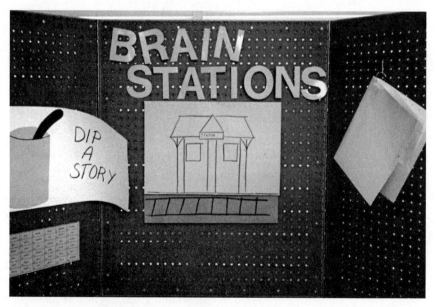

High expectations and creative assignments can result in heightened student performance.

the achievement of these skills? Are students successfully learning curricular information? What additional modifications are necessary?

It is difficult for anyone to be motivated to work hard if there is no clarity as to why the outcomes of that work are important. However, if students realize what skills need remedial work and why their improvement will be personally helpful in the future, they are more likely to try.

It is important to be honest with students during these discussions, yet sensitive to their feelings about past failure. John might create a remedial writing group in his class for students who need additional assistance in basic skills. Before beginning instruction, he might meet with students to discuss specific goals, such as improving use of certain areas of punctuation. He can help students fill in a contract about the type and amount of weekly writing practice they can complete successfully to earn a specified reward.

Students should participate also in the ongoing evaluation of their work. Under teacher supervision, checking their own work and that of peers will provide reinforcement for skill-building as well as a sense of accomplishment as they watch their own abilities improve. Self-assessment can be highly meaningful for most students because it affords opportunities for direct involvement in the progress of their work efforts, rather than having an external evaluator, the teacher, respond judgmentally.

Everyone likes learning to be fun. When teachers try something new, they have a stake in the outcome and tend to put more energy into the process. The very announcement, "We're going to do something different today" to a class of students often is enough to spark their curiosity and enthusiasm. When teachers become too comfortable with their style and method of presentation, they tend to teach worn-out lessons from the past. Trying new grouping patterns, different materials, or working together in teams with other teachers can provide enough change to motivate teachers and students alike.

## MANAGING SUBGROUPS OF LEARNERS

"I don't see where I'm going to have time for all this," notes John. "How can I provide new and interesting activities and differentiate instruction for students at a variety of levels when I teach five classes every day? What can simplify this process?"

John's questions are important; if teachers feel overwhelmed, they will be ineffective and begin to experience "burn-out." Since there is rarely enough time to work individually with each students, teachers need to develop small-group arrangements with which they are comfortable.

While types of grouping arrangements were discussed in previous chapters, teachers need to develop personal guidelines for scheduling and managing learners. Careful planning allows for groups to be supportive of instructional efforts, freeing teachers to be more creative and meet the needs of a variety of learners.

Idol, Nevin, and Paolucci-Whitcomb (1994) discuss a number of managerial strategies to provide successful small-group outcomes. Assessment of each learner's skill levels within the curriculum provides teachers with information to use in grouping students appropriately. Creating a **flexible grouping system** allows students to rotate easily among groups, especially as skill levels improve. Ongoing use of reinforcements provides motivation and encourages students to complete their work. These reinforcements should vary between individual and group incentives. The latter helps to develop a sense of camaraderie among group members as they work towards a mutual goal.

Careful group scheduling can help create a sense of orderliness and discipline in the classroom. Teachers should have a structured time when each subject area meets. Not only does this provide constancy for students who tend to be disorganized, it allows for everyone to have their assignments and materials prepared in advance. At the secondary level, within content areas where both skill building and more creative, thought-filled work are required, teachers should structure the class session carefully.

As they enter the room, through the use of preplanned instructions or work contained in folders, students should know if they are to begin independently

*flexible grouping system*— dividing the class into groups that are easily rotated as skill levels improve and content units change.

---

**Table 10–3**
**Guidelines for Scheduling and Managing Groups**

By following these guidelines, teachers should be able to use small groups as a supportive mechanism for academic learning.

- Assess each learner's proficiency level within the curriculum.
- Create a flexible system allowing for students to move easily between groups, dependent on skill levels.
- Use reinforcements when motivation is not inherent in the lesson.
- Have a structured time when each subject area meets daily.
- Arrange work in advance through weekly assignments and folders, so students can begin independently.
- Allow enough time for direct teacher instruction and student practice to attain skill mastery.

(*Source:* Adapted from Idol, Nevin, & Paolucci-Whitcomb, 1994)

or move directly into groups. Completion of worksheets and other assignments in folders should be established at the beginning of the week and agreed upon by both teacher and student. In this way, the student will understand work expectations and try to fulfill them because of having had a voice in their design (Waldron, 1992a).

While group work is essential for providing a basis for discussion and elaboration of ideas, teachers should be sure to allow enough time for direct instruction and student practice of skills. Overuse of groups may prevent students from having the opportunity to ask questions regarding information they do not understand, or to participate in guided practice where the teachers provide feedback and corrective teaching. As with any type of instructional arrangement, it is used most successfully when in fulfillment of teacher goals.

## MANAGING LARGE GROUPS

Maura asks, "While I'm learning from these discussions that working in small groups is favorable, there are times when I want to present some information to the entire class or to have a large-group discussion. What can I do to keep students on-task and to be sure that students are actively involved?"

Scruggs and Mastropieri (1992) discuss important strategies for using large grouping effectively. They emphasize the provision of positive and encouraging feedback for student responses to teacher questions. This positive attitude by the teacher reinforces student risk-taking and encourages additional involvement in the future. It is important to refrain from criticizing any student responses, even when the answers do not seem considered carefully. Instead, the teacher should provide clarifying feedback when students answer incorrectly.

Many problems occur during transitional, or noninstructional periods, where students tend to become discipline problems or waste time. By minimizing transitions, teachers can direct students more effectively. As suggested for streamlining small groups, the use of folders and posted schedules helps students go from one task to another more quickly. To have students organize themselves quickly for work as they enter the room, the teacher may write a problem on the blackboard for them to begin immediately.

At all times, students should be working with instructional materials and learning tasks that they can complete at a low error rate, with 80 percent or more performed correctly (Larrivee, 1989). When materials are more difficult, students lose the benefits of independent reinforcement and become frustrated. Subsequently, they may refuse to complete assignments or may become disciplinary problems.

# TECHNIQUES FOR ACTIVELY INVOLVING STUDENTS

"What do you do to get students involved on a daily basis?" asks John. "If I'm trying to vary the way I teach, I can't just put students in small groups every day or they'll become bored with that too. What are some teaching techniques that will heighten interest in learning?"

Klumb (1992) and Waldron (1992a) list a series of strategies for increasing students' opportunity to learn through active involvement. Brief directions, often just verbal cues, can set students into immediate action. The teacher should ask those who have difficulty integrating directions to repeat them. From the beginning of the year, students should practice how to change between activities quickly and with a minimum of disruption.

Pacing appears to be particularly important in keeping students actively involved. When the class moves slowly, students tend to become disinterested and off-task. When teachers break larger conceptual areas into small segments and present activities at a brisk pace, students become more directly involved. Guided reinforcement that students complete individually or in groups should be similarly segmented allowing for shorter attention spans.

"The balance of rapid pacing can be tricky when you are teaching students with disabilities," adds Teresa. "Some students learn more slowly than their peers. They need more time and practice for reinforcement. Yet, they can become as bored as anyone else when their attention span is stretched

## Table 10–4
## Strategies for Increasing Student Involvement in the Classroom

Since involved students tend to benefit more from instruction, the following strategies should be helpful in engaging all students academically:

- speak briefly and clearly, avoiding lengthy directions
- have students with learning problems repeat directions verbally and write them for homework assignments
- employ rapid instruction and practice
- alternate preferred and nonpreferred activities
- divide long assignments into small segments
- as needed, allow more time or shortened assignments
- schedule practice in short time periods
- pace instruction to allow time to cover information as well as for student practice

(*Source:* Adapted from Klumb, 1992; Waldron, 1992a)

too far. I've learned that brisk pacing is an attitude, a feeling of enthusiasm combined with daily practice in small doses.

"Classes of teachers who pace instruction well are fun to visit because they feel busy without giving the appearance of busy-work. Students move to their assigned work areas or learning centers, take out their materials, and begin. They know how long they need to work, when it is acceptable to notify the teacher if they have questions or problems, and when it is time to change. In this environment, students with disabilities are difficult to identify because they're moving about and doing their work just like their peers."

Part of the ability of students with academic difficulties to be full participants is based on teachers' willingness to allow more time or a shortened assignment as the need arises. The pace of instruction should include direct teaching or discussion in the presentation of information, with time for reinforcement activities to provide mastery.

Students with short attention spans benefit from short assignments, or longer ones interspersed with brief breaks. If Kevin needs extensive practice in phonics but attends for only a few minutes at a time, he takes his phonics worksheets from his folder during reading time and completes the number agreed upon in advance with his teacher. When he finishes those, he carries them to the teacher or a designated peer for correction. He then returns to his desk and completes more work. The physical movement across the room affords him enough of a break that he is now ready to return to work.

As indicated in Table 10–4, it is also important to schedule activities so preferred ones immediately follow the less preferred. Students will be more willing to complete an assignment that is difficult for them if they feel there will be an immediate reward or activity that they enjoy (Premack, 1959).

"Sounds like *Grandma's Rule* to me," comments Maura. "First you eat your peas, then you get dessert. Or in school, first you complete your math drill, then you get to practice spelling words with a friend. Many times students tell us which subject area they prefer. I've learned to listen carefully and use that subject area as reinforcement. I much prefer this system to giving students external rewards for doing their work. I save the externals for the really difficult situations and use preferred work reinforcers daily."

Additional ways teachers can help students become more attentive and actively involved in the classroom are to add unanticipated changes, for example, through telling a joke or having students stand and stretch. Introducing a quick educational game or announcing, "Think about that; I'm going to call on someone in a minute," tends to bring students back into focus.

Klumb (1992) also suggests having students share with a peer guidelines or rules for performing a skill correctly, such as writing a complex sentence, completing a science experiment, or sequencing steps in arithmetic. Or as they finish reading assignments, they can write down a few questions or ideas to share with the class. Teachers should vary their rate and volume during discussions, sometimes talking more quickly or slowly, loudly or softly. This variation tends to cause others to respond more closely.

"What about giving quizzes?" asks John. "I didn't like them when I was a student, and I can tell that my students don't like them either. Yet, without a purpose, such as a test or a paper, I find that most just don't study that thoroughly."

Frequent quizzes encourage students to attend more closely to details and to review important material when they would not be motivated otherwise. They tend to be more concerned about their work. While no one enjoys taking tests, students have less anxiety when they are prepared. Stress may be avoided by telling students in advance that there will be a quiz and helping them prepare for it. Additionally, frequent quizzes provide a number of opportunities for teachers to obtain not only student grades, but an awareness of those skills students have mastered and those that still need to be developed.

Special educators in Resource Rooms routinely have read exams to students to measure knowledge without penalizing students with problems in reading and written expression. When students respond orally, these exams are given individually. When students have strong enough skills to respond in writing, teachers can administer tests orally to small groups. In either case, most often the regular education teacher does not have time to provide oral exams, but is dependent upon the specialist for support. These exams can be administered in the regular classroom.

Some students with learning differences may not be able to complete exams in the allotted time. Two options are possible: Extend the amount of time or shorten the exam. If only a few minutes of additional time are needed, there should not be a problem. However, when extensive time allotments are necessary, it may be preferable to abbreviate the exam. If the student is capable of answering all the questions, then items removed should afford a balance between easy and more difficult items, in fairness to others in the class. If the cognitive level of some of the questions is beyond the student's capability level, those questions should not be included.

# TECHNIQUES FOR DIRECTING
# THE INCLUSIVE CLASSROOM

Teresa adds, "We have been talking about a number of techniques for motivating students and including them actively in the classroom. Let's add some additional basic strategies that will help inclusion work on a daily basis."

***Intervene Immediately when Problems Arise.*** When any student in the class begins to demonstrate academic or behavioral problems, teachers should intervene immediately. If the problem is serious, such as concerns over

**Table 10–5**
**Techniques for Directing the Inclusive Class**

There are general techniques that can be highly effective for teaching students with varied academic and behavioral needs:

1. Intervene immediately when problems arise.

2. Have students read, speak, and write daily.

3. Provide additional time for learning whenever necessary:
   - Students can complete work when peers are involved in a different academic activity
   - Special education teachers can provide direct teaching and guided reinforcement activities within the regular education classroom
   - Teachers can provide additional reinforcement activities for parents to supervise at home.

4. Monitor student success continuously.

5. Insist that students complete their work.

6. Require all students to demonstrate appropriate group behavior.

7. Assist students in relating information to their own life (Klumb, 1992):
   - Have students paraphrase information in their own words
   - Encourage students to verbalize their opinions
   - Provide direct, hand-on experiences to integrate information first-hand
   - Prompt students in asking questions of teachers and peers
   - Allow students to select topics that relate to their own interests
   - Use students' names or familiar events as examples basic to problem-solving.

8. Design activities that are different from the way the student was taught previously.

gang membership or substance abuse, the collaborative team of teachers should meet to discuss intervention strategies. If the problem is developmental, such as the student falling behind academically, the regular and special education teachers should meet. They should consider the nature of the problem and possible teaching methods and modifications that would support student skill improvement.

"That really worked for me when Shane started to fall behind in math skills," interjects Maura. "He needed much more reinforcement than the others to learn multiplication. I just didn't have the time to spend with him, and I didn't want to slow the rest of the class down. When I discussed it with Teresa, she gave me additional math materials for Shane to use during the day. When students were doing their independent seatwork in a variety of areas, from spelling to handwriting, I shortened these assignments for Shane and gave him an overdose of multiplication through Teresa's materials. I told Shane that we all need more practice in different areas, and right then his was math. I kept folders of multiplication problems for his additional practice. When he came to class in the morning or had a few extra minutes during the day, he went to these folders and found his seatwork. He received a reward at the end of each day for additional sheets completed. He was so proud when he caught up with the rest of the class, because he knew it had been through his own efforts."

The best time to deal with problems is early. Immediate intervention may not only prevent a concern from worsening, it may provide the opportunity for educators to work in teams to establish precedents for avoiding or dealing with difficulties in the future.

*Practice Academic Skills Daily.* Teachers should provide students with opportunities to read, speak, and write daily. When a learning problem exists, students tend to avoid related academic areas, clearly because the work is difficult and they feel a sense of embarrassment when they do not perform well.

Yet, students with reading problems gain fluency by reading, as others with math difficulties improve skills through practice. Teachers should set the stage for reinforcement activities through daily scheduling. Even problem areas will not seem so onerous to students if their peers are similarly involved in practice. Students should have the chance to be involved in discussions on a daily basis as well, affording them the opportunity to develop their own ideas and gain self-confidence expressing them to others. Equally important is the development of listening skills, where with teacher modeling and direction, students learn to give the ideas of others equal attention to their own.

*Provide Additional Time to Learn.* Some students with disabilities learn more slowly than their peers. It is important to allow additional time, especially in skill and conceptual development areas, so that they may "overlearn" information. Emphasis on continuous integration allows basic knowledge to become automatic when higher abstractions are studied.

However, it is difficult for teachers to provide additional time for some students to continue their practice when others are finished. Maura handled the situation very capably when Shane needed extra reinforcement to learn arithmetic facts. She provided practice time when peers were involved in other activities.

It is important to note that she did not penalize Shane by viewing extra time as a punishment. Traditionally, teachers have kept students from recess or after school if work is not completed. While punishment may seem justifiable if the student has refused to complete the work, certainly it cannot be used on a student who is exerting full effort but simply learns slowly or requires more practice for content integration.

Teresa adds, "The co-teaching model provides extra support through the special educator being available to review material and provide additional direct teaching when students have not mastered the information. As with Shane, when students need additional time to learn, often I provide the teacher with extra remedial materials for practice. Then, even when I'm not in the room, the student can work in areas he needs."

Most parents like to help their children succeed in school. They should not be excluded when their child needs additional time and practice to learn schoolwork. Teachers should talk to parents and give them information on how to help provide additional practice at home. The teacher should provide books and supportive worksheets, along with direction on how much intervention should come from the parent.

***Monitor Student Success.*** Whether a student requires remedial or advanced work, teacher observation can provide the most accurate evaluation of progress. While quizzes and exams are formal means of responding to student skills in curriculum mastery, overseeing daily work efforts affords teachers the opportunity to stop students encountering a problem and ask them to explain the process. Whether students have been practicing reading and spelling sight words in second grade or conjugating French verbs in high school, teachers can quietly observe improvement and accelerated rate of performance, indicating clearly that learning is taking place.

***Insist that Students Complete their Work.*** "I'm confused about how to be understanding about differentiating assignments and allotting enough time to students, while being sure they're not using their disability as an excuse to get away with something," comments John.

The first step in ensuring that students meet their responsibilities is to give them work at their level. Often, students with disabilities are called "lazy" for not attempting assignments or for working slowly. When teachers assess student skills and assign work they feel to be individually appropriate, they can discuss with students their expectation that the work will be completed as quickly as possible.

At first, students may refuse to try if they have a history of failure. In this instance, it is better to give students work that is slightly below their level that they know they can complete in order to encourage any response. Once students begin to experience a sense of success, they will be more willing to try more difficult assignments in that teacher's class. Teachers should insist that all students complete their work. While most educators are sympathetic towards students with disabilities, a student's placement in special education should never be used as an excuse to not complete an assignment. Special education students should be held to the same class rules and outcomes as anyone else.

***Student Behavior in Groups.*** Similar to expectations for academic self-discipline, teachers should have standards for student behavior in groups. Students with disabilities need to follow these rules since any misbehavior on their part will disrupt the progress of others. If a student begins to behave inappropriately, the teacher should provide a reminder of the rule that is being broken and the correct behavior. If behavior does not change, the teacher should remove the student from group activity and discuss appropriate performance for the future. Each class member should earn the right to participate in the group through successful completion of assigned seatwork and good conduct when working alone. Before beginning the next group assignment, students should recite the rules for participation.

*Make Information Relevant.* A common complaint of students at-risk academically is that schoolwork has no relevance to their lives. For the main part of their day they are asked to attend to and memorize information that they may never need again, or at least whose usefulness they do not understand. Since students tend to concentrate on present time and their own immediate lives, it becomes the teacher's responsibility to help them draw parallels between what they know and what they need to learn. Once students perceive some value in school-related information, they tend to become more motivated in their efforts.

As indicated in Table 10–5, Klumb (1992) suggests some important techniques to help students appreciate the relative value of schoolwork. Teachers should encourage students to paraphrase instead of reciting by rote, requiring them to elaborate on their understanding. When students use their own vocabularies, they are more apt to relate the information to their own experiences. When teachers hear how students have interpreted information, it helps them prevent misunderstanding and indicates where elaboration is necessary.

Similarly, teachers should encourage students to verbalize opinions, providing the opportunity to relate new information to what they already know. Students should ask questions of the teacher and peers. In small-group discussions, they can elaborate on varied opinions, allowing for understanding of alternate viewpoints.

When students select topics of interest they tend to perceive relevance. Allowing them to choose from a limited variety of assignments, or to work on supplementary areas of interest provides motivation to enjoy the task. To expand awareness, teachers may introduce new, but related, information with direct questions that encourage students to explore relationships between ideas.

Teachers should start with the familiar. When exploring new concepts, students enjoy the teacher's use of their names or of significant events. When information begins with accepted or interesting ideas, students have more of a tendency to treat it as relevant.

"That really is true," reflects John. "I had a class last year that I was just going to give up on. Their favorite word was 'boring,' and I admit that I felt that way about them too! One day I was trying to give them an example of great poetry and the features that distinguish it from poor poetry. I looked at Josh tapping away at a song on his desk. Normally, his tapping made me angry, but that day it gave me an idea.

"I asked him to name a few of his favorite songs. After he realized that I wasn't going to embarrass him for not having paid attention, he smiled and named several. Immediately a few others agreed or disagreed loudly that

MY PORTFOLIO

a

ARizona

navada

montana

nubbraska

nevbraska

b

poland          Bolivia

Italy

somalia

Sadi arabca

saudi arabia

In skill areas, such as spelling, teaching students through the familiar results both in motivation and application.

*(Continued)*

MY PORTFOLIO

*(Continued)*

zombea     spaing  sweder

zambia   germany

vietnam        ♥  england

canada

india     IRan  Rusia

c

the ones named were 'great' songs. With my questions directing the discussion, the students gave varied and very heated opinions about which songs had some lyrics or music that even their grandchildren would appreciate. We considered which songs most of them agreed upon and the elements that would make these songs 'great.' Their homework assignment was to read two poems and determine if they were great or not, based upon the criteria we had discussed in class. The next day they came to class excited and ready to argue some more. When Josh raised his hand at the beginning of class, Tom complained, 'Don't call on him. He got to talk a lot yesterday. Call on me.' I never viewed that class the same way again. My expectations for them and myself changed. If I could make the information relevant, they could make the discussion exciting!"

## VARYING METHODS OF INSTRUCTION

John was successful with his "boring" class because he tried something new. He made ideas relevant to their interests and directed the discussion to combine new and familiar information. If he had continued to try to lecture about poetry, it is unlikely that class response would have been as favorable.

Variety is important in teaching, especially for students who have performed poorly in the past in traditional classrooms. If lecture and reading are the bases for learning, students who have difficulty processing oral language or have disabilities in reading will fail. When teachers use alternate methods, they open up new avenues for learning and students see opportunities for success where they have failed before.

Table 10–6 includes a number of options for varying instruction to make it more interesting as well as more responsive to students with varied learning styles (Laurie, Buchwach, Silverman, & Zigmond, 1978; Waldron, 1996). Ranging across a spectrum of activities, these alternate methods can provide "something for everyone," and add excitement to the classroom.

Considered in the previous chapter, the more traditional techniques of lecture and discussion will always have a place as teachers present new information for student consideration. The key is not to avoid using them, but to have specific teaching-learning goals in mind for selecting them. While students who learn well through receptive and expressive verbal language tend to do quite well with these methods, students with visual or experiential learning styles often do not integrate information and become inattentive.

Also highly traditional, basal readers are relied upon for elementary reading instruction, and textbooks for content areas. Above-average readers with good attentional skills do well in obtaining information from books. However, students with reading problems in word analysis or in comprehension rarely perform well if a text-reliant teaching method is emphasized. Similarly, many students with Attention Deficit Hyperactivity Disorder do not have the attentional or organizational skills to read independently for long periods of time and retain information.

---

### Table 10–6
### Options for Varying Instruction

When teaching students with diverse learning needs, educators should employ a variety of alternate methods:

| | |
|---|---|
| • Lecture and discussion | • Educational games |
| • Basals, texts, worksheets | • Technology |
| • Guided independent study | • Learning centers |
| • Demonstration | • Unit study |
| • Simulation and role-playing | • Reports |

(*Source:* Laurie, Buchwach, Silverman, & Zigmond, 1978; Waldron, 1996)

**guided independent study**—student completes assignments under teacher supervision to ensure correctness of response.

These students perform well with **guided independent study**, where they complete reading assignments and worksheets under teacher supervision. They can ask questions concerning details that are unclear, or processes they have not fully integrated, such as in mathematics and science.

Demonstration provides the opportunity for students to observe information first-hand so they can integrate it more thoroughly. This method is particularly effective when there are a series of steps to follow in an ordered sequence, ranging from arithmetic problems to science experiments and sentence syntax in a foreign language. While students who are visual learners benefit most from demonstration, when accompanied by discussion, all will follow processes more easily.

When students perform learning activities themselves, experiences are heightened. Whether through simulation, role-playing, or dramatization, enacting the processes affords the opportunity for long-term recall. These methods are particularly effective when students are experiencing social stigmatization from peers and need to understand improved methods of interacting.

For example, if a student in Maura's class is excluded socially by peers because he has poor interactive skills, he may not know how to behave appropriately to win peer acceptance. Maura must first observe the specific behaviors that are interfering socially. Once she has listed these behaviors, she can develop a role-playing circumstance in which a similar situation occurs. She can have the student participate and discuss appropriate behaviors, asking questions about how each person feels in the situation and ways to treat each other to show mutual respect. In this way, she teaches two lessons: appropriate behaviors and concerns for the feelings of others.

Teachers can use educational games to support student growth in skill knowledge. While games can be played by pairs of students involved in learning centers, they are most effectively used as reinforcement for completion of less-favored tasks. Foreign language teachers wanting to improve vocabulary can have students play *Monopoly* or *Scrabble* after completion of other assignments. The students enjoy the opportunity to play a game during class, and teachers are satisfied that student time is not wasted.

This policy of providing motivational reinforcement is far more beneficial than the policy of "free time" many teachers employ. Allowing students to talk with friends or complete work for other classes once their primary assignment is completed, "free time" becomes wasted time, signaling that class is over even to those who have not completed their work. It also encourages students to become disruptive, creating discipline problems. Through a venue such as educational games that provide additional activities supportive of concepts being studied, teachers can provide more time on task.

Additionally, technology has become increasingly important in supporting the learning of all learners. Perhaps the result of a generation of students arriving at school expecting rapid entertainment similar to television and videogames, more than ever technology has become a viable means of engaging students in learning. Ranging from audiotapes and videotapes to computers, students enjoy varied methods of reinforcement and often attend more fully during their use. While supportive technology will be discussed more extensively in Chapters 11 and 12, it is important to note that it holds the key for successful inclusion of students with deafness, blindness, and physical impairments.

learning centers—areas in a classroom that contain numerous activities and instructional materials organized around a common theme.

Additionally, learning centers provide the opportunity for students to develop and explore concepts under study and to reinforce skill development. They contain numerous activities and instructional materials organized around a common theme. Activities should be directed toward a variety of learning styles as well as independent work by individuals or small groups of students.

"What types of materials would I include in a reading center?" asks Maura. "I'm afraid they would be destroyed or that students wouldn't work well independently."

Materials should be ones that students can handle with comfort. In her reading center, Maura might include a language master for students to compare their reading or spelling of sight words with the model on the tape. High-interest, low-vocabulary books provide an opportunity for independent reading for those students needing reinforcement of sight words, phonics skills, or general reading rate and fluency.

She can have audiotapes to which students listen as they read along with the text, with questioning points where students stop and respond to taped questions. Inexpensive materials such as newspapers, magazines, cartoons, and even travel pamphlets provide students with the opportunity to practice skills. There could be games reinforcing phonics or syllabication skills, played by pairs of students. Boxes of Dolch sight words could be available for students to practice in pairs, recording on checklists which words were read easily and which require further work.

Close to the reading center should be the writing center, where individual and groups of students are prompted to write stories, poetry, even songs, through the use of topic cards, and suggestions listed by the teacher or by students in previous years. Letters to Ann Landers, the President, or the Chamber of Commerce in another state usually provide motivation as well as the opportunity for practice. Questions posed to students about themselves, their interests, and their opinions usually provide incentive for students to express their views. Creative students can write dramas while students with good interpersonal skills can design and conduct interviews on specified topics. Group outcomes from these projects might involve compilations such as a book or newspaper or a school project.

"One of our political science teachers, Clay Harding, had a small project blossom in just that way," commented John. "He started out with a learning center on World War II. The students had helped him gather some of the materials for the center, including folders of articles by categories such as 'Pearl

Harbor,' 'Concentration Camps,' and 'Impact on the American Economy.' The task cards suggested debate topics, such as whether or not we should have bombed Hiroshima. Students who elected these topics conducted their own research. Other students in the learning center read files of newspapers published during the war, describing daily events. They designed their own one-act play about the impact of the war on Americans back home. Learning packets in the center directed students through a series of questions they needed to consider in their debate, play, or discussion.

"The class became really energized with students busily working together in their research. Those with reading problems watched videos about the war and heard taped conversations from men and women who had fought or worked in the factories back home. When Clay assigned task cards for student choice, he was careful to direct the more experiential towards students who need extra input.

"The project went on everyday for three weeks. They asked the teacher if they could share their 'World War II' information with other students in the school. They wanted to present their debate, one-act play, discussion of critical issues, and conclusions about the war. After finding his history colleagues enthused about this experience for their own students, Clay decided that for two days, during history, students from other classes could come to the room and learn about the war. The outcome was excellent. His students were able to show off what they had learned, and the other students benefitted from the information. While his colleagues contemplated how they could use the unit study method in their own rooms, he began to plan the next topic in the curriculum."

This teacher had initiated the study of World War II in the learning center. When students became strongly involved, he expanded to unit study. Emphasizing a broad concept while having a series of subtopics for students to explore, units allow for a more global understanding of a subject. They also permit heterogeneous grouping of students, where interest in a particular area is more important than skill level.

unit study—teaching a broad concept with a series of subtopics for students to explore and allow for global understanding of a subject.

"Clay mentioned an important outcome," noted John. "He included a student with a severe learning disability, a nonreader, in the group studying Pearl Harbor. He was concerned about her ability to research the background of the attack, since she was unable to read most of the library texts. He asked her how she would like to conduct her research, and she asked if there was anyone around who had been at Pearl Harbor. She wanted to conduct an interview on tape and then report orally.

"It made a lot of sense to Clay to have her group work originate through her stronger learning style. After having students in the class ask their grandparents, they actually located a woman who had been there with her husband and children during the attack. She was delighted to recall her experiences for the student, who was fascinated by the details. The oral presentation to the larger group went well, with many students asking interesting questions." In this instance unit study provided a means for everyone to excel.

The teacher realized that learning styles differ and varied activities allowed for all students' needs.

An important outcome of Clay's unit on World War II was involving students in reports on their research or group discussions. Reports provide a directive to students regarding outcomes expected from their work, and lend a sense of direction and significance to assignments.

However, it is important that teachers provide alternate means of reporting information than the traditional method of one student speaking to the entire group. In addition to instilling fear in the student making the presentation, peers are frequently bored and inattentive. Since student-read reports are even more unappealing than teacher lectures, any information to be shared is superseded by the wish that a tortured peer be allowed to return to his seat!

Clay's design of the history unit, allowing students to provide debates, to role-play, to discuss first-hand interviews with others, creates an interesting format for students to share information. Before beginning the unit of study, teachers should consider varied ways students can report their outcomes so the process will decrease anxiety for the presenter while increasing total class knowledge and enjoyment.

Table 10–7 lists a series of activities that students can perform both in group and unit work. All of these allow for an interesting and non-threatening reporting of information to the larger group of peers at the completion of the unit.

Ones such as creating an exhibit allow for a variety of activities. Students can begin with a field trip to a natural history museum to understand the idea of an exhibit and its components. Afterwards, within the content of their unit they can discuss which areas to include in the exhibit. In doing so, they are planning the topical areas of interest to them. For example, within a unit on Native Americans, after selecting which tribes to study, the students might decide to investigate tribal food, homes, hunting, fighting, and religions. This planning session serves several purposes. It promotes motivation through choice of area of study, as well as delineating specific content to be covered and how it will be presented to the class in its final form.

When students have completed the unit of study, by presenting their research through an exhibit for their peers, not only do they experientially summarize their research, supporting long-term memory of information, but they also allow other students to visualize and better integrate research from the entire class.

Other varied reporting methods listed in Table 10–7 include writing a story instead of a formal essay discussing information gathered, affording students creativity in their discussion. Sharing magazine pictures and photos with peers, discussing relevance to the topic discussed, allows students visual supports for conceptual clarity. Use of newspapers, ranging from data on current events to stock market fluctuations, encourages the intermeshing of the theoretical and the real. The alternative of having students create their own newspaper provides the opportunity for varied activities, ranging from interviewing

**Table 10–7**
**Activities for Varying Instruction**

There are numerous activities beyond traditional reading and lecture that teachers can use to motivate and involve learners:

- create an exhibit around an expanded unit or topic

- perform an experiment

- cut out magazine pictures and discuss relationship to topic

- conduct a survey or interview

- write a story or letter in place of a report

- draw a map of familiar locations such as the neighborhood

- after a field visit, combine group experiences into a report on most interesting observations

- take photographs and use them as basis for the report

- write newspaper headlines for classroom experiences or discussion, encompassing main occurrences and ideas

- discuss a personal event with a peer who then summarizes the discussion for the class

- use mail-order catalogs for basic arithmetic instruction

- follow selected stocks, bonds, and funds in the stock market, noting changes and predicting economic directions

- rate independently read books on a "best-seller list"

- make a newspaper for class/school distribution

(*Source:* Adapted from Klumb, 1992)

school and community figures, to creating the layout for final copy, and practicing objectivity in reporting school-related events. Mail-order catalogs provide reinforcement activities for arithmetic facts, such as computation of item costs including taxes and postage.

## TEACHING FACTUAL INFORMATION

"All this sounds good," observes John, "but I'm still concerned about how to teach students the facts and skills they need. Activities such as creating a newspaper or reporting research within a story format are motivational and fun. If inclusion is going to work in my class, I need to be sure students are acquiring all the basic information they need."

Table 10–8, on page 349, includes a list of techniques for teaching factual information effectively (Howell, Fox, & Morehead, 1993; Klumb, 1992;

Unit study can result in exhibits on a variety of topics.

Scruggs & Mastropieri, 1992). While many of these strategies are implemented individually, they have greatest impact when combined and directed toward the goal of building specific skills.

Certain techniques listed may differ from common instructional practices. For example, teaching a series of brief lessons around related skills will have a greater impact than longer lessons encompassing more information. When each of the shorter lessons is followed by drill and practice, students have the opportunity to master information.

The concept of distributed practice (Klumb, 1992), where students apply the information from the lesson over a number of short periods, allows time for integration of new concepts as well as review. While teachers may expect students who learn more slowly to respond more slowly, it is important to have everyone drill and practice until they respond rapidly and automatically. During these periods, teachers should provide feedback on the accuracy and rate of student responses, encouraging personal improvement instead of group competition.

"I can see where this would be really useful," comments Maura. "I have a large number of students in my class who have 'splinter skills,' ones where they know some of this process and some of another, but whose overall abilities are incomplete. For example, Kate is a strong auditory and weak visual learner. She's really good at phonics, but rarely reads or spells common words that can't be analyzed, such as *the, when, that, who*. She has seen these words many times and occasionally guesses correctly from context, but she could use some of those brief lessons with lots of practice, maybe with a language master or a tracing approach. Learning them automatically would improve her reading greatly."

The technique of separating the teaching of material that is frequently confused is not new to special educators. Since students such as Kate may have problems reading and remembering whole words because they misperceive letters, such as *b/d, c/o, m/n, l/i, m/w,* and *m/n,* it is important to overteach one skill, such as reading the letter *b* and then to teach dissimilar letters, such as *l, m,* and *r.* Only when the student has overlearned *b* to the point of automaticity should the teacher introduce the letter *d.* Practicing other letters that are significantly different in appearance while providing daily practice in reading and writing *b* allows the student to fully integrate the shape and sound of this letter. When the student has mastered one of the similar pair of letters, he is ready to begin the second. This method is far more effective than teaching the students rules or tricks to indicate the difference in similar letters. Students tend to spend time trying to remember the trick instead of identifying the letter.

Table 10–8 includes practice strategies to help students learn new or difficult information permanently. While they would find it tedious to read or repeat aloud all information they study, students should verbalize difficult material audibly and then read it silently. They should repeat this verbalization until they recall the information easily and automatically. This technique is especially effective for data that is necessary to learn by rote, such as facts in addition, subtraction, and multiplication; vocabulary and conjugations in a foreign language; definitions of terms or formulas in advanced mathematics and science; terminology basic to content fields and the arts.

They should also use memory strategies such as categorizing similar information with previous experiences and vocabulary. Mnemonic devices allowing for association with familiar material are highly effective, especially when humorous. Students remember the connection, which in turn helps them recall the facts.

Students have a tendency to restrict the application of information to the situation in which it has been learned. Mathematical content is particularly vulnerable to lack of connection with real-life situations. Students tend to memorize data to complete computational problems as if these were an end in themselves. When asked to complete "word problems," often they complain because of the difficulty of applying facts. It is important for teachers to present questions and problem-solving situations that allow for association of basic skills with broader concepts. Often students are more motivated to practice drill activities when they know the information will help them be more competent in the future. When teachers enjoy the process, using student names and school-based situations, they bridge the gap between having students use rote memory to pass a test and long-term memory for important information.

## Table 10–8
## Techniques for Teaching Factual Information

When teaching basic skills and facts, teachers should follow these guidelines:

- review prior knowledge before beginning the lesson

- lessons should be brief and targeted toward specific skills

- when skills have a number of steps, teachers should conduct several short lessons instead of one long one

- encourage rapid responses from students

- provide drill and practice until mastery is obtained

- use "distributed practice"

- when information is easily confused, separate its presentation over long periods of time

- use systematic procedures, such as flashcards, for reinforcement

- pair students who have similar skill needs

- relate basic facts to students' practical experiences

- have students verbalize information aloud and then silently to themselves as they study

- encourage use of memory strategies (e.g., rehearsal and categorization)

- use parents as tutors

- have students use skills in a variety of situations beyond ones initially studied

- as students learn basic facts, apply the information to broader conceptual knowledge to encourage understanding of application

- as students master skills, gradually introduce new ones

- after skills have been practiced, check periodically to assure mastery

(*Source:* Adapted from Howell, Fox, & Morehead, 1993; Klumb, 1992; Scruggs & Mastropieri, 1992)

Another motivational tool for teaching facts is to have students work together to drill in systematic ways such as flash cards or checking each other's oral and written practice. Often pairs of students are more effective than larger groups for skill-building, since each student is afforded more time to practice instead of waiting for others to complete their recitation.

However, as discussed earlier in creating grouping arrangements, paired students should be at approximately the same level of skill needs (Scruggs & Mastropieri, 1992). When students who are more advanced are asked to listen to another student perform drill or practice activities, they become bored, unmotivated, and often initiate behavior problems. When both students need to learn the information, they are more motivated and benefit equally.

As students practice skills, teachers should observe rate and accuracy and supply frequent feedback through praise and corrections. When students master one skill, teachers should gradually introduce the next, carefully integrating skills and demonstrating how each builds on the other.

To ensure that students place new skills in their long-term memory store, teachers should carefully examine ongoing work products for correctness. They should review basic information periodically if they feel that it has not been overlearned. Many times this review requires only minutes of the teacher providing reminders about application of skills, ranging from writing correct sentences and performing a musical piece to the use of laboratory equipment or a mathematical formula.

# TEACHING CONCEPTS

The teaching of concepts is far more sophisticated than skills development. Students require time to integrate information into their pre-existing knowledge base and use it as a springboard into additional abstractions and generalizations. When concepts are taught carefully and hierarchically, affording multiple reinforcement opportunities, they become basic to future cognitive development.

"Conceptual development is an area in which teachers tend to underrate the potential of students with disabilities," notes Teresa. "In my discussions with classroom teachers, I hear comments that a student won't be able to understand higher-order information. I believe this is true only if the teacher uses the lecture format or does not allow enough time and practice for integration. However, it has been my experience that most students can integrate concepts if we guide them through the process."

Table 10–9 includes a number of techniques for effectively teaching concepts. Instead of solely using lecture and discussion of ideas as they occur, teachers should have a structured plan before introducing the lesson. They should review prior knowledge of related areas to form the foundation for new input. Students should not encounter new or technical vocabulary for the first time as they read. Before beginning the assignment, teachers should introduce words critical to the passage. With direction, often the class can attain meaning through analyzing the word structurally. Teachers can attach explanations and memory devices such as mnemonics to encourage long-term retention.

In addition to vocabulary, teachers should introduce significant concepts before beginning the lesson. Concepts taught should be a part of the total curriculum, a structure allowing for continuous content integration as the year continues. Concepts selected for current instruction should form a smaller conceptual unit and be sequenced in order of their difficulty.

To avoid confusion, from the onset teachers should specifically name the concepts under study and continue to use the same name throughout the unit. For example, if Maura is teaching arithmetic, she might carefully define terms

**Table 10–9**
**Techniques for Teaching Concepts**

When teaching significant concepts, teachers should follow these guidelines:

- review prior knowledge before beginning the lesson

- introduce vocabulary, especially technical terms

- overview important main ideas and topics before beginning the lesson

- plan units of instruction in large, related conceptual blocks

- divide blocks into smaller conceptual units and sequence in order of difficulty for individual lessons

- name the concept at the onset and use the same name throughout all lessons; introduce synonyms later when students are comfortable with the topic

- draw cognitive maps of concepts with students

- provide multiple examples of the concept

- ask students why something is or is not an example of the concept

- have students identify things that are/are not examples of the concept

- discuss how an example of the concept can be changed to a non-example

- ask frequent questions when presenting new information

- ask students to support their answers

- explain clearly why an answer is correct or incorrect

- play "devil's advocate"

- over an extended period of time, afford frequent opportunities for practice in using concepts

- help students apply knowledge beyond the situation and examples studied; apply to their real-life experiences whenever possible

- through verbalizing, writing, reading, interacting, provide continuous opportunities for students to integrate new concepts

- actively involve students in reinforcement techniques:
   ReQuest: teacher and student (student and student) take turns asking each other about the text or information studied
   Concept Maps: displays and diagrams of an idea are visible during class
   DTRA (Directed Thinking-Reading Activity): students predict what will happen and read to confirm predictions
   Focus Journals: teacher poses a different "focus question" each day and students write a brief comment in response

(*Sources:* Adapted from Howell, Fox, & Morehead, 1993; Klumb, 1992; Morsink, 1984)

such as subtraction and multiplication, avoiding terms such as "take away" or "times" in her teaching. Once students have mastered the process, she can allow the use of colloquialisms or synonyms.

The use of examples is critical to understanding concepts. Teachers should provide multiple examples of a concept, then ask students why something is or is not an example. Subsequently, on their own or in groups, students should be asked to identify things that are or are not examples of the

The Environment is something that we need. Some living things you can eat, other things you can't. Everything needs respect and some people do not know that and that is not good.

**All students should have the opportunity to express their ideas concerning significant issues.** Reprinted with permission, Winston School, San Antonio.

concept. Finally, students and teachers should work together to explore how examples can be changed to nonexamples.

In a class studying the tenets of freedom, the teacher might begin by giving students examples of how the United States Constitution guarantees all citizens freedom of speech and the right to vote. The teacher could then provide multiple examples from American history that have supported or denied freedom to individuals, ranging from slavery before the Civil War to the recent *Americans with Disabilities Act.* In large and small groups, students should be asked to discuss how the noted situations or laws are examples or nonexamples of freedom. They can then identify their own examples of freedom, giving reasons for their selection. Finally, under the teacher's direction, they should consider how the specific examples they have discussed could be changed to non-examples (e.g., return to governmental policies of segregation; denial of the right of free speech to certain political and ethnic groups).

As teachers present new information, they should ask frequent questions and require students to support answers. Teachers should explain clearly why an answer is correct or incorrect. Playing "devil's advocate" at times by espousing an alternate view to that stated by a student can be highly effective. Students enjoy this process when they understand that the teacher is not expressing a personal opinion but is encouraging them to think more broadly and use logic to support their own ideas.

As with skill building for facts, teachers need to provide numerous opportunities for students to practice applying and expanding on the ideas they are learning. Spaced over time, reinforcement can be conducted through teacher questions in large and small group discussions, as well as student reading and writing assignments. The previous example of teaching freedom as a concept can be expanded across content areas, into considerations of history and politics, literature, and the arts. While secondary teachers have a designated content area, they broaden student awarenesses immeasurably when they refer to concepts outside the usual realm of their subject area.

This cross-application of information helps students understand how concepts relate to their daily lives and interactions with others, resulting in increased motivation for learning. The more often they apply newly studied ideas, the better their appreciation of the complexity of daily life. By teaching the increased use of logic, educators are expanding students' knowledge base and ability to make sound judgments.

ReQuest—a paired question-answer technique in which the teacher and student, or pairs of students, take time asking each other about information from the text.

Additionally, Table 10–9 lists specific techniques for introducing and reinforcing concepts. Summarized by Klumb (1992), educators and students alike find these to be both effective and motivational. **ReQuest** is a paired question-answer technique in which the teacher and student take time asking each other about information from the text. Often teachers are too busy with the larger group to work individually with students. In these instances, pairs of students working together can design questions. Before using this technique, students should be directed in asking inferential and main idea questions instead of those solely pertaining to facts.

Directed Thinking-Reading Activities (DTRA)—a method of teaching in which students make predictions and support their predictions with logic and association.

**Directed thinking-reading activities (DTRA)** can form the basis for interesting discussions relying on logic and insight. In this method, students predict what will happen next in a story (or mathematics problem, or scientific experiment). In defending their prediction, they need to use logic and association to support its validity. These classroom discussions can be lively and can encourage students to listen to and challenge each other's viewpoints. Then they read or perform the activity to see if their prediction is correct.

Focus Journals—students write a brief comment in response to a teacher's daily "journal focus" question, including support for their opinion or response.

**Focus Journals** provide an excellent opportunity for students to apply concepts they have studied to the reality of their daily lives. The teacher asks a "journal focus" question that varies each day. Students write a brief comment in response, including support for their opinion or response. While this activity need only take a few minutes, it requires students to go outside their personal world and consider situations different from their own.

"That's an interesting idea," reflects John. "I find my students tend to be very egocentric, as if their personal reality is the only one that exists. Unfortunately they tend not to read much outside of school, and too often they lack an awareness of important world events, as well as information in science and in the arts. I could enjoy asking them to read an article in the day's paper on a political issue, such as whether the U.S. should sell arms to warring nations, and then have them write their opinion the next day. Another day it would be fun to ask if citizens should save snail darters from extinction when it will mean loss of jobs in that geographical location for thousands of people. I could ask economic questions, or have them regard a print of a modernistic work of art in their texts and ask them to support why they feel the piece should or should not be considered art. The use of these focus journals could be fun for me too."

To save John's time and encourage students to use logic and the concepts they are discussing, peers might read each other's journal entries on a particular topic and discuss differences or similarities in responses. Small groups could consider journal writings and compare and contrast opinions.

The teaching of concepts can be interesting for teachers as well as students. Key issues involve relating new information to prior knowledge, using extensive examples and indepth questioning, and giving students the opportunity to practice over an extended time period.

# SUMMARY

Chapter 10 included a number of strategies for improving student learning in the classroom. Techniques for motivating students to learn ranged from using varied methods and interesting activities to effective use of praise. Since many students refuse to try because they have a history of failure, it is important for teachers to create a risk-free environment. Rewarding effort and giving students enough time to complete their work affords a sense of success.

Teachers should examine their own behaviors and how they may impact student performance. Including all students in discussions through asking questions at a varied range of difficulty improves student academic esteem. Heightened expectations for time on task and individual performance creates a sense that everyone can be productive. Including students in discussing their learning problems and evaluating their progress gives a feeling of openness and acceptance to student-teacher interactions.

There are a series of guidelines for conducting small groups effectively. Groups should be flexible, allowing students to move freely as academic levels and interests vary. Scheduling all work closely helps students begin independently. If teachers use folders containing weekly assignments, they help students follow their own progress. Time is another critical element. Teachers should allow sufficient time for direct teaching, guided and independent practice, so students can gain skill mastery.

A number of strategies were discussed for use in engaging all students academically. Teachers should give directions, explanations, and clarifications in brief statements, having students repeat the most important. Instruction and practice should move along rapidly to lessen opportunities for misbehavior. Practice activities should be short and brisk, with a sense of commitment to the task.

In the inclusive class, there are a number of general techniques that allow teachers to meet the needs of all learners. Immediate intervention for learning or behavior problems prevents their escalation. All students should be required to demonstrate appropriate group behavior. Specialist teachers can provide additional work in the classroom when students need much reinforcement.

When students attach personal meaning to information, they tend to understand and recall it far better. They should be directed to express their opinions, ask questions, and select topics of interest for projects.

Teachers can vary instruction from typical lecture and reading to a number of alternate formats that are more motivational. Students enjoy demonstrations and hands-on experiential learning. Educational games with peers provide good skills reinforcement, as do computers. Learning centers allow students to work independently and at varied levels. Unit study supports heterogeneous grouping where all students can participate and support each other's learning.

Activities to promote learning should be varied and fun. Students enjoy creating exhibits to demonstrate learning from unit study. They are motivated when actively involved, such as in taking photographs, participating in a skit or simulation, and conducting interviews. In mathematics they learn more experientially through using mail-order catalogs and following favored stocks.

When teaching basic skills and facts, teachers should carefully review previous learning to be sure prerequisite skills are in place. They should separate the teaching of skills that may be confused, and encourage use of memory strategies. Teachers should encourage students to apply skills to their broader experiences, using real-life examples. Practice activities should include generalization to new areas of interest to the student.

When teaching concepts, teachers should introduce technical or unusual vocabulary in advance of reading. Units should be planned conceptually, with students frequently being asked to discuss relationships between concepts. Information should be sequenced in order of difficulty so that students build one concept upon another. Questioning should be frequent and require application of ideas. Playing "devil's advocate" encourages students to consider alternate viewpoints. Activities such as directed thinking and reading activities engage students in predicting outcomes. Others such as Focus Journals provide students the opportunity to write daily responses to teacher questions. Learners are encouraged to go beyond their daily activities to consider situations outside their usual experiences.

**CASE STUDY:** *Elementary*

Jane is a student in your fifth-grade class. She has a history of school failure, especially in the basic skills areas of word recognition and analysis, as well as arithmetic facts. Never having mastered these areas, her academic difficulties have compounded. Currently she is unable to read content area texts. She cannot understand fractions and decimals as well as peers since she has never mastered addition through division facts.

Last year she complained of headaches and stomach aches before school each day. At school she refused to participate in any academic work, also withdrawing from peers. When tested for special education services, she was diagnosed as having a severe anxiety disorder.

As your school year begins, you have a number of goals for Jane:

1. to improve her basic skills in decoding words and completing arithmetic facts;

2. to have her interact with peers in class activities; and

3. to decrease her negative response to school and learning.

Based on the ideas suggested in Chapter 10, list specific ways you will achieve all of these goals.

CASE STUDY: *Secondary*

Perhaps you've been teaching too long. Could this be "burn-out," or just that you're in a rut? Both you and your students lack enthusiasm daily. You lecture. They talk to each other and pass notes. You cover the curriculum, but their test scores indicated that they haven't learned it. While you used to be excited by teaching, you're feeling bored these days—and so are your students. You want to see if you can stem this tide and gain back your pleasure in teaching.

1. In your content area, what are specific ways that you can vary instruction so that you lecture less often?

2. What types of small-grouping arrangements are best suited to your subject? To enhance classroom motivation, how will you vary them to incorporate areas of personal interest to students?

3. Which of the techniques in Table 10–8 can you use to teach and reinforce factual information without boring students?

4. Which techniques in Table 10–9 apply to your content area as possible ways to teach critical concepts?

# TEACHING TECHNIQUES AND CURRICULUM MODIFICATION

# 11

# TECHNIQUES FOR STUDENTS WITH LEARNING AND BEHAVIORAL DIFFERENCES

While Westside teachers were feeling more confident about their ability to work with classes of diverse learners, Alex wanted to be sure they were comfortable instructing individual students with unique needs. "It's one thing to know how to motivate a class to learn, but quite another to teach reading to a student who missequences letter order in words. There will always be some learners who require specialized techniques, modified curricula and materials."

Teresa agreed. "Teachers have to know how to teach students with hearing or visual impairments as well as ones who are learning disabled or behaviorally disordered. It's a type of 'security blanket' for making inclusion work. It's hard to go too far wrong if you know in advance how to teach to a particular student's needs."

# STUDENTS FROM MINORITY LANGUAGE BACKGROUNDS

John responded, "I'd like to start by discussing specialized techniques to use with ESL students. We have so many new students who are learning English as a second language and also have disabilities. While we discussed earlier how to assess and sort out cultural factors, I don't understand the best way to teach ESL students yet. Do I emphasize facts or concepts? What type of systems are strongest for improving spoken and written language? I need some direction."

In their use of the Assessment and Intervention Model for the Bilingual Exceptional Student (AIM for the BESt), Ortiz and Wilkinson (1991) discuss optimal strategies for ESL instruction. They note the lack of success of commonly used teaching approaches emphasizing task analysis, sequential instruction ranging from simple to complex activities, and direct instruction focusing on drills and practice (Cummins, 1984). They observe that while drill may appear to improve student language structure, it is an unnatural way to learn because it treats developmental or overgeneralization problems as if they are errors. Additionally, direct instruction de-emphasizes higher-order thinking skills in order to simplify teaching activities relying on automaticity of student response.

reciprocal interaction—a teaching approach in which the teacher creates spoken and written dialog with the student, emphasizing higher-order thinking instead of basic skills.

Ortiz and Wilkinson (1991) underscore the use of **reciprocal interaction** teaching approaches for language minority students with disabilities. The teacher creates a dialog with the student, emphasizing higher-order thinking instead of basic skills. This interchange should involve both spoken and written communication, affording the student motivation to express ideas instead of performing rote memory activities.

While specific approaches differ, reciprocal interaction emphasizes reading comprehension over word attack skills, and written expression of ideas over correct punctuation. The assumption is not that skills are unimportant, since a student needs to be able to read fluently to attain full comprehension and to use grammatic elements correctly for clarity of expression. The underlying premise is that the purpose of language is to share ideas mutually and in a relaxed, unstructured format. When students are motivated to say something important to them, they work harder to find the words.

Teachers should integrate language throughout the curriculum and not treat it as a separate subject. The more students hear English, the more quickly they learn to use it appropriately. Within the school environment, language opportunities abound. In class daily, teachers should emphasize new vocabulary critical to understanding content areas, while at recess or between class periods, they should have informal discussions with students. Language experience approaches and writing in personal journals afford opportunities for students to express themselves without fear of criticism.

Students tend to learn language more quickly when they want membership in a significant peer group. Teachers can structure the classroom to expedite interactions through cooperative learning and peer tutoring. Conversational partnerships with peers help limited-English-proficient students expand their content knowledge as well as improve their overall interactive language structure to express themselves optimally.

**shared literature units**—students in the class participate in a different thematic unit every few weeks in which the teacher provides introductory activities for units and books.

Ortiz and Wilkinson (1991) recommend the use of **shared literature units**. All students in the class participate in a different thematic unit every few weeks. Teachers are provided guides including introductory activities for units and books. After these activities, they read a picture book to elementary students or a content chapter to secondary students. Teachers then ask students a series of questions and record their responses on a chart. Considerations should include higher-order questions about the reading, with varied follow-up activities to enhance language skills, including writing, drama, art, and simulations. The combination of award-winning literature or supportive content coverage followed by a language experience approach stimulates ESL students through creative exercises.

**Graves Writing Workshop**—a system in which students write daily and hold conferences with the teacher and peers to discuss content; writing efforts are finalized into books.

The **Graves Writing Workshop** (Graves, 1983) also relies upon reciprocal interaction as a means of improving language skills through activities that are beneficial to the entire class. Based on individually chosen topics, students write daily. Teachers hold individual conferences with students, asking questions about writing content and evaluating basic skills. At times students meet with peers to discuss their content. These dialogues afford opportunities for teachers and students to interact verbally, supporting the development both of academic and conversational skills. Additionally, as teachers observe the need for skill instruction in areas such as spelling and punctuation, they can review information for the student or the class. After editing their work, students finalize their writing into books that are placed in the classroom for other students to read.

"What do you do in any of these systems if a student has a more severe reading or writing problem requiring extensive remediation?"

When a student's progress is hindered by significant lapses in basic skills, teachers should list the specific areas where remedial instruction is required. Relying on informal review of student work products from class or indepth assessment by school psychologists, deficit areas should be identified. Then special educators can work individually with the student in identified need areas, or with small groups of students with similar problems. Additionally, the consultant teacher model can be used, where the specialist provides the regular classroom teacher with techniques, and additional or modified materials to support student gains. It is critical to offer a combined program of enriched language opportunities with supportive skills instruction for ESL students.

# STUDENTS WITH COGNITIVE AND LEARNING DISABILITIES

Students with cognitive and learning disabilities may demonstrate a large number of varied behaviors. Some students' problems may be an outgrowth of not perceiving information correctly as they process it initially. Others may have difficulty examining new information at higher levels of abstraction, demonstrating problems with association and classification of ideas. For other students, short- or long-term memory deficits may be present, hindering recall and application of information covered in classes.

Some students' problems may be a result of an inability to attend well, to concentrate on readings and lectures in order to process school-related information. They may be disorganized, demonstrating poor use of time in advance planning or studying. While their actual disability may not be caused by a cognitive loss, they are experiencing behaviors counterproductive to the learning process and to achieving their potential.

While the type of behavior may vary, there are some general techniques that work well with students demonstrating cognitive and learning problems. Listed in Table 11–1, these strategies rely on the use of appropriateness and transferability of information to students' personal lives and experiences. When students can relate new information to things they know, they tend to understand and recall it more extensively.

When teachers present information outside the experiences of their students, they should use media, discussion, stories, and simulation to help students visualize and integrate meaning. As a means of assuring understanding, they should afford students the opportunity to talk, discussing their ideas with the teacher and peers. A student's nods and smiles during a lesson may be indicative of the presence of a social behavior to avoid appearing foolish, but should not be taken to indicate understanding of content. When the student explains the information to the teacher's satisfaction, the teacher may feel confident in proceeding.

Since many students with learning disabilities read below grade level, teachers may tend to provide materials for younger children. It is very important to provide content that is age-appropriate. Not only does it contain information of significantly greater interest, but it sends the important message that the student is on a social level acceptable to peers. Studying information written for younger children tells students that they must be developmentally delayed since they cannot read, further supporting the concept of inadequacy.

Teachers should also attempt to have learners apply class information to their daily lives on a continuous basis. Having students watch the evening news and write their responses to a particular social or political issue increases their awareness as world citizens while considering how outside events impact them personally. Requiring students to watch a sunrise on a school day or study the seasonal changes in plants assists them in applying science to their daily lives. Taking them to a classical concert or a museum

**Table 11–1**
**Techniques for Students with Cognitive and Learning Disabilities**

Teachers should:

- use concrete objects and personal experiences whenever possible

- relate all learning to students' personal experiences, making the relationship evident through discussion

- practice transfer of new information to situations beyond those initially studied through experiential tasks such as role-playing and simulation

- review, and re-teach if necessary, prerequisite information for new material

- teach material that is meaningful to students' lives and has immediate application

- question students about their understanding of all new information as it is being taught, making clarifications immediately and re-questioning student understanding

- provide additional opportunities to practice information, beyond that required by the rest of the class

- outline material using primary headings and subheadings, indicating relationships between ideas

- assess each student's optimal learning modality before beginning instruction, and direct information towards each learning style

- eliminate irrelevant details and information and focus on essential knowledge in any lesson

- avoid activities that require copying from the blackboard or overhead projector

- through highlighting, use color whenever possible to underscore ideas; to demonstrate relationships, use one color for main topics and another for secondary

- have students explain a process while it is being learned, assuring understanding of individual steps

- teach brief lessons at a rapid pace to sustain student interest

(*Source:* Adapted from Scruggs & Mastropieri, 1992; Waldron, 1996)

on a field trip may initiate a lifetime love of the arts. Showing videos of life in other countries motivates them to study other languages and explore their world. Students tend to view things from a perspective centered on their own experiences. To make information meaningful, it is necessary to study those experiences and expand them gradually into new arenas.

"What about basic skills instruction?" asks Maura. "How can I be sure that students are ready to learn the information and are really understanding it as we go along? I'm asking this because of a bad teaching year with Joey, a third-grader last year. From the beginning of the year, everything we studied seemed to be over his head. He was lacking some reading and math skills that made it really difficult for him to be successful as we progressed. He didn't seem to understand many of the concepts we covered and by the end of the year both he and I felt a sense of failure. I worried that I had wasted a year of his life, but frankly, I just didn't know how to teach him."

Maura's frustration is expressed by many teachers. Traditionally, educators were able to focus more time on developing academic skills, remaining closer to curricular demands. Yet with increasingly difficult social problems children and adolescents bring to school, the academic focus has been lessened because of more encompassing problems diverting teachers' attention. As a result, many students outside of special education lack specific skills basic to their academic success. Teachers may find that a large percentage of their class needs specialized techniques to support their learning of curriculum content.

The skills techniques listed in Table 11–1 will be helpful for those students who are behind academically, even if they do not have cognitive or learning disabilities. When students such as Joey demonstrate difficulty from the onset, teachers should informally assess their skill levels using the techniques discussed previously. During assessment they should note if the student is an auditory or visual learner, aiding their later approach to teaching.

For example, Maura might determine that Joey has some problems recalling sight words common to reading, as well as basic arithmetic facts, but is good at phonics and recalling multiplication tables he has practiced aloud. This information would not only tell her what he needed to learn as prerequisite skills to be successful in her class, but that she needs to teach him through primarily auditory channels.

She should begin the year with a review of background information he will need to progress in the year's curriculum. Since there will always be other students requiring similar remediation, she should form a small skills group, or pair students together, where they can work in areas of common need. This group should meet as often and as long as possible so that students will receive intensive training at the beginning of the year, enabling them to progress into the required curriculum.

"How will I ever teach them the entire curriculum if they have to spend so much of my time on review?"

Teachers express this concern frequently. However, it is important to realize that if students do not have prerequisite skills, they cannot progress and understand new curricular content. With Joey as a case in point, the entire year can be spent covering the curriculum without him ever learning the curriculum. Early, intense training in skills areas lays the groundwork for students having the capacity to progress.

"If the student's skills are so low that a large portion of the year will be spent in remediation instead of curricular progress?"

It becomes necessary to bring the special education teacher into the classroom daily to meet with the group of students in a direct-teaching model. If students still cannot learn the basic skills quickly enough to be of use that year, both teachers should use compensatory techniques. These will bypass basic skills when possible and instead allow students to concentrate on primary curricular concepts. For example, if a student cannot read the text, the teacher can use taped books. Students with handwriting or spelling problems can use a computer word processor with spelling correction. When compensation is used, it should accompany ongoing remediation by specialists in areas where the student can demonstrate progress.

Additionally, teachers can use some of these compensatory techniques in their daily teaching to ensure that all students are learning critical information.

Use of charts and behavioral reminders supports students in fulfilling teacher expectations.

Listed in Table 11–1, strategies focus on emphasizing critical concepts and elimination of irrelevant details and information. Teachers should use the questioning techniques discussed in earlier chapters, assuring that students have an ongoing understanding of content. During lessons, teachers should call on all students, asking them questions about information being studied. When student response indicates a lack of understanding, teachers should either re-explain or demonstrate the information in another way, such as through media use or hands-on experience. The teacher should always keep in mind whether the student's primary learning style is visual, auditory, or kinesthetic, and provide practice through that modality.

The way practice is provided is also critical to success. Some students with cognitive disabilities require more time to integrate information. This time is best spent performing reinforcement activities such as listening to tapes of information, writing new content down and saying it aloud, or pairing with another student at the same level, using a language master or flashcards when rote is necessary. Joey can practice his sight words and basic arithmetic facts with another student daily, increasing both their retention.

Secondary students appreciate reading texts where important information is highlighted or underscored, directing them toward essential facts. Many schools now use taped texts, permitting students with reading problems to gain the same curricular information as peers. Teachers should avoid overuse of blackboards or overhead projectors, since many students copy information incorrectly.

"True," comments John. "In the past I've had my students copy vocabulary words for their Friday test. I've held them responsible for correct spelling as well as definition. Although they had defined it correctly, when several students lost points consistently for misspelling the word, I decided to check their copying skills. Sure enough, they were missequencing or omitting letters and syllables when rewriting the word. They were studying it as they had misspelled it and then reporting it back to me incorrectly on the test. When I started giving them a printed sheet with their words on it, having them practice from the correct model, they had few spelling problems."

# PERCEPTION

These students may have had perceptual problems common to students with cognitive and learning disabilities. Their visual difficulties with sequencing and correctly discriminating letters are indicative of only one type of perceptual disorder. Students may have difficulties perceiving information correctly through any area of the auditory, visual, or kinesthetic channels.

MY PORTFOLIO

> The BrBr Gav heR a
> checup.

Students with visual memory problems have difficulty recalling the correct spelling of words.
Reprinted with permission, Winston School, San Antonio.

Perceptual skills are critical to academic success, because when information is not taken in correctly, it becomes almost impossible for students to respond with any degree of accuracy.

For example, if Carl missequences letter order and perceives the word *perfect* to be *prefect*, he will have difficulty gaining any meaning as he reads the sentence "It was a prefect time for him to leave." If he has visual-spatial problems, causing him to invert the letter *p* into *b*, he will find it impossible to decode or comprehend the sentence "It was a brefect time for him to leave." Or if he cannot recall certain sounds that accompany letters, he may be unable to analyze the consonant blend *pr* at all.

Some students with perceptual problems have difficulty distinguishing or sequencing sounds and letters accurately or blending sounds into words. Others have spatial problems, preventing them from tracking a line of print in reading and writing. Each of these problems can have a profound impact on the way that students understand information that they see and hear, as well as the responses they provide in their reading, speaking, writing, and computing. Faulty input results in faulty output.

Faulty input also results in faulty memory. For example, if Maura gives directions to the class to take out their books and papers, write their name and the date on the top left corner, and answer arithmetic questions on page 42, a student with an auditory sequencing problem will not be able to follow all these directions accurately. He may write the name and date on the wrong section of the paper or begin arithmetic problems on a different page than directed. Instead of becoming angry or frustrated at the student, it is important for Maura to prevent the problem before it happens. Many times students are blamed for being lazy or inattentive when in actuality they did not understand or recall the information correctly.

Table 11–2 lists a number of problems commonly encountered by students with perceptual problems and techniques teachers can use to help them. Sadly,

**Table 11–2**
**Techniques for Students with Perception Problems**

*Problems Distinguishing Between Similar-Appearing Letters and Numbers (e.g., i/l, c/o, m/n, b/d, 3/8, 1/7)*

- Overteach one letter or number until the student masters it. Teach dissimilar ones next.
- Use a multisensory technique, having student trace letter/number in sand or salt. Have student place a screen under a sheet of paper and write the letter, number, or word on the paper in crayon. Remove the screen and have the student trace the raised image while saying the name.
- Write the confused letter or number oversized and in a bright color so the student will attend to it more carefully.
- Pair the student with another student with similar needs. Have them check the accuracy of each other's work.

*Missequences Letters in Words (e.g., broad/board, pre/per, scald/sclad)*

- Emphasize the use of cursive handwriting.
- Combine consonant blends and digraphs (e.g., *bl; pr; th; sm*) with consistent spelling patterns (e.g., *-ed; -an; -ing; -op*), so students can recall frequent letter combinations as whole units.
- Teach students to divide words into syllables, saying the syllable aloud when writing.
- Have students match cards with similar words through games such as "Concentration."

*Skips Words or Lines When Reading*

- Initially allow student to point with finger.
- Train student to place blank index card under a line of print. When teaching recall of context clues for earlier sentences, instruct students to put the card above the line of text. Use a slot card when avoiding having other lines of print interfere.
- Emphasize reading for meaning.

*Spacial Difficulties When Writing on a Line of Print or Remaining in Correct Column in Arithmetic Problem*

- Use lined paper for writing assignments.
- Start with broadly lined paper, going over lines with a brightly colored magic marker for easy visibility.
- Use glue on lines if student has fine motor problems.
- Draw brightly colored vertical lines in arithmetic problems, indicating correct column for reading and writing numbers.
- Use graph paper with large squares for arithmetic problems, placing a number within each square.

*(Continued)*

**Table 11–2**    *(Continued)*

---

*Reads/Writes from Right to Left*

- Place a green mark at the beginning and a red mark at the end of each line.
- Have student follow along line of print with finger, dramatically picking it up at the end of the line and placing it down at the beginning of the next line.
- Have the student draw an arrow from left to right across the top of the page before beginning written work.
- Teach directionality in reading and in arithmetic separately.
- Place arrows in arithmetic problems, indicating the direction to be followed during the operation.
- If the student produces mirror-writing, use a multisensory technique, tracing on a screen or sand while viewing a correctly written model.

*Unable to Consistently Relate the Letter to the Correct Sound When Studying Phonics*

- Have the student say the sound, not the name, of the letter each time it is written.
- Move students from individual consonants to consistent letter combinations as quickly as possible.
- Pair a sound with an object beginning with that letter.
- Avoid teaching similar sounds together: *p/b, k/g, t/v, f/v/th*, and *sh/ch*.
- Do not teach vowel sounds in isolation. Initially teach them in rhyming words and consistent spelling patterns, such as *-an, -at, -ed, -ent, -ip*, and *-ing*.

*Problems Recalling Sight Words and Basic Arithmetic Computation*

- Wherever possible, teach by spelling patterns instead of individual words. Try to relate new words to patterns already learned, such as *may/day/say; song/long/wrong; light/fight/tight*.
- Have students practice saying words and arithmetic problems aloud.
- Pair students to practice sight words and arithmetic problems written on flashcards.
- Use a language master for reinforcement.
- Keep a box of index cards with sight words and another with basic computation facts for students to review daily, individually or in pairs.

---

(*Source:* Adapted from Mann, Suiter & McClung, 1987; Mercer, & Mercer, 1989; Waldron, 1996)

many teachers believe it is impossible to help students with these difficulties. To the contrary, students can be trained to overcome or to compensate for perceptual problems. Often the techniques simply include alternative ways to practice deficient skills.

## Visual Discrimination Problems

The first perceptual category in Table 11–2 lists ways of teaching students with problems discriminating between similar-appearing letters and numbers. Most effective is a multisensory technique, in which the student says the sounds of the letter or word while tracing it on a raised surface. An extended time period between teaching similar letters such as *b/d* allows students to integrate the first letter completely with a great deal of practice before proceeding to the confused letter.

Cruickshank (1961) suggests that because the following letters are similar in appearance they are difficult for students to discriminate. Therefore, they should be taught separately to avoid confusion:

| | | | | |
|---|---|---|---|---|
| *b/d* | *r/h* | *n/u* | *i/l* | *i/j* |
| *b/p* | *t/f* | *a/s* | *e/c* | *h/n* |
| *o/e* | *o/c* | *m/w* | *m/n* | *h/k* |

One of students' most immediate responses is to color. If there is a letter or number that the student has difficulty with consistently, the teacher might write it very large and in color to attract the learner's full attention. Students tend to find this technique amusing and respond quickly.

## Missequences Letter Order

When students missequence letter order, a tracing technique can be effective as well. However, since it can be time-consuming to trace words separately, learning will proceed much more quickly when students use cursive writing consistently. The flow of cursive encourages the student to perceive the word as a whole instead of as a series of individual letters to be learned separately. Additionally, the word becomes a part of a student's **motor memory**, aiding in recall when it is written in the future.

motor memory—using repetitious motor functions to help recall.

"The idea of motor memory as a basis for learning can be really important," adds Alex. "I've observed myself use it when I'm spelling an unusual word in a letter or report. For example, if I can't remember how many *t*'s are in "commitment," I write it out with one or two *t*'s in the middle of the word, and select the one that feels right. Similarly, when students with perceptual problems have difficulty recalling words, if they have practiced writing the word in a flowing cursive movement, they are more likely to recall it correctly."

Students tend to missequence letter order more often when they view each letter as a separate unit. Therefore, it can be very helpful to instruct them to read by letter combinations, especially when they are consistent. For example, teaching students to read common spelling patterns, such as *-ed, -ing,*

-an, and -op, will help them perceive these as whole units and avoid mis-sequencing letters to other parts of the word. At the same time, teachers can instruct students in the use of beginning blends and digraphs (sl-, br-, th-, st-) to attach to these spelling patterns. For example, instead of analyzing by individual sound units, it is easier to read the word bring if a student can read br- and -ing as units and blend them. This perception of consistent units assists students in sequencing letters correctly through the repetition of seeing them together frequently.

Teachers should move next to emphasizing reading individual words structurally. Starting with division of compound words, then prefixes and suffixes, and finally, syllables, the student learns to read by larger, often meaningful, parts. Encouraging students to spell by syllables instead of individual letters supports the perception of consistency among letter units encountered frequently.

"It's fine to urge students to read by syllables, but I've found that they don't do it naturally and need a good deal of practice before you can assume they will do it automatically and independently," observes Teresa. "Pairing students and having them play games that support these skills is a fun way to provide reinforcement. They love 'Concentration,' in which they have to match similar words from a multitude of cards turned over on a table. The one to match the greatest number of pairs wins. This game improves a number of skills: visual discrimination and sequencing of letters; use of blends and digraphs as well as syllables; and certainly, sight words that require additional practice.

## Visual Tracking Problems

tracking—following with the eye.

Other students with perceptual problems have difficulty tracking a line of print correctly as they read. They omit punctuation and smaller words, such as conjunctions and some prepositions. At times they skip whole lines of print, clearly impacting their comprehension of the passage.

Teachers of young students can assist by allowing them to point with their finger as they read. They can teach older students to place a blank index card under a line of print, forcing the reading of the appropriate line of print. As students finish each line of print, they move the card down the page. When emphasizing context clues, teachers may advise students to place the card above the line of print. The student can then use knowledge gained from previous information to decode new words. Teachers can also give students a card with a rectangular slot cut out in the center, so neither the lines above or below can interfere with the line being read.

Additionally, teachers should emphasize reading comprehension, alerting students to attend to meaning as they read each sentence. When a word or longer unit is not meaningful, the student should stop reading at that point and review the words and lines to check for correctness.

## Spatial Problems when Writing

Students with spatial problems in reading also tend to experience them in writing and computation. Caused by perceptual or motor problems, they find it difficult to remain on a line of print, sometimes forming letters far above and below the line while writing a single word. They may misjudge the amount of space remaining on a line, not leaving enough room to finish a word, resulting in their crushing letters togethers illegibly or continuing them just below the line. Some students may even continue off the page, writing on the desktop in their need for additional space.

As listed in Table 11–2, there are some strategies teachers can use to help students with these problems. Students should write only on lined paper, providing visual guidance for letter size. Younger students or those with motor problems should use paper with larger spaces between lines. If students inappropriately write above and below lines, teachers should trace over lines in a brightly colored, wide-tipped magic marker. Again, the use of color will make the process more apparent to students. If students continue to cross lines, ones raised by glue tend to stop the motion, indicating an error to students. To save preparation time, teachers may want to purchase commercially produced paper with raised lines.

In arithmetic, students with visual-spatial problems have difficulties staying on a horizontal or vertical row of numbers. In operations such as division, when there are frequent horizontal and vertical changes within the

MY PORTFOLIO

Visual-sptial problems can hinder full understanding of students' ideas. With corrections, the student states, "We should respect our environment, because it (is) the only one we have, and the ozone layer is wearing down. We should not pollute the environment. We should not dump oil." Reprinted with permission, Winston School, San Antonio.

computation, students may experience extreme difficulty with spatial integration. It is important for the teacher to train students in appropriate visualization of columns early in their arithmetic studies. Otherwise, by the time they reach multidirectional problems such as division and fractions, not only will they have failed to master basic processes, but they will find integrating spatial changes all the more difficult.

When instructing students in writing in the correct column when computing basic problems, the teacher, and eventually the student, can draw vertical lines in bright colors between columns. If necessary, the student can place a checkmark above the column in which he is working, to further draw his attention to the appropriate area. If he still crosses columns, he can write each number in the square of large graph paper and trace the squares vertically. A "tic-tac-toe" form is also effective for number placement.

## Problems with Directionality

Reading from left to right is not a natural act. If a student were reading Hebrew or Arabic, right to left would be the required direction. For students with visual-spatial problems, proceeding across a line of print may present many problems.

"Reading direction is so reflexive once learned, that it is difficult for me to realize that some students have real problems," commented Teresa. "A few years ago, I was referred a second-grader who had no understanding of how to read a line of print. I encouraged him to ask me questions about what he didn't know. I couldn't believe how difficult the concept was for him to learn. While he was a very bright young man, certainly these directionality problems had turned him into a nonreader.

"He asked me, *On which side of the paper do I start reading? Which way do the words go? When I get to the end of a line of print, where do I start with the next line?* Of course, he couldn't read! You can just imagine what the results were when I assessed his math skills. He went up, down, left, and right indiscriminately. He just didn't understand the system. I equated it with my trying to drive a car without comprehending which way to turn the steering wheel. And I could only imagine how I would feel if everyone else around me understood the system and had no problems!"

Perceptual difficulties such as this can be so overwhelming that no progress can be made until they are solved. Yet, providing practice as part of the content areas studied instead of in isolation can support student learning. It will not help a student to sequence beads or copy a pattern from a model if he does not understand the subsequent application to reading. However, from the onset, if directionality involves writing letters and numbers, the student will integrate the process through ongoing practice and reinforcment.

Intervening using remedial strategies, teachers can overcome this problem. Since students attend immediately when color is used, teachers should place a green mark at the beginning and a red mark at the end of each line. Teachers should explain that the process is like a traffic light, with green indicating movement starting and red noting where it ends. They should instruct that in reading, students may only begin at the green color. Therefore, when finishing a line of print, the student must return to green to begin the next line. This explanation allows students to understand that they should not proceed down to the end of the next line from the end of the previous one. If they still attempt to read from right to left, the teacher should have them draw an arrow in brightly colored magic marker from left to right across the top of the page.

If reading a textbook that would be ruined by marking lines or margins with color, the teacher can tape paper onto the student's desk with green and red lines on appropriate sides, as well as one with an arrow across the top. Over time, this ongoing visual reminder helps students integrate directionality.

directionality—integration and application of spatial concepts, such as *left* and *right*.

As previously indicated for students with letter sequencing problems, motor memory can be an important support for integrating directionality. When students need reinforcement for left-to-right reading, they should place their finger under each word as they read. When reaching the end of the line, they should pick the finger up dramatically and place it back at the beginning of the next line. Students tend to find this process amusing, thereby supporting its recall.

mirror-writing—writing from right to left, rather than left to right.

If students perform mirror-writing, in which they write from right to left, a multisensory approach can be effective. Using a medium such as window screen, crayons, and paper can result in a raised model for the student to trace. The teacher places a piece of screen larger than 8 1/2" x 11" *under* the sheet of paper. Students write on the paper with crayon using large movements. They then remove the screen and trace the raised word, saying it aloud. Sand or salt trays and sandpaper letters also are effective, as well as the use of green and red marks and arrows to indicate proper directionality. Students who perform mirror-writing should never be allowed independent practice until the teacher is sure they can copy models correctly. They should practice brief exercises, with the teacher or a peer examining their correctness before being allowed to continue. When the class is performing a large-group lesson, the teacher should check the student's work at intervals to be sure that he is not writing in the wrong direction. Teachers should view mirror-writing as a habit that can be changed with constant modeling and frequent correction.

Students with confused directionality may have problems separating spacial concepts in reading and arithmetic. It is important to teach these processes separately, using different techniques when possible. For example, if the student is learning basic arithmetic using single digits, the teacher should emphasize top-to-bottom problem solving until it is overlearned. When approaching double digits, the teacher should draw brightly colored vertical lines between columns, noting "Start here, where you did before, and move from top to bottom." Explanations such as "In reading we go from left to right, but in these math problems we go from right to left," will only confuse students. This confusion will be heightened when more sophisticated algorithms such as division are learned, and the student is expected to begin at the right side of the problem.

## Sound-Symbol Association Problems

"Often my beginning readers have problems relating individual or clusters of letters to the sounds they represent," comments Teresa. "It can be really frustrating for teachers to review a sound frequently and still find their students unable to identify it in reading. There's a few tricks that I've learned to help them associate sounds and symbols more easily.

"It doesn't always make sense to have students learn the letter name first, since they try to read the letter by its name on the page and become confused when they're inaccurate. Students should say the sound of the letter, not its name, each time they encounter it. Even in spelling, when I like to reinforce correctness by having students say the spelling aloud, I have them spell by sounds. Of course, this works best with phonetic words, since their sound-symbol association is very consistent. When I'm having them practice non-phonetic sight words that range from *the* to *although*, I still have them spell by sound. This can be really effective when paired with the multisensory technique, where student trace the words on a rough surface at the same time. I'm convinced that emphasizing sounds is the key.

"When students still have problems recalling the sound of a letter, I pair it with an object they know and say the name of the object whenever the students encounter the letter to be sounded out. If students have cognitive problems, this concrete approach really helps. The sound of *p* is identified when I say *pizza*, and *j*, when I say *jelly*. We move onto letter combinations, the blends and digraphs, with associations such as *black* for *bl* and *thumb* for *th*. Through repetition and reinforcement of these letters, eventually students don't need the associated object.

"It is important to separate the teaching of letters that have similar sounds. For example, students tend to confuse the sounds of *p/b; k/g; t/v; f/v/th; sh/ch*. Teachers can provide practice in just one of those confused sounds and have many instances of reinforcement so the student can overlearn it. Then the teacher can move to a number of totally different sounds, only much later beginning the one that could be confused.

"A final point that I feel is really important is to avoid teaching vowel sounds in isolation. Vowels are not as consistent as consonants, especially when followed by an *r* or other letters that change their sound. Additionally, vowels have long and short sounds requiring rule memorization. Often our students with learning problems have a difficult time relating rules to words as they read."

## Teaching Reading and Spelling through Consistent Phonetic Patterns

"How do we incorporate vowel sounds into phonics?" asks Maura. "Obviously we have to include them."

"The very best way is to teach them initially is through their use in spelling patterns at the end of words. Figure 11–1 contains an instructional plan with a series of steps for incorporating consonants and vowels consistently so students learn many words at the same time.

"First teachers instruct in the sounds of individual consonants, such as *f, h, l, m, n, r, s,* and *v,* the differences are easy to hear. They teach these through relating them to objects, names, and activities with which students are familiar (e.g., *f/fan, fish, finger, fight, fly, Frank, first*). Where possible, they post beginning sounds and words around the room for reference. They then teach the additional consonants listed in Figure 11–1.

Once students learn beginning consonants, teachers should instruct them in basic spelling patterns to be used with the consonants. This avoids teaching vowel sounds separately. For example, when students learn *-an, -ed, -it, -op, -un,* they are learning vowel sounds and useful letter combinations simultaneously. The key is consistency. The vowel always has the same sound in these combinations. Students like rhyming words, probably because they have a musical quality. In practicing, when students add individual consonants to these patterns, they can create numerous words (e.g., *man, pan, ban, can, Dan, fan, Nan, ran, tan, van*). The student learns to read a dozen words at a sitting, practices integration of a consistent sound unit, reinforces the use of beginning consonants, and does not have to learn any rules that may change.

As indicated in Figure 11–1, the next step is to broaden individual consonants into *blends,* consistent combinations where letters maintain their individual sounds, such as *bl-, cr-, st-, tr-.* Other consonant combinations are called *digraphs,* where letters combine to make a new sound, such as *ch-, sh-, th-, ph-, wh-, -ng.* Teachers provide practice for these letter combinations by placing them with the same spelling patterns they used with individual consonants (for example, *plan, Stan, bran, Fran, scan, span*).

"These spelling patterns become rhyming words for students, and progressively they add longer units together, both at the beginning and ending of words. This continues through common phonics principles, such as the "Silent-e Rule," in which patterns afford practice for students.

"I love these spelling patterns. When students graduate to using them in longer, more sophisticated words, they rarely have any trouble (e.g., *many; banish; can't; fantastic; vanish; thank*). They read the spelling pattern as a unit and apply phonics or syllabication to the rest of the word. Then when vowel sounds vary slightly between words, such as *than* and *thank,* I tell them to say the word quickly, and they read the word easily because the difference is not that pronounced."

| INSTRUCTIONAL PLAN | PHONICS PATTERNS |
|---|---|
| Teach sounds of individual consonants. | Consonants:<br>First, teach *f, h, l, m, n, r, s, v*<br>Next, teach *b, g, t, d, p*<br>Finally teach *c, j, k, q, w, y, z* |
| Do not teach vowel sounds in isolation, but as part of a final, consistent spelling pattern. | Spellinng Patterns (Consonant-Vowel-Consonant):<br><table><tr><td>Pattern</td><td>Examples</td></tr><tr><td>*-an*</td><td>fan, man, ran, van, tan, pan, can</td></tr><tr><td>*-ap*</td><td>lap, map, nap, tap, cap, rap, sap</td></tr><tr><td>*-ed*</td><td>fed, led, red, bed, wed</td></tr><tr><td>*-en*</td><td>men, ten, hen, den, pen</td></tr></table> |
| Place beginning consonants in front of spelling patterns. | Add consonants to additional spelling patterns: *-at, -ab, -ad, -ag, -am, -ed, -eg, -em, -et, -id, -ig, -im, -in, -ip, -it, -ob, -od, -om, -on, -op, -ot, -ub, -ud, -ug, -um, -un, -up, -ut* |
| Once the student learns beginning consonant sounds, combine consonants into blends and digraphs. | Consonant Blends:<br><table><tr><td>Pattern</td><td>Examples</td></tr><tr><td>L</td><td>*bl-, cl-, fl-, gl-, pl-, sl-*</td></tr><tr><td>R</td><td>*br-, cr-, dr-, fr-, gr-, pr-, tr-, str-, thr-*</td></tr><tr><td>S</td><td>*sc-, sk-/-sk,* sm-, sn-, sp-/sp,* sw-, sch-, scr-, spl-, spr-, str-*</td></tr><tr><td>T</td><td>*tw-, -ft,* -lt,* -nt,* -st**</td></tr><tr><td>D</td><td>*-ld,* -nd**</td></tr></table><br>Consonant Digraphs:<br><table><tr><td>Pattern</td><td>Examples</td></tr><tr><td>H</td><td>*ch-/-ch,* sh-/-sh,* wh-, th-/-th,* ph-/-ph**</td></tr><tr><td>N</td><td>*-ng**</td></tr></table>*pattern appears at the end of the word |
| Add consonant blends and digraphs to spelling patterns. | Spelling Patterns (Consonant-Consonant-Vowel-Consonants)<br><table><tr><td>Pattern</td><td>Examples</td></tr><tr><td>*-an*</td><td>clan, plan, bran, scan, span</td></tr><tr><td>*-at*</td><td>flat, slat, scat, spat, chat, that</td></tr><tr><td>*-ap*</td><td>flap, slap, trap, strap, snap, chap</td></tr><tr><td>*-ed*</td><td>bled, fled, sled, bread, sped, shed</td></tr><tr><td>*-op*</td><td>clop, flop, plop, slop, drop, stop, shop, chop</td></tr></table><br>Add consonant blends and digraphs to additional spelling patterns: *-at, -ab, -ad, -ag, -am, -ed, -em, -et, -id, -ig, -im, -in, -ip, -it, -ob, -od, -om, -on, -op, -ot, -ub, -ud, -ug, -um, -un, -up, -ut* |
| Add consonants, blends, and digraphs to longer spelling patterns. | Spelling Patterns (Varied)<br><table><tr><td>Pattern</td><td>Examples</td></tr><tr><td>*-ang*</td><td>fang, hang, rang, sang, bang, gang, clang, slang, twang</td></tr><tr><td>*-ing*</td><td>king, ping, ring, wing, fling, sling, bring, string, sting, swing, spring, wring, thing</td></tr></table> |

*(Continued)*

| | |
|---|---|
| *-ack* | lack, rack, back, tack, pack, jack, black, slack, crack, track, smack, snack, stack |
| *-ick* | lick, nick, tick, pick, kick, wick, click, stick, brick, trick, stick, thick |
| *-ash* | dash, hash, lash, mash, rash, cash, clash, flash, slash, brash, trash, splash, smash |

Additional longer spelling patterns include:

| Pattern | Examples |
|---|---|
| A | -ath, -ack, -aff, -all, -ask, -asp, -atch, -ange, -aste |
| E | -eck, -ell, -ess, -est, -eed, -eep, -eam, -eak, -eal, -eap, -etch |
| I | -ick, -ill, -iss, -itch, -ight, -iff |
| O | -oth, -ong, -oll, -oss, -oad, -oat, -ount |

| | |
|---|---|
| Teach the "Silent-e Rule." (The final *-e* is silent while the vowel represents its own long sound.) | Contrast the word without -e with the word with -e: |

| Pattern | Examples |
|---|---|
| *-at(e)* | hat/hate, mat/mate, fat/fate, rat/rate |
| *-im(e)* | dim/dime, Tim/time, grim/grime |
| *-an(e)* | pan/pane, can/cane, man/mane |
| *-in(e)* | fin/fine, win/wine, pin/pine |

Additional sounds influenced by a silent -e at the end of the word include:
*-et(e), -it(e), -ir(e), -op(e), -od(e), -ut(e), -us(e), -ub(e)*

**Figure 11–1**   Teaching Reading and Spelling Through Consistent Phonetic Patterns (*Sources:* Adapted from Mann, Suiter, & McClung, 1987; Burmeister, 1975; Waldron, 1996)

## Visual Memory Problems

Words frequently encountered or ones that do not fit as easily into spelling patterns are called *sight words.* Routinely, sight words fall into two categories: (1) words that cannot be analyzed phonetically (e.g., *enough, although*) or (2) words that are encountered so often that they should be read automatically to increase rate and fluency (e.g., *then, an, mother*).

While teachers may tend to have students learn these words individually and by rote memory, an overview indicates that in some instances there are consistent spelling patterns to assist recall. For example, the word *might* appears on many sight word lists. Under analysis, the teacher realizes that it is part of the spelling pattern *-ight,* encouraging the teaching of *light, fight, night, right, sight, flight, plight, fright* at the same time. Not only should students learn to read these words, but as discussed earlier, they should write them while saying the sound of the spelling pattern aloud. While the *-ight* sound is nonphonetic, students tend to enjoy stretching it over a prolonged period as they write it. This process aids later recall. Once they have mastered it when copying from a model provided by the teacher, they should write it independently. Finally, they should practice writing it in a sentence.

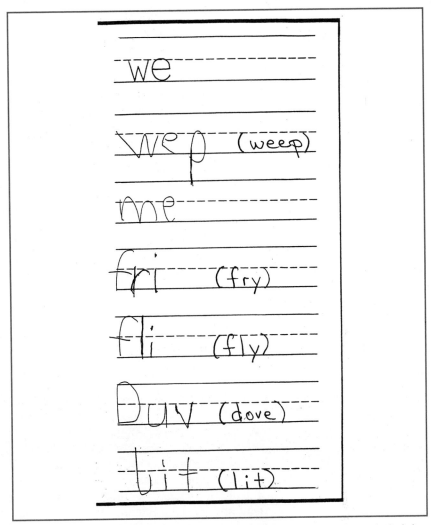

When visual-perceptual skills are poor, students may attempt to use phonics exclusively in spelling. Reprinted with permission, Winston School, San Antonio.

Other sight words on the list might serve a similar function of introducing important spelling patterns (*last: -ast; than: -an; took: -ook*). When students understand the generalizability of spelling patterns, they tend to look for them and use them accurately.

Students experiencing difficulty in long-term visual memory for words often experience problems recalling basic computation problems learned by sight. For example, they tend to forget sums such as 13 + 8; 15 + 9; 6 + 5; 9 + 7. Students may have even more difficulty recalling common subtraction facts, as with 22 – 8; 14 – 9; 16 – 7; 9 – 3.

Interestingly, students may have a better facility with multiplication facts than with addition or subtraction, because they tend to practice multiplication aloud. Since these facts are in patterns and sequences, students use a variety of modalities to learn them, including visual, auditory, and motor. Teachers realize that rote memory for the numerous multiplication facts can be improved by multisensory instruction.

Teachers should use the oral-written method for teaching sight words and other arithmetic facts or formulas. Students can work with each other in pairs, practicing reading, writing, and checking each other's work for additional reinforcement. Traditional methods such as flashcards can be effective, and students can record their words and facts on a language master after listening to a model taped by the teacher.

Additionally, students should keep separate boxes of index cards with sight words and computation facts for daily review. Again, pairs of students can be successful, and the teacher can pull cards randomly from the boxes, informally quizzing students as time permits. Daily practice should take place for optimal reinforcement.

## STUDENTS WITH MEMORY PROBLEMS

retrieval disorder—difficulty recalling information.

Problems in visual memory for words and computational facts may be indicative of a larger problem, such as a **retrieval disorder** for previously learned information. Many students with cognitive and learning disabilities have extreme difficulty recalling school-related information, particularly on a long-term basis. As a result, their information store is low, resulting in difficulty dealing with higher-order concepts.

Table 11–3 contains a number of techniques educators can use to help students improve their retention of school-related information. During lectures and discussions, teachers should ask questions requiring student application of information studied. When student responses are unclear or confused, teachers should clarify information through additional explanation and discussion until student comprehension is assured.

Before beginning a class or unit predicated on mastery of previous learning, teachers should have a review of any difficult information. Not only will this review help them recall facts and concepts, but it will provide a springboard for reference in studying new information.

"I can attest to the importance of review," reflects John. "When students in my English class finish studying a story or novel, they tend to forget they've ever read it. Not only can't they recall significant themes or motives, many times they don't even remember the plot!

"I've found that before studying a new literary work or genre, if I hold

**Table 11–3**
**Techniques for Students with Memory Problems**

Teachers should:

- emphasize important information through intensive questioning and repetition by students

- have a brief daily class review of previously studied information that is difficult to recall

- encourage students to use memory supports whenever possible (e.g., calculator, important phone numbers carried in wallet, class schedules taped to notebook)

- use advance organizers and introduce content vocabulary before the lesson so students can begin to associate and categorize information

- help students develop mnemonic devices, forming strong associations between new information and their prior knowledge

- use structural analysis techniques in teaching new vocabulary, showing students how to examine prefixes, suffixes, and word roots in order to support understanding and recall

- relate new information to students' experiences

- encourage students to read material aloud when it is difficult to recall

- pair students who need similar practice, using flashcards or educational games for reinforcement

- use media, activities, and experiences so students can integrate and recall difficult material

(*Source:* Adapted from Klumb, 1992; Waldron, 1996)

a brief discussion reviewing previous themes and alerting students to compare and contrast writings by a new author with previous authors studied, they have much better recall. While I don't need to consider earlier works daily as we read, I find that referring to them throughout the year as we move on helps students see relationships they might otherwise miss.

"Yet, when we study grammar, I find a daily review of facts to be very helpful. For example, if we're working to avoid comma splices or overuse of colloquial terms in formal writing, a few examples of either of these as we begin the lesson serves to remind students of our goal and sets the stage for new information. My colleagues in math and foreign language, and in sciences such as Chemistry and Physics, integrate previous factual and conceptual information daily because their disciplines are so hierarchical. Otherwise students would view the information as segmented instead of integrated. And in the arts and physical education, practice as a means of review and integration is critical."

As noted in Table 11–3, teachers can encourage students to use specific memory supports for difficult-to-recall information. Calculators and class schedules, as well as copies of locker combinations and important phone numbers or personal information, not only facilitate memory needs, but relieve the student's emotional stress at potentially forgetting something important. They also help prevent embarrassment in social situations.

Alex notes, "One of our psychologists has been counseling a small group of high school students who lack some of the adaptive behaviors and social skills so important to acceptance by peers. One day the discussion included appropriate dating behavior. A few of the students admitted that even when they could afford to take someone to a restaurant, they usually didn't because of being unable to figure out how much to leave as a tip. One young man described his embarrassment as his friends watched him closely when he counted on his fingers laboriously. He had never tried to calculate the tip again, tending to just leave several dollars. He added that he felt angry when he recomputed the amount at home and realized that he usually tipped too much, wasting money in order to avoid being teased.

"The school psychologist gave each of the students a small card with a variety of frequent expenditure totals. The students were amazed when they learned that they just had to glance at the closest amount on the card in order to leave the right tip. The irony was that after he told us how he had given these cards to the students, teachers wanted them too! Sometimes I think we all appreciate these supports."

Another way to improve students' memory for important information is to begin the lesson with an overview demonstrating relationships among concepts to be presented and relating them to students' previous experiences. Additionally, teachers should introduce specialized vocabulary *before* students encounter it in their reading. If teachers use structural analysis to introduce the meaning of prefixes, suffixes, and word roots, not only will they delineate target vocabulary, but they will prepare students to understand related concepts in the future.

Earlier, in the discussion of techniques for improving students' recall of basic facts, mnemonics was mentioned as a popular method. While most students enjoy these often-humorous devices to support recall of important information, if the memory loss is severe, they may require some cues or training to remember the device itself. Therefore, instructors should gauge when the recall support is easy for the student and when it requires additional work. If it can be formed through easily derived relationships with students' past experiences, then it may serve a broad memory purpose.

As a teaching method, lecture may be the most difficult for students with retrieval disorders to recall. Verbal information tends to rely on a strong auditory learning style as well as an ability to revisualize concepts symbolized by words. For students with conceptual or language disabilities and students distracted by emotional concerns, significant information in a teacher's lecture may be lost.

To assist students, teachers should use varied media, hands-on activities, and in-depth experiences to support attaining information through a variety of learning styles. The use of multisensory presentations affords students the opportunity to integrate concepts through stronger modalities. Direct experience allows them to explore and ask questions as they learn.

# TECHNOLOGY FOR USE WITH STUDENTS

Since students with learning problems experience a wide array of difficulty, the assistive technology of choice will vary with individual needs. Rarely is technology designed for a particular category of disability. Instead, its use is defined by a specified need within the individual. Therefore, often there is an overlap of equipment for students with varying differences.

**Talking Books**—literature that comes with audio support.

For example, students with reading problems can benefit from Talking Books, as can students with visual disabilities. As previously discussed, the modifications necessitated by perceptual differences or difficulties with memory can be supported by alternate classroom methods. Talking Books are recordings of texts or other significant works to aid student who are disabled readers. They are supplied if the student is documented as having perceptual or language disabilities strongly impeding word retrieval or analysis. Unfortunately, many teachers are not aware of these supports, assuming they are available only for students who are blind or partially sighted. Ways to obtain these materials are described in Chapter 12.

**Kurzweil**—a microcomputer with voice character recognition to support students as they learn to read.

Other students with reading problems benefit from the Kurzweil, a microcomputer with voice character recognition to support students as they learn to read. Students see the visual character combined with the auditory, providing multisensory input to meet a variety of learning modalities.

Additional materials such as classroom texts can be taped for nonreaders. Talking computers and talking calculators that note the factors in an arithmetic problem support student gains in an informative, nonthreatening manner.

When students experience difficulties in writing and spelling, computer word processors provide invaluable support. In addition to grammatical programs that offer suggestions to clarify written meaning, spell-checkers respond to the correctness of individual words as well as total documents. Students are freed to consider their ideas and organization of content once grammar and spelling are no longer a consideration. When students experience handwriting difficulties, assistive technology such as the Talking Pen, based on fiber optics, indicate auditorily when students move off a line of print.

**Talking Pen**—a device based on fiber optics that indicates auditorily when students move off a line of print.

Calculators have become a critical support to students with disabilities in arithmetic. While it is important to teach basic mathematics skills to everyone, when students are impeded by memory or learning delays, the

Word processors can be invaluable for teaching writing and spelling skills.

calculator allows them to perform at a level much closer to peers. Teachers should introduce calculators when they feel the student cannot progress further without ongoing support. Students using calculators should be exposed to a variety of life experiences to enhance their application, such as use in grocery stores and restaurants.

The use of technology with students who learn differently has allowed them to avoid embarrassment daily through maintaining their skill level with peers. Additionally, supporting their ability to perform tasks basic to daily survival such as the correct use of money, it provides the opportunity for normalization.

## STUDENTS WITH LANGUAGE DISORDERS

Many students with learning and cognitive disabilities experience disorders in communication. Clearly, the outcomes from a language disorder are far-reaching and have profound impact on students' school performance and social interactions.

When they have problems understanding or expressing verbal and written information, understandably students may experience both failure and frustration in the classroom. Students with receptive language problems may have problems perceiving differences between pitch levels of two tones or discriminating or blending sounds of letters (Lerner, 1993). Some may not comprehend the meaning of individual vocabulary. Others can understand individual words, but not in combination. These students may misunderstand the syntax of longer units such as sentences and paragraphs. They have difficulty with subtle meanings, colloquialisms, and unusual structures such as passive voice. Teachers may think they are lazy because they do not respond correctly to directions. During lectures and discussions they may become inattentive and distractible because they cannot follow the context easily.

**expressive language**—the ability to communicate in speech and writing.

Other students have difficulty with **expressive language**. While they are able to understand spoken and written language, they encounter problems remembering and using vocabulary correctly or expressing themselves fluently. While not necessarily experiencing speech problems such as articulation or voice pitch, some students have difficulty communicating their meaning clearly because they cannot arrange words in the appropriate syntax (Johnson & Mykelbust, 1967).

They may speak in shorter sentences, gesturing frequently and rarely using adjectives and adverbs. Students may substitute words like *that* or *thing* when their vocabulary is faulty, and they may use general phrases such as *over there* or *a long time ago* when they lack ability to express specific meaning easily.

While their intelligence level may be above average, they may be classified as slow learners because of language delays. Often these students are quiet in class and appear shy socially because of fear of ridicule. Usually they avoid situations that will bring attention to their inability to express themselves. Since humans rely so much on verbal interactions, these behaviors may serve to cut them off from academic and social situations with peers.

Alex adds, "I saw this problem so clearly in Travis, a middle school student we were asked to assess for psychological problems. He seemed like a really fine young man, more observant and reflective than most students his age. At least that was my first impression. Then I realized I was using terms like *observant* and *reflective* to describe his extreme quietness and lengthy pauses before response. Yet, I would certainly consider him very intelligent because of his easy ability to understand everything going on around him.

"When students appear so withdrawn, we begin our appraisal informally to observe behavior patterns and help them relax before formal assessment begins. Travis's behavior didn't relax, as he avoided anything other than cursory responses. I noticed a very interesting pattern. He hesitated for a long time when I asked him a question. Then he gestured and responded in a short sentence or two. When asked to elaborate, he spoke in a soft voice, barely intelligible. Any required explanation trailed off while he shook his head and appeared embarrassed.

"Psychological tests indicated that he had a very low self-esteem. Aside from having to rely more on nonverbal assessments, he did not appear to have a behavioral disorder. His language test scores were average and above in comprehending what he heard and read, but far below expectancy in expressing his ideas verbally and in writing. The cause of the lowered esteem was very apparent: Any of us would feel badly about ourselves if we were unable to express our ideas and feelings to others. Because of his high intelligence, Travis has a good deal to say. He just can't put the words together to say it correctly. His response has been to be a passive rather than active participant in academic and social arenas so that he won't embarrass himself."

Travis and other students demonstrating language disorders should benefit from the techniques listed in Table 11–4. Because the classroom provides an excellent milieu for combining receptive and expressive language

---

**Table 11–4**
**Techniques for Students with Language Disorders**

Teachers should:

- allow students sufficient time to consider and answer questions
- provide a cue for the class, indicating that students must listen
- speak in brief sentences, omitting unnecessary information and words
- integrate new vocabulary studied into the context of ongoing information f
- have students rename vocabulary important to the lesson, describing its meaning
- use pictures and concrete objects to support learning of meaningful vocabulary
- provide numerous opportunities daily for students to speak and listen
- ask students to sequence events in a story, history or scientific unit, or arithmetic word problem after they have heard or read the information
- have students practice prepositions or directional word (e.g., *over, under, around, through, on top of, next to*) to fully understand their meaning
- model good grammar by repeating a sentence correctly when a student makes an error
- ask students to make up the title for a story or content area reading assignment, encouraging understanding of main ideas
- read a story or content area section of a text and ask the student to complete the rest based on details given
- use model sentences to encourage practice with structure. Each time, the teacher should omit a different type of word in the model (e.g., verb, adjective, noun) and ask the student to suggest an appropriate word while repeating the entire sentence (*The _____ walked quickly; The man _____ quickly; The man walked _____*)

(*Source:* Adapted from Lerner, 1993; Waldron, 1996)

training, an integrated approach incorporating both areas may be superior. It is not necessary or even preferable to teach language activities separately when working to improve communications skills. Incorporating them throughout informal and formal lessons provides continuous reinforcement for all students. Teachers can also provide language models and use teaching strategies that encourage understanding and usage.

Earlier chapters considered the importance of asking appropriate questions as a critical teaching tool. While it was noted that teachers should wait for students to have the opportunity to consider responses carefully, sufficient time is a critical variable when students have receptive language problems. If students do not understand the question, the teacher should rephrase it using different language. Using the same words and sentences will not clarify meaning if students did not understand it the first time.

However, attentional problems can worsen a language disorder if students do not focus on the task. Teachers should provide a cue for the class before giving directions. Flashing the lights a few times or ringing a bell can indicate that everyone is to become silent and attend to the teacher. Harsh sounds or yelling should be avoided when trying to gain attention, since they tend to be negative and to encourage avoidance.

When teachers have student attention, they should speak briefly and directly, avoiding excess words that can cloud sentence meaning. For example, a teacher might say to the quiet class, "You need to return to your desk and put away your notebook." Once students are at their desks, the teacher could then say, "Line up quickly for the assembly." These brief messages are far easier to understand than one longer one that attempts to give all instructions at once: "OK now. We're about done, so it would be a good idea to go back to your desks. When you get there, put away your notebooks so we can get ready for the school assembly that starts in a few minutes. Please hurry so we won't be late." While the second message provides more information, it also affords more opportunities for confusion to students with receptive language problems.

When students such as Travis have problems expressing themselves, many times their difficulties arise from a lack of integration of previously studied vocabulary into their language store. They cannot remember a particular word because they did not store it in long-term memory. The development of good receptive language provides the basis for good expressive language. Therefore, teachers should take particular care to have students repeat, define, read, and use content vocabulary daily. The greater frequency of use, the more opportunities for reinforcement and overlearning. As students integrate vocabulary thoroughly, both their receptive and expressive language are improved. Teachers can use pictures and concrete objects and experiences to support full comprehension of vocabulary during initial teaching. As students progress through unit study, they should be encouraged to rename significant vocabulary, including discussion of its meaning and application.

Students also need to use language to comprehend and speak fluently. Teachers should provide opportunities for students to speak and listen on a daily basis. Since Travis and others with expressive problems might be embarrassed by speaking to the entire class, pairs and small groups of students working together can provide less threatening interactions that afford practice. In small groups, after reading or listening to information, students can respond to printed questions provided by teachers. These questions might require students to sequence events in any content area, to summarize ideas stated into a cohesive whole, or to provide a written response to previously viewed material.

Often younger students with language problems experience difficulties with basic directional words such as *below, behind, next to, around, above.* Older students confuse more sophisticated directional terms such as *west, southeast, left, right.* It is important for teachers to provide instruction when students demonstrate directional confusion. Integration of spatial terms is not only necessary, but supports safety needs in areas such as driving and reading road signs correctly. Teachers can reinforce these concepts best through practice in content area subjects. For example, whether performing map-reading in history and geography, studying graphs in arithmetic, measurements in science, teachers can use directional terms with students and require their use in student responses. When difficulty arises, the use of brightly colored arrows drawn in appropriate directions on blackboards and student papers provides good support for memory.

Stories and content area sections discussing major concepts provide an excellent opportunity to encourage comprehension of main ideas. Critical to the growth of students with language disabilities, teachers must instruct how to summarize and compile individual bits of information into meaningful conceptual units. They can do this by having students entitle stories or content area reading assignments. To support conceptualization in areas such as mathematics or science, teachers should begin problem-solving with students and then provide questions so students can complete the activity individually or in small groups.

When students have problems with expressive vocabulary and complex sentence syntax, teachers provide model sentences to encourage practice within a clear structure. Younger students benefit from the practice suggested in the final technique on Table 11–4. Here the teacher provides basic model sentences with a particular element of grammar missing, such as an adjective, adverb, or verb. When in large group, students complete the sentence in a round-robin manner, supplying variations on the same missing word.

For example, in the sentence *The old house was dark and* _____, students can take turns adding a colorful descriptor. Students developing their language skills may supply words such as *broken, scary,* or *awful,* while those using language more creatively might suggest *dilapidated, archaic,* or *seasoned.* In this way, all students get to consider appropriate vocabulary while listening to a variety of suggestions from others. The next time the teacher uses this

MY PORTFOLIO

> All About Weather
>
> Ch1. What I learned about weather. In since I learnd hight and low precher systems are and how tornados are form. I also learnt what those little tornados are called dust devil. Also I learned that their are three types of tornados.

Students with expressive language problems may express themselves best when allowed to weave art into their writing. Reprinted with permission, Winston School, San Antonio.

modeling technique, she might provide a sentence such as *The old _____ was dark and frightening,* providing students the opportunity to consider nouns that might be meaningful in this context.

Older students such as Travis can receive similar instruction in pairs or small groups in the regular classroom. Usually students with his degree of difficulty require direct input from a language therapist. In order not to single out Travis for further embarrassment, teachers should consider other students who may require similar instruction. For instance, even if they are not experiencing a language disability, students from non-English backgrounds can expand their vocabulary and syntax use through this type of practice.

# TECHNOLOGY FOR STUDENTS WITH COMMUNICATIONS DISORDERS

Alex interjects, "In my years of working with students with learning differences, I have observed the most frustration among those with language disabilities. Few things must be as limiting as the inability to discuss ideas and personal needs with others. Yet many students with communications disorders experience daily failure in expressing themselves, impacting a range of areas from friendships to self-esteem. I've been pleased to note the technological advances for individuals with speech and language problems. They afford the opportunity to participate so much more fully, not only in school but in daily living activities."

While specialized equipment may not be needed with students with mild language problems, there are a number of technological devices that can assist students with severe language disabilities.

pitch—production of the appropriate tone, speaking in a voice that is not too high or too low.

articulation—the ability to correctly produce speech sounds.

***Speech Disabilities.***  Levitt (1989) notes several devices to assist students with speech disorders in fluency, pitch, and articulation. Serving the purpose of providing feedback, they range from videotapes to tape recorders, meters measuring pitch and sound articulation, language masters, and phonic mirrors. With this equipment, students are able to observe correct models of speech production and work on replication, comparing their efforts with those of the therapist.

Additionally, computer software is available to teach and reinforce correct sound production. Especially in a time of interactive computers and CD-Rom, students practice sounds independently, allowing for generalization of therapeutic instruction. Computer software includes games affording practice of students modeling correct pitch, rhythm, and loudness. Students are reinforced for approximating model sounds within drill and practice formats.

***Language Disorders.***  In their overview of supportive technology for students with disabilities, Wisniewski and Sedlak (1992) describe three levels of assistance. The first does not involve actual physical devices, but affords unaided basic communication. In this category are included nonverbal indicators of needs or ideas, such as gestures, pointing, nodding agreement or disagreement, signing, or writing messages. Unless the student signs or writes fluently, the other modes limit discussion and tend to exclude the student from participation in group activities.

communication boards—devices that allow students to convey basic messages by pressing certain responses indicated on the board.

The second level of assistance incorporates basic aids such as **communication boards** that permit the student to convey basic messages, again primarily about personal wants and needs. Traditionally, language books containing a series of words or pictures are carried by the individual, who indicates the message through pointing at the appropriate symbol. Within the classroom, the student may use a lap or table board with important messages included. Even when physical mobility is limited, the student is able to communicate through the use of devices such as a pointer attached to the head or other stable limb, such as an arm or leg. He can direct the pointer to the correct message to make needs known.

The third level of assistance is far more technological and has allowed individuals with language disorders to express themselves with unusual breadth. Small, portable microprocessor-based electronic devices convert text into sound, providing the opportunity to engage in fuller conversations than with gestures and communications boards. The student types the complete message and the microprocessor transforms it into voice output. The vocabularies on these devices are extensive. Their use is adaptable to a variety of physically limiting disabilities as well, through the use of systems involving pictures and symbols for conversion when spelling and written expression are a problem for the individual. Students with limited range of motion can use pointers or switches to indicate their meaning.

The sophistication of modern technology enhances everyone's ability to communicate.

In all, technology for individuals with language disabilities continues to progress from the cumbersome equipment available even ten years ago to more portable systems allowing for diversity within users' cognitive and physical abilities.

# STUDENTS WITH BEHAVIORAL DISORDERS

It is important to note that regular and special education teachers express the same tolerance level for student behavior in the classroom (Landon & Mesinger, 1989). Teachers regard certain behaviors as more disturbing and serious than others. Of no surprise was the finding that teachers are most concerned about physically threatening behaviors, followed in order by disruption to classroom learning, challenge of the teacher's authority, violation of social standards, ignoring the rights of others, and illegal behaviors. Teachers found socially defiant behavior to be more disturbing than immature, delinquent, or physically disruptive actions (Baer, Goodall, & Brown, 1983).

Cangelosi (1988) notes two broad categories of behaviors considered inappropriate by teachers. The first includes behaviors disruptive to the learning environment, such as disorganization, inattentiveness during class, incomplete or sloppy work, poor time management, and failure to follow directions. The second category includes blatantly overt behaviors disruptive to class, such as calling out, swearing, arguing, and noncompliance with teacher requests.

## Avoiding Potential Behavior Problems

Smith and Misra (1992) observe that behavior problems rarely result from one factor, but from a combination of causes working together. At times students are not aware of appropriate methods to obtain teacher attention. Other times they may be unable to complete the assignment and uses noncompliance or apathy to avoid that realization by peers.

"That's interesting," comments John. "Last year I had a student, Jennifer, who rarely turned in homework assignments and literally put her head down and went to sleep during my class. Needless to say, I felt frustrated. On several occasions, when I confronted her she became verbally aggressive, saying that she hated the class and the work was *boring*. Understandably, I tried to avoid confrontations because she would yell and the rest of the class

Rewards for appropriate behavior can be highly motivational, especially at the preventative level.

would be disturbed, waiting to see who would win the battle. She failed the first two grading periods, and her anger toward me accelerated to the point where I didn't have to challenge her. She confronted me over anything, and didn't seem fazed by trips to the office. She even used that as an opportunity to tell Elena what a terrible teacher I was."

"An interesting lesson for all of us," interjected Elena. "She was bent on convincing me about John's personal cruelty to her and how boring his teaching style was. When I told her John was one of the teachers in the entire high school who cared most about students, she became angry and stared swearing at me! While I try not to hide behind my administrative role, I was amazed at the chutzpah of a young person who would swear at the school principal. While I was certainly within rights to suspend her for her treatment of both John and me, I called Alex for his advice, suspecting that a deeper problem might be present."

"Clearly there was more to the story," added Alex. "We called Jennifer's mother to request written permission for assessment. At first the mother refused, but when we told her the alternative was Jennifer's school suspension, she gave in. Test results showed Jennifer was more than two years below other students in reading and she had a learning disability in written expression, ranging from exceptionally weak spelling to poor organization of ideas. Because

Jennifer was from a military family that had moved frequently, the problem had been overlooked. Everyone felt it had been school change that had slowed her down.

"Affective testing showed that these moves had indeed had an effect. However, the impact was more on her emotional status. She was afraid to make friends, felt angry about relocations, and had a generalized sense of hostility toward adults. Since she couldn't read the text in John's class, he was the recipient of her feelings toward another adult who had let her down."

"I felt very badly about my lack of awareness of Jennifer's weak academic skills," commented John. "At that time I didn't know to give an informal skills inventory at the beginning of the term. I assumed if a student was into work refusal, it was through choice, not an avoidance of embarrassment.

"At the conclusion of the testing, I met with her and told her that I would do anything I could to help her learn if she would treat me respectfully and tell me when assignments were too difficult. While she was wary at first, she agreed to try. To avoid embarrassment in front of peers, I let her keep the class text, but found her content material at a lower level. I modified my assessment of her writing assignments, grading primarily on ideas and to a lesser degree on grammar. She handed in assignments and her grades improved. We turned a potential disaster into a successful experience after all. She stops in to see me and chats amicably this year. She's continuing to do better since I alerted her new teachers to the problem."

---

**Table 11–5**
**Techniques for Avoiding Behavior Problems**

Teachers should:

- afford all students the opportunity to be successful in their class
- establish rules that indicate expectations for behavior and consequences for misbehavior
- select material that is meaningful and age-appropriate
- display a daily schedule so students routinely move from one task to another
- arrange functional seating, but do not allow students to distract each other from the main task
- maintain a rapid pace to well-ordered lessons
- demonstrate ongoing consistency in administering rules and consequences

(*Source:* Adapted from Smith & Misra, 1992)

Jennifer's reaction to failure is typical of that of many students. It becomes easier to avoid tasks than confront them and to strike out at others when forced to perform. As frustration and failure grow, so do anger.

Table 11–5 includes techniques for averting likely behavior problems. Adapted from Smith and Misra (1992), these strategies emphasize student success as critical to degree of performance. When teachers are aware of at-risk students and work with them instead of against them, students respond with increased respect and effort.

Additionally, teachers must convey specific rules that indicate their expectations for behavior and class performance. By establishing positive and negative consequences for student behavior, they set the stage for what is acceptable in their rooms. The rules should be posted in the classroom so that the teacher can refer to them with ease. Rules should be positively stated, concretely describing what students are expected to do (e.g., "Raise your hand to speak" rather than "Don't call out in class").

Teachers should limit the number of rules and prioritize their importance. Such emphasis should result in students' understanding their significance. Teachers should afford students a chance to practice class rules. If students break a rule, the teacher should have a simple signal to make the student aware of the infraction, as part of the redirection to task. Students should never have to guess about a teacher's standards. Rules should be discussed at the beginning of school to clarify results for everyone. Teachers should monitor student progress, rewarding students for behaving appropriately (Waldron, 1996).

As Table 11–5 indicates, material studied should be at the student's level so responses such as Jennifer's can be avoided. As discussed in Chapter 6, teachers can have students complete informal inventories at the beginning of the school year in order to ensure they can read the text and complete assigned work. Material should be motivational through its meaningfulness to their lives. When students find a book interesting and at their reading and conceptual levels, rarely do they avoid assignments.

Class routines are critical to avoiding behavior problems because they structure the way tasks are to be completed. For example, all students should know how to indicate they have completed their assignment when the teacher is working with another student or small group. There are routines for using learning centers, for collecting and distributing materials, and for changing from one assignment to another.

In nonacademic areas, students will behave more correctly if they know procedures for acquiring a hall pass, obtaining permission to use the restroom, or using the library. Routines are established by the adults in the school. There is no way students can follow them successfully without direction.

A daily schedule affords a routine that many students may not have in their personal lives. When posted in the room, they can anticipate their day,

A daily schedule provides a routine that many students value in its consistency.

providing a sense of security and control. Teachers should avoid changing the classroom schedule unless absolutely necessary, since students enjoy the predictability of knowing what activity comes next.

Some students may need modified schedules because of additional activities such as physical therapy or meeting with the school counselor. They can write their schedules on index cards and tape them to their desk or inside their notebooks (Smith & Misra, 1992). Teachers should schedule less-preferred activities (i.e., vocabulary practice or skill-building) before preferred ones (i.e., music or physical education), so students will complete their work to begin the more motivational task. Teachers should also alternate active and passive activities, so as not to overstimulate or to go beyond attention spans.

Additional considerations of the physical layout of the room should emphasize seating and work areas. If teachers do not assign seats, naturally students will sit by their friends, who are likely to be of similar interest and skill levels. Since teachers tend to direct most of their attention to individuals who sit in the front of the room, usually the most academically capable students take those seats because of their enjoyment in class participation. Unfortunately, students with academic difficulties tend to sit in the back or along the side of the room, where teachers are less likely to notice them. In selecting seating arrangements, teachers should scatter high achievers randomly throughout the room so they can provide an example for students with academic difficulties. This pattern also encourages teachers to interact with students throughout the classroom (Smith & Misra, 1992).

"Some of the more popular seating patterns may encourage behavior problems," commented Teresa. "As I work with regular educators, I see the recent tendency to arrange desks in groups, usually containing four students. Most of the time this seating is random, but viewed as requiring less movement when students need to work with each other, as in Cooperative Learning. At times these arrangements encourage discipline problems. It's difficult for a distractible student not to notice peers sitting right next to him or to read the paper of a student sitting across the table. In many rooms, part of the class at these tables have their backs to the teacher. Certainly this isn't encouraging attention and participation."

Lessons should be fast-paced allowing little transition time or off-task opportunities. If students need to move along quickly, they tend to be less able to be involved in diversionary activities. Teachers can further encourage student efforts by creating a friendly atmosphere where students are willing to take risks because they know their responses will be treated with respect. To demonstrate appropriate behaviors, teachers should comment on peers' responses to situations difficult for the student. Modeling is one of the benefits of the inclusive classroom, and should be underscored whenever possible.

modeling—demonstrating first-hand.

## Monitoring the Physical Environment

Teachers may underrate the significance of the physical environment to ensuring success and avoiding behavior problems. Yet, especially for many students with sensory and physical disabilities, personal comfort is critical to their attention, concentration, and ability to produce quality work. Room temperature should be appropriate to the season, with adequate heating, cooling, and ventilation so students are comfortable.

Avoidance of glare in lighting is particularly significant for students with visual and auditory impairments. Students should be able to see each other at all times. The student with a hearing loss should be seated for full view of the teacher and peers and allowed to move freely to improve visual access. Desk size and height should be appropriate for students' physical needs. If students are left-handed, it is critical that they not have to move their body into an uncomfortable position to write. Alternate height tables should be available for students in wheelchairs, as well as adequate cushioning for long school days (Heimstra & Sisco, 1990).

Students with Attention Deficit Hyperactivity Disorder need to be placed away from distractions of any kind. Their work areas should be uncluttered, containing only the materials of immediate use. They should be permitted to move flexibly within their desk or table space, as long as they do not provide a distraction to others. Younger students may attach a folder to the back of their chairs or sides of their desk to hold papers.

# MANAGING STUDENT BEHAVIORS

Regardless of the existence of a diagnosed behavioral disorder, all students in the class benefit from a careful plan of rules, schedules, and consequences. Instead of initially singling out individual students for behavioral change, teachers will prevent problems through following certain techniques with all students. Then, if certain students go beyond the boundaries of the plan, teachers can provide specific interventions.

As indicated in Table 11–6, there are an extensive number of techniques that are effective in managing student behaviors. The most effective is Premack's Principle (1959), previously referred to as *Grandma's Rule,* in which the teacher establishes what task the student needs to complete before moving on to a preferred activity. Stating the reward along with the task provides motivation for students to complete work that is difficult for them. It is important that teachers not be coaxed into giving the reward if the task is incompletely or poorly accomplished. Instead, the teacher should check for satisfactory completion, praise the student, and then give the reward.

Organization and avoidance of distractions are important to supporting positive behaviors. Students should be seated away from peers when necessary, in areas secluded visually by a bookshelf or file cabinet. If they feel themselves becoming frustrated, they should have a place to calm down. Assignment sheets or books should contain daily homework and indicate materials necessary for its completion. Parents can sign assignment sheets at home after reviewing student work completion. Dividing notebooks' pockets for completed work and homework allows for better organization.

Teachers should use verbal cues to signify upcoming directions or information that is particularly important. They should say distracted students' names before giving instructions, with student repetition of directions when necessary. If written, students should highlight or underline important statements. Teachers should establish eye contact and sequence directions carefully, not giving more than two at any one time.

Many teachers prefer a contingency system where they reward students for work completed or acceptable behaviors. While some teachers may use tokens, checkmarks, or objects to signify goal attainment, most prefer activity rewards since they are easier to monitor and less expensive.

Students should be told their potential reward in advance of a particular lesson in order to provide optimal motivation. Motivators can be taken

**Table 11–6**
**Techniques for Managing Student Behaviors**

Teachers should:

- use Premack's Principle: "First you do what I need you to do. Then you get to do what you want to do" (Premack, 1959)
- give the student a note card to place under the line of print being read; this prevents distractions by other words on the page
- provide students with a private place to calm down when they are frustrated or angry
- give students an "office," a desk in a visually secluded area where they will not distract or be distracted by others
- have students organize their desk or work space so it is uncluttered
- to avoid distractions, seat students with behavioral problems in the front of the room with back to peers
- seat students away from visual and auditory stimuli (windows, pencil sharpeners)
- divide notebooks into pockets for completed work and pockets for homework
- check completed work for accuracy before permitting the student to begin next assignment
- prepare an assignment sheet to be signed daily by parents
- use charts that show student progress and instill personal motivation
- explain appropriate behavior before special occasions such as schoolwide assemblies
- highlight or underline directions on the page
- use a special sound or signal to attract attention for directions
- plan potentially overstimulating activities for "down" times of the day
- vary voice tone and loudness to keep students' attention
- break activities down into shorter units varying from quiet to lively, supporting ongoing interest
- once they have completed a difficult assignment, allow students to move to a preferred task, such as computer time
- use concrete and visual materials
- give cues that identify particularly significant information: "This is important"
- before giving directions, say the names of students who are distracted
- present directions in a series of steps, with students completing one section before moving on to the next
- have students repeat oral directions, underline or highlight written ones
- while giving directions, establish eye contact with students who have attentional difficulties
- require an assignment book for all students, including space for daily homework and required texts
- have a different notebook for each subject, with color-coded covers if necessary

*(Continued)*

**Table 11–6**   *(Continued)*

- when assigning homework, list necessary materials
- keep all handouts in a folder so that students can replace lost items
- review the correctness of any assignments copied from the chalkboard
- list steps when giving an independent assignment; check progress at frequent intervals
- avoid giving homework assignments verbally
- reward positive statements about self and peers
- name the specific behavior when praising the student
- provide frequent opportunities for daily success
- when appropriate, in addition to praise, add nonverbal cues such as smiling and nodding
- have behavioral contracts in which students work toward specified outcomes
- ignore negative behavior whenever possible
- speak directly and briefly to students during negative encounters
- give positive attention to students demonstrating effort
- be non-confrontational, giving more "I-messages" than "You-messages"
- provide immediate attention to students demonstrating an academic difficulty in order to avoid frustration
- use charts and graphs to demonstrate student progress
- reward student effort through tokens or preferred activities
- work with parents to reward the same behaviors at school and home
- include planned interruptions in which students have opportunities for movement and relaxation
- state the rule, but never debate or argue with students
- provide in-class time-out for infractions or time-away for reflection
- send notes regarding positive behavior home to parents

*(Sources:* Adapted from Klumb, 1992; Moskowitz, 1988; Lerner, 1993; Waldron, 1992a; Waldron, 1996)

from those activities students most prefer. Ones enjoyed both by elementary and secondary students include: a positive note home to parents; listening to tapes through headphones; being group leader; studying with a friend; acknowledgment by the principal; being excused from tests; tutoring peers or younger children; helping a student with disabilities; not having homework that night; watching a video; running errands; collecting or distributing materials; having outdoor lessons; decorating bulletin boards; performing a skit for the class based on content studied (Andersen, 1974).

If students begin to misbehave, teachers should have a warning system that indicates that the behavior is unacceptable. This signal should be established in advance so that there is no doubt of its meaning and so the teacher does not have to stop the class. Even for minor infractions, teachers should give only one warning before taking action. If they hesitate or give several, the message to the student is that the behavior is acceptable or not serious.

## Time-Out

A time-out area has become standard in many classrooms. It should be located in an area where the student cannot see the class or teacher and cannot gain attention, such as a back corner of the room. The student should not be located outside the classroom or in a public area where additional attention is obtained. When student behavior is beyond boundaries, the teacher should point to the student and then to time-out. As previously instructed, the student should move there immediately with no discussion. The teacher who confronts may initiate an argument or an attempt by the student to gain attention. Once in the corner, the student begins a timer for a designated, usually brief, period of time. At the conclusion of that period, the student may rejoin the class, unless needing more time to calm down personally. For major infractions, some teachers direct students to write down what happened, step-by-step, before being placed in time-out. Students should be held accountable for all assignments their peers are completing so they do not view their removal from class as a means of work avoidance.

In advance, students should know the punishment for refusing to go to time-out (i.e., remain in class during recess for elementary students or a lowered grade or missed activity for secondary). When choosing these punishments, teachers should consider those activities students most enjoy so that their absence will be impactful.

## Verbal Interactions with Students

Many students with behavioral problems learn to "bait" teachers through personal, negative comments. Teachers respond with anger or immediate punishment, not realizing that the student has won the battle through receiving attention. Teachers should ignore what they can, and redirect students when the behavior goes too far. It is critical to have a plan in advance so that teachers do not become goaded into negative interactions that students control.

Ignoring the comment, the teacher should quietly but firmly state the task the student should be performing at that moment, and move on to make positive comments to students who are demonstrating appropriate behavior. If the student follows the teacher or persists in making negative statements, the "broken-record technique" is usually effective. Here, the teacher repeats the same direction given previously, in the exact same words ("Joe, I need

**"I" statements**—a style of communicating in which the teacher is not blaming the student or even commenting on the misbehavior, but is stating and restating the expectations.

for you to finish your math assignment"; "Kelly, I need your spelling words in five minutes"). Both of these comments are **"I" statements** in which the teacher is not blaming the student or even commenting on the misbehavior, but is stating and restating the expectation.

Teachers should avoid the tendency to say too much when redirecting students. A short verbal statement is far more effective than a lengthy explanation. They should make eye contact and speak both softly and directly. There should be no doubt that the teacher is in charge and consequences will follow if the student does not perform as directed. Teachers should never yell or physically approach a student. They should not threaten outcomes that they are unwilling or unable to pursue. It is far better to have consequences discussed and posted in advance of potential infractions so the students are aware of responses to negative behaviors. If student behavior escalates and is threatening to become out of control, the teacher can remind the student of the outcome. ("Joe, you may choose to return to your seat or go to time-out.") If the teacher turns her back and walks away after reminding the student of the behavioral choice, she avoids a stronger confrontation.

When responding to infractions, it is important for teachers to remember not to take challenges personally and to become angry with the student, but to objectify the situation and work to change the behavior. When the teacher refuses to participate in a power struggle with the student, she diffuses the interchange quickly.

# SUMMARY

Chapter 11 included a large number of teaching techniques for students with language, cognitive, and behavioral differences. Optimal strategies for teaching English as a second language (ESL) emphasize reciprocal interaction instead of drills and practice. As teachers have dialogues with students in which they emphasize higher-order thinking skills, they provide the groundwork for improved language use. Reading comprehension is emphasized instead of word attack skills and written expression over mechanics. Students are encouraged to use spoken and written skills across the curriculum, expanding content vocabulary and generalizing application. Because they are motivational, informal discussions with peers further broaden language skills.

Within thematic units teachers provide questions at varied levels for student consideration. The combination of literature use followed by writing, drama, and art stimulates students to use language thoughtfully and creatively.

If students from different language backgrounds demonstrate disabilities, teachers should use the informal oral proficiency scale from Chapter 7 to gauge stronger and problematic areas. A consultant teacher model is often effective where the ESL and special education teachers provide the regular educators with modified materials to support students

When students demonstrate cognitive and learning disabilities, teachers should relate new ideas to concrete objects and personal experiences. Students should complete activities requiring them to transfer new information to new situations through role-playing and simulations. Teachers should help them outline material using primary headings and subheadings, indicating relationships between ideas. Copying should be avoided, with a greater reliance on discussions in which students explain processes studied, providing additional opportunities for integration.

Table 11–2 contains numerous activities for use if students have peceptual problems. They emphasize multisensory techniques, color for emphasis, cursive handwriting, and arrows to demonstrate appropriate directionality. Consistent spelling patterns should be preceded by consonants, blends, and digraphs to emphasize regularity of sound-symbol association.

Students should always say the sound of the letter, not its name, as they spell. Sounds commonly confused should not be taught together. One should be overlearned before beginning the next. Students should use syllables as early as possible in order read by larger sound units. Students should practice sight words and arithmetic facts on flashcards with peers who are at the same level and need reinforcement.

If students demonstrate memory problems, teacher review of previously studied information as well as careful questioning provides the opportunity for students to relate to concepts and later recall them. Structural analysis of new words supports meaning through prefixes, suffixes, and roots. Application to content vocabulary improves recall across content areas.

If a language disorder is present, teachers should alter their own verbal patterns. They should speak in brief sentences and allow extra time for student response. Their modeling of good grammar and encouragement of opportunities for students to verbalize encourages a language-supportive environment. Students should discuss new vocabulary and practice sequencing content and story material.

Behavior problems should be prevented before they escalate. When students are successful and enjoy lessons and materials, they attend better. Physical arrangements that place them away from potential student or environmental distractors are optimal. Teachers can encourage behavior through Premack's Principle (1959), "First you do what I need you to do. Then you get to do what you want to do." When students complete less desired tasks to participate in more appealing work, their behavior is usually cooperative.

Teachers should design behavioral contracts specifying outcomes and consequences. If misbehavior begins, they should give a warning signal to the student or use physical proximity to avoid disturbing the class. Never arguing, teachers should direct students to time-out if the misbehavior continues. If the student refuses to go, the teacher should state a pre-established choice allowing the student to compare a brief stay in time-out with a stronger consequence.

## CASE STUDY: *Elementary*

"My role as a special educator has really changed these days," comments Teresa. "Whereas I used to have my own Resource classes in a separate room all day, now I do most of my work co-teaching or working with small groups of students in regular classrooms. At first I thought I would miss my autonomy and classes, but I've found it can be fun to participate on collaborative teams and consult with teachers about students experiencing learning and behavior problems. I've never worked with so many teachers and children before. My job has gained an acceptance I love. Everyone is so happy when I help them!

"This success rate is not always easy. For example, I'm currently trying to help Maura teach Keith, a student with severe perceptual problems. Usually, I would start by observing for his stronger learning modality for instructional purposes, and suggest ways to provide remedial work for his weaker areas. Unfortunately, Keith is experiencing problems in the visual, auditory, and fine motor areas.

"He's a fourth-grader who reads on a first-grade level. He has problems discriminating between similar-appearing letters and numbers. When he reads or copies words, often he missequences letter order, slowing his reading and writing progress. He does attempt to read from left to right, but he skips small words and sometimes even whole lines of print. His phonics are poor. While he knows most of his beginning consonant sounds, he has real problems with beginning letter combinations (i.e., *st - / gr - / bl - / ch - / tr - / th -*). He just can't seem to recall the sounds they represent.

"When he tries to write, he has problems holding the pencil correctly, resulting in poor letter formation. I was going to rely on a multisensory technique where he traces the word, says its sounds aloud, and sees what it looks like. I can't rely on this technique alone, since he takes forever to copy things!

"Keith's recall of sight words and arithmetic facts is poor. Even after saying the word or fact aloud and then writing it, he doesn't remember it the next day. He never seems able to relate vocabulary or math facts to anything in real life. I'm starting to be concerned that his memory problems may be a result of language and reading comprehension difficulties, not just with difficulties analyzing letters and numbers."

1. From Table 11–2, what are specific teaching techniques that can be adapted to help Keith overcome his perceptual problems?

2. How can Teresa assess if Keith has language and reading comprehension problems in addition to difficulties with perception?

3. Considering that his reading level is extremely low, how should Teresa adapt techniques in Tables 11–3 and 11–4 for use with Keith?

4. How should Teresa best structure her time with Keith? Direct instruction? As a consultant to Maura? Teaching to the larger class? To a small group?

CASE STUDY: *Secondary*

John remembers Leslie from his ninth-grade class. She was somewhat quiet, rarely raising her hand or participating eagerly in discussions. While she was never highly motivated, she always did her homework and studied for exams. Her performance was average for the class. She was respectful of him but never overly friendly.

Two years later, in his Junior class, she's an entirely different person. She acts angry and hostile all the time. John can sense her emotions simmering as she sits at her desk. She rarely participates in small group work, instead talking to others and distracting them from the topic. In large group she makes very negative comments about John and his teaching, which the other students find comical. She mimics his gestures, knowing that he can see her. She repeats his sentences in a sarcastic manner to everyone around her and in a voice loud enough for John to hear. She turns in no homework and does not appear to study for exams. Her attitude is "Fail me. Who cares?"

John called a parent conference with Leslie's mother. Canceled twice without explanation, when they finally met, the mother told John that she and Leslie's father had gone through a lengthy and bitter divorce last year. Elaborating many overly-personal negatives about the father, she said that she and Leslie "hate him" for having left them both. After a few attempts at getting together, Leslie has refused to see him. She explained how happy they both were when he took a job in another state.

The mother said that while Leslie seemed unhappy at home, she had not demonstrated the negativism she was showing in John's class. The mother asked John to be patient with Leslie, since she had been through a difficult time which was likely reflected in her behavior. She felt that with time the situation would rectify itself.

John came away from the meeting extremely dissatisfied. "She may advise patience, but she doesn't have to teach a class disrupted by a student making fun of her. I find Leslie's behavior personally intolerable."

1. What are specific things John can do to involve Leslie positively in the class, diverting her from negative behaviors?

2. Design a system for John to use that will provide boundaries for her behavior. How should he explain the system to Leslie? Specifically, what should he do when she makes fun of him to classmates?

3. How can he work together with her other teachers to give her positive support through this difficult period?

4. How can he redirect the attention of other students in the class so that they do not reinforce her behavior?

5. What can he do to have her complete her homework and to prepare more for exams?

# TECHNIQUES FOR STUDENTS WITH SENSORY AND PHYSICAL CHALLENGES

**12**

"It's interesting to watch reactions to inclusion from our community," observes Mort. "While there hasn't been too much negativism about including students with learning and language difficulties, people seem to react more strongly to physical impairments. Although students actually may require fewer accommodations, if they are deaf or blind, or happen to need a wheelchair, the difference seems so much more pronounced that everyone notices.

"Maybe that's the problem," responded Dr. Mirales. "Everyone notices. While a student can get away with a mild vision or hearing loss, the minute she wears a hearing aid or needs magnification to see, somehow she stands out much more. Perhaps it's the need for that equipment that makes people feel somewhat overwhelmed about working with students with physical challenges. They see the wheelchair before they notice the student who sits in it. They see the white cane before they get to know the person holding it. It's ironic and sad that the very ways we have embraced technology for normalization may be part of the reason students are not fully accepted."

Mort added, "I think there's more to it than just our concerns about how to work the equipment. Students with more severe disabilities tend to require additional alternative instructional and curricular modifications. While teachers may grapple with students who can't read the textbook, they are understandably more concerned with students who can't see the book. Students with fine motor disabilities may experience difficulties with handwriting, but what does a teacher do with a student who can't hold a pencil?"

"True, Mort. I think its also significant that students with physical challenges, including orthopedic, vision, and hearing, are of low incidence. In many states certification requirements for teachers in these fields remains totally separate. Therefore, universities that train other specialists may not even offer courses in working with these students. It's often the case that teachers who are certified in special education don't know anything about deafness or blindness or teaching a student with cerebral palsy. If the specialists in our schools don't know, how can we expect the regular educators to be successful?

"In Westside we're contracting with the regional service center to add consultants for students with low-incidence disabilities. Anytime one of our students is included in regular education, we want to be sure the teachers in that school are fully prepared to be successful.

"In addition to providing ongoing consultation and support by the district and service center working together, we will continue inservices such as this so all teachers in the school receive appropriate planning and program implementation information. Through working together before placement and providing ongoing supportive consultation, we can furnish an appropriate setting for the student without overburdening the teacher."

# TECHNIQUES FOR STUDENTS WITH HEARING IMPAIRMENTS

"Can we review some ways to work with students with hearing impairments?" asked Maura. "In just a few weeks Jeff will be joining our class. I'm a bit nervous this time, because frankly, I don't know what to expect, especially concerning types of specialized equipment we'll need. I'm not sure if the consultation model is best or if there actually will be someone in the class with him most of the time. Primarily I'm concerned about how to give directions and verbal information to the class and be sure he understands it."

## Resource Provision

As listed in Table 12–1, White (1981) suggests a number of questions the collaborative team at Jackson should consider before placing Jeff in Maura's class. An important member of this team should be a specialist in designing programs for students with hearing impairments. It is optimal to have this specialist be the person who will interact with Maura after Jeff is in her class. If this is not possible, a special education supervisor can participate on the team, outlining typical procedures and information that Maura needs to know to smoothly integrate Jeff.

However, identification of the person with whom she will meet should be initiated as quickly as possible. This will allow her to gain confidence through having a specialist on whom she can rely to ask questions and gain ongoing support through consultation.

---

**Table 12–1**
**Questions Before Placement of Students with Hearing Impairments**

The prereferral team should consider the following:

- Who is the consultant and resource person for ongoing support?
- What amplification equipment will the student use? The teacher use?
- Does the student wear a hearing aid? Who will check and replace the batteries?
- Will media be adapted for student use?
- Who will demonstrate and maintain specialized equipment?

(*Source:* Adapted from White, 1981)

Depending on the nature and extent of the student's hearing loss, the specialist should indicate the type of amplification that the student and Maura will use. Once in place, the specialist should demonstrate how to operate this equipment optimally without interfering with Maura's teaching or her flexibility in working with all students in the class.

She will want to know if any other equipment or materials are needed to support Jeff. Does he wear a hearing aid? Whose responsibility is it to check and replace batteries, since they have such an abbreviated life span? Will captions be available when she is showing videos to the class? If not, are there amplifiers and headsets to improve his receiving as undistorted sounds as are possible?

**American Sign Language (ASL)** —an alternate communication system that uses hand gestures to express words and thoughts.

**finger spelling** —using the fingers to form the letters of the words.

**total communication** —students rely on residual hearing with amplification whenever possible, and use a manual approach such as sign language as a complement whenever necessary.

Many individuals with hearing impairments prefer the support of alternate communication systems, such as **American Sign Language (ASL)** and **finger spelling**. While manual systems may be easier to learn, they have difficulty clearly expressing specifics such as tenses and plurals (Morsink, 1984). The use of manual communication is also limited by others who are aware of appropriate signs to initiate or respond to conversations and discussions. Students who use only sign language and finger spelling may be excluded daily from interactions with peers.

Often a system of **total communication** is the most effective. Students rely on residual hearing with amplification whenever possible, and use a manual approach such as sign language as a complement whenever necessary. Usually total communication develops over a period of years as students sort out differences in auditory and visual language and receive systematic instruction in ASL. Much depends on the language used in the home and the training of teachers.

## Student Behaviors

Once the level of assistance is established, Maura needs more information about Jeff. She can obtain this by meeting with him informally after she has read his records and reports of previous assessments. Then she should have him attend her class for critical subject areas such as reading and arithmetic. During these visits she can employ some of the observation techniques discussed in Chapter 6.

Without additional formal testing, there are a number of areas Maura can observe regarding Jeff's learning styles and abilities. As indicated in Table 12–2, she can note how much hearing appears to be present during conversations. While she will have a better idea of his acuity once he participates fully in her class, she will be more at ease initially with at least a general idea of his skills.

Since students with hearing disabilities may not be able to understand verbal information when noise levels in the room are high, the teacher will want

## Table 12–2
## Questions Concerning Students with Hearing Impairments

For proper instruction, teachers should ask:

- How much hearing is present?
- How much classroom noise can the student tolerate and still understand information?
- Does the student express personal needs and ideas clearly?
- Can the student interpret nuances of verbal and written information?
- Is there an ability to relate new information to past experiences?
- How clear are the student's speech patterns? Do they allow for easy interactions with others?
- What level are decoding skills in reading, including word recognition and analysis?
- What level is reading comprehension of passages in content areas?
- Is written expression clear? What is the student's level of conceptual discussions when compared with peers?
- Does the student demonstrate appropriate social skills or merely imitate behaviors of peers?
- Is the student accepted by peers? If not, what interpersonal skills are needed?
- Are there any behavioral concerns such as a tendency to become inattentive and daydream?

to observe the student carefully to see the impact of a busy class and optimal seat placement.

As important as his hearing is his verbal language. Can he express his ideas and needs completely? Since many students with hearing disabilities may have distorted speech through difficulties with articulation, Maura will have to consider his clarity of expression and how encumbered he will be when interacting with others.

Since language is tied intricately to conceptual skills, Maura will listen carefully as Jeff answers questions about inferences in academic discussions and social conversations. How well does he understand language, especially subtleties? Is he satisfied with his ability to verbalize his response, or does he seem frustrated by not being able to express ideas easily? How well has he integrated past experiences in order to use them as a basis for assimilating additional knowledge?

It is important to focus on his level of socialized language as well. Often peers do not respond negatively to his hearing loss, since it is neither visible nor related to immediate interactions. However, often they focus on the quality of language, especially its fluency and articulation. If Jeff is difficult

Participating as an important group member allows a student with a hearing impairment to experience group acceptance.

for peers to understand, he may become isolated because of lack of communication with others who find conversation with him challenging.

Because of predictable problems in learning phonics, many students with hearing disabilities have difficulty with word recognition and analysis. Their reading and spelling are impacted by an inability to "sound out" words common to others. As a result, they are forced to memorize many more words than peers, slowing their reading progress. Maura will need to listen to Jeff read from class texts informally to note progress in the level of his skill development.

Additionally, receptive language skills that limit a student's ability to understand spoken language may hinder reading comprehension similarly. Although the student is not dependent on hearing what is said when reading, difficulty understanding sophisticated concepts may occur due to delayed language development. As Maura observes Jeff in her room, she will need to question him concerning the meaning of main ideas and inferences in the passages he reads.

Jeff's written work is also very important. Maura may have to look beyond problems in spelling to examine depth and clarity of ideas. In com-

MY PORTFOLIO

> *We should be nice to amials bocase the brids carry seed to the forests that were biernd done and then fly over and the seeds fall on the grond and then it rains and they grow a new frorst. Cows give us milk. And we play with dogs and cats if leve a message and thell get bock to you.*

Teachers should carefully examine student organization and clarity of ideas to determine the full impact of the disability. With correction, this student notes, "We should be nice to animals because the birds carry seed to the forests that were burned down and they fly over and the seeds fall on the ground. And then it rains and they grow a new forest. Cows give us milk and we play with dogs and cats. We leave a message and they'll get back to you." Here the student demonstrates problems with letter sequencing (brids/birds; frorst/forest). More significantly, in the last sentence he is cognitively distracted from the topic. Reprinted with permission, Winston School, San Antonio.

parison with peers, what is the level of conceptual expression? Is he able to organize his thoughts? Is his syntax good? Does he write in expanded sentence form, fluently using descriptors such as adjectives and adverbs? Does he express ideas more clearly in speaking or writing?

Maura should consider Jeff's behavior in her class, since it will directly impact the effectiveness of her instruction with him and others. She should observe for behaviors such as daydreaming when others are talking, outbursts indicating frustration, or withdrawal tendencies. Many of these behaviors will be modulated by his acceptance from peers. If his social skills are appropriate and if he initiates interactions with others, he will gain more immediate acceptance.

## Teaching Techniques

To assimilate students with hearing disabilities into their classes, teachers can use a variety of techniques. Listed in Table 12–3, these strategies modify the learning environment to afford students the opportunity to become active members of the class instead of passive observers.

Ross (1982) suggests that students sit in locations away from ambient noise in order to use their residual hearing optimally. Common distractors include heaters and air conditioners, windows by busy streets, and learning centers

**Table 12–3**
**Techniques for Students with Hearing Impairments**

Teachers should:

- seat students away from sources of background noise (e.g., windows, doors, learning centers, heating and cooling systems)

- place students in front of room with desks turned at an angle so they can see peers' faces

- permit students to change seating easily in order to see speakers' faces

- allow for flexible seating arrangements in groupwork

- be sure speakers' faces are illuminated even when the room is darkened for media

- vary teaching formats to include exhibits, demonstrations, experiments, simulations

- write directions in short statements

- use pictures for visualization of abstract concepts

- use advance organizers to underscore important ideas in lectures and texts

- face students when using an overhead projector or blackboard

- avoid moving around the room constantly

- use gestures, body language, and facial expression to emphasize ideas

- require all students to raise their hands before addressing the class

- call the speaker's name for identification

- modify written materials through use of visuals such as diagrams, charts, and graphs

- de-emphasize reading and lecture as the primary means of teaching

- assign a peer to take notes

- use concrete words and sentences, basing information on student's past experiences or content studied

- ask the student questions to assure understanding

- avoid speaking rapidly

- emphasize visual, non-phonetic methods in teaching reading

(*Sources:* Adapted from Ross, 1982; Waldron, Diebold, & Rose, 1985; Kampfe, 1984; Palmer, 1988; Morsink, 1984; Waldron, 1996)

fostering talking by others. Students are thereby afforded the opportunity to attend more fully to teacher and classmate discussions.

It is best to place a student with a hearing impairment in the front of the room with the desk slightly angled to allow the student to observe peers' faces as they speak. However, in an active classroom where students change groups frequently, the student should be permitted to change seats without special permission. Moving quietly to a spot where speakers can be more clearly observed gives the student the responsibility, while it assures the teacher that the student is comfortably placed.

Even when the room is darkened for media use, if a speaker is addressing the group, there should be enough light for the student to see the speaker's face in order to **lip-read**. Students are very dependent on seeing whomever is speaking to receive the message. When the teacher or peers are talking in a darkened room, the student with a hearing impairment is removed from the discussion.

**lip-read**—to understand what a person is saying by distinguishing the movement of the person's lips.

Waldron, Diebold, and Rose (1985) discuss the need to use a variety of teaching formats. If teachers rely on lecture and reading, students with hearing impairments may not learn to their optimal potential. Hands-on methods are easier for students to comprehend than are lessons reliant on verbal language. When instructors use methods allowing students to experience new situations or at least observe demonstrations, they understand and retain information better.

In addition to verbalizing information as succinctly as possible, teachers should write directions in short statements. Pictures are very helpful when more expanded explanations are necessary or when abstract concepts are considered. They highlight meaning, and even for secondary students, may provide new insights into basic information.

Kampfe (1984) and Palmer (1988) suggest preparation of students for understanding new ideas in lectures and texts through the use of advance organizers such as outlines or sheets listing primary topics and associated subareas, in order to demonstrate relationships. Presented before the lecture, discussion, or reading, advance organizers alert students to the most important concepts.

When teachers use an overhead projector, they should face the class. Students with hearing impairments benefit from having information listed visually, but miss out on important discussion when the teacher's back is turned. Similarly, it is important to never discuss information while writing on the blackboard. Although this tendency is natural, if hearing impaired students cannot see the instructor, they try to obtain this information from peers, posing a potential disruption to the class.

While teachers should not feel the necessity to stand in one place, they should avoid constant movement that forces students with hearing impairments to work harder to see them. Students with more severe hearing difficulties benefit from the teacher's use of gestures and body language. While facial expressions also help provide meaning, teachers should not exaggerate their lip movements since this tends to interfere with the students' interpretation of meaning and to distort sounds.

At times it can be difficult for students to follow a discussion if they are unsure who will be speaking next. They have to visually search the room to note who is talking. By the time they identify the speaker, usually they have missed the beginning comments, placing them at a disadvantage. Teachers should require students to raise their hands before speaking to the class, and call on the speaker by name. Use of a hand gesture or a turn of the teacher's body also helps identify who will speak next.

While some students with hearing impairments find reading content information easier than attending to lectures, they may not read as fluently as peers. Their rate may be slower and their comprehension poor. In elementary grades they should receive additional reading instruction to expedite skill-building. In secondary school, they can benefit from texts where the specialist teacher has highlighted important information, allowing them to concentrate on the most significant content. When reading of highly conceptual material is required, teachers can provide visual supports such as diagrams or charts to make information more easily understood.

Morsink (1984) suggests assigning a peer to take notes when the teacher has to lecture. This permits the student with the hearing impairment to concentrate on content instead of having to look down at the notebook or consider how to structure incoming information. The note-taker should be a student who has volunteered and who has a good facility with the subject area. It is important to give status to the role of note-taker as an honor in the classroom. The teacher can ease the process and avoid students' recopying notes by providing carbon paper. The note-taker should be praised both for demonstrating good listening and organization skills as well as being willing to help a classmate.

Teachers may need to modify their teaching style to incorporate the needs of students with hearing impairments (Morsink, 1984). They should not speak too rapidly so students can follow lectures and discussions more easily. Instructors should question all students about their understanding, overcoming students' tendency to nod compliantly even when information has not been integrated fully. When providing initial explanations of new information, they should use specific and concrete examples relating the newly presented to previous content.

Whether at elementary or secondary levels, they should emphasize less auditory means of reading new words. For example, instead of encouraging Jeff to sound out words, Maura can teach the spelling patterns (-*at*, -*ing*, -*ed*) to demonstrate constancy in whole units. Then when she shows him how to preface the spelling patterns with consonant blends and digraphs (*th*-, *str*-, *fl*-) Jeff will have a broader array of words than he would if trying to memorize each separately.

Phonics cannot be avoided in learning to read fluently, but its importance can be lessened for students with auditory difficulties. It is important to note that a number of the suggestions provided in Chapter 11 for auditory perception problems will work equally well with students demonstrating hearing impairments.

At the upper elementary and secondary levels, teachers should continue reading instruction in their content area through placing emphasis on structural analysis and syllabication skills. Reading *penta-*, *ana-*, and *-ism* provides a basis for integrating larger units that add consistency in sound and meaning. Reading by syllables allows students to gain in speed and fluency while discouraging their reliance on individual sounds that may be difficult for them because of the hearing difference.

# TECHNOLOGY FOR USE WITH THE HEARING IMPAIRED

hearing aids—devices used by the hearing impaired to amplify specified sound frequencies to a volume permitting improved use of residual hearing.

residual hearing—available hearing capabilities.

"Again, let's discuss technology," comments Maura. "What are some of the assistive devices that will help Jeff become a class member? I don't want to exclude something that's available just because I'm not aware of it."

Individuals with hearing impairments who prefer to use an oral approach to communication rely on residual hearing and speech, or lip, reading. However, only about 20 percent of English sounds can be distinguished by lip and facial movements, the most difficult being high-frequency consonant sounds such as *s, sh, th, ch, f* (Morsink, 1984). These factors make an oral approach especially difficult for students with severe losses.

Clearly **hearing aids** are the most commonly used devices available. They amplify specified sound frequencies to a volume permitting improved use of **residual hearing**. There are a variety of hearing aids available, depending on the nature and degree of the loss. While often ineffective for sensorineural losses, they are more successful with conductive hearing problems.

However, hearing aids are limited at times because they may distort some sounds. When the amplification is increased to improve certain sound input, other sounds may be diminished. The result can be difficulty in following conversations, radio and television shows, and speakers in large rooms such as an auditorium (Wisniewski & Sedlak, 1992).

Teachers should be aware of the effects of background noise on students with hearing aids. Loud sounds are amplified and take precedence over individual voices. Therefore, students should be seated as far away from noisy work areas as possible if any listening to teachers or individuals is required.

For hearing aids to be effective, they must be functioning correctly.

Batteries should be changed regularly and volume checked daily to assure correctness of setting for the student. This is especially critical for younger children who may not have facility with adjustments or awareness of optimal settings. Parents should be trained by specialists in checking the working status and adjustments of their children's hearing aids daily. Often teachers are too busy or subject to distractions by other students to be able to perform these tasks. If the parents do not check the hearing aid, a classroom assistant should be trained to examine it daily with the student. As students become older, they can check batteries and settings daily as part of their independent skill building.

Additional supports for the hearing impaired have improved their ability to use telephones as part of their daily lives. State-supported services allow individuals to call a toll-free number and tell an assigned operator their message. In turn, the operator immediately relays the message to the specified individual. The operator becomes the conduit for information sharing.

The teletypewriter and printer (TTY) allow the individual to communicate by using a typewriter that converts messages into electrical signals in different frequencies. Transmitted over the phone, these frequencies are converted back to print on the receiving end.

Now available in most public facilities and in many homes, the Telecommunications Device for the Deaf (TDD) has expanded these systems. The individual types the message on a keyboard through a word processor. The modem connection is similar to an on-line communication in Internet. The responder must have a compatible system to receive the message. The "conversation" can be ongoing, with messages appearing in print on a screen. As visual to auditory translations are enhanced, this technology will become even more important and useful.

# STUDENTS WITH VISUAL IMPAIRMENTS

Alex interjects, "While sensory losses are infrequent, it's important for us to know how to design programs for and teach students with these disabilities. It's so inexcusable to have students isolated from peers because they happen to be hearing or visually impaired. As we've been discussing, it's really critical that teachers and supportive staff have the full range of resources in order to meet these students' needs without feeling overwhelmed."

"Very true," responds John. "But you'll need to give us some guidelines for working with students who are partially sighted or blind. If I'm to be honest, I'd have to admit that including these students worries me, since I know that they need specialized materials and methods and I haven't been trained in this area."

## Resource Provision

Programming for students with visual impairments begins the same way as planning for students with any type of disability. The collaborative team needs to meet and consider a series of questions before the placement of a partially-sighted or blind student.

As indicated in Table 12–4, the initial concern should be the appointment of a specialist in the area of visual impairment. As with planning efforts for students with other disabilities, this specialist should work as an important member of the collaborative team. While larger school districts may have a full-time person, smaller districts may share a specialist or use a consultant from the regional service center.

Appropriate materials and equipment are particularly important to working successfully with visually impaired students. Therefore, the specialist should have catalogues of materials for the teacher to review as well as suggestions for appropriate equipment to enhance the student's class participation. Supports for teaching the student to read are of concern to most teachers. The planning team will need to rely on the specialist's input concerning the most suitable materials and the process for ordering them. Often the addition of specialized equipment and materials allows the student to progress through the same curriculum as peers.

**mobility instruction**—training relating to movement around a location.

The planning team should also question how much **mobility instruction** the student will require to move about the school and vicinity. The specialist teacher may provide this training directly. If not, he should be responsible for contacting the school district or regional service center to arrange for mobility training within the student's schedule. Optimally the trainer should meet with the student before placement in the regular classroom to assure the student's orientation to the building and campus, especially necessary facilities such as the cafeteria and restrooms. Extensive mobility training is

---

**Table 12–4**
**Questions Before Placement of Students with Visual Impairments**

The prereferral team should consider the following:

- Who is the consultant and resource person for ongoing support?

- What specialized reading materials will the student require? Large-print? Braille? Talking books?

- How much mobility training will the student require to move freely around the classroom and school campus?

- When will the student require a full-time teaching assistant in the classroom vs. be able to work independently?

especially important at the secondary level, where buildings are large and students suffer great embarrassment at becoming lost.

The collaborative team should also consider instances when the student will require full-time support in the classroom so the regular educator will not be overburdened. For example, if the student is totally blind and the class is involved in content area reading or an exam, a visual training specialist should bring braille materials to the room and stay with the student if direct reading training is necessary. Eventually, the student will be able to perform braille activities independently. If the student learns primarily auditorially, recordings will provide information and the specialist need not remain. It will be important for the teacher to share lesson plans weekly with the vision specialist to ensure that necessary personnel, materials, and equipment are available.

## Student Behaviors

Once the teacher is satisfied that resources are in place, it is time to continue to obtain more information about the student. As indicated in Table 12–5, the teacher needs some background to understand the nature of any learning differences. This input can be gained from meeting with the specialist assigned to this student. It is important to understand the history and prognosis of the disability without creating embarrassment for the young person.

While some of these concerns will have been discussed at the collaborative session before placement, the teacher can ask the specialist a number of the questions in Table 12–5 and gain answers to the remainder by direct observation of the student. A critical concern is whether the student possesses any vision or is totally blind, since the follow-up programming techniques, equipment, and materials will differ. If the student is sighted, the degree of vision is important since print size and magnification needs vary depending on acuity levels.

Age of occurrence of the disability is significant in indicating the level of conceptual development. For example, students who have been blind since birth lack the ability to create visual images of the world about them. Their ideas of object appearance, size, distance, and motion are totally based on their prior success with internalizing what they have learned through touch, what they have heard personally, or what others have told them.

Some students possessed sight at birth but became blind or partially sighted later through an accident or progressive disease. Unless these students were very young when they lost their sight, they would have created permanent images that may be maintained despite the visual loss. Students who have access to the seeing world either through partial sightedness or recallable visual experiences have an easier time developing concepts because they have a broader experiential base on which to build. Usually their

## Table 12–5
## Questions Concerning Students with Visual Impairments

For proper instruction, teachers should ask:

- Is the student partially-sighted or blind? If partially-sighted, what degree of visual acuity is present?
- At what age did the visual loss occur?
- Is the student's vision stable or will it become progressively worse?
- Does the student have visual-spatial concepts such as distance?
- What is the student's level of conceptual development when compared with peers?
- Does the student require large-print materials? Braille?
- What additional equipment will the student need (e.g., magnifiers; scanner; raised-surface globes and maps; talking calculator)?
- To what extent has the student been exposed to a variety of previous social and educational experiences?
- If braille is necessary, how much previous instruction has the student received?
- How much independent mobility does the student have?
- Whether in braille or large print, at what level are the student's decoding skills?
- At what level is reading comprehension in content areas?
- Does the student have any habits ("blindisms") that will distract other students?
- Are appropriate social skills present, or is the student isolated from peers?
- Do peers accept the student?
- Does the student have behavioral problems, such as speaking loudly in class to get attention?

oral receptive and expressive language as well as their reading comprehension are at a higher level than if they had been blind from birth.

Blind students can attain a high level of abstraction, but it may take longer because they lack the visual associative ability their peers have. Especially in visual-spatial concepts such as distance and size, students tend to learn relationships through discussions with others. In each content subject teachers should ask students with visual impairments direct questions measuring their depth of knowledge in that area. Does the student understand fractions and proportions in mathematics? Geography and concepts such as city, state, and nation in social studies? Biological and environmental concerns in science? All of these areas are impacted by previous experiential learning.

After assessing visual acuity, the consultant should determine the optimal reading medium for the student. In Table 12–6, Koenig and Holbrook (1989) list the factors teachers should consider in selecting print versus

**Table 12–6**
**Selecting the Reading Medium for Students with Visual Impairments**

The selection of large print or braille as a medium for teaching reading should be made carefully. The following student characteristics should be reviewed by the collaborative team, including a specialist in visual impairment.

Students who might benefit most from reading **print:**

- have stable eye conditions
- have intact central visual fields
- are able to use vision for near-distance tasks
- can understand the content of pictures
- have already used print in reading readiness skills such as discriminating different shapes and forms
- show progress in using vision efficiently to read print
- do not possess additional disabilities that would hinder progress in a developmental reading program

Students who might benefit most from reading **braille:**

- have unstable eye conditions with a prognosis of additional visual loss in the future
- have a reduced central visual field that decreases efficient reading of print
- prefer exploring the environment through the tactual sense
- have the ability to identify small objects tactually
- have made progress in developing tactual skills necessary to read braille
- have demonstrated readiness to associate braille with meaning through identification of symbols such as a personal name
- do not possess additional disabilities that would hinder progress in a braille reading program

(*Source:* Adapted from Koenig & Holbrook, 1989)

braille reading materials. Including the stability of the eye condition and intact central visual field, as well as demonstrating a previous history of success with print or tactile media, once this selection process is complete, the consultant can order appropriate reading materials.

Additionally, the teacher and consultant should observe informally how much independent mobility the student has, both within the classroom and around campus. As discussed above, the consultant should provide initial mobility training as the student enters the campus. However, if mobility training will require an extended period of time, the student should be placed in the classroom while it continues. The teacher and peers can manage introducing the student to in-class physical arrangements. At first the student should walk with peers to areas outside the class, learning over time to be independently mobile.

Blind students tend to be excluded from peer interactions more than many students with disabilities, often because others do not know how to handle the differences they associate with blindness. Peers may be afraid of saying the wrong thing and embarrassing themselves. It is difficult for blind students to initiate conversations because they may not be fully aware of who is close by or what is happening in the room. As a result, they may feel the need to wait for others to begin talking to them. Unfortunately, to avoid a situation they view as difficult, peers may talk among themselves, avoiding involvements with the student.

"blindisms"—personal or behavioral habits a blind person exhibits.

There may be some personal or behavioral habits that encourage further isolation of the blind student. From the onset, the teacher can help the student by quietly explaining how some blindisms may affect others negatively. For example, the student may rock back and forth in his seat. He may tap on his hand or the desk incessantly. He may make a certain quiet sound frequently. All of these behaviors may be comfortable habits to the student, ones that provide stimulation and diversion, since he does not have the ability others do to look around when he gets bored. Many times the behavior is so ingrained the student does not realize he is doing it or that it is affecting others. If teachers observe negative behaviors, they should explain to the student their impact on others in order to enhance opportunities for positive social interactions.

## Techniques for Working with Blind Students

As listed in Table 12–7, there are additional things teachers can do to enhance the learning of blind students in their classes. To simplify mobility, they can place students' desks close to the door and be sure that desks and backpacks are not placed in traffic patterns to learning centers or discussion areas. As changes are made in the physical arrangement of the classroom, teachers can ask a peer to help the blind student walk through the new traffic patterns. It is helpful to provide explanations of where the student's equipment and materials are located for easy and independent access.

Peer awareness of the physical arrangements of the classroom on the mobility of a blind student is critical. Their heightened involvement will not only encourage acts of support and helpfulness, but will prevent accidents. For example, teachers can instruct students that doors should be completely open or closed, avoiding an accident though walking into the door inadvertently. Lab work and field trips present novel situations each time. Voluntary support by others in the class in these situations allows for friendships and acceptance of the blind student as a peer instead of as someone who is different. As students spend time with peers with

**Table 12–7**
**Techniques for Working with Blind Students**

Teachers should:

- place desks close to completely opened or closed door
- keep traffic patterns open with furniture out of the way
- reorient students any time room is rearranged or groups are working in different areas
- have peers volunteer to be a partner during field trips, lab work, or activities in different campus locations
- touch objects to students' hand instead of having them grope for things
- provide thorough oral descriptions, using specific words (not "this" or "over there")
- explain what the student cannot see when the class is viewing media; if media are used extensively, a teaching assistant should sit close by and explain
- when calling on peers during class, use students' names
- speak to blind students frequently and encourage peers to do the same; if the encounter with blind students is unexpected, provide names of speakers so they know with whom they are talking
- review catalogs of special materials from the American Printing House for the Blind, asking the specialist to order them
- work together to explain to students which blindisms are distracting to others and how to avoid them
- notify the assistant when specialized materials and equipment are needed so the student can participate fully in the class
- have the specialist contact Recordings for the Blind for availability of taped books
- call on blind students during lectures and discussions
- expect blind students to follow all class rules and behavioral policies

(*Sources:* Adapted from Koenig & Holbrook, 1989; Morsink, 1984; Waldron, 1996)

disabilities, they come to know them as real people and to see beyond even those disabilities that may at first distract from the individual.

Teachers can support the dignity of the student through inclusion in large- and small-group discussions, always calling his name and those of others speaking so that he can gain familiarity with voices and speaking mannerisms. If teachers chat and interact in an informally friendly way with the student, peers will model on this behavior and not ignore him.

Teachers might encourage peers to note their names initially as they begin informal conversations with the blind student so that he will recognize them in the future. In lectures and discussions, teachers can model using specific language to describe meaning instead of overly frequent use of pronouns referring to visual objects. If media or visuals are part of the lesson, the teacher or a peer can provide descriptions for the student. If the class is viewing a lengthy video or visual performance, an assistant should be present to sit with the student and provide auditory descriptions and information.

## Techniques for Working with Students Who Are Partially-Sighted

"What about students with partial vision?" asks Maura. "Our first-grade teachers report that they have a student who is partially-sighted, but who is going to need a number of modifications, particularly for reading. Do we modify as much for students with partial vision as for blind students, or are the modifications just different?"

There can be a tremendous difference between teaching students who are blind and those who are partially sighted. The latter tend to become part of the class more easily because they read printed texts and can view classroom activities and peers. The degree of their visual loss sets the stage for the extent of modifications necessary in the classroom.

Table 12–8 lists a series of suggested techniques for successful teaching of students with partial sightedness. As with blind students, initial orientation to the setting is critical for developing complete mobility. With their desks as a focal point, they can integrate the direction or location of important areas in the room. This orientation will help their moving to alternate classroom areas for groupwork or materials. Similarly, depending on the degree of assistance their visual loss necessitates, they should receive some mobility training supporting their orientation to significant areas in the school. Once familiarized, students with partial sightedness can become independent in the room and on campus very quickly.

Glare and light settings strongly impact the student's ability to follow lectures, read, and write. As the day progresses and light filtering into the room changes, teachers should adjust the settings on window shades and blinds to avoid glare, and avoid standing in front of light sources when addressing the class.

Wherever possible, the teacher should allow students to establish their own threshold for correct lighting, training independence and refocusing the locus of responsibility. To do this, students should be allowed to change their seat flexibly if glare interferes with their ability to perform. They should be instructed to move quietly to a place in the room where they see best. Students are usually appreciative of the opportunity and rarely misbehave when changing seats.

The student's primary seat should be near the blackboard, on which the teacher writes with white chalk for accentuation. Providing paper in a buff color helps the student avoid glare as he writes. When in use, the student

**Table 12–8**
**Techniques for Students Who Are Partially Sighted**

Teachers should:

- orient students to the physical arrangement of the room, using their desks as the central point
- familiarize students with school surroundings, allowing them eventual complete independence
- change setting on windowshades and blinds to avoid glare on objects or people in the students' visual fields
- allow students flexibility in changing seats to see better or avoid glare
- avoid placing students in locations where they face light directly or have light fall on books and papers they are reading
- locate student desks close to the blackboard
- write on the blackboard with white chalk for accentuation
- avoid standing in front of light sources when speaking
- allow students to sit next to the overhead projector and make notes from the copy instead of the projection
- allow students to hold materials they read close to their faces or at odd angles
- use audiotapes whenever possible
- provide verbal explanations of any materials or media that may be difficult for students to see
- provide remedial handwriting instruction if students have problems reading what they write
- allow students additional time for reading and writing assignments
- explore the use of technology for developing reading and writing skills beyond the use of large print or braille

(*Sources:*  Adapted from Harley & Lawrence, 1984; Morsink, 1984; Koenig & Holbrook, 1989; Waldron, 1996)

should be allowed to sit next to the overhead projector and take notes from the transparency instead of the screen. Any time the teacher notes that the student is having difficulty seeing materials or media, he can provide a verbal explanation to supplement visual input.

Students may tend to turn their papers to an angle or place their heads close to the paper when reading. Since they are trying to accommodate their visual condition to the fullest, the teacher should ignore these behaviors. If the problem in reading arises from difficulty in reading their own handwriting, the vision specialist can be asked to provide a remedial handwriting program when working in the classroom.

Teachers can expect the student with partial sightedness to require additional time for reading and writing assignments. If extra time is not

In addition to books for typical students, classrooms should contain a variety of manipulatives for students who are partially sighted.

possible because of class schedules, the teacher might shorten the task by selecting out those items critical to understanding the information. If reading and writing performance are discernibly slower, it becomes important to consider the length of homework assignments so the student is not overwhelmed each evening. Additionally, the teacher should consider the potential shortage of supportive materials and equipment at home. The specialist teacher should talk with the family regarding resources available in the home to sustain student academic efforts. Where permissible, the student might be allowed to use some of the materials at home, such as audiotapes. Avoiding possible eyestrain or headaches from a daily overload of reading will allow the student to learn more from homework assignments instead of regarding them as an additional chore.

## TECHNOLOGY FOR USE WITH THE VISUALLY IMPAIRED

Available technology provides tremendous support for students with visual disabilities. Taped books allow following along with peers during assignments and participating in subsequent discussions. Before the school year begins, the teacher should contact the specialist about ordering tapes of all texts that will be used during the year. Regardless of the content area studied, recordings are free and often provide additional support for others in the class who may have reading disabilities. Taped educational books are available from:

> Recording for the Blind Inc.
> 215 East Fifty-Eighth Street
> New York, NY   10022

For large-print materials, magnifiers, and lined paper, specialists should contact the services for the visually disabled in their state Department of Education. Other sources, such as the American Printing House for the Blind and the Library of Congress provide records and audiotapes, not only of textbooks but of a variety of printed matter for pleasure reading.

While traditional audiotapes have supported the availability of information, they are limited in their use with blind students. While reading rates for sighted persons are at approximately 250 to 450 words per minute, listening rates from recorded materials average 150 words per minute (Wisniewski & Sedlak, 1992). Therefore, modifications still need to be made if the student is to keep up with peers. Additionally, not all books are available on tape because of limited resources.

Newer tape recordings employ changes in technology to help students organize information as they listen. Normally certain clues that support printed information are lacking when information is presented on audiotapes. These might include indicators of paragraphs, headings and subheadings, italicized or underlined words, pictures, charts, and graphs. Therefore, when listening, students have a tendency to take in details and memorize bits of information without understanding relationships among ideas. Since their experiential base is limited from the onset, most blind students require direction toward developing abstractions.

Adaptations to the tape player include organizational modifications for students as they listen. Cues are imbedded in the tape, indicating categories and subcategories of information, improving student understanding of relationships within the material. Definitions of vocabulary words may appear on one track, with expanded discussions recorded on another. The student selects the track based on desire to hear the information for the first time, review areas of confusion, explore certain areas in more depth, or prepare for an exam.

**speech compression**—a method of altering the speech of a recording without affecting its pitch.

With speed still a concern, **speech compression** is a method of altering the speed of a recording without affecting its pitch. With training, students can learn to listen at a dramatically increased rate. Mellor (1981) notes that a student can listen to a 60-minute tape in less than 30 minutes, at approximately 375 words a minute or 2 1/2 times normal speaking rates. As skills advance, speed can increase dramatically beyond this level.

Microcomputers have revolutionized the delivery of information to individuals with visual impairments. At their most basic word processing level, computerized print can be produced in a variety of sizes and shapes, in order to find the one most legible to the student. The specialist, classroom teaching assistant, or a student in a computer class can prepare basic large-print materials.

There are tremendous storage and retrieval possibilities of vast libraries of information from the daily newspaper to encyclopedias. Information can be downloaded and stored for future use, permitting extreme flexibility. Microcomputers with voice output capability can "read" designated materials. This capacity affords an expanded access to printed information, not only for individuals who are visually impaired, but also for those with a variety of disabilities impacting reading and cognition (Beevers & Hallinan, 1990).

**Optacon**—a portable, hand-held camera that converts printed material into tactile stimuli.

The **Optacon** offers access to materials that are not recorded or that are personally significant to the individual. Reading letters, daily local newspapers, magazines, and even menus in restaurants afford more normalized flexibility in dealing with change. Its easy portability does not bring attention from others and allows the individual to carry it everywhere.

The Optacon is a hand-held camera that converts printed material into tactile stimuli. The student places an index finger into a slot on the scanner. When the visual message is changed into a specific vibrating sensation, the student feels the output on his finger. While intensive training is necessary for students to avail themselves fully of the Optacon, with practice they begin to use it more easily and fluently. Not only in class but in their personal lives, they quickly grow to appreciate its support in their developing independence (Mellor, 1981).

The Kurzweil Reading Machine was described previously as supporting students with learning disabilities. However, its use of synthetic speech to convert printed material into spoken language has also become supportive of the needs of students with visual impairments.

## Assistive Mobility Devices

John interjects, "I see how I can work with the vision specialist in our district to order recordings and equipment to help students academically. I'm also concerned about mobility. Peers and I may not always be available to help students with visual impairments make their way around the building or school grounds. We have such a large school that I'm afraid students with visual impairments might become disoriented, or worse, injured. What types of technology are available to help them become more independent without embarrassing them in front of peers?"

As Wisniewski and Sedlak (1992) note, individuals with visual impairments indicate lack of easy mobility as the most severe outcome of their

white cane—used by individuals with visual impairments to feel objects in the environment as a support for mobility.

disability. John mirrors their concerns about injury, since most environments are filled with potential hazards. Ranging from stairways to curbs, from water fountains to telephones placed midway on walls, hazards await even those blind individuals very schooled in **white cane** use. The cane is only practical when it touches an object or a change in the environment. If the object is at a different level, such as a telephone or water fountain, it may cause injury to the individual.

Several electronic devices have been developed to do away with many of the shortfalls of the white cane. The most basic is the Pathsounder (Heyes, 1984). It is helpful for young students who need to develop spatial skills, as well as for cognitively impaired and/or deaf-blind students. In front of the student's chest, the **Pathsounder** emits ultrasonic pulses that are then converted into a sound or vibration. Through this signal, the blind person becomes aware of an obstacle directly in his path. As he comes closer to the object, the intensity of the signal increases. The tactile output enhances its use with deaf-blind students. The location of the vibration indicates the distance the object is from the individual.

Pathsounder—a guiding device for individuals with visual impairment; an electronic device worn in front of the chest that emits ultrasonic pulses, which are then converted into a sound or vibration to tell where obstacles are.

Laser Cane—a cane used by individuals with visual impairment; used in a sweeping motion while walking to maximize the field it explores for obstructions.

The **Laser Cane** (Goldie, 1977) is used in a sweeping motion while walking to maximize the field it explores for obstructions. It uses three light beams, one probing straight ahead, another upward at head height, the third, downward, detecting dropoffs of more than five inches. This multidimensionality permits it to be more accurate than the Pathsounder in its report of the location of the obstruction, as well as safer because of the ability of the beams to focus on objects at heights normally injurious to the body.

The Laser Cane can be an important training device for orientation and mobility with its built-in indicators of spatial relationships and distance. As students practice with the cane, they become very skilled in approximating not only object intervals and general size, but depth, width, and height. The development of these concepts assists both with their mobility improvement as well as increased understanding of concepts such as distance and spatial relationships. Understandably difficult abstractions for the blind, this awareness improves their language comprehension and expression.

Sonicguide—worn by students with visual impairments, this electronic device looks like sunglasses; emits inaudible impulses when its ultrasonic scanner indicates the presence of objects.

A unique device that affords an expanded perceptual awareness of the environment, the **Sonicguide** (Heyes, 1984) looks like sunglasses. It emits inaudible impulses when its ultrasonic scanner indicates the presence of objects. Sophisticated in its output, the Sonicguide provides information about the immediate environment: *How far away is the object? What is its direction? Its texture?* The latter capability is particularly interesting. Each surface has its own sound imprint that becomes familiar through practice (Wisniewski & Sedlak, 1992). Hot or cold liquids, solid versus hollow objects, all resound differently. The user gains personal mobility as well as a skillful sense of object recognition, affording a more normalized lifestyle.

# STUDENTS WITH PHYSICAL CHALLENGES
# AND HEALTH IMPAIRMENTS

"I'm a little embarrassed to admit that I listen to Curt O'Hare on the radio as I drive home every day," commented John. After the inservice group laughter and several admissions that others were listening also, John continued. "He's discussing inclusion even more these days. He's scaring everyone to death with his tales of how students will be wheeled on hospital beds into our classrooms, that soon teachers will be giving injections to infectious students, and that students who can't walk or talk will be commanding all our time and attention. Mike Gonzales was on the show again the other day, commenting how his son was more likely to be assigned to tutor students with disabilities than to be given work at an advanced level.

With assistance, students with physical impairments can gain
new skills toward personal independence.

"I feel I've benefitted a great deal from our inservices and by experiencing personal success with students newly included in my classes. I need to know if Curt is close to the truth for once. As we start including more and more students with physical and health impairments, will we remain teachers or become caretakers?"

Alex responds, "Perhaps because many physical conditions require specialized medical treatment, educators react with a degree of concern or even alarm because they feel the student will require treatments or modifications outside their personal training. If students are to be included successfully, it's critical to provide information for teachers on how to handle academic and social needs. They should also know whom to contact to provide ongoing assistance for meeting students' physical and personal care needs.

nonambulatory—not able to walk.

"For example, if a student does need an injection of insulin, it is the nurse's responsibility to administer it. If a student is **nonambulatory**, there must be an assistant provided to move the student between locations. This assistant should remain with any student whose needs are so extreme as to require one-on-one attention. The inclusive movement has never intended that a teacher should spend all of his time with one student, to the detriment of the rest of the class.

"John, the latter point that Mike Gonzales made on the talkshow deserves to be addressed. When he noted concerns about his son's needs being put aside to have him help students with disabilities in his class, he was expressing the fears of many parents about inclusion. It's critical that all students be given as full an opportunity as possible to develop their potential. In a way, Mike is right. His gifted son deserves as much attention as anyone else and should not have his needs sacrificed. On the other hand, his son needs to learn compassion for others. The best way to learn that is through students being together and helping each other.

"Students with physical or multiple impairments may have tremendous needs. As a result, planning and working together as a team is even more critical than for students with lesser needs. While the team concept most often means working with colleagues and specialists to support a more diverse student, other times the team does include students in the class who may volunteer or earn the right to assist a peer. No student should ever be permanently assigned to another in place of a specialist or assistant because resources are lacking. Every student should have the right to benefit academically and socially in the school environment."

## Physical Impairments

health impairments—bodily systems are affected by diseases or conditions that are debilitating or life-threatening.

While there are hundreds of conditions within the term physical impairment (Morsink, 1984), the most common can be included within the area of orthopedic/neurological disorders or within **health impairments**. The first category includes students experiencing skeletal, muscular, and joint disorders that impair mobility, coordination, balance, posture, and at times, communication.

cerebral palsy—a condition caused by damage to the brain's motor control center; includes restrictions on muscle activities that may limit fine and gross motor behaviors and academic learning.

Demonstrative of these problems is **cerebral palsy**, in which motor control and muscle use may be impacted so strongly as to prevent writing, or even walking, as well as verbal expression. However, the degree of cerebral palsy can vary tremendously, affording different levels of group participation. While the cognitive level differs among children with cerebral palsy, all students can benefit from instruction. The most important aspect of teaching many students with cerebral palsy may be modification of equipment to allow them to communicate ideas and needs despite the existence of physical limitations.

scoliosis—curvature of the spine.

**Scoliosis**, or curvature of the spine, can be treated most successfully when identified early. Often the student requires a brace and surgery. However, except for limitations on physical movement, the student can proceed normally. The family physician should provide a listing of any specific activities the student should avoid.

spina bifida—a congenital malformation characterized by incomplete closure of the spinal column and often resulting in hydrocephalus, paralysis, and a lack of bladder and bowel control.

spinal cord injuries—damage, usually accidental, to the spinal column; extent of injury is usually determined by its location and the degree of neurological damage.

**Spina bifida** results from a nonclosure of vertebrae in the spine as the fetus develops, while **spinal cord injuries** occur most often in adolescents and young adults as the result of accidents. The extent of injury is usually determined by its location and the degree of neurological damage. When the lower spinal cord has been damaged, the student's legs are paralyzed, and frequent incontinence occurs, requiring surgery or catheterization for control. When the upper spinal cord is damaged, the student may become a quadriplegic, losing function of the arms, legs, and body trunk. Some students suffer lowered cognitive function, while others have average or above intelligence. Often present are lessened use of fine motor skills, and learning disabilities, including perceptual problems (Bigge, 1991).

muscular dystrophy (MD)—a hereditary disorder that is progressive; causes loss of energy and deterioration of the body as muscle tissue is replaced with fatty tissue.

An inherited condition usually found in males, **muscular dystrophy (MD)** is marked progressive muscular degeneration. While students may walk awkwardly at first, their balance continues to worsen until confinement to a wheelchair becomes necessary. As other muscles in the body degenerate, the student becomes totally dependent. When the condition worsens, he will need the support of a teaching assistant to meet his needs.

## Health Impairments

Some students have chronic conditions or diseases that affect their living and learning. As a result, their stamina may be decreased, limiting class participation, or they may experience ongoing pain. Sometimes a condition such as juvenile rheumatoid arthritis can overlap into the health impairment area by not only limiting mobility, but causing pain or requiring the use of medications dramatic enough to diminish the student's attention to schoolwork.

asthma—a chronic respiratory condition that causes periodic breathing difficulty.

allergies—a hypersensitivity to a certain substance.

**Asthma** and **allergies** are very common health conditions that can strongly impact student performance. Asthma affects about 6 percent of the population and is responsible for more school absences, emergency room visits, and hospital admissions than any other chronic childhood disease (Silkworth and Jones, 1988). It is a result of inflamed airways that make breathing extremely difficult. It is caused by infections and responses to allergens, with attacks often occurring during physical overexertion or emotional stress. It is important for teachers to be aware of any restrictions on students' physical activities in order to prevent asthma attacks from occurring.

Allergies occur when an individual reacts negatively to a substance such as an airborne substance or food. While responses are usually mild and demonstrated by cold-like symptoms, strong reactions can be serious. Most allergies can be controlled by medications. Yet, similar to asthma, they result in numerous school absences.

While medication may be the solution to symptoms from asthma and allergies, often it has side effects that cause student drowsiness and lack of responsiveness. If teachers observe these problems they should contact the school nurse and parents so the medication can be modified to allow increased school attention.

cystic fibrosis—an hereditary condition in which the person experiences problems breathing due to the build-up of thick mucus in the lungs.

In **cystic fibrosis**, students also experience problems breathing due to the build-up of thick mucus in the lungs. Parents usually help students with physical therapy daily at home as they cough up the mucus to keep airways clear. It is an hereditary disorder in which the pancreas does not break down food correctly, digestive problems occur and the student may need an alternate diet. The school can be most helpful by allowing the student to sit in an area where frequent coughing will not disturb others, and where he is allowed more frequent bathroom breaks. Again, physical limitations should be discussed with parents (Bigge, 1991).

Heart conditions are uncommon in children, with necessary surgery usually occurring before school age. Few classroom modifications are necessary except to allow for rest periods as necessary and restrict involvement in physical activities. However, it is important to consider the emotional impact on students when they are deprived of full participation with their peers in a range of activities, from recess to sports.

human immunodeficiency virus (HIV)—a virus that affects the individual's ability to ward off infections.

**Human immunodeficiency virus (HIV)** and acquired immunodeficiency virus (AIDS) have become the subject of much controversy. When the HIV virus is present, individuals may face progressive breakdown of the immune system's ability to combat diseases. While HIV-infected individuals may contract the AIDS virus eventually, many never do. Therefore, it is important to note that the presence of the HIV virus does not mean the existence of AIDS. Students with these conditions experience frequent school absences and may need medication or additional food and fluids. Teachers should follow district guidelines for disease management and encourage strong hygienic methods such as handwashing (Frazer, 1989).

## Resource Provision

"All of this can be a bit overwhelming if you haven't worked with students with physical impairments before," observes Alex. "Between adaptive equipment and teaching assistance, there are so many resources available that everyone here can be successful. The key is in knowing the questions to ask in order to begin the process."

Table 12–9 includes a number of questions the collaborative team should consider before placing a student. As with learners demonstrating vision or hearing differences, advance planning can be the key to success. A physical therapist should be a member of the collaborative team. This specialist should be familiar with the student and able to discuss motoric limitations that will impact schoolwork. The therapist should be aware of available specialized equipment, as well as exercises and body positioning needs. The occupational therapist can provide background on family living needs, such as toileting, feeding, and equipment in these areas. If appropriate, the speech/language therapist should also participate, in charge of designing

---

**Table 12–9**
**Questions Concerning Students with Physical Impairments**

Before initiating instruction, teachers should ask:

- What type of self-help will the student require? Who will provide this care?

- What specialized equipment will the student need in the classroom and to gain mobility around the school? Who will be responsible for providing and maintaining this equipment?

- Are there special seating or positioning aids that will make the student more comfortable in the classroom?

- What degree of communications skills does the student have? How will personal needs be expressed? Does the student write or type? Has the student been trained previously to use computers or communications devices? If additional training is necessary, who will provide it?

- Is the student on medication? What side effects will be demonstrated in the classroom? Is the medication to be administered in school? If so, how often and by whom?

- Does the student ever experience major responses to the condition, such as seizures or insulin shock? If so, what is the proper immediate procedure? Who should be contacted?

- What is the degree of the student's stamina? Should physical activities be restricted?

(*Source:* Adapted from Lewis & Doorlag, 1987)

the best communication system to help the student express needs and ideas. The school nurse can be an important team member, acting as a liaison person between the family and school, administering medications or procedures as approved, and responding on a daily basis to any questions the teacher may have.

While planning teams discussed earlier included predominately regular educators, teams for students with physical disabilities may be comprised primarily of specialists because of the demands of daily medical or equipment-based needs. The student's parents and regular education teachers also play critical roles.

The initial questions in Table 12–9 are concerned with meeting the student's basic needs in areas such as feeding and toileting, and who will provide this care. Clearly the classroom teacher will not have time to perform these tasks, so it becomes critical for personnel to be assigned before the student enters the classroom.

Additionally, team members involved in physical and occupational therapy and in communications should note necessary equipment. One or more individuals should be assigned the task of equipment acquisition and maintenance. Critical issues are student comfort and ability to participate as fully as possible. Therefore, specialists on the planning team should provide the teacher with information on optimal positioning and seating. Communications devices ranging from basic language boards to computers should be considered before the student enters the class. If the teacher is not familiar with the equipment, a specialist should be appointed to familiarize or provide indepth instruction as warranted.

The team member authorized to administer medication should be receive a daily schedule and become aware of potential side effects. Additional responses to health conditions should be made known in advance so as to provide preventative measures. For example, parents should discuss physical symptoms indicating that a student may be overly fatigued or in physical distress. They should elaborate emergency procedures and contact persons. Educators feel a sense of relief instead of concern when they know exactly what to expect in advance of a situation. Parents should be encouraged to be as open as possible in discussing their child's needs.

Part of this discussion should include the physical energy level and degree of participation teachers can anticipate in classroom activities. If a student has rheumatoid arthritis or asthma, conditions that may vary weekly, or even daily, in the degree of their limitations, the parent should send a note to the school indicating that the student is having a difficult time or is in pain. Older elementary and secondary students should be encouraged to tell the teacher or school nurse if they are in particular discomfort at any given time. The situation can be managed most easily if collaborative team members have discussed back-up plans in advance, such as whether the student is to remain in class, go to the nurse, or return home.

## Techniques for Students with Physical Impairments

Table 12–10 includes a number of techniques educators can employ when including students with physical impairments in the regular classroom. Many of these involve managerial tasks that assure support of physical needs and involvement of appropriate assistants and therapists. The teacher should informally assess the status of all equipment, and notify the contact person if maintenance is necessary. While the district usually has someone assigned for repairs and modifications, the family should be involved if the student outgrows equipment they own, such as a wheelchair or crutches.

Part of equipment concerns include mobility within the classroom provided by pathways for student access. Since concerns regarding furniture arrangement are paramount for students with visual disabilities as well, teachers become very attuned to the physical layout of their room as they include more students with disabilities. Simple rearrangement of a few desks or of

### Table 12–10
### Techniques for Students with Physical Impairments

Teachers should:

- observe that all equipment is in working order, and contact the specialist if any maintenance or modification is necessary

- note the times of the day when an assistant is needed to help the student with personal and academic needs

- consider the physical arrangements in the classroom and any restrictions they may impose on the mobility of students

- meet with the communications specialist to determine devices to allow the student to express needs most completely

- watch for any changes in the student's condition

- meet with the physical therapist to determine how to reinforce therapeutic intervention in the classroom

- include the student in all social and academic activities, allowing for the development of friendships

- have a predetermined rest area if the student demonstrates chronic fatigue or strong medication response

- ask the parent to let the teacher or school nurse know if the student needs special modifications on a given day

- discuss with the parents and the school nurse any particular school activities that may stress the student's condition

- ask the parent to inform them if the student will miss school for an extended period of time

(*Source:* Waldron, 1996)

a learning center can allow for participation by a student who was previously excluded, enhancing his self-esteem and supporting academic gains.

If the student appears to be sitting alone away from the central learning area of the classroom, the teacher should observe why the isolation is occurring. Many times it may be logistical, such as difficulty in relocating the student from one place to another. In this case, brainstorming with specialists on how to make equipment more mobile may solve the problem. Other times it may be that the student is not able to communicate his ideas enough to become a group participant. When this occurs, the teacher and communications specialist need to explore additional equipment or adaptations that will allow broader language expression.

## Responding to Seizures

epilepsy—disorder of the nervous system characterized by varying types and degrees of seizures.

absence seizures (petit mal)—brief and nondisruptive seizures in which the student stares straight ahead; may go unrecognized but cause delays in acquiring school-related information.

complex partial (psychomotor)—seizures in which individual loses consciousness and demonstrates numerous body convulsions.

generalized tonic-clonic (grand mal)—seizures in which individual loses consciousness and demonstrates numerous body convulsions.

Perhaps more than with other conditions, teachers tend to be concerned when a student has **epilepsy**. A type of disorder resulting from dysfunctions of the central nervous system, epilepsy can result in a range of types of seizures, all of which affect the student's academic progress and personal interactions. While **absence seizures (petit mal)** are brief and nondisruptive enough to go unnoticed by the teacher, their recurrence may cause the student to miss significant amounts of work. During these seizures, the student may stare straight ahead quietly. However, since students may experience many, even hundreds in a day, they will fall further behind if the seizures are not recognized and medicated. **Complex partial (psychomotor)** may result in uncontrolled motor activities such as excessive movement or wandering. Of greatest concern to the student is the **generalized tonic-clonic (grand mal)**. Familiar to many, the individual loses consciousness and demonstrates numerous body convulsions (Epilepsy Foundation of America, 1989).

"Great. I can really see this happening in my high school English class," says John. "That scares me. Is there any way to prevent the seizures? What do I do if a student actually has one in my class?"

In particular, grand mal seizures are startling. However, students with epilepsy have participated in regular classrooms for years with few negative outcomes, since most seizures can be controlled with medication. An important consideration for the teacher and planning team is to have someone interact with the family to be sure the medication is correct and the student takes it as prescribed. If the student or family are inconsistent, the school nurse can administer the medication daily. Usually this is not a problem, since students do not want to have seizures. They are physically and personally upsetting and cause peers to avoid the student with epilepsy. The key is for the student to have regular exams to ensure that the dosage and type of medication remain appropriate.

Table 12–11 contains the listing of procedures for a teacher to follow if a student has a grand mal seizure in class. It is critically important for the teacher

**Table 12–11**
**Seizure Recognition and Response**

| Seizure Type | Characteristics | Appropriate Response | Inappropriate Response |
|---|---|---|---|
| Grand Mal | • Lasts several minutes.<br>• A sudden cry, followed by a fall, rigidity, and muscle jerks.<br>• Breathing becomes shallow or temporarily suspended, but resumes.<br>• Confusion is followed by a return to full consciousness. | • Protect from nearby hazards.<br>• Loosen tight collars.<br>• Turn on side to assist breathing.<br>• Reassure student when consciousness returns.<br>• Immediately call school nurse.<br>• Remain calm.<br>• Reassure peers. | • Do not put anything in student's mouth.<br>• Do not try to suppress tongue.<br>• Do not restrain.<br>• Do not give liquids.<br>• Do not use artificial respiration unless breathing does not resume after muscle jerks subside, or unless student has inhaled water. |
| Petit Mal | • Student has a blank stare that begins and ends abruptly, and lasts a few seconds.<br>• Rapid blinking may occur, along with chewing movements.<br>• Student appears to be daydreaming or inattentive.<br>• Student ignores adult directions.<br>• Student is totally unaware of what happens during the seizure.<br>• Once the seizure is complete, student quickly returns to full awareness.<br>• Learning difficulties may arise if not recognized and treated. | • No first aid required.<br>• When first recognized student should receive a neurological evaluation.<br>• Developmental academic skills should be reviewed and remedial instruction provided wherever necessary. | • Avoid labeling the student as inattentive.<br>• Do not ignore the existence of the seizures. |

(*Source:* Adapted from Epilepsy Foundation of America, 1989; Waldron, 1996)

to be informed in advance that a student may have a seizure. The teacher should be knowledgeable about preventing certain classroom activities that might inadvertently prompt a seizure to occur. He should have a place for the student to rest or a designated location, such as the nurse's station, if a convulsion appears imminent. The teacher and nurse should discuss specific procedures to be followed after a seizure occurs.

## Supportive Service Provision

Teachers may resent having students with disabilities in their classrooms if they do not have enough assistance. If a student's physical needs are extreme, such as in some forms of cerebral palsy or advanced stages of muscular dystrophy, an assistant may be assigned on a one-to-one basis all day. This arrangement frees the teacher to work with other students while ensuring that the students' needs are met. Whenever possible, the assistant should be assigned a small group including the specific student so that peer interactions will be fostered.

However, when the disability is less individually demanding, the student may be able to remain in class without an assistant or with partial-day help. For example, students with asthma, heart conditions, diabetes, and epilepsy rarely require assistance at all except for careful monitoring of their condition and consistency of their medications. A student with spina bifida may participate independently for part of the day, with an assistant helping with toileting needs or repositioning. Another with a spinal cord injury may require ongoing sessions with a physical therapist, but otherwise be able to participate independently. A student having suffered a head trauma may require daily instruction from a communications therapist and a reading specialist. Yet, he may be able to participate without assistance for part of the day.

"How can I be sure of this?" asks John. "I'm afraid that the student will be placed in my class, the door closed, and I'm on my own to teach Shakespeare and remedial reading while worrying about a student's ability to operate a computer. Can I trust the system?"

"Let me respond to that, John," comments Elena. "Wonderful teachers like you are in the classroom just trying to make students' lives better daily. You can't do everything, although some days I'm sure it feels like that's what we expect. As a principal, I'm supposed to support you and make your job easier. In an era of inclusion, that support has never been more important.

"While teachers are on the firing lines everyday, Rich Villa (1995) reports that more than 85 percent say the most critical factors for success include principals' feelings about inclusion and their ability to gain resources to sustain students' participation in class. If I don't get you the help you need, you can't be successful. If you fail, the student fails, and certainly our efforts along with it. It is the job of the school administrator to assure that teachers have all the supports they need to include the student without disrupting the teaching process for others in the class."

# TECHNOLOGY FOR USE WITH THE PHYSICALLY IMPAIRED

## Academic Supports

Part of the resources Elena mentioned involve necessary equipment. The teacher's job is facilitated tremendously when necessary supports are present. Hale (1979) suggests adaptations for allowing the student to write independently, some of which the teacher can initiate without assistance. For example, students have an easier time when writing on a pad of paper instead of using loose sheets. When loose papers are necessary, they can be taped to a clipboard or affixed by magnets to a cookie sheet.

Students can use felt tip pens or pencils, because they require less pressure on the page. If students have difficulty grasping the pen, placing a sponge ball or golf practice ball over the pen makes it easier to hold. If a smaller modification is necessary, a commercial rubber pencil holder or a twisted rubber band should work well.

Computerization has opened a new world of communication options to students with physical limitations. However, the most significant obstacle may be the computer keyboard. **Keyguards** with large finger holes cover the computer keyboard and allow student access to a variety of software. Avoiding inadvertently resting hands on keyboards and pressing multiple keys, students have improved access to the system. When student physical needs are more intense, alternate keyboards can be used, with multifunction keys, large touch-sensitive squares, or the most frequently used keys placed closest to the student.

A variety of **control switches** allow access using head pointers, mouthsticks, arm/hand, and leg movements and may bypass the keyboard completely. The more localized the type of movement (e.g., eye or foot), the greater the cognitive skills necessary to work the equipment. If students have lower conceptual skills, switches requiring only a touch pattern may be more effective (Esposito & Campbell, 1985).

There are a number of computerized **communication aids** to support oral and written expression of students with physical impairments. Software packages may include scanning systems or keyboards that provide verbal as well as visual output. The ability to improve receptive language through the availability of tremendous stores of information has been supported by CD-Rom. Possessing a huge storage capability, CD-Rom is used by libraries and industries alike. While noninteractive, it affords persons with limited mobility and reading (e.g., physically limited; blind) access to extensive bodies of information. Computer-based speech recognition programs for students with communications disorders are equally supportive when a physical impairment is present. While still in developmental stages, voice activation and interactive technology may provide a strong basis for allowing greater access to information as well as enhancing individual capacity to communicate needs and ideas.

**keyguards**—adaptive devices for computer keyboards that have large finger holes that cover the keyboard and allow student access to a variety of software.

**control switches**—manipulative controls for working the computer; varieties include head pointers, mouthsticks, arm/hand, and leg movements that may bypass the keyboard completely.

**communication aids**—devices used to support oral and written expression of students with physical limitations.

## Mobility Aids

The wheelchair remains the primary mobility device for students who are nonambulatory. Over the years its modernization has increased safety factors and afforded flexibility of use. Redesigned cushions have eased the process

Mobility aids permit students to be included with their peers.

of sitting for long periods, and lighter weight has eased portability. Electric wheelchairs with battery power allow ease of movement when the individual has other health impairments limiting physical strength. They can be operated with a joy-stick type of control and may have a chin and head positioner for the student with greater physical limitations. More effective braking systems allow for maintenance of constant speed and self-corrective steering prevents the individual from swerving from side-to-side (Wisniewski & Sedlak, 1992).

prostheses—artificial limbs.

**Prostheses,** artificial limbs, can greatly normalize the involvement of students missing limbs (Bigge, 1991). While some limb deficiencies are congenital, many are caused by accidents or surgical responses to disease or tumors. While initial prostheses may have been clumsy or cumbersome to use, new designs allow for excellent flexibility and control of gross and fine motor movements. With their use, students with foot, ankle, and knee amputations are able to run and participate in sports. Others missing hands and elbows are able to use artificial limbs that support writing skills. Ones such as the myoelectric hand are responsive to muscular contractions in the remaining part of the limb. The appearance of these prostheses is very natural.

"The latter point about appearance can be very important," notes Alex. "Often teachers worry a good deal about how they will learn to use certain software or monitor students' equipment needs because they feel uncertainty about technology. Yet the most important factor for these students' success is the very thing that teachers provide best: Sensitivity to their needs as young people, not as disabled people.

"While mobility technology has enabled students with physical limitations to participate in activities far more easily, they may still suffer restrictions, especially if wheelchair-dependent. When they have grown up missing a limb or recently faced an amputation, their response may be one of anger or grief. It is important to remember that they carry their physical difference with them everywhere they go and can never escape it.

"Your understanding of their need to be accepted and have friends and creating a classroom environment where they can thrive emotionally is the most important thing you can do. You can always ask a visiting consultant how to use the equipment, but you'll be the expert in helping a student belong in your class."

# SUMMARY

Chapter 12 included discussion of specific teaching techniques and use of supportive services for students with sensory and physical impairments. Advancement in technology has afforded tremendous opportunities for students to participate fully in the classroom environment.

Initial discussion reviewed methods for working with students with hearing impairments. While placements are being considered, the school planning team should consider which specialist will provide support for the student and act as a consultant to the teacher. If specialized equipment is necessary, ranging from hearing aids to amplification systems for generalized classroom interactions, maintenance provisions should be considered by the team.

After the committee has determined the logistics of resource provision, the teacher should ask a variety of questions concerning the student's individual needs. Listed in Table 12–2, these questions include concerns regarding skills in verbal and written expression, as well as decoding and comprehending words in reading. Does the student express needs well? Are speech patterns distinct enough to be understood by the teacher and peers? Importantly, other considerations include the student's social acceptance based on interpersonal skill levels as well as attentional skills in the classroom.

This chapter included a number of teaching techniques for students with hearing losses. The physical arrangement of the room was a predominant factor, with students being seated away from background noise and always in a position to see the faces of the teacher and other students. The use of visuals is very important as a supplement to auditory instruction.

Pictures and use of varied teaching formats including exhibits, demonstrations, experiments, and role-playing afford students the opportunity to maximize visual input. The teacher should call on students by name and use body language more extensively when addressing students. De-emphasis on reading and lecture and modification of materials through increased use of diagrams, charts, and graphs encourages student comprehension and recall.

The teacher can avoid speaking rapidly, and relate new concepts to past experiences to build on concrete knowledge. The teacher should informally question the student's understanding. Written directions will help guide students correctly through assignments. Importantly, the teacher will notice that a number of these techniques will improve the learning of all students in the class by providing input through more channels than the traditional reading and class lecture.

Technology for students with hearing impairments includes ongoing reliance on hearing aids. Through amplification of specific sound frequencies to a volume permitting improved use of residual hearing, they enable the user to participate more fully in communication with others. Their use may be limited because of sound distortions or background noise. Their batteries and volume should be checked daily to ensure effectiveness. Parents should be taught how to perform these tasks, gradually turning responsibility over to students in order to encourage independence.

The second section of Chapter 12 considered the needs of students with visual impairments. The steps in the planning and intervention process are similar to those with hearing disabilities. Before placement the collaborative team should consider consultant availability and student need for mobility training to ensure personal safety. The student's degree of visual impairment will determine the type of equipment and materials necessary to support the highest level of independent work in the classroom.

Specialists should supply teachers with background information to support full understanding of students' needs. Knowledge of the degree of visual acuity, when the vision loss occurred, and whether the disability is progressive will sensitize teachers to potential emotional and behavioral responses. Observation of social skills and habits with the goal of encouraging interpersonal behaviors supports students' acceptance by peers.

A number of techniques are included for working with students who are blind or partially-sighted. Ranging from physical arrangements in the classroom to supports while students use specialized equipment, the strategies allow the student access to information while not interfering with instruction for the entire class. As when teaching students with hearing impairments, teacher and material location plays an important role in responding to limitations imposed by a visual loss.

Methods of selecting the appropriate reading medium included a review of the characteristics of students who will benefit most from print versus those who will benefit from braille. When students have enough vision for near-distance tasks, have stable eye conditions with intact central vision fields, and successfully complete reading readiness tasks, print is the appropriate means of teaching reading. Students with unstable eye conditions and reduced central vision field may benefit more from braille instruction, especially if they have shown an adeptness with tactual identification.

There have been significant improvements in classroom-based technology for students with visual impairments. Within the arena of taped books, students have access to numerous textbooks as well as pleasure reading. To increase listening rate, compressed speech alters the speed of a recording without impacting pitch. Typically the words are at $2^1/2$ times the normal speaking rate, although with training and practice this rate can increase considerably.

Student comprehension and retention of auditory information increase with their ability to understand vocabulary, categories, and subcategories of information. Many tapes now have imbedded cues to alert students to this information, as well as expanded discussion on alternate tape tracks.

Microcomputers have provided print in a variety of sizes and shapes to meet the needs of learners with visual impairments, affording the opportunity to design large-print materials right in the classroom. Additional storage and retrieval capabilities of vast libraries of information and the ongoing development of voice output capability provide an almost endless supply of accessible information. For informal information such as reading newspapers and menus, the Optacon is available to change visual messages into tactile stimuli.

For mobility improvement, there are several electronic devices that emit impulses or sounds to alert the individual to immediate hazards, such as objects in their path. While their sophistication varies, the most developed even permit information about the impending object, such as its texture.

The final section of Chapter 12 explored methods of including students with physical disabilities and other health impairments. While there are hundreds of conditions in this area, there are common ways to respond to students and develop their academic program. In the planning stage, collaborative team members should consider issues such as degree of self-help skills and who will provide any needed assistance.

Ordering and maintenance of equipment should be discussed before the student ever enters the classroom. Equipment needs will vary, but can support students' ability to become mobile and respond to the curriculum. Student communication skills and needs should dictate the type of equipment and materials modifications necessary.

For students with ongoing health needs, teachers should be informed of any medication responses they may evidence in class. If the medication is to be administered in school, it will be important to inform the teacher of the schedule and the adult assigned. As a precaution, teachers should receive written instructions regarding any restrictions on physical activities.

Chapter 12 included discussion of techniques to support students with physical limitations. Teachers should note activities requiring an assistant to be present. Ongoing interaction with a communications specialist, occupational and physical therapist, will result in all professionals working together to develop a total program. The more extensive the disability, the broader specialist participation.

Wherever possible, the student should be included in all social and academic activities, allowing for development of peer relationships. Parents should be viewed as partners in discussing changes in the student's condition and how to have maximal input even if the student experiences frequent absences.

While minor modifications to writing implements facilitate daily performance for some students, more technological input is needed for others. Computer use has facilitated the ability of students to express not only their needs but their ideas. Varied keyguards and control switches allow access using head pointers, mouthsticks, arm/hand/leg movements. Computerized communication aids support oral and written expression. CD ROM has brought huge storage capabilities for providing libraries of information. Voice activation and interactive technology are developing rapidly as means of enhancing individual ability to communicate.

Mobility technology has resulted in a streamlined and updated wheelchair, with new safety and comfort factors. Electric wheelchairs allow for ease of movement and can be operated by a joy-stick type of control. Improved braking systems and self-correcting steering prevent swerving and potential accidents.

Protheses have allowed many students to participate in activities from which they would have been isolated otherwise. New designs permit flexibility and improved fine and gross motor control. Yet teachers should be responsive to the emotional and social needs of students with missing limbs. They should be particularly sensitive to how students feel about physical limitations or equipment-based needs that make their condition more obvious to others. The student desires to be accepted, to develop positive relationships with peers, and to experience success along with the rest of the class should dictate programming directions.

## CASE STUDY: *Elementary*

You have been attending the inservices at Westside regularly and feel the information on inclusion has been helpful. As a matter of fact, the students with learning problems in your fifth-grade class seem to be doing much better since you've been implementing some of the modifications suggested.

But a blind student? Can you really be helpful here or will you be spending all of your time trying to prevent accidents and discover ways to teach her? You'll give it a try before you ask Mort to find another room, but you're simply afraid this student may be too much for you to handle.

Jenny is 10 years old and will be entering Westside District and Jackson Elementary for the first time in a few weeks. She has been blind since birth, the result of a genetic condition.

You haven't met her yet, but your planning team had its first session this morning. The vision specialist indicated Jenny has average intelligence, but lacks a number of higher-order concepts because she has not had the experiences of sighted students.

She reads braille, but somewhat slowly. Her understanding of what she hears is strong, although she has a number of ongoing questions as she tries to interpret information that comes easily to the sighted world. She uses a white cane for mobility. She appears to make her way adequately around her current school building.

Records indicate Jenny is a quiet student who has difficulty making friends, primarily because she tends to wait for others to address her first. She has a number of "blindisms," such as rocking and nodding her head, that also make peers avoid her.

1. You do not know how to read or create braille materials. Given this limitation, how can Jenny use braille in your class? What are additional methods and technology you may want to use to supplement braille instruction?

2. How will you include her in ongoing academic activities in your class so she participates in large- and small-group discussions?

3. How can you expand her limited store of concepts?

4. What can be done to make the classroom safe? To provide for independent mobility in class and in the school?

5. What will you do to help her interactions with others so that she develops friendships?

CASE STUDY: *Secondary*

John Robinson's greatest concern has come true. (Maybe Curt O'Hare can say, "I told you so!") Chris, a student with moderate cerebral palsy, will soon be entering John's third period English class. The student is nonambulatory, spending his day in a wheelchair. He has difficulty with speech production, laboring over the articulation of many sounds, resulting in difficulty being understood. Chris has a mild level of arm and hand spasticity that make it impossible for him to write accurately. Training has recently begun to have him use a computer with a keyguard.

Chris is somewhat below peers cognitively, having difficulty grasping main ideas and inferential information. His auditory learning skills are better than visual. While he can read, his level of understanding is approximately three years below that of peers. His listening skills are higher. It has been difficult to accurately assess his reading skills because of his speech problems.

Chris's attitude is excellent. He and his parents are so excited at his first opportunity to attend a "real class," that John could not refuse. Yet, John is now afraid of the reaction of the other students, hoping they won't make fun of Chris or just ignore him.

Chris is going to need help with self-help skills such as toileting. The district has promised a teaching assistant to help Chris in these areas and to work with him if there are instructional tasks that he cannot perform. Yet, due to limited resources, the assistant can only be there for 30 minutes of each class period.

You are on John's planning team for Chris and he is looking to you for new ideas.

1. John wants to continue using the same books with his class, but is afraid Chris won't be able to read the information. How can he teach Chris the curricular material?

2. Which equipment should John request from the district to support Chris' learning needs? When will this equipment be most helpful?

3. Chris is just beginning to use a computer, including learning keyboard skills. For what type of information should he use the computer as he improves his accuracy?

4. If John can only have a teaching assistant for 30 minutes each class period, what types of tasks should the assistant perform with Chris to make the time most worthwhile?

5. What can John do to have peers respond positively to Chris and include him in class activities on their own initiative?

# 13

# CURRICULUM AND MATERIAL MODIFICATIONS

"Until recently I thought my job was strictly administrative,"comments Dr. Andrea Mirales. "As Special Education Director, I've spent a good deal of time supporting staff development and 'putting out fires' as best I could. I've never really thought of myself as an instructional leader because I spend so much of the time in meetings ranging from program development to settling litigation.

"My role has been changing dramatically as we've initiated inclusion in Westside. I'm spending much more of my time working together with administrators in regular education. When Mort, Elena, and I met early in the semester to explore how inclusion was proceeding in their schools, we were all surprised at the early support some of the regular and special education teachers gave the program. But we were equally taken with the magnitude of the task of adapting the regular education curriculum to meet the needs of special learners. Mort and Elena pointed out to me very clearly that if regular education teachers did not know how to adapt content and materials, they would not be able to teach a diverse population of learners."

Concerns about teaching curricular material are of paramount importance. Traditionally, regular educators have used a statewide or school district curriculum deemed appropriate to their specific instructional area and grade level. Often these curricular materials include goals, objectives, and essential elements of instruction. Usually teachers receive a formal listing of topics and subareas to teach during the year.

Curricular concerns in special education have been different. When needs have been extreme or unique, such as for students with multiple involvements or severe behavioral disorders, separate curricula have been available. However, for the majority of students receiving special services, there has not been a curriculum. Special educators have chosen materials in isolation from the larger school program. Often they have used texts that do not correspond to the topics covered by typical peers (Gloeckler, 1991). It is no wonder that at times their work in Resource classrooms and separate settings has slowed their progress in learning content instead of given them more concentrated instruction.

# MATCHING THE STUDENT AND THE CURRICULUM

"What if the student isn't able to do the work?" asks John. "It doesn't seem to matter much if we use the same curriculum with all learners. We have to be most concerned about who can learn the prescribed content."

John expresses the concern of many regular education teachers. Yet, it is important to note that all students can benefit from curricular information if it is taught in a manner directed toward their learning style or needs. Before beginning instruction, teachers can explore the match between the learner and the curriculum in order to make any modifications necessary to assure success.

Table 13–1 lists a series of questions that the regular educator should ask before beginning instruction. Of initial concern is how well the student has mastered prerequisite skills in preparation for more advanced content. These areas usually include reading, computation, and writing competence, as well as a body of knowledge in content areas that forms the basis for additional learning. For example, if a student is to enter the second year of Spanish, specific vocabulary and sentence patterns, as well as varied tenses and plurals, should have been learned to prepare the student to move to greater fluency. Before a student can study fractions, it is important that basic computational skills and equivalency be mastered.

If the student is missing skills in prerequisite areas, the collaborative team should consider what supports will be necessary to ensure success. If skills are substantially below those of peers, the special educator might work with

---

**Table 13–1**
**Matching the Student and Curriculum**

Teachers should ask the following questions:

- Has the student mastered prerequisite skills basic to learning the new information? If not, what skills does the student need? How will any necessary supports be provided?

- Can the student read the information necessary to learn curricular content?

- What is the student's attention span for reading? For listening?

- Can the student work in a large group? In a small group?

- Can the student work independently? If not, what types of assistance will be necessary so the teacher is not overburdened?

- What is the student's optimal learning style? How can instructional strategies be modified to teach content to coincide with this style?

- Is the student motivated to learn the information?

Sometimes only a bit of additional practice is needed to allow students full curricular participation.

the student in the classroom to provide necessary practice or remediation. Since rarely is the student alone in needing supports, the specialist might work with a small group of students with similar needs. When the skill deficiency is not extreme, teachers might modify materials, allow a longer time period for completion of the assignment, or provide questions reinforcing earlier skills.

Teachers should be aware of students' ability to read the material. Informal reading inventories discussed earlier provide important information both at elementary and secondary levels. Text adaptations for students with reading problems are discussed in the following sections.

A number of student characteristics listed in Table 13–1 are important for curriculum-student matches. The length of students' attention and their ability to work independently are significant. Students' abilities to work with others in pairs and small groups, as well as to participate in larger group work, signal the teacher that behavior is conducive to learning through interaction. Importantly, the teacher should note students' learning styles in order to adapt instruction to include elements of success. While a number of teaching techniques specific to students with physical and sensory impairments were discussed in the previous chapter, teachers can also note if student recall improves through experiential or multisensory involvement. Finally, student degree of motivation provides the key for curricular success. If the student wants to learn the material and works attentively toward mastery, the teacher is more willing to make modifications to enhance learning.

## RELATIONSHIPS BETWEEN CURRICULUM AND INSTRUCTION

It is impossible to separate curriculum from instruction. Student integration of the most significant content is dependent upon the success of the teaching method selected. Yet variations in method can be extreme, depending on the preference or expertise of the teacher.

Carnine (1991) discusses a spectrum of methods for organizing instruction. The expanse of teaching methods is depicted in Figure 13–1. Child-centered approaches consider the needs of each student individually. These methods emphasize one-on-one interactions between student and teacher, with instruction directed to the student's learning style. They are difficult to enact in the regular classroom because teachers have too many students to focus their attention for more than minutes on any one child. This problem is true especially at the secondary level because teachers have well over 100 students daily, meeting large classes at any given time.

**children-centered approaches—** methods for organizing instruction that rely on students taking responsibility for teaching and supporting each other; may incorporate strategies such as cooperative learning and peer tutoring.

The middle of the spectrum includes **children-centered approaches,** incorporating strategies such as cooperative learning and peer tutoring. They are more efficient than child-centered approaches because they are not dependent on teachers freeing time to work with individuals. They rely on students taking responsibility for teaching and supporting each other. This method is effective when students have the capacity to work together well. Assignments must be structured carefully so that students concentrate on task and are able to perform designated group roles without ongoing teacher supervision.

**lecture-only approach—**the teacher provides information and students occasionally ask questions.

Teacher-centered approaches are at the other end of the spectrum. The most extreme version is the **lecture-only approach,** in which the teacher provides information and students occasionally ask questions. This method is the least

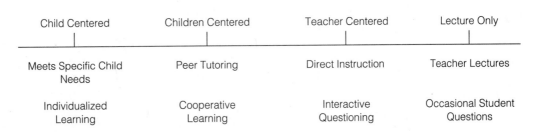

Figure 13–1   Methods for Organizing Instruction (*Source:* Adapted from Carnine, 1991).

interactive and the most difficult for students with learning differences. It depends on auditory memory for facts and information, an area of frequent difficulty. Unfortunately, this method is used often at high school and university levels.

However, not all teacher-centered approaches involve the lecture-only format. Others are more interactive, involving carefully-designed questions by teachers, often resulting in animated student answers. This direct instruction method can be responsive to the needs of individual students since teachers can focus on the level of student comprehension, ranging from factual to evaluative.

It is important to note that while the child-centered and children-centered approaches have benefitted from recent popularity, the direct instruction approach may be the best for many students with disabilities (Scruggs & Mastropieri, 1992). It allows teachers to respond to the needs of the individual while ensuring that all students in the class are being challenged.

"Don't we all use a variety of these methods at one time or another?" asks Maura. "Even with my third-graders, there are times when I lecture for a few minutes, telling them information they all need to know. Yet a short time later, my students are involved in cooperative learning or peer tutoring. While those groups proceed, I may give a few minutes of individualized instruction in skill-building to a student falling behind the rest of the class. Immediately after that, I may direct a discussion summarizing what students learned in their groups, trying to engage a variety of students. My selection of method depends on what I'm trying to teach."

Maura's comments mirror those of good teachers who do not rely on any particular method of instruction but who understand the effects of their considered combination. The determinants of the method selected should involve the characteristics and needs of the students and the curricular content to be studied.

## Efficient Teaching

Carnine (1991) discusses two factors that are basic to good instruction, regardless of the approach selected. The first involves careful structuring of activities toward productive outcomes. Such structuring results in the second outcome of minimizing wasted time. He gives the example of an unproductive activity as teaching students to use manipulatives when dividing with two-digit divisors.

"I don't understand," responds Maura. "I thought that using concrete objects whenever we can is basic to teaching many students with special needs."

While teachers have been encouraged to use hands-on activities and objects wherever appropriate, they should first consider whether the outcome will ensure enhanced student learning. Passing out and collecting manipulatives can consume a good deal of time. If students have attentional problems, they may begin to play with or concentrate on the manipulatives, distracting themselves from the lesson. In the example of teaching two-digit divisors, breaking blocks of 100 into groups of 10, or those of 10 into individual units is tedious and wrought with opportunities to count incorrectly, drop the blocks, or lose one's place in the problem. The student may leave the exercise believing that the blocks were the activity instead of the concept.

Other ways to avoid wasting time have been mentioned in describing specific instructional and behavioral methods. These time enhancers include monitoring of student attention to task and immediate redirection if off-task behavior occurs; proximity control; frequent questioning of all students; quick transitions between tasks; careful consideration of student seating arrangements to avoid distractions; avoidance of using free time as a reward for work completed; and using posted charts or schedules so students know where they are to be at all times and can begin work independently.

# CORE CURRICULUM

**core curriculum**—skills and subject matter in the curriculum are designed to meet student needs through units of relevant content study.

The **core curriculum** has developed in response to problems in more traditional curricula, especially fragmentation of information occurring from an over-reliance on individual facts without demonstrating their relationship. The concept of core curriculum begins with analyzing students and the society in which they live. Skills and subject matter in the curriculum are designed to meet perceived needs through units of study relevant to students.

As depicted in Table 13–2, Vars (1991) considers three different ways of organizing school staff to provide a core curriculum. In the **total staff approach**, teachers select a single theme to teach for a brief, but intense, period. Topics such as the environment or African-American heritage become part of each class as teachers relate the theme to their content area.

**total staff approach**—teachers select a single theme to teach for a brief, but intense, period; every teacher in the school relates the theme to the content area he or she teaches.

**interdisciplinary team approach**—teachers from several different subject areas instructing the same group of students work together to organize around the topic suggested; students are exposed to theme content in certain grade levels, but not across the entire school.

The **interdisciplinary team approach** is also thematic, with teachers from several different subject areas instructing the same group of students. Content area teachers work together to organize around the topic suggested. Therefore, students are exposed to theme content in certain grade levels, but not across the entire school, as in the total staff approach. Teachers select themes they feel are relevant to student needs in understanding their society.

**block time approach**—individual teachers design and instruct several subject areas within a related theme.

The **block time approach** involves single teachers designing and instructing several subject areas within a related theme. More reliant on the teacher than the theme, this method involves students remaining with the same instructor for a longer period of time as they study multiple content fields, such as language arts and arithmetic, or English and history. The intensity of integration of content is reliant on the teacher.

**Table 13–2**
**Integrated Curriculum**

| Approach | Characteristics |
| --- | --- |
| Total Staff | Teachers develop an all-school theme for a brief period of time. Students encounter some degree of theme learning in every class. |
| Interdisciplinary Team | Teachers of different content areas are assigned a single group of students. They plan together and relate unitary themes across subject areas. |
| Block Time | Individual teacher instructs students in several different content areas across an extended period of time. Degree of integration between subjects is dependent on the teacher. |

(*Source:* Adapted from Vars, 1991)

## CONCERNS REGARDING TEXTBOOKS

"Maybe I'm too traditional in my teaching," comments John, "but I rely on my textbooks a great deal. One of the problems I'm having is that some of the students with special needs can't read the book. I understand that I can ask for occasional assistance from the special education teacher, but it doesn't seem a productive use of his time to have him come to the room a few times a week to help a student read. I'd like to use his support better as well as move along quickly with assignments, not being slowed by extended explanations of information students can't read. What can I do?"

John's concern is widespread. The majority of teachers at both elementary and secondary levels rely on texts to teach curricular information. As instruction cannot be separated from curriculum, neither can supportive textbooks. Guerin (1991) reports that elementary teachers spend more than 90 percent of their reading instruction time using basal texts. More than 90 percent of all science teachers use a text for 95 percent of their teaching (Penick & Yager, 1986, in Guerin, 1991), and the textbook is the dominant teaching medium in social studies. Researchers report that social studies texts are likely to be written at the highest reading levels of all content areas, and may provide superficial coverage of information while using highly complex language (Woodward, Elliott, & Nagel, 1986, in Guerin, 1991).

## Teaching for Exposure

**"teaching for exposure"**—presenting information to students in a broad or general way without covering content in any depth; surface content coverage.

In many classrooms, textbooks tend to define content and teaching methods. A major flaw that has begun to impact student knowledge basis is the frequent tendency of texts to cover a broad number of critical topics, but in a surface manner. Carnine (1991) calls this **"teaching for exposure,"** where on the average, educators spend less than 30 minutes of instructional time during the entire year on 70 percent of the topics they cover. When considering the reliance higher education and even societal advancement place on basic skill development as well as sophisticated problem solving abilities, it becomes clear that surface teaching results in surface learning. Yet, using the text as their guide, teachers may introduce topics too quickly, before others have been mastered, moving constantly on to more advanced area in a perceived need to "cover" material. When material is only covered, it may not be learned, hindering student abilities to perform higher-order tasks.

Teachers are not unaware of the surface quality of many texts. Frequently, they complain about the lack of practice activities suggested as well as the seemingly random presentation of ideas, lacking coherence, explanation, and demonstration of relationships among concepts. Educators are all too familiar with advanced reading levels that do not take student skills into account, confusing students and lessening their motivation to read the material. A common complaint in basic skills texts such as basal readers, arithmetic workbooks, and secondary texts in most areas, is that there are not enough practice activities to allow students to fully integrate concepts.

## State-Adopted Texts

"Yet some of the new texts are beautiful to look at," observes Elena. "The biology books we bought last year are some of the most colorful I've seen. They have intricate diagrams in them that would be instructive in most medical schools. They cost a fortune for the district, but we felt that students would only benefit in the long run.

"At the end of the semester, we were very surprised at student grades being far lower than any of the biology teachers remembered. We began to receive complaints from students and their parents that biology was too hard. Since none of the teachers were new and the same group of students were performing capably in other areas, we couldn't figure out what was happening.

"Gradually the teachers realized they were continuing to rely on the text for exams and quizzes. While the test information was in the books, they reported that even some of their best students were not able to understand what they were reading. They were memorizing distinct facts without perceiving relationships. The previous text was not as attractive, but it included primary and secondary headings in bold, highlighted questions for study that required students to relate and apply information, and follow-up activities for class performance and discussion. It has been a costly mistake for us to realize that publishers often rely on a book's appearance as a major selling point to adult purchasers, but they do not always include sound pedagogy to help student mastery."

state-adoption textbooks— states select texts to be used in all of their schools.

Nowhere is this clearer than when **state-adoption textbooks** are involved. States such as California, Florida, and Texas spend millions of dollars each year purchasing texts to use in all of their schools. The size of this market has strongly encouraged publishers to be highly responsive to the preferences of the state adoption committees. Often these committee members are not educators and are unfamiliar with pedagogy or research, rarely even considering issues such as clarity of information presentation or depth of coverage of important topics (Powell, 1985). The tremendous political pressures they face from statewide organizations and religious groups impact strongly the final texts selected.

Because separate text production is expensive and time consuming, publishers prefer marketing to all states those texts most likely to be approved by state adoption committees. Therefore, the decisions of these committees has a powerful impact on curriculum and instruction. In their attempt to provide standardized texts and curricula across their state, they have in fact instituted a uniformity of curricula across the country (Tulley & Farr, 1985).

## Effects of Uniform Texts

These issues of noneducational criteria for textbook selection and the extensive daily reliance of teachers on approved books have significant impact on the instruction of diverse learners. Wood (1989) notes that implications go beyond the problem of reading. Student learning styles differ, often requiring extended explanation or practice activities. Students who have difficulty with complex language require diagrams and graphs. Others with memory difficulty require associative devices such as cognitive mapping to demonstrate relationships.

The use of a single text implies that "...the only legitimate learner is a text-book learner" (Guerin, 1991, p. 12), and all students read and integrate information in the same way. This progressive standardization of curricula through textbook reliance is especially significant at the secondary level, where instructional techniques tend to be more traditional.

Included in Table 13–3, Blankenship (1985) lists aspects of typical middle and high school instruction and reasons they may actually increase student potential for failure. Many teachers rely on a single text to impart curricular content as well as to provide a framework and sequence for their academic year. Generally, all students receive and read the same text, including information basic to successful completion of classroom and homework assignments. In-class teaching involves lecture and discussion of subject matter,

**Table 13–3**
**Traditional Secondary School Practices**

Typical secondary school instruction involves

- use of a single text for all students in the class
- lecture and discussion of curricular content
- an assignment for students to complete individually, usually from the text

In this environment, students at risk may fail because

- the text content may not be appropriate for their needs
- concepts and skills may not be ordered logically or sequentially, lessening student understanding
- they require more examples to support mastery
- there is insufficient review of previously studied or newly acquired material
- they cannot read the textbook
- they have not mastered the prerequisite concepts or skills to understand the textbook
- they lack behaviors supporting independent work and participation in group discussions

(*Sources:* Adapted from Blankenship, 1985; in Klumb, 1992)

often using the text as a basis. Students then complete an individual assignment reliant on information from reading and lecture.

The pitfalls of this method appear in Table 13–3. For students with disabilities, the text content may not be appropriate to their needs, resulting in lack of motivation and generalization. It is important for teachers to realize that textbooks are only a support for their content area instruction. They can modify or change the direction of the unit at any time, going beyond restraints of the book.

In Table 13–3, Blankenship (1985) also suggests that there may not be an organized method of information sequencing. Teachers tend to rely on the text for a hierarchical structure of when to teach a particular concept. They usually move from one chapter to the next, assuming that progression has been planned for a pedagogical purpose. In actuality, the order is random at times, lacking a logical purpose.

As part of understanding through conceptual relationships, it is important for instruction to provide multiple examples of the same concept so that student can associate and integrate new information with previous experiences.

Students will fail if they are not provided review of previously studied information. They tend to forget information quickly if it is not discussed and related to newer concepts studied. Workbooks that provide insufficient activities for reinforcement can hinder student learning. The teacher may assume that the student is ready to move on because the chapter is completed, when actually, much additional practice is necessary.

Lack of student skills in the reading-lecture-discussion environment can also hinder learning. Students may need prerequisite work before they can understand content. They must be able to read the text in order to be successful in assignments subsequent to its use.

Behavioral concerns may diminish students' ability to benefit from participation in large and small groups. If teachers rely on student questions to indicate a lack of understanding, they may find that students feel others will think less of them for asking too many questions or indicating they are having trouble with content. Students with attentional problems will experience difficulty completing assignments independently, especially from a text that is difficult for them to read.

## SELECTION OF APPROPRIATE TEXTBOOKS AND MATERIALS

"As a result of these problems, we've been developing guidelines for our teachers to use in choosing textbooks. We're trying to avoid costly errors in the future and also to be sure that we have materials that can be used by all of our learners. We feel that if we select appropriate books based on our knowledge of good teaching instead of solely by appearance, we'll stand a better chance of meeting our goals."

Table 13–4 contains a guidelines for textbook selection. Adapted from Gall (1981), they provide practical considerations that afford improved learning for all students. The suggestions include an initial statement of objectives and purposes for studying content. Many times students read a lesson with no goal in mind except to complete an assignment. If they understand that the information may be of significance to them, they are more motivated to study content. Since students tend not to read introductory information or that contained in chapter margins, it is important for teachers to review it with them before independent reading.

A text that contains an outline of information as well as advanced organizers provides a framework for relationships among ideas. Students are introduced to upcoming concepts, establishing a basis and sequence for details. Questions at the beginning and end of the chapter should help students understand relevance of information to their own lives (e.g., *Have you ever wondered why it rains? Given the current reproductive rate, how long do you think it will take the world population to double? If you were living in Zimbabwe, what do you think you would be studying in school today? What would happen if all use of punctuation were canceled in any future writing?*) Questions should be phrased to encourage curiosity and interest in the upcoming reading assignment.

**Table 13–4**
**Considerations in Selecting Curricular Materials**

Teachers should select materials that include

- a statement of goals for the unit so students are aware of skills that need to be mastered

- a discussion of the importance of the information, stating reasons for study

- an outline summarizing main ideas

- questions at the beginning and end of the chapter to assess knowledge of the skill area

- placement of questions in margins to encourage students to consider ideas during reading

- headings, margin notes, and contrasting fonts to cue important information and aid retention

- an interactive writing style, with phrasing and expressions appropriate to the age of the reader

- advanced organizers to introduce significant concepts and to provide the learner with a framework of information to follow

- presentation of concepts in understandable vocabulary and at an appropriate reading level

- frequent examples of facts and abstract ideas

- diagrams, illustrations, and graphs to clarify concepts

- practice activities appropriate for the learner's level, such as problem-solving situations and case studies

- an assessment process within the chapter allowing the learner to check personal level of mastery

- exercises for the learner to practice skills and concepts

- a glossary of unfamiliar or technical terms with readable explanations so the learner can understand them more fully

(*Source:* Adapted from Gall, 1981; Waldron, 1996)

Whether in the instructor's manual or directly in the student text, there should be an explanation of the prerequisite skills and knowledge students should master in order to be able to understand and use the information. The manual should include additional activities to bolster student mastery of mandatory skills (e.g., *The student should create a series of vocabulary note-cards with words not mastered from previous lessons. These words can be practiced in pairs with other students requiring similar reinforcement.* Another might be *Students should spend 10 minutes daily solving word problems integrating information from the previous lesson. Several of such problems accompany each chapter.*)

Whether as a basis for class discussion or when reading texts, carefully formulated questions guide students through comprehension of content. Teachers and students should review these questions together before reading the chapter, in order to establish in advance the most important content. Teachers should also underscore significant vocabulary and discuss its meaning in advance of reading. Encountering new words in the chapter will then serve as reinforcement instead of confusion.

Clarity of language, choice of vocabulary, and explanation of concepts should be among the highest priorities in material selection. A personalized writing style that appeals to reader interest helps to engage students in content and motivate them to want to read the selection. The readability level should be appropriate to the grade level of students. Frequent use of visuals such as tables, diagrams, and pictures provides additional explanation for material at higher conceptual levels.

In selecting books, it is important to have students as part of the process. They can respond most accurately to the instructional difficulty, clarity of content, organization, and degree of helpfulness of information at the beginning and end of the chapter. Including learners with diverse needs in the process provides teachers advance notice about strengths and drawbacks, avoiding negative surprises in later use.

Textbooks should provide learners the opportunity to practice content application as they read each chapter. Students can benefit from self-checking questions that refer to specific pages for review if answers are incorrect. These questions are most effective when they are part of the ongoing narrative or material in the margins. They should de-emphasize memorization of facts and emphasize understanding of main idea in each passage.

# MODIFICATION OF EXISTING TEXTBOOKS AND MATERIALS

"I'd love to have the flexibility to select my own materials," comments Maura. "I'm afraid we rarely seem to order new basals or content area texts. Because of the expense, we tend to keep the same books as long as we can. What can I do to modify the materials I have to make them more useful for diverse learners?"

## Modification Considerations

An area that concerns teachers is the potential time consumption of preparing or modifying materials. With the numerous tasks confronting them daily, understandably they are reluctant to take on more work. Therefore, if modifications are to be successful, teachers should set boundaries about the amount of time they are able to spend and the amount of effort they are willing to devote toward material development.

Lambie (1980) suggests that teachers should consider some basic guidelines for material modification. Listed in Table 13–5, they help teachers approach students and their needs in a practical manner. The first two considerations are basic: Teachers should combine ease with efficiency in selecting adaptations. The most simple change is preferable to the more complex, time-consumptive method.

Teachers should know the material and the student well. Based on a task analysis approach, they should examine the material for obvious pitfalls such as pages that are organized in a cluttered fashion or a readability level that is too high. Examining the student's learning style, they should then consider additional factors that might impact learning, such as attention span and distractibility. Based on this combined knowledge of material and student, they are ready to alter the text or material.

Once teachers have made the changes, such as covering all but one row of arithmetic problems or vocabulary words on the page, or re-phrasing assignment directions for improved clarity, they should try the modifications with the student immediately. They should give the student time to practice using the material independently, observing for success and problems.

While teachers will have to take charge of the modification process since they have a broad view of problems matching material and learner styles, they should consult with students. Teachers can ask, "You seem to be having trouble reading this book. What in particular bothers you about it?" A

### Table 13–5
### Considerations in Modifying Curricular Materials

Teachers should

- keep changes as simple as possible for teacher efficiency and effective use by students
- choose the change requiring the least amount of teacher time if two modifications will be equally effective
- examine the material for potential problems and make changes before using it with students
- observe students' learning strengths and problems; consider the types of material changes that will most enable learners to work independently
- try parts of the modified material with learners to make adjustments
- discuss the changes with learners as input for other necessary modifications
- to avoid students' boredom, use several types of materials and modifications

(*Source:* Adapted from Lambie, 1980)

student response such as "I don't understand what it says" or "There are too many spelling words for me to learn at once" will help the teacher understand the learner's difficulty.

The teacher can then modify further if necessary (e.g., providing an outline of material to be covered in the chapter; having the students learn one-half of the spelling words). To avoid any boredom that might develop through the overuse of a particular modification, teachers should change types of adaptations as frequently as possible.

## Techniques in Material Modifications

While many educators rely on instructional modifications when working with students with disabilities, material modification can strongly support the teaching-learning process. From their review of the literature, Idol, Nevin, and Paolucci-Whitcomb (1994), Scruggs and Mastropieri (1992), Cheney (1989), and Blankenship (1985) suggest a number of specific modifications that may be helpful to regular and special educators.

Listed in Table 13–6, use of these techniques should be within the framework of simplicity and ease for the teacher wherever possible. As noting earlier, highlighting important information works well with all students. If the regular education teacher does not have time to do this, the specialist can highlight one text and have a parent, student, or office volunteer highlight others, using the original as a model.

If the chapter does not contain advanced organizers or good preview questions, the teacher can prepare these for the class. As with a number of the modifications, many students will benefit from their implementation, not just a student with disabilities. If the teacher discusses the preview questions with the entire class as well as the meaning of technical vocabulary, text comprehension will be enhanced for everyone.

Similarly, all students can benefit from increased use of pictures, diagrams, and graphs. Many students become inattentive during long reading assignments, but carefully examine visuals that enhance meaning. As part of the lesson the teacher can ask students to prepare graphs or cognitive maps of relationships among ideas. Students can provide explanation for their peers of the content of visuals. These materials can be saved for future use with other students.

If a student cannot read the text, the teacher will have to de-emphasize its use as a primary information source. Providing students books written on an easier level of difficulty but discussing the same content will allow them to follow along with class discussions. If these supportive texts are not available, teachers can used audiotapes of chapters for students to listen to on headphones as they attempt to read the book. Often, teachers do not have time to prepare these materials. If the student has a visual perceptual disability or a visual impairment, taped books can be ordered from Recordings for the

**Table 13–6**
**Techniques for Modifying Materials**

Teachers should

- highlight specific paragraphs containing important information
- create advanced organizers of material to be read
- add pictures, graphs, and diagrams to elaborate meaning
- de-emphasize reading from textbooks, placing emphasis on activities-oriented methods
- have specialist or volunteers create audiotapes of textbook chapters
- provide additional reinforcements through extra worksheets or practice activities
- rewrite unclear explanations and directions
- reduce the number of problems by covering part of the page with a note card
- provide reading materials that cover the same content but at an easier level of difficulty
- offer alternative assignments that demonstrate knowledge but do not require reading or writing
- create vocabulary lists and discuss meaning of significant words before teaching the lesson
- use music, rhyming, and movement to reinforce information
- if coordination is a problem, fasten papers to the student's desk
- if time is a factor, give the student a smaller amount of material to complete

(*Sources:*  Adapted from Idol, Nevin, & Paolucci-Whitcomb, 1994; Klumb, 1992; Waldron, 1996)

Blind. Otherwise, volunteers such as parents, grandparents, and older students can record the text.

Most students can learn content if given enough time and practice. Extra worksheets and practice materials kept in folders afford any student the opportunity to reinforce a problematic concept. If stored over the years, they also reduce the amount of new material preparation for teachers.

"I have a system that has really worked well for me," comments Maura. "Even before Westside initiated inclusion, I've had students who just needed more practice. Before I discard old workbooks, I cut out pages and file them. The Jackson teachers save everything, including old texts, workbooks, and worksheets. If I have a student who is exceptionally low in reading and math and I need to provide material from first or second grade, I contact those teachers and they go to their files for me. In turn, I save everything in case I need it or the fourth and fifth grade teachers do. When we run out of materials, we contact Teresa and she goes to her supply of remedial reading or math books and gives us additional materials. Rarely do we have to create our own. With all of us working together it has turned out to be easier than I thought."

Those worksheets can be cut into rows of paragraphs or arithmetic problems, especially if on separate sheets. When the text has cannot be cut or written upon, teachers can use a blank index card to cover information that may be overwhelming to the student, or limit the amount of work at any moment. If teachers note to the entire class at the beginning of the year that everyone will be doing practice activities in different areas throughout the year, it will lessen the impact of remedial work for any one student.

Some students may require ongoing daily remedial assistance to develop skills basic to content mastery. To avoid a sense of adding to their instructional tasks, teachers might allow them to choose which of the remedial tasks to work on that day as well as their order. In this way, students have choices and task completion is viewed more positively.

If technical vocabulary is part of the reading and explanations or glossaries are poor, teachers can create vocabulary lists before students begin the lesson or unit. While they may want to discuss the most critical terms initially in order to have students understand the information more easily from the onset, they may also post these lists and instruct students to seek out the meaning of these words based on context. Instead of having students memorize the words, their meaning should be discussed with emphasis on examples of information they already know.

If students seem able to complete the work but require more time, teachers should allow additional minutes. However, if excessive amounts of time are necessary, the teacher should shorten the assignment so that students are not kept from other class activities.

## Motivation for Task Completion

"I have a real problem with students not being motivated if they feel the work is going to be difficult," notes John. "I can understand their fear of failure, but it's really debilitating to walk into a classroom where students are apathetic and don't seem to care. If I'm going to use all these techniques to make them more successful, how can I get them to want to try?"

John's comments are very significant. Teachers need to convince students that they can be successful. The best way to do this is to encourage them to complete the work, underscoring positive outcomes. While teachers prefer careful work products for **intrinsic rewards**, it is unlikely that students with a history of failure have experienced a sense of personal success critical to future efforts. Therefore, at first teachers may need to offer external contingencies as a reward for effort, gradually fading them as students become more motivated.

Cheney (1989) suggests additional ways that teachers can motivate students to attempt assignments and to participate in classroom activities.

intrinsic rewards—a sense of personal success and subsequent gratification.

A field trip, such as a tour of a football stadium, can motivate everyone to write. Reprinted with permission, Winston School, San Antonio.

MY PORTFOLIO

> I lvrunD That The FußoII Plar heb theer Nem is on lokn

"I learned that the football players have their names on the lockers."

> I Lrind that waier the Nes paper pealpil see the game,

"I learned (that) where the newspaper people see the game."

> I LrhD Wut The CAW Lockrs Loock Lick.

"I learned what the Cow(boys) lockers look like."

Contracts for completion of a designated amount of work can have students earn a preferred activity. Completion of a weekly contract can result in students taking a positive note to parents. Additionally, extra credit may motivate students to work for higher grades than they have earned in the past.

Students enjoy completing daily graphs to chart their progress and to compete against their own previous performance. If they are involved in personal goal-setting, they have a commitment to seeing improvement in their own performance. Students also are motivated by personal choice concerning where to sit and the order in which they complete tasks. While these issues may seem insignificant to the teacher, they are important modifications for the student as they make the learning environment more welcome. However, they should not serve as distractors from the academic performance of students or peers.

All students enjoy high-status materials such as newspapers, magazines, mail-order catalogs, and driver's manuals, since they represent habits of the adult world. Reinforcement activities such as calculating the costs of outfits of clothing to following the stock market can involve students who are usually passive.

John observes, "One of our math teachers developed a really interesting unit with the health teacher last year. We were concerned about the increase in pregnancies and drop-outs at Apter. They designed a module to meet the needs of both their curricula, but especially relative to student concerns.

"In health the students played a game where they were married to another student in the class and had a young child. They had to drop out of school and go to work at minimum-wage jobs. Their daily problem-solving included instances where the baby became ill and needed expensive medicine. Of course, the car needed repairs around the time the husband was laid off from work. While the students laughed at first, when their own parents refused to watch the baby and they had to find a good babysitter, their approach became more serious. When the wife wanted to go back to school to get a degree, she knew she needed to work to support the family. Throughout all this, they read classified ads for jobs daily, even contacting some of the advertisers to find out educational prerequisites and scheduled hours. When they went into debt over stereos and clothing and even began to put food on their charge card, their math lessons evolved.

"In his class, Steve Cheng first used budget sheets to continue the unit. His students created formal budgets after calling to find out the cost of apartments, phone hook-ups, and utilities. They had to go to the grocery store on their own time, list their favorite products, and with the support of the health teacher devise nutritional meals for themselves and the baby. They computed weekly food costs in Steve's class and added that total onto other expenses.

"Next Steve gave them mock checkbooks. Their daily problem-solving included bills arriving from credit card companies, the doctor, and the car dealer. They had to balance out the checkbooks, learning their needs and desires outstripped their incomes. They had no money for rock concerts or CDs. They were amazed that they couldn't even pay the rent.

"Both teachers agreed this was one of their most exciting and motivational units. But student responses were the most compelling. They had not considered the degree of responsibility and the cost of daily life before. Having to research rents, utilities, and food costs, as well as medical expenses without health insurance taught them more than any lecture or text. At the end of the unit, one student commented to Steve that it 'feels good to be a kid again.'"

# CONCEPTUAL ORGANIZATION WITHIN THE CURRICULUM

"That sounds like a lot of fun, John," responded Maura. "You and I both know there are so many skills that have to be taught along with curricular content that we can't always emphasize their daily experiences. "I have to teach word attack and spelling rules and you have to teach Shakespeare. How can we organize within our curriculum to have students understand and recall this information?"

Carnine (1991) underscores the importance of students building cognitive structures based on interrelated concepts. He summarizes research supporting sameness as a critical teaching variable for conceptual organization. Based upon the work of Nobel prize winner Gerald Edelman (1987), moment-to-moment integration of similarities is a basic human neuro-function. The result of this reliance on similarities is the categorization and recategorization of information by the brain. These ongoing processes strongly impact primary brain processes in perception, recognition, and memory. They explain the interconnectedness of knowledge, the degree of an individual's conceptual skill as based upon the ability to perceive similarities, to note samenesses.

In mathematics and science, the use of significant samenesses results in the development of formulae and underlying laws and principles. In beginning reading, the child learns that -ad has the same sound regardless of its placement in a word. The use of iambic pentameter in poetry results in the same cadence no matter where it appears. Rules and patterns are based on generalizations from samenesses.

The organization of curricular instruction around significant samenesses can strongly influence student understanding and retention. Many textbooks tend to cover a series of topics in a superficial manner, fragmenting instead of relating information. When curricular content emphasizes relationships among concepts, students build cognitive structures. The more expansive and sophisticated the samenesses, the more advanced the level of problem solving.

Simplistically, this principle involves an individual teacher using examples and nonexamples of content being studied in an individual lesson, in order to formalize student understanding. Holistically it means teachers working together within and across subject areas to relate information and broaden student integration of relationships.

For example, Carnine (1991) recommends the teaching of history within a problem-solution-effect model. If students see trends in causes of historical problems (e.g., economics or human rights) and solutions (e.g., expansionism, war, inventions, or litigation), they have developed a framework for explaining events in their own lives. Their recall of historical information will be improved because it is organized in relationship to series of events. In this environment, memorization of isolated facts is far less necessary.

Teachers can take the sameness concept even further by helping students relate developing cognitive structures to their own surroundings. In John's class, *Romeo and Juliet* becomes the basis for discussion of gangs. As students view the video and that from *West Side Story*, they conclude samenesses of experience that are cross-generational. In collaboration with the history teacher, the unit can be expanded to consider how the cancellation of the draft and the breakdown of many families have impacted gang growth in America. The current period can be related to the Roosevelt era and the growth of the Works Progress Administration (WPA). Students can then participate in groups to debate if a similar program would be effective today and how it might be structured.

## INCORPORATING BASIC SKILLS

When designing broader units of curricular study, teachers must be careful to include basic skills development. Often they and students alike are more interested in expansive topics related to their experiences than to practicing skills that may be tedious to develop. Literature can be more compelling than grammar, or environmental studies more interesting than labwork.

The best curricula provide a balance between required skills to master the learning process and significant concepts to enhance the meaningfulness of life. The student who does not memorize French vocabulary will never speak the language fluently. The student who is not fluent with chords may not become the great musician. All of these areas require practice. Unfortunately, repetition usually results in boredom.

On a broader scale the primary concept of teaching by samenesses applies equally well to conceptual and factual information. The principles of phonics are based on sameness when applying sounds to letters. Arithmetic computation is based on algorithms using the same steps to solve operations. The grammar of a language has a pattern. Music composition relies on sound combinations within a range, while primary and secondary colors result in predictable outcomes when mixed.

Skills must be taught or students would never learn to read, write, or compute. When taught in isolation they result in fragmented learning without the powerful generalizations that can result from studying their samenesses. Often teachers comment that students begin to read fluently after they generalize the process of breaking words into larger sound units, or syllables. They speak a foreign language with greater ease after they learn model sentence patterns within which to structure their syntax. They move into higher mathematics after they practice the common application of a formula.

Scruggs and Mastropieri (1992) emphasize the importance of direct instruction in teaching basic skills to students with disabilities. Yet teacher-directed does not have to mean lecture or passive learning by students. At its best it involves the careful questioning of students, encouraging them to perceive samenesses within the skills being practiced. Students who learn the constancy of sound-symbol association in phonetically analyzing words are on their way to becoming independent readers.

In addition, Simmons, Fuchs, and Fuchs (1991) point out the limitations of many traditional curricula and textbooks through provision of inadequate numbers of examples from which students can generalize. At times, students with disabilities may not master a concept before the text or material moves on to the next. Within this setting, it is important for teachers to provide examples for students to discuss and practice.

Similarly, teachers should model skills to be learned, discussing the appropriate sequence of steps in skill-building. They should ask questions as they demonstrate procedures, guiding students into predicting specific outcomes. Next, teachers and students should solve practice problems together, so teachers can see where difficulties might develop. They can correct errors immediately, explaining and modeling the correct process for any steps with which the student is experiencing difficulty.

In preparation for independent practice, teachers again set the stage when they help students complete the initial problem. As students continue to work, teachers can circulate around the room and provide feedback. Students should continue to practice until they master the particular skill under study. At the end of the lesson and throughout the year, teachers should review new skills to promote generalization to other environments (Simmons, Fuchs, & Fuchs, 1991).

feedback—a process in which a response is provided concerning personal efforts toward a goal.

## HOMEWORK

"Speaking of generalization of school-related skills, let's discuss homework," added John. "I'm really frustrated that students complete my home-

Spring fever is a distraction, piled on top of complete boredom and need for major brain surgery. As you look around everything is a blur, indeed. Distractions are abundant as thoughts move in out and through your mind. Concentration is stretched to its limit fortunately you're to distracted to notice where the double brick stick your last thought went and why you forgot it, Hugh? tap tap tap tapping is very faint it is enough to cause intense upheaval of the thought process. Intresting how easily one can be distracted. I never stopped to think how simply even the soundest person can be sent on a tangent, like this I right now, perplexing is this metamorphis of this paper starting out on spring fever and the distraction arising from it to analyzing the logic or illogic behind the thought process distracting me from this distracting page about distraction the amazing human brain everybody! not 9.95 but more for the amazing low price of 9.95 you can have your very own sales tax applies to california residents only,

work assignments in such a sloppy manner. Or worse yet, they don't do them at all. If they're ever going to learn to write well, they need to practice in order to gain ease and fluency. And they should be reading more in order to build skills and gain general information. What can I do to develop good homework habits?"

Homework has become a source of confusion for many teachers. They appreciate its benefits of providing additional practice and reinforcement for important concepts. However, as John notes, too often it becomes a source of contention between the home and school.

Table 13–7 includes ways teachers can establish successful homework practices for their students (Mims, Harper, Armstrong, & Savage, 1991). When teachers view homework positively, student attitudes tend to improve. The initial suggestion listed is the most important. Homework is practice, not punishment. When teachers become angry with class misbehaviors and assign extensive homework, students come to view the work as extra and punitive. Coaches who want to encourage track participation do not assign "laps" as punishment. The principle is the same.

Everyone can remember instances in which a homework assignment seemed impossible to complete. Generally this happens when students encounter the ideas for the first time as they read the text or are asked to solve problems for which they are unprepared. The teacher should introduce and discuss new information, providing guided and independent practice as previously discussed. Only after demonstrating that they can perform competently should students be asked to complete the homework assignment. Since many texts include only surface content coverage, this provides an excellent opportunity for additional work to insure competency.

MY PORTFOLIO

A highly-gifted 15-year-old boy with a visual-perceptual learning disability analyzes his Attention Deficit Disorder, especially his distractibility. In this remarkable essay, as he writes he demonstrates many characteristics of higher abstract thinking associated with Piaget's "Formal Operations" stage. Yet, he expresses an overreaction to both external and internal distractions.

With corrections, it reads, "Spring fever antsily is a distraction, piled on top of complete boredom and need for major brain surgery. As you look around everything is a blur, indeed. Distractors are abundant, as thoughts race in, out, and through your mind. Concentration is stretched to its limit. Fortunately, you're too distracted to notice where the "H-E-double chopstick" your last thought went and why you forgot it. Nifty, Huh? Tap, tap, tap. Someone in the distance is hammering something. Although the tap, tap, tap, tapping is very faint it is enough to cause intense upheaval of the thought process.

"Interesting how easily one can be distracted! I never stopped to think how simply even the soundest person can be sent on a tangent, like this one right now. Perplexing is the metamorphosis of this paper. Starting out on spring fever and distractions arising from it, to analyzing the logic of thought behind the thought process distracting me from this distracting paper about distraction. The amazing human brains everybody! Now for $19.95, not for $9.95, but for the amazing low price of $19.95, you can have your very own. Sales tax applies to California residents only." Reprinted with parental permission.

**Table 13–7**
**Guidelines for Establishing Homework Practices**

- Never give homework as punishment.

- Do not give homework that requires new knowledge or skills not previously covered in class.

- Homework should provide an ongoing review of skills and concepts.

- To avoid frustration, always be sure homework is at the student's level.

- If time permits, allow students to begin homework in class so teachers can answer any questions and observe potential areas of difficulty.

- Homework should not exceed two hours. Younger students and learners with short attention spans should receive less homework.

- Assign a grade to most homework assignments, encouraging effort. If students have performed poorly on tests, homework can bolster their grades.

- All students should have an assignment notebook or specially-designed form from each class. Parents should sign the assignment sheet to indicate the student has completed the work.

- Tell parents and students in advance if any special materials or resources will be required to complete the assignment.

- Send home information discussing "homework policies," so parents will understand their role in the process.

(*Source:* Adapted from Mims, Harper, Armstrong, & Savage, 1991; Waldron, 1996)

Teachers should only give homework that is on the student's level. In the inclusive classroom, some adjustments may be needed, such as a shortened or differentiated assignment. Some students may be responding to conceptual questions while others are reinforcing their skills. If students are working in small groups for instruction, teachers can give homework reinforcing content studied by the group that day. If the teacher explains from the beginning of the year that at times there will be different homework assignments to reinforce different needs, there should be no questions about fairness. The important issue to students is that all students receive or do not receive an assignment. There is less concern about what the assignment contains.

To ensure that all students can complete the homework independently, as appropriate teachers should encourage beginning the assignment in class. Within a few minutes of observing student efforts, teachers realize which students may encounter problems. They should provide guided practice with explanation before allowing these students to continue the work at home independently.

It is important for teachers to consider the amount of time their assignment will require each evening. Many high school students despair over hours of homework nightly, resulting in haphazard performance and a negative attitude. The maximum amount of combined assignments should not require more than two hours on any evening for secondary students. For younger students or those with shorter attention span, the assignment should be abbreviated to no more than an hour. After fatigue sets in, little learning takes place.

Homework should be graded, demonstrating that the teacher feels it is important. Students with low test scores are afforded an additional opportunity to improve their grades for the class. Since students have more time to respond and greater control over the information, they may become more positive toward homework completion.

To organize homework assignments, a special notebook or form should indicate the date, the assignment pages or materials, and an area for parental signature indicating its completion. If students with special needs have difficulty copying an assignment from the blackboard, the teacher might check for accuracy. In the elementary grades, if students tend to be disorganized, they should visit the office of an assigned counselor before going home each day. The counselor can check to see that the student has all the necessary books and materials to complete the assignment correctly. At the secondary level, while students' backpacks may become heavy, most prefer to have students carry all of their books and materials. This avoids materials left in the locker or at home and assures that students carry their academic needs with them, regardless of the location.

## Parents and Homework

Homework can place a tremendous pressure on parents, especially if the student is encountering difficulty with the content. Should parents help their child with the assignment? If so, how much? Every teacher has a homework policy, but may need to express it more clearly for both parents and students. At the beginning of the school year, sending home a statement of homework expectations clarifies the teacher's intent. In this statement, the teacher should indicate if the student is to complete the work independently or in conjunction with parents. Teachers should state approximately how often they will assign homework and how it will be graded. They should indicate its weight in comparison with other grades in the class.

"I finally understood how important having a stated policy can be," comments Maura. "I always send a letter home indicating that in my class homework is a contract between the teacher and the student. I explain that I want the students to perform the work independently, reinforcing daily class activities. Parents can answer their child's questions if there are problems. But on the whole, I like homework to be the student's responsibility.

"Well, my own ninth-grade daughter came home needing to design a project for the school district Science Fair. My husband was full of ideas that really excited him and even my daughter, who is normally nonresponsive to anything scientific.

"Together they created a giant eyeball with a cataract. They demonstrated the difference in visual acuity before and after surgery was performed. For weeks our house was ablaze with plastic models and diagrams. It was fun for me to hear them talk about the project over dinner. Of course, the inevitable happened, as my husband brought more books home and the project became incredibly sophisticated beyond my daughter's understanding. We laughed one evening as she commented quietly that she hoped her Dad won the prize.

"After they set it up for the judges at the competition, my husband waited by his office phone all day. She was to answer questions about the project, describing not only its method of composition, but most importantly, the theory behind it. When she finally called, disappointedly she told him that one of the judges had asked if either of her parents was involved in a related field. The judge said that her dad, an optometrist, deserved an A, but she would have to settle for less.

"While they were both upset, I had to reflect on the irony of my own position about assignments. I probably would have given the same response that the judge did if an overly sophisticated project came my way. But in fairness to my family, I asked that the district provide a written policy statement for the following year about degree of parental involvement in assigned projects."

Maura's example underscores how parents may take over student assignments, either through personal interest or because their child is experiencing difficulty. Their role needs to be clarified from the onset. Since many parents want to help their children, they should not be discouraged, but given direction in ways that will be supportive to school learning.

For example, the policy statement at the beginning of the year might encourage parents to review school material with their children before an exam in order to discuss difficult concepts. Or parents can be asked to review student homework once it is completed and explain problem areas without giving students the answer. Teachers can check to see if the parent is receiving the grade instead of the student by matching exams and daily work products to homework output. If the difference is dramatic, the teacher can review the homework policy with the parent.

## THE ROLE OF THE PARENT

There are other ways parents can help their children perform well in school. These go far beyond internalizing curricular content or completing homework. Instead, they involve a series of attitudes and structures that create the environment for academic success.

Table 13–8 includes a listing of informal ways parents can support student learning and overall development during formative years (Waldron,

**Table 13–8**
**Guidelines for Parents**

- Talk to your child.

- Create a quiet place for homework, away from television and telephones.

- Have an established time for meals, bedtime, homework, and reading.

- Limit the amount of television, music, and video games.

- Have children read daily. Model behaviors through personal involvement in reading books and newspapers.

- Establish a feeling of being "world citizens" through discussing news and events outside the daily life of the child.

- Do not say anything negative about the school or teacher in front of the child.

- Create a sense that school is the child's workplace and requires attitudes of promptness, attention, and disciplined behavior.

- Encourage acceptance of diversity.

- Develop a sense of helpfulness towards others through shared responsibility in the home and volunteerism to support those outside the home.

- Model and teach responsibility, respect, and discipline.

(*Source:* Waldron, 1995)

1995). Usually parents feel they can best help by working with their children as Maura's husband did, by supervising homework daily. There are more significant ways with long-term impact.

The initial suggestion in the Table 13–8 indicates parents should talk to children. Most parents would say they do. Yet, most often interactions involve parents telling children to brush their teeth or go to bed. A real conversation involves both individuals sharing their ideas or feelings. Talking to young children encourages their language development as well as a sense of affection and closeness when adults indicate that children's ideas are important.

Talking with adolescents gives them the opportunity to explore their own thoughts and opinions, as well as to test values. As they consider newly discovered abstract ideas ranging from evolution to abortion, they are forced to comprehend how others may feel differently, but just as strongly. This intellectual expansion during a period of personal egocentrism can result in highly charged interactions with each person coming away emotionally reactive. While parents may not always enjoy these conversations, they are a critical part of young people's intellectual and personal development.

Because youth tend to be most concerned with their own daily lives, often they lack a sense of world citizenship. In conversations, it is important for parents and teachers to discuss world events and their impact. Students should be asked their opinions about issues ranging from politics to social services.

Their initial response of "I don't know" often changes to a strong conviction when they expand their information base.

If students have language delays, vision or hearing losses, discussions become even more important. Not only are students given models of language expression, but the opportunity to let others know that they have good ideas too.

"That was really brought home to us a few years ago," reflects Dr. Mirales. "We had a young man who had multiple disabilities caused by cerebral palsy. He was unable to walk and he interacted with others by a communication board. He would point to squares or their combination indicating that he wanted something to eat or to sit in a particular location. Everyone around him was kind and friendly and immediately met his needs.

"When he entered high school, we put him on a computer. His teachers were all amazed at the speed with which he learned some really advanced skills when he had specialized switches and keyboard. But it was his motivation that surprised us most. He worked at communicating all day. He wrote messages to everyone on his word processor. His parents bought a computer for him to use at home, his mother reporting that it was like getting to know her own son for the first time. The following year he became addicted to the Internet system, interacting in a way that showed all of us how very bright he is.

"I was visiting his room one day and asked him what he liked best about the computer. Using it to respond, he told me that it allowed him to discuss his feelings and ideas with others, not just his basic needs. 'Now I feel like a real person,' he said. 'I can tell people more than that I'm hungry. I can tell them how I feel about world hunger.' For perhaps the first time, I fully understood how important being able to communicate with parents, teachers, and peers can be."

## Structuring the Home

In the course of daily life, many things parents provide are more practical than cognitive. They create the environment for academic success. A quiet place for homework, away from television, telephones, and household distractions helps young people focus on reinforcing academic tasks. A structured schedule for bedtime and meals as well as television or videogames provides a sense of organization to students with cognitive differences who may be experiencing a chronic sense of confusion.

Smith (1981) explains that the disorganization students demonstrate when they lose their assignments or have trouble planning time is indicative of the cognitive confusion they experience daily. The best way parents and teachers can help students become organized is to provide a structured environment daily. While most homes are subject to the schedules of working parents and busy children, a sense of hurriedness should be exchanged for a sense of stability.

Students of all grade levels can suffer from a sense of "change overload" (Elkind, 1988); they move constantly from one location or activity to another. When children and adolescents are experiencing disabilities, this sense of being overwhelmed can be compounded. Frequent changes in classes and teachers with differing expectations can be difficult. When before and after-school time becomes similarly rushed, the student has no chance to escape

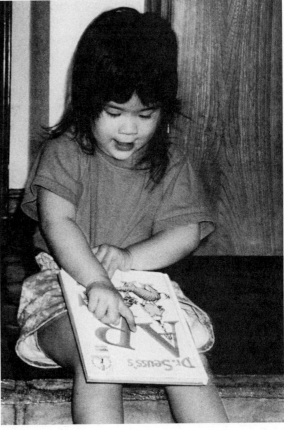

Parents who encourage young children to read can set the stage for a lifetime love of books.

demands. If relaxation becomes reliant on television or "hard rock" music, there may be additional stress from viewing or listening to violence.

It becomes the job of parents to monitor the student's day so there are periods of quiet and family interaction. They can create a sense of priorities by indicating that school is the child's workplace and requires attitudes of attention and discipline. Children should not be sent to school tired or hungry. Parents should insist on a reasonable bedtime and breakfast before leaving the house. The usual response of "I'm not hungry" may mean that the child does not have time for food. Parents should wake children 15 minutes earlier so they go to school fully prepared to learn. Such monitoring becomes especially important for adolescents, who may tend to stay up late and rush off to school unprepared the next day. Parents must structure children's evenings so school tasks are completed with care.

It is also important for parents to read to young children, encouraging their responsiveness to books. As children read independently, there should be a designated time each evening, away from the television and distractions. By the time they reach adolescence, reading will be a natural and enjoyable part of their lives. Parents can model this behavior by reading newspapers and books themselves and discussing new ideas. It is very difficult for the school to bear the full responsibility for students becoming avid readers if no one reads at home.

## Teacher-Parent Cooperation

If the child complains about the teacher, while listening carefully the parent should explain the teacher's viewpoint about the situation. Students tend to be egocentric and bring home their side of the story. If parents criticize the teacher without understanding fully what has happened, their children may become adversarial to the school. If students hear their parents blame the school, they will adopt a similar attitude of negativism.

Parents of students with disabilities may have developed a strong sense of antagonism toward the school if they have experienced difficulties with placement or teacher acceptance. It is important for teachers to understand that parents may have reasons for feeling negatively. Teachers should approach parents with a positive, "We..." attitude, indicating a willingness to work together to help the child succeed. When parents feel that teachers are not opposed to having their child in class and will help as much as possible, they tend to become much more school supportive.

## Parents and the Community

"What do we do with really negative parents such as Mike Gonzales?" asks Elena. "He has done so much to hurt the development of our inclusion program. He doesn't want any students with disabilities in his son's class. He really feels his son will be harmed instead of helped by exposure to diversity."

The best way to change the attitudes of parents and community members is to have the program be successful despite their concerns. Once they observe first-hand that all students are benefitting, they will put the issue aside. It is important to realize that they believe the negative outcomes will outweigh the positives. If the pattern changes, they tend to become more accepting.

However, despite all best efforts, some parents remain negative, convinced that they are right. School personnel may be unable to change their views, but often their own children can be more successful. When parents do not teach acceptance of diversity and helpfulness towards others, their children will rarely demonstrate these behaviors without encouragement at school.

Aware of his father's apprehensions, teachers can have Greg Gonzales be part of a classroom that embraces difference. As teachers model acceptance, students observe. When grouped with a student who happens to be visually or hearing impaired, they learn the peer is still a "regular" person. As Greg watches others volunteer to help the student, he learns kindness. If he does not volunteer to work with the student or to be supportive in other ways, he should never be forced to be involved. However, as time progresses, the issue will fade and he will come to view diversity as acceptable.

Importantly, Greg and his classmates will be most accepting of others' needs if their own are being met. Are they all being given work at their level? Challenged by academics? Afforded the chance to be creative and go beyond expectations? Inclusion encompasses the educational and social needs of all students, creating an environment that supports the opportunity for success.

## SUMMARY

Chapter 13 discussed optimal methods of curriculum and materials modification. Many teachers express concern that included students will be unable to complete curricular work. To assure student readiness, teachers should ask a variety of questions before beginning instruction. A review of factors such as the student's mastery of prerequisite skills, reading level, and ability to work in small groups, information gathered will prepare teachers to make necessary modifications. If adaptations are more extreme, they can involve specialists in direct assistance or in consultation.

Teachers tend to move along a spectrum, ranging from child-centered to teacher-centered instruction. The middle range includes children-centered approaches, where groups of students support each other's learning. No one of these organizational methods is effective all the time, but depends on the learning needs of the individual student and the information to be taught.

The integrated, or "core," curriculum is an attempt to present information holistically instead of relying on individual facts. Skills and subject matter are designed around perceived students' needs to learn specific societal information. It can be presented in a total staff format, where teachers develop an all-school theme for a concentrated time period. Every class provides information to reinforce the theme. The interdisciplinary team model involves teachers of different content areas who are assigned a single group of students. They plan together to relate their information across subject areas. Block time involves an individual teacher instructing students in several content areas across an extended time period. The teacher is responsible for integrating the information.

Chapter 13 next included discussion of concerns regarding textbooks. Traditionally teachers have relied upon the use of a single text for all students, adding lecture, discussion, and individual assignments for reinforcement. Students at-risk may fail in this environment because they may have difficulty reading and understanding the book or lack behaviors supportive of attention in large or small groups.

Table 13–3 contains a series of considerations in selecting optimal texts to meet varied learner needs. Prominent placement of unit goals and an outline presenting a hierarchy of topics gives direction to the chapter. Headings, margin notes, and contrasting fonts cue important information and support retention. Diagrams, tables, and illustrations afford visual supports for abstract material. Practice exercises allow for skill and concept reinforcement.

When teachers must use existing materials, certain modifications can be helpful. With specialist assistance, they can highlight certain paragraphs or content, provide additional practice activities, and reduce the visual field through using a notecard to cover information not being read. They can expand text directions, reduce the amount of reading, and create vocabulary lists for concept explanation.

Teacher concerns about homework can be ameliorated by following additional guidelines. Homework should never be viewed as punishment, but as reinforcement for information already covered in class. Students should have an assignment book for all subjects. When possible, they should begin homework completion in class so teachers can see that students are performing correctly.

Parents should support school learning through having a quiet place for homework and reviewing its completion. They should have established times for meals, bedtime, and reading. Parents should support the school through positive comments about teachers and learning, creating a sense that school is the child's workplace and requires attitudes of promptness, attention, and disciplined behavior. Above all, they should model and teach responsibility, respect, and discipline.

## CASE STUDY: *Elementary*

You are about to start your first year of teaching. You've been told that you will be able to order some new materials next year, but school policy is that new teachers use existing materials until they decide personal preferences for the future. In other words, "Good luck with what we have." Since the school seems really fine otherwise, you've decided to make the best of it.

You're eager to see what's in the cupboard. You understand the priority of reviewing student records first to see what their academic levels will be.

Bad news, but no one ever said teaching was going to be easy. You have three students whose reading skills are so low they will not be able to read the text without modifications. Two of the students have disabilities in cognitive areas, demonstrating problems with understanding directions and content beyond the factual level. One has serious problems with word analysis, and is basically unable to decode the words. This student requires basic skill building, ranging from phonics to sight words, far below the class. As you approach the cupboard with available materials, you have some questions.

1. Given their problems with reading and understanding the text, these students may have other difficulties you'll want to examine from the onset. Based on the questions in Table 13–1, how will you determine the prerequisite skills of each student, as well as their ability to work within groups or independently?

2. Reviewing the suggestions in Table 13–4 and 13–5, what can you do to ensure that the materials are examined for any modifications needed? What specific materials modifications will you make for (a) the students who have difficulty understanding directions and material content? (b) the student with problems decoding the information on the page?

3. If these students demonstrate additional behaviors including short attention span and distractibility to cluttered materials, which modifications should be most successful?

4. You're concerned that these three students will not be motivated to complete assignments because of their learning problems. How will you engage them to be full participants in your class?

## CASE STUDY: *Secondary*

One class, one text. They warned you in college about districts and even states where textbooks were determined first and students needed to adapt. Yet there's more than just the book: It's the entire curriculum that scares you. You've decided to include a few new students this year, ones who have been tracked into "slower" classes in the past. As a result, the principal has given you a modest budget to support additional materials. Not enough, but at least an acknowledgment that you'll need to differentiate. It's time to plan which materials to order. The broader question is how to adapt the curriculum to meet their needs.

1. Reviewing the questions in Table 13–1, which are the most important for considering the needs of students with cognitive disabilities who may lack abstraction abilities as well as organized study habits?

2. In selecting new materials, you'll need to review the considerations in Table 13–4. Which of the suggestions may be most beneficial to these students? To ones with short attention spans? Poor memory for previously studied material?

3. Whether the materials are new or existing, there are a number of considerations for modifying them to better meet learner needs. From Tables 13–5 and 13–6, which modifications may be most appropriate for students with cognitive differences?

4. In your classroom teaching, how can you introduce textbooks and materials to students so that they use them optimally? Which specialists in the school can help you by completing some of the materials modifications that require extra time? Additionally, how can these specialists provide direct or consultant assistance to support your teaching of students with cognitive disabilities in the regular classroom?

# EPILOGUE

John comments, "In the vernacular, I want to ask, 'Are we having fun yet?' I had an important realization the other day in class: I've been having fun all along. The challenge of schooling for diversity has given new life to my teaching. Before, I was primarily concerned about Shakespeare and teaching the writing of fluid sentences. Now I'm more interested in *students.* How can I help them learn to love Shakespeare and to communicate better? How can I improve their understanding and support of each other? Not only has my shift from content to people provided more meaningfulness to my teaching, but it's added a human concern to my classes."

"I'm amazed by the responsiveness in the school and broader community," added Maura. "We've started having inservices for peers in classes where we're including students with disabilities or from different cultures. Before we place new students, we're trying to cultivate understanding and a sense of helpfulness and responsibility for others. Then we ask students to volunteer to be a 'buddy.' We can't handle all the students who want to help. What a wonderful problem!"

Mort notes, "An interesting outcome of teacher and student support has been a total attitude change at Jackson. When parents are concerned that their child won't get enough attention because of inclusion, we have them talk to the teacher, who most often brims with enthusiasm based on success. Our greatest supporters have been the children themselves. They carry home the message that diversity is interesting, adds a dimension to their lives, and that parents' concerns are unfounded.

"I've finally scheduled that interview with Curt O'Hare for next week. I'm bringing a few students and parents with me to discuss their reactions to our changes this year. We're going to ask Curt to be on our Advisory Board. Want to take bets?"

Reprinted with permission, Winston School, San Antonio.

# GLOSSARY

**absence seizures (petit mal)**—brief and nondisruptive seizures in which the student stares straight ahead; may go unrecognized but cause delays in acquiring school-related information.

**academic functioning level**—the instructional level of the student in each subject area.

**active learner**—a student who shows genuine involvement and understanding during the lesson.

**active listening**—a technique in which people show interest and understanding in what others are saying; often exhibited by using eye contact and gestures of acknowledgment.

**adaptive software**—computer programming made to suit a particular need.

**advocacy**—efforts, usually by parents or educators, to establish services for students.

**allergies**—a hypersensitivity to a certain substance.

**American Sign Language (ASL)**—an alternate communication system that uses hand gestures to express words and thoughts.

**anecdotal records**—observations of a student written in a narrative form.

**antecedents**—things that happen before or prior to a behavior.

**anticipated student outcomes**—expected results or achievement of a student.

**aphasia**—a disability in which the student has difficulty understanding or speaking oral language.

**areas of need**—specific conditions in which there is a deficiency.

**articulation**—the ability to correctly produce speech sounds.

**assessment**—collecting a broad variety of data that provides an extensive picture of the student's achievement and behavior.

**assessment stages**—the steps taken to determine a student's abilities.

**asthma**—a chronic respiratory condition that causes periodic breathing difficulty.

**at risk**—refers to children who do not demonstrate disabilities, but who for environmental or biological reasons may develop such delays.

**Attention Deficit Disorder (ADD)**—a conduct disorder characterized by difficulty in sustaining attention and by impulsiveness.

**Attention Deficit Hyperactivity Disorder (ADHD)**—a disorder characterized by difficulty in sustaining attention, impulsivity, distractibility, and excessive movement.

**attribution training**—understanding exactly why efforts succeeded or failed.

**audiologist**—a specialist who assesses hearing acuity at different frequency ranges and decibel levels.

**auditory perception**—the process by which sound gains meaning.

**auditory sequencing**—recalling multiple units of information in the correct order.

**authentic assessment**—assessment based on examples of students' work in a particular subject area over an extended period of time.

**baseline data**—collection of facts taken, usually through observation and assessment, before intervention strategies are implemented, with the purpose of determining effectiveness of the intervention.

**behavior management**—skillfully directing a student's conduct in a positive direction.

**behavioral functioning level**—the student's ability to demonstrate predetermined appropriate behaviors individually and in group settings.

**behavioral objective**—a description of the task to be learned including specific behaviors demonstrating its acquisition.

**"blindisms"**—personal or behavioral habits a blind person exhibits.

**block time approach**—individual teachers design and instruct several subject areas within a related theme.

**cerebral palsy**—a condition caused by damage to the brain's motor control center; includes restrictions on muscle activities that may limit fine and gross motor behaviors and academic learning.

**child-centered approach**—instruction is designed to meet the needs of the children.

**children-centered approaches**—methods for organizing instruction that rely on students taking responsibility for teaching and supporting each other; may incorporate strategies such as cooperative learning and peer tutoring.

**classroom discussion model**—teaching-training structure in which discussion stimulates consideration of multiple answers to the same question and may lead to additional considerations not in the initial questions; the purpose is to consider a wealth of responses and expand one's original ideas through contemplating ideas offered by others.

**clinical assessment**—assessment performed in a professional setting.

**clinical teaching**—analyzing the learning or behavior problem, and using information gathered in developing a specific intervention plan to help the student.

**closure**—finality; drawing an activity or lesson to an end.

**cognitive functioning level**—the student's ability to use logic and analysis, to associate and categorize information to perform inductive and deductive reasoning.

**collaboration**—when educators interact to solve problems relating to student needs.

**common schools**—schools for the general population of children.

**communication aids**—devices used to support oral and written expression of students with physical limitations.

**communication boards**—devices that allow students to convey basic messages by pressing certain responses indicated on the board.

**complex partial (psychomotor)**—seizures in which individual loses consciousness and demonstrates numerous body convulsions.

**conduct disorder**—students who exhibit bold, negative actions and behaviors.

**confidentiality**—privacy and secrecy, restricting sharing of information without approval.

**consequences**—things that happen as a result of a behavior.

**Consulting Teacher**—educators who are trained to interact with and advise regular classroom teachers and others involved in instructing or working with exceptional children.

**Content Mastery Center**—educational setting designed for students experiencing occasional difficulty in understanding the content or being able to perform assignments; this placement provides supportive instruction.

**content validity**—a test's provision of an adequate sample of skills, abilities, or attributes in a specified area.

**content-based**—directed toward developing content knowledge at the appropriate level for integrating curricular information.

**contingencies**—effective consequences used to deter or encourage certain behaviors.

**continuum of services**—instructional and placement options available to serve students with disabilities.

**control switches**—manipulative controls for working the computer; varieties include head pointers, mouthsticks, arm/hand, and leg movements that may bypass the keyboard completely.

**convergent questions**—encourage factual, "right or wrong" responses, usually with only one correct answer; encourage little classroom interacting.

**cooperative learning**—an approach based on children working in teams combining students with disabilities with typical peers.

**cooperative teaching (co-teaching)**—based on regular and special educators jointly planning, teaching, and evaluating all learners in the integrated classroom.

**core curriculum**—skills and subject matter in the curriculum are designed to meet student needs through units of relevant content study.

**criterion-referenced tests**—assessment of a student's performance that is not based on comparison to other students, but to an absolute level of mastery.

**cultural bias**—prejudging a student's abilities based on preconceptions or stereotypes regarding cultural background.

**cultural identity**—the feeling of belonging to a group with the same cultural background and having some of the same characteristics of that group.

**curriculum-based assessment (CBA)**—a procedure that uses curricular content as a basis for determining students' instructional needs.

**curriculum-based measurement (CBM)**—prescribed system of appraisal that considers students' long-term goals.

**cystic fibrosis**—hereditary condition in which the person experiences problems breathing due to the build-up of thick mucus in the lungs.

decentralization—keeping children with exceptional needs close to their home communities.

decoding skills—the ability to recognize and analyze words.

deductive—reasoning from a known general statement to an unknown.

deinstitutionalization—a movement toward removing individuals with disabilities from hospital-like buildings to community-based group homes.

developmental motor activities—functions of motion that normally develop in a sequence, such as standing and walking.

diagnosis—determining the nature of the problem by examiniation or assessment.

diagnostic teaching—planning activities based on the needs of the students.

difficulty level—the skill level necessary to complete the work successfully.

direct instruction model—teaching method in which the teacher reviews previously learned material, states objectives for the lesson, presents new material, provides guided practice with feedback, provides independent practice with feedback, and reviews all concepts before beginning any new material; most effective in teaching skills that can be broken up into discrete segments.

Directed Thinking-Reading Activities (DTRA)—a method of teaching in which students make predictions and support their predictions with logic and association.

directionality—integration and application of spatial concepts, such as *left* and *right*.

discovery learning—understanding through integrating varied experiences; arriving at new concepts gradually as a result of independently understanding relationships among ideas.

discrimination—denying equal opportunity due to physical or personal characteristics.

divergent questions—encourage open-ended responses, permitting multiple answers, generating discussion, and encouraging creativity and critical thinking.

diversity—a characteristic that makes someone dissimilar or different.

drills—repeated practice.

due process—legal proceedings and policies that establish rules; in education, designed to ensure equal opportunities in education for all students with disabilities.

duration recording—keeping track of the amount of time spent involved in a specific behavior.

dysfunctional—abnormal; not providing the nurturing and support needed by family members.

eclectic—based on integration of a variety of approaches.

effective communication—interactions that produce the intended results or outcomes.

English as a Second Language (ESL)—programming support for non-native speakers as they learn English.

entry level behaviors—how a student behaves or performs before the intervention strategies are implemented.

epilepsy—disorder of the nervous system characterized by various types and degrees of seizures.

equal opportunity for success—the ability of all students to contribute to team success by improving their own past performance.

equity vs. excellence—the fear that the education of average and gifted learners will become "watered down" to meet the needs of atypical learners.

evaluation stage—teachers review stated objectives and the student's success in meeting them.

event recording—making a tally each time the behavior being observed occurs.

expressive language—the ability to communicate in speed and writing.

extraneous stimuli—external distractions.

facilitators—trained specialists.

family practice physicians—generalist doctors who deal with all aspects of medicine.

feedback—a process in which a response is provided concerning personal efforts toward a goal.

fifth-order level—research and development directed toward educational change.

finger spelling—using the fingers to form the letters of words.

first-order level—trained teachers in regular education classes who are prepared to work with all types of students.

flexible grouping system—dividing the class into groups that are easily rotated as skill levels improve and content units change.

flexible rules—regulations that are capable of modification to suit the needs of the student and teacher.

Focus Journals—students write a brief comment in response to a teacher's daily "journal focus" question, including support for their opinion or response.

formal assessment—use of specified standardized tests to determine performance levels or the existence of a disability.

fourth-order level—college and university programs for the preparation of personnel at all levels.

**full inclusionists**—those who believe all students should participate in regular education classes.

**functional analysis**—examination of a problem within the context of the classroom to determine necessary changes to impact student behavior.

**generalization data**—information indicating how well modified behavior continues in other environments.

**generalized tonic-clonic (grand mal)**—seizures in which individual loses consciousness and demonstrates numerous body convulsions.

**"golden mean"**—the average.

**Graves Writing Workshop**—a system in which students write daily and hold conferences with the teacher and peers to discuss content; writing efforts are finalized into books.

**guided independent study**—student completes assignments under teacher supervision to ensure correctness of response.

**habilitation**—efforts made to improve a student's skills and abilities.

**hands-on activities**—lessons that include the student's getting involved actively.

**health impairments**—bodily systems are affected by diseases or conditions that are debilitating or life-threatening.

**hearing aids**—devices used by the hearing impaired to amplify specified sound frequencies to a volume permitting improved use of residual hearing.

**hearing**—the process by which individuals take in raw auditory stimuli and convert them to sound.

**heterogeneously**—grouping low and high achievers together.

**history**—the interactive patterns that develop as the year progresses.

**hospital-homebound**—students who are removed from their regular school environment for brief periods of time due to needed recovery from an accident, intensive medical treatment, or a physically or emotionally disabling condition.

**human immunodeficiency virus (HIV)**—a virus that affects the individual's ability to ward off infections.

**hyperactive**—excessive movement that usually interferes with a student's learning ability.

**IEP committee**—team that reviews special education assessment data, and plans and evaluates the effectiveness of subsequent interventions.

**immediacy**—the occurrence of classroom demands that require quick responses, not always allowing for full reflection.

**impartial hearing**—an appearance before a judge in which no party has undue advantage.

**inappropriate behaviors**—actions that are not proper for the present circumstances.

**inclusion**—providing a normalized education experience for all children with disabilities.

**individual accountability**—each member of the group has a certain responsibility toward the group.

**individual contracts**—agreements with the teacher in which the student promises to perform or behave a certain way in exchange for an agreed-upon reward from the teacher.

**Individualized Educational Plan (IEP)**—specific goals, strategies, and evaluative measures for meeting a particular child's learning and behavioral needs.

**individualized instruction**—teaching strategies based on the idea that a student's program should be tailored to meet the student's specific needs.

**Individuals with Disabilities Education Act (IDEA)**—formerly The Education of All Handicapped Children Act (PL 142); a law that eliminated the exclusion of children with disabilities from the education system.

**inductive**—pulling separate facts together to prove a general statement.

**informal assessment**—use of nonstandardized information, such as curriculum-based measures and student work products, to determine performance levels.

**inservice**—training given to teachers to help them continuously develop new professional skills.

**instructional level**—the level at which the teacher should present lessons; the student should experience success as well as learning.

**instructional models**—methods of teaching based on student learning styles, the demands of the content, and teacher preference.

**instrument**—in assessment, the chosen test.

**integrated curriculum**—combining the content areas within a meaningful context.

**interdependence**—students are responsible for others' successful learning as well as their own.

**interdisciplinary team approach**—teachers from several different subject areas instructing the same group of students work together to organize around the topic suggested; students are exposed to theme content in certain grade levels, but not across the entire school.

**interpret**—rephrase for practical use.

**interval recording**—the teacher divides the observation period and notes the appropriateness of student behaviors within subunits of the total time.

**intervention**—input directed toward change.

**intervention data**—a collection of facts that substantiates which antecedents and consequences are most effective in shaping student behaviors in the desired direction.

**intervention methods**—preventive, remedial, or compensatory efforts to educate students.

**intervention plan**—steps of action to be taken to interrupt the current pattern of behavior or learning taking place.

**intervention stages**—the teaching time; the critical period when the student receives academic and/or behavioral assistance, and specialists and generalists work together to support improved learning and behavior.

**intrinsic rewards**—a sense of personal success and subsequent gratification.

**inventory**—test including a sampling of skills across a variety of areas.

**IQ (intelligence quotient)**—a number that indicates intelligence as measured on a standardized instrument.

**Itinerant Teacher**—an educator trained to provide direct services to students with disabilities and their teachers, visiting them in their classroom on a regular basis.

**"I" statements**—a style of communicating in which the teacher is not blaming the student or even commenting on the misbehavior, but is stating and restating the expectations.

**keyguards**—adaptive devices for computer keyboards that have large finger holes that cover the keyboard and allow student access to a variety of software.

**Kurzweil**—a microcomputer with voice character recognition to support students as they learn to read.

**labeling**—figuratively attaching a name that categorizes a student as demonstrating a designated disability.

**Laser Cane**—a cane used by the individuals with visual impairment; used in a sweeping motion while walking to maximize the field it explores for obstructions.

**latency recording**—noting the amount of time a student takes to respond to a particular stimulus.

**learning aptitude**—ability to learn or understand new information.

**learning centers**—areas in a classroom that contain numerous activities and instructional materials organized around a common theme.

**learning modality**—the means through which a student best learns: visually, auditorily, or motorically.

**least restrictive environment**—the most normalized educational setting appropriate for a student.

**lecture-only approach**—the teacher provides information and students occasionally ask questions.

**life-skills training**—teaching a student the skills needed to work and live independently.

**lip-read**—to understand what a person is saying by distinguishing the movement of the person's lips.

*Literacy Development Checklist*—a checklist of reading processes, such as skills, interests, applications, and strategies, that can provide valuable information to a teacher about a student's reading skills.

**long-term goal**—an objective set to work toward over an extended period of time.

**low-incidence**—not occurring often.

**Mainstream Assistance Team**—consultants visit the classroom to help guide teachers through identifying student problems, analyzing intervention strategies, and providing feedback.

**mainstream**—the typical educational milieu.

**media/materials centers**—a library of supportive educational materials.

**mentors**—advisors.

**mirror-writing**—writing from right to left, rather than left to right.

**mission statement**—a declaration of the special function of a group; how a group perceives its duty.

**mobility instruction**—training relating to movement around a location.

**modality processing level**—considers how the student performs psychomotor or information processing.

**modality testing**—assessing through which modality the student best learns.

**modeling**—demonstrating first-hand.

**momentary time sampling**—the teacher observes a student at a given time to note if the specified behavior is occurring.

**motor memory**—using repetitious motor functions to help recall.

**multidimensionality**—the coexistence of many tasks and events occurring at the same time in the same classroom.

**multidisciplinary teams**—fulfill legal placement and review requirements for students in special education.

muscular dystrophy (MD)—a hereditary disorder that is progressive; causes loss of energy and deterioration of the body as muscle tissue is replaced with fatty tissue.

neurologists—specialists trained to diagnose problems with motor and integration skills or behaviors.

nonambulatory—not able to walk.

norm—average or normal.

norm-referencing—information on the population used as the standardization group when a specific test was developed.

normalization—the belief that all individuals with disabilities should be provided the opportunity to live as normally as possible in daily society.

nurturing attitude—encouraging and warm disposition.

observe—to watch a student and document specific occurrences of a particular behavior.

occupational therapist—a specialist who works with the family to determine the behaviors the student must master to facilitate participation in daily life.

off-task behavior—when attention is distracted from the activity or task at hand; results in nonproductive classroom time.

ophthalmologist—a doctor who treats the diseases and functions of the eye.

Optacon—a portable, hand-held camera that converts printed material into tactile stimuli.

opticians—concerned with correct eye function; trained to prescribe series of eye exercises to help improve areas such as muscular balance and coordination; not a medical doctor.

optometrists—trained to deal with measurement and correction of visual disorders, not diseases; not a medical doctor.

oral miscue analysis—observations about how a student uses word attack and analysis skills, repetition, omission, and substitutions of words and sounds, use of phonics and syllabication.

oral receptive language disability—a language disorder in which the student has difficulty understanding spoken language.

otitis media—middle ear inflammation that may cause fever and pain, and subsequently affect hearing; impact may reduce student's ability to use phonics in learning to read.

otolaryngology—the study of ear, nose, and throat diseases.

otologist—a physician who diagnoses and treats conditions and diseases of the auditory system.

paired learning—two students work together on a particular task.

paraprofessionals—staff who assist the teacher in the classroom.

parental consent—permission from the parents for special education assessment.

Pathsounder—a guiding device for individuals with visual impairment; an electronic device worn in front of the chest that emits ultrasonic pulses, which are then converted into a sound or vibration to tell where obstacles are.

peer interaction skills—ability to act reciprocally and appropriately with peers.

peer tutoring—a method for providing one-to-one instruction in which peers work individually with students with disabilities to help them learn, practice, or review academic information.

physical therapists—professionals who assess the motor abilities of the student and provide input for educators on approriate body positioning, exercise for specific problem areas, and the correct use of adaptive equipment.

pitch—production of the appropriate tone, speaking in a voice that is not too high or too low.

planning teams—groups of educators directed toward identifying developing student problems and recommending specific techniques for intervention.

portfolio assessment—a collection of samples of student work in a specified subject area.

portfolio—a selection of representative work compiled over an extended period to indicate gains in student performance.

POWER model—a tool used to determine students' spoken and written language skills; based on a comparison between skills in the native language and English.

"practice effect"—once a student takes a test a number of times, or even more than once in a brief time period, it becomes unreliable because of familiarity with the questions.

prereferral—early intervention in response to an observable, developing problem; may preclude the need for later placement in special education.

preservice—receiving training to eventually become a teacher.

pretest—test to determine how much the student already knows about a skill; used to determine where to begin teaching.

procedural follow-up—the involved teacher has ongoing contact with a member of the Teacher Support Team.

procedural safeguards—precautions taken to protect the rights of students and their families during referral for special education assessment and programming.

processing skills—the ability to interpret incoming stimuli into usable information.

professional development schools—schools that implement the collaboration of school and university educators through mutual supports.

program-centered approach—instruction is designed to meet general programmatic goals.

prostheses—artificial limbs.

psychiatrists—medical specialists who examine the relationship between psychodynamic and organic factors, considering how the physiological aspects of an individual student may interface with psychological behaviors and experiences.

psychologists—nonmedical specialists who work with students and their families to uncover the reasons for behaviors and ways to redirect student actions productively.

psychometric—measuring mental processes.

publicness—being on display; having one's behaviors judged by others.

pull-in programs—educators work with special education students in the regular classroom.

pupil-teacher ratio—the comparative number of students for whom a teacher is responsible.

questioning—prompting student comprehension and application of information by asking for responses and directing students toward the development of new ideas.

readiness—the background skills necessary to perform a task.

reciprocal interaction—a teaching approach in which the teacher creates a spoken and written dialog with the student, emphasizing higher-order thinking instead of basic skills.

redirection—introducing a new behavior to guide the student toward the appropriate task.

referral—a request for consideration of special services.

regional service center—federally and state-funded resources and consultants available to educators in a designated geographic area.

Regular Education Initiative—national movement toward combining special and regular education into one educational system for all children.

reinforcement—a consequence that encourages or discourages the continuance of a behavior.

reliable—provides results consistent with the individual's performance over an extended time.

remedial services—efforts made to correct a deficiency through education.

ReQuest—a paired question-answer technique in which the teacher and student, or pairs of students, take turns asking each other about information from the text.

residential care facility—placement that removes the student from home because of the assessed need for a totally therapeutic environment.

residual hearing—available hearing capabilities.

Resource Room—a separate classroom in which the student receives remedial or compensatory assistance from a specialist one to three hours daily.

resources—materials and equipment available for use.

retrieval disorder—difficulty recalling information.

risk-free environment—an atmosphere in which students feel free to take chances and are not afraid others will laugh at them or tease them.

scantron tests—machine-scored answer sheets.

school counselor—works directly with individuals and groups of students, as well as serving as a liaison with families; primary function is to guide towards responsible decision-making.

school nurses—nurses in a school setting who are responsible for administration of medications, catheterization, and consulting with teachers, parents, and community social services on health issues pertaining to the students.

school psychologists—psychologists who perform primarily assessment functions, identifying learning and behavioral differences that may be contributing to school-related problems.

scoliosis—curvature of the spine.

screening—testing students in a variety of subject areas to identify those who may need special services.

second-order level—provides assistance to regular educators through direct in-class support by special and compensatory education teachers with additional expertise in teaching methods and curricular adaptations.

segregation—separating because of differences.

self-assessment—students evaluate their own work.

self-contained—a placement separate from the regular classroom in which the student spends most of the day with the special education teacher.

**self-esteem**—how a person feels about himself or herself.

**self-fulfilling prophecy**—brought to fulfillment as an effect of having been expected or predicted.

**service delivery**—providing instruction.

**shared literature units**—students in the class participate in a different thematic unit every few weeks in which the teacher provides introductory activities for units and books.

**short-term objectives**—small steps within goals to be worked on and achieved in a short span of time, such as 3 to 6 months.

**sight words**—words a reader commits to memory rather than having to analyze them each time they are encountered.

**simultaneity**—the teacher's ability to direct and monitor a number of ongoing variables at any one time.

**site-based**—taking place on the school campus.

**skill deficits**—areas that lack specific ability.

**skill groups**—a number of students collected together for intensive reinforcement of prerequisite information.

**skill-based**—directed toward developing skills at the appropriate level for completion of school tasks.

**small class size**—limited number of students in class; allows all students to receive attention.

**social workers**—professionals who are involved with families needing school and community support in areas such as counseling, social services, and health care.

**socially appropriate**—acceptable based on the norms of society.

**"soft signs"**—observable indicators that neurological problems may be present.

**Sonicguide**—worn by students with visual impairments, this electronic device looks like sunglasses; emits inaudible impulses when its ultrasonic scanner indicates the presence of objects.

**sound-symbol association**—the ability to match the correct sound and letter.

**spatial assimilation**—allows students to write and compute properly, to manipulate the body and objects correctly in the surrounding environment, and to understand relationships among distances in mathematics, science, and geography.

**special educator**—a professional trained in meeting the needs of students with disabilities.

**special school**—a separate school campus for students with more severe disabilities.

**speech and language specialists**—diagnose and provide remediation for a variety of communication disorders.

**speech compression**—a method of altering the speech of a recording without affecting its pitch.

**spina bifida**—a congenital malformation characterized by incomplete closure of the spinal column and often resulting in hydrocephalus, paralysis, and a lack of bladder and bowel control.

**spinal cord injuries**—damage, usually accidental, to the spinal column; extent of injury is usually determined by its location and the degree of neurological damage.

**splinter skills**—student knows certain operations well but has never learned others completely.

**standardized scores**—valid and reliable scores for which norms are available.

**state-adoption textbooks**—states select texts to be used in all of their schools.

**stereotypes**—critical judgment; categorizing expectations based on generalizable preconceptions about specific groups.

**Student Oral Proficiency Scale**—an instrument used to measure students' abilities to use English in five areas: comprehension, fluency, vocabulary, pronunciation, and grammar.

**stuttering**—a language disorder in which the student repeats words or parts of words involuntarily.

**supportive personnel**—provide assistance to regular educators through direct in-class support by special and compensatory education teachers with additional expertise in teaching methods and curricular adaptations.

**supportive services**—special services, such as physical therapy, occupational therapy, and speech therapy, that may be appropriate for a student.

**syntax**—the meaningful arrangement of words in a sentence.

**Talking Books**—literature that comes with audio support.

**Talking Pen**—a device based on fiber optics that indicates auditorily when students move off a line of print.

**teachable moment**—an immediate opportunity to explain a concept.

**Teacher Assistance Teams**—teachers work together to brainstorm ideas; the regular education teacher requesting help with a particular student joins the team for as long as the assistance is needed.

**Teacher Resource Model**—a consultant trains selected regular classroom teachers and building-level special educators to provide inservice training, ongoing consultation, and technical assistance to regular classroom teachers with students at risk.

**teaching assistants**—people trained to support instruction in an educational situation.

**"teaching for exposure"**—presenting information to students in a broad or general way without covering content in any depth; surface content coverage.

**team leader**—the person who coordinates the team and runs the meetings.

**team rewards**—reinforcers based on combined outcomes of individual members, not competition with other teams.

**team-teach**—to work together to instruct students.

**test anxiety**—a fear of taking tests.

**test manual**—information and directions concerning an evaluation instrument.

**testing**—the acquisition of data or information in specific areas of concern.

**third-order level**—specialized consultant training staff serving a particular region or total school district; especially appropriate in school districts where schools are geographically distant.

**time out**—isolating the student from the group as a consequence.

**"top-down"**—directives from others who are perceived as having more input because of greater job status.

**total communication**—students rely on residual hearing with amplification whenever possible, and use a manual approach such as sign language as a complement whenever necessary.

**total staff approach**—teachers select a single theme to teach for a brief, but intense, period; every teacher in the school relates the theme to the content area he or she teaches.

**tracking**—ability grouping.

**trained assessors**—people educated in the process of testing students.

**trial-and-error**—making attempts that are steered by failures and successes.

**Unified School**—schooling option in which students are considered special education for state and federal reporting and funding purposes, meeting legal requirements; yet in every other way they participate daily with their typical peers.

**unit study**—teaching a broad concept with a series of subtopics for students to explore and allow for global understanding of a subject.

**unpredictability**—occurring unexpectedly.

**valid**—measures accurately what it is supposed to measure.

**verbal redirections**—verbally guiding the student back to on-task, purposeful behavior.

**vision**—a measure of acuity, or how accurately a person takes in raw visual stimuli from the environment.

**visual perception**—analyzing and giving meaning to visual information.

**visual-spatial perception**—the ability to correctly perceive the spatial arrangement of objects or symbols such as letters and numbers.

**white cane**—used by individuals with visual impairments to feel objects in the environment as a support for mobility.

**whole language activities**—lessons based on the integration of writing, reading, and oral language skills.

**word analysis**—use of strategies such as phonics or structural clues (prefixes, suffixes, or syllables) to obtain word meaning.

# REFERENCES

Airasian, P. W. (Spring, 1991). Perspectives on measurement and instruction. *Educational Measurement: Issues and Practice, 13–26.*

Allen, J. P., & Turner, E. (August, 1990). Diversity reigns. *American Demographics, 34–39.*

American Psychological Association (1994). *Diagnostic and statistical manual of mental disorders: IV—Revised.* Washington, DC.

Anderlini, L. S. (1983). An inservice program for improving team participation in educational decision making. *School Psychology Review, 12,* 160–167.

Andringa, J. W., & Keller, A. R. (April, 1991). *Prereferral collaboration helps ensure that only students with exceptionalities are referred for case study evaluation.* Paper presented at the Annual Council for Exceptional Children Conference, Atlanta, GA.

Audette, B., & Algozzine, B. (November/December, 1992). Free and appropriate education for all students: Total quality and the transformation of American public education. *Remedial and Special Education, 13*(6), 8–18.

Baca, L., & Cervantes, H. T. (1989). *The bilingual special education interface* (2nd ed.). Columbus, OH: Merrill Publishing.

Baca, L. M., & Almanza, E. (1992). *Language minority students with disabilities.* Reston, VA: Council for Exceptional Children.

Baer, G. T., Goodall, R., & Brown, L. (1983). Discipline in the classroom: Perceptions of middle grade teachers. *The Clearing House, 57,* 139–142.

Barsch, R. (1965). Six factors in learning. In J. Helmuth (Ed.), *Learning disorders,* Vol.1. Seattle, WA: Special Child Publications.

Batshaw, M., & Perret, Y. (1981). *Children with handicaps: A medical primer.* Baltimore: Paul Brookes.

Beevers, R., & Hallinan, P. (1990). Talking word processors and text editing for visually impaired children: A pilot case study. *Journal of Visual Impairment and Blindness, 84,* 552–555.

Bicklen, D., & Zollers, N. (1986). The focus of advocacy in the learning disabilities field. *The Journal of Learning Disabilities, 19,* 579–586.

Bigge, J. L. (1991). *Teaching individuals with physical and multiple disabilities* (3rd ed.). Columbus, OH: Merrill.

Birch, J., & Reynolds, M. (1982). The proposed role of special educators. *Exceptional Children Quarterly, 2*(4).

Blankenship, C. S. (1985). Individualizing mathematics instruction for students with learning problems. In J. F. Cawley (Ed.), *Secondary school mathematics for the learning disabled.* Rockville, MD: Aspen.

Blatt, B., & Kaplan, F. (1966). *Christmas in Purgatory: A photographic essay.* MA: Scituate Harbor Press.

Bogdan, R., & Bicklen, D. (1977). Handicapism. *Social Policy, 7*(5), 15–19.

Boyer, E. (May 17, 1993). Comments at Trinity University, San Antonio, TX.

Burmeister, L. E. (1975). *Words: From print to meaning.* Reading, MA: Addison–Wesley Publishing Co.

Burrello, L. C., & McLaughlin, M. J. (April, 1993). *Policy issues and options for inclusion.* Paper presented at the Annual Council for Exceptional Children Conference, San Antonio, TX.

Cangelosi, J. S. (1988). *Classroom management strategies: Gaining and maintaining students' cooperation.* White Plains, NY: Longman.

Carman, R. A., & Adams, W. R. (1972). *Study skills: A student's guide for survival.* New York: Wiley.

Carnine, D. (1991). Curricular interventions for teaching higher order thinking to all students: Introduction to the special series. *Journal of Learning Disabilities, 24*(5), 261–269.

Chalfant, J. C., & Pysh, M. V. (1985). *Teacher assistance team report: State of Maryland.* Baltimore, MD.

Chalfant, J. C., & Pysh, M. V. (1989). Teacher assistance teams: Five descriptive studies on 96 teams. *Remedial and Special education, 10*(6), 49–58.

Chalfant, J. C., Pysh, M. V., & Moultrie, R. (1979) Teacher

assistance teams: A model for within-building problem solving. *Learning Disability Quarterly, 2,* 85–95.

Chapman, C. (1990). *Authentic writing assessment.* Washington, DC: Office of Educational Research and Improvement.

Cheney, C. O. (1989). The systematic adaptation of instructional materials and techniques for problem learners. *Academic Therapy, 25*(1), 25–30.

Christiansen, S. L., Ysseldyke, J. E., & Thurlow, M. L. (1989). Critical instructional factors for students with mild handicaps: An integrative review. *Remedial and Special Education, 10*(5), 21–31.

Cosden, M., Pearl, R., & Bryan, T. H. (1985). The effects of cooperative and individual goal structures on learning disabled and nondisabled students. *Exceptional Children, 52,* 103–114.

Council for Children with Behavioral Disorders (1989). Position statement on the regular education initiative. *Behavioral Disorders, 14,* 201–208.

Cruickshank, W. M., Bentzen, F. A., Ratzeburg, F. H., & Tannhauser, M. T. (1961). *A teaching method for brain-injured and hyperactive children.* Syracuse, NY: Syracuse University Press.

Cruickshank, W. M. (1977). Guest Editorial. *Journal of Learning Disabilities, 10,* 193–194.

Cummins, J. (1984). *Bilingualism and special education: Issues in assessment and pedagogy.* San Diego, CA: College Hill Press.

Dardig, J. C. (1981). Helping teachers integrate handicapped students into the regular classroom. *Educational Horizons, 59,* 124–130.

Davis, W. E. (1989). The regular education initiative debate: Its promises and problems. *Exceptional Children, 55*(5), 440–446.

DeGeorge, G. P. (1989). Assessment and placement of language minority students. *Equity and Excellence, 23*(4), 44–56.

Deno, E. (1970). Special education as developmental capital. *Exceptional children, 37,* 229–237.

Deno, S. L. (1985). Curriculum-based measurement: The emerging alternative. *Exceptional Children, 52,* 219–232.

Deno, S. L. (1986). Formative evaluation of individual student programs: A new role for school psychologists. *School Psychology Review, 15,* 358–374.

Development Associates (1987). *Student Oral Proficiency Rating.* Arlington, VA.

Doyle, W. (1980). *Classroom management.* West Lafayette, IN: Kappa Delta Pi.

Edelman, G. (1987). *Neural Darwinism: The theory of neuronal group selection.* NY: Basic Books.

Elkind, D. (1988). *The hurried child.* Reading, MA: Addison–Wesley.

Epilepsy Foundation of America (1989). *Seizure recognition and first aid.* Landover, MD.

Esposito, L., & Campbell, P. H. (1985). *Use of computer programs to train switch activation skills with young children with handicaps.* Presentation at 8th Annual RESNA Conference, Memphis, TN.

Fifteenth Annual Report to Congress on the Implementation of the Education of the Handicapped Act (1993). Washington, DC.

Fradd, S. H., & Bermudez, A. B. (1991). POWER: A process for meeting the instructional needs of handicapped language-minority students. *Teacher Education and Special Education, 14*(1), 19–24.

Fradd, S. H., & Weismantel, M. J. (1989). Developing and evaluating goals. In S. H. Fradd & M. J. Weismantel (Eds.), *Meeting the needs of culturally and linguistically diverse students: A handbook for educators* (pp. 340–362). Boston: Little Brown.

Frazee, B. M., & Rudnitski, R. A. (1995). *Integrated teaching methods; Theory, classroom applications,* and *field-based connections.* Albany, NY: Delmar.

Frazer, K. (1989). *Someone at school has AIDS: A guide to developing policies for students and school staff members who are infected with HIV.* Alexandria, VA: National Association of State Boards of Education.

Fuchs, D., Fuchs, L. S., & Bahr, M. W. (1990). Mainstream assistance teams: A scientific basis for the art of consultation. *Exceptional Children, 57*(2), 128–139.

Fuchs, D., Fuchs, L. S., & Fernstrom, P. (1992). Case-by-case reintegration of students with learning disabilities. *The Elementary School Journal, 92*(3), 261–281.

Fuchs, L. S., & Fuchs, D. (1988). Curriculum-based measurement: A methodology for evaluating and improving student programs. *Diagnostique, 14*(1), 3–13.

Fuchs, L. S., Fuchs, D., & Hamlett, C. L. (1990). Curriculum-based measurement: A standardized, long-term goal approach to monitoring student progress. *Academic Therapy, 25*(5), 615–633.

Gable, R. A., Hendrickson, J. M., Meeks, J. W., Evans, S. S., & Evans, W. H. (1990). Curriculum-based measurement of oral reading. *Preventing School Failure, 35*(1), 37–42.

Gall, M. D. (1981). *Handbook for evaluating and selecting curriculum materials.* NY: Allyn & Bacon.

Garcia, S. B., & Ortiz, A. A. (1988). Preventing inappropriate referrals of language minority students to special education. *New Focus, No. 5.* Wheaton, MD: National Clearinghouse for Bilingual Education.

Garcia, G. E. & Pearson, P. D. (1991). Literacy assessment in a diverse society. *Technical Report No. 525.* Washington, DC: Office of Educational Research and Improvement. (ERIC document Reproduction Service No. ED 329 918)

Gartner, A., & Lipsky, D. K. (1987). Beyond special education: Toward a quality education for all students. *Harvard Educational Review, 57*(4), 367–395.

Gerber, M. M., & Semmel, M. I. (1985). The microeconomics of referral and reintegration: A paradigm for evaluation of special education. *Studies in Educational Evaluation, 11,* 13–29.

Gloeckler, L. C. (Spring, 1991). Fostering integration through curriculum development. *Teaching Exceptional Children,* 52–53.

Goldie, D. (1977). Use of the C-5 Laser Cane by school age children. *Journal of Visual Impairment and Blindness, 71*(8), 346–348.

Graves, D. H. (1983). *Writing: Teachers and children at work.* Exeter, NH: Heinemann Books.

Guerin, G. R. (1991). *Critical step in curriculum reform: Regular education materials and special needs students.* Sacramento, CA: California State Department of Education.

Gunter, M. A., Estes, T. H., & Schwab, J. H. (1990). *Instruction: A models approach.* Boston: Allyn & Bacon.

Hale, G. (1979). *The source book for the disabled.* Philadelphia: Saunders.

Hall, V. (1975). *Managing behavior: Part 1.* Austin, TX: PRO:ED.

Hallahan, D. P., & Kauffman, J. M. (1991). *Exceptional children* (5th ed.). Englewood Cliffs, NJ: Prentice-Hall.

Halliday, M. A. K. (1978). *Language as social semeiotic.* Baltimore: University Park Press.

Harley, R. K., & Lawrence, G. A. (1984). *Visual impairment in the schools* (2nd ed.). Springfield, IL: Charles C. Thomas.

Heiss, W. (March, 1977). Relating educational assessment to instructional planning. *Focus on Exceptional Children, 9*(1), 1–11.

Hewett, F. M. (1968). *The emotionally disturbed child in the classroom.* Boston: Allyn & Bacon.

Heyes, A. D. (1984). The Sonic Pathfinder: A new electronic travel aid. *Journal of Visual Impairment and Blindness, 78*(5), 200–202.

Hiemstra, R., & Sisco, B. (1990). *Individualizing instruction.* San Francisco, CA: Jossey-Bass.

Hoover, J. J., & Collier, C. (1991). Meeting the needs of culturally and linguistically diverse exceptional learners. *Teacher education and special education, 14*(1), 30–34.

Howard, J., & Hammond, R. (1985). Rumors of inferiority. In L. Fenson & J. Fenson, Eds., *Human Development.* Guilford, CN: Dushkin.

Howell, K. W., Fox, S. L., & Morehead, M. K. (1993). *Curriculum-based evaluation.* Pacific Grove, CA: Brooks/Cole Publishing Company.

Idol, L., & West, J. F. (1993). *Effective instruction of difficult-to-teach students: An inservice and preservice professional development program for classroom, remedial, and special education teachers.* Austin, TX: PRO-ED.

Idol, L., Nevin, A., & Paolucci-Whitcomb, P. (1994). *Collaborative consultation* (2nd ed.). Austin, TX: PRO-ED.

Itard, J. M. G. (1962). *The wild boy of Aveyron* (Trans. George & Muriel Humphrey). Englewood Cliffs, NJ: Prentice-Hall.

Jobes, N. K., & Hawthorne, L. W. (1977). Informal assessment for the classroom. *Focus on Exceptional Children, 9*(2), 1–13.

Johnson, D. W., & Johnson, R. T. (1975). *Learning together and alone: Cooperation, competition, and individualization.* Englewood Cliffs, NJ: Prentice-Hall.

Johnson, D. W., & Johnson, R. T. (1986). Mainstreaming and cooperative learning strategies. *Exceptional Children, 52,* 553–561.

Johnson, D. W., & Johnson, R. T. (1989). Toward a cooperative effort: A response to Slavin. *Educational Leadership, 46,* 93–97.

Johnson, D. W., Johnson, R. T., Warring, D., & Maruyama, G. (1986). Different cooperative learning procedures and cross-handicap relationships. *Exceptional Children, 53,* 247–252.

Kagan, S., & Kagan, M. (1994). The structural approach: Six keys to cooperative learning. In S. Sharan (Ed.), *Handbook of cooperative learning methods.* Westport, CN: Greenwood Press.

Kampfe, C. M. (1984). Mainstreaming: Some practical suggestions for teachers and administrators. In R. H. Hull & K. L. Dilka (Eds.), *The hearing-impaired child in school.* Orlando, FL: Grune & Stratton.

Kauffman, J. M. (1988). Revolution can also mean returning to the starting point: Will school psychology help special education complete the circuit? *School Psychology Review, 17,* 490–494.

Kauffman, J. M., Gerber, M. M., & Semmel, M. I. (1988). Arguable assumptions underlying the regular education initiative. *Journal of Learning Disabilities, 21*(1), 6–11.

Kauffman, J. M., & Hallahan, D. P. (1993). Toward a

comprehensive delivery system for special education. In Goodlad, J. I., & Lovitt, T. C., Eds., *Integrating general and special education.* NY: Macmillan Publishing Co.

Kennedy, D. A., & Thompson, I. (1967). Use of reinforcement techniques with a first grade boy. *The Personnel and Guidance Journal, 46,* 366–370.

Klumb, K. (1992). *Generic considerations in adjusting curriculum and instruction for at-risk students.* CA: Lucerne Valley Unified School District.

Koenig, A. J., & Holbrook, M. C. (1989). Determining the reading medium for students with visual impairments: A diagnostic teaching approach. *Journal of Visual Impairment and Blindness,* 296–302.

Kounin, J. (1977). *Discipline and group management in classrooms.* NY: Holt, Rinehart & Winston, 1977.

Kuhn, T .S. (Ed.) (1970). *The structure of scientific revolutions* (2nd ed.). Chicago: University of Chicago Press.

Lambie, R. A. (1980). A systematic approach for changing materials, instruction, and assignments to meet individual needs. *Focus on Exceptional Children, 13*(1), 1–12.

Landon, R., & Mesinger, J. F. (1989). Teacher tolerance ratings on problem behaviors. *Behavioral Disorders, 14,* 236–249.

Larrivee, B. (1989). Effective strategies for academically handicapped students in the regular classroom. In R. E. Slavin, N. L. Karweit, & N. A. Madden (Eds.), *Effective programs for students at risk.* Boston: Allyn and Bacon.

Larson, J., McIntire, J. C., & Muoio, G. T. (April, 1993). *Inclusion—Successes and issues.* Comments presented at the Council for Exceptional Children Annual Conference, San Antonio, TX.

Laurie, T. E., Buchwach, L., Silverman, R., & Zigmond, N. (1978). Teaching secondary learning disabled students in the mainstream. *Learning Disability Quarterly 1*(4), 62– 72.

Lerner, J. (1993). *Learning disabilities: Theories, diagnosis, and teaching strategies* (6th ed.). Dallas: Houghton-Mifflin.

Levitt, H. (1989). Technology and speech training: An affair to remember. *Volta Review, 91*(5), 1–6.

Lewis, R. B., & Doorlag, D. H. (1987). *Teaching special students in the mainstream.* Columbus, OH: Charles E. Merrill.

Licht, B. G. (1983). Cognitive-motivational factors that contribute to the achievement of learning disabled children. *Journal of Learning Disabilities, 16,* 403–409.

Lieberman, L. M. (1985). Special education and regular education: A merger made in heaven? *Exceptional Children, 51*(6), 513–516.

Lilly, M. S. (1986). The relationship between general and special education: A new face on an old issue. *Counterpoint, 6*(1), 33–43.

Lipsky, D. K., & Gartner, A. (1987). Capable of achievement and worthy of respect: Education for handicapped students as if they were full-fledged human beings. *Exceptional Children, 54*(1), 69–74.

Lloyd, J. W., Crowley, E. P., Kohler, F. W., & Strain, P. S. (1988). Redefining the applied research agenda: Cooperative learning, prereferral, teacher consultation, and peer-mediated interventions. *Journal of Learning Disabilities, 21*(1), 43–52.

Lyon, S., & Lyon, G. (1980). Team functioning and staff development: A role release approach to providing integrated educational services for severely handicapped students. *Journal of the Association for the Severely Handicapped, 5,* 250–263.

Macmillan, D. L., & Hendrick, I. G. (1993). Evolution and legacies. In Goodlad, J. I., & Lovitt, T. C., Eds., *Integrating general and special education.* NY: Macmillan Publishing Co.

Madden, N., & Slavin, R. (1983). Effects of cooperative learning on the social acceptance of mainstreamed academically handicapped students. *The Journal of Special Education, 17,* 171–182.

Mann, P. H., Suiter, P. A., & McClung, R. M. (1987). *Handbook in diagnostic-prescriptive teaching* (3rd ed.). NY: Allyn & Bacon.

Matthews, M. K. (1992). Gifted students talk about cooperative learning. *Educational Leadership,* 48–50.

McRobbie, J. (1992). *Using portfolios to assess student performance.* Washington, DC: Office of Educational Research and Improvement.

Mellor, C. M. (1981). *Aids for the 80s: What they are and what they do.* NY: American Foundation for the Blind.

Mercer, C., & Mercer, A. *Teaching students with learning problems.* Dallas: Merrill, 1988.

Mims, A., Harper, C., Armstrong, S. W., & Savage, S. (Fall, 1991). Effective instruction in homework for students with disabilities. *Teaching Exceptional Children,* 42–44.

Moran, M. R. (1976). The teacher's role in referral for testing and interpretation of reports. *Focus on Exceptional Children 8*(6), 1–15.

Moran, M. R. (1978). *Assessment of the exceptional learner in the regular classroom.* Denver, CO: Love Publishing Co.

Morrow, L. M. (1989). Using story retelling to develop comprehension. In K. D. Muth (Ed.), *Children's comprehension of text: Research into practice*. Newark, DE: International Reading Association.

Morsink, C. V. (1984) *Teaching special needs students in regular classrooms*. Boston: Little, Brown & Co.

Morsink, C. V., & Lenk, L. L. (1992). The delivery of special education programs and services. *Remedial and Special Education, 13*(6), 33–43.

Morton, J. L. (1991). *What teachers want to know about portfolio assessment*. Tahlequah, OK: Northeastern State University.

Moskowitz, F. C. (1988). Success strategies: Help for struggling students. *Learning, 88,* July/August.

Mykelbust, H. D. (1965). *Development and disorders of written language*. NY: Grune and Stratton.

Olson, P. (1991). *Referring language minority students to special education*. Washington, DC: Office of Educational Research and Improvement (ERIC Doc. 329 131.)

Omaggio, A. C. (1986). *Teaching language in context*. Boston, MA: Heinle & Heinle.

Ortiz, A., & Wilkinson, C.Y. (1991). Assessment and intervention model for the bilingual exceptional student. *Teacher Education and Special Education, 14*(1), 35–42.

Ortiz, A., Wilkinson, C. Y., & Rivera, C. (1991). AIM for the BESt: Assessment and intervention model for the bilingual exceptional student. Washington, DC: Technical Report for the U.S. Department of Education, Office of Bilingual Education and Minority Languages Affairs. (ERIC Document Reproduction Service No. ED 300 867).

Palmer, L. (1988). Speechreading as communication. *The Volta Review, 90,* 33–42.

Penick, J. E., & Yager, R. E. (1986). Science education: New concerns and issues. *Science Education, 70,* 427–431.

Pierce, L. V. (Ed.) (1992). *Cooperative learning in the secondary school: Maximizing language acquisition, academic achievement, and social development*. Washington, DC: National Clearinghouse for Bilingual Education.

Pierce, L. V., & O'Malley, J. M. (1992). Performance and portfolio assessment for language minority students. *Program Information Guide, Series 9*. Washington, DC: National Clearinghouse for Bilingual Education. (ERIC Document Reproduction Service No. ED346 747).

Powell, D. (1985). Selection of reading textbooks at the district level: Is this a rational process? *Book Research Quarterly,* 24–35.

Premack, D. (1959). Toward empirical laws: I. Positive reinforcement. *Psychological Review, 66,* 219–233.

Putnam, M. L. (1992). The testing practices of mainstream secondary classroom teachers. *Remedial and Special Education, 13*(5), 11–21.

Reynolds, M. C. (1984). Classification of students with handicaps. In E. W. Gordon (Ed.), *Review of Research in Education (Vol. II)*. Washington, DC: American Educational Research Association.

Reynolds, M. C., & Wang, M. C. (1983). Restructuring "special" school programs: A position paper. *Policy Studies Review, 2*(1), 189–212.

Reynolds, M. C., Wang, M. C., & Walberg, H. J. (1987). The necessary restructuring of special and regular education. *Exceptional Children, 53*(5), 391–398.

Riesberg, L., & Wolf, R. (1988). Instructional strategies for special education consultants. *Remedial and Special Education, 9*(6), 29–40.

Rosenshine, B., & Stevens, R. (1986). Teaching functions. In M.C. Wittrock (Ed.), *Handbook of research on teaching (3rd ed.)*. NY: Macmillan.

Ross, M. (1982). *Hard of hearing children in regular schools*. Englewood Cliffs, NJ: Prentice-Hall.

Sage, D. D. (1970). How we got here from there. *A Study of the Special Education Program*. MD: Montgomery County Public Schools.

Sapon-Shevin, M. (1988). Working towards merger together: Seeing beyond distrust and fear. *Teacher Education and Special Education, 11*(3), 103–110.

Schumaker, J. B. & Deshler, D. D. (1988). Implementing the regular education initiative in secondary schools: A different ball game. *The Journal of Learning Disabilities, 21*(1), 36–42.

Scruggs, T. E., & Mastropieri, M. A. (1992). Effective mainstreaming strategies for mildly handicapped students. *The Elementary School Journal, 92*(3), 389–409.

Shinn, M. R. (Ed.) (1989). *Curriculum-based measurement: Assessing special children*. New York: Guilford.

Silkworth, C. S., & Jones, D. (1988). Helping the student with asthma. In F. Larson (Ed.), *Managing the school age child with a chronic health condition*. Minneapolis, MN: DCI.

Simmons, D. C., Fuchs, D., & Fuchs, L. S. (1990). Instructional and curricular requisites of mainstreamed students with learning disabilities. *Journal of Learning Disabilities, 24*(6), 354–360.

Skrtic, T. M. (1986). The crisis in special education knowledge: A perspective on perspective. *Focus on Exceptional Children, 18*(7), 1–16.

Skrtic, T. M. (1991). The special education paradox:

Equity as the way to excellence. *Harvard Educational Review, 61*(2), 148–206.

Slavin, R. E. (1983). *Cooperative learning.* NY: Longman.

Slavin, R. E. (1991). Synthesis of research on cooperative learning. *Educational Leadership, 48,* 71–82.

Smith, C. (March, 1992). *Different hats, different questions, assessment audiences/questions/answers.* Paper presented at a Conference of School Principals, NY.

Smith, S. (1981). *No easy answers.* NY: Bantam Books.

Smith, M. A., & Misra, A. (1992). A comprehensive management system for students in regular classrooms. *The Elementary School Journal, 92*(3), 353–369.

Smith, J. R., Smith, D. J., Taylor, L., Dodd, J. M., & Reavis, K. (1991). Prereferral intervention: A review of the research. *Education and treatment of children, 14*(3), 243–253.

Stager, J. (1990). *At-risk students in regular education. Structuring the schools for student success.* Quincy MA: Massachusetts Department of Education. (ERIC Document Reproduction Service No. ED 342 849).

Stainback, S., & Stainback, W. (1984). A rationale for the merger of special and regular education. *Exceptional Children, 51*(2), 102–111.

Sugai, G. (1988). *Educational assessment of the culturally diverse and behavior disordered student: An examination of critical effect.* Paper presented at the Ethnic and Multicultural Symposia, Dallas, TX. (ERIC Document Reproduction Service No. ED 288 706).

Taylor, R. L. (1989). *Assessment of exceptional students* (2nd. ed.). Englewood Cliffs, NJ: Prentice Hall.

Thousand, J., Villa, R., Paolucci-Whitcomb, P., & Nevin, A. (1992). A rationale for collaborative consultation. In W. Stainback & S. Stainback (Eds.), *Divergent perspectives in special education.* Boston: Allyn & Bacon, 223–232.

Thousand, J. S. (1990). Organizational perspectives on teacher education and renewal: A conversation with Tom Skrtic. *Teacher Education and Special Education, 13*(1), 30–35.

Tikunoff, W. (1985). *Applying significant bilingual instructional features in the classroom.* Wheaton, MD: National Clearinghouse for Bilingual Education.

Tucker, J. (1987). Curriculum–based assessment is not a fad. *The Collaborative Educator, 1*(4), 4–10.

Tulley, M., & Farr, R. (1985). The purpose of state level textbook adoption: What does the legislation reveal? *Journal of Research and Development in Education, 18*(2), 1–6.

Tyack, D., & Hansot, E. (1982). *Managers of virtue.* NY: Basic Books Inc.

Vars, G. (October, 1991). Integrated curriculum in historical perspective. *Educational Leadership,* 14–15.

Vasquez-Chairez, M. (1988). *Bilingual and special education: Procedural manual for program administrators. Cross-cultural Special Education series, Vol. 1.* Sacramento, CA: California State Department of Education.

Villa, R. (January, 1995). *Making inclusion work.* Presentation for the Trinity University Education Lecture Series, San Antonio, TX.

Vygotsky, L. M. (1978). *Mind in society: The development of higher psychological processes.* Cambridge, MA: Harvard University Press.

Wagner, M. (September, 1991). *Drop outs with disabilities: What do we know? What can we do?* Menlo Park: SRI International. (In *Supplement to Teaching Exceptional Children,* January, 1994) Reston, VA: The Council for Exceptional Children.

Waldron, K. A. (1980). Toward effective inservice delivery. *Pointer, 24,* 68–75.

Waldron, K. A. (1992a). *Teaching students with learning disabilities: Strategies for success.* San Diego, CA: Singular Press.

Waldron, K. A. (1992b). The teaching-learning environment: Adaptations for mainstreaming. In K. A. Waldron, A. E. Riester, & J. H. Moore, Eds., *Special Education: The challenge of the future.* San Francisco: Mellen Research University Press.

Waldron, K. A. (October, 1995). *Parenting students with learning differences.* Paper presented at the Winston School Symposium, San Antonio, TX.

Waldron, K. A. (Ed.) (1996). *The inclusion handbook.* Austin, TX: Texas Education Agency: Center for Educational Development and Excellence.

Waldron, M. B., Diebold, T. J., & Rose, S. (1985). Hearing impaired students in regular classrooms: A cognitive model for educational services. *Exceptional Children, 52,* 39–43.

Walker, L. J. (1987). Procedural rights in the wrong system: Special education is not enough. In Gartner, A. & Joe, T. (Eds.) *Images of the disabled/disabling images.* NY: Praeger, 98–102.

Walker, W., & Buckley, N. K. (1968). The use of positive reinforcement in conditioning attending behavior. *Journal of Applied Behavior Analysis, 1,* 245–250.

Wang, M. C., Reynolds, M. C., & Walberg, H. J. (December, 1985). *Rethinking special education.* Paper presented at the Wingspread Conference on the Education of Students with Special Needs: Research Findings and Implications for Policy and Practice, Racine, WI.

Wang, M. C., Walberg, H., & Reynolds, M. C. (October, 1992). A scenario for better—not separate—special education. *Educational Leadership,* 35–38.

West, J. F., & Cannon, G. S. (1988). Essential collaborative consultation competencies for regular and special educators. *Journal of Learning Disabilities, 21*(1), 56–63.

White, N. A. (1981). The role of the regular classroom teacher. In V. J. Froehlinger (Ed.), *Today's hearing-impaired child: Into the mainstream of education.* Washington, DC: Alexander Graham Bell Association for the Deaf.

Wiener, R. (March, 1992). The REI movement. *Electronic Learning,* 12.

Will, M. C. (1984). Let us pause and reflect—but not too long. *Exceptional Children, 51*(1), 11–16.

Will, M. C. (1986). Educating children with learning problems: A shared responsibility. *Exceptional Children, 52,* 411–415.

Willis, S. (1990). Cooperative learning fallout? *ASCD Update, 6,* 8.

Wisniewski, L., & Sedlak, R. S. (1992). Assistive devices for students with disabilities. *The Elementary School Journal, 92*(3), 297–314.

Wolfensberger, W. (1971). *The principle of normalization in human services.* Toronto: National Institute on Mental Retardation.

Wood, H. W. (1989). *Mainstreaming: A practical approach for teachers.* Columbus, OH: Merrill Publishing Co.

Woodward, A., Elliott, D. L., & Nagel, K. C. (1986). Beyond textbooks in elementary social studies. *Social Education, 50*(1), 50–53.

Yates, H. R. (1992). Special education futures: Implications of national trends and forces. In K. A. Waldron, A. E. Riester, & J. H. Moore, Eds., *Special education: The challenge of the future.* San Francisco: Mellen Research University Press.

Ysseldyke, J. E., Thurlow, M., Graden, J., Wesson, C., Algozzine, B., & Deno, S. (1983). Generalizations from five years of research on assessment and decision-making. *Exceptional Education Quarterly, 4,* 75–93.

# AUTHOR/NAME INDEX

# SUBJECT INDEX